PATTERNS
OF
POWER

Social Foundations of Education

Pitman Education Series

Rychard Fink, GENERAL EDITOR

PATTERNS
OF
POWER

Social Foundations of Education

THOMAS E. LINTON
UNIVERSITY OF WISCONSIN, MILWAUKEE

JACK L. NELSON
STATE UNIVERSITY OF NEW YORK AT BUFFALO

Pitman Publishing Corporation

NEW YORK / TORONTO / LONDON

To Clover and Gwen

LA
209.2
L5

Preface

THE EDUCATIONAL system of a country is influenced by various social forces and cultural values that are present in that society. For this reason, it is important for the student to gain an understanding of major social issues that affect the operation of the school and an awareness of the broad-based social questions which underlie educational decisions. Selected material from the social sciences has been utilized for this purpose. This social foundations text is to provide the student with an introduction to the major social, cultural, and economic forces that exert a direct influence upon our educational system.

The articles should be used as a basis for further reading and discussion. All of the areas considered contain both factual and theoretical material in the selected articles. Each section has an introduction which specifically relates the articles to a major educational theme. Preceding every article is a short statement, providing continuity for the reader throughout the book. Since the text is meant to serve as an introduction to the issues discussed, the reader will find a bibliography for further reading at the end of the text.

Throughout the text the student should keep a central goal in mind: to understand the material in terms of its implications and significance for the classroom, the teacher, and the school in society. The text provides selections from the social sciences which are directly applicable to educational problems. Another goal of basic importance is nonpersonalized involvement. Many of the topics presented are commonly discussed in homes, among friends, and in the mass media, with the result that nearly everyone has a definite opinion or belief about the problems considered. Throughout the course and in reading the material, the student should try to maintain what might be called an attitude of scientific detachment. This does not mean that the student should abandon his traditional values and beliefs, nor does it follow that he should adopt the values expressed in the articles. Rather he should read the material carefully and critically, trying constantly to evaluate the truth and relevance of the issues in an objective manner.

The opinions and ideas expressed in the articles do not necessarily represent those held by the editors of these readings; but they do represent a wide spectrum of attitudes and perceptions regarding social and educational conditions in the United States.

INTRODUCTION:
THE SCHOOL IN SOCIETY

As the Preface indicates, the direction of this book is toward encouraging the student to become more aware of the historical, social, cultural, and economic forces which affect the educational process. The education system reflects and reacts to those forces which are important during particular historical periods. Further, the school system, like other major institutions in the society, develops its own momentum and inertia which can be analyzed as an internal social system, apart from the social forces and institutions which are external to the schools. Both the external forces and the internal culture of the school system will be presented in the text.

The educational institution should be studied in terms of its historical development and in relation to the social problems which characterize a particular society. The schools are not isolated from the major social forces which are dominant in the total society. They are influenced by these forces as well as by the national values of the period.

At the present time American society is vitally concerned with such issues as peaceful coexistence with Russia and China, maintaining our international "commitments," production for national defense, the civil rights movement, the reduction of poverty, the effects of automation, and the breakdown of the large metropolitan centers. These issues are important for the teacher in two ways. On the one hand, the educational choices the schools make are directly influenced by the major national concerns of the period. These choices are reflected in the school curriculum, the Boards of Education, the choice of textbooks, and within the accepted value system of the schoolteacher's life. Secondly, the teacher, as a transmitter of the national culture, is able to perform more competently when he understands the major problems and issues confronting the general society. For the teacher not only passes on information and the values of his society, but he also analyzes the meaning of these national problems. The interpretive part of the role relates directly to the teacher's depth of understanding of these various social questions. When he is aware that these issues are complex, he will be less inclined to present the culture in an overly simplified and doctrinaire fashion.

In order to examine the schools as an institution in the larger society, it is necessary for the student to develop an objective frame of reference concerning the educational process. Social science has studied such institutions as the family, the labor union, big business, organized religion, and the social-class structure in our society. This has been done in an analytical manner, avoiding personalized judgments which make it difficult to evaluate the effectiveness of the institution being studied. The student should attempt to view the total educational system, and its various aspects, as parts within a whole. Some of these parts would include the history and traditions of the profession, theoretical issues and educational choices, the operational structure of the system, and the subculture of the school itself.

The behavioral sciences have developed an extensive body of information and theory about the various institutional systems in our society. These have been studied individually and as they relate to each other. Some of the educational critics have argued that teachers often lack a substantive knowledge of this background material from the social sciences. This text presents a broad selection of major contributors to the behavioral sciences, as well as the social problems that currently confront the society and the educational system.

The student and the instructor may wish to use these issues, which are often controversial, as points of reference for analyzing the role of the school and the teacher. This text does not offer a complete range of answers for the questions that are raised. With the complexity of modern day society and the wide range of answers to most major questions, it would be difficult to present all sides of an issue, or even all of the important problems. However, it is possible to present some of the major scholars of the period, dealing with some of the most important questions of their time.

The School as a Social Force

It may be assumed that the schools are a highly conservative institutional force in the society. One does not generally associate the concept of dynamic social change with public education. Yet the fact is, that the schools have served as an important agent of social change in the growth of the American economy. It is important for teachers to understand the school's role as a change agent in dealing with national problems. This understanding should help the teacher to assess the school's position in relation to major issues presently confronting the educational system. The following are some of the important goals which the American system of public education has helped to achieve.

Developing a National Identity

The schools have served to integrate and consistently maintain certain democratic value themes which are characteristic of American life. These themes such as egalitarianism, personal freedom, and civic responsibility are presently viewed as basic to daily life in our society. But these conditions were not accepted by many groups and institutions in the nation's formative years. The public education movement represented in its early development those individuals who favored an enlargement of social and economic opportunity, rather than limiting these to a select minority.

Those individuals who desired free public education available to everyone were forced to commit themselves to a long-term political struggle. There was a general feeling for a long period that education was not to be given freely to the mass of children in the society. Further, while some admitted the importance of a free common school for a few years in the child's life, very few accepted the idea of free secondary education. Many people felt that the majority of children could not benefit from secondary education, and would be rendered unfit for factory service by raising their level of social and intellectual understanding.

On the other hand, those individuals and groups who wanted compulsory, free secondary education believed that the schools were an extremely important force in developing and maintaining a free and democratic society. Their argument was that freedom required understanding and social responsibility which could best be developed in a free and compulsory public school setting. They felt that diverse ethnic and social groups attending a common school and experiencing a core of accepted values and traditions was essential for the effective maintenance of a pluralistic and democratic state.

Mass Versus Elite Educational Choices

When a nation chooses to restrict the opportunity for secondary and university education to a selective minority, one usually finds that the society as a whole has made certain assumptions about human ability in terms of what has been called a mass versus elite approach to education.

In the elite approach the social system is structured to limit the social and economic opportunities available to the majority. The European countries have historically promoted the aristocratic and meritocratic patterns in their economic, social, and industrial arrangements. The aristocratic assumption holds that both intellectual and social achievement are found primarily in the ruling classes. The meritocratic assumption holds that high academic ability, while narrowly distributed, is found at all socio-economic levels. In the meritocratic approach the education system seeks to identify the child of "merit" and assists him financially and academically toward the fulfillment of his high intellectual capacities.

In contrast to the aristocratic and meritocratic ideology, which has characterized European education, the American approach may be viewed as democratically based. Since the early 1900's the schools have been viewed as institutions serving the mass of citizens rather than attempting to restrict the educational development of this majority. As the society continued to grow in social and economic opportunity, the schools became one of the main avenues for advancement into the expanding economy.

The main values of American culture, such as egalitarianism, individual choice, and pragmatism, have been important factors in the success story of this society. It is a pluralistic society which offers a wide latitude of choice; however, this privilege of choice is exercised within a framework of social and human responsibility. These values and traditions were the working intellectual foundations of the public education movement. Hence the role of the school as a cultural force is a comprehensive and active one.

Human Understanding and Educational Development

There has been an extensive application of the ideas from the behavioral sciences to the process of education. Underlying this process was the value premise that education did not have to be ritualistic and dreary. It was felt by Dewey and others in the 1920's that learning could be related to the needs, interests, and abilities of the children attending schools. It was believed that the traditional and authoritarian role of the teacher and the school could be altered. The entire meaning of the school was changed drastically, so that the school milieu and the learning process were to become interesting and attractive rather than punitive and rigidly arbitrary.

The concerns for individual worth and equality were basic to this educational revolution. It would have been difficult to provide the same curriculum for the great diversity of students attending the schools while the society provided multiple social and vocational opportunities. From this adjustment of the schools to the realities of the social and ethnic differences in the student population, there developed an attempt to scientifically understand the educational process. This understanding involved a study of human development, child psychology, learning theory, and curriculum alternatives.

As a result of these changes and advances, education has moved a long way from the prescribed approach which was utilized by the schools during the eighteenth and nineteenth centuries. The movement toward the scientific study of education has progressed to a point where there is a large body of information which may be viewed as educational technology. Much of this material is taken from the social sciences and adapted for educational use. However, it is important for the student to consider the value premise from which most of the educational technology is developed. The technology itself is based on several value assumptions about the goals and purposes of American education. And, as in many areas of human knowledge, the technology itself may become a primary end. When this occurs the educational process becomes heavily involved with technique and the actual purpose and function of education is often overlooked or not carefully examined.

This is especially important to consider at the present time, for the schools are currently faced with major social problems which involve value choices rather than primarily questions of educational technology. Since much educational research is based on social-science findings, it is important to consider the nature of behavioral-science research. Educational research, like that of psychology and sociology, is at the present time extensively involved with the accumulation of data and the statistical manipulation of this same material. If one examines the leading journals in psychology, education, and sociology, it becomes apparent that scientific methodology and mathematical concerns are of primary importance. Humanistic values and basic social questions, which are of major importance to the general society, are often ignored or not considered germane to the researcher's role. The authors of this text do not mean to repudiate the importance and worth of empirical and statistical data. In fact, readings have been selected which are based on extensive research and comprehensive compilations of information. It is from the analysis of these data that theory is developed and tested. However, the essential position of this book is that the theories and their implications for society and education are of prime significance. Values and value conflicts continue to be basic to decisions in education and the culture.

The following article by Professor Berger, titled "A Humanistic Perspective" examines the work and role of the sociologist in American society. Most of his comments may be readily extended to the other social sciences, as well as to education. The article considers the relationship between social-science research and the major social issues which are important to the larger society. Fundamentally, the question involved is, What is the purpose of knowledge? Is it intelligent to gather data and publish an endless series of articles which remain on library shelves and are too technical for public use? Further, and of central importance, is the question, What is the actual purpose of much of the research that is undertaken?

A Humanistic Perspective

PETER L. BERGER

The political and economic structure of American academic life encourages this pattern, and not only in sociology. Colleges and universities are
normally administered by very busy people with little time or inclination
to delve into the esoterica produced by their scholarly employees. Yet
these administrators are called upon to make decisions concerning the hiring and firing, promotion and tenure of their faculty personnel. What
criteria should they use in these decisions? They cannot be expected to
read what their professors write, having no time for such activities and,
especially in the more technical disciplines, lacking the necessary qualifications to judge the material. The opinions of immediate colleagues of the
professors in question are suspect "a priori," the normal academic institution being a jungle of bitter warfare between faculty factions, none of
which can be relied upon for an objective judgment of members of either
his own or an opposing group. To ask the views of students would be even
more uncertain procedure. Thus the administrators are left with a number
of equally unsatisfactory options. They can go on the principle that the
institution is one happy family, in which every member advances steadily
up the status ladder regardless of merit. This has been tried often enough,
but becomes ever more difficult in an age of competition for the favor
of the public and the funds of foundations. Another option is to rely
on the advice of one clique, chosen on some more or less rational basis.
This creates obvious political difficulties for the administrator of a group
chronically defensive about its independence. The third option, the one
most common today, is to fall back on the criterion of productivity as
used in the business world. Since it is very difficult indeed to judge the
productivity of a scholar with whose field one is not well acquainted, one
must somehow try to find out how acceptable the scholar is to unprejudiced colleagues in his field. It is then assumed that such acceptability can
be deduced from the number of books or articles that publishers or editors
of professional publications are willing to accept from the man in question.
This forces scholars to concentrate on work that can easily and speedily
be converted into a respectable little article likely to be accepted for publication in a professional journal. For sociologists this means some little
empirical study of a narrowly confined topic. In most instances such

studies will require the application of statistical techniques. Since most professional journals in the field are suspicious of articles that do not contain at least some statistical material this tendency is further strengthened. And so eager young sociologists stranded somewhere in hinterland institutions, yearning for the richer pastures of the better universities, supply us with a steady stream of little statistical studies of the dating habits of their students, the political opinions of the surrounding natives or the class system of some hamlet within commuting distance of their campus. It might be added here that this system is not quite so terrible as it may seem to the newcomer to the field, since its ritual requirements are well known to all concerned. As a result, the sensible person reads the sociological journals mainly for the book reviews and the obituaries, and goes to sociological meetings only if he is looking for a job or has other intrigues to carry on.

The prominence of statistical techniques in American sociology today has, then, certain ritual functions that are readily understandable in view of the power system within which most sociologists have to make a career. In fact, most sociologists have little more than a cookbook knowledge of statistics, treating it with about the same mixture of awe, ignorance and timid manipulation as a poor village priest would the mighty Latin cadences of Thomist theology. Once one has realized these things, however, it should be clear that sociology ought not to be judged by these aberrations. One then becomes, as it were, sociologically sophisticated about sociology, and enabled to look beyond the outward signs to whatever inward grace may be hidden behind them.

Statistical data by themselves do not make sociology. They become sociology only when they are sociologically interpreted, put within a theoretical frame of reference that is sociological. Simple counting, or even correlating different items that one counts, is not sociology. There is almost no sociology in the Kinsey reports. This does not mean that the data in these studies are not true or that they cannot be relevant to sociological understanding. They are, taken by themselves, raw materials that can be used in sociological interpretation. The interpretation, however, must be broader than the data themselves. So the sociologist cannot arrest himself at the frequency tables of premarital petting or extramarital pederasty. These enumerations are meaningful to him only in terms of their much broader implications for an understanding of institutions and values in our society. To arrive at such understanding the sociologist will often have to apply statistical techniques, especially when he is dealing with the mass phenomena of modern social life. But sociology consists of statistics as little as philology consists of conjugating irregular verbs or chemistry of making nasty smells in test tubes.

Another image of the sociologist current today and rather closely related to that of statistician is the one that sees him as a man mainly concerned in developing a scientific methodology that he can impose on human phenomena. This image is frequently held by people in the humanities and presented as proof that sociology is a form of intellectual barbarism. One part of this criticism of sociology by the "litterateurs" is often a scathing commentary on the outlandish jargon in which much sociological writing is couched. By contrast, of course, the one who makes these criticisms offers himself as a guardian of the classical traditions of humane learning.

It would be quite possible to meet such criticism by an argument "ad hominem." Intellectual barbarism seems to be fairly evenly distributed in the main scholarly disciplines dealing with the phenomenon "man." However, it is undignified to argue "ad hominem," so we shall readily admit that, indeed, there is much that passes today under the heading of sociology that is justly called barbarian, if that word is intended to denote an ignorance of history and philosophy, narrow expertise without wider horizons, a preoccupation with technical skills, and total insensitivity to the uses of language. Once more, these elements can themselves be understood sociologically in terms of certain characteristics of contemporary academic life. The competition for prestige and jobs in fields rapidly becoming more and more complex forces specialization that all too frequently leads to a depressing parochialism of interests. But it would again be inaccurate to identify sociology with this much more pervasive intellectual trend.

Sociology has, from its beginnings, understood itself as a science. There has been much controversy about the precise meaning of this self-definition. For instance, German sociologists have emphasized the difference between the social and the natural sciences much more strongly than their French or American colleagues. But the allegiance of sociologists to the scientific ethos has meant everywhere a willingness to be bound by certain scientific canons of procedure. If the sociologist remains faithful to his calling, his statements must be arrived at through the observation of certain rules of evidence that allow others to check on or to repeat or to develop his findings further. It is this scientific discipline that often supplies the motive for reading a sociological work as against, say, a novel on the same topic that might describe matters in much more impressive and convincing language. As sociologists tried to develop their scientific rules of evidence, they were compelled to reflect upon methodological problems. This is why methodology is a necessary and valid part of the sociological enterprise.

At the same time it is quite true that some sociologists, especially in America, have become so preoccupied with methodological questions that they have ceased to be interested in society at all. As a result, they have found out nothing of significance about any aspect of social life, since in science as in love a concentration on technique is quite likely to lead to impotence. Much of this fixation on methodology can be explained in terms of the urge of a relatively new discipline to find acceptance on the academic scene. Since science is an almost sacred entity among Americans in general and American academicians in particular, the desire to emulate the procedures of the older natural sciences is very strong among the new-comers in the marketplace of erudition. Giving in to this desire, the experimental psychologists, for instance, have commonly nothing more to do with anything that human beings are or do. The irony of this process lies in the fact that natural scientists themselves have been giving up the very positivistic dogmatism that their emulators are still straining to adopt. But this is not our concern here. Suffice it to say that sociologists have succeeded in avoiding some of the more grotesque exaggerations of this "methodism," as compared with some fields close by. As they become more secure in their academic status, it may be expected that this methodological inferiority complex will diminish even further.

The charge that many sociologists write in a barbaric dialect must also be admitted with similar reservations. Any scientific discipline must develop a terminology. This is self-evident for a discipline such as, say, nuclear physics that deals with matters unknown to most people and for which no words exist in common speech. However, terminology is possibly even more important for the social sciences, just because their subject matter "is" familiar and just because words "do" exist to denote it. Because we are well acquainted with the social institutions that surround us, our perception of them is imprecise and often erroneous. In very much the same way most of us have considerable difficulty giving an accurate description of our parents, husbands or wives, children or close friends. Also, our language is often (and perhaps blessedly) vague and confusing in its references to social reality. Take for an example the concept of "class," a very important one in sociology. There must be dozens of meanings that this term may have in common speech—income brackets, races, ethnic groups, power cliques, intelligence ratings, and many others. It is obvious that the sociologist must have a precise, unambiguous definition of the concept if his work is to proceed with any degree of scientific rigor. In view of these facts, one can understand that some sociologists have been tempted to invent altogether new words to avoid the semantic traps of the vernacular usage. We would contend, then, that some of these neologisms have been necessary. We would also contend, however, that most sociology can be presented in intelligible English with but a little effort and that a good deal of contemporary "sociologese" can be understood as a self-conscious mystification. Here again, however, we are confronted with an intellectual phenomenon that affects other fields as well. There may be a connection with the strong influence of German academic life in a formative period in the development of American universities. Scientific profundity was gauged by the ponderousness of scientific language. If scientific prose was unintelligible to any but the narrow circle of initiates to the field in question, this was "ipso facto" proof of its intellectual respectability. Much American scholarly writing still reads like a translation from the German. This is certainly regrettable. It has little to do, however, with the legitimacy of the sociological enterprise as such.

Contents

PART 3

Dissent and Agreement in Society and Education

Contents

PART 4

Education in a Metropolitan Society

PART 5

Teaching as a Social and Professional Vocation

Contents

PART 1

The School
as an Institution of
the Culture

CONTEMPORARY EDUCATION: HISTORICAL PERSPECTIVE AND CONFLICTING VALUES

There are many avenues for viewing the schools as institutions not only in, but of the culture in which they operate. One obvious method of study to determine the respective roles of school and society is provided by history. An analysis and interpretation of past events from systematic and knowledgeable exploration of documents and artifacts can provide the student of education with a perspective of the school in contemporary society. One needn't study the relation of education to culture in ancient times to perceive the strong link of social factors to a socializing agency. Indeed, the understanding of modern education is not contingent upon a knowledge of prior attempts to enculturate the youth of a society, but surely the lack of historical perspective limits the vision of the student, the critic, and the defender of an educational system.

A study of schools in a cultural context over time indicates the close ties which have continually existed as societies have developed the means for formally transmitting their heritage. The intent of a society to perpetuate its traditions, mores, and values through a formal structure of education is well known to educational historians and to many who as students and teachers are acutely aware of this relationship.

Of course, informal education which existed prior to the establishment of schools, and which still accounts for a large share of educational effort in every culture today, is also demonstrably entwined with the values, mores, and traditions of a society. In America the child, prior to entering school, has learned a great deal about his culture. He is toilet trained; he understands that boys wear trousers; he uses knife, fork, and spoon; he believes his father to be the head of the house; he has developed specific material desires. These are cultural characteristics that have not been gained in formal schooling. It is much the same as it was in prehistoric and in early periods of history when the child learned from the parent to operate within the culture—as a berry-picker, a hunter, a cook, a fisherman. These skills were necessary to the culture and to the individual.

In recent and more complex times, the formalization of education as a social institution reflects the formalization and sophistication of contemporary society. Whether the school leads or follows society is a question to be analyzed as this text is used. In either case there is an indisputable school-society relationship which is expressed historically in the first reading in this section. Without dwelling on the detail of history, the reading shows the depth of confluence between the schools of American society and the values of that society at a period in time.

Following Lawrence Cremin's excellent setting for a view of contemporary education are two readings presented to approach the problem of values. Granting the close relationship of the school and society, the need to study the values of a society is an important part of a study of the schools of that society. The first of these readings on values is a broad, sweeping indictment of lack of consistent values and its resulting bewilderment; the second is a denial of absolutism in democracy. In each of these the search for values is apparent.

What does the search for values mean to an educational system? Are the schools heading from progressivism in social direction to relativism or beyond to nihilism? Is it a movement that is contrary to perennial education which is based on beliefs in absolutism and eternal truths? Can confusion and conflict in educational purposes be explained by confusion and conflict in social purposes, or have the schools created social bewilderment? These questions are worthy of considerable thought.

The Progressive Movement
in Education

Progressivism in American society has been a pervading influence during the twentieth century. The strength of the progressive movement has affected intellectual, political, economic, and social thought. By no means has progressivism been the only social theme, but it has been one of the most significant, if not the most embattled. The schools, as cultural institutions, have been involved in the thrust and parry of conflicting social ideas. The progressive movement in education has been the center of the greatest conflict in contemporary educational dialogue. Many selections in this text treat different aspects of this conflict in ideas. The first history of progressivism in American education is to be found in an outstanding book written by Lawrence Cremin and titled The Transformation of the School. *Cremin, a noteworthy educational historian whose previous works are standards in the field, has shown in his chronicle of the progressive move-*

*ment that a study of education has profound value for understanding a
culture.*

*In this selection from Professor Cremin's book, the story of progressive
education's general acceptance, its growing pains of dissension, and the
resulting crisis is told with clarity, sensitivity, and scholarliness. This story
lays the foundation for an understanding of contemporary American education and its cultural involvement.*

The Crisis in Popular Education

LAWRENCE A. CREMIN

There is a "conventional wisdom," to borrow from John Kenneth Galbraith,
in education as well as in economics, and by the end of World War II
progressivism had come to be that conventional wisdom. Discussions of
educational policy were liberally spiced with phrases like "recognizing individual differences," "personality development," "the whole child," "social
and emotional growth," "creative self-expression," "the needs of learners,"
"intrinsic motivation," "persistent life situations," "bridging the gap between home and school," "teaching children, not subjects," "adjusting the
school to the child," "real life experiences," "teacher-pupil relationships,"
and "staff planning." Such phrases were a cant, to be sure, the peculiar jargon of the pedagogues. But they were more than that, for they signified
that Dewey's forecast of a day when *progressive* education would eventually be accepted as *good* education had now finally come to pass.

The sources that document this view are legion: professional journals,
education textbooks, school board reports, and the various publications of
the Office of Education. Few are more significant, however, than a series
of pronouncements issued during the middle forties by the Educational
Policies Commission: *Education for All American Youth* (1944), *Educational Services for Young Children* (1945), and *Education for All American Children* (1948). Since its creation in 1936 the Commission had
spoken boldly and authoritatively as the responsible voice of the teaching
profession. Its membership in 1944 included the presidents of Harvard and
Cornell, along with such leading pedagogical lights as George Stoddard,
George Strayer, and Pearl Wanamaker; Commissioner John Studebaker
and his predecessor, George Zook, were advisory members. Anything these
people had to say would undoubtedly have been of interest, but their
formulations as members of the Commission took on added weight because

From *The Transformation of the School*, by Lawrence A. Cremin. Copyright © 1961
by Lawrence Cremin. Reprinted by permission of Alfred A. Knopf, Inc.

of the high prestige that body had come to command in the councils of American teachers.

The Commission's three volumes set forth a comprehensive blueprint of postwar education in Farmville and American City, both in the mythical state of Columbia.[1] The message of the analysis is clear. Americans must organize a comprehensive public school system concerned with all young people from the age of three through twenty, those in school as well as those outside. Public nursery schools in Columbia are followed by six-year elementary schools and then by eight-year secondary schools, organized as single units with three subdivisions: a junior high school, a senior high school, and a community institute. All these schools are unreservedly dedicated to the proposition that "every youth in these United States—regardless of sex, economic status, geographic location, or race—should experience a broad and balanced education which will (1) equip him to enter an occupation suited to his abilities and offering reasonable opportunity for personal growth and social usefulness; (2) prepare him to assume the full responsibilities of American citizenship; (3) give him a fair chance to exercise his right to the pursuit of happiness; (4) stimulate intellectual curiosity, engender satisfaction in intellectual achievement, and cultivate an ability to think rationally; and (5) help him to develop an appreciation of the ethical values which should undergird all life in a democratic society."

The nursery school, a unit defined as "an extension of educational services to include children too young for the customary reading program of grade one," is a regular part of the public school system, providing children with a supervised program of "work-play indoors and out." The youngsters experiment with clay, paints, and crayons, use simple tools, play and listen to the phonograph, and examine books and pictures. They dance and dramatize, explore the wonderland of nature and science, and make frequent trips to local stores and nearby farms. From the beginning they work at the business of learning how to behave as "participating members of a democratic group." The staff of the nursery school includes teachers, family life consultants, nursing and medical personnel, and mental hygiene and nutrition experts. Parents too, of course, play a central role in the program.

The elementary school strives toward "the discovery and full development of all the humane and constructive talents of each individual" at the same time as it nurtures "social responsibility and the cooperative skills necessary to the progressive improvement of social institutions." The staff works constantly at designing a curriculum to meet "the total needs of children." Not only the three R's, but physical well-being and mental health are prime educational responsibilities. Above all, both children and

---

[1] The Commission insisted that it was not drawing any blueprint but rather sketching "samples of the many different possible solutions to the problem of meeting the educational needs of all American youth." What emerged, though, was willy-nilly a blueprint.

teachers are freed from a "narrow and unimaginative daily routine." The description of a typical day at "Oak Hill School" is revealing. During the early morning the six- and seven-year-olds "play house" in an alcove, imaginatively recreating the life of the world they know, using a collection of child-sized toys, dolls, and furniture. Another group of younger children are in the midst of a project on animal life in the Oak Hill neighborhood, and use the time to answer questions aided by a variety of reference books. Several ten- and eleven-year-olds duplicate programs for a Neighborhood Night scheduled for the coming Friday. After the mid-morning break most of the children work individually or in small groups on arithmetic skills. Lunch hour means not only a nutritious meal but the eager pursuit of various committee responsibilities. In the afternoon there is reading, followed by a half-hour of physical activity, and then a final period of group work and community singing.

In Farmville's secondary school, a new consolidated school created through the union of five formerly independent school districts, some 800 boys and girls participate in a "common secondary program" from grades seven through nine, and a "partially differentiated program" from grades ten through fourteen—differentiated, that is, with respect to occupation, intellectual pursuit, and recreational interest. New courses have been worked out cooperatively by the Farmville faculty. For example, the tenth-grade offering in "The World at Work" not only acquaints students with the economic system in Farmville and American City, but also helps them "to become familiar with the facts about the chief occupational fields, among which their choices are likely to be made." And cutting across the whole program is a continuing concern with guidance, "personal assistance to individual boys and girls in making their plans and decisions about careers, education, employment, and all sorts of personal problems." Four special counselors give full time to such assistance, but the entire staff participates. Finally, a community institute provides continuing education and services, full-time or part-time, for those adults who desire them. Needless to say, the schools of American City, making due allowances for cultural and environmental differences, reflect many of the same emphases.

Supporting these educational services are a variety of local citizens' groups that help in the formulation of educational policy, an interested legislature willing to contribute a larger share of state tax funds to equalize educational opportunity, and, at the same time, a Congress ready to use federal money to neutralize vast inequalities among the states. The mistakes of the thirties, in which federal educational programs circumvented the schools rather than assisting them, are now past history. Local, state, and federal authorities work hand in hand at maintaining the schools as a bulwark of American democracy.

Education in the Commission's world of the fifties is patently the logical outcome of the progressive education movement. In effect, the Commission was projecting the "schools of tomorrow" that the United States might have if it was willing to buy the progressive dream. The Commission's pronouncements were discussed and checked with the American Vocational Association, the National Association of Secondary School Principals, the American Association of Health, Physical Education, and Recreation, the NEA's National Department of Elementary School Principals, and a host of individual experts in and out of the educational world. Once they appeared, they were quickly incorporated into education syllabi across the nation. In retrospect, there is little doubt but that they summed up as well as any contemporary publications the best-laid plans of the teaching profession for American education in the postwar decades.

The conventional wisdom, Galbraith tells us, is articulated at all levels of sophistication. At the highest level, that of scholarship, some novelty of statement or formulation is always encouraged, since the very vigor of minor debate preserves an aura of continuing criticism while effectively excluding any fundamental challenge. So it happened with progressive education after World War II. The movement had lost its intellectual vitality, but not its reformist thrust;[2] the presence of the one without the other resulted in a short-lived Alexandrian period in which refinements were elaborated one upon the other, but in which insistent realities were studiously ignored. What eventuated was a complex pedagogical mystique, mastered by the initiates but virtually incomprehensible to laymen concerned with the making of educational policy.

Of all the postwar refinements of progressive education—and they were legion, ranging from the preoccupation with group dynamics in the teachers colleges to the preoccupation with guidance in the schools—none achieved the publicity, or indeed the notoriety, of the so-called life-adjustment movement. The ill-fated effort originated in the activities of the Vocational Education Division of the United States Office of Education. Early in 1944 that Division undertook a study of "Vocational Education in the Years Ahead"; and as part of the usual regimen of committee and consultant activities, a conference was organized for May 31 and June 1, 1945, at the Wardman Park Hotel in Washington. For two days there was much talk about the problems of high school students whose needs seemed to be served neither by vocational nor by college-preparatory programs; and toward the very end of the sessions Dr. Charles Prosser, the able lobbyist of the National Society for the Promotion of Industrial Education

2 The clearest restatement of the progressive philosophy was John L. Childs: *Education and Morals,* Appleton-Century-Crofts, New York, 1950. The principal theoretical reformulations came in the works of Theodore Brameld and Isaac B. Berkson. For Brameld's assessment of the progressive education movement, see *Philosophies of Education in Cultural Perspective,* Holt, Rinehart & Winston, New York, 1955, Chaps. iv–vi; for his own "reconstructionism," see *Ends and Means in Education,* Harper & Row, New York, 1950 and *Toward Reconstructed Philosophy of Education,* New York, 1956. For Berkson's assessment of the progressive education movement, see *Education Faces the Future,* New York, 1943, Chaps. vi–xi; for his own reformulation, see *The Ideal and the Community,* New York, 1958.

who had subsequently gone on to head the Dunwoody Institute in Minneapolis, introduced the following resolution:

It is the belief of this conference that, with the aid of this report in final form [the report on "Vocational Education in the Years Ahead"], the vocational school of a community will be able better to prepare 20 percent of the youth of secondary school age for entrance upon desirable skilled occupations; and that the high school will continue to prepare another 20 percent for entrance to college. We do not believe that the remaining 60 percent of our youth of secondary school age will receive the life adjustment training they need and to which they are entitled as American citizens—unless and until the administrators of public education with the assistance of the vocational education leaders formulate a similar program for this group.

We therefore request the U.S. Commissioner of Education and the Assistant Commissioner for Vocational Education to call at some early date a conference or a series of regional conferences between an equal number of representatives of general and of vocational education—to consider this problem and to take such initial steps as may be found advisable for its solution.[3]

The resolution was unanimously adopted by the conferees.

Commissioner Studebaker was agreeable, and the Office of Education began to lay plans for the proposed series of conferences. Five regional gatherings were held between April and November, 1946, bringing together secondary school principals, school superintendents, state directors and supervisors of vocational education, representatives of state departments of education, administrators and professors of teacher education institutions, and officers of national professional associations. (No arts and science professors from the universities were included.) In all, thirty-five states and the District of Columbia were represented. It was the consensus of these regional conferences (1) that secondary education was "failing to provide adequately and properly for the life adjustment of perhaps a major fraction of the persons of secondary school age"; (2) that "functional experiences in the areas of practical arts, home and family life, health and physical fitness, and civic competence" were fundamental to any educational program designed to meet the needs of youth; (3) that a supervised program of work experience was essential for most high school youngsters; (4) that those entrusted with the education of teachers needed "a broadened viewpoint and a genuine desire to serve all youth"; and (5) that sufficient public interest could be mobilized to support a nationwide program of life-adjustment education. These propositions were brought before a national conference the following May, which recommended in turn that a Commission on Life Adjustment Education for Youth be created, and that a vigorous program be inaugurated to promote the purposes of life-adjustment education at the state and local levels. Commissioner Studebaker asked various professional associations to sub-

[3] United States Office of Education: *Life Adjustment Education for Every Youth* (Washington, n.d.), p. 15.

mit nominees for the Commission, and eventually a nine-member body was formed under the chairmanship of Superintendent Benjamin Willis of Yonkers.

From the beginning, the Commission saw its prime task as one of translating conventional progressive wisdom into contemporary educational practice. "National committees," stated an early report, "have been developing and extending basic theses for the past thirty years, and they have made progress in clarifying thought and securing consensus. It is the conviction of the Commission that there is available such a wealth of sound theory by which to achieve effective educational programs that at this time the great need is for action which translates the theory into school practice." Based on its own reading of these reports, the Commission defined its goal as an education "designed to equip all American youth to live democratically with satisfaction to themselves and profit to society as home members, workers, and citizens."

In spelling this out, the Commission reiterated most of the now time-honored phrases: life-adjustment education was concerned with "physical, mental, and emotional health," and with "the present problems of youth as well as their preparation for future living"; it recognized "the educational value of responsible work experience in the life of the community" as well as "the importance of personal satisfactions and achievements for each individual within the limits of his abilities." And as if in anticipation of the torrent of criticism that would later descend, the Commission noted that life-adjustment education "emphasizes active and creative achievements as well as an adjustment to existing conditions; it places a high premium upon learning to make wise choices, since the very concept of American democracy demands the appropriate revising of aims and the means of attaining them." But the disclaimer was of little avail. The terribly unfortunate choice of name—"life-adjustment education"—coupled with the unmistakable emphasis on adjustment *to* existing conditions, was more than enough to damn the movement in the eyes of a generation increasingly concerned with conformity in American life and thought.

The first Commission on Life Adjustment Education for Youth worked for three years, and turned in a report in 1951; a second Commission followed and issued its report in 1954. A study of these two documents reveals that aided by the Office of Education, the movement made substantial headway in school systems throughout the nation, and probably represented the most forceful thrust of progressivism at the secondary level. The first Commission sponsored a number of regional and national conferences; it initiated cooperative efforts with several influential organizations like the National Association of Secondary School Principals and the National Catholic Education Association; and it sponsored publications that were widely distributed by the Government Printing Office. Most important, perhaps, the Commission eagerly encouraged state and local effort, and by 1950 it could report a plethora of workshops, conferences, surveys, and pilot programs in public and private schools. (At least five of the 122 Roman Catholic diocesan school systems, for example, were reorganizing in light of "life-adjustment principles" during the 1949-50 academic year.)

The second Commission, enlarged to include representatives of the American Association of Colleges for Teacher Education, the National Congress of Parents and Teachers, and the National School Boards Association, also pressed ahead at the state and local levels, and its 1954 report devoted most of its space to describing the more effective programs to date. The report ended with a section on "unfinished business" that pointed to the need for continuing study and experiment. "One may conclude," the Commission contended, "that an enormous and necessary task undertaken during the 20th century is but half finished. This is the task of providing universal secondary education for all youth that they may live in a society which must make full utilization of scientific discovery. The speed with which this assignment is completed depends in part on the resources which the public through public funds, individually or through foundations are willing to devote to the unfinished business of providing education for all American youth."

No new commission was appointed in 1954, and no new funds were forthcoming, for the life-adjustment movement had come under sharp attack by the critics of progressive education. For all their fanfare, the two Commissions had come up with precious little in the way of original thinking or new programs; their self-appointed mission was propaganda and implementation. Yet at a time when the Progressive Education Association was rapidly disintegrating, the critics were undoubtedly accurate in their sense that here was the place to concentrate their fire. A fusillade of books and articles slammed into the various pronouncements of the Commissions, with devastating effect. The life-adjustment movement quickly disappeared, as much the victim of its own ill-chosen name as of the deeper attacks on its principles and practices.

The attack on the life-adjustment movement was no isolated phenomenon; it came rather as part of a much larger crisis in American education that had been brewing at least since the early 1940's. There were, to begin, the prosaic problems of buildings, budgets, and enrollments created by the war: few schools had been built since 1941; teachers had deserted the profession in droves; inflation was rampant; and the first of a flood of "war babies" began to enter the elementary grades as early as 1946. Then too, there were the multifarious difficulties associated with deepening public concern over communist expansionism at home and abroad. And finally, though perhaps less visibly, there were the voracious demands of an expanding industrial economy for trained and intelligent manpower. Any one of these in and of itself would have loosed fantastic pressures on the schools. Taken together, however, and compounded by a growing dissatisfaction among the intelligentsia, they held the makings of the deepest educational crisis in the nation's history. A spate of books, articles, pamphlets, radio programs, and television panels burst upon the pedagogical scene, airing every conceivable ailment of the schools, real and imaginary. One result was the most vigorous, searching, and fundamental attack on progressive education since the beginning of the movement.

The assault during the immediate postwar years was essentially continuous with the criticism of the early forties. Bernard Iddings Bell's book *Crisis in Education* and Mortimer Smith's polemic *And Madly Teach*— both of them published in 1949—furnish excellent examples.[4] Bell's stated intention was to disturb a "pseudopatriotic complacency" by asking to what extent American educational theory and practice were responsible for "the unsatisfactory state of our life and culture." His answer was a sweeping indictment of mass education for the perennial adolescence of the American people. The elementary schools had failed to transmit the elemental wisdom of the race; the high schools seemed far more interested in coddling young minds than in strengthening them; and the colleges, by surrendering to a vague utilitarian mediocrity, had deprived the nation of a humanely educated leadership. From kindergarten through the university, the school system suffered from misplaced emphases: it had taken over domestic functions that were properly parental, and it had excluded religion, without which education could have no ultimate purpose. To remedy these defects, Bell proposed a drastic series of reforms: teachers would have to be better trained, better paid, and better organized; educational opportunity would have to be extended by a vast program of scholarships; the school system would need to be thoroughly overhauled to remove wasteful overlap; parental responsibilities would have to be returned to parents; and religion would have to be given a central place in the curriculum, in publicly supported denominational schools if necessary.

At first glance, Smith's book seemed closely similar to Bell's. Carrying an introduction by Bell himself, it was a pointed attack on the principles and practices of "modern education." The writings of Dewey, the pronouncements of the Educational Policies Commission, and the Teachers College catalogue all came under Smith's pungent criticism. Not surprisingly, many of Bell's charges were reiterated: the schools had failed miserably in teaching the most elementary skills, and education itself had been systematically divested of its moral and intellectual content. But there were crucial differences as well; for whereas Bell sought to strengthen the teaching profession, Smith directed his ultimate indictment against it. He wrote: "... if anyone will take the trouble to investigate, it will be found that those who make up the staffs of the schools and colleges of education, and the administrators and teachers whom they train to run

---

[4] Bell wrote as an experienced educator; Smith wrote as a " 'layman and amateur' whose eyes were opened when he happened to serve as a member of a board of education in Connecticut."

the system, have a truly amazing uniformity of opinion regarding the aims, the content, and the methods of education. They constitute a cohesive body of believers with a clearly formulated set of dogmas and doctrines, and they are perpetuating the faith by seeing to it, through state laws and the rules of state departments of education, that only those teachers and administrators are certified who have been trained in correct dogma."[5] While Bell contended in his introduction that "the fault lies not in our pedagogues but in ourselves," Smith's plea was that parents rise up in righteous indignation against the pedagogues and insist on "education's historic role as moral and intellectual teacher." It was a plea destined to resound through discussions of educational policy for at least a decade.

In retrospect, the Bell and Smith books represented the intellectual thrust of a polyglot political movement that managed to gain considerable headway during the later 1940's. Yet citizens and educators alike remained only vaguely aware of what was going on until *This Happened in Pasadena* burst upon the educational scene early in 1951. Written by David Hulburd, a professional journalist, the book described the political demise of Willard Goslin, the progressive superintendent of Pasadena's progressive schools. President of the American Association of School Administrators, and widely respected among educators, Goslin had been forced out of one of the showcases of modern education by a vigorous coalition of citizens opposed to school taxes, radicalism, and progressive pedagogy. Hulburd's warning—and the warning of many who reviewed the book— was insistent: good education had been successfully subverted in one American community; it could happen in any American community; now was the time for all interested citizens to come to the aid of the schools. "Most of the people constituting Goslin's opposition," proclaimed the book jacket, "were well-intentioned and sincere, and quite unaware of their true roles in a calculated, far-reaching plot. Fantastic? It can't happen here? Read this book . . . It has happened here."

The notion of "a calculated, far-reaching plot" was quickly taken up by progressives, and became the leitmotif of their counterattack during the next few years. A rash of pamphlets and articles appeared directing attention to a new genre of ultra-rightist, frequently rabble-rousing citizens' group that had entered the arena of educational policymaking. Armed with charges of soft pedagogy, waste, and subversion, and cloaked with the mantle of superpatriotism, self-styled school improvement organizations like Allen Zoll's National Council for American Education and Milo McDonald's American Education Association were busily spreading the poison of pedagogical reaction in school districts across the nation. From Englewood, New Jersey, to Denver, Colorado, to Eugene, Oregon, the pattern seemed the same. A few citizens eager to keep taxes down would form a "school development council" and demand that "fads and frills" be

[5] Mortimer Smith, *And Madly Teach,* Regnery, Chicago, Ill., 1949, p. 7.

eliminated from the system. Under the aegis of the council, the community would be showered with leaflets proclaiming the evils of modern education. Mass meetings would be held demanding immediate action. Teachers would be intimidated and the board coerced. In the end, the victims would be the nursery school, the guidance program, the teacher workshop—and almost inevitably, community morale.

Whence the support for such efforts? Writing in the January, 1952, issue of *Progressive Education,* editor Archibald W. Anderson of the University of Illinois ventured an explanation. Local critics, he suggested, might be divided into two groups. One of these was composed of "honest and sincere critics" generally interested in public education. "Some of these critics take the trouble to keep themselves well informed about educational matters, are willing to work with the schools, *and generally favor the same lines of progress as the educators.* Such critics are not likely to join an organized attack." Others in this first group were generally well disposed toward public education but not so well informed. Their criticisms were usually "very specific in nature and based on some specific instances which they do not see in their total educational context." The second group of critics Anderson described as a motley assortment of "chronic tax conservationists," "congenital reactionaries," "witch hunters," "super-patriots," "dogma peddlers," "race haters," and last but not least, "academic conservatives."[6]

Anderson's explanation fit many of the facts, but not all of them; for he ignored the growing number of citizens who were taking the trouble to keep themselves well informed about educational matters, but who did *not* generally favor the same lines of progress as the educators. What was already apparent in 1952, and what became ever more apparent as the decade progressed, was the presence of a large and articulate public ready for educational reform of a nonprogressive variety. Dean Hollis L. Caswell of Teachers College put his finger on this phenomenon in his Steinmetz Memorial Lecture of May, 1952, when he laid the "plot theory" aside and contended instead that what was happening was not merely a subversive attack on the schools but rather a searching reappraisal of the whole philosophy of progressive education.

Events of the next few years generally bore out the Caswell thesis. The year 1953 brought Albert Lynd's *Quackery in the Public Schools,* Arthur Bestor's *Educational Wastelands,* Robert Hutchins's *The Conflict in Education,* and Paul Woodring's *Let's Talk Sense about Our Schools.* A year later Mortimer Smith published *The Diminished Mind.* The character of these volumes varied considerably, from Smith's uncompromising diatribe against life-adjustment education to Woodring's more moderate efforts at eclecticism; but all were fundamentally critical of progressive education.

[6] Archibald W. Anderson, "The Cloak of Respectability: The Attackers and Their Methods," *Progressive Education,* Vol. 29, 1951–52, pp. 69–70. Italics are authors.

Of the four, it was Bestor whose attacks were destined to exert the most telling impact on the progressive movement.

Bestor was an American historian who had taught for a number of years at Teachers College, Columbia, before going on to professorships first at Stanford and then at the University of Illinois. His criticisms of American education date from a 1952 article in *The American Scholar*, a piece on "Liberal Education and a Liberal Nation" that only vaguely foreshadowed the sharpness of subsequent writings. There followed a series of brilliantly polemical essays in *The New Republic, The Scientific Monthly*, and the *American Association of University Professors Bulletin* that ripped savagely into the theory and practice of the life-adjustment movement—and then in 1953, *·Educational Wastelands*. The book was widely reviewed and commented upon, both within the profession and without, and a revised and enlarged version was published in 1955 under the title *The Restoration of Learning*. Taken together, these writings constituted by far the most serious, searching, and influential criticisms of progressive education to appear during the fifties.

Bestor's general argument may be summed up under four broad headings: a theory of education, a conception of the historic role of the public school, a notion of the "great subversion" of American education, and a proposal for reform. In Bestor's view, the ultimate purpose of all education is intellectual training, "the deliberate cultivation of the ability to think." To think may not be the most important function in life, but it is the most important concern of the schools; likewise, intellectual training may not be the only function of the schools, but in the last analysis it is their *raison d'etre*. How is intellectual training given? Through the academic disciplines. These, Bestor argued, have developed historically as systematic methods for solving problems. To conceive of problem-solving apart from the disciplines is to abandon man's best hope for using systematic intelligence in confronting the difficulties that beset him. True education, then, is the deliberate cultivation of the ability to think through training in the basic academic disciplines: history, English, science, mathematics, and foreign languages.

The function of the public school, Bestor continued, is to give such a basic education to all citizens. Democratic education differs from aristocratic education only in the number of persons with whom it deals, not in the values it seeks to impart. To convert the education of the common man into something other than systematic intellectual training is to rob him of his birthright; it is to vulgarize culture under the guise of democratizing it. By training all in the ability to think, the schools distribute intellectual power widely among the people. This and this alone is their distinctive way of contributing to social progress.

The great subversion of American education, Bestor contended, had been the divorce of the schools from scholarship and of teacher training from the arts and sciences. The subversives were a powerfully entrenched "interlocking directorate" composed of professors of education, the school administrators they trained, and the state departments of education that required their courses for teacher certification. Bestor pointedly attempted to distinguish between the progressive education Dewey espoused, and that he himself had received at the Lincoln School, and the life-adjustment program he so sharply criticized; but there is no denying that his attack was ultimately on the whole progressive movement and the profession that had come to support it.

Finally, there was Bestor's threefold program of reform: first, the organization of a coalition of parents and liberal arts professors who would remove the schools from the control of the "interlocking directorate"; second, the redrawing of certification requirements to strengthen academic learning and deemphasize pedagogy; and, finally, the return of teacher training to the control of the larger university. Professional schools and departments of education had an important role as repositories of wisdom on the methods and techniques of pedagogy, Bestor granted; but it was the university as a whole that needed to determine and provide the proper education of a teacher.

It is interesting to note that in a little over half a century, Bestor had come full circle from the early progressives. Whereas Joseph Mayer Rice in the nineties had called upon the public to reform the schools by creating a new class of professionals who would manage education according to scientific principles, Bestor was now calling upon that same public to undo the damage of the professionals by returning the schools to the arts and science professors. And whereas Rice had railed against the narrowness and formalism of the curriculum, Bestor was now contending that the schools, in attempting to do everything, had ended up forsaking their own distinctive function: intellectual training. Thus swung the pendulum of reform.

For many reasons, Bestor's arguments found considerable support among the intelligentsia.[7] The academic community, long critical of goings-on in the department of education, was quite ready to blame the educationists for the crisis in the schools, particularly as the tensions of popularization began to affect the colleges. So, too, were the editors of *Life* and *U.S. News & World Report*. And so, too, was the public. When the Russians launched the first space satellite in the autumn of 1957, a shocked and humbled nation embarked on a bitter orgy of pedagogical soul-searching. "None of us is without guilt," wrote Admiral Hyman G. Rickover the following year. "But now that the people have awakened to

[7] A Council for Basic Education was founded in 1956 to advance the view that "schools exist to provide the essential skills of language, numbers, and orderly thought, and to transmit in a reasoned pattern the intellectual, moral, and aesthetic heritage of civilized man." *The Main Job of the Schools*, Washington, n.d. Arthur Bestor and Mortimer Smith were among the first directors.

the need for reform, I doubt whether reams of propaganda pamphlets, endless reiteration that all is well with our schools, or even pressure tactics will again fool the American people into believing that education can safely be left to the 'professional' educators.... The mood of America has changed. Our technological supremacy has been called in question and we know we have to deal with a formidable competitor. Parents are no longer satisfied with life-adjustment schools. Parental objectives no longer coincide with those professed by the progressive educationists. I doubt we can again be silenced."[8]

The surprising thing about the progressive response to the assault of the fifties is not that the movement collapsed, but that it collapsed so readily. True, the Progressive Education Association had never been able to recoup its fortunes after the war, and slid steadily downhill after 1947. True, too, the phrase *progressive education* had itself fallen into disfavor among professionals, though progressive ideas continued to command wide assent. But even so, one is shocked by the rapidity of the decline. Why this abrupt and rather dismal end of a movement that had for more than a half-century commanded the loyalty of influential segments of the American public? A number of reasons suggest themselves.

First, distortion. As frequently happens with social movements, success brought schism in the ranks. The pluralism of the nineties became the bitter ideological fragmentation of the thirties and forties. Factions developed, and within the factions cults, cliques, and fanatics. The movement became strife-ridden, given to bandwagon behavior, dominated by the feuding of minorities. The strife made headlines, and within these headlines lay the seeds of many a cartoon version of progressive education.

Second, there was the negativism inherent in this and all social reform movements. Like many protestors against injustice, the early progressives knew better what they were against than what they were for. And when one gets a true picture of the inequities of American schools during the half-century before World War I, he realizes they had much to be against; the physical and pedagogical conditions in many schools were indescribably bad, an effrontery to the mildest humanitarian sentiments. Yet, granted this, a protest is not a program. Shibboleths like "the whole child" or "creative self-expression" stirred the faithful to action and served as powerful battering rams against the old order, but in classroom practice they were not very good guides to positive action. At least the generation that invented them had an idea of what they meant. The generation that

[8] H. G. Rickover, *Education and Freedom*, Dutton, New York, 1959, pp. 189–90. Like Bestor, Rickover too had come full circle from the early progressives. Whereas they had argued that the national interest demanded an *extension* of the school's functions, he was contending that the national interest demanded a *contraction* of those functions. Both arguments tell us a good deal about the politics of American education and the kind of rhetoric it has traditionally stimulated. [Quotation used by permission of E. P. Dutton & Co., Inc.]

followed adopted them as a collection of ready-made clichés—clichés which were not very helpful when the public began to raise searching questions about the schools.

Third, what the progressives did prescribe made inordinate demands on the teacher's time and ability. "Integrated studies" required familiarity with a fantastic range of knowledge and teaching materials; while the commitment to build upon student needs and interests demanded extra-ordinary feats of pedagogical ingenuity. In the hands of first-rate instructors, the innovations worked wonders; in the hands of too many average teachers, however, they led to chaos. Like the proverbial little girl with the curl right in the middle of her forehead, progressive education done well was very good indeed; done badly, it was abominable—worse, perhaps, than the formalism it had sought to supplant.

Fourth, and this too is a common phenomenon of social reform, the movement became a victim of its own success. Much of what it preached was simply incorporated into the schools at large. Once the schools did change, however, progressives too often found themselves wedded to specific programs, unable to formulate next steps. Like some liberals who continued to fight for the right of labor to organize long after the Wagner Act had done its work, many progressives continued to fight against stationary desks in schools where movable desks were already in use. For some young people in the post-World War II generation the ideas of the progressives became inert—in Whitehead's sense of "right thinking" that no longer moves to action. Dewey in the very last essay he ever published on education likened these progressive ideas gone stale to mustard plasters taken out of the medicine cabinet and applied externally as the need arose. Other young people of this same generation simply developed different preoccupations, different concerns, different rallying points. The old war cries, whatever their validity or lack of it, rang a bit hollow; they no longer generated enthusiasm. Like any legacy from a prior generation, they were too easily and too carelessly spent; rarely perhaps were they lovingly invested in something new. In the end, the result was intellectual bankruptcy.

Fifth, there was the impact of the more general swing toward conservatism in postwar political and social thought. If progressive education arose as part of Progressivism writ large, it should not be surprising that a reaction to it came as a phase of Conservatism writ large. When the reaction did come, too many educators thought they would be progressives in education and conservatives in everything else. The combination, of course, is not entirely impossible, though it may well be intellectually untenable. John Dewey addressed himself to the point in *Characters and Events*. "Let us admit the case of the conservative," he wrote; "if we once start thinking no one can guarantee what will be the outcome, except that many objects, ends and institutions will be surely doomed. Every thinker puts some portion of an apparently stable world in peril, and no one can wholly predict what will emerge in its place." Dewey's comment, by the way, makes incomparably clear what he thought was progressive about good education, and gives the lie to a good deal of nonsense about his philosophy being anti-intellectual.

Sixth, there was the price the movement paid for its own professionalization; for given the political realities of American education, no program can survive that ceases assiduously to cultivate lay support. Progressives were undoubtedly right in contending that teachers needed to be better educated and better paid, and that professionalization would ultimately serve these ends. And they were right, too, in assuming that once teachers had been converted to their cause, half the battle would be won. But they committed a supreme political blunder during the thirties when they allowed the movement itself to become professionalized; for in the process the political coalition of businessmen, trade unionists, farmers, and intellectuals that had supported them in their early efforts was simply permitted to crumble. The resultant lack of nonprofessional support during the fifties was a crucial factor in the high vulnerability of the movement to widespread criticism of its policies and procedures.

Seventh, and most important, progressive education collapsed because it failed to keep pace with the continuing transformation of American society. The ultimate enemy of the conventional wisdom, Galbraith points out, is not so much ideas as the march of events. For the conventional wisdom accommodates itself not to the world that it is meant to interpret, but to the audience's view of that world. And since audiences tend to prefer the comfortable and the familiar, while the world moves on, the conventional wisdom is ever in danger of obsolescence.

The fact is that postwar America was a very different nation from the one that had given birth to progressive education. The great immigrations were over, and a flow of publications by David Riesman, William H. Whyte, Jr., Will Herberg, and others wrestled insistently with a redefinition of community.[9] The search for *Gemeinschaft* of the nineties had become the quest for pluralism of the fifties, while the rampant individualism that Dewey so earnestly feared was now widely applauded as nonconformity. The economy had entered upon an era marked by the harnessing of vast new sources of energy and the rapid extension of automatic controls in production, a prodigious advance that quickly outmoded earlier notions of vocational education. And new information was being generated at a phenomenal pace, thrusting to the fore the school's traditional responsibility for organizing and transmitting knowledge of every sort and variety.

Most fundamental of all, perhaps, the continued advance of the mass

---

[9] See for example David Riesman *et al.*, *The Lonely Crowd*, Yale University Press, New Haven, 1950; William H. Whyte, Jr., *The Organization Man*, Doubleday, New York, 1956; Will Herberg, *Protestant-Catholic-Jew*, Doubleday, New York, 1955. For Riesman's "counter-cyclical" theory of education, see *Constraint and Variety in American Education*, University of Nebraska Press, Lincoln, Neb., 1956, Chap. iii.

media, the proliferation of social welfare agencies under public and quasi-public sponsorship, and the rapid extension of industry-sponsored education programs—the "classrooms in the factories" that Harold Clark and Harold Sloan labelled the real pedagogical revolution of the time—had literally transformed the balance of forces in education.[10] Whereas the central thrust of progressivism had been expansionist—it revolted against formalism and sought to extend the functions of the school—the central effort of the fifties was rather to define more precisely the school's responsibilities, to delineate those things that the school needed to do because if the school did not do them they would not get done. It was this problem more than any, perhaps, that stood at the heart of the argument over educational priorities that dominated the citizens' conferences of the decade.

Granted this, however, and granted the collapse of progressive education as an organized movement, there remained a timelessness about many of the problems the progressives raised and the solutions they proposed. John Dewey once wrote in the Preface to *Schools of To-Morrow*: "This is not a text book of education, nor yet an exposition of a new method of school teaching, aimed to show the weary teacher or the discontented parent how education should be carried on. We have tried to show what actually happens when schools start to put into practice, each in its own way, some of the theories that have been pointed to as the soundest and best ever since Plato, to be then laid politely away as precious portions of our 'intellectual heritage.'"

However much progressive education had become the conventional wisdom of the fifties, there were still slum schools that could take profitable lessons from Jacob Riis, rural schools that had much to learn from the Country Life Commission, and colleges that had yet to discover that the natural curiosity of the young could be a magnificent propellant to learning. Glaring educational inequalities along race and class lines cried out for alleviation, and the vision of a democracy of culture retained a nobility all its own—Lyman Bryson restated it brilliantly in *The Next America* (1953), a book that never received the attention it deserved. As knowledge proliferated, the need to humanize it only intensified;[11] while the awesome imminence of atomic war merely dramatized the difference between knowledge and intelligence. Finally, the rapid transformation of the so-called underdeveloped nations lent new meaning and new urgency

[10] Harold F. Clark and Harold S. Sloan: *Classrooms in the Factories*, Institute of Research, Rutherford, N.J., 1958. Martin S. Dworkin has written perceptively about the educational impact of the modern film in a number of critical essays; see especially "The Family of Man," *Fundamental and Adult Education*, X (1958), pp. 177–80, and a review of *Films in Psychiatry, Psychology, and Mental Health* in the *Teachers College Record*, LVI (1954–5), pp. 50–52.

[11] I am using the term as James Harvey Robinson used it in *The Humanizing of Knowledge*, George H. Doran Co., New York, 1923, to indicate the need to reorder, restate, and resynthesize new knowledge so that the average person can understand it.

to Jane Addams's caveat that "unless all men and all classes contribute to a good, we cannot even be sure that it is worth having"—the point was compellingly made in C. P. Snow's widely read lecture, *The Two Cultures and the Scientific Revolution* (1959).

The Progressive Education Association had died, and progressive education itself needed drastic reappraisal. Yet the transformation they had wrought in the schools was in many ways as irreversible as the larger industrial transformation of which it had been part. And for all the talk about pedagogical breakthroughs and crash programs, the authentic progressive vision remained strangely pertinent to the problems of mid-century America.[12] Perhaps it only awaited the reformulation and resuscitation that would ultimately derive from a larger resurgence of reform in American life and thought.

The Reconsideration of Educational Values

The suggestion of moral decay as a result of loss of direction or values by a society can be traced throughout written history. The dynamics of man and of society propel the society into consideration and reconsideration of its values, and each revaluation poses some threat to an existing value system. The obvious reaction is for the values of an earlier time to appear more solid and the moral structure to appear more stable. Thus, the alteration of values, although a constant occurrence, is viewed with skepticism. This is not to suggest that all value change is improvement, but only to describe an interaction of values which leads to the bewilderment described in the following article by Professor Ginsberg.

The portrayal of moral bewilderment posed in this selection is basically a concern of philosophers who attempt to analyze the problems of relativism and absolutism. The problem has importance, however, for the social sciences and for education in several areas, including decisions on the type of school which fits a morally bewildered society. Professor Ginsberg expresses the confusion between the search for absolute answers to social-scientific questions and the relative nature of answers acceptable to science through nonvalue empirical studies.

A totalitarian society is readily adapted to a firm set of common values.

[12] Despite the sharpness of the assault on progressive education, public opinion polls revealed a good deal of latent public support for the progressive program.

Can an open society justify a single-value system? On the other hand, without some basic accepted values, can a society avoid moral decay, or at the least, moral bewilderment? Or, are the conflicts and tensions resulting from moral bewilderment necessary to a thriving and viable culture? Even without attempting answers to these broad and significant questions, the student of education is confronted with educational bewilderment over values. The schools as implementing agents for a society necessarily transmit the overriding values of that society. If there is moral bewilderment in social direction, the schools suffer in like manner. The dilemma between absolute and relative values in society, in knowledge, in the social sciences, and in education is an increasingly complex and important consideration in contemporary times.

Moral Bewilderment

MORRIS GINSBERG

A hundred years ago Auguste Comte attributed the troubles of his day to what he called "intellectual anarchy" that is, the lack of any agreement on the fundamental principles of political and social action. He drew attention to the fact that the greatest measure of agreement was to be found in those spheres in which the stage of positive science had been reached. This was not the case in dealing with social problems. Hence a state of mental confusion, "half conviction and half will," a condition in which men, in Guizot's phrase, "will feebly but desire immensely" and in which in consequence, they become the ready victims of political quackery and illusion.

In the twenties of this century, in a very different setting from that in which Comte was writing, similar complaints or diagnoses were frequently made. In Germany the decay of Western civilization was propounded elaborately by Spengler and others, and in many other countries also the peoples of Western Europe were alleged to be suffering from decay, moral and intellectual. In politics there was growing skepticism regarding the efficacy of democratic forms of government. The arts, it was alleged, reflected a sense of the aimlessness of existence and the futility of ideals. The buoyant belief in science and in its power to give a complete explanation of the structure of the world, which had characterized the nineteenth century, was weakened, it was argued, by the increasing influence of the idea that all knowledge was relative. On like grounds the claims of

Reprinted from *Social Forces*, Vol. 34, October, 1955, pp. 5–10, by permission of the publisher, University of North Carolina Press, Chapel Hill, N.C.

religion and morals to absolute validity were challenged and believed to be seriously shaken.

Just now we are going through a similar phase. We are told on all sides that we have lost the sense of direction, that the world is torn by irreconcilable ideologies, that there is moral decay, a lack of zeal and alertness, lack of confidence in their future and in the future of civilization, among the masses of the people, and that the intellectuals are suffering from what the French call a sort of "moral Hamletism," a state of irresolution, in which "conscience makes cowards of us all."

Comte, it will be remembered, attributed the intellectual anarchy of his day to two things, the failure of the social sciences to attain the stage of positive knowledge, and the "dispersive" effect of the division of labor in the sciences, or, in other words, the excessive specialization which makes it impossible for any one to obtain a general or over-all view of the problems with which mankind is confronted.

These difficulties persist and are even greater than in Comte's time. The gaps between the natural sciences and the social sciences remain and many would say are unbridgeable. If the social sciences are to be judged by the degree of agreement among their exponents, they would seem to be very far from having reached the positive stage. The opinion is even gaining ground that the assumption that social phenomena are subject to laws analogous to those which govern the processes of nature, upon which the positivist conception of sociology was based, was fundamentally mistaken, and that the two spheres of knowledge call for different kinds of insight and interpretation. The evils arising from excessive specialization in their application to our own times have been powerfully described by A. N. Whitehead, whose words I should like to quote:

> The dangers arising from this aspect of professionalism are great, particularly in our democratic societies. The directive force of reason is weakened. The leading intellects lack balance. They see this set of circumstances, or that set, but not both sets together. The task of coordination is left to those who lack either the force or the character to succeed in some definite career. In short the specialized functions of the community, are performed better and more progressively, but the generalized direction lacks vision. The progressiveness in detail only adds to the danger produced by the feebleness of coordination.[1]

It remains to be added that the progress of knowledge itself from which Comte expected so much has brought with it its own dangers and perplexities. The growth of communications has brought the peoples of the world nearer to one another politically and economically, but it has also produced the result that a disturbance at any one point has repercussions which may be quickly felt everywhere else. Again advances in technology

[1] A. N. Whitehead, *Science and the Modern World,* The New American Library of World Literature, New York, 1948, p. 276.

have enormously increased the rate at which areas can be urbanized and industrialized. On the other hand, our knowledge of psychology and sociology is as yet too slight to enable us to secure the necessary adjustments in social institutions and habits of life. The result is an increase of restlessness and nervousness which is a danger to the communities involved and to the rest of the world. Rapidity of urbanization and industrialization was by all accounts one of the most important factors affecting the mentality of modern Germany. The industrialization and urbanization now occurring in hitherto underdeveloped areas of the world may well have similar results. Finally, the development of weapons of mass destruction has led to a terrifying concentration of power which now threatens the entire structure of civilization. In all these ways and no doubt many others, science has brought with it its own problems.

These reflections suggest a number of very difficult questions. Is there any evidence of a general moral decline or decay? Are the differences now dividing mankind moral in character? If so, are they important or are they only reflections of a struggle for mastery between rival powers, in itself strictly amoral? If the moral differences do count what precisely do they consist in, and where is the dividing line to be drawn?

Charges of general moral decay are, I think, always to be taken *cum grano salis*. Every age has had its Jeremiad, and if they are all to be believed, mankind has been steadily getting worse since the days of Hesiod and should by now be without a vestige of goodness. The scale of wickedness and the means at its disposal have undoubtedly grown to terrifying dimensions. But has not the scale of goodness similarly grown? The barbarities of modern warfare are obvious enough. But has not the experience of the world wars brought to light the existence of astonishing powers of devotion, readiness for self-sacrifice and indomitable courage and endurance, in millions of ordinary men and women all over the world? Difficult as it may be to balance gains and losses, there seems but little evidence for the view that the men and women of our generation are particularly lacking in moral fiber.

Are the conflicts of our time strictly amoral, a struggle for power utterly indifferent to moral values and using the moral appeal only to disguise the real motives at work? This is the view of those who pride themselves on being "realists"; but it is not borne out by the facts. No doubt the mass movements of our time give power maniacs their opportunity and the havoc they work is terrifying. But equally dangerous are the moral fanatics who are so convinced of the righteousness of their cause and its supreme value that all ordinary moral considerations are brushed aside and who thus destroy morality in the name of morality. Neither type can get very far without the capacity to inspire devotion. The capacity again sometimes rests, no doubt, on nonmoral qualities, but in the main it relies on moral sentiments. In the Nazi propaganda, appeal was constantly made to justice, fairness, reasonableness. Communist writings abound in uncontrolled and savage moral condemnation; they are inspired by and seek to inspire a relentless hatred of tyranny and injustice. They know that people will not in the long run be ready for extreme sacrifices unless they are convinced that right is on their side. The moral factor is thus, to put it mildly, not negligible.

Is the appeal then to one and the same set of moral principles or values, or is there a fundamental divergence in moral outlook? That there is such a divergence is widely held, though there is much difference of opinion about its precise nature. According to some the division is between those who attach ultimate value to the individual and those who attach ultimate value to the community. According to others the difference is between those who accept a universalist morality binding on all mankind and those who believe that moral rules are relative. Others again think that the difference is not about ultimate ends but about the way in which ends and means are related in the shaping of policy.

On the purely theoretical level, the alignment indicated by these distinctions is far from clear. In theory, communist writers will certainly deny that they reject the values of individual personality: they will maintain, as socialists have always done, that their ultimate aim is the liberation of the individual. Nor is there any logically necessary connection between totalitarianism in politics and relativism in ethics. Relativist theories have been used in defense of both democratic and totalitarian rule. Again in theory communist philosophers deny that in their view the end justifies the means always and without qualifications. Means and ends are, as they put it, in the Hegelian jargon, dialectically interdependent and therefore, again in theory, the means adopted must be such as not to distort or corrupt the end aimed at. They would thus agree with "bourgeois" philosophers that in any evaluation of policy ends and means must be considered together.

Is there then no moral difference? I think there is, but it has its roots not so much in a difference of theory regarding ultimate ends as in what I should describe as a difference of moral temper and above all in ideological differences in the analysis and interpretation of the facts.

I can best describe what I mean by a difference of moral temper by contrasting the liberal with the totalitarian type of mentality. The liberal mind is characterized by an abhorrence of fanaticism, a greater readiness to count the cost in terms of human happiness and human lives, a profounder awareness of the corroding and demoralizing effects of violence both on those who employ it and those who suffer from it. The totalitarian, on the other hand, in whatever camp he may be found, is single-minded and fanatical, moved to desperation by the inertia of the masses and the dilatory habits which he associates with the liberal spirit. Above all the totalitarian ignores the distance between the final end he sets himself, which though in fact vague and cloudy, is to him vivid and compelling, and the means which are needed to bring it about. The result is that the means turn into ends, power comes to be sought for its own sake, and as usual, grows by what it feeds on. The final end then tends to be pushed farther and farther into the future, whilst it is represented at the same time as just round the corner, given sufficiently thorough and drastic action. In this way, ordinary moral standards are set aside. The substance of morality is destroyed in the supposed service of an apocalyptic good, and the barriers against arbitrary power are broken down in the name of freedom.

The root of the trouble is to be found, if this analysis is on the right lines, on the one hand, in a species of moral fanaticism and, on the other, in a distorted interpretation of the relevant facts, which in turn leads to a further distortion of the moral judgment. As a result of moral fanaticism the end sought is transfigured into an ideal so lofty that by comparison all ordinary moral ideals fade into insignificance. In these circumstances the moral issues are obscured. The ultimate ends sought, in fact obscure, are psychologically compelling. The means become all important and are pursued fanatically without any consideration of their relevance to the ends. Under the influence of this moral fanaticism the facts are distorted and provide food for further intensified fanaticism. It is taken as established that the end *can* be attained by violent revolution and that it is the *only* method by which it can be attained. It is assumed that the interests of the social classes are irreconcilably opposed and that the classless society can be attained and can only be attained by revolutionary, that is violent, means. Ordinary moral standards then become inapplicable, and the operative code is that of war. Does this involve a conflict of ideologies between the communists and their opponents? Clearly, the answer is "yes." Does the conflict involve a difference of moral outlook? The answer again must be "yes," though the difference turns ultimately on a difference in the interpretation of the facts.

This applies also, I think, to the international situation. Here also moral judgments are affected by sociological theories of the dynamics of social development. The most plausible hypothesis seems to be that apart from the possible influence of some power maniacs, those who are concerned with the making of policy in the U.S.S.R. are influenced by the belief that a conflict between them and the capitalist world is, in accordance with Marxist doctrine, inevitable. It follows that in the interest of self-defense they must have control over the neighboring countries and that they must draw within their orbit more distant areas likely to support them in the coming struggle. It is easy to see how in this way, communist faith and the policy of expansion fuse, so that it is difficult to distinguish between them. The belief that a war between the communist states and the rest of the world is inevitable, soon passes into the belief that the world is already at war. The lofty morality of the classless age is relegated to the millennium; the interim ethic of the class struggle is called into action and this justifies everything that is required by revolutionary tactics and strategy.

Thus, the moral conflicts involved rest in part on conflicting interpretations of the facts and the predictions based on them.

I have argued above that there was no evidence of any general moral decay. The conflict of ideologies which I have just briefly analyzed, however, shows that there is a good deal of moral bewilderment. It seems to me important to sort out the different forms of this bewilderment or malaise which is by no means confined to the particular issues involved in the struggle between liberal democracy and totalitarianism.

This moral malaise is not yet quite articulate, yet certain elements in it can, I think, be discerned and disentangled by analysis. In the first place there is an uneasy feeling which arises from the difficulty of applying the highly general principles taught by the great religions or formulated by the philosophers to the immensely complicated problems of modern life. A wide gulf separates such a principle as, say, "love ye one another" and the principles which should govern, say, the distribution of property or the treatment of criminals. The ultimate principles may be accepted in theory, but the disagreement about the secondary or tertiary principles which are needed to give them concrete expression makes it easy for the former to remain at a safe level of abstraction or else to be used in defense of contradictory policies.

Consider as an example the attitude of Christianity to war. There is not one but several views about war all of which claim to be Christian. There is, first, the view—of ancient standing—which considers all war to be sinful. There is a second view early formulated by St. Augustine and later by Aquinas and adopted in the main by the Protestant churches, which distinguished between just wars and unjust wars. On this view further important differences of opinion naturally arise as to the criteria to be used in distinguishing between just and unjust wars. There is, thirdly, the view of those who think that normally it is the duty of the Christian to obey the orders given to him by a duly constituted authority and that, therefore, if he is commanded to fight, then fight he must, though some authorities would admit that even so, individuals may feel justified in refusing, if they are convinced that the fighting is in a wrong cause. In a conference of Christian churches held at Oxford in 1920, the difficulties of the problem were felt to be overwhelming and were in the end taken as a sign of the sins in which the members of the Church were implicated. There are similar perplexities in recent discussions of atomic warfare. These difficulties are not peculiar to Christianity. They arise equally in respect of the teaching of other great religions or for that matter of philosophical ethics. The distance between the categorical imperative, the principle of the greatest happiness and the problems of modern political and social organization is too great for people to see the connections between them. The principles may not be denied, but they remain ineffectual and this cannot but generate a feeling of uneasiness.

A second source of moral malaise is to be traced to the tendency to confuse questions of fact with questions of value. It is sometimes thought that it is easier to get agreement about facts than about values. But this is often not the case. A wrong sense of values may lead to a distorted view of the facts and conversely ignorance or distortion of the facts may generate false or distorted moral judgments. Examples of this were given above in the analysis of the conflicts of ideologies between totalitarianism and liberal democracy. But there are plenty of examples from other spheres of social life as in discussions about sex equality or race equality, in which the distortions of relevant fact are as difficult to remove as the divergence in moral outlook. The result of this confusion of facts and values is that people often think they differ about ethics, while in all probability the root of the difference lies in the obscurity or complexity of the relevant facts. In this way a skeptical attitude about ethics is generated which might perhaps be dispelled on a fuller or more penetrating analysis of the sources of disagreement.

A third tendency which appears in many forms is a manifestation not so much of moral skepticism as of moral fanaticism. But fanaticism and skepticism are near akin and the fanatic is often the man who hunts his own doubts in the doubts of others, or who attaches himself to some one who can decide for him and free him from hesitation and irresolution. The trouble with fanaticism is its ready association with violence, its intolerance of opposition, its impatience with the liberal methods of eliciting consent by persuasion and argument. We have already seen that from one point of view the problem of the use of violence raises the general problem of the relation between ends and means, and I have a feeling that here the moral perplexities of our time are felt most acutely. In what circumstances and for what ends is the use of force justified? Can we distinguish between just and unjust rebellions as we can distinguish between just and unjust wars? These are problems of great difficulty which must for long continue to be a source of bewilderment to the reflective mind.

A fourth source of perplexity at the present time has its origin in the discrepancy between public morals and private morals. The ordinary man must be greatly puzzled when he finds statesmen justifying acts which in the relations between individuals would be condemned. Is there one morality for states and another for individuals? Is there such a thing as justice among nations and how is it related to justice among individuals? The ordinary man is told that he is responsible for what statesmen do in his name, but a person is only responsible when he knows what he is doing and whether what he is doing is right or wrong. The question arises whether the ordinary individual can ever know enough of the forces at work to form an intelligent estimate of the consequences likely to follow from the course of action recommended by those acting in his name. Then there is the further question whether there are any generally agreed principles to guide him in his choice and if there are whether he is in a position to apply them intelligently to the highly complex problems of world politics. In dealing with these difficulties it is no wonder that the ordinary man is often led to accept the view, by no means confined to the cynical and disillusioned of our generation, that politics and morals have nothing to do with one another, or that if there is a morality of state action, it cannot be the same as the morality governing the relations of individuals. Doubts such as these tend to shape the whole structure of morals.

Finally the bewilderment is intensified by the use made of the moral appeal in modern propaganda. Marxist propaganda is generally infused with passionate moral idealism: it owes its success to the appeal which it makes to the sense of justice. Yet in the same breath it proclaims that morals like religion are just an opiate for the people, designed to inculcate submission to the powers that be. The contradiction was even more blatant in Nazi and fascist propaganda. There was continual talk of justice, righteousness and reasonableness, whilst in the same breath the fundamental principles of humanity and justice were derided and rejected. Equally disconcerting is the effect of war propaganda. In war, both sides claim to be fighting for the highest ideals, and whilst in the midst of war most people come to feel that right is on their side. The political disillusion that follows wars is, however, only too apt to raise doubts which during a war are latent or suppressed. The slogans that were inspiring during a war then strike us as insincere, as spiritual traps to catch the unwary. The "realist" then tends to dismiss what is described as the "moralistic" approach to politics, and this by an easy transition raises doubts whether there are universally valid ethical principles at all.

Comte thought that the remedy for the intellectual anarchy of his day was to be found in what he called positive knowledge. Positive science would overcome the limitations of the specialists, give us an all-round view of the world and at the same time provide us with an ethic which would define the goals or ends to be aimed at. Nowadays we are not so sanguine. It is only too obvious that knowledge can be used for evil purposes and that this applies to the social as much as to the natural sciences.

Furthermore, I doubt whether Comte's view that positive science can of itself yield an ethic would now gain wide acceptance. It is difficult to see how statements of what ought to be can be derived from statements of what is, has been, or is coming to be. Social science cannot, it seems to me, take the place of social philosophy. Yet taken together they ought to make it possible for us to get clearer insight into the nature of the disagreements that divide men. Political differences are sometimes alleged to turn on difference of views regarding the basic values of life, or the fundamental principles of justice. Nevertheless, supporters of this position are hard put to it when challenged to define the differences with some precision. That conservatives want freedom without welfare, socialists welfare without freedom, and communists neither freedom nor welfare are statements that each might make about the others, but hardly about themselves. Analysis might show that there is much more agreement about primary valuations than is commonly thought. But as we have seen there is much confusion and bewilderment about the secondary principles which are needed to mediate the transition from first principles to the detail of life. This is further increased by confusion between questions of fact and questions of values, by the difficulty of foreseeing the consequences of human interactions in large scale societies or grasping the complicated relations of ends and means involved in the shaping of policy.

It is perhaps reasonable to hope with Comte that the growth of positive knowledge in the sphere of human relations would help in reducing the area of disagreement or at least in giving fuller insight into what the disagreements are about. From this point of view ethical thought stands to gain from the development of the social sciences. But the problems involved cannot be resolved by the social sciences alone. There is needed in addition philosophical analysis designed to bring out the latent assumptions underlying the divergencies of outlook and to inquire how far they can be reconciled or transcended. Whether any fundamental divergencies will remain when the facts have been clarified and the ideals elucidated remains to be seen. The rationalist assumption is that ideals like facts come within the scope of rational inquiry and that we must proceed in the hope that sufficient agreements can be reached in those spheres at least which call for collective action.

Democracy and Educational Purpose

This short treatment of the dilemma of absolutism and relativism in a democracy presents the opinion that a fixed democratic ideology is an internal contradiction. It would follow that the search for an official educational ideology in the democracy Professor Kaplan supports would be equally contradictory. Educational purpose may rest in the same greatness of journey—the continuous pursuit of freedom—described in this article.

On the compass of democratic civilization and its corollary educational system, are there any fixed points? If there are, who decides them and who accepts them? If there are none, is there no set direction for the schools? Social values, as diverse and perplexing as they are, are a necessary consideration of the student of education.

The Great Journey

ABRAHAM KAPLAN

For some time Americans have been expressing concern over what is felt
to be a loss of national purpose, and there are desperate pleas for its
recovery. People ask: How can we exercise leadership of the free world
if we have nowhere to lead it? How can we appeal to the uncommitted
nations to join our side if we cannot say *what* side it is beyond the fact
that it is ours? Our enemies know where they are going and they know
how to get there; we are groping and unsure. How can we hope to win?

Many Americans, though not convinced that the end of the world is at
hand, nevertheless anxiously await the apocalyptic moment when our fate
will be revealed once for all. Outside the backyard shelters and the vigilante hideouts, we search for a sign in which to conquer. To meet the challenge of Communism, it is said over and over again, we must make of
democracy a faith as unshakable as theirs: we need not choose between
red and dead, but if we have no absolutes of our own the choice will not
be ours to make.

I have never been persuaded by this logic. An official democratic ideology is a contradiction in terms. Only the totalitarians can have a mission. If this puts us at a disadvantage we must meet it head on. Democracy
does not and cannot have a commitment to an absolute goal. It is a *way*
of arriving at social policy and not a fixed set of social arrangements. The
liberty provided by democratic institutions is a form to which content can
be given only by the free spirit of the individual citizen. A belief is rational, not because it embodies a truth—for who is to say?—but because it
was rationally arrived at.

Such freedom does not come cheap, and rationality has its price. It is
the price paid by medicine to quackery and by science to superstition.
The other side claims to cure everything and to explain everything, while
we can present only something piecemeal and provisional. Democracy cannot offer any guarantees. To live with democracy a man must have the
courage to put at stake his life, his fortune, and his sacred honor for something less than an ironclad absolute.

We must look, not to the Day of Judgment, but to the issue of the day;
not to ultimate destinations, but to the next step we are to take. The
ideology we confront has the appeal of a full-color travel folder—and as

Reprinted from *Saturday Review*, Vol. 24, December 23, 1961, p. 26, by permission of
the publisher and author.

little worth. There is no need for us to produce an alluring picture of our own. What is needed is no picture but a map, a map to show us and all the world where we are and what roads lie open before us. Statesmanship is equated with vision; in democracy it is the vision not of a predestined end but of the greatness of the journey.

The clamorous search for national goals does not stem from democracy's loss of purpose but from our loss of faith in its citizens. We are characters in search of an author, while the greatness of the drama lies just in this: that the characters themselves take over the plot. Democracy means that you carry no banner but your own.

The leadership that is ours to give—to other countries or in our own— can mean nothing to those who want only to follow. If we do have a mission to proclaim, it can only be that man is the master of his own fate— regardless of history or the Bomb, armies or governments, leaders or ideologies. We need not search for values that will sell to those nations who are still in the market to buy; we are not dedicated to the dream of a world rich and creamy with a homogenized goodness of American manufacture. Our dedication is to a world where no man is a stranger or afraid, because he knows it as a world of his own making.

The real disadvantage which we suffer from the Communist ideology is the disadvantage of life as it confronts the death that stalks it. Once dead always dead, but to survive one bout with death means only to prepare for the next. A people that has fallen to Communism has lost its freedom irrevocably; a free people must struggle endlessly to preserve its freedom. Nothing we can do will solve this problem for us once for all; we must simply learn to live with it. Not to *solve* our problems, but to cope with them and survive for the next—that is our task. What we need is not a mission, but the courage to do without. What we need is to believe in ourselves.

CULTURE, NATIONAL
CHARACTER, AND EDUCATION

The term *culture* has many facets. It is often used to denote enlightened or refined taste acquired by intellectual and aesthetic training, hence, the cultured person. It also is used in a scientific sense to describe the environment and growth of certain substances as in mold cultures. The referent used in this section is more inclusive than exclusive. It includes the total man-made environment. Social institutions, traditions, mores, artifacts, interactions, taboos, tools, and all other mental and physical phenomena attributable to man are a part of culture as used herein. It is this usage which incorporates a popular education system, its teachers, its pupils, its textbooks, its critics, its problems, its peer groups, and other forms of subcultures.

There is no doubt that inquiry into the nature, function, and operation of culture as related to individuals within it has high social and personal value for any member of that culture. The realization that cultural influences on personality are great is important to anyone undertaking to understand himself. Beyond that, the need for students of education to perceive the interrelation of man and culture as a means for understanding behavior of students, administrators, parents, peer teachers, and the school in the social setting is apparent.

A cultural pattern includes roles portrayed by its members with generally limited variance. To paraphrase Shakespeare, the world is a stage—the culture the play, its members the players. It is the inquiry of the behavioral sciences that attempts the description of cultures. One of the most important aspects of this description is an analysis of the life style of individuals in the culture. The values of a culture as manifested in the beliefs, attitudes, and behaviors of persons of that society may be studied in a number of ways. Objective, firsthand descriptions of physical occurrences; analyses of rituals, writings, and cultural artifacts; introspective descriptions of feelings and attitudes; comparison and contrast studies from the viewpoint of an alien culture are all means by which culture and life style can be presented. Major themes, as revealed in national-character studies, are another way of providing insight into cultural patterns.

There is disagreement as to the value of pursuing national-character studies. Indeed, Oliver Goldsmith in the eighteenth century decried the tendency to describe national character as a provincial and limited-version approach to understanding man. Yet, as some of the articles in this section show, national character is a topic of interest in contemporary times. Is there a national character? How does a description of national character assist or hinder an understanding of a culture? What does national character mean for education? Does national character lose its descriptive power and become prescriptive over a period of time?

This section is structured to view initially two ways of describing cultural values by analysis of national character. Both rely on observations of the American scene made by those who are not directly involved in it, but each takes a different form of inquiry—one supports a position, the other uses pure description. It has been suggested that a prime characteristic of Americans is a love of character analysis. As the first two selections demonstrate, national-character descriptions abound. The third treatment gives a clear picture of the use of the schools to develop a national character based on selected cultural values. The final piece presents the problems of a Western European cultural tradition in terms of sickness, diagnosis, and potential remedy.

Public Education and

National Character

If you were asked to propose the two major cultural themes in America, what would they be? Would you agree with the two stated in the following article by Seymour Lipset?

The themes are presented and discussed in light of modern education. Mass education is shown as a positive influence in the establishment and continued development of dominant cultural values. The family as another social institution is given credit for the propagation of equalitarian and achievement-motivated values in American society. The influence of national wealth and its relation to the life styles of affected individuals is viewed as a means of distinguishing between European and American class structures.

One of the most interesting problems in modern society and education is that presented by mass culture. A later section of this text treats the subject more fully, but Professor Lipset poses the predicament of a culture which values and strives to improve common man, yet is the heir to and believer in some attributes of elite societies. Education, the means by which a society is mass or elite in orientation, is directly involved in this cultural value conflict. Is the conflict detrimental to the society? Not according to the concluding lines of the following article.

Constant Values in American Society

SEYMOUR M. LIPSET

It seems to me that in many areas of American society there has been less change over the past century than many people believe.

I do not mean to imply that our society is basically static. Clearly, there have been great changes—industrialization, bureaucratization, and urbanization—which have profoundly affected other aspects of the social structure. There have been changes in work habits, leisure, personality, and family patterns. But concentration on the obvious social change in a society that has spanned a continent in a century and moved from a predominantly rural to a metropolitan culture tends to obscure what has been relatively constant and unchanging.

Two basic values, equalitarianism and achievement, are dominant in American culture, and they are now as they have been in the past expressed in various institutional structures. Though they have certain contradictory features, neither seems to be weakening. The value equalitarianism still largely determines the nature of our status system; and, in spite of dire predictions that the growth of large corporations has meant a decline of upward mobility and a consequent fall in achievement motivation, American society is still characterized by a high level of actual achievement in the population as a whole.

EQUALITARIANISM

The feature of American life which most impressed the foreign travelers in the 19th century was the way in which Americans behaved toward each other. A summary of the writings of hundreds of British travelers in America before the Civil War reports:

> Most prominent of the many impressions that Britons took back with them [between 1836 and 1860] was the aggressive egalitarianism of the people.[1]

Reprinted from *Children*, November–December, 1959, U.S. Department of Health, Education and Welfare, Social Security Administration, Children's Bureau, by permission of the publisher and the author.

[1] Max Berger, *The British Traveller in America, 1836–1860*, Columbia University Press, New York, 1943.

Frances Trollope, visiting in America in 1830, complained about the "coarse familiarity, untempered by any shadow of respect, which is assumed by the grossest and the lowest in their intercourse with the highest and most refined."[2]

In 1837 Harriet Martineau, a sympathizer with republican institutions, found the same phenomenon but evaluated it quite differently:

Nothing in American civilization struck me so forcibly and so pleasureably as the invariable respect paid to man, as man.[3]

Similar observations were made by the two best-known foreign commentators on 19th century society, Alexis de Tocqueville and James Bryce.

What impressed the typically upper class European travelers in the past has also deeply affected the high status Europeans who have come to America in recent years. One observer has commented:

With his deep sense of class and status, integration in American society is not easy for the émigré. . . . I met several young Croatian doctors in the Los Angeles area who were earning $25,000 to $35,000 a year, but still felt *declassed*.[4]

An eminent sociologist at one of the leading universities in the Communist world when asked at a private gathering what in America most surprised him as compared with his expectations replied without hesitation: "Equality. There just is no country in Europe, Communist or capitalist, in which men treat social inferiors with as much respect, and in which inferiors show as little fear of those higher than themselves."

The strength of equalitarianism may be seen in the internal structure of many other institutions such as the family and the school. For example, reports of pre-Civil War British travelers were almost unanimous in commenting on unique patterns of the American family in terms which read like contemporary analyses:

The independence and maturity of American children furnished another surprise for the British visitor. Children ripened early. . . . But such precocity, some visitors feared, was too often achieved at the loss of parental control. Combe claimed that discipline was lacking in the home, and children did as they pleased. . . . The child was too early his own master, agreed Mrs. Maury. No sooner could he sit at a table than he chose his own food; no sooner speak than he argued with his parents. Bad as this might be, countered Thomson, American children were still far more affectionate and respectful towards their parents than was true in British poor or middle-class families. Children were not whipped here, but treated like rational beings.[5]

[2] Frances M. Trollope, *Domestic Manners of the Americans*, Howard Wilford Bell, New York, 1904.

[3] Harriet Martineau, *Society in America*, Vol. 3, Saunders and Otley, London, 1837.

[4] Bogdan Raditsa, "Clash of Two Immigrant Generations," *Commentary*, January, 1958.

[5] Berger, *op. cit.*

Harriet Martineau's report on child rearing in Andrew Jackson's day also sounds contemporary:

My friend observed that the only thing to be done [in child rearing] is to avoid to the utmost the exercise of authority, and to make children friends from the beginning. . . . They [the parents] do not lay aside their democratic principles in this relation, more than in others. . . . They watch and guard: they remove stumbling-blocks: they manifest approbation and disapprobation: they express wishes, but, at the same time, study the wishes of their little people: they leave as much as possible to natural retribution: they impose no opinions and they quarrel with none: in short, they exercise the tenderest friendship without presuming upon it. . . . the children of America have the advantage of the best possible early discipline; that of activity and self-dependence.[6]

What struck Harriet Martineau as progressive was interpreted differently by Anthony Trollope:

I must protest that American babies are an unhappy race. They eat and drink just as they please; they are never punished; they are never banished, snubbed, and kept in the background as children are kept with us.[7]

Another Englishman's description of New York schools in 1833 also has a contemporary ring:

The pupils are entirely independent of their teacher. No correction, no coercion, no manner of restraint is permitted to be used. . . . corporal punishment has almost disappeared from American day schools; and a teacher who should now have recourse to such means of enforcing instruction would meet with reprehension from the parents, and perhaps retaliation from his scholars.[8]

This emphasis on equalitarianism as a dominant feature of American values and behavior, past and present, is seemingly contradicted by the widespread existence of status differences. The American value system has never denied existing differences in rank and authority. But as Alexis de Tocqueville and others noted, Americans believe that such differences are accidental, not essential attributes of man, which it is not good taste to emphasize publicly.

ACHIEVEMENT

Achievement, as a dominant value, shown by Americans' efforts to improve their lot in life and by the belief that the most able should be rewarded by high position, is also strongly rooted in American society. It

---

[6] Martineau, *op. cit.*

[7] Anthony Trollope, *North America*, Alfred A. Knopf, New York, 1951.

[8] Isaac Fidler, *Observations on Professions, Literature, Manners, and Emigration, in the United States and Canada, Made During a Residence There in 1832*, Wittaker, Treacher, and Co., London, 1833.

may, in fact, be a necessary concomitant of the stress on equality. Thus Americans as compared to Europeans are more willing to acknowledge their lowly origins. This enables the man of humble birth to regard upward mobility as an attainable goal for himself or his children; while it has fostered in existing elites the persuasion (however mistaken) that their eminence is the result of individual effort.

Though there does not seem to be more social mobility in the United States than in Western Europe, in America the modest social origins of men of prominence are given widespread publicity, while comparable backgrounds in Europe are more likely to be conveniently forgotten. A [1950] study of social mobility in France reports that "it is precisely among those who have experienced the greatest social mobility that reticence [in the interview] may be of the most significance."⁹ Similarly, British corporation directors have been found to be less likely than American executives to report menial jobs in their career histories.

But even in a completely egalitarian society, only a few can reach the top of the ladder. What is more important for the average person are his experiences with and consequent perception of more modest opportunities for social mobility: the extent to which he sees sons of manual workers and poor farmers becoming teachers, government officials, engineers, clerks, and businessmen.

The most constant source of social mobility throughout American history has been the recurrent waves of mass immigration which over the years brought the depressed strata of other lands to fill vacancies at the bottom of the social structure, thus enabling native-born Americans to rise. The early pre-Civil War foreign travelers in America were struck with the fact that "it was left to the free Negro, the Irish immigrant, and to a lesser extent the Chinese 'coolie' (in California) to be the hewers of wood and the drawers of water."¹⁰

If the immigrants felt aggrieved with their position in the New World, their lot was materially better than it had been in Europe, so that they could think of their situation as an improvement even though they were at the bottom of the social ladder in this country.

If mass immigration has contributed to the existence of widespread social mobility and the perpetuation of the American value system, then it may be asked why its ending after World War I did not reduce mobility, and give rise to a native American working class which would have less faith in the "promise of America." The answer probably lies in two factors: (1) the changing character of the occupational distribution, as more of the total labor force is employed in higher paid and higher status white-collar, professional, and managerial positions; (2) the replacement of immigration from Europe with migration to the industrial centers from

⁹ Marcel Bresard, "Social Mobility and Size of the Family," *Population*, July–September, 1950.
¹⁰ Berger, *op. cit.*

"underdeveloped" parts of this continent—of Negroes, Puerto Ricans, Mexicans, French Canadians, and "poor whites" from the rural South.

These ethnic groups, which comprise over 20 million people, earn a disproportionately low share of the national income; they have little political power, and no social prestige. Many of them live in ethnic neighborhoods and have little social contact with native white Americans higher up on the social scale. The recent "flight" of middle-class whites from cities to suburbs is but a recent example of a longtime pattern of similar flights from areas of immigrant settlement. The only difference today is that color as well as ethnicity is involved.

As in the past, there are now two working classes in America, an upper skilled level composed largely of native white Americans, and a lower less skilled one composed largely of Negroes, Mexicans, and Puerto Ricans. The social and economic cleavage between them diminishes the chances for the development of solidarity along class lines.

Despite the deprivations experienced by immigrants and minority groups, thus far each group entering the system has been able to move up. In late 19th century America there was a strong occupational differentiation between Catholics and Protestants. Catholics were largely immigrants in manual occupations, while Protestants were mostly native born and thus in relatively high status jobs. But today Catholics whose families have been in this country for three generations show no difference in occupational structure as a group than white Protestants of comparable background.

While the Negroes, Puerto Ricans, and Mexicans have a long way to go to achieve the status of descendants of European immigrants, there is evidence that they too are on the road upward economically as well as legally and socially.

CONSEQUENCES OF NATIONAL WEALTH

The emphases on equality and achievement in the American value system have been perpetuated by our increasing national wealth.

Through industrialization and advancing technology America in the latter part of the 19th century became the wealthiest country in the world, a position it has never relinquished. Between 1869 and 1953, per capita income (standardized to 1929 prices) rose from $215 to $1,043. As the size of the national income has increased the distribution of consumers' goods has tended to become more equitable. This in turn has considerable effects on patterns of class relations.

Gideon Sjoberg has pointed out that with increasing national wealth has come a great gain in the income of manual workers relative to the incomes derived from many middle-class occupations. And he argues that with a rise in relative income status manual workers have achieved a rise in social status as well. The status difference between skilled manual workers and at least the lower sections of the middle class has become less well defined, since manual workers like middle-class people have been able to purchase goods which confer prestige on the purchaser—clothing, cars, homes, and television sets.[11]

Such improvements in income and style of life undoubtedly help to preserve the belief in equality of opportunity. A manual worker who can buy his own house, or a new car, will feel that he has moved up in the world even though he has not changed his occupational position.

To some Europeans, different classes mean distinct ways of life with little overlapping of the goods they own or can afford to purchase, even though in many European countries rates of individual mobility across class lines may be quite high. The greater the inequities, the more the upper classes have the need for a rationalization of their claim to privilege. In part, this need becomes resolved by a value system which defines the lower classes as congenitally inferior and worthless.

In America, by contrast, the mildness of differences in distribution of consumers' goods enables the wealthy and poor alike to see differences among the classes as relatively unimportant, reflecting differences in rewards for greater ability or luck, and encourages many to feel that they can improve their lot.

EFFECTS OF MASS EDUCATION

The strong and continuing interest of Americans in equality of opportunity is perhaps nowhere as vividly expressed as in the constant pressures to expand educational opportunities. Since the winning of the fight for free public schools before the Civil War, there has been a steady growth in school attendance at primary, secondary, college, and adult levels. By 1954 more than half of all high school graduates continued their education. Today about 1 in 4 of those in the college age group (18 to 21) are attending college, compared to 1 in 25 in 1900.

Today college teachers are not only the fastest growing major profession, but now far outnumber lawyers, physicians, dentists, clergymen, and military officers. These data belie the contention that Americans are not willing to pay for education. In fact, the percentage increase of expenditures on education by American consumers in the period from 1935 to 1948 was far higher than the percentage change in all other categories of consumer expenditure.

In providing opportunities for education America far outranks every country in the world. This means that a large proportion of our young people have the formal prerequisites to achieve the highest positions in

[11] Gideon Sjoberg, "Are Social Classes in America Becoming More Rigid?" *American Sociological Review*, December, 1951.

society. Over 30 percent of college students in the United States are the sons of manual workers.

The gradual equalization of educational opportunities in America has reduced the previously marked discrepancy between the educational attainments of manual and nonmanual workers. Today high school graduation has practically become the working-class norm.

Mass education has also had effects on the quality of education. The notion is common today that the strictness of past educational methods resulted in a superior output. But present-day students do as well or better than past generations on comparable examinations in the same subjects even though the schools have been serving increasing proportions of students from lower cultural backgrounds and of less intellectual aptitude.

Mass education has also resulted in raising the level of taste and culture among the population. Recent years have brought an extraordinary rise in the sales of classical records, a growth of "serious" radio stations, a shift in paperback book sales from "lowbrow" to "highbrow" literature, and the emergence of more than 100 literary magazines, 1,100 community symphony orchestras, and much greater numbers of little theater groups.

Sociological and public opinion research indicate that education is also a liberalizing force which may be bringing about increasing national consensus on questions of public policy, since increased education is highly correlated with support for equal rights for ethnic minorities and civil liberties for dissident political views.

CHANGE IN FAMILY PATTERNS

The theory that our society's dominant values continue to be equality and achievement are supported by certain patterns and trends in family life: the relative weakness of parental authority; child-centeredness (reflecting the orientation toward future achievement); a decline in the "double standard" of sexual behavior; the growth of equality in husband-wife relations; the ever increasing proportion of married women who work. However, some recent changes in family behavior do not seem to confirm this assumption, at least within the family.

Perhaps the most surprising change is the rise in the birth rate. Demographic experts had expected in the later postwar years a continuation of the long-term decline in the birth rate which has been characteristic of all developed industrial societies. The crude birth rate had jumped from a low of 16.6 per 1,000 in 1933 to 25.8 in 1947, reflecting the deferred "demand" of the war years. But instead of dropping sharply from this high figure as was anticipated, birth rates have continued to run at about 25.0 during the past decade.

The earlier decline in the birth rate had been explained in part by the thesis that since the intimate obligations of family relations hold people back in occupational success, there will be a strong tendency in an achievement oriented society to restrict the family to the smallest possible unit consistent with the performance of the major function of producing and socializing the young. The "baby boom" of the fifties does not fit into this thesis. Perhaps, the earlier pattern of restricted family size involved serious strains which induced a reversal of the trend, for a solitary family group provides the social intimacy and psychic security needed for personal stability. Moreover, increasing wealth and the fact that movement up industry's bureaucratic ladder does not require the accumulation of personal savings have lessened the conflict between occupational and family requirements in middle-class families.

Demographically speaking, the recent increase in fertility has been produced by a number of factors: Americans are getting married at younger ages, more people are marrying at some time in their lives; the number of families having three and four children has increased.

Birth rates have increased more among the better educated groups than among manual workers. While the lower status groups are still producing more children than the middle classes, higher status individuals are contributing a much larger share of today's offspring than they did in the past. A study made during the depression found that among families who deliberately planned for each child a large family size was correlated directly with higher income, occupational status, and education.

The trend toward a more familistic culture in the United States is also reflected in the stabilization of divorce rates. In 1900 there were 4 divorces for every 1,000 married women over 15. Although by 1946 this rate had climbed to 17.8, there has been a steady decline in the divorce rate since the peak reached at the end of the war. This had fallen to 9.2 in 1957, still the highest for any major country in the world but almost down to prewar levels. [It has stabilized at around 9.5 since 1957.]

BY-PRODUCTS

Many problems in American life which are the source of considerable anxiety and controversy may actually be concomitants of an egalitarian and achievement orientation. For example, the same patterns of status distinction which some people regard today as evidence of the decline of equalitarianism were reported by various foreign travelers in the 19th century. Some of these observers regarded Americans as more status conscious than Europeans and suggested that this was the result of a lack of a well-defined deference structure in which there is no question about social rankings.

The great concern with family background (which generation made the money?) that observers from Harriet Martineau to Lloyd Warner have shown to be characteristic of parts of American society may be a reaction to the feelings of uncertainty about social position engendered in a society whose basic values deny anyone the legitimate right to claim higher status by birth than his neighbor.

The problem of conformity which so troubles many Americans today has also been noted as a major aspect of American culture by observers from Alexis de Tocqueville to David Riesman. Such analysts have repeatedly stressed the extent to which Americans are sensitive to the judgments of others. Never secure in their own status, they are concerned with "public opinion" in a way that aristocrats do not have to be. Harriet Martineau almost seems to be paraphrasing Riesman's own description of today's "other-directed" man in her picture of the early 19th-century American:

> Americans may travel over the world, and find no society but their own which will submit [as much] to the restraint of perpetual caution, and reference to the opinions of others. . . . where the youth of society determines in silence what opinions they shall bring forward, and what avow only in the family circle . . . and where elderly people seem to lack almost universally that faith in principles which inspires a free expression of them at any time, and under all circumstances.[12]

In a situation of "status anarchy," when people are encouraged to struggle upward, but in which there are no clearly defined reference points to mark their arrival and where their success in achieving status is determined by the good opinion of others, this kind of caution and intense study of other people's opinions is natural.

A society which emphasizes achievement and which resists status claims based solely on ancestry must necessarily be a society in which men are sensitively oriented toward others. And precisely as we become more equalitarian, as more people are able to take part in the status race within the large industrial bureaucracies of the impersonal metropolises, so we become more American in the Tocquevillian sense.

The same point may be made in regard to much of the discussion about the negative consequences of mass culture. Increased access by the mass of the population to the culture market necessarily means a leveling of cultural taste as compared with a time or a country in which only the well-to-do and the well-educated have access to the creators of culture. The "Americanization" of European culture, which disturbs so many European intellectuals, may reflect not the power of American dollars but rather the Americanization of the class structure of Europe.

Many in this country who believe in equalitarianism would also like to secure some of the attributes of an elitist society. Today perhaps we need to remember the maxim that you cannot have your cake and eat it too. You cannot have special public schools for the elite in a society which stresses equality; you cannot produce for a cultural elite without regard to public opinion and mass taste in a society which emphasizes the value

[12] Martineau, *op. cit.*

of popular judgment; you cannot have a low divorce rate and an end to differentiation in the roles of the sexes; you cannot expect to have secure adolescents in a culture which offers no definitive path from adolescence to adulthood.

But we are not necessarily in a vicious circle. In fact, there is considerable evidence to suggest that higher education, greater economic security, and higher standards of living result in strengthening the level of culture and democratic freedom. The market for good books, good paintings, and good music is at a high point in American history. There is evidence that tolerance for ethnic minorities is also at a high point. More people are receiving a good education in America today than ever before. Many people, to be sure, buy good paintings, records, books, or well-designed furniture in order to "keep up with the Joneses," but this means that their children will grow up in homes in which good taste is part of the environment.

I would like to emphasize again what most of the foreign travelers to 19th-century America took for granted: that this country has been the most radical Nation on earth in terms of social relationships. American cultural radicalism consists of breaking down the barriers of class, of inherited background, and opening the doors of real culture to the entire population.

I do not predict a coming egalitarian and cultural utopia. Some of our values will always turn out to be incompatible. As we cope with various problems, we create others. But problems and conflict and even despair are the lifeblood of democracy.

An Analysis of American Culture

The great interest we Americans have in seeing ourselves as others see us, coupled with the sometimes perceptive, always provocative, analyses of the American character that noted foreign travelers delight to engage in, has produced a flood of descriptions of the nature of American life styles. Certainly, one of the first inquiries made of visitors to any region is, "What are the people like?" Character studies based on sense impressions of a very limited sampling of people, organized case studies of selected individuals, comprehensive statements based on longitudinal studies using behavioral-science methods of observation, or detailed perusal of the arti-

*facts of a society, make available a wide variety of information which can
be studied for common threads and obvious divergencies. Perhaps the
areas of general agreement by foreign observers of the American society
present some accurate measure of American character. The following
analysis of literature about Americans is an attempt to show these dominant cultural themes.*

   *How much of the following is an accurate portrayal of the American
character as you have experienced it? Which of these themes are dominant
today? Of the themes, which have important connotations for the classroom teacher? Several contradictions appear in the themes presented. Are
these reconcilable? Should the schools make a conscious effort to recognize
and to encourage or discourage any of the themes described?*

American Cultures Themes: An Analysis
of Foreign Observer Literature

WILLIAM TORRENCE
AND
PAUL MEADOWS

The general purpose of this paper is to present a thematic analysis of the
observations of American culture by certain foreign observers. Specifically,
this study identifies, by means of a given definition, prevailing culture
themes of American society selected from the works of these foreign observers.

   It is, of course, a commonplace that the task of culture analysis becomes
more complicated when one turns to the more industrialized, heterogeneous national societies. A suggestion to meet this problem has been advanced by Opler. He asserts:

   In every culture are found a limited number of dynamic affirmations, called
themes, which control behavior or stimulate activity. The activities, prohibition
of activities, or references which result from the acceptance of a theme are its
expressions. Such expressions may be formalized or unformalized. Limiting factors, often the existence of other opposed or circumscribing themes and their
extensions, control the number, force, and variety of a theme's expressions. The
interplay of theme and counter-theme is the key to the equilibrium achieved in a
culture, and structure in culture is essentially their interrelation and balance.[1]

Reprinted from *Sociology and Social Research,* Vol. 43, September–October, 1958,
pp. 3–7, by permission of the publisher.
   [1] Morris E. Opler, "Themes as Dynamic Forces in Culture," *American Journal of
Sociology,* No. 51, p. 198.

It is proposed here to examine a sample of foreign traveler literature in terms of the preceding suggestion of culture themes. Such an investigation represents, it must be pointed out, a type of culture analysis. Two very general approaches are available for use in the content analysis of any given media. These are the a priori and the a posteriori departures. According to McGranahan, the a priori approach is one "which sets up logical categories (of culture characterizations) in advance." The a posteriori approach is one "which derives categories from the specific material examined."[2] The latter method has been chosen for this study. The frame of reference used in establishing the a posteriori categories has been suggested by Opler's definition of culture themes as previously noted. The specific categories of analysis were obtained by induction from the culture theme assertions of these foreign observers. These culture theme assertions constitute the collected data of this study.

Eleven foreign traveler reports were consulted.[3] Initially, in the case of each book every statement considered to be within the scope of culture themes as defined above was abstracted from the text. For example, from Andre Siegfried's *America Comes of Age* there are these assertions:

Organization appeals to the American, for he loves teamwork and cooperation with machinery. He is perfectly at home wherever it is possible to use machinery, and if he is aware that his excessive division of labor limits his personal interest in the final achievement, he does not seem to regret it.[4]

The themes were then examined in order to determine the presence of similarities; these made possible a tentative list of classes of themes. At this point the "sort" was examined for overlapping, ambiguities, and misfits. The final classification thus derived and elaborated and offered below is not regarded as definitive but only as tenable because empirical; it is an inductive, derivationally a posteriori classification.

The class (a) is given first in the summary that follows and is italicized; after the class statement the codal summary (b) appears.

[2] Donald V. McGranahan, "Content Analysis of the Mass Media of Communication," in M. Jahoda, M. Deutsch, and S. Cook, editors, *Research Methods in Social Relations: with Especial Reference to Prejudice*, Part Two, *Selected Techniques*, The Dryden Press, New York, 1952, p. 554.

[3] The eleven reports were: Hilaire Belloc, *The Contrast* (1924); Paul de Constant, *America and Her Problems* (1915); Walter L. George, *Hail, Columbia* (1921); Geoffrey Gorer, *The American People* (1948); Hermann Keyserling, *America Set Free* (1929); Wyndham Lewis, *America and the Cosmic Man* (1949); Hugo Munsterberg, *The Americans* (1904); Lucien Romier, *Who Will Be Master, Europe or America?* (1928); Andre Siegfried, *America Comes of Age* (1928); Peter Vay De Vaya, *The Inner Life of the United States* (1908); Tingfang Wu, *America, Through the Spectacles of an Oriental Diplomat* (1914). A survey was made of reviews written by American authors about these books. Of 88 critiques, approximately three fourths were favorable toward them.

[4] Andre Siegfried, *America Comes of Age*, Harcourt, Brace & World, New York, 1928, p. 152.

I. (a) *Americans love practicality.* (b) Theory is discounted by Americans; intellectual activities seem inconsequential; only self-expression in tangible ways is acceptable.

II. (a) *Mechanization, organization, and efficiency appeal to Americans.* (b) Cooperative or organized effort is a good thing per se; the mechanical is prized; the machine is the embodiment of impersonal control.

III. (a) *Americans insist on standardization.* (b) If it can't be mass produced, it loses its appeal; unity and uniformity are equated; conformity is prized above creativity.

IV. (a) *Americans prefer individualism and freedom from authority.* (b) It is displayed in the repugnance felt toward authority, which is regarded as per se bad, in the fear or contempt for holders of authority.

V. (a) *Americans are fond of bigness and quantity.* (b) Americans love excess, power, superlatives, size, headlines; quantity is a measure of achievement; monopoly is admired though resented.

VI. (a) *Americans demand competitive effort.* (b) America is the land of new chances; American qualities are products of competition, status should be competitively earned, unearned status is scorned.

VII. (a) *Some superior-inferior relationships are acceptable.* (b) Isolationism reflects disdain for the rest of the world; customers are properly objects of deception; Americans accept or assume the authority of American civilization.

VIII. (a) *Americans admire productivity.* (b) Trade and industry are admired because they are productive; production sets a premium on all things; (production) takes priority over all things.

IX. (a) *Americans prize creature comforts.* (b) Americanism is equated with goods; tangible gain is a supreme goal; acquiring goods leads to no further drives, no other motivations are really necessary.

X. (a) *Americans love to moralize their economic interests.* (b) Moral values are abstract terms, attached freely and dogmatically to concrete realities; the business frame of reference is the social frame of reference; exploitation of resources is legitimized into terms of civic value.

XI. (a) *Work is regarded as of moral value.* (b) Worklessness is embarrassing and immoral; work is a value in itself; unworked-for status is despised.

XII. (a) *The achievement of wealth is held to be a test of worth.* (b) Wealth is a path to distinction; wealth is equated with superiority; the greater the wealth, the greater the achievement.

The reader will have noted that each of the major classes of culture themes covers, within each class, a range of theme statements. It was thought that a subgrouping of theme statements within each class would prove to be a useful method of further summarizing the observations of these foreign observers. In other words, it was hypothesized that modalities could be established within each class, just as modalities, in the form of major classes, had been established for the entire collection of culture themes. This, as a phase of the study, was done.[5]

Next, the rank-order distribution of the theme classes and the original numbering of the theme classes (in Roman numerals and in parentheses), followed by the frequency of each class, appear below:

1. Americans prefer individualism and freedom from authority (IV), 76.
2. Some superior-inferior relationships are acceptable (VII), 39.
3. Americans love to moralize their economic interests (X), 32.
4. The achievement of wealth is held to be a test of worth (XII), 26.
5. Americans demand competitive effort (VI), 25.
6. Americans insist on standardization (III), 23.
7. Work is regarded as of moral value (XI), 18.
8. Mechanization, organization, and efficiency appeal to Americans (II), 17.
9. Americans love practicality (I), 17.
10. Americans are fond of bigness and quantity (V), 13.
11. Americans prize creature comforts (IX), 12.
12. Americans admire productivity (VIII), 9.

It would be too much to expect of any report of a modern culture that it be free from contradictions and conflicts in the material reported. Even a casual examination of the culture themes which our foreign observers have noted will locate major disagreements among the themes of American culture. Because of these disagreements, the authors have sought to present some of the more obvious contradictions as follows: (1) conformity versus autonomy, (2) egalitarianism versus inegalitarianism, (3) antiracism versus racism, (4) American superiority versus American protectionism, (5) materialism versus antimaterialism, (6) isolationism versus intervention.

On the basis of the study, it appears that culture themes may, by using the definition advanced by Opler and certain of the methodological tools used in content analysis, be identified in a sample of foreign observer literature. There were 307 culture theme assertions identified in the works of the eleven foreign observers selected for this study. It was possible to sort this group of culture theme statements into 12 general classes. Each general class was conceptualized in terms of similarities of statement. Finally, it proved to be possible at this point to determine subcategories of culture themes within each general class. This subcategorization developed 36 distinct subclasses. It seems, therefore, that the general methodology of content analysis, with the refinements posed in this study,

---

[5] Because of space limitations the 36 subcategories are not presented here. Interested readers can secure copies by writing to the authors. It should be understood, however, that this identification of intraclass modalities does not involve the assumption of a continuum of culture theme statements within each class; instead, the identification involves only clusters based upon obvious similarities.

can be used as a method of identifying culture themes in literature dealing with American or other culture phenomena.

Some definite future research projects appear feasible on the basis of the present study. Thus, content analysis, using the theme as the dimensional unit, can be applied to the material of native American writers in order to determine the extent of agreement or disagreement with the theme assertions found in this study. In addition, a desirable investigation involves the construction of a precoded or uncoded questionnaire or interview schedule followed by a fielding of such an instrument in order to determine, among a representative sample of Americans, the extent of their acceptance or rejection of the theme assertions found in this study. Such a fielded instrument would, without question, disclose many other culture themes held by Americans but not apparent to foreign observers, however well trained and observant they might be. That such data would be enormously useful to institutional leaders as well as culture theorists goes without saying.

The Schoolbook Image of
National Character

The final question preceding the last selection centered on the problem that arises out of the schools' attempt to develop specific life styles and cultural values. The question was posed as a hypothetical point for deciding the wisdom ·of consciously encouraging or discouraging selected cultural themes. In the following presentation, J. Merton England analyzes American schoolbooks used from 1783 to 1860 to determine the cultural values proposed and denounced. As Mr. England ably points out, a remarkable tendency to show polarities like good-bad, right-wrong, freedom-tyranny, was a predominant occurrence in these works. This article illustrates an apparently conscious attempt to inculcate selected social values through the schools. It is a look at practice, not hypotheses.

The relation of culture to education is brilliantly illuminated as book after book is exemplified. The ethic of Puritanism as a cultural force in education is clearly shown. In the development of culture idols, moral themes, and traditional values, the books described conveyed a cultural heritage, whether fact or fiction, to a young society which had a need for direction. This is shown in the wide acceptance of the ideals proclaimed, if not by the elders, at least by the youth.

Is it possible to produce nonculturally biased materials for schools? Is it wise? What effects of culturally biased materials are noticeable in contemporary society? Does the school influence the culture as much as the culture influences the school? What criteria should serve as a basis for deciding which values to encourage and which to discourage?

The Democratic Faith in American Schoolbooks, 1783–1860

J. MERTON ENGLAND

From Noah Webster in the 1780s to Emma Willard in 1860, the authors of American school textbooks emphatically believed that there was such a thing as national character and that they had a duty to help form and preserve it. They set out to create a usable past for republican America— an agreed-upon national myth, we might say now. Fundamental elements in the canon they constructed were the enduring shibboleths of the American democratic faith—liberty, equality, morality. Taken together, their schoolbooks present a composite picture of a chosen people and a unique nation, especially favored by Providence and endowed with a world mission to spread democratic government and pure religion.

In the rhetoric of schoolbook patriotism, the words liberty and freedom appear more often perhaps than any others, unless it be their antonyms, tyranny and oppression. (Indeed, one of the most striking characteristics of schoolbook authors is the habit of polarization, the tendency to see things in terms of their opposites.) Nowhere are the dimensions of "liberty" defined. It does not seem to have meant simply the absence of restraints upon the individual, since the authors themselves wove a tight net of moral constrictions around individual conduct. Essentially, liberty seems to have meant release from foreign monarchic rule and a dictated religion. Once "crown and crosier rul'd a coward world," a Fourth of July poem said, but then the Pilgrim Fathers, "by faith impell'd, by freedom fir'd,/By hope supported, and by God inspir'd," helped to break the "vile chains" which had bound "earth's torpid children."[1] "The principles of civil and religious liberty," Benson J. Lossing wrote, were asserted before Columbus made his first voyage, and "had shaken thrones and overturned dynasties before Charles the First was brought to the block."

Reprinted from *American Quarterly*, Vol. 15, No. 2, Pt. 1, Summer, 1963, pp. 191–99, by permission of the publisher and the author.
[1] Montgomery Robert Bartlett, *The Juvenile Orator*, Philadelphia, 1839, p. 139.

In Europe the "love of liberty . . . germinated beneath the heat of persecution." In America it "budded and blossomed. . . . Here king-craft and priest-craft never had an abiding place, and their ministers were always weak in the majestic presence of the popular will."[2]

Although schoolbook "liberty" was primarily political or religious, occasionally it also meant economic free enterprise. In 1800 Mathew Carey linked "liberty and the security of property."[3] To a politician whose Fourth of July speech in 1837 was anthologized in a school reader, freedom was a creative power. He called the "magic changes" since 1776—growth "in population, in wealth, and in all that constitutes individual prosperity and national power"—"the natural results of that perfect freedom of enterprise, and security of person and property" guaranteed by our political institutions. He asked: "Will any one tell me that these, instead of being the legitimate fruits of free government and free institutions, are the result of the native energies of the country?"[4] This idea was exceptional. The texts usually did attribute the growth of the United States to the "native energies" of the people as well as to their freedom; and freedom was a boon they deserved because they had won it by their determination and valor. Yet it was essentially a negative boon, an escape from the injustice of "a tyrant king"[5] and from "the curse of moral and political despotism" like that which still prevailed in Hispanic America.[6]

Equality, not liberty, Tocqueville considered the great passion of democratic America. A prolific author and editor of school texts, Samuel Griswold Goodrich ("Peter Parley"), agreed: "The tendency to exclusiveness [in America] is checked and repressed by public opinion, which is exercised more to secure equality than even liberty."[7] Nevertheless, equality received much less emphasis than freedom in school texts; and much more than liberty, it was a negative value, a safeguard against relapse into monarchy. William Grimshaw, the author of an early school history of the United States, commented:

. . . although . . . aristocratic customs are so generally denounced by the laws, they are eagerly followed by the people. . . . There are in the United States more nominal nobility, than any country in the world exhibits, of legitimate creation. Every governor is Excellent; every judge, senator, and representative, is Honourable; and every justice of the peace, distinguished by the chivalric title of Esquire. These frivolities should be carefully discouraged, and the dangerous assumptions,

[2] Benson J. Lossing, A Pictorial History of the United States for Schools and Families, New York, 1854, pp. 158–59.

[3] The School of Wisdom: or American Monitor, ed. Mathew Carey, Philadelphia, 1800, p. 3.

[4] Lyman Cobb, Cobb's New North American Reader; or, Fifth Reading Book, New York, 1852, p. 340.

[5] William S. Cardell, The Middle Class Reader, new ed., Philadelphia, 1853, p. 57.

[6] Lossing, op. cit., p. 33.

[7] Samuel G. Goodrich, Manners and Customs of the Principal Nations of the Globe, Boston, 1845, p. 21.

by every real friend of liberty, opposed. They are the first robes in which a republic advances to aristocracy; thence, to monarchy; and, from monarchy, to oppression and extravagance.[8]

In the texts equality is a lackluster hero to whom the authors pay canting tribute. The villains of the piece, kings and nobles, are lusty and colorful. There is, perhaps, unacknowledged envy in the words of latter-day Puritans as they denounce "proud and haughty" English aristocrats who "live in great castles and palace-like halls" and revel in sensual pleasures. As rulers, Jacob Abbott wrote, "instead of being the wise and the good, they are only cunning and wicked. It is not possible for the imagination to conceive of characters more selfish, profligate, and vile, than the line of English kings, with two or three doubtful exceptions, have uniformly exhibited from the earliest periods to the present day."[9]

One of the foreign aristocrat's worst vices, Abbott thought, was "to look with scorn on every species of peaceful industry."[10] Similarly, other Yankee authors disparaged Southern slaveowners as aristocratic scorners of the secular Puritan ethic—industry, thrift and sobriety—which the textbooks sought to make universal. Southerners were "haughty and imperious," Nathaniel Dwight wrote, and "attached strongly to pleasure and dissipation."[11] They were indolent, the author of a geography said, and self-indulgent devotees of "dancing, horse-racing, cock-fighting, and chiefly hunting."[12]

Rarely does one find in the schoolbooks of pre-Civil War America an ardent plea for equality as a moving force for democratic development. William H. Seward, in a Fourth of July speech in 1839 that soon found its way into a school reader, struck this rare positive note:

Our institutions, excellent as they are, have hitherto produced but a small portion of the beneficent results they are calculated to bestow upon the People. The chief of these benefits is EQUALITY. We do indeed enjoy equality of civil rights. But we have not yet attained, we have only approximated toward, EQUALITY OF SOCIAL CONDITION. . . . [Aristocracy unfortunately exists even in America.] We should be degenerate descendants of our heroic forefathers, did we not assail this aristocracy, remove the barriers between the rich and the poor, break the control of the few over the many, extend the largest liberty to the greatest number, and strengthen in every way the democratic principles of our constitution.

[8] William Grimshaw, *History of the United States*, rev. ed., Philadelphia, 1826, p. 193.
[9] Jacob Abbott, *Narrative of the General Course of History from the Earliest Periods to the Establishment of the American Constitution*, New York, 1856, pp. 300, 388–89.
[10] *Ibid.*, p. 315.
[11] Nathaniel Dwight, *A Short but Comprehensive System of the Geography of the World*, 2nd Conn. ed., Hartford [1797?], pp. 183, 186. The American Antiquarian Society copy of this book gives the publication date [1795?]. But it tells of the admission of Tennessee to the Union.
[12] Daniel Adams, *Geography; or, a Description of the World in Three Parts, for the Use of Schools and Academies*, 5th ed., Boston, 1820, pp. 136–37, 140–41, 145, 150.

In this great work, he told his audience at a Sunday School celebration on Staten Island, "Sunday Schools and Common Schools are the great levelling institutions of the age."[13]

"Levelling institutions"! On the "levelling" role of the schools, most textbook authors of Jacksonian America agreed with Seward. Their opposition to aristocracy extended even to an aristocracy of brains. They valued creativity less than uniformity, trained intelligence less than the spreading of useful knowledge and the cultivation of virtue.[14] After quoting Benjamin F. Butler on "The Necessities and Advantages of the General Diffusion of Knowledge," the compiler of a reader asked: "Will all remember, however, that it would be better for the community to have all the children and youth of our country grow up in UTTER IGNORANCE, if they are not *morally* educated at the same time that they are *intellectually* educated, so as to become GOOD, MORAL, and VIRTUOUS citizens as well as WISE and LEARNED men, as a *learned* wicked man can do *ten* times as much mischief in society as an *ignorant* wicked man?"[15] "We have, indeed, been desirous to cultivate the memory, the intellect, and the taste," Emma Willard wrote. "But much more anxious have we been to sow the seeds of virtue."[16]

Education meant indoctrination—indoctrination in the familiar catalogue of moral virtues of Protestant, agrarian-commercial America: industry, thrift, practicality, temperance, honesty, plain living, patriotism and piety. These moral values were the props of the state. Without them the flourishing republic of the New World could not endure.

The incarnation of all these virtues was George Washington, the gigantic hero-figure of pre-Civil War America. American schoolbooks often called the Revolution the supreme event in human history, and Washington dwarfed all its other heroes. In writing of him, bombastic authors drew upon their lushest prose. The compiler of *The Juvenile Orator* wrote:

The history of the Old World records the names of those whose deeds and daring cast a passing glare upon the age in which they lived, and whose memory yet survive[s] the waste of time; but to the New World was reserved the glory of giving existence to one, the lustre of whose virtues lighted the habitable globe with a noon-tide splendor, that can subside only with subsiding nature. Upon the broad page of the history of man, GEORGE WASHINGTON stands in unclouded sublimity, an unmatched model of self-created greatness.[17]

[13] Cobb, *op. cit.*, p. 286.

[14] "The primary intellectual value embodied in these books is that the only important knowledge is that which is 'useful.' " Ruth Miller Elson, "American Schoolbooks and 'Culture' in the Nineteenth Century," *Mississippi Valley Historical Review*, Vol. 46, December, 1959, p. 413.

[15] Cobb, *op. cit.*, p. 253.

[16] Emma Willard, *Abridged History of the United States, or Republic of America*, new ed., New York, 1860, p. 5.

[17] Bartlett, *op. cit.*, pp. 149–50.

Washington stood alone in the American pantheon, but much can be inferred about the nation's culture merely from a listing of other school-book heroes: Christopher Columbus, intrepid discoverer; John Smith, successful colonizer; Benjamin Franklin, practical philosopher; Israel Putnam, patriotic Cincinnatus; Patrick Henry, eloquent agitator; Robert Fulton, useful inventor. Sometimes their virtues may now sound strange. In Noah Webster's *Little Reader's Assistant* we read: "What a *hero* was Capt. Smith! How many Turks and Indians did he slay! How often was he upon the brink of death, and how bravely did he encounter every danger! Such a man affords a noble example for all to follow, when they resolve to be *good* and *brave*."[18]

Even fictitious heroes were mustered to illustrate the schoolbook virtues of industry, patriotism and piety. Jack Halyard, the "Sailor Boy" of William Cardell's *Middle Class Reader*, was a rural American prototype of the popular version of the Gilded Age Alger hero. Jack's father, a sailor turned farmer, died when the boy was young, leaving a destitute, invalid widow and four children. The family soon lost its New Jersey farm and moved to New York. Jack, the elder son, went to sea, and in his letters home told his family of the strange places and people he saw on his travels. On one of his voyages Jack was shipwrecked just off the American coast. Although most of the passengers and crew lost their lives, Jack saved a young English girl, Harriet Temple, and her mother was also rescued. Mrs. Halyard and Mrs. Temple became fast friends, and Jack and Harriet were married. By the end of the book, Jack has retired from seafaring, bought back the old family farm and settled there with his bride. His prospects are bright. In summing up Jack's career, the author tells us that the young man had made his way in the world "by persevering industry and upright conduct." He had always been honest and trustworthy, always "the dutiful son, the kind brother, the sincere friend, the lover of his country, and of his fellow-men." Jack, "the Christian hero," had at all times kept "two prime objects in view: to gain useful knowledge and to practice right." His life served as an example "that there is no real greatness on earth, but the will and power of being greatly good." The Halyards were among "the virtuous poor" who possess "that inward peace which the sons of vice, with all their power and state, can never find." The author assured his schoolchildren readers: "Bad men cannot be happy. If the wicked appear sometimes to prosper, their deceitful success must soon come to an end; and the good, though their day may be clouded with misfortune for a while, will surely have their reward; for truth and virtue are from the beginning, and, unchanging, shall last as long as the throne of God endures."[19]

Other textbook writers agreed with the chronicler of the Halyards in

[18] Noah Webster Jr., *The Little Reader's Assistant*, 2nd ed., Hartford, 1791, p. 12.
[19] Cardell, *op. cit.*, pp. 205–6, and *passim*.

emphasizing "the throne of GOD." Morality depended upon religion—more specifically, Protestant Christianity. The zealous spirit of anti-Catholic evangelical religion permeated the schoolbooks of nineteenth-century America.[20]

Pious textbook authors, many of them ministers, had no doubt that God was on the side of the United States, indeed had a special mission for His "American Israel." "God hath not dealt so with *any* other people," said Hall and Baker's *School History of the United States.*[21] The Puritan idea of a chosen people's "city on a hill" and the idea of inevitable progress gained new vigor and momentum with the rise of millennialism in the religious revivals of the nineteenth century. "God did not design this continent to remain a wilderness," Lossing wrote.[22] Here was a new Eden: "The great garden of the western world needed tillers, and white men came."[23] Before the occupation of New England, a plague annihilated local Indian tribes. "Thus," Emma Willard wrote, "Divine Providence prepared the way for another and more civilized race."[24] The coming of the settlers "opened a new era in the history of man— . . . the dawn of a *new civilization,* higher and more perfect than had yet been born," wrote Jesse Olney on New Year's Day 1851, in the preface to his school history of the United States. He continued:

In these United States, the great Republic of the World, lies the grand and impos-ing theatre of the *future* progress of the race. We are to work out, not alone our destiny, but that of the whole world. . . . Here, for the first time in human history, man will be *truly* man. . . . Here shall be realized the long-prophesied, long-expected *Golden Age.* . . . From this Free and Happy Land shall go forth the power to perfect the Civilization of the World. . . . The arts of Freedom and of Peace shall be brought home to the ancient cradle of the race, and the deserts of Asia made to rejoice and blossom with the fruits of the highest culture. . . . The inferior races shall be educated . . . and made fellow-laborers in the great work of human progress. To the portal of this Golden Future, the consummation of man's earthly destiny, *America* holds the key. *She* only can accomplish the work to which she is pledged, and thus make the sublimest prophecies and aspirations of the Past the bright *realities* of the Present, and the foundation for a yet nobler Future.[25]

[20] Anti-Catholic bias shows especially in comments in geographies on Spain, Portugal, Italy and Ireland. For example: "The Roman Catholic religion, to the exclusion of all others, is the religion of the Spanish monarchy; and it is, in these countries, of the most bigoted [sic], superstitious, and tyrannical character." Jedidiah Morse, *The American Geography* . . . , 2nd ed., London, 1792, p. 496.

[21] Samuel Read Hall and A. R. Baker, *School History of the United States,* new ed., Andover, Mass., 1839, p. 4.

[22] Benson J. Lossing, *A Common-School History of the United States,* New York, 1864, p. 9.

[23] Lossing, *Pictorial History of the United States,* p. 12.

[24] Willard, *op. cit.,* p. 19.

[25] Jesse Olney, *A History of the United States, for the Use of Schools and Academies,* rev. ed., New Haven, 1851, pp. 5–7.

Yet under such brave words of millennial vision lay anxieties and fears. If one reads beneath the surface of the schoolbooks, he can feel insecurity and tension, which were no doubt personal with the authors but also part of the culture. There was the habit of polarization referred to before—for example, the contrasts between England and America: age and youth, smallness and bigness, past and future, oppression and liberty, aristocracy and equality, a state church and religious freedom, decay and vigor, depravity and innocence. This simple black-and-white way of seeing things did not, one feels, reflect the assurance of certitude. It reveals tautness, not relaxation—a kind of whistling in the dark to keep up one's courage. Textbook emphasis upon self-control through the exercise of will power resulted in part from the abundant evidence of rampaging, often violent individualism in romantic mid-century America, a society of hectic growth and change. But perhaps it also sprang from the authors' personal, unconscious straining against the built-in bonds of the culture.

What is called "millennial hope" can just as easily be felt as a hovering apocalyptic despair. Throughout the texts recur such phrases as "to the end of time," "when time is no more," "the last shock of time." Over and over the schoolbooks recount the decay and death of glorious empires of the past and point the cautionary moral. The New World empire would last only so long as it kept its youthful innocence and virtue. Caleb Bingham's *Columbian Orator* brought to the attention of schoolboys the words of a Harvard commencement speaker: "Warned by the fate of her predecessors, may she [the United States] escape those quicksands of vice, which have ever proved the bane of empire. May her glory and her felicity increase with each revolving year, till the last trump shall announce the catastrophe of nature, and time shall immerge in the ocean of eternity."[26] "Protect us from evil!" the texts cry out. The subject was America, but the feelings, one suspects, were often personal and morbid.

European travelers in Jacksonian America marveled at the way New World citizens lived in the future. By some incredible alchemy, the swaggering backwoods booster transformed a sleepy village into a bustling city —and he actually saw it! But progress created anxiety. If the divine event toward which creation moves is far off, one can contemplate its advent calmly. But what if it is at hand, may come at any moment in a blinding flash? If I read the schoolbooks right, boastful Americans were shouting down inner voices of doubt and fear. Vaunting optimism had an undertone of desperation. This was cultural, and it was personal. America was beautiful, and so was life. For Young America it was a dawning time, but perhaps, whispered *timor mortis*, a dying time too.

A favorite poem of the American schoolbook anthologist was Bishop Berkeley's "The Muse's Hopes for America." It prophesied that

[26] Caleb Bingham, *The Columbian Orator*, Boston, 1797, p. 34.

> In happy climes, the seat of innocence,
>
> . . . .
>
> There shall be sung another golden age,
>
> . . . .
>
> Westward the course of empire takes its way;
>   The first four acts already past,
> A fifth shall close the drama with the day:
>   Time's noblest offspring is the last.[27]

Of similar theme was Timothy Dwight's poem "Columbia." The first stanza has the line: "Thy reign is the last and the noblest of time."[28]

Planet Earth's great drama began, the textbooks said, in 4004 B.C. America was the fifth and final act. It was an exciting but an awesome thought.

One must hesitate before equating the democratic faith of Young America with the schoolbook interpretations of liberty, equality and morality. Nor can we assume that the texts performed a dominant role in shaping the minds of their readers. Although reflecting opinions widely held in American society, the texts did not faithfully mirror republican sentiments, if we may trust other sources that indicate more positive democratic beliefs and a happier, more carefree spirit.

Few of the textbook authors were representative men of their age or of their sprawling country. Most of them spoke with the twang of the New England town, not the drawl of the Southern plantation or the careless slurring of the Western farm. Heirs of the Puritans, whose memory they perpetuated, they had accepted a modified Calvinism, in that they believed that man could by his own efforts curb his inherent sinfulness and follow the narrow path of virtue, but they could not stomach Methodist Arminianism or a Jeffersonian confidence in the essential goodness of human nature. Diehard Federalists, many of them, they wrung their hands over the passing of antique values—and of their own former status—in the pushy society of Jacksonian America. Soft breezes from the South, murmuring of aristocratic ease in the land of slavery, and hurly-burly gales from Western clearings, carrying the raucous shouts of coonskin democracy, did not moderate but made more bitter the winter of their discontent.

In such persons of the "Mugwump" type an anxious temper would prevail. They would incline toward a negative view of the trinity of democratic values: Liberty was release from slavery, not opportunity to develop one's talents to the full; equality was a barrier against aristocratic privilege, not a force to promote universal respect for human dignity; morality was a checkrein upon vice, not a spirit to motivate the development of free, responsible individuals living in harmony in an open society.

In what ways, then, did the schoolbooks reflect, transmit and shape

[27] Cobb, *op. cit.*, pp. 419–20.
[28] Caleb Bingham, *Young American's Speaker*, Philadelphia, 1857, p. 44.

popular culture? Most important, perhaps, they imposed restraints upon a people who lacked them. They helped to establish and maintain a tradition in a society that tended to forget or scorn the past. They perpetuated the secular ethic of Puritanism, emphasizing work, thrift and earnestness, and made it seem as fresh and valid for urban-industrial America as for the simpler agrarian republic. They intensified the concern of the age with individual morality, under the guidance of religion, and the belief in man's capacity and responsibility to do good. And they reaffirmed the general belief in the superiority of American institutions and in America's unique mission in the world.

Diagnosing the Ills of Society

The analogy of society's life style to an individual's life style has been suggested several times. Some sociologists have portrayed society as a group of individuals having collective needs, wants, problems, and growth processes. A society, like an individual, generalizes nondirected activity in infancy, and develops strength and vitality in childhood, rebelliousness in adolescence, striving ambition in young adulthood, status quo continuance in middle age, and finally senility and retrospection in old age. No analogy is completely accurate, but this idea of individual and society has contemplative merit.

Consider the sick individual, as Lawrence K. Frank does in the following selection. Can we view a society in need of therapy in the same way we view an individual? Is the diagnosis of social ills accurate? What about the prescription suggested? Is Western European culture in the midst of decay? What does this portend for the schools of the culture? Are the schools perpetuating the social myths described? If society and not the individual is the patient, what role should the schools undertake—uncritical cultural transmission, critical social reconstruction, or social therapy?

Society as the Patient

LAWRENCE K. FRANK

There is a growing realization among thoughtful persons that our culture is sick, mentally disordered, and in need of treatment. This belief finds expression in many different forms and from a variety of professions. We have had, for example, *The Sickness of an Acquisitive Society*, by Tawney, and *Modern Education*, by Rank, wherein society, not merely the individual, is portrayed as the patient.

Anyone who reflects upon the present situation in which our Western European culture finds itself cannot fail to see that we have passed from the condition in which deviations from a social norm could be regarded as *ab*normal. Today we have so many deviations and maladjustments that the term "normal" has lost almost all significance. Indeed, we see efforts being made to erect many of the previously considered abnormalities into cultural patterns for general social adoption.

The disintegration of our traditional culture, with the decay of those ideas, conceptions, and beliefs upon which our social and individual lives were organized, brings us face to face with the problem of treating society, since individual therapy or punishment no longer has any value beyond mere alleviation of our symptoms. No one can complain that we in America lack self-appointed physicians who are ready, nay eager, to doctor our own society; and abroad we can see various treatments in progress which we are being invited to emulate.

The conception of a sick society in need of treatment has many advantages for diagnosis of our individual and social difficulties and for constructive therapy, although we may find it necessary to prescribe a long period of preparation before the patient will be ready for the remedies indicated. Perhaps the most immediate gain from adopting this conception is the simplification it brings. Instead of thinking in terms of a multiplicity of so-called social problems, each demanding special attention and a different remedy, we can view all of them as different symptoms of the same disease. That would be a real gain even if we cannot entirely agree upon the exact nature of the disease. If, for example, we could regard crime, mental disorders, family disorganization, juvenile delinquency, prostitution and sex offenses, and much that now passes as the result of pathological processes (e.g., gastric ulcer) as evidence, not of individual

From *Society as the Patient*, by Lawrence K. Frank, 1948, pp. 1–6. Reprinted by permission of the publisher, the Rutgers University Press, New Brunswick, N.J.

wickedness, incompetence, perversity, or pathology, but as human reactions to cultural disintegration, a forward step would be taken. At present we cherish a belief in a normal, intact society against which we see these criminals, these psychopaths, these warring husbands and wives, these recalcitrant adolescents, these shameless prostitutes and vicious sex offenders, as so many rebels who threaten society and so must be punished, disciplined, or otherwise individually treated. This assumption of individual depravity or perversity gives us a comfortable feeling that all is well socially, but that certain individuals are outrageously violating the laws and customs that all decent people uphold.

It is, indeed, interesting to see how this conception of a social norm, with individuals as violators and frustrators of normality, runs through so much of our thinking. In political life we cherish a fond belief in the essential soundness and efficacy of representative government. The cumulative evidence of social injustice, of corruption in office, of legislative "deals" and intrigues—the whole slimy trail of graft and misfeasance is treated as the vicious practices of dishonest politicians. We save our belief in democracy and in our representative political organization by imputing all their faults and shortcomings to individual malefactors. The remedy for political chicane is then viewed as investigation and prosecution: "Turn the rascals out."

In our economic affairs we follow a similar practice. Rugged individualism, free enterprise, the money and credit economy, the price system with its supposed free play of economic forces and the law of supply and demand—all these are considered as naturally sound, effective economic practices based upon the very nature of society; if perverse and selfish individuals did not interfere with these natural forces, frustrate competition, and break these laws, we should have no economic troubles. When our industry and banking and commerce are crippled or paralyzed, we begin to look for the guilty persons who have interfered with normality. Some blame the stifling of competition, others the excess of competition, while others aim their accusations against this or that individual or organized group of individuals whose conduct is deemed to be uneconomic and therefore responsible for our troubles. The confusion over the nature and the perpetrators of these economic misdeeds provides occasion for vivacious, sometimes vituperative, argument, but we generally agree that the trouble comes from individual misdeeds that must be curbed by more laws, more regulation, and more severe punishment.

Likewise, in family life, difficulties are similarly treated in terms of individual wickedness and guilt, to be corrected by severe moral instruction and legal adjudication on a semicriminal basis, as in divorce. Similarly, the admitted inadequacy of the courts, both civil and criminal, is blamed upon individuals, corrupt judges, unprincipled shysters, and unethical practitioners, whose disloyalty to their high duty has stained the bright garments of Justice and prevented honest administration of the laws.

In every department and aspect of our social life we find the same pattern of thought about our society: that our social ills come from individual misconduct that must be corrected and punished so that these supposed underlying social forces and social laws can operate without hindrance, thereby solving our social problems. Nor is this point of view confined merely to the man in the street and the unscrupulous manipulator who has learned to utilize these social myths for his own purposes. Our social scientists, with few exceptions, are strong believers in these supposed social forces and laws and underlying natural processes that, if left unhindered, would operate smoothly. Much of our social research is a persistent search for these underlying social, political, and economic systems, the discovery of which will, it is expected, bring social progress, just as physical science revealed the underlying physical-chemical processes that gave us our modern industry and technology. Indeed, these conceptions of normality and inherent order in society have dominated both lay and professional thinking for many generations.

If, then, we abandon this social mythology, as a growing number of individuals are urging, for another view of the situation, what have we as an alternative? The term "society as the patient" is a good analogy for discussion, but we need something more than a clever phrase as a basis for reconsidering our social theory and revising our social objectives. The conception of culture and personality, emphasizing the patterned behavior of man toward his group and toward other individuals, offers some promise of help, for it indicates at once that our society is only one of numerous ways of patterning and organizing human life and that what individuals do, for good or evil, is in response to the cultural demands and opportunities offered them.

This cultural conception reveals human conduct, not as whimsical or volitionally controlled, but as the way the individual takes over the ideas, beliefs, and practices of the traditional group life and, under their guidance, carries out his life-processes. In a secluded group where, over a long period of time, men have worked out a unified culture with appropriate sanctions and beliefs, the individual ordinarily finds the pattern of his life prepared for him and, within the permissions and restrictions it offers, he can achieve his life goals and fulfil his social responsibility. His culture dictates what he will be aware of, how he will respond to it and explain it, and what he can and must do with his organic needs and functions. In homogeneous cultures individuals of aberrant temperaments are less likely to find it difficult to conform to the patterns laid down by their culture; when forced to do so, they can adapt themselves with a minimum of strain because their culture does not offer conflicting choices. In some cultures it is the practice even to give specific exemptions to an individual whose temperament makes it difficult for him to conform to the patterns that are recognized as socially normal; such exemption saves the individual deviant from anxiety or guilt.

When we regard Western European culture, which has emerged from an almost incredible background of conflict and confusion and mixture of peoples, and see that for centuries it has not been unified either in ideas and beliefs or in socially approved practices, we can begin to understand the etiology of the sickness of our society. Our culture has no unanimity of individual or social aims, no generally accepted sanctions, and no common patterns of ideas or conduct. All our basic ideas, conceptions, and beliefs have been in process of revision for the last three hundred years or more, beginning with the displacement of the older notions of the universe and man's place therein and going on now to the supersedure of the traditional animistic, voluntaristic conceptions of human nature and conduct and man's relation to his society. The American scene, moreover, has been successively invaded by representatives of widely different nationalities, who have accelerated the decay of the early American tradition that our changing industry has made inevitable. The picture is sufficiently familiar and has been adequately described so that no prolonged description is needed here.

If we bear in mind this disintegration of culture, then our socalled social problems and the seeming perversity of individuals become intelligible. They are to be viewed as arising from the frantic efforts of individuals, lacking any sure direction and sanctions or guiding conception of life, to find some way of protecting themselves or of merely existing on any terms they can manage in a society being remade by scientific research and technology. Having no strong loyalties and no consistent values or realizable ideals to cherish, the individual's conduct is naturally conflicting, confused, neurotic, and antisocial, if that term has any meaning in the absence of an established community purpose and ideal. The more skilful contrive to profit from the social confusion and their own lack of scruples, while others evade or break laws, become mentally disordered or diseased, or otherwise violate the older codes of conduct, damaging themselves and those whose lives they touch. No one is happy, it is apparent; the successful are driven as relentlessly as the failures by their sense of guilt, their compulsions, and their frustrations.

We see, then, that continued faith in the myths regarding an underlying social system comes from a need to cling to something that offers some sense and meaning in the social confusion and keeps alive the hope that things may be better. Cynicism is, of course, the refuge of the majority of successful men, especially professional men, who shrug their shoulders, acknowledge the decay of their professional scruples, but go on "getting theirs." There is, apparently, no profession or occupation that has not succumbed to the current practice of racketeering, which means that the traditional ethics and senses of responsibility are breaking down, leaving each one to pursue his own personal ends. It is neither fair nor useful to upbraid the individual who could not singly maintain the old standards, even if they were workable, or withstand the competitive pressure to adopt the unscrupulous practices of the others. Campaigns for social reforms are unavailing since there are no new patterns or sanctions to which we can give allegiance, and we cannot return to the old since they offer no meaningful answers to our present perplexities. The only common faith we share at present is this social mythology which we cling to with increasing difficulty as the absurdity of such beliefs and the futility of our efforts to restore normality become more evident.

Where, then, does the cultural view help beyond providing another apt theory of social confusion which is useful as a point of vantage from which the intellectual can contemplate the vulgar scene? It transfers the focus of attention from the seemingly recalcitrant or perverse individual to the cultural patterns and sanctions. This revision of our thinking will modify the doctrine of individual responsibility and guilt that is not only an active factor in the growing criminality and insanity, but also a complete block to any understanding of the problem or any attempt at modification. If we accept the conception of society as the patient, absolve the individual from guilt, and regard these various social problems as symptoms of progressive cultural change, we can at least relieve some of our anxiety since we then have a definite and possibly manageable problem.

PART 2

Poverty, Deprivation,
and Social Class:
Their Impact
on Education

THE EFFECTS OF SOCIAL
CLASS ON EDUCATION

The concept of social class has become common knowledge during the past three decades as sociologists have analyzed similarities and differences in life styles in societies. Descriptive and hierarchic titles have been used to differentiate one class from another, for example, working class and leisure class; lower, middle, and upper class. Just as in the development of scientific knowledge, sociologists have first described, then classified phenomena in an attempt to understand and to predict social happenings. Analyzing social structures includes this process, as social classes are established to assist in understanding the dynamics of a society.

To perceive the relation between social class and caste one needs to understand social mobility. An individual who is allowed, by social sanction, to move upward or downward within a single class or from one class to another is considered socially mobile. When this mobility is curtailed, as happened when a child was born to a Negro slave and was not allowed to change his social status because of social and, at the time, legal pressures, the result is a caste situation. Thus, class systems vary in amount of mobility, but provide some means for rising or falling in social station. An example of a means for falling social status is alcoholism in a middle-class environment. Similarly, marriage can be used as a means for moving up or down in social class.

One of the most prominent avenues of social mobility in American society has been education. In earlier periods education was limited to an elite socio-economic group. As democracy became more important as a social and political form, the need to educate larger segments of the population was acknowledged. Although initially the idea of mass education was religious in purpose—protecting the souls of children by teaching them to read the Bible—the move toward educating all levels of society was mainly a recognition of social and political necessity. This tended to alter the concept of education as something worthy only of leisure classes. Practical education, public schools, compulsory attendance laws, and related popular education movements gained; the schools became a major force in social mobility. The proportion of students from other than the upper class now enrolled in high school and college has increased in the past fifty years to the extent that more college students now come from working-class homes than from upper-class homes, an indication of the larger number of working-class people in society. Even this very important influence of social class on education is not the only impact of class on school.

This section is concerned with the study of social class as it affects the school, and as it relates to the problems of poverty, deprivation, and alienation. The characteristics and dynamics of social class are a valuable study for persons interested in education in a society. It is often maintained that teachers are from middle-class backgrounds, that upper-class children do not attend public education facilities, and that lower-class children do not have innate abilities. None of these is demonstrably true, but an understanding of social class, social status, and social mobility is an important part of understanding a society and its schools. Sociologists have classified the various socio-economic levels in society by several criteria. The major means for determining social class include occupation, income, education, friends, property and its location, family background, and self-perception. The concern of educators is not that of classifying individuals by class, but of knowing the relative-value systems that pervade the separate classes and being able to adapt the school situation to account for these varying values.

The schools have been accused of indoctrinating youth with a middle-class morality. If this is true, is it wise; if not, why does it seem to occur? Can a school system designed to accommodate average students be useful in depressed areas? What values are in conflict? How can they be resolved to the benefit of the child and the society? What can the school do for a child who comes from a background which does not value education? In a society where education plays an increasing role in personal attainment, how do the primary purposes of education change?

How can the school account for the conflict of encouraged creativity and overbearing conformity to attain grades? Are the schools the most appropriate agency for social mobility?

On Defining Equality

In an earlier selection by Seymour Lipset, the two American cultural traits analyzed were equalitarianism and achievement. In the following article, Lawrence A. Cremin points to the paradox of equalitarianism in a class structure. The democratic ideal of equal men and the inequality of social class are both tempered in what Cremin describes as the "social reality." Are the roots of social class economic as the Marxian position holds? If

*they are, should social class be socially controlled by economic means—a
redistribution of wealth or a reward system based on prior wealth? What
social factors, such as achievement, ambition, and initiative, alter the
Marxian view? How can the schools stress ideals of equality and at the
same time recognize inequalities in students? What distinctions exist between equality of condition and equality of opportunity?*

"Some Are More Equal Than Others...."*

LAWRENCE A. CREMIN

Most Americans cherish and affirm their time-honored ideals of equality.
They point with pride to the Declaration of Independence, the Constitution, and the other great documents of their Republic which have traditionally proclaimed this principle to the peoples of the world. Yet most
Americans are well aware that all men are not equal, that there exist distinct ranks in society, in a word, that "some men are more equal than
others." Not only are they aware of such social stratification, they will vigorously assert that anyone with the proper initiative and capabilities can
get ahead of his fellows and reach the top. The innumerable rags-to-riches
stories of American history serve only too well to document their faith.

The roots of this interesting paradox are to be found in the American
social class system, the analysis and definition of which have occupied the
primary attentions of sociologist W. Lloyd Warner and his associates during the past ten years. Working with representative communities in many
parts of the United States, this group has sought to apply the methodological tools of the social scientist to the study of this class system and its
impact on American life. Their findings today provide a rich source of
knowledge and procedures for anyone seeking to understand the complex
organization of our democratic society.

HOW SOCIAL CLASSES ARE DEFINED

Warner defines a social class system as "two or more orders of people
who are believed to be, and are accordingly ranked by members of the
community, in socially superior or inferior positions."[1] Essentially, mem-

Reprinted from *Progressive Education*, Vol. 27, No. 4, February, 1950, pp. 97–100, by
permission of the John Dewey Society.
* Quote taken from George Orwell's *Animal Farm*.
 [1] W. Lloyd Warner and Paul S. Lunt, *The Social Life of a Modern Community*,
Vol. 1, "Yankee City Series," Yale University Press, New Haven, 1941, p. 82.

bers of a given social class will possess similar status by virtue of common social characteristics. They tend to be grouped together in ordinary parlance by such terms as "the 400," "the country club set," "the poor but respectable," "the tobacco road crowd," or any number of other phrases used to rank people socially. Although variations occur, members of a social class tend to marry one another, to associate with one another in the same or similar schools, churches, and clubs, to evidence similar tastes, and to feel at ease in each other's company.

The clue to Warner's method of determining the class structure of a community is also implicit in his definition quoted above. It is that these superior and inferior groups of people are accordingly ranked as such by members of the community themselves. In effect, this provides the key to Warner's *Evaluated Participation* technique of measuring social status. By this method, members of a community are asked to evaluate the social behavior of individuals whom they know or know of, and to rank these in relation to one another. By comparing the ratings of a number of persons, ratings which inevitably show a degree of agreement far above that which might be expected by chance, the investigator is able to set up certain status or class divisions for the community as a whole. Thus, for instance, raters Jones and Smith may both agree that lawyer Brown is certainly among the cream of Elmville society, while carpenter Williams is a shiftless, "no account" pauper. Similarly, both might agree that banker Johnson is on a close plane with lawyer Brown, while plumber Stone is not far removed from carpenter Williams in social worth. Furthermore, both might agree that schoolteacher Evans, while not among the cream of Elmville society, is certainly a "better citizen" than either Williams or Stone. Given enough of such information and agreement, one has the basis for outlining the class structure of Elmville.

Once the broad outlines of a community's social structure have been determined through *Evaluated Participation,* the investigator has at his disposal a far less complicated method for measuring the social status of other individuals. The Warner group has found that certain economic and other prestige factors are closely correlated with social status, and that information concerning these factors will yield a fairly accurate picture of an individual's social class. Principal among these are occupation, source of income, type of house, and dwelling area. When an individual is rated for each of these factors, and these ratings are properly weighted according to importance, the investigator is provided with an index number—an *Index of Status Characteristics*—which is easily converted to social-class terms. Thus, for example, the fact that an individual is a banker, receives most of his income from securities, and lives on a large estate in the community's best residential area, may be translated into an index number which, when converted, will inevitably place that individual in the highest social class.

WHAT SOCIAL CLASSES HAVE BEEN ASCERTAINED?

Given these methods of measuring social class, what have been the find-ings of the Warner group? Basically, they have discovered that although American class patterns vary from region to region and from community to community, definite class levels do exist and are consciously recognized by most people. Generally, they have distinguished five distinct classes which may be briefly described as follows:

The Upper Class: Wealth and lineage, Hollingshead states, have com-bined through the economic, legal, and family systems to make member-ship in this class rather stabilized from generation to generation. Embrac-ing only a small percentage of the community (*e.g.* 3% in *Yankee City*), members of this class are colloquially referred to as "the 400," "the fancy crowd," "high class people," "the aristocracy," or "the wealthy and promi-nent." As a rule, families in this class boast the highest incomes in the com-munity and wield much of its power. Inherited wealth makes leisure, as opposed to making a living, their prime concern; and much of such leisure is spent in exclusive clique associations with other members of their class. In the South and in New England, this upper class tends to split into two groups: an upper upper group composed of old families who have enjoyed their status for generations, and a lower upper group who, though secure in their status, have not enjoyed it as long as their hierarchical superiors. Where this split occurs a six-class system evolves. In the West, on the other hand, and in other more recently populated regions, time has not allowed this definite split of the upper class to take place, and the five-class system prevails.

The Upper Middle Class: Members of this class either have achieved their status by virtue of their own efforts, or have inherited their wealth but been prevented from further social rise by questions of time and lin-eage. Embracing roughly a tenth of the community (*e.g.* 10% in *Yankee City*), the upper middle class is composed primarily of professional men, salaried executives, and owners of well established businesses. They are not only the community's most educated group, but also its most active participants in the leadership of political, civic, religious, and patriotic affairs. A critical factor in community organization is the tendency of this class to identify closely with the upper classes, and to emphasize in turn the gap between themselves and the class below them.

The Lower Middle Class: Warner conceives of the upper and upper middle classes as constituting the social groups "above the common man." The lower middle class, embracing roughly a quarter of the community (*e.g.* 28% in *Yankee City*), composes the upper level of the "common man" group. Realizing the gap between themselves and the groups above them, they are a highly class conscious group. Made up largely of small businessmen, and skilled or white collar wage earners, they are aware of some superiority to the group below them, yet cognizant of their many ties with this group. Much of their effort goes into emphasizing this superiority through the purchase of prestige symbols—press notices, memberships (especially in churches), clothes, cars, etc. Comparatively few members of this class finish college, many finish high school, and most have completed at least eight grades of grammar school.

The Upper Lower Class: Composing the lower reaches of the "common man" group, this class embraces about a third of the community (*e.g.* 34% in *Yankee City*). Well aware of their inferior social status, they pride themselves in being "poor but respectable"—thus emphasizing their distance from the class below them. As a rule, they are wage earners in the local factories and businesses, with many of the women working to supplement family incomes. Their formal education is usually confined to grammar school, perhaps with some high school courses added. As Hollingshead has aptly pictured their life: "Neither the men nor the women are expected to do more than work hard, pay their bills, raise their family in a manner expected of this class, vote 'right' in elections, and, above all, eschew any radical or 'bolshevik' ideas."

The Lower Lower Class: At the bottom of the social scale, considered by Warner as below the "common man" level, is roughly the final quarter of the community (*e.g.* 25% in *Yankee City*). Referred to colloquially as "river-rats," "hill-billies," "tobacco roaders," or "peckerwoods," these people are thought by their social superiors to be lazy, shiftless, lawless, immoral, licentious, and animal-like. Their incomes are meagre, their surroundings dingy, their education limited, their families unstable, and their prospects drab. Yet, as Warner has indicated, research shows many of them guilty of no more than being poor and simply lacking in the desire to get ahead.

SOCIAL MOBILITY IN THE CLASS STRUCTURE

Within the reality of such a class structure, much of the meaning of our American ideal of equality would center in equality of opportunity, and at least one aspect of such equality would be the opportunity to move from one of these social levels to another. What of such social mobility in the American class structure? The Warner group has found this to be a critically important factor. They have discovered that through such instruments as education, marriage, money, talent, changes in individual behavior, changes in group membership, and changes in occupation, an individual or a family may move from one class to another. Such movement of course may be either up or down the social ladder.

We all know instances of persons who have made "good marriages," of members of the lower classes who have used scholarships to become outstanding academic specialists, of former newsboys or stock clerks who have become industrial tycoons. While more often than not, a combination of factors rather than any single one is involved in such social movement, illustrative cases are not difficult to find. Thus, the preservation of meaningful social democracy involves more than simple understanding of our American class structure. It involves the maintenance of social fluidity—of channels by which we may continue to utilize Jefferson's natural aristocracy of virtue and talent for the maximum benefit of society. To the extent that such fluidity is preserved, democracy flourishes; to the extent that class lines harden, democracy is weakened and attenuated.

IS THE AMERICAN CLASS SYSTEM MARXIAN?

A few words seem a propos at this point concerning the differences between Warner's conception of social class and the older Marxian conception. There is little doubt but that the early thinking of the Warner group was directly influenced by the latter conception. For instance, in the "Yankee City" study, Warner stated concerning his initial assumptions: "It was believed that the fundamental structure of our society, that which ultimately controls and dominates the thinking and actions of our people, is economic, and that the most vital and far-reaching value systems which motivate Americans are to be ultimately traced to an economic order."[2] This notion of economic first causes is, of course, at the heart of the Marxian conception. Yet, as the Yankee City research continued, and as other studies were conducted over the years, significant differences emerged.

First, as implied above, the Marxians see economic forces as the ultimate determining factors of class structure. Classes emerge out of the common relations of men to the tools of production. The Warner group, on the other hand, sees the economic as important, but as only one among many factors determining social class. A doctor, for instance, may earn less than a skilled electrician, yet he will inevitably be assigned higher social status. Second, the Marxians hold that the presence of classes implies class conflict, struggle, and violence. The Warner group holds that relations among social classes can not only be non-violent, but are often peaceful and amicable. Third, the Marxians view class organization teleologically; that is, as a struggle of classes moving inevitably toward an ultimate "classless society." The Warner group views class organization functionally as it operates today—holding not only that a classless society is incompatible with the complexity of modern industrial society, but also that changes in class structures are neither determined nor inevitably predestined to move toward given ends.

One may be tempted to inquire after surveying Warner's findings whether the paradox posed in the introductory remarks is not resolved

[2] *Ibid.*, p. 81.

simply by concluding that there is no equality in America—that our ideals of equality are meaningless. Such a resolution ignores completely the genuinely equalitarian aspects of American life. Far too many have resolved the paradox by blinding themselves to one half or the other. Is it not rather the task of Americans to make maximum use of the knowledge at their command in understanding their society, in giving new meaning to their ideals of equality and equality of opportunity, and, as Warner himself has urged, in fitting their dreams and aspirations to the possibilities of social reality? Certainly, in light of their responsibilities to the young, this would seem a central task for American teachers.

The Effect of Social Class
on the School

The social-status system is a recognition of the place of a given individual within the framework of social class. The social status of a child is determined by applying criteria of social class to his family origins, his playmates, and his family's present environment. Establishing the social status of a teacher includes consideration of family background, but emphasizes the teacher's present situation—income, housing, friends, education, and general life style. Other indicators of status involve the population's view of the occupation and the individual's own perception of his class status. The family that lives in the large estate on the edge of town and after whom the town was named is considered upper class by the populace of the community. The bank teller going to night school and working for a degree in accounting recognizes the characteristics of classes below and above him and is able to fix his own social status.

W. Lloyd Warner, Marchia Meeker, and Kenneth E. Eells have conducted considerable and profound investigations into social structure. In this article they suggest the same problem discussed earlier in the paradox of equality and social class, and propose some ideas as to how education might deal with social status. How does social mobility affect social status? Are there finite limits to mobility that constrict the attainment of certain social-status positions? What dangers appear if the schools teach youngsters to be aware of their own social status?

Social Status in Education

W. LLOYD WARNER,
MARCHIA MEEKER, AND
KENNETH E. EELLS

In the bright glow and warm presence of the American dream all men are born free and equal. Everyone in that dream has the right and often the duty to try to succeed and to do his best to reach the top. Its two fundamental themes and propositions, that all of us are equal and that each of us has the right to the chance of reaching the top, are mutually contradictory: for if all men are equal there can be no top level to aim for, no bottom one to get away from; there can be no superior or inferior positions, but only one common level into which all Americans are born and in which all of them will spend their lives. We all know such perfect equality of position and opportunity does not exist.

When some men learn that *all* the American Dream does not fit *all* that is true about the realities of our life they denounce the Dream and deny the truth of *any* of it. Fortunately most of us are wiser and better adjusted to social reality; we recognize that, though it is called a dream and though some of it is false, by virtue of our firm belief in it we have made some of it true. Despite the presence of social hierarchies which place people at higher and lower levels in American communities, the principles of democracy do operate; the Christian dogma that all men are equal in the sight of God because He is our Father and we are His spiritual children, buttressed by the democratic faith in the equality of men and the insistence on their equal rights as citizens, is a powerful influence in the daily life of America.

EQUALITY IS WELL TAUGHT

From grade school on we have learned to cite chapter and verse proving from the lives of many of the great men of American history that we can start at the bottom and climb to the highest peaks of achievement when we have a few brains and a will to do. Our mass magazines and newspapers print and reprint the legendary story of rags to riches and tell over and over again the Ellis-Island-to-Park-Avenue saga in the actual lives of

Reprinted from *Phi Delta Kappan*, Vol. 30, 1948–49, pp. 113–19, by permission of the editor.

contemporary successful immigrant men and women. From mere repetition it might be thought the public would tire of the theme; the names are all that vary and stories, like those of children, remain the same. But we never do tire of this theme, for it says what we need to know and what we want to hear.

Among people around us we sometimes recognize men who have got ahead, who have been successfully upward mobile, and who have reached levels of achievement beyond even the dreams of most men. Many Americans by their own success have learned that for them enough of the Dream is true to make all of it real. The examples from history, from the world around us, and from our own experience provide convincing evidence that, although full equality is absent, opportunity for advancement is present sufficiently to permit the rise of a few from the bottom and a still larger number from the middle to the higher economic and social levels. Although we know the statement that everyone is equal but that some men are higher than others is contradictory, and although some of us smile or become angry when we hear that "all of us are equal but some are more equal than others," we still accept both parts of this proposition either by understressing one part of the proposition or by letting all of it go as a paradox we feel to be true.

INFORMATION OF SOCIAL STATUS IS NEEDED, TOO

Our society does an excellent job in giving us an explicit knowledge of, and good argument for, the equalitarian aspects of our life. We have much scholarly knowledge about these workings of democracy; but we have little scientific knowledge about the powerful presence of social status and how it works for good and evil in the lives of all of us. Yet to live successfully and adaptively in America each of us must adjust his life to each of these contradictions, not just one of them, and we must make the most of each. Our knowledge of the democratic aspects of America is learned directly as part of our social heritage, but our understanding of the principle of social status tends to be implicit and to be learned obliquely and through hard and sometimes bitter experience. The lives of many are destroyed because they do not understand the workings of social class.[1]

Our great state papers, the orations of great men, and the principles and pronouncements of politicians and statesmen tell us of the equality of all men. Each school boy learns and relearns it; but most of us are dependent

[1] Jurgen Ruesch *et al., Chronic Diseases and Psychological Invalidism, a Psychosomatic Study*, American Society for Research in Psychosomatic Medicine, New York, 1946. A research at the University of California Hospital by Ruesch and others which demonstrates that this can be literally true; their results show how certain serious physical and mental ailments are directly attributable to social class and mobility strivings and anxieties.

upon experience and indirect statement to learn about "the wrong side of the tracks," "the Gold Coast and the slums," and "the top and bottom of the social heap." We are proud of those facts of American life that fit the pattern we are taught, but somehow we are often ashamed of those equally important social facts which demonstrate the presence of social class. Consequently we tend to deny them, or, worse, denounce them and by so doing deny their existence and magically make them disappear from consciousness. We use such expressions as the Century of the Common Man to insist on our democratic faith; but we know that ordinarily for Common Men to exist as a class uncommon superior and inferior men also exist.

CLASS ORDER IS PERVASIVE INFLUENCE

Recent scientific studies of social class in the several regions of the United States demonstrate that it is a major determinant of individual decisions and social actions; that every major area of American life is directly and indirectly influenced by our class order; and that the major decisions of most individuals are partly controlled by it. To act intelligently and know consciously how this basic factor in American life affects us and our society it is essential and necessary that we have an explicit understanding of what our class order is, how it works, and what it does to the lives and personalities who live in it. Our most democratic institutions, including our schools, churches, business organizations, government, and even our family life are molded by its all-pervading and exceedingly subtle but powerful influence.

DIVISION OF LABOR BRINGS CLASS ORDERS

When societies are complex and service large populations they always possess some kind of status system which, by its own values, places people in higher or lower positions. Only the very simple hunting and gathering tribes, with very small populations and very simple social problems, are without systems of rank; but when a society is complex, when there are large numbers of individuals in it pursuing diverse and complex activities and functioning in a multiplicity of ways, such positions and behaviors are evaluated and ranked. This happens primarily because, to maintain itself, the society must coordinate the efforts of all its members into common enterprises necessary for the preservation of the group, and it must solidify and integrate all these enterprises into a working whole. In other words, as the division of labor increases and the social units become more numerous and diverse, the need for coordination and integration also increases, and, when satisfied, enables the larger group to survive and develop.

Those who occupy coordinating positions acquire power and prestige. They do so because their actions partly control the behavior of the individuals who look to them for direction. Within this simple control there is simple power. Those who exercise such power either acquire prestige directly from it, or have gained it from other sources sufficiently to be raised to a coordinating position. For example, among many primitive peoples a simple fishing expedition may be organized so that the men who fish and handle each boat are under the direction of one leader. The efforts of each boat are directed by the leader and, in turn, each boat is integrated into the total enterprise by its leader's taking orders from his superior. The same situation prevails in a modern factory. Small plants with a small working force and simple problems possess a limited hierarchy, perhaps no more than an owner who bosses all the workers. But a large industrial enterprise, with complex activities and problems, like General Motors, needs an elaborate hierarchy of supervision. The position in a great industrial empire which integrates and coordinates all of the positions beneath it throughout all the supervising levels down to the workers has great power and prestige. The same holds true for political, religious, educational, and other social institutions; the more complex the group and the more diverse the functions and activities, the more elaborate its status system is likely to be. We will amplify this point later.

The studies of other societies have demonstrated one other basic point; the more complex the technological and economic structure, the more complex the social structure, so that some (The Marxians and many classical economists) argue that technological advancement is the cause of social complexity and all class and status systems. It cannot be denied that economic and technological factors are important in the determination of class and status orders. We must not lose sight of the fact, however, that the social system, with its beliefs, values, and rules, which governs human behavior may well determine what kind of technology and what kind of economic institutions will survive or thrive in any given tribe or nation. In any case, social complexity is necessary for economic advancement. Furthermore, social complexity is a basic factor determining the presence or absence of class.

CLASS ORDERS IN RUSSIA

The Marxians have argued that the economic changes our society is undergoing always result in a class war in which "the proletariat" will be triumphant and out of which a "classless society" will result. The authors do not agree with them for several reasons. The principal reasons are: (1) the presence of a class order does not necessarily mean class conflict—the relations of the classes can be and often are amiable and peaceful; (2) classless societies (without differential status systems) are impossible where there is complexity for the reasons previously given. Russia's Communistic system, supposedly designed to produce a pure equalitarian society, necessarily has citizens who are ranked above and below each other. Generals there outrank privates; commissars outrank the rank and file; and members of the Politburo, the ordinary comrade. Occupants of these higher ranks in Russia tend to associate together; those of the lower ranks form their own groups. Their children are trained according to the rank of their parents. This means that the younger generation learns these status differences, thereby strengthening status differences between levels and fostering the further development of social class in Communistic Russia.

All this has occurred despite the fact the Russians have removed the means of production from private hands and placed them under the control of the State ("the people"). The economic factor which by Marxian doctrine produced social classes is largely absent; yet social hierarchies and social class are present for the reason that Russia is a complex society and needs them to survive.

These status trends in Russia will undoubtedly continue, for her population is vast, her people diverse, her problems immensely complex, and elaborate systems of coordination and control are necessary for such a nation to maintain itself. The Communist ideals of economic and political equality cannot produce perfect equality within the complexities of Russian life.

THE STATUS SYSTEM IS PART OF A COMPLEX SOCIETY

But let us return to the United States. We, too, have a complex, highly diverse society. We, too, possess an elaborate division of labor and a ramified technology; and we, too, possess a variety of rank orders built on the need of maintaining unity and cohesion in making our common enterprises successful. Men occupying high and low positions possess families. Their families and their activities are identified with their social position. Families of the same position tend to associate together. They do this informally or through cliques, associations, or other institutions. This social matrix provides the structure of our class system. Children are always born to their families' position. Through life they may increase or decrease their status. The family thereby strengthens and helps maintain our class order. Social status in America is somewhat like man's alimentary canal; he may not like the way it works and he may want to forget that certain parts of it are part of him, but he knows it is necessary for his very existence. So the status system, often an object of our disapproval, is present and necessary in our complex social world.

If we cannot eliminate the system of status, we can and must work to keep it as democratic and equalitarian as possible. To be successful, we

must see to it that each American is given his chance to move in the social scale. This ideal of equality of opportunity is essential for our democracy. To do this intelligently, we must know what our class order is and
what can be done to make it conform most closely to the needs of the
American people.

MORE THAN ECONOMIC FACTORS
DETERMINE CLASS

   Economic factors are significant and important in determining the class
position of any family or person, influencing the kind of behavior we find
in any class, and contributing their share to the present form of our status
system. But, while significant and necessary, the economic factors are not
sufficient to predict where a particular family or individual will be or to
explain completely the phenomena of social class. Something more than a
large income is necessary for high social position. Money must be translated into socially approved behavior and possessions, and they in turn
must be translated into intimate participation with, and acceptance by,
members of a superior class.

   This is well illustrated by what is supposed to be a true story of what
happened to a Mr. John Smith, a newly rich man in a far-western community. He wanted to get into a particular social club of some distinction
and significance in the city. By indirection he let it be known and was told
by his friends in the club they had submitted his name to the membership
committee.

   Mr. Abner Grey, one of the leading members of the club and active on
its membership committee, was a warm supporter of an important philanthropy in this city. It was brought to his attention that Mr. Smith, rather
than contributing the large donation that had been expected of him, had
given only a nominal sum to the charity.

   When Mr. Smith heard nothing more about his application, he again
approached one of the board members. After much evasion he was told
that Mr. Grey was the most influential man on the Board and he would
be wise to see that gentleman. After trying several times to make an ap-
pointment with Mr. Grey, he burst into Grey's office unannounced.

   "Why the hell, Abner, am I being kept out of the X club?"

   Mr. Grey politely evaded the question. He asked Mr. Smith to be seated.
He inquired after Mr. Smith's health, about the health of his wife, and inquired about other matters of simple convention.

   Finally, Mr. Smith said, "Ab, why the hell am I being kept out of
your club?"

   "But, John, you're not. Everyone in the X club thinks you're a fine fellow."

   "Well, what's wrong?"

"Well, John, we don't think you've got the *kind* of money necessary for being a good member of the X club. We don't think you'd be happy in the X club."

"Like hell, I haven't. I could buy and sell a half dozen of some of your board members."

"I know that, John, but that isn't what I said. I did not say the amount of money. I said the kind of money."

"What do you mean?"

"Well, John, my co-workers on the charity drive tell me you only gave a few dollars to our campaign and we had you down for a few thousand."

For a moment Mr. Smith was silent. Then he grinned. So did Mr. Grey. Smith took out his fountain pen and checkbook. "How much?"

At the next meeting of the X club Mr. Smith was unanimously elected to its membership.

Mr. Smith translated his money into philanthropy acceptable to the dominant group, he received their sponsorship, and finally became a participant in the X club. The "right" kind of house, the "right" neighborhood, the "right" furniture, the proper behavior, all are symbols of status that can ultimately be translated into social acceptance by those who have sufficient money to aspire to higher levels than they presently enjoy.

To belong to a particular level in the social-class system of America means that a family or individual has gained acceptance as an equal by those who belong in the class. The behavior in this class and the participation of those in it must be rated by the rest of the community as being at a particular place in the social scale.

Although our democratic heritage makes us disapprove, our class order helps control a number of important functions. It unequally divides the highly and lowly valued things of our society among the several classes according to their rank. Our marriage rules conform to the rules of class, for the majority of marriages are between people of the same class. No class system is so rigid that it completely prohibits marriages above and below one's own class. Furthermore an open class system such as ours permits a person through his lifetime to move up or down from the level into which he was born. Vertical social mobility for individuals or families is characteristic of all class systems. The principal forms of mobility in this country are through the use of money, education, occupation, talent, skill, philanthropy, sex, and marriage.

PEOPLE MOVE HIGHER BY EDUCATION

Although economic mobility is still important, it seems likely now that more people move to higher positions by education than by any other route. We have indicated before this that the mere possession of money is insufficient for gaining and keeping a higher social position. This is equally true of all other forms of mobility. In every case there must be social acceptance.

Class varies from community to community. The new city is less likely than an old one to have a well organized class order; this is also true for cities whose growth has been rapid as compared with those which have not been disturbed by huge increases in population from other regions or countries by the rapid displacement of old industries by new ones. The mill town's status hierarchy is more likely to follow the occupational hierarchy of the mill than the levels of evaluated participation found in market towns or those with diversified industries. Suburbs of large metropolises tend to respond to selective factors which reduce the number of classes to one or a very few. They do not represent or express all the cultural factors which make up the social pattern of an ordinary city.

Yet systematic studies from coast to coast, in cities large and small and of many economic types, indicate that, despite the variations and diversity, class levels do exist and that they conform to a particular pattern of organization.

Education is now competing with economic mobility as the principal route to success. Fewer men today rise from the bottom to the top places in industry and business than a generation ago. More and more the sons of executives are replacing their fathers in such positions, leaving fewer positions into which the sons of those farther down can climb from the ranks. Captains of industry educate their sons to take their places or to occupy similar places in other industries. Also, more and more top jobs in industry are being filled by men coming from the technical and engineering schools or from the universities. The route up for them is no longer through a hierarchy of increasing skill to management and ownership as it was two generations ago. The prudent mobile man today must prepare himself by education if he wishes to fill an important job and provide his family with the money and prestige necessary to get "the better things of life."

IT IS HARD FOR LOWER-CLASS CHILDREN
TO GET SCHOOLING

Social-class research demonstrates that our educational system performs the dual task of aiding social mobility and, at the same time, working effectively to hinder it. This ceases to be a paradox when all the facts are examined.

In the lower grades our public schools are filled by children from all walks of life. Since education is free in the public schools, since everyone has a right to it and our laws try to keep children in school, and since it is common knowledge that "if you want to get ahead you must get an education," it would be assumed that children at, and below, the Common

Man level would stay in school and equip themselves for mobility. Such is not the case. The social and educational systems work to eliminate the majority of them and permit only a few to get through.

It has been estimated that, whereas 80 per cent of the upper and upper-middle-class children actually go to college, only 20 per cent of the lower-middle and five per cent of the lower-class children get there. The evidence indicates that most, if not all, of the children of the top classes complete their preparation and go on to college, whereas those from the lower classes start dropping out in the grade schools and continue to do so in increasing numbers in high school. Only a very few of them go on to college. The educational conveyor belt drops lower-class children at the beginning and bottom of the educational route and carries those from the higher classes a longer distance, nearly all the upper-class children going to the end of the line.

PREDICTIVE VALUES OF STATUS RANKING

If the teachers and school administrators in grade and high schools know the class positions of the children who enter their schools they can predict who will and who will not get to college. Furthermore, with such knowledge the educator can act to change a negative prediction to a positive one for the bright, ambitious, lower and lower-middle-class children whose chances for higher education are now very slight.

The reason for the high mortality rate among the lower-class children becomes apparent when one examines the relation of the teachers and the other children to them. We now know that the intelligence of all lower-class children is not responsible for their failures in school for some of their I.Q.'s are equal to those higher up. Although inferior intelligence has been the most frequent and plausible explanation,[2] I.Q. tests equated to social class demonstrate that differential intelligence is not the answer.

TEACHERS TRY TO BE DEMOCRATIC, BUT—!

The teacher, it must be said, although one of the most democratically minded people in America, tends to favor the children of the classes Above the Common Man and to show less interest in those below that level. Studies in the Deep South, New England, and the Middlewest indicate

[2] The unpublished studies of Allison Davis, Robert J. Havighurst, and their collaborators in the class bias *within* the I.Q. tests themselves provide powerful evidence to show that the tests are not "culture free" but reflect the middle- and upper-class cultural bias of those who fabricate them. For example, the tests, being largely products of upper-middle-class people, reflect their biases and only middle- and higher-class children are properly prepared to take them.

that they rate the school work of children from the higher classes in accordance with their family's social position and conversely give low ratings to the work of the lower-class children.

How can this be? The answer is that most of it is done through ignorance about social class and how it operates in our lives. To be more specific, part of the general answer lies within the teacher as a product of our class system. The teacher conscientiously applies his own best values to his rating of the child. The middle-class teacher, and over three-fourths of them are middle-class, applies middle-class values. For the upper and upper-middle-class children possess traits that rank high and are positive; lower-class children have characteristics that are negative and are ranked low.

CHILDREN JUDGE EACH OTHER

Perhaps the most powerful influence of social class on the educational careers of our children, and certainly one of the most decisive and crucial situations in settling the ultimate class position of children from the Common Man and lower-class levels, is the influence of other children on the child's desire to stay in school. If the world of the child is pleasant, rewarding and increases his self-esteem, he is likely to want to stay and do well. If it is punishing and decreases his self-respect, he is likely to do poorly and want to quit.

In a study of children's ratings of other children in a middle-western community, Neugarten found that the children of the upper and upper-middle classes were rated high by all other children for such traits as good looks, liking for school, leadership, friendship, and many other favorable personal traits; lower-class children were ranked low or, more often than not, were given a negative rating and were said to be bad looking, dirty, and "people you would not want for friends."[3] When it is remembered that these children were only in the fifth and sixth grades and that each child in these grades was supposedly rated by all other children with no reference to status, we can see how quickly class values influence behavior and have their decisive effect in molding the personalities and influencing the life careers of Americans from their earliest years.

School for the children of the populous lower classes is not the satisfactory place it is for the middle and upper classes. Given children of equal intellect, ability, and interest, it can be predicted by the use of class analysis that a large percentage of those from the lower classes will be out of school before the sophomore year in high school and none of the upper-class children except those physically or mentally handicapped will quit school.

[3] Bernice L. Neugarten, "Social Class and Friendship among School Children," *American Journal of Sociology*, Vol. 41, No. 4, January, 1946.

Studies of the relations of workers and managers in business and industry demonstrate how class continues to operate selectively when the young people leave school. Management is bringing college-trained men into the lower ranks of supervisors and promoting fewer from the ranks because it finds that the workers, while good men technically, do not have the necessary knowledge about handling men and relating themselves effectively to the higher reaches of management. Their education is often insufficient to make them good prospects for continuing advancement. The hiring of formally educated men effectively puts a ceiling over the legitimate aspirations of workers who expect to rise in the ranks. The blocking of the worker's mobility and the encouragement of college-trained men is the ultimate payoff of what began in the grade schools. Mobility for workers is becoming more difficult; this means for the United States generally that the American Dream is becoming less real.

UNDERSTANDING OF THE STATUS SYSTEM CAN HELP

If our society is to use more effectively the brains and native talent of this great army of young people, it must learn how to train them. To do this it must keep them in school for a sufficient time to equip them with the skills and disciplines necessary for them to function satisfactorily in our economic and social world. Children as well as teachers and school administrators must have a conscious and explicit understanding of social class and a simple and easy way to use such knowledge in solving problems. Personality and I.Q. tests are important instruments to guide the teacher, but unless they are supplemented with instruments to measure and count the effects of social class they are insufficient.

Teaching Conflicting Values

The teaching of values is implicit in virtually every aspect of education. Requiring bookcovers for schoolbooks, imposing punishments for tardiness to class, locker inspections for cleanliness and orderliness, marking papers for spelling errors, examining for right answers, imposing clothing requirements, and the very necessity of attendance by law are all examples of value-laden education. It is not the question of whether to teach values or not, but rather, which values and why.

A major problem discussed in the following treatment of class biases is the predicament of opposing student-teacher values that results from differing social-class backgrounds. Should a teacher send a pupil to the principal for smoking? When a student swears in class what value systems are in conflict? How should the teacher deal with the student who underlines and writes in the margins of his schoolbook?

Class Biases in the Teaching of Values

CELIA BURNS STENDLER

The process of socialization, by which the child is brought under control of society, has been of considerable interest to psychiatrists and child guidance experts for many years. It is also a process which concerns teachers, for bringing the child under control of society is part and parcel of sound character and wholesome personality development, long accepted as ends toward which the schools should work. Because they are implicated in the socialization of the child it is important for teachers to be informed concerning the factors which affect the process. One of these factors which is being increasingly recognized as significant is that of social class. How social class may influence the socialization of the child will be discussed in this article.

It is generally recognized that the years from two to six constitute an important part of the socialization process. In the infant and young baby stage, the child is regarded as "cute" and "darling" regardless of what he does. But once he begins to walk, to go outside the home, perhaps to mingle with other children, he is made subject to pressures designed to make him conform to the mores of our society. He receives instruction, deliberate or incidental, from adults and from peer groups, which builds up in him certain attitudes toward property, authority, aggression, sex, achievement, and his role in his peer group. This instruction is enforced by rewards and punishments so that the child gradually builds inside himself a system of values which guides his choice of conduct even when adults are not present. At three he may refrain from hitting a playmate over the head because Mother is looking and he knows he will be punished for his aggression; the socialization process is much farther along when he wants to hit but refrains, even when no adults are near, because he has taken inside himself the warning voice of his parents and society.

Reprinted from *Progressive Education,* Vol. 27, No. 4, February, 1950, pp. 123–26, by permission of the John Dewey Society.

HOW THE CHILD LEARNS VALUES

A consideration of how the child learns values, of how socialization takes place, is necessary at this point. While much light still needs to be shed on the process, it seems clear that socialization in the preschool years is facilitated by two factors: (1) a consistent discipline, and (2) the child's desire to be like his parents. Through identification with his parents, the child takes inside himself their values and begins to acquire a conscience which will guide him in doing good or bad regardless of whether he is observed or not. Two conditions are proposed by Davis as necessary if socialization is going to take place.

First, the child should receive complete love from his parents or from his parent substitutes; second, he should receive socially appropriate prohibitions from them. The love relationship seems to be necessary as a basis of the best type of identification. The prohibitions are necessary in order that the child may take into himself a warning and punishing voice. Thus, parents who never punish their children (either by corporal punishment or by withdrawing affection from them) would not be able to instill a warning, punishing conscience in them. On the other hand, parents who never show affection to their children would not instill a conscience in them, either, no matter how much they punish them, because their children would not love them enough to want to be good. (There is some evidence that some children can identify with cruel repressive parents on the basis of fear. But this identification probably leads to pathological results.)[1]

But socialization is not necessarily completed by six years of age. Even after the child enters public school the process continues, with the teacher becoming an important socializing agent. In addition to reading, writing and arithmetic, she also teaches, directly or indirectly, a system of values which may or may not become a part of the character structure of her pupils.

It is at this point that a consideration of social class becomes important. As some sociologists have pointed out, we live in a society which is stratified into social classes, distinguished one from the other by such factors as income, ancestors, housing, occupation, social activities and mores. But even more fundamental as far as this particular problem goes is the possibility that social classes may also differ among each other in the values which each class cherishes. This may have particularly significance for teachers of lower- and upper-class children, for such teachers, as members of a middle class, may be trying to impart their class values to the children of other social classes.

[1] Davis, Allison, and Havighurst, Robert, *Father of the Man*. Houghton Mifflin, Boston, 1947, pp. 177–78.

WHOSE VALUES DOES THE SCHOOL RECOGNIZE?

Perhaps a look at what values the school does attempt to teach is in order here. While there is no research which bears directly on this question, some light on the subject is shed by two studies primarily designed to answer other questions. These studies have been concerned with the kinds of child behavior which teachers regard as serious. From the results, it would appear that children who answer back, who fight, who are tardy, who swear or use toilet talk, who are dirty, who do not respect property, who bully, are the problem children as far as the school is concerned. One might infer from these findings that the teachers hold in high esteem such values as respect for authority and property, work, non-aggression, promptness, cleanliness, and sexlessness.

But while the middle-class teacher may teach her group that "nice" people don't swear, a lower-class pupil (or an upper-class) in her room may not accept her judgment; indeed, his parents may have a rich and varied vocabulary and still be "nice" people in his eyes. The middle-class teacher may teach, "We don't fight" to children who are taught at home that we do, and that they had better fight to stick up for their rights. Respect for authority may be drilled into the middle-class child, whereas the lower-class may suspect the respectful child as an apple polisher. In "Father of the Man" the conflict in values is well illustrated in the case studies of the two Washington children.

> Mary, who is praised by her middle-class teacher for being quiet and anxious to please, is criticized by most of her family for the same behavior. Her softness and compliancy are regarded by Hazel and all her sisters as traits of a schemer and of an apple polisher. Most of her family believe that she is designing . . .
>
> Paulette's aggression, on the other hand, seems to her mother and Hazel to prove her honesty. . . . In her slum community, where a curse and a blow—, a readiness to "tell people off" and let them "like it or lump it"—are highly admired, Paulette is popular.[2]

What happens when the school attempts to teach values which run counter to those of its pupils?

Several possibilities suggest themselves. For one, the pupils may learn two or more patterns for behaving. He may learn that in school one talks and acts in a particular way but that outside of school one acts in a different way. He may discontinue fighting on the playgrounds but fight when a block away from the school; or he may refrain from cursing in the boys' locker room because someone may squeal but continue to do so when playing in his neighborhood. Children who adopt this pattern have not taken within themselves the values the school is teaching; they are actually

[2] Davis and Havighurst, *op. cit.*, pp. 14–15.

rejecting these values. They are like the three-year-old in that they are learning a method of adjustment in order to avoid punishment.

A second possible outcome of a conflict in values is that the pupil may reject the values of the school openly as well as privately. Such pupils will continue to exhibit in school the kinds of behavior based upon values learned outside the school. They fight and swear; they are disrespectful of people and property. They are the pupils who are continually in trouble with school authorities and who drop out of school when they reach the legal leaving age. However, in their out-of-school life, they may be the Paulette Washingtons, accepted and liked by their own social class, and secure in their feeling of belonging to such a group.

A third possibility is that the pupil may accept the values which the school is teaching, and may substitute these for the values of his own sub-culture group. These are the pupils who become socially mobile; who will eventually leave their own social class and move on to the middle class as they become more and more like the middle class in their ways of thinking, speaking and acting. But such children in accepting middle-class values wholeheartedly may find themselves rejected and regarded with suspicion by those in their own culture. The case of Mary Washington, to which reference has already been made, illustrates the point. While moving into the middle class may bring with it the advantages that go with middle-class membership, it also imposes a penalty, the penalty of growing up without a feeling of belongingness. The socially mobile child may find himself an outcast from his own class before he has made the grade with a higher social class group.

HOW TO TEACH VALUES WHICH ARE IN CONFLICT WITH THE PUPIL'S VALUES

If the schools are going to be effective agents in building sound character and wholesome personality, the last choice mentioned in the above paragraph where the child accepts the values of the school is obviously the goal toward which we should be working. But in order to build values effectively, and with less cost to the socially mobile, several important steps need to be taken. First it would seem necessary for schools to re-examine the values which they are attempting to teach. While middle-class values of cleanliness, respect for authority and property, and others already indicated are important to a degree, one might question the compulsiveness of the middle-class adherence to them and also the extent to which they are advocated. While a certain standard of cleanliness is necessary for health reasons, one might raise questions about making a fetish out of clean finger nails. While a certain amount of respect for authority is necessary, one might question the teacher who holds this value so rigidly that she becomes emotionally upset when a youngster threatens her authority or her control of the group. Again, while proper use of school materials is something schools should be teaching, one might question the extreme emphasis teachers place on the use of two paper towels to dry the hands instead of one. What we are arguing for here is that teachers develop more insight into the origin of their own values. When a teacher finds herself unduly disturbed by pupil conduct—that is, disturbed out of proportion to the actual deed when she stands off and looks at herself objectively, she might well see if the misdeed is one which grates upon her middle-class personality. The next step for the teacher to take is to see whether the particular value being violated by the pupil deserves the prestige she has placed upon it.

Not only the extent to which middle-class values are advocated, but also the choice of values to be emphasized needs to be examined critically. In *Adolescent Character and Personality*, the authors point out, "The influence of the school affects primarily the sense of responsibility and honesty; it is less effective as far as loyalty, moral courage and friendliness are concerned."[3] A recommendation from the authors is to the effect that "They (boys and girls) should learn to make distinctions between the lesser mores of eating, drinking, amusement, clothing, and marriage customs, which differ from one social group to another, and the more basic moral qualities such as honesty, loyalty, kindness, and courage, which are very nearly universal."[4] Readers, too, will no doubt be in agreement that these basic qualities are more important than saying "Excuse me" when one walks in front of the teacher, yet they are receiving far less attention in our schools than the lesser mores. Such a reevaluation of our teaching of values may result in a program which will make better sense to lower class children and therefore stand a better chance of being accepted by them.

A third step necessary for schools to take if they are to be effective in teaching values is to establish a warm emotional climate in the classroom. This means that teachers must accept all pupils regardless of social class background, for the child who feels himself rejected by the teacher will not accept the values for which she stands. This means that teachers must watch their own emotional reactions to child behavior to see to what extent these may be class conditioned. For a horrible example of class-biased attitudes toward pupils, the reader is referred to *Elmtown's Youth*. Here we have an account of how a superintendent of schools and a high school principal excuse upper-class youngsters who evade staying after school for being late. This is contrasted with their shocking treatment of "Boney" Johnson, a lower-class member who is also tardy:

When school was out that afternoon, the Superintendent stood in the hall near the side exit, Mr. White, a teacher, watched the front door, while the principal

[3] Robert J. Havighurst and Hilda Taba, *Adolescent Character and Personality*, Wiley & Sons, New York, 1949, p. 94.
[4] *Ibid.*, p. 201.

patrolled the building. Mr. Gardner, another teacher, was in the detention room. After the building was cleared of students and most of the teachers had gone home, the Superintendent walked back to his office, but the principal stood outside the front door. Suddenly the door was thrown open from the outside, and angry voices were heard. The Superintendent rushed out of his office and stood at the head of the stairs. The principal pushed and shoved "Boney" up the stairs as he repeated, "You can't get away with that stuff." As they neared the top, "Boney" broke from his grasp and started down the hall toward the side door. The Superintendent leaped and grabbed him by the coat collar with his left hand. "Boney" turned and started to fight. The principal spun him around, seized the visor of his cap with his right hand and yanked it down over his eyes. While "Boney" was fighting to get the cap off his face, the principal hit him three times with the heel of his hand on the back of the neck near the base of the skull. "Boney" cursed, struggled, and hit in all directions. Soon he broke free and ran toward the Superintendent, who shook and slapped him three or four times. Both men then grabbed him by the arms and shook him vigorously. The Superintendent angrily screeched, "You're going out of this building. You're never coming back until you bring your father and we talk this over." By this time, the three had reached the front door. "Boney" was shoved outside. He stood there, cursing and threatening both men with violence. In a few minutes he composed himself, straightened his clothes, and walked away, muttering to himself.[5]

Obviously, teachers and administrators who are hoping to build the basic moral qualities of honesty, kindliness, loyalty and courage cannot do so in such a fashion. If we want children to accept the values we are attempting to teach, it is necessary for children to feel that we like them and accept them.

Still a fourth step for teachers to take in facilitating the socialization process is to work on group structure in the classroom. In addition to being liked and accepted, children should have a feeling of belonging in order to accept more readily the values that the school is attempting to teach. By the use of socio-metric measures the teacher can discover which children are isolates and then work to bring those youngsters into the group. She can also find out about the cliques operating in her room, and through the use of projects give children in school at least the opportunity to know intimately and to work with different social classes.

The measures that have been suggested so far have been in line with current thinking on the problem. The fifth suggestion, however, goes much deeper. It suggests that teachers should carefully open up the problem of social class with older children and help them see class differences in values in so far as we know them. Research has shown that by the time the children reach the eighth grade (indeed, in some cases, the sixth) they are pretty well aware of the fact that a class structure exists in their particular community. Perhaps then, at the junior high school level teachers could profitably explore this issue with their pupils. There is no beaten path for teachers to follow in this connection, but experimentally-minded

[5] A. B. Hollingshead, *Elmtown's Youth*, Wiley & Sons, New York, 1949, pp. 190–91.

teachers might cull from some of the case studies in the numerous volumes on social class, material to be presented in social studies, or English, or problems of living classes. Pupils might analyze and discuss the case studies and in so doing, develop keener insight into their own value systems. It is to be hoped also, that with their new insights, pupils will be helped to build a system of values that will contribute to the moral fibre of our democracy.

Class Patterns Within the School

This excerpt from Democracy in Jonesville, *a classic study of society in microcosm, describes the operation of social classes in the field of education. Although the study is nearly twenty-years-old and the numerical data are no longer accurate, the essence of the study still has validity. The student of education and society can easily see the contemporary significance of the statements made. In light of your firsthand knowledge of the schools, gained from the experiences of attendance and observation, the following descriptions can be judged as to their relevancy to education today.*

Do social classes have the same influence today on education as they had in Jonesville? Is the Board of Education essentially representative of the same classes noted? In what ways are the teachers, administrators, and students of this decade similar to or different from those depicted in the following?

Democracy in Jonesville

W. LLOYD WARNER

School districts are not required to maintain a high school; none of the rural districts within the communal area has established one. In accordance with the statutes, all land in Abraham County, not in a high school district, is organized into a non-high-school district and a tax is

Pp. 194–96, 198–99, 204–13 from *Democracy in Jonesville* by W. Lloyd Warner. Copyright 1949 by Harper & Row, Publishers, Incorporated. Reprinted by permission of Harper & Row, Publishers.

levied to pay for the tuition of pupils who attend high schools elsewhere. Since Jonesville has the only high school in the community the pupils from the non-high-school district come to Jonesville High School. Thus, the families in rural territory are in two districts—the common school district and the non-high district—and pay two taxes. The Jonesville school system is organized into one district under the jurisdiction of a Board of Education.

THE BOARD OF EDUCATION

Responsibility for the operation of the school system rests in a seven man Board of Education. The president of the Board is elected annually in April along with two members elected for three year terms. Theoretically, any adult citizen who is a resident of the district may be a candidate for the school board. In practice, the members of the Board of Education come from the two upper classes and have to qualify under three strictly administered ground rules: first, only men are eligible; second, Catholics, Jews, Irish, and Democrats are informally disqualified; and third, the Board is "nonpolitical." To become a member of the Board a man has to be a Protestant, a Republican, a property owner, and a Rotarian or, at the very least, approved by the Rotarians. Rotarians are proud of the way they have controlled the selection of the Board for "more than twenty-five years."

The selection of a candidate to fill a vacancy is left to the president of the Board. He discusses possible candidates with his friends on the Board and in Rotary. Generally he invites a fellow Rotarian with whom he believes he can work to become a candidate. The president then files this man's name with the election clerk; nothing is said publicly about the impending vacancy or the forthcoming election until after the last date for filing has passed. Then the *Jonesville Eagle* runs a news item which notes that the date for filing for the school election has passed, and that such-and-such men have filed as candidates for the Board of Education, and Mr. X has filed again for president of the Board. Little additional publicity is given to the election until the *Eagle* carries the necessary legal notices of the polling places and names of candidates. When election day comes only a handful of voters go to the polls to elect the handpicked candidates. In 1940, 132 votes were cast; 114 in 1941; and 84 in 1942.

This carefully controlled system for the selection of Board members has resulted in the election of middle-aged business and professional men from the top two classes who possess a highly developed sense of responsibility to these classes especially with respect to the preservation of economic interests, power, and prestige. The policies they have followed in the administration of the school system have reflected the community interests of their own social classes and, to a less extent, those of the little business and professional people in the lower-middle class. The relationship between their official positions as Board members and the education of approximately four-fifths of the children is not comprehended by either the Board members themselves or the rank and file of adults in the classes they represented.

Members of the Board have intimate and coordinate relations almost exclusively with people in their own classes who tend to think more or less alike on educational questions, particularly those that might raise the tax rate. They are out of touch with the opinions, beliefs, prejudices, and aspirations of some 75 percent of the people in the community. Contacts outside their class groups are largely superficial; their social positions make it difficult, even if they so desired, to bridge the gap between themselves and persons in the lower classes. People in the upper classes do not believe it wise or necessary to know what the common people are thinking. If they pick up information through gossip and chance remarks indicative of hostility or unrest, they tend to ignore it and consider the person voicing it as irresponsible, "radical," or "a local red." Persons in the Level Above the Common Man are satisfied with the Board since it represents the "finest people," "the good element," "the refined interests"; but, as one moves lower in the social structure, criticism of the Board of Education and its members is encountered with increasing frequency until the lower-lower class where the question of the school is ignored or avoided by most adults.

The Board of Education has been concerned primarily with two things: the operation of the schools as economically as possible, and conformity by teachers to conservative economic, political, religious, and moral doctrines, both in the classroom and in their private lives. The school is viewed as an indispensable but expensive institution by the members of the Board. They believe it should reflect in its administration and teaching all that is traditionally good and wholesome in Middle Western American small-town life—if it does not cost too much. The question of cost comes first whenever an innovation is suggested. Throughout its thinking on educational questions the Board compares the cost with the alleged value of the item or the program under consideration. Cost versus value is acute whenever an item that touches the high school enters the picture.

High school education is far more expensive than elementary; moreover, members of the Board are of the opinion that not everyone of high school age should have a high school education. No Board member was found who believed it was the responsibility of the community to provide educational facilities for *all* high school adolescents. They believed there are many boys and girls in high school who would be better off "on the farm" or "down at The Mill." They are interested, however, in seeing that "everyone who can profit by a high school education is provided with the necessary facilities," but they are not clear in the conception of who "can profit by a high school education." In general, they mean the sons and daughters

of the three higher classes, and those in Class IV, if they "behave themselves." Adolescents in Class V are not considered to have enough ability
"to profit from a high school education." . . .

PROFESSIONAL PERSONNEL

Educational policies formulated by the Board are executed by the Superintendent of Schools, a professionally trained, licensed administrator
hired by the Board from year to year and responsible directly to it. His
contact with the community is professional and contractual, but his social
relationships are far more important to his success or failure locally than
his professional or contractual ones. The superintendent comes into a pre-
existing socio-cultural complex with all its local values, beliefs, prejudices,
and ground rules of what "to do" and "not to do." He must adjust to, and
become a part of, a social system he did not help create. He is compelled
by the pressures around him to organize his thoughts and activities in
accordance with the demands made upon him by the people who wield the
power in the community.

The superintendent's first responsibility is to the Board that hired him,
and to which he must answer for his actions, as well as the actions of his
teachers, and the pupils in the school system. He acts as liaison between
the principals, teachers, and pupils, on the one hand, and, on the other,
the Board and the schools' patrons. The superintendent is subject to many
types of demands from the community as they relate to him as a person,
the school system, and the Board, and from students and teachers. He
knows that what teachers do in the classroom and community, especially
what they are alleged to do, reflects on his standing with the Board. He
is hired to keep the school system functioning smoothly, and his success
depends upon the avoidance of criticism, rather than upon how well he
educates the students.

The principals of the elementary schools and the high school are immediately subordinate to the superintendent. The elementary principal has
jurisdiction over the four grammar schools and their 22 teachers. The high
school principal is in charge of the high school and its 15 teachers.

The Board followed different employment policies in the two parts of
the system. "Outsiders" were procured for all administrative positions and
for positions in the high school; local girls were hired in the elementary
schools whenever they were available. About three-fourths of the elementary teachers had been born, reared, and educated in the community.
After high school they had gone away to teachers' colleges or universities
for their professional training, then appointed back into the system. These
women generally came from lower-middle-class families, with a few from
upper-middle status; none was from the other classes. Local girls usually
followed one of two paths: they either taught a few years, then married

and raised a family, or stayed on year after year to become "maiden ladies." The local teachers lived with their parents, if they were living, or in the family home. Turnover in this group was in marked contrast to the outside teachers who left the system as soon as possible. . . .

WHO GOES TO HIGH SCHOOL

"Learning things from books and life" in a friendly atmosphere was the ideal stressed in Jonesville High. Perhaps this preoccupation with friendliness on the part of the superintendent, principal, and teachers was related to the lack of friendliness in the student body, the schisms between class and religious groups, the club members and the nonmembers, the "rich kids" and the "poor kids," the "Americans" and the "Poles." Perhaps the students were learning about the business of life from their teachers and fellow students a little too realistically.

During the school year, 1941–42, there were 735 adolescents of high school age in the community who might have been in high school if they had all conformed to legal requirements or the ideal that the society should provide its members with a high school education at public expense. In the course of the year, 437 were enrolled in the high school at one time or another. The peak enrollment was reached early in September when 423 pupils crowded into the little rooms and narrow halls. By early June, through drop-outs, withdrawals, and transfers, which overbalanced the children enrolled from new families, the number had dwindled to 390, or 53 percent of the potential high school population.

Who was in school and who was out of school? Was there any relationship between age or place of residence and enrollment? What are the conditions under which some students persist in school and others withdraw?

It is a common belief in Jonesville that country children quit school oftener than town youngsters, but the facts refute this belief. Almost 75 percent of the 735 adolescents of high school age live in town and 25 percent in the country. The 390 who finished high school in 1941–42 were in almost the same proportion as the total: 75.9 percent lived in Jonesville and 24.1 percent in the rural area.

A second local myth is built around compulsory attendance. It is believed the authorities "make the children go to school" until they are sixteen years of age. Seventy-four percent of the 345 adolescents out of school in the spring of 1942 had withdrawn from school before they were sixteen years of age.

The people of Jonesville, both within and outside the school system, are unaware of the number or the proportion of young people of high school age who are not in school. The superintendent knew there were "some"; the president of the Board stated, "Certainly, there are a few youngsters not in school, but you will find that in any town."

Analysis of the data showed a high correlation between class position and continuance in, or dropping out of, school. All the young people in the classes Above the Common Man Level were in school; over 9 out of 10 in the lower-middle class; 6 out of 10 in the upper-lower class; but only 1 out of 10 in the lower-lower class.

We must conclude that the class to which a child belongs is a significant factor in his relations to the high school.

TABLE 1

Social Class and School Attendance

Social Class	In School		Out of School	
	No.	Percent	No.	Percent
U	4*	100.0	..	..
UM	31	100.0	..	..
LM	146	92.4	12	7.6
UL	183	58.7	129	41.3
LL	26	11.3	204	88.7
	390	53.1	·345	46.9

* Hereafter, the 4 cases in the upper class are combined with the 31 in the upper-middle class.

We believe this is a two-way relationship. On the one hand, the class culture of the child provides him with certain beliefs and values about the high school and what it has to offer. On the other, the institutional values of the school, represented by the Board of Education, the professional administrators and teachers, as well as the students, develop differential attitudes toward persons in different positions in the social structure which act as attractive or repellent agents to keep the adolescent in, or to force him out of, school.

WHO TAKES WHAT

The high school curriculum is built around three courses: College Preparatory, General, and Commercial. The entire College Preparatory Course is designed to meet the requirements for entrance into the State University. The General Course requires six units—three years of English, one of United States history, one of mathematics, one of some kind of science—and 10 units of electives. The Commercial Course is divided into two sections, General-Commercial and Secretarial-Commercial. Students enrolled in the College Preparatory Courses are placed in different classes from those taking General and Commercial subjects. College

Preparatory English is different from the English given to other classes. The College Preparatory students are given traditional algebra and geometry, whereas the other students receive what is called "Practical Mathematics," composed largely of problems in arithmetic.

Teachers in the College Preparatory Course consider it to be of higher educational value than the General or Commercial Courses. Those who teach both College Preparatory students and General students believe there is more ability in the former. They prefer to teach College Preparatory students because they are "more interested" and "do better work." These contentions may be true, but a more probable reason is that teaching the College Preparatory group satisfies the urge to teach the children who reflect the same academic values as one's own. Most teachers regard students in the General Courses as persons who do not have anything better to do with their time, mediocre in ability, and lacking motivation and interest in their subjects. Students in the Commercial Courses are rated even lower in ability than those in the General Course.

The students reflect attitudes held by the teachers in their evaluation of the three courses. Those who take the College Preparatory Course believe themselves to be on a higher intellectual level than the General students; the Commercial students, as we would expect, are placed on the bottom rung of the value ladder. A 1941 graduate, and a leader in her class, summarized the views of the students:

If you take a College Preparatory Course, you're better than those who take a General Course. Those who take a General Course are neither here nor there. If you take a Commercial Course, you just don't rate. It's a funny thing, those who take College Preparatory set themselves up as better than the other kids. Those that take the College Preparatory Course run the place. I remember when I was a freshman, mother wanted me to take Home Economics, but I didn't want to. I knew I couldn't rate. You could take typing and shorthand and still rate, but if you took a straight Commercial Course, you couldn't rate. You see, you're rated by the teachers according to the course you take. They rate you in the first six weeks. The teachers type you in a small school and you're made in classes before you get there. College Preparatory kids get good grades and the others take what's left. The teachers get together and talk and if you are not in College Preparatory, you haven't got a chance.

Enrollment in the three courses is associated significantly with class: The adolescents from Above the Common Man Level concentrate in the College Preparatory Course (64.3 percent) and ignore the Commercial Course. The lower-middles are divided unequally: 51.4 percent are in the General, 27.4 percent in the College Preparatory, and 21.2 percent in the Commercial. The upper-lower children enter the General (58.5 percent) and Commercial (32.8 percent) Courses and avoid the College Preparatory (only 8.7 percent). The pattern for the lower-lowers is similar to the upper-lowers, but the number is too small to allow generalization.

The class bias in the different courses is particularly clear among the girls. For instance, 71 percent of the girls from the top class are in the College Preparatory Course, none in the Secretarial Division of the Commerical Course, and only one in the General Commercial Course. Girls from the upper-lower are concentrated in the Commercial Course with the greatest number in the Secretarial Division. Sixty-two percent of the girls in the Secretarial Division are from the upper-lower class and 38 percent from lower-middle. Most girls trained in the Secretarial Division find jobs in local offices as secretaries and clerks. The high school provides these girls with a specialized terminal education.

GRADES AND GRADING

The semester grades each student received were averaged, and the arithmetic mean used as an index of school performance. Individual mean grades were then tabulated on a three division scale: 85–100, 70–84, and 50–69. Distribution of grades by class is shown in the following table:

TABLE 2
Grade Distribution in Percents

Social Class	85–100	70–84	50–69
U + UM	51.4	48.6	..
LM	33.5	65.2	1.3
UL	18.4	69.1	12.4
LL	8.3	66.7	25.0
Total	23.8	66.3	9.9

Two points are clear here: (1) the grade distribution varies significantly from one class to another, and (2) the better grades go to the higher classes and the poorer grades to the lower classes.

Behind these figures lies the intricate pattern of human relationships, motives, and desires as they function in the class system. The struggle of the family to maintain a favorable prestige position is connected with the grades a child receives since grades are accepted in the culture as a symbol of intellectual worth. High grades are tantamount to quality and low grades to inferiority. Only a few may achieve high grades in a grading system where the teacher is constrained by the requirements of the normal curve to limit high grades to seven percent of a class. There are few boys and girls from the top classes, just as there are few high grades; there are more students from the lower than upper-middle class, likewise, more grades in a lower category; and so on down to the bottom where most of the boys and girls have dropped out of school. There are few students from these "poorer families," but what is more natural, the society being what it is, than that these students should receive the poor grades.

In the local system offices, prestige positions, committee memberships, and exercise of power are accepted as the rightful due of the two higher classes. Teachers soon learn who is who and what must be done to satisfy the requirements of proper public relations in their associations with these people and their children. In the same informal way, they hear about families whose reputations are symbolic of all that is considered evil in the communal value system. They are told the children of these people "have to be watched," or, "you cannot expect anything from that tribe." Teachers experienced in the system warn the newcomers about this and that boy or girl, "their parents are touchy," "John comes from one of the best families here," "her mother expects her to make all A's," "all of Veronica's sisters have turned out to be prostitutes," "Jeannie's father was electrocuted a few years ago for murdering a prominent farmer; she's mean like he was." Narratives, gossip, a hint here, and a warning there give the teacher a feel of the situation. Remarks in teachers' meetings such as "we can't do anything there," said in relation to an upper-class boy caught copying an algebra problem on an examination, or "don't send her to detention [an upper-middle-class girl]—if you do our whole discipline program will be discussed in Board meeting"—in these none too subtle ways teachers learn to act judiciously in their relations with the children of the powerful.

It was believed widely in the lower classes and, to a somewhat less extent, in the lower-middle that the grades a high school student received were determined by who his parents were rather than by his ability or effort. This had some foundation, as one would expect, in a belief that has persisted over a number of years and is documented by one story after another. In the stories, each case was personalized around the relations between the teacher, principal, superintendent, and the adolescent or his family. If the stories could be believed in their entirety, the honors in the graduating classes, from both the elementary and high schools, were deliberately given to the prominent families' children. It was charged that grades were changed, teachers threatened with dismissal, and examinations rigged. Several families in the top classes were alleged to have brought pressure on the superintendent or principal, through the Board of Education, to have grades changed after graduation so the child could enter college. We doubt that the process was as deliberate as we have been led to believe by some parents, but it undoubtedly happened in a few cases.

There is little question that the stories were rooted in fact, for the teachers did cater to the prominent families. The one teacher who had been in the high school for more than four years was highly regarded by the parents from the higher classes but hated and distrusted by many in the Common Man Level who were convinced she graded "with one eye on the social register and the other on her own advantage." An old lady who was often referred to as "the most powerful person in Jonesville" once told us, with reference to this teacher, that the town "is very fortunate to be able to keep 'Miss X.' She is such a wonderful teacher. She teaches every child in a different way; she knows each one's background and treats it accordingly."

EXTRA-CURRICULAR ACTIVITIES

An elaborate extra-curricular program brings the school's activities before the public on a broader front than its teaching functions. This, the circus side of school, entertains both student and adults in their leisure time. These entertainment activities are emphasized by the Board, the superintendent, the principal, teachers, and students. They want their athletic teams to win games, musical organizations to perform publicly at all possible times in a creditable manner, and the dramatics group to produce plays no one will criticize, but all will enjoy.

Extra-curricular activities that do not have spectator appeal or broad public relations value receive little emphasis. Girls' athletics, student government, school clubs, and dances are tolerated, but not encouraged. These minor·programs are approved, and the administration "goes along" with the teachers and students interested in them, but they receive little support from the Board or the community. Clubs are fostered by the teachers in their departments and developed under their interest and leadership rather than through student interest. Any teacher can organize a departmental club if she is interested enough to take the time or trouble. For instance, the French teacher has a French Club; the domestic science teacher, the Homemaking Club; one English teacher developed a Library Club; and the agriculture teacher started a chapter of the Future Farmers of America for the boys in his classes.

Twenty-three extra-curricular activities ranging from organized athletics to the school paper are actively supported by the student body. They tend to be severely sex-graded, but some, such as the Dramatics Club, are composed of both boys and girls. It is possible for a boy to belong to eleven different organizations and a girl to twelve. In spite of the large number of activities and the wide range of interests they represent, one student out of three does not participate. Participation or nonparticipation is associated very strongly with class position as the following table shows:

TABLE 3

Social Class and Participation in School

Social Class	Participation	Nonparticipation
U + UM	100.0	. . .
LM	75.3	24.7
UL	57.4	42.6
LL	27.0	73.0
Total	65.9	34.1

Adolescents from the higher classes are found in far more activities than those from the lower classes, and the girls are in more than the boys.

TABLE 4

Mean Number of Extra-Curricular Activities
Participated in by Sex and Class

Social Class	Boys	Girls
U + UM	1.8	3.9
LM	1.1	2.0
UL	.8	1.0
LL	.6	.1
Total	1.0	1.4

In the two middle classes, the girls are in twice as many activities as the boys, but the difference is negligible in upper-lower, and in the lowest class the boys are more strongly represented than the girls. Eighteen girls are in six activities and seven in seven activities. Nine are upper-middle, six lower-middle, and three upper-lower. Since there are only fourteen girls in the upper-middle class, it is easy to see these girls enter as many activities as possible and give the impression to the other girls "they are in everything" as they, indeed, tend to be. The few hyperactive lower-middle-class girls represent only 11 percent of the girls in this class; moreover, they tend to be scattered in more activities so their presence in an activity is not so conspicuous. The three upper-lower girls in either six or seven activities represent less than four percent of the girls in the class; therefore, the roles they play are really different from the average girl in the class below. Boys do not allow themselves to become involved in as many activities as the girls. No boy participates in more than four, and only two are in this many—one, upper-middle, the other, upper-lower. Nevertheless, the upper-middle boys are in almost twice as many activities on the average as the lower-middle-class boys.

Participation in all extra-curricular activities except boys' athletics is biased in favor of some classes and against others. Boys' athletics is the one area where no association between class position and participation appears. The boys from the several classes turn out for all athletic teams in the approximate proportion represented by each class in the student body.

The invisible lines between the classes channelize the activities of an increasing proportion of the boys and girls out of extra-curricular activities as one moves through successive strata toward the bottom class, where the adolescents who are still in school are left out of the things that would give them vital training in getting along with persons in the other classes. As it is, each social class goes its way without paying too much attention to what is happening, simply as a result of the general indifference that characterizes the society.

THE MEANING OF POVERTY

Despite the increased gross national product, improved general living conditions, raised average income levels, and other positive signs of an affluent society, there still exists the social problem of poverty and its resulting deprivation and disparity in social class. While poverty apparently is in evidence in some form or another in virtually every culture, the problem is not alleviated by ignoring its existence or by assigning it to fatalism and nonsolubility. The failure of an open society to acknowledge conditions of poverty has repercussions throughout that culture. As the range between rich and poor widens, the equality of opportunity for productive life style decreases and the conditions of caste more than class expand. Although equality of condition is not a tradition in American society, equality of opportunity is surely an ideal toward which the society has striven. The theory of a free enterprise economic system which attempts to reward merit, not caste, depends upon an equality of opportunity to demonstrate merit. The extent to which poverty denies opportunity is the extent to which members of poverty classes are denied social mobility and become members of a caste.

The fact that larger numbers of members of a society are becoming more affluent does not account for the tragedy of poverty which remains hard core. Many answers to the poverty problem have been suggested, including social concern without program, program without financial support, financial support without social concern, and denial of the problem as a function of natural selection. Examples of these are the poverty ghetto moralists who decry conditions, but offer no suggestions, the various charities on shoestring budgets, the poverty war, and the older answer of debtor's prisons. There apparently is no simple solution, but there is a complex problem which affects many areas of the culture.

Education has gained increased status as a potential partial solution to the problems of poverty. Surely the deprivation of members of a society as a result of poverty is directly felt in the schools of a system which requires attendance and rewards educational achievement. The cultural deprivation accompanying poverty is a striking influence on the level of opportunity and attainment available through education. If a democracy depends on an intelligent, enlightened citizenry, as Thomas Jefferson indicated, the agents of democracy which accept primary responsibility for this enlightenment must be concerned about the cultural level of all strata of a society. The schools, then, have a distinct relation to the problem since poverty and deprivation create a wide disparity in the life styles of citizens.

Problems of the Poor

*By the middle of the 1960's, average family income in the United States
had risen above $6,000 annually. Yet over five million families had incomes
of less than $2,000—the initially established income to qualify for federal
assistance. Income in dollars is no indication of rich or poor until it is related to standards of adequate life in a society. As Sargent Shriver points
out in the first reading in this section, a 1959 criterion established for
"adequate standard of living" for a family of four in an urban area was
$2,500.*

*Problems of the poor include health, housing, education, and related
psycho-social problems of motivation, incentive, will, desire, and status.
The answers to these problems have not been discovered. Education has
been suggested as one of the primary means for alleviating problems of the
poor. Are the schools, as presently organized, capable of this kind of social
reform? What effects will increased educational opportunities have on the
depressed areas of the country? How can the schools alter a social problem
as long-standing as poverty? If the schools do not attempt the alteration,
what courses remain?*

Poverty

SARGENT SHRIVER

The United States in the 1960's was the richest and most powerful nation
in the world. Thanks to ample natural resources and a highly developed
technology, most of its citizens lived lives of comfort and affluence unimaginable a century before. It was also a nation with a record of generosity
to other nations. It had lent and given billions of dollars to western Europe
and to newly born and have-not countries all around the globe.

Yet in the midst of unprecedented American prosperity there existed—
although often invisible to visitors from foreign lands—the paradox of
poverty. It was estimated that 35 million persons, or one fifth of the population, existed in conditions of want, or near want. Of these, 11 million were

Reprinted from the *Encyclopedia Americana*, by permission of the publishers, Grolier
Incorporated, New York, and the author.

children. Although statisticians disagreed on definitions of poverty, there was ample evidence that 6 million families were attempting to feed, shelter, and educate their youngsters on grossly inadequate incomes.

Older Americans remembered the Great Depression of the 1930's when, in President Franklin D. Roosevelt's words, one third of the nation was "ill-housed, ill-clad, ill-nourished." There was nothing invisible about poverty then. There were long lines outside employment offices. There were apple sellers in Wall Street. It was during this period that the government introduced federal programs for health and welfare, social insurance, and unemployment compensation.

The tremendous industrial effort that began with World War II expanded production to peaks previously unknown. And, despite minor recessions, production continued to expand. By the mid-1960's, for example, there were estimated to be 71 million automobiles in the United States.

But in its 1964 annual report to the President, the Council of Economic Advisers said:

There will always be some Americans who are better off than others. . . . In the United States today we can see on the horizon a society of abundance, free of much of the misery and degradation that have been the old fate of man. Steadily rising productivity, together with an improving network of private and social insurance and assistance, has been eroding mass poverty in America. But the process is far too slow. It is high time to redouble and to concentrate our efforts to eliminate poverty.

Shortly after the report was issued, President Lyndon B. Johnson called for an "all-out war on poverty." In August, 1964, Congress passed legislation setting up the Office of Economic Opportunity—with the authority of the White House behind it—to direct and coordinate the efforts of many government and private agencies toward this end. On Oct. 8, 1964, Congress provided the money, $800 million, to start the attack.

It was a bold and imaginative program that commanded worldwide attention. Sponsors of the legislation knew that it would not end poverty overnight. But it was a beginning.

THE MEANING OF POVERTY

From Biblical to modern times the great majority of people were poor. They were poor, however, in *things* rather than in *food*. Except in times of regional crop failures or plague or disastrous wars, there was generally enough food to go around. But even the few who enjoyed great riches—the barons, the great landowners, the aristocracy—might be considered "poor" by today's standards. None of them enjoyed free education through college, expert medical care, or the chance for worldwide travel. None of them knew such conveniences as central heating, hot running water, electricity, or the automobile—all of which are now available to families with modest incomes throughout the United States.

Origins. Poverty as a social problem first came to be recognized in Europe and the United States during the Industrial Revolution at the end of the 1700's. A slow, stately agricultural economy gave way to the hustle and bustle of factories. Soot and smoke blackened the skies. Working people abandoned the spaciousness of farms for the day wages and distempers of factories and slums. The Industrial Revolution transformed the Western world, created great private fortunes, and permitted giant steps in man's material progress. But it accomplished all this at a considerable price in human misery.

Under feudalism, in theory at least, the landowner had been responsible for the welfare of his tenants. Often rural landowners had little more education than their inferiors and shared with them a crudity of manners and a love of blood sports. Henry Fielding's novel *Tom Jones,* written in the 1700's, gives an excellent, rollicking picture of the rough justice and paternalism of the rural squire.

The landowner's sense of personal responsibility for his workers did not carry over to the factory owner in England, the coal operator in Wales, or, later, the steel magnate in the United States. Their behavior was consistent with the laissez-faire theory of economics as expounded by Adam Smith.

This may seem paradoxical, for in his time Adam Smith was a reformer, a fact that many people now overlook. He wanted to take away the special privileges that had been granted to favored subjects by British kings. When such privileges and restraints are abolished, he wrote, "the obvious and simple system of natural liberty establishes itself of its own accord."

The system he believed in was based on the "free market." It was a market of self-interest and competition. The factory owner would buy as cheaply as he could and sell as profitably as he could. Adam Smith believed in a free market for labor as well as for materials. He wrote that competition also existed for labor: if the factory owner would not pay enough, workingmen would move on for higher wages.

But the supply of cheap labor seemed endless. The population expanded at an unprecedented rate during the Industrial Revolution. Workers migrated to the cities from farms that would no longer feed their large families.

For the most part, these transplanted country people were ignorant and untutored. Whatever country skills they possessed no longer availed them in the slums in which they settled. Whole families worked 14 hours a day in dark, airless mills. They did not move on for higher wages because they were too many to command higher wages. Jobs were scarcer than people.

Both in England and in the United States, there was concern for these transplanted people. But it was moral concern rather than concern for their material needs. In their villages, they had been subject to the spiritual authority of a church. In the cities, many of them were without anchor or direction. Drunkenness and depravity became more common in the streets as distilled liquors became cheaper. Scenes of such debauchery were dramatically documented by William Hogarth, the English artist.

Educated people were slow to connect the sins of the slum poor with the misery of their lot. Richard Cobden, for example, was a reformer and a friend of the laboring classes. Yet, as Stuart Chase pointed out, as late as 1847 Cobden voted in Parliament against the 10-hour working day because he believed workers needed "the discipline of the factory."

Caste-conscious society seemed to be afflicted with double vision when it looked at poverty. On the one hand, poverty was regarded as a spiritually elevating condition. Jesus Christ had said: "Sell all thou hast and follow me." St. Francis of Assisi and the founders of many Christian orders took vows of poverty so that they might be concerned with things of the spirit rather than with worldly things. On the other hand, poverty was regarded as something disgraceful. In some way, it was thought, the poor man must be responsible himself for the wretchedness of his condition. This ambiguity still survives in some archaic minds.

George Bernard Shaw attacked the callousness of the governing classes in the introduction to his play *Major Barbara* in 1905. He wrote:

We tolerate poverty as if it were either a wholesome tonic for lazy people or else a virtue to be embraced as St. Francis embraced it. If a man is indolent, let him be poor. If he is addicted to the fine arts or to pure science instead of to trade and finance, let him be poor. If he chooses to spend his urban eighteen shillings a week or his agricultural thirteen shillings a week on beer and his family instead of saving it up for his old age, let him be poor. Let nothing be done for 'the undeserving': Let him be poor. . . .

Now what does this Let Him Be Poor mean? It means let him be weak. Let him be ignorant. Let him become a nucleus of disease. Let him be a standing exhibition and example of ugliness and dirt. Let him have rickety children. . . . Let his habitations turn our cities into poisonous congeries of slums. . . . Let the undeserving become still less deserving.

Kinds of Poverty. Economists differ in their definition and classification of poverty. In his book *The Affluent Society,* John Kenneth Galbraith described three types of poverty in the United States: generalized poverty, island poverty, and case poverty. Other economists, viewing the problem in worldwide terms, have spoken of *collective* poverty, *cyclical* poverty, and *individual* poverty.

(1) *Collective poverty* exists in nations or regions where economic resources do not meet the needs of the population. India, where millions live on a diet just above starvation level, is a prime example. China, which turned to communist leaders in vain hope of relief, is another. The peasants of some South American countries have existed on an almost permanent level of privation. Ignorance and exploitation have contributed to their poor condition.

(2) *Cyclical poverty* is widespread but periodic. In an industrial econ-

omy, it is usually caused by lack of purchasing power. A memorable example is the Great Depression of the 1930's, with its mass unemployment. In an agricultural economy, it usually occurs with failure of crops. Pearl Buck in her novel *The Good Earth* presented a moving account of hordes of starving peasants migrating from a land stricken by famine.

(3) *Individual poverty* is harder to define. It can be loosely classified as poverty that is not caused by general economic trends.

Every culture has wrestled with the problem of individual poverty. There have always been widows and orphans, the sick and the aged, the dull, the incapable, and the intemperate. In the past, their care usually fell upon the local community, the church, or private charity. Almost forgotten today is the almshouse or poor farm where towns and counties sheltered their paupers. To many of the needy, it represented the last step down in personal defeat.

Central governments began to assume at least some responsibility for the relief of the poor in the late 1800's. This movement began in Germany under the authoritarian Chancellor Otto von Bismarck. Systems of social insurance were formulated. The poor began to be treated more like people and less like convicts. This, however, did not solve the problem of individual poverty in the midst of general prosperity.

In the United States and elsewhere, a strong back and a willingness to work cheap were once ample qualifications for employment. Manual laborers dug the ditches and constructed the transcontinental railroads. They picked cotton and fired the steel furnaces. But now the automation of industry and the mechanization of agriculture have made employment scarcer for the unskilled and the poorly educated.

PROBLEMS OF POVERTY

Between the depression years of the 1930's and the war on poverty of the 1960's, there was relatively little investigation into the causes of poverty in the United States. Because of a lack of information, a number of misconceptions about this complex problem became widespread. Some persons denied the problem on the ground that even those at the bottom of an affluent society were better off than members of most other societies, past or present. Others acknowledged the problem but dismissed it as one that would automatically disappear as national wealth increased. A few called for drastic revisions in the economy to achieve a redistribution of wealth. Still others continued to see poverty as a sign of lack of initiative by the poor.

Problems of Wealth Distribution. How much real purchasing power does an average family have? In terms of dollars, the average family income in the United States in 1963 was $6,249. But did this amount represent more or less purchasing power than that of families in other major nations?

Although such comparisons are difficult, one study did shed some light on the subject. Economists calculated the cost at retail prices of an adequate meal for a family of four in several countries. Then they translated the cost into the number of hours an industrial employee in each of the countries would have to work to pay for it. In the United States he had to work one hour, in Denmark an hour and a half, in West Germany and Great Britain two hours, and in Italy five hours.

Such comparisons, of course, could not be made in the Orient, the Middle East, and other underdeveloped areas. There a day's work often provided the peasant with only enough sustenance to prevent hunger pains.

There were also inadequate data for comparison with communist nations. A walk from democratic West Berlin to communist East Berlin, however, seemed to many tourists to take them from urban prosperity to urban desolation. Unquestionably the Soviet Union had become a great military and nuclear power by the mid-20th century. But its extraordinary effort was obtained through the harsh regimentation of the Russian people by a monolithic government. Only limited facilities were put to producing consumer goods.

Do the rich get a larger share of the total income in the United States than in other countries? Many Europeans believe they do, perhaps remembering sensational stories about the luxurious living of American multimillionaires. But this is not true, according to data collected by Professor Simon Kuznets of Harvard University, an authority on income distribution. Income distribution is about the same in the United States as it is in Denmark, Sweden, and Britain. And it is much more nearly equal in the United States than in most other countries for which such information is available.

Why then is there poverty in the United States? It seems clear that the nation has enormous wealth in terms of real purchasing power, and that its wealth is comparatively evenly divided. But poverty still does exist. It exists because the prosperity that raised the living standards of most of the people has not reached the really poor.

Who Are the Poor? Opinions vary about the income necessary to maintain an "adequate standard of living" for an urban family of four. In 1959, Professor Robert Lampman of the University of Wisconsin put it at $2,500. A few years later, this amount was probably no longer adequate. But in 1962 there were 5.4 million families with income *below* $2,000. More than a million children were being reared in large families, with six or more children each, on less than $2,000 a year. For this group, hairsplitting about the statistics of poverty was unnecessary. These Americans were poor, and there could be no doubt in anyone's mind about it.

The poor also included many who lived alone or, without family ties, in boarding houses and drab hotels. The Council of Economic Advisers reported that 5 million of these "unrelated individuals" had incomes below $1,500. Of these, 3 million had incomes below $1,000.

In the main, the unrelated individuals were aged or aging people who subsisted on small pensions, small savings, or public relief. In their working years, some had not been eligible for Social Security. Others had always worked for low pay. They received none of the benefits of the increasing strength of labor unions because they worked in nonunionized fields. And many were employed in service industries, where the federal minimum wage law did not apply.

Problems of the Poor. "Poverty breeds poverty," in the words of the Council of Economic Advisers' report. "A poor individual or family has a high probability of staying poor. Low incomes carry with them high risks of illness; limitations on mobility; and limited access to education, information, and training. Poor parents cannot give their children the opportunities for better health and education needed to improve their lot. Lack of motivation, hope, and incentive is a more subtle but no less powerful barrier than lack of financial means. Thus the cruel legacy of poverty is passed from parents to children."

A sample study of recipients of aid to families with dependent children showed that more than 40 percent of the parents had been reared in families receiving public assistance. And other statistics showed that 61 percent of poor families were headed by persons who had completed no more than elementary school. By contrast, less than 7 percent of poor families were headed by persons with some college education.

The rise in juvenile delinquency has justifiably excited newspaper editorial writers. But few of them associate the rise with the scarcity of jobs available to teenagers. In 1964 national unemployment had been reduced to 5 percent. But among youngsters between the ages of 16 and 21 who were not in school, the unemployment rate was 15 percent. Among Negro teenage boys and girls, the rate was 25 percent.

This was the kind of discouraging evidence uncovered when the national problem of poverty was examined in the middle 1960's.

THE WAR ON POVERTY

Both President John F. Kennedy and President Lyndon B. Johnson undertook a varied attack on the problem of poverty. Three major parts of their attack focused on tax reduction, civil rights, and the poverty program.

With a growing population, the United States would need an accelerated growth of national production to maintain high employment. To effect this growth, President Kennedy recommended a tax reduction. After President

Kennedy's death in November, 1963, President Johnson carried on the administration's legislative program. The tax reduction bill was passed by Congress in the spring of 1964.

Civil rights legislation also had a direct bearing on the problem of poverty. It was clear that the poor included a disproportionate number of Negroes and other nonwhite minorities, largely because of discrimination practiced against them. The 1964 Civil Rights Act, designed to correct some of these injustices, was passed in June, 1964.

President Johnson initiated his own bill to augment the fight against poverty. Called the Economic Opportunity Act, it was passed by Congress in August, 1964. Approximately $800 million was appropriated in October, 1964, to finance its first year's operation.

Civil Rights. The 1964 Civil Rights Act had both social and economic aims. In effect, it was a moderate law. It provided Negroes and others with legal means of achieving the rights already guaranteed them by the Constitution of the United States.

It had been amply demonstrated that discrimination against Negroes, Indians, and Latin Americans, including Puerto Ricans, reduced their employment opportunities. But discrimination did more than that. It instilled in minority groups a hopelessness that inhibited ambition and limited educational advance. Almost half of nonwhite Americans were poor. Infant mortality was twice as high for them as for whites. Maternal deaths were four times as frequent.

In addition to being a moral issue, discrimination is costly to the economy. Both labor unions and industry have been guilty of discriminating because of race and color. By doing so, they robbed society of the potential talents of about one ninth of the population.

The Poverty Program. President Johnson's poverty program had the following objectives: (1) improving regional economies in cooperation with states; (2) rehabilitating urban and rural communities; (3) expanding educational and job opportunities for youth; (4) promoting adult education and training; and (5) providing community help for the growing numbers of aged poor.

In the past, there was a conviction that economic growth alone would take care of the problem of poverty. But in 1964 the Council of Economic Advisers thought otherwise. "We cannot leave the further wearing away of poverty," the council said in its report, "solely to the general progress of the economy. A faster reduction of poverty will require that the lower fifth of our families be able to earn a larger share of national output."

The administrators of the Office of Economic Opportunity, set up by the 1964 Economic Opportunity Act, gave immediate attention to the young. It seemed to them that without adequate education the sons and daughters of the poor would never break through economic barriers. Out of this conviction, the Job Corps was established. The Job Corps sought to remove youngsters from both city and rural slum environments, give them useful labor in Job Corps Centers, and provide basic education in reading, writing, and arithmetic.

Work-training and work-study programs were also provided. The work-training program sought to give both jobs and job-training to young men and women in their home towns. The work-study program gave children of poor families a chance to work their way through college.

The Economic Opportunity Act emphasized local initiative in the struggle against poverty. It encouraged local leaders to produce blueprints for action in their own cities and communities. When the local programs were approved by the Office of Economic Opportunity, the federal government assumed 90 percent of the cost for a period of two years.

These local projects included educational programs, such as preschool programs, remedial reading, and special classes for school dropouts. There were also job-training projects for youth and adults. Other projects included health clinics, guidance and counseling for poor families, and programs for the aged.

Under the Economic Opportunity Act, loans of $2,500 could be extended to rural families to help them toward self-sufficiency. Loans up to $25,000 were made available to help small businessmen. For migrant workers, there were programs for housing, sanitation, education, and child care. To help unemployed fathers get off relief rolls, work experience programs were provided for them. And a unique organization, which was called Vista Volunteers (Volunteers in Service to America), was created. This organization encouraged Americans to volunteer their full-time services in the war against penury and want.

The ultimate aim of the government's drive against poverty was once described in these words:

to provide the young with the opportunity to learn, the able bodied with the opportunity to work, the poor with the opportunity to live in decency and dignity.

President Lyndon Johnson spoke firmly of the future in his message on poverty to Congress on March 16, 1964:

. . . this program is much more than a beginning. Rather it is a commitment. It is a total commitment by this President, and this Congress and this nation, to pursue victory over the most ancient of mankind's enemies.

On many historic occasions the President has requested from Congress the authority to move against forces which were endangering the wellbeing of our country.

This is such an occasion.

On similar occasions in the past we have often been called upon to wage war against foreign enemies which threatened our freedom. Today we are asked to declare war on a domestic enemy which threatens the strength of our nation and the welfare of our people. If we now move forward against this enemy—if we can bring to the challenges of peace the same determination and strength which has brought us victory in war—then this day and this Congress will have won a secure and honorable place in the history of the nation, and the enduring gratitude of generations of Americans yet to come.

HISTORY OF POVERTY IN THE UNITED STATES

The United States has had several unique advantages in satisfying the material needs of its citizens. For a hundred years, its rich western frontier offered the promise of another chance to those who felt limited by local conditions either within the United States or elsewhere. Policies of open immigration brought to the United States the talents of all the world's peoples. American technological ingenuity created undreamed of prosperity.

But each of these advantages has brought accompanying problems. The frontier inspired a tradition of individualism that sometimes made the needed social action difficult to achieve. Immigration raised problems of discrimination against minorities. And prosperity has often blinded Americans to the plight of their poor. Until recently, legislation on behalf of the poor has seldom been advanced in the United States except in times of economic crisis.

Early Economic Growth. The rise of industrialism caused far less social dislocation in the United States than it had caused in Europe. One reason was that the American population consisted largely of immigrants and pioneers.

In the beginning, the American republic welcomed immigration from the Old World. It was not only a matter of democratic principle—there was also a vast empty continent to populate.

The prospect of free land in western United States was a magnet to the adventurous. It produced a vigorous citizenry, that seemed always on the move. Many Americans retained their independence even though they were poor. Instead of accepting the regimentation of the mill and the furnace, they chose the gamble and the freedom of the western frontier.

With its seemingly limitless frontier, the United States remained a land of labor scarcity for more than a hundred years. The growth of heavy industry in the 1800's created an increasing demand for labor that could not be satisfied by local markets.

The national policy of unrestricted immigration lasted until the end of World War I. More than 8 million persons emigrated across the Atlantic in the decade from 1901 to 1910 alone. The floods of new recruits from foreign countries were willing to accept the hard work and long hours of factory life. At first, many of these immigrants were docile and immune to labor union organization. Even if wages were low, the immigrant was still better off financially than he had been in southern or eastern Europe.

Meanwhile, ingenious American artisans and mechanics were introducing important technological innovations. Self-taught engineers harnessed brooks and rivers for waterpower to run mills. Eli Whitney invented the cotton gin, which made a rich plantation empire of the American South. Whitney also introduced the practice of making interchangeable parts for machinery, which in itself revolutionized technology. Later, Henry Ford developed this idea still further. He introduced the assembly line in his automobile factories and thus became the father of modern mass production.

The Great Depression. In his book *The Future as History*, Robert Heilbroner wrote: "In the folklore of our country we still look back to 1929 not only as a year of great business prosperity but as a year of widespread and fundamental wellbeing. But when we examine the economy of 1929 critically, we find that the facade of business prosperity concealed an inner structure of widespread economic frailty."

The crash of the stock market in 1929 and the depression of the 1930's occasioned a profound disillusionment in the United States. Many Americans felt a confusion and a sense of despair such as never had been known before.

The United States was no longer a land of labor scarcity. Moreover, the people lost faith in the country's financial leadership. One after another, banks failed and what were supposed to be solid corporate structures fell apart. Unemployment reached a peak of 15 million.

President Franklin D. Roosevelt suggested a wide pattern of legislation to bolster the economy and relieve the distressed. Congress passed the Social Security Act in 1935. The same year, the Wagner Act was enacted to protect the rights of labor. The Securities and Exchange Commission was created to police unbridled speculation in the stock market. Federal programs of public works were inaugurated and federal spending was increased to create jobs for the idle.

World War II and After. Full recovery from the depression did not come until World War II, when American industry went into high gear producing war materiel. Technological miracles were achieved to enable the Allied armed services to win a conflict in two hemispheres.

During the war years, there was a tremendous growth in family incomes. High wages were earned as factories worked around the clock, but prices were government-controlled. Because few consumer goods were available, much of the money went into savings. Measured in dollars of constant purchasing power, or what economists call "real income," average yearly take-home pay of families rose by about $800 in the five years from 1941 to 1946—an increase of about $160 a year.

Although mass unemployment at the end of the war had been widely predicted, industry remained in high gear. As price controls were removed, industry returned to a peacetime economy and began meeting the huge backlog of demand for consumer goods.

There were recessions in the postwar period. But, in the words of Herman P. Miller of the U.S. Census Bureau, who contributed much to the study of poverty in his analyses of statistical data, these recessions were "minor economic ripples compared with the national depressions each previous generation of Americans experienced." By 1960 real family income per year had risen by $1,000 over family income in 1946.

The Present and the Future. Professional economists have their own measurement of national well-being. They call it Gross National Product—the total value of all goods and services produced in a year. The Gross National Product measurement is admittedly inexact, but it does satisfactorily reflect currents and trends in the economy. Valued in 1963 prices the Gross National Product in 1929 was $214 billion. In 1933 it had fallen to $150 billion. In 1964 it rose to an unprecedented $600 billion. And there was every indication that it would continue to rise still higher.

There could be no doubt that this tremendously increased national income was distributed widely. As late as 1947 almost a third of the nation's population had incomes below a $3,000-a-year family annual level in terms of today's purchasing power. In 1962 less than one fifth of the population had incomes below that level. Plainly a considerable section of the people had climbed the economic ladder from penury to good living.

But there was an American consensus that *no one* should starve in a land of plenty. It was widely believed that federal aid should be given to the needy within the United States just as it had been given to those in foreign countries. Direct relief for the poor had obviously been necessary during the depression of the 1930's, and for many it was still necessary. To those who studied the problem, however, it seemed clear that alleviation of distress was not enough. Greater emphasis had to be placed on prevention, rehabilitation, and economic opportunity if an ugly and disheartening progression—poverty breeding poverty—was to be ended.

The Rich and the Poor

In the preceding article Sargent Shriver contended that the distribution of income in America was no more disparate than in other western countries. Gabriel Kolko, in the following treatment of the rich and poor in society, suggests that distribution of income and wealth in America has not changed essentially in the past fifty years. He ties the social-class structure to an economic base and discusses the factors responsible for the continued gap between the two classes. In describing economic and social distinc-

tions among the classes, Kolko says that the advantages of selective higher education are one of the ways of perpetuating class structure.

If educational opportunity is actually equal, what accounts for greater losses in talent-development among lower-income classes than among higher? What responsibilities does the society and its educational system have toward the poor as children, as youth, as productive or potential workers, as retirees, as members of the general culture?

Selections from *Wealth and Power in America*

GABRIEL KOLKO

Most recent studies of American society assume that since the end of the Great Depression, in 1939, the nation's wealth has been redistributed and prosperity has been extended to the vast majority of the population. The authors of these works—popular and academic alike—are virtually unanimous in their conviction that our society has attained a substantial measure of social and economic democracy. They hail our economy for its triumphs in eliminating poverty and in creating the life of abundance for the many, not the few.

This assumption of economic equality has become the foundation of broad new theories in the social sciences, the common impression of millions of intelligent laymen—and even the basis of specific political and social policies on taxes, aid to the elderly, poverty, and other areas of economic significance.

But this assumption is nonetheless fallacious, for despite the obvious increase in prosperity since the abysmal years of the Great Depression, the basic distribution of income and wealth in the United States is essentially the same now as it was in 1939, or even 1910. Most low-income groups live substantially better today, but even though their real wages have mounted, their percentage of the national income has not changed. . . .

Insofar as economic power in the United States derives from savings and income, it is dominated by a small class, comprising not more than one-tenth of the population, whose interests and style of life mark them off from the rest of American society. And within this class, a very small elite controls the corporate structure, the major sector of our economy, and through it makes basic price and investment decisions that directly affect the entire nation.

From *Wealth and Power in America*, by Gabriel Kolko, 1962, pp. 127–32. Reprinted by permission of the publisher, Frederick A. Praeger, Inc., New York.

"The historic ethos of American life" may be "its bourgeois hungers, its classlessness, the spirit of equality," as Louis Hartz suggests in *The Liberal Tradition in America* (1955), but these are surely not the dominant realities in its social and economic structure. American society is based on a class structure, and it pervades most of the crucial facets of life.

More than any other factor, the American class structure is determined by the great inequality in the distribution of income, an inequality that has not lessened although the economy's unemployment total has dropped from 12 million to a much smaller but still substantial figure. A sharp inequality of income has remained despite a generation of encroachments by laws, wars, and crises at home and abroad. If the form this inequality takes has been modified by expense accounts, undistributed profits, undeclared income, and similar complex measures, the nature of the phenomenon has not been altered.

The economically determined class lines in American society have been reinforced by the failure of the lowest-paid groups (largely blue-collar workers) to increase their relative income share since 1939—contrary to the common academic notion that they have. Their occasional ascents to a higher-income bracket usually result from the entry of wife or child into the labor market. And, perhaps most significant of all, the movement of the children of blue-collar workers into white-collar occupations is not necessarily a step upward, since white-collar workers are losing ground in their income standing.

Inequality of income is reflected in inequality of consumption, an inequality so great that contemporary social theories on the "democratization" or "massification" of symbols of economic status hold little relevance to the America of this decade. On the one hand, nearly one-half of the population is financially able to meet only its immediate physical needs, and the larger part of this group, nearly one-third of the nation, are in want of even basic necessities. On the other hand, a small section of the population, at most the top tenth, lives in the prosperous and frequently sumptuous manner that most social commentators ascribe to the large majority of Americans. And within this small section, there exists an economic elite variously described as the "sports-car," "country-club," or "Ivy League" set, depending on its particular tastes. Here are found the major owners of stock and the corporate managers, sharing the same social life and the same set of values.

Sharp inequalities in consumption are the pervasive fact of the American class structure. Privacy and comfort in housing are privileges of the well-to-do, and an increasing number of $250,000-and-up homes are being built throughout the United States—at a time when the few old mansions of the Astors and Morgans are being sold, purportedly because of loss of wealth, but actually because of changes in taste. The type of car one drives is a fairly accurate index of social class; the expensive sports car is purchased when an ordinary car will no longer impart sufficient prestige. Steaks are standard fare in the upper-income ranks; hamburger—which now accounts for one-quarter of beef consumption as opposed to one-tenth before World War II—is the staple of the luckier among the lower-income groups. Life is longer for the wealthy, whose money spares them from some diseases and in general gives them superior medical care. Last of all, higher education at the best institutions perpetuates the advantages of wealth in succeeding generations, while among the poor, vast reservoirs of talent and creativity go unexploited.

The basic economic fact of life for a majority of the population is insecurity. This is the logical outgrowth of their lack of ready savings; a very large majority of the low- and middle-income population have no more than a few months' income saved for financial emergencies.

Yet such emergencies are frequent among low-income families—in part because they are low-income families. The resultant increased rate of illness not only drains their meager finances, even with hospitalization insurance, but often has the disastrous effect of cutting off the earnings of the breadwinner.

Another common emergency for the low-income family is recurring unemployment, a by-product of the business cycle. If the family is covered by unemployment insurance—and over one-third of workers are not—the loss of income during this period is compensated for only very inadequately. If unemployment is very brief, the average family weathers it, although not without suffering reductions in consumption and other difficulties. If unemployment lasts more than several months, it eliminates the average family's savings, and causes a sharp reduction in consumption and perhaps some credit defaults. If unemployment compensation ends, relief is often the only recourse. For millions of Americans, this sequence of events is more than academic; they have experienced the necessity of having to live on $20 or $30 a week.

The insecurity caused by the ever-present possibility of unemployment, illness, or some other cause of financial emergency is made more ominous by the suddenness with which these crises occur. Perhaps more important is the expectation, growing out of personal experience and the observation of family and friends, that there is never enough money with which to meet predictable, certain responsibilities. Children add to the financial burdens of the average worker during the period when his income is greatest. By the time his financial responsibility for his children is ended, his peak earning period is past, and for himself and his wife, there is only the prospect of a continuation of the inadequate living standards of their late youth and early middle age. During the plateau between the children's attaining financial independence and the start of retirement, the average worker may save, but after retirement, he ends his life in want. If, before old age, he lived slightly below the maintenance level, he now drops below the emergency level.

For nearly half the population, these are the harsh facts of economic life—and for most, these facts limit their freedom to conceive or attain noneconomic goals.

It is true, as John Kenneth Galbraith suggests, that poverty is an "afterthought" in the contemporary American economy, but it is not true that the nation is so well off that we should "escape from the obsolete and contrived preoccupation associated with the assumption of poverty." Poverty is an afterthought not because it *has* disappeared, but because social scientists *believe* it has.

In the coming decades, certain conditions giving rise to poverty will grow in importance, and if they meet the same response in future years as they have since World War II, the percentages of the population living at submaintenance and subemergency standards will climb, despite the increase in real income for some occupations. One such factor is the simultaneous numerical growth and relative economic decline of the white-collar class. This trend is a crucial aspect of a group that many social scientists thought would join that "classless" and nebulous category the middle class. Another element is the mounting number of families headed by women, a low-income group—in part because of wage prejudice. But, above all, there is the persistent growth in the population aged sixty-five and over, most of whom live on penurious Social Security payments or other meager funds.

It is conceivable that the termination of the business cycle, plus a substantial rise in real income, could end poverty in the United States caused by unemployment and low wages. But realization of these two goals is quite unlikely. Too many factors are operating to assure a continuing sequence of recessions, or even worse.

One difficulty in the way of full employment is the rising productivity per man-hour, and it is certain to become more formidable as automation spreads. The solution obviously is to expand consumption greatly, but only a decisive shift in the distribution of income and purchasing power can accomplish this. A self-defeating factor in wage boosts is the almost invariable business practice of passing along the cost of pay increases to the public. Raising legal minimum wages and extending the coverage to more people will not increase real purchasing power unless accompanied by direct control of prices.

Thus, eliminating poverty caused by unemployment and low wages requires the sweeping sort of political decisions concerning the economy which no administration has proposed or practiced, except during World War II. For this reason, it is probable that the very substantial importance of poverty caused by unemployment and low wages will not diminish in the near future. This static position, plus the rising new trends toward poverty discussed above, and the instability inherent in an extensive credit system—all these factors indicate that poverty will continue to be a basic aspect of the American social and class structure so long as no fundamental changes are made in the distribution of wealth and the autonomous control of the corporate machinery.

Poverty and low incomes in the United States are not, as in underdeveloped nations, an inevitable consequence of deficient industry. In 1958, only three-quarters of the nation's industrial capacity was utilized, and 5 million workers were unemployed. This was true in large part because the poorer half of the nation was not seriously in the market for new automobiles, refrigerators, houses, and goods of every other type. The problem was not in technology, but in economic organization, and at the bottom of this economic inadequacy was the sharply unequal distribution of income and wealth.

Let us ignore for the moment the tremendous industrial development that would be stimulated by the growth of the consumer-goods market among the poorer half of the population. Let us consider only that if the existing industrial machinery were fully exploited, its production would be sufficient to raise markedly the standard of living of those now living below the maintenance level.

Any valid social theory must be based on a reasonably correct empirical analysis. But it is impossible not to conclude that the social theories now dominant in the United States are dependent less on a valid analysis of American society than on illusion—the illusion that "economic equalitarianism" is a reality in the United States. But as my study has shown, the evidence refutes the basic assumption of universal abundance in America, which figures so centrally in current social thought.

ALIENATION AND THE
DEPRIVED CHILD

Alienation is a social phenomenon which has become more widespread as life in the twentieth century has become more complex. Although variously described in psychological terms, alienation amounts to the separation of individuals from their society. The alienated feels a lack of continuity with his own culture, in much the same manner that a "man without a country" feels alien to any society. It is a sense of dislocation from environment caused by multiple factors, including individual personality, social status; conflicting social values, lack of means to become involved in social life, social ostracism, and continuing neglect by society. In contrast to lepers who were forcibly alienated from their society, today's psychologically alienated often carry a lack of identification with any group. The assembly-line worker who fails to perceive his relation to the final product is similar to the individual who is unable to see his own status in society.

Much alienation is socially derived. Large urban centers which display greater concern for commerce or street cleaning than for their inhabitants; quiet, secluded suburbs with rigid class lines, high fences, and noncommunicative families; rural poor areas bypassed by superhighways, supported by welfare checks, and economically depleted of resources; the factory partially automated, providing air-conditioned rooms for computers and name tags to identify employees; and the schools, packed with thirty or more students per room per teacher per hour, piled with mimeographed notices, lists, and details, burdened with test scores, health records, and teaching machines, have all become sources of alienation.

An additional factor in alienation as a social problem is deprivation. Whether the deprivation be economic, social, political, emotional, or intellectual, it creates feelings of alienation. Dissociation may occur as one result of compensation for deprivation. The three readings in this section treat alienation and the deprived child as social and cultural problems. Both pose demands on the school to accommodate the disadvantaged. Can the schools offset deprivation imposed by family conditions? What means can be used to identify the other than economically deprived? What responsibilities does the school have for producing the security lacking in alienation? Has the school contributed to increasing deprivation and alienation by imposing middle-class standards and mores on all students? What changes must be effected in the schools if they are to deal with these problems?

The Nature of Alienation

The schools are a basic social institution for the propagation of values, morals, and attitudes. If the society is of a type that produces alienated individuals, what role does the school play in this process? To what extent should teachers be social analysts? Are the values expressed in school in opposition to the values practiced in life? In what specific ways are the schools responsible for alienation?

In the following article, Professor Besag summarizes the main theories defining alienation and describes the symptoms of an alienated society. The conflict in values (the direct cause of these symptoms) expressed in this piece is consistent with the concern for social and educational value conflicts upon which this text is based.

What Is Alienation?

FRANK P. BESAG

During the past ten years the concept of alienation has been revived as a handy label to be used in the explanation of most of the ills of the society. One of the apparent reasons for the success of this revival is that as long as alienation is not too closely defined, it can be used to explain most things. For example, alienation has been used to explain criminal behavior, sexual deviance, the quest for love, the history of man, etc. It is obvious that no one concept, if it is well defined, could explain them all.

It is the purpose of this paper, then, to define alienation by formulating useful constructs from which can be drawn hypotheses. The major authors used in this theoretical formulation are: Karl Marx, Emile Durkheim, Thomas Merton, and Eric Fromm. The first three are social theorists while the latter is a psychologist. All are interested in the influence of the society upon the individual.

An original article prepared especially for this text.

Theories of alienation fall generally into one of two classes: 1. estrangement from the self, or, 2. estrangement from the society. Karl Marx is the primary exponent of the former theory. It is based upon the concept that the degree of alienation of the individual is determined by the relationship of the individual to his economy. The process is as follows: In the non-complex society, each man owns the things necessary to his own survival and he is by and large the master of his own labor and time. As societies become more complex, there is need for a division of labor. Rather than one man following a product from its inception to its completion, different men complete various parts of the product and no one man might ever see the finished product as a whole. Even more to the point is the fact that no one man could fully care for himself and his family without the aid of others. He has to go to experts (doctors, farmers, etc.) when he is in need of a particular commodity. With the division of labor, private ownership increases. Further, as some people come to own large parts of the economy, they come to employ others, that is, they come to own labor as well as products. Both the owner and the laborer become estranged from their work, their product, and themselves as a result of the separation of themselves from their work. As this estrangement increases, the employer and the employee become dislocated and estranged from their families, society, and the norms and values which hold work as their basis.

The basic concept here is that as commercialism rises and the value of money increases, the value of the men who make commercialism possible, decreases. These men become alienated and have little or no respect for the norms of the society or for themselves. Their work seems purposeless and the norms of society are meaningless. Men become isolated within themselves.

Marx's construct of alienation seems to have value for the present day since it has been postulated by many authors that the modern man is estranged from his work, his product, and himself. Through this process of dislocation and lack of pride in self has also come the estrangement from family and society. A feeling of powerlessness and meaninglessness has resulted.

Durkheim's construct is somewhat different. Durkheim also begins with the concept of the changing society from the stable feudal society to the industrial society characterized by the division of labor. However, Durkheim is not interested in individuals. As a point of fact, Durkheim does not think that individuals exist outside of their social milieu. He begins and ends with two types of societies as opposed to two types of individuals. The stable form of society is that one characterized by mechanical solidarity, the society in which the patterns of existence are given. For example, the son follows the father's trade, the role of women is stated and understood, etc.

With the rise of the division of labor, the family unit breaks down, as does the entire society. For now the society is characterized by individual morality; each member of the society can and does set up his own set of mores and norms for his own behavior. In this state, no one is ever sure of what is expected of him (normlessness). For one thing, there are no limits to his desires since no one knew what he was capable of in terms of upward social mobility. Further, there is a great tendency, since there are no limits to the desires of man, that he feels that he can never achieve all that he is capable of (powerlessness). In this way, with the advent of the division of labor, man's desires become insatiable and his ability to meet these insatiable desires is, by definition, inadequate for the task.

Durkheim was able to show that with the increase in this feeling of normlessness and powerlessness, there was a corresponding increase in the suicide rate. He called this form of suicide *anomic*. It is usually described as a feeling of depression due to the lack of ability to cope with modern society or its problems.

The distinction between Marx and Durkheim should be kept in mind, namely, Marx bases his theories of estrangement on the worker becoming estranged from himself, whereas Durkheim bases his concept of *anomie* upon the individual's lack of continuity with the society of which he is a member. Further, while Marx discusses an individual who finds the mores of the society meaningless and who feels that he is powerless to do anything about it, Durkheim discusses the society which has broken down to the extent that the individual has nothing to hang on to, *i.e.*, normlessness.

Fromm's basic contribution to the study of alienation has been the construct of the "socially patterned defect." His basic postulate is that the society attempts to make us insatiable so that we will continue to consume vast quantities of commercial material. If, as Durkheim postulated, insatiability is one sign of alienation, then it would appear that the society attempts to make us more alienated. Further, the only individuals who are not alienated from themselves in the sense that their desires are not insatiable, are of necessity alienated from the society which expects them to be insatiable. Fromm attempts to prove that things are in such a bad way that the only solution is to eliminate the insatiability of our society, the "sick society."

All three of the previously mentioned theorists dealt with the etiology of alienation. They were as interested, if not more interested, in the causes of alienation. Merton's construct differs in this regard in that he was less interested in the etiology of alienation than he was in the overt forms of behavior which it caused.

Merton begins with the twin constructs of the cultural structure (the goals which the society defines as good) and the social structure (the means which the society defines as good in the attainment of these goals). Merton assumes that there would always be some conflict between these two and that in our society where the pecuniary value is supreme, the conflict would be greater. In Merton's terminology, the cultural structure (money) outweighs the social structure (honesty, prudence, etc.). The problem for Merton is not the cause of the conflict but rather the method of adaptation to the stress caused by the conflict.

Assuming that the individual is in conflict with the society, there are five modes of adaptation which are open to him. The first is conformity. Here, when the individual realizes that he is in conflict with the society, he attempts as far as possible to completely eliminate the conflict by overtly assuming both the cultural and social structure of the ruling culture. Total and complete assumption of the ideal norms of society is rare, but varying degrees of conformity characterize many members of our society.

Ritualism is characterized by the complete assumption of the social structure (conventional means) but incomplete assimilation of the cultural structure (goals). This is the person who is often mistaken for the conformist, but who in our society just goes through the motions of making money while he really has not assumed that goal.

Retreatism is characterized by negating both the cultural and the social structure. Here the individual accepts neither the goal of moneymaking nor the conventional methods of indicating a desire for making money. Often this person becomes a beatnik.

The rebellious individual may or may not accept either the cultural or the social reforms. His basic interest is in removing the powers that be and replacing them with those who are more like himself.

The most common form of adaptation in our society is innovation. Here the individual accepts the cultural structure (money) but is less interested in the social structure (the means to attain money). The emphasis is on the goal and since money is the goal, cheating on one's income tax forms (dishonesty) is acceptable; built-in inefficiency (lack of pride in workmanship) is acceptable; "white collar crime" generally becomes a way of attaining the goal.

Alienation, for Merton, is defined in terms of how well the individual assimilates the cultural and social structure of the society; the availability of the necessary social structures so that the cultural structures are attainable; and the availability of alternate solutions which are still within the general framework of the cultural and social structures. There can be degrees of alienation (since there are degrees of assimilation) and, therefore, there can be degrees of response to the alienation in terms of the modes of adaptation. The basic assumption, however, is that we all suffer from some alienation and we all use one or more of the modes of adaptation in order to reestablish some sort of equilibrium.

On the basis of what Marx, Durkheim, and Merton, and Fromm have said, what are the parameters of alienation? In general, the parameters of the *alienated society* can be stated as follows:

1. The society in which the ideal values are no longer practiced by the majority of the members of the society, but where these values are still held as ideals;

2. The society characterized by individual morality, where it is assumed that each individual should be his own judge and jury;

3. The society which indicates the goals which are to be desired, but which does not give all of its members the means available to attain these goals;

4. The sick society in which certain deviant patterns are inculcated in the individual.

The parameters of the *alienated individual* are:

1. The individual who feels a lack of orientation to the values of society;

2. The individual who feels that there is little opportunity for him to succeed in the society;

3. The individual who feels that if he is to succeed in the society the only means available to him are those of deviance, *e.g.*, crime;

4. The subject who has unlimited desires or the inability to achieve success for his desires;

5. The subject who does not understand the norms of society;

6. The subject who feels that there are few alternatives open to him.

What is alienation from a sociological perspective? It is a feeling of conflict between opposing and strongly held values. Whether the conflict is, for example, between the Victorian values which are held as ideal and the values practiced in the marketplace, or between the pecuniary values established as the only legitimate goal without the means to achieve these values, is not the point. What is of interest is that the conflict causes basic changes in the patterns of behavior of the individuals involved. There is a decided increase in the feelings of powerlessness, normlessness, lack of faith in the future, meaninglessness, and isolation. When these symptoms, or any one of them, appear in an individual we say that he is alienated. When these symptoms, or any one of them, appear in a society, we say that the society is alienated. Durkheim pointed out that the alienated person had a greater proclivity to commit suicide. Whether or not the alienated society has the same proclivity remains to be seen.

Deprivation and the Problem Child

Are all forms of deprivation the same? Are the problem children in school readily identifiable? What social pathology (deviant behavior) is found in those at the "bottom of the social heap"?

Robert J. Havighurst presents here an analysis of the forms and types of problem youth, deprivation, and social class. He describes the behavior of a few students to show characteristics of differing forms of deprivation. Which of the illustrated cases involves alienation? On what bases does Professor Havighurst state that the theory of lower-class susceptibility to delinquency is misleading? Can there be an alienated class in society?

Problem Children and Social Class Differences in the Schools

ROBERT J. HAVIGHURST

I suppose that every child is a problem at one time or another or to one person or another. But when we speak about problem children, we are talking about categories. I'm going to recognize four categories of problem children and talk mainly about two of them. I suppose we could say there are four major categories of problem children as they appear to us in the schools. One is the mentally handicapped group, i.e., ones with I.Q.'s below 75 or something like that. Another is the physically crippled or physically handicapped group. A third is the emotionally disturbed group. In this latter group I include those who are fearful, intimidated, and pathologically· shy. We often call them the withdrawn group. A fourth is the aggressive group, i.e., the ones who, if they carry their aggression beyond a certain point, are what we call delinquent.

These first two groups we have a fairly good way of handling. There

From a presentation at the Thirtieth Annual Summer Conference of the School of Education at the University of Michigan, July 13, 1959. Reprinted by permission of the author.

isn't very much question about how to work with these children. You put them in special classrooms as far as they need it and you give them specially trained teachers. For this reason I am going to limit my discussion to the other two problem groups—the withdrawn, pathologically shy and intimidated, or fearful type of youngster and the aggressive type.

The aggressive type causes the most difficulty. I think we're most aware of them as a difficult group. The other group, the withdrawn group, we can overlook and we often do overlook. But they are just as difficult a group to work with and just as important a group to give special attention to because they, if they don't get better, but get worse, come into the mental hospital with a diagnosis of a schizophrenia. These two groups of children can be found anywhere in our society, at any economic level; nevertheless, they seem to be found disproportionately in the lower working class. We find that there is a statistically over-large group of aggressive youngsters and also of withdrawn youngsters in the lower working class.

Now here I have to make what is really a major point about social class. I'm not going to talk as much about social class this morning as I thought when I first accepted this topic and as perhaps the people in charge of the program thought. But I'm going to try to make one extremely important point about social class which is that most of the social pathology in our society is found concentrated in the lower lower class or the lower working class. So we're not here primarily concerned with the distinction between white collar and blue collar or with middle class and working class when we're talking about the prevalence of problem behavior in children. Rather, there is a small group at the bottom of the social heap and it is in this small group that we find most of the social pathology.

My own views about social class in America have been modified somewhat as I have seen more of America and more of social class phenomena. I now tend to talk less of the distinction between middle class and working class. I think this distinction is becoming less and less apparent in our society. The real difference between working class and middle class is decreasing not only in the United States but in all of the modern societies partly because the difference in income is decreasing. There's not much difference in income now between a person at the top of the manual labor group and a person at the bottom of the white collar group. There is some difference in social prestige still, I might say, but I think that even this is tending to disappear. We can think of our class structure as consisting of four groups. An upper and upper middle class we usually put together because the upper class are so hard to discover and so few in number that for most purposes we combine them with the group just below. Anybody who was specially interested in social class would of course not want to combine the upper and the upper middle. That makes it about 10% of the population. Then there is a lower middle group of about 30%, an upper working class of about 40%, a lower working class of about 20%. Now it is in this lower 20% that most of our social pathology occurs. But even this lower 20% is not 100% pathological by any means. I suppose that in our society, perhaps 5% of the population or of the families present the real pathology. And most of these 5%, say 4 of the 5% anyway, are found in this lower working class. This has been found again and again in recent studies. For example, in one study in Minneapolis they found that a very small number of families was making an inordinate demand upon the social service facilities of the city. A particular family might be known to ten different social service agencies. And if you simply added up their figures on the number of people they served, you would get maybe five or ten times as many families as were actually being served when you counted the duplications. There's a heavy concentration in the lower working class of social pathology and this is true with respect to these particular children I'm talking about. Though they can be found all through the social structure, they tend to be found in this lower working class group. But even there, they don't make up over maybe one fourth or one fifth of the lower working class. This is important because there has been a tendency, and I suspect that I've had something to do with this, to suppose that a working class person was a different kind of animal than a middle class person. Culturally there is some difference but the cultural difference between lower middle class and upper lower class is relatively small and growing smaller. Consequently the task of the teacher is, I think, not so much to learn the different cultures in our society but at least as far as problem behavior is concerned, to learn how to recognize and deal with problem behavior wherever it is found.

These problem groups that I've spoken about, the aggressive group and the withdrawn group, have somewhat similar causes. They are the result of deprivation. In my judgment, a large part of the problem behavior is caused by deprivation in the environment perhaps supplementing some inadequacy of heredity. There are four kinds of deprivation that we can speak of. One is affectional deprivation, where the person is deprived of an adequate amount of affection, love, attention, emotional support. The second is what we might call model person deprivation, the absence of model persons in the child's life who present a good example for imitation by the child as he grows up—for example the absence of a good model in the father and the mother or the grandparents. A child who grows up without a father is disadvantaged, of course. A child who grows up with a father or mother who present a very bad example is also at a disadvantage and we can say that, in this case, the child suffers from deprivation in the model person. Then there is intellectual deprivation—a child who grows up in a family where nobody reads or what little reading is done is confined to the headlines of the newspaper; a child who grows up in a family where nobody talks about music, or nobody talks about books or nobody talks about the political affairs of the day. This child is deprived intellectually—deprived of the kind of stimulus that comes of being with parents and with other people who direct the child to things intellectual. Then there is a fourth kind of deprivation—nutritional, which I am using in a rather general sense here. I think it is not as important as it was but it still exists in some measure, where actually the child is not given an adequate amount and kind of food. But it is the first three, the affectional, the model person, and the intellectual deprivation that I think are the main causal factors of aggressive maladjustment or of the withdrawn type of maladjustment.

Let me give you examples of youngsters from this particular lower working class group to illustrate these kinds of deprivation. The first one I will take is a girl whom I will call Catherine—a girl whom my colleagues and I studied from the time she was about 10 until she was 17 or 18. This little girl, I say little because she was always small—in fact one of the first things she said to the interviewer who visited the family and talked to her was, "I've always been the smallest. I've always been the smallest in my class and I'm the smallest in my family." She was a tiny, slender youngster with stringy hair. She was near-sighted and had glasses with thick lenses. Her clothes were ill fitting. This was more and more noticeable to the boys and girls as she moved up through the grades. On sociometric tests, she was seen as a person who was unkempt, and occasionally a person who was mean and spiteful. If she made any impression, it was one of being mean and spiteful. The father was spasmodically present and not present in the home. He hadn't been working regularly for some years. The family was on relief most of the time.

The mother was holding the family together. There were ten children in the family. When she wasn't having a child, or raising a young child, she tended to go out and work. I think this was partly an escape for the mother. She liked to be "with people" as she said, and I guess "people" were not her own children. So, whenever possible, she would go out and get a job as a dishwasher or something like that and let the older children take care of the younger ones. In fact that's what happened to Catherine as she reached age 13 or so and was able to be trusted with the younger children. The mother would go out and get a job and Catherine would have to hustle home from school at noon to get lunch for the children. The mother would leave at about 12 o'clock to go to work. Catherine would have to hustle home, get lunch, and look after the children a bit. Then she would have to run back to school, and run back home right after school and take care of the children the rest of the day while her mother was at work again. She had no chance to associate with other youngsters after about age 12 or 13. Her mother was using her as a mother substitute for the younger children.

Catherine had an I.Q. of about 85 or 90 and she did not learn very well. She didn't learn even as well as this might have suggested. There were other youngsters with similar I.Q.'s who were doing much better in school than she was. She just drifted through school. She was kept back one year and then allowed to move up on a social promotion basis. By the time she got to high school, she was just about out of things—hardly in touch with her classes although she did find a little something in home economics that aroused a spark in her. She told the interviewer how she'd been making an apron and was very proud of this fact. This would have represented a possibility I think for the school to make contact with her, through the home economics teacher. But she was already 15, I think, when she entered the ninth grade. Almost before she was 16 her mother took her out of school and said she was needed at home.

So this little girl grew up on the fringe of the social group becoming less and less a part of it as she moved into high school. At the age of 17 she was then a small, shy, rather fearful creature, and had no contact with boys. About once a week (she did have a girl friend in the neighborhood), she and the girl friend would go to a skating rink and skate together hoping that some boys would notice them but nothing like this had happened yet by the age of 17. You see this person then, making no impression really on the surroundings, being increasingly withdrawn and having a fairly poor chance of being anything more than a kind of domestic servant-type all of her life. The one good possibility is that a man or boy who wants a domestic or servant type as a wife will find her and will marry her and will give her a chance to go through life at least having her own home. Because she had a mother with ten children who did not care much about children anyway and a father out of the home and not really contributing in any important way, she had suffered from affectional deprivation. She also suffered from model person deprivation in that the mother was not a good model for this girl to grow up by. There was an older sister, the oldest girl in the family, who had a good deal of spunk, had left school at the age of 16, had left town, and was on her own so that she was not available as a model person for Catherine. She certainly suffered from intellectual deprivation. There was no intellectual stimulus in the family.

Now I'll take a boy whom I will call Dick who represents the aggressive type of problem. This boy was studied from about the fourth grade on. In the fourth grade, he emerged as a highly aggressive youngster as seen through sociometric tests and seen through the eyes of the teacher. He was a tough youngster and known as that already in the fourth grade. He was already a year older than his classmates, having been kept back one year. He was known as a bully and a constant source of irritation to his teacher. He had an I.Q. of 90. The teacher felt he was somewhat brighter than this indicated. He showed sparks of brightness but nothing consistent enough to register in terms of school achievement. His father was a truck driver— often away from home and when he was at home was a rather cruel and punitive father who beat the boy a good deal. The mother worked in a tavern as a waitress a good deal of the time. Dick had two older brothers and none younger. The mother turned the boy over to the older brothers and went off to have her life in the tavern—leaving the little boy pretty much in the hands of the brothers to get him to school when they got to school.

He was a very much neglected youngster and his reaction to this kind of deprivation was the one of the two possible ones—either you fight in this kind of situation i.e., thresh around and cause trouble, or you withdraw i.e., become a daydreamer and withdraw from the world. The girl, Catherine, withdrew; the boy, Dick, became a fighter. By the time he was in junior high, he was one of a group that were troublesome. In junior high, the main troublesome group is this group of rather tough hostile boys and some girls of the same type. He was quite clear about his hostility to the school and what it stood for. He was becoming increasingly truant and by the time he was in the ninth grade, he was becoming a member of a gang of boys a year or two older than he—some of them old enough to be able to have the license to drive a car. They would get rattletrap cars, fix them up as best they could, and ride around town trying to qualify for the club which they called the "Heaven Hounds." The members in good standing were supposed to drive at least fifty miles an hour inside the city limits and they also had a favorite game which they called "Chicken." They would get their cars into a vacant field on a bluff overlooking the river and the game was to drive the cars right to the edge of the bluff. The one who stopped first was "chicken." In the course of time, several cars went over the bluff but the boys were quite skillful at jumping out of the car just in time to save their own skins. Well, this was the group that this boy, Dick, was now going with. When he wasn't quite sixteen, he and another boy borrowed a car one night which they found in the neighborhood, picked up two girls and went riding. They wound up in a ditch. Although nobody was hurt, the police came along, examined the situation, and found that Dick had a stolen gun in his possession. They took him into the court. There was quite a lot of publicity about it. He thrived on the publicity, became quite a hero with a certain sub-group in the school, and became more hostile and unruly than ever. Three or four months later, he was sent to the state reform school for delinquent boys.

Now here was a boy who again suffered from affectional deprivation. His father was absent much of the time and when he was home he showed his attention to the boy by beating him. He was not a good model person for the boy and there was no other man in the boy's life who could serve as a model person. He also suffered intellectual deprivation.

These are examples, then, of these two major problem groups, and they come from this lower working class that I have spoken of. But I have to keep reminding myself that there are more children who come out all right in this same lower working class so we cannot regard this as essentially a working class phenomenon. There has been a certain misleading theory of delinquency—the so-called "lower class theory." This is a cultural theory of delinquency which is to the effect that the delinquent as a member of a lower class culture becomes hostile to the middle class and what it represents because the middle class frustrates and keeps the lower class down. Therefore a person with any spunk at all should naturally become an aggressive person and a delinquent in this kind of a situation. Now there is a certain amount of truth in this, but the fact is still that for every one boy or girl who becomes delinquent in this situation, there are three or four who do not. Therefore one can hardly say that the natural thing is to become delinquent in this situation. There are three or four of his neighbors who do not become delinquent, so I think we should be hesitant about subscribing in a simple way to the hypothesis that delinquency is a natural thing for lower class youngsters. It is one way out for some of them but there are other ways out which are more acceptable to society and even to them.

Here is an example of a person who did find this other way out, and I think we might call him a pseudo-problem. He was a problem all right, as you will see, to his teachers, and yet at least the problem didn't turn out to be a problem in the category of social pathology. This is a boy whom I will call Roy. When he was in the fifth grade, he emerged sociometrically as one of the most aggressive boys in the community, as seen by his age mates and seen by the teachers. He had an I.Q. of about 80 and had a lot of trouble with reading. He dropped out of school just at 16 when he became of age to do so. At this point, we had the first interview with the boy and then an interview with the mother. The interviewer asked him about his teachers and whom he liked best and whom he liked least and he begins to expand on the one he liked least, "Albright, he was the one I liked the least. I still don't care for him. It all started over at Garfield. I was helping the principal with some tables in the gym. He sent a few of us down to do the job. They had a new floor on the gym. Anyway, I had trouble with Albright before and he held a grudge against me. I was always smarting off to him. Well, some kids were playing basketball on this new floor with shoes on. Albright came in there and yelled at me to get out of the gym. He blew his stack. And I said, you tell these other guys to get out and I'll get out. He grabbed me by the neck and arm, about broke my arm off and I knocked him on his rump down three or four steps. I went up to the office and told the principal to call him off me or I'd kill Albright. (This was in the sixth grade.) Later on, Albright started smarting off and I got mad and threw some books at him. Later he accused me of putting paint on his car on Halloween. It was two of his pets and the most sissified kids in the class that did it." So you see how this boy might have earned a reputation of being one of the most aggressive boys.

Now here are bits of the report from the home visit at the time the boy had just quit school at sixteen. This was three or four years after this first episode. "The Cranston family lives in a small deteriorating brick house with apparently two rooms downstairs and possibly one or two rooms upstairs under a small gable roof. The house is closely hemmed in by sub-

standard dwellings on either side. Several large elm trees near the street
shade the front yard which is small and without grass. Roots from the elm
trees have spread through the surface of the front yard causing the brick
walks across the front of the house and the house to buckle in places.
There is no landscaping in the front yard. The brick walk leads past the
east side of the house and one long cement step runs across two doors—
one at an entrance to the front room and the other to the kitchen. There's
a screen at the kitchen door. The screen is rusty and the door frame and
door both have dirty chipped gray paint. Roy was home alone when I
called the first time. He was combing his slick black hair at the kitchen
sink. The kitchen looked dark and dingy with the table piled with dirty
dishes and cereal boxes. Roy did not bother to come to the door. He talked
to me from the sink, apparently thinking I was a school representative trying to talk him into returning to school. He told me to come back late in
the day to see his mother. . . . When I found her at home, it was difficult
to explain my purpose. She is a short, plump woman, rather sloppy in
dress with black kinky hair parted on the side. She has big brown eyes and
a round, rather friendly face. Her smile exposed large gaps between her
upper front teeth. She wore a blue cotton housedress and black house slip-
pers. She thought I was trying to urge Roy into returning to school. She
said that she thought he should go too, but she wasn't going to force him.
After I explained that I was not here for that purpose, she could see no
special reason for our spending time on an interview as long as the boy is
no longer in school. She finally agreed for me to return on a Saturday
morning and concluded by saying that if she was present, we would talk
and if she wasn't, we would just forget it. Therefore I hardly expected her
to be home when I called on Saturday but she was there. She did not take
me into the house and she suggested it might be cooler back on the long
picnic table in the rear yard and she led the way back to a shaded spot.
The rear yard was cluttered somewhat with old types of metal including
an old lawn mower and parts of a car motor, an old style Ford parked in
the back yard and a fenced area with several Mallard ducks caged up.
Mrs. Cranston says that her husband uses them for decoys although they
are not legal in hunting. There were some hoop fishing nets suspended
over the fencing. She said that her husband has done quite a bit of commercial fishing on the side. She said that he works as a construction worker
for the union. She means that the union gets him employment on construction jobs from time to time.

What kind of a day does Roy have at the present time? By that I mean
just how does he get along with everybody at different times of the day
like breakfast, mealtime, and bedtime? (This is the question the interviewer asks.)

She said, "Well, right now I don't even know where he is. I guess he's
at some boyfriend's house. He must have gone there last night but he

didn't let us know. He talked to me a few weeks ago about staying over-night with a boy on the farm and then working the next day to earn a little money. I told him that I didn't think he should and he said, 'Why? I did that before,' and that was the first time I knew about it. He doesn't always tell me what he's doing. I suppose he was out at the farm last night or at one of his friend's in town. When they get to be about 16 years old, you just don't know where they are. And I can understand it. I was married when I was 16 years old and my hubby is the kind that went on his own pretty young. He thinks it's all right for a boy to be that way. But Roy is a pretty good boy. He will scrub the floor, wash clothes, iron his own clothes. I always say he will make a pretty good woman for somebody."

"Do you find that he loses his temper around the house pretty easily?"

"Oh yes. He's hot headed and if he gets against us, he's fighting mad."

"Did this happen much when he was in school?"

"Yes, I think it did. Now he's helped out at the Washington Laundry the past week." (This is where she was working.) "He came home the other night and said that someone was flipping an old towel at him and he had a notion to tell him off. He's a boy who won't be run over. I don't know about Roy in school. I just don't know why he didn't take to it. He was in St. Joseph's Parochial School until about the fourth or fifth grade and then he went to Garfield, a public school. They didn't seem to think they could do much for him at St. Joseph's. He couldn't get the reading and they weren't very anxious for him to go on there."

"What sort of things does he do that you wish he wouldn't?"

"Well, like at night we think he ought to be in by 10:30 but he don't usually get in then. Of course his father has the idea that at his age he should be pretty much on his own. Then, I think he ought to let us know when he stays over night. We should know a little more about him and what he is doing."

"What sort of things is Roy rather successful at?"

"Well, he's pretty good at jobs like cleaning up yards. He also has helped deliver papers for two of his buddies though he didn't have a paper route of his own."

"Has Mr. Cranston been able to help you much in raising the kids or have you had most of the responsibility?"

"Well, he thinks I'm the one who should tell the kids what to do because I'm here with them most of the time or at least have been until I started to work. But I can't get them to do things very easy. When he is home, he will tell them and flog them quicker than I will. They sort of wear me down."

"Do you mean he is more quick tempered than you are?"

"No, he isn't quick tempered, but he will just boot them quicker to get them to move." She laughed and said, "He hasn't killed any of them yet. Then they sort of hold it against me. It's that old grind of telling them too many times to do something and they sort of blame me for having to tell them. I've told Roy and Patsy so many times and when they don't do it, I tell my husband and then they had better do it."

"What does your hubby do in his spare time?"

"Oh, he hunts and fishes and goes to car races." While we were talking about him, Mr. Cranston backed another old model car into the yard from the alley. He was a husky guy of medium height with a large flushed face. He was neatly dressed wearing a summer cap, a tan sport shirt, blue wash pants, and cloth shoes. He pushed the little two year old girl a bit in the swing near our bench and then he sat down with us.

"What do you think of the schools? Do you think there's anything the schools might have done to make Roy enjoy it a little more?"

She said, "Well, he just didn't seem to care for school except arithmetic. He had trouble with reading when he was real young and he never did learn to read very well. And then he would get disgusted and lose interest. Somehow he missed something where Patsy seemed to get it. (Patsy was a younger sister.) Roy did better though since he left St. Joseph's."

"Are you and Mrs. Cranston active in any organizations or church auxiliaries?"

"Well, I belong to the St. Joseph's church. Me and the kids belong but my husband doesn't. I don't belong to the auxiliary and anything like that. I guess I could but I just never did."

"What do you enjoy doing, Mrs. Cranston?"

"Oh, I like to go to shows, I like to have parties for the kids. I enjoy getting with other people a little bit ..."

Here is a boy who was a problem in school and he finally quit school as soon as he could. Now two years later, he's eighteen, and was married about a year ago. He married a sixteen-year-old girl. He has a fairly good job and a job that has some training possibilities. He has settled down and I think there is no question but what he will make a very good adjustment at the father's level or a little above the father's economic level. There is no affectional deprivation. The father has time for the youngsters. He takes the boy hunting and fishing. He pushes the two year old in the swing. He's not a very aggressive energetic man in our competitive economic system, but he's probably a rather good father to produce boys who themselves are going to be a little on the tough side but nevertheless have a fair amount of self-discipline. The mother is a person who has had plenty of affection for the children. She did not work out of the home until they were pretty well along. She stayed home and looked after them. She complains that she doesn't know where Roy is, as a sixteen year old. But this is probably evidence that she was keeping tab on him when he was younger pretty much and knew who his friends were. So here we have no affectional deprivation.

Model person deprivation? No, I think not. The father has made a fairly good adjustment in working class life—at least it's one that's well within

the law and so we see this boy who was a problem in school but nevertheless who has not become delinquent and who's going to make a fairly good
adult adjustment.

Certainly a good deal of intellectual deprivation. This is a family that's
not intellectual at all and the boy himself had trouble with reading early.
This has stood in his way and, I think, it was probably the cause of a good
deal of his misbehavior in school. He wasn't doing well and one of the
things for a boy like this when he's not doing well is to do other things
that call attention to him, get him status if he can't do well in his studies.
This is one, therefore, who will cause a lot of trouble to teachers. There's
no question about that. But nevertheless, not really a problem in our
society as compared with the kind who have affectional deprivation and
have model person deprivation and make a lot of difficulty for themselves
and for other people too as they grow up.

Now what about the school for these kinds of problem children? It
seems to me there are two major things for the school to do. The first is
to do a much better job of discovering these children and working with
them in the kindergarten and primary years. If I had a certain amount of
money to dispose of in the ordinary community so as to reduce the amount
of real problem behavior, I would put most of it at the kindergarten and
primary level. I would try to find the children who obviously, or very
likely, will suffer from affectional and model person deprivation and intellectual deprivation. I would place them in relatively small classes with
excellent teachers and count on these classes getting them over that first
barrier—the barrier of learning to read. There is enough evidence now to
indicate fairly definitely that you can do a great deal for this kind of
youngster if you take it easy, take it slow, patiently, in these early years.

I give you one example, one in which we've been working. We picked
out eighteen youngsters who had been failures in the first grade in one of
the slum schools. Six of them were being passed on probation and the
other twelve were being kept back because they hadn't even gotten
through a pre-primer. The other six, it was thought, might make a go of
it in the second grade. So they were put into a class of eighteen—a small
class. The teacher assigned to work with them for two years was given
facilities (she could buy special equipment, special books, and so on if
she needed them) and had the help of one of our staff. They visited the
homes, they studied each child. At the end of two years ... five of these
eighteen had left town. These people are likely to be geographically mobile. Of the remaining thirteen, I think all but three were ready to go into
the third grade—they were up with their grade in terms of both reading
and arithmetic at the end of two years. I think if they had either been
simply put back into a regular first grade, only a few of them probably
would have picked it up because the teacher would have been busy with
the others and been paying more attention to the "regular" first graders.
If they had been put in the second grade, things might have moved too

rapidly for them. I believe that during this crucial period, this kind of child needs a lot of special attention and needs to be carried ahead fairly slowly.

One of my students came in the other day and proposed a master's thesis along this line. I was rather interested in her observation. She said, "I'm teaching now in the fourth grade, I have noticed that I have got some children who were three semesters in a 1-C." (1-C in Chicago means a slow first grade. They keep them an extra semester because they were not reading reasonably well at the end of the second semester.) She said, "I believe that most of these youngsters are doing all right in the fourth grade, and I've got some others who are not doing well and I've checked back and found they were rushed through (as she put it) the first grade." Well, there may be something to this. I encouraged her to go ahead and make it a more systematic study.

My general notion is that perhaps the school can begin to make up for intellectual deprivation by taking it "slow and easy" with these youngsters. It can supply some of the affectional deprivation through a teacher who is a warm motherly type of person who deliberately tries to supply this and will talk with the mother to try to get the mother to understand and accept more of her responsibilities.

Then the other place to work would be at the junior high level. By now these youngsters are a real problem, but still some kind of treatment is possible. In my judgment the best solution of this now is to put these youngsters in special groups. I know there are disadvantages to this. Most junior high principals and teachers would be happy to put them off in this special group if they didn't have to deal with them themselves. But I believe that a special grouping of the youngsters who've done poorly in school and have evidence of either aggressive behavior or withdrawn behavior has some possibilities. We've tried this in this one community. We haven't felt we had anywhere near the amount of success that we had with this first grade group but it is true that the youngsters who were put in the special room reduced their truancy—in other words, school became more tolerable to them so they quit being truant. There was less delinquency in this group than in the control group whom we left in the regular schoolroom situation. There was less actual delinquency during the two years they were in this special room. There was not much gain in the academic skills and this doesn't surprise me very much. These youngsters were reading at fourth or fifth grade level when they were up in eighth or ninth and they're probably past the time when they could do very much about the academic skills. But this kind of program ought to emphasize moral habits and social adjustment. It ought to try to get these youngsters into some kind of work experience where they can begin to pick up reasonably good work habits and it ought to try to get them to the point where they have more confidence in themselves and can carry on in the social group.

This would be my prescription for work at the junior high level. It is not preventive, it is a matter of treatment.

The numbers involved here are between five and ten percent of the total age group. They tend to fall, as I said, in the lower part of the working class because that's where deprivation tends to appear most frequently. To a limited extent, the school can do something for them by making up for the deprivation. The earlier we start, the better. Kindergarten and first grade are best but some kind of treatment is possible at the junior high level.

The Disadvantaged and Deviant
Classroom Behavior

Diagnosis of a person's ills is a difficult process in the medical profession. It becomes more complicated as more exotic symptoms are uncovered. Diagnosis of social ills is even more complicated because of their scope, their variabilities, and the lack of systematic experience by the diagnosticians. Conflicting diagnoses by medical experts are not uncommon, but most individual sickness has identifying symptoms. Experts in the study of society differ widely in diagnosing social ills since the symptoms are often more subtle and the interpretations more diverse. Some see increased average income as a positive sign, others negative. Some view the poor as incurable, others prescribe massive financing, others special work camps, and others education.

Diagnosing cultural deprivation and alienation is also difficult since they are matters of degree and not kind. In effect, everyone suffers in one way or another from cultural deprivation and alienation. The following reading concerns itself with deviant classroom behavior that is a direct consequence of this illness. If IQ scores are not acceptable measures of deprivation, what yardstick can be applied? How can determining the motivation level and value systems of youngsters assist in alleviating the deprivation that causes classroom behavior problems? What approaches to teaching are necessary to treat alienation and deprivation? Can a middle-class school provide adequately for children of lower classes? What factors are responsible for deviant behavior? To what extent can causality be established for deviation from social norms? Which classroom norms differ from social norms?

Social and Cultural Factors in Deviant Classroom Behavior

THOMAS E. LINTON

Currently there is a great deal of concern in both Canada and the United States for the culturally deprived and socially maladjusted child. In the U.S., this concern has caused the federal government to provide millions of dollars for various kinds of school programs in deprived areas. Another aspect of this concern is expressed in the government's large appropriations for mental health, including the emotionally disturbed child.

Historically, it may be argued that the conditions of poverty, social maladjustment, and emotional disturbance in children are not new or particularly different, in terms of their influence on the pathology of personality. There has been ample evidence to demonstrate the relationship between personality dysfunction and poor social conditions. Why, then, this sudden and rapidly escalating interest in financial support for deprived and disturbed children?

This support probably has been initiated by several social forces. Among these are the large-scale physical decay of cities, the abandoning of the center of cities by the more affluent citizens, discrimination and racial strife, large-scale growth of slum populations, and unemployment effects of automation.

Poverty studies indicate that vast segments of the population are economically and culturally deprived. Kolko states that:

Since 1947, one-half of the nation's families and unattached individuals have had an income too small to provide them with a maintenance standard of living and one-third have had an income too small to provide even an emergency standard of living.[1]

Harrington writes:

Tens of millions of Americans are at this moment maimed in body and spirit, existing at levels beneath those necessary for human decency . . . This poverty twists and deforms the spirit. The American poor are pessimistic and defeated and they are victimized by mental suffering to a degree unknown in Suburbia.[2]

Reprinted from _Canada's Mental Health_, Supplement No. 52, July–August, 1966, by permission of the publisher, Department of National Health and Welfare, Ottawa, Canada.

[1] Gabriel Kolko, _Wealth and Power in America_, Praeger, New York, 1964, p. 101.
[2] Michael Harrington, _The Other America_, Penguin Books, Baltimore, Md., 1962, pp. 9–10.

This large-scale poverty is directly involved in limiting the social, moral, and intellectual development of millions. The largest group of school failures, the highest crime rate, the narcotics addiction problem, alcoholism and large-scale mental illness are all problems closely tied in with hard-core poverty. It has long been recognized that poverty has extremely detrimental effects on human development. Yet we continue to focus on individual pathology and family dynamics, deliberately avoiding an examination of the real factors producing the large-scale disruption of our cities.

The fact of urban social disruption is probably the most important force in motivating governments to spend funds for programs for the disadvantaged in urban areas. It has reached the point where many major cities such as Montreal, Toronto, Chicago, and New York are viewed as unsafe by many of their inhabitants. They feel a continuous sense of anxiety. And with good reason, since the crime rate in these and many other cities is excessively high.

The feeling of anxiety and panic operates on two levels. First, there is a simple denial of the problem, an attempt to avoid a realistic confrontation of these dangerous social issues. This is commonly seen when school boards and their officials deny the validity of some of the most minor criticisms of their policies. Officials have openly and flatly denied that there are favored schools, or that they cater to middle-class students. And of course, this only furthers the causes of social disruption.

The second level of anxiety is the brutal and obvious one: the specific physical dangers of living in large urban cities. It is illegal to walk in some city parks after nightfall. Some of them are dangerous even in mid-day. Many metropolitan beaches are not safe for children or adults. Large sections of most major cities are considered "out of bounds" by the suburban set, not only for their children but for themselves as well. These sections are the already huge and growing slum districts which characterize most large cities. They are the breeding ground for crime, delinquency, narcotics, and the social alienation that leads to physical retaliation against other parts of the community. It is quite common for the slum dweller's child to experience parental rejection, school failure, police hostility, family and street violence, the apathy and patronizing callousness of public officials, and eventually the reality of being an unwanted commodity on the labor market. Social alienation is not a unique or individual problem. As Harrington points out, it is the simple reality of daily existence for "40 to 50 million citizens of this land."[3]

THE PROBLEM

What are the social and cultural factors which produce a mass-based form of deviant classroom behavior? Broad-scale social deviancy and failure to "succeed" in school is primarily the direct result of social and other

[3] *Ibid.*

factors which perpetuate these conditions. Deviant classroom behavior, as such, is really not deviant, but normal for the area in which it occurs. It is deviant only when considered from an academic and very traditional point of view. This, it seems to me, is the core of the problem. Vast numbers of disadvantaged children are being approached with obsolescent and rigid curriculum standards. The teacher-selection and classroom methods for the poor are essentially the same as for the well-to-do. The common cry of school people is that disadvantaged children are not motivated or concerned with achieving as are suburban children. But rarely does one see a radical revamping of the traditional school approach for disadvantaged children. What one does see, however, is the standard clinical approach to "deviant behavior," as long emphasized by education, social work, and psychology.

This widespread clinical approach is seriously in error. The problem, by and large, is not one of pathological behavior of the child. If anything it is pathological behavior of the adult authorities. These authorities—political leaders, board members, school officials and teachers—frequently deny the seriousness of the problems and refuse to openly examine the basis for deviant classroom behavior. This retreat from reality is indicative of a kind of social pathology which characterizes many of the social and civic leaders of our time. More importantly, most of the professionals directly involved with maladjusted and delinquent children refuse to examine the implications of the social and psychological deficits imprinted on millions of children. School officials, teachers, psychologists and psychiatrists are fond of detailing a child's deviations from acceptable social and classroom behavior. One has only to attend conferences of the American Orthopsychiatric Association to observe the extreme emphasis which is placed on individual pathology. It is common for these meetings to deal with maladjustment and social deviancy, but they rarely emphasize the social causes of these conditions.

There is a great involvement with clinical measurement and personality evaluation of deviant children, many of whom display behavior which is mass-based and not unique to the particular child. By endeavoring to rescue with therapeutic techniques a few children from the mass, we are, of course, able to enlarge our occupational domain. We train more and more specialists who focus on the clinical personality needs of the child, but we carefully manage to avoid any involvement with the conditions which breed the mass-based social maladjustment!

INTELLIGENCE AND ENVIRONMENT

What, then, are some of the major theoretical formulations in support of the argument that deviant behavior is not a clinical entity but a mass-based social condition?

It is common knowledge that the largest group of "educable" children in most urban areas come from what is often termed the "inner city." This area is usually the most socially fragmented, the most decayed, and the lowest income section of the city. Many of the residents of these areas are Negroes, immigrants, and migrants from rural communities. They are usually minority group members who have been prevented from normal participation in the "main stream" of Canadian and American life. They have been contained in ghettoes, and socially ridiculed. They have been utilized as inexpensive labor by concerns not required or able to avoid paying the standard wage. In slack periods they are the first to lose their jobs; as conditions improve, they are the last to be hired. In essence, their potential has been far from utilized. They have been treated as unwanted, rejected members of society, lacking education, employment, housing, and healthy social activities.

Yet, despite these conditions the schools apply standard I.Q. and achievement tests to a population that has difficulty in producing normal-range results. There is abundant evidence that intelligence is strongly affected by environmental factors. And not only is intelligence affected in this way but so is motivation, language development, interest patterns, cognitive growth, and perceptual patterning of one's environment.

The relationship between social class and I.Q. has been clearly established in numerous studies showing that, as social class rises, so does I.Q. and school achievement. For example, in a study by the author of a Canadian population there was established a clear and significant relationship between income and occupation, on the one hand, and school achievement on the other.[4] The research examined 525 boys in the ninth grade who, at this point in their schooling, were required to take an examination which would determine their school placement in subsequent years. The sample was divided into three groups: those who failed, those who received average passing marks, and those obtaining honors. With few exceptions, the failing group of 120 boys were from lower-income working-class families. With some exceptions, the honors group were from the more affluent families of higher status occupations. As the status of the fathers' occupations rose, so did the boys' results. Thus these ninth-grade examinations, instead of acting as a means of screening students on the basis of intellectual ability and achievement, served to reinforce pre-existing social prejudices against lower-income groups.

This study was concerned with why lower class students test at lower levels, not merely with establishing the already well known fact that I.Q. varies with the rise in social class. The IPAT (Institute for Personality and Ability Testing) test of nonverbal reasoning was used as a measure against the standard verbal and quantitative measures used in the examination.

[4] Thomas E. Linton and Donald F. Swift, "Social Class and Ninth Grade Educational Achievement," *The Alberta Journal of Educational Research*, September, 1963, pp. 157–67.

While the IPAT results were not significant, they did reflect a higher student capacity than that indicated by the examination marks. In several cases, the scores were higher than would be expected by the students' examination results. Personality testing of the students, as well as parent interviews, further substantiated the importance of lower social-class conditioning as a key determinant in school failure.

In an extensive review of the research on the relationship between intelligence and environment, it was concluded that I.Q. scores were not valid measures of intelligence:

The I.Q. is unstable over time, cannot be reliably measured by any agreed upon single instrument and has strong environmental determinants, and that its genetic determinants are sufficiently multi-factorial that they do not lend themselves to existing techniques of genetic research.[5]

The "multi-factorial" aspect referred to is taken from Guilford's studies which elicited forty factors involving differing intellectual functions. This researcher comments: "The question: 'Is intelligence inherited or is it acquired?' makes less sense than it ever did. Such a question must be asked regarding each and every factor."[6]

Schools commonly look upon achievement and intelligence tests as fair measures of academic potential. They seldom alter their curriculum, teaching methods, or counselling approach to benefit a disadvantaged lower-class population and act as though only a few of the many factors involved in intelligence have to do with education. Yet many of these factors are the very ones utilized frequently by the more successful members of the community and are deliberately articulated and fostered by parents of the more successful students. When the latter come to school they experience a pattern of behavioral expectation which is very similar to what they already learned at home. Hence, the transition is from acceptable behavior to acceptable behavior. But the disadvantaged child moves from acceptable to nonacceptable behavior in the eyes of school authorities who see the way he behaves and acts as "socially deviant." Thus the problem is not classroom management of behavior deviance, but a radical change of approach to educating culturally and intellectually deprived children.

Schools have also tended to associate intelligence and achievement with a very narrow range of human abilities. School teachers and officials are inclined to believe that the higher achievement results found in suburban schools are the product of essentially superior genetic endowment. They may not say this in public, but they express it in private. For example, suburban area high school superintendents like to quote their low drop-out statistics, the high percentage of their students who graduate, or the large number who go on to college, seemingly unaware that the social condition-

---

[5] Richard Masland, Seymour B. Sarason, and Thomas G. Gladwin, *Mental Subnormality,* Basic Books, Inc., New York, 1958, p. 211.
[6] *Ibid.*

ing factors, rather than the school's effort, are mainly responsible for these figures.

MOTIVATION AND VALUES

Considerable research has been done on cultural values and personal motivation. Studies by McClelland, Strodtbeck, Davis, Atkinson, and Hollingshead have indicated that cultural factors play an important part in determining academic achievement. McClelland, for example, evaluated intellectual motivation as measured by an analysis of student responses to selected cards from the Thematic Apperception Test which are assigned numerical weights and related to assumed motivational states. Using this approach he found that specific groups such as Italians, Irish, and Negroes have lower achievement motivation than do Jews, Greek Orthodox, and white Protestants.

McClelland's thesis is that subcultural value themes produce differing kinds of motivational systems. When the subculture shares the values held by the "main stream" group in Canada and the U.S., academic achievement is enhanced. When the cultural orientation is antithetical to the school's expectations, the child experiences failure. This is not the school's fault but the result of years of value conditioning by the child's family.

Strodtbeck and Kluckhohn have written that these subcultural themes may be analyzed in terms of specific types of "value orientations." Such orientations are derived from examining the ways in which many cultures approach such behavioral themes as: active vs. passive; dependent vs. independent; the use of time and personal relationships. These values may be measured by specific questions developed by these researchers which attempt to measure the individual's approach to these choices. It has been found, for example, that some lower income, subcultural groups are passive, dependent, and relationship oriented. These qualities run counter to the value expectations held by the schools. The problem is one of conflict between family-held and fostered values, and the schools attempt to provide a new value orientation.

In specific subcultural groups, like the Mexican-American, the value orientation is strongly in conflict with the behavioral choices permitted and rewarded by the schools. With most Jewish and Japanese groups, the family value themes reinforce the school expectations. It has been shown that if these three ethnic groups start at an equally low socio-economic position, the Jewish and Japanese groups eventually outdistance the Mexican-American group in terms of school achievement and upward social mobility. Hence, poverty or low-status occupation are not necessarily the big determinants in school failure. The specific values demanded by the parents are very significant in predicting school success or failure.

Children whose values are not congruent with those of the teacher or the school are inclined to become classroom behavior problems. Such children are not likely to enjoy sitting passively through hours of carefully structured factually-orientated material. Yet the school day is made up of six to seven periods of tightly scheduled, highly organized blocks of time. Also, in about the fifth grade, an increasing number of rules begin to be introduced having to do with student behavior, infractions of which result in some form of disciplinary action for the deviant student.

On the other hand, the 'good' student is one whose values are congruent with the teacher and other school authorities. He conforms to the rules, is passive before authority, and quiet when the teacher speaks. He comes from a home where he has been brought up to learn the rules as they are now being played in school. His use of time has been structured, actively used, and controlled by his parents. He has been rewarded for conforming. His independence, play, study habits, even his choice of friends, have been heavily influenced by his parents and their values.

But the 'deviant' child often comes from a home where the parents' values are inconsistent and fragmentary. In many cases his parents are absent from home all day and he has had to learn to fend for himself. His time has been unstructured, passively experienced, and subjected to a minimum of adult control. Often he is managed by peers and adults who have little or no personal involvement in his life. It is not surprising, therefore, that controls, structure, and a carefully organized school day may be viewed by him as further evidence of the restrictive and punitive nature of the adult world.

Children's motivation and values are largely a product of conditioning experiences learned in the home. Parental expectations which are similar to those of the school result in adaptive and successful school performance. Even if the school is restrictive, uninteresting, and essentially a boring kind of learning situation for the 'good' child, he will likely conform and not be a behavior problem—at least in school. He internalizes his resistance to adults and rarely displays his real feelings about school. However, the 'deviant' student has not learned to passively accept the structure and the efficiency of the "achievement motivation" necessary for effective school work. Inner satisfaction and rewards from school participation and achievement are absent. In fact, it is even dubious whether they are obtained by the 'good' student, for the adaptive and congruent responses in school probably reflect a continuation of parental controls for the middle-class child, rather than evidencing the value of the school as a catalytic, motivating force in the child's experience.

HUMAN DEVELOPMENT AND PERSONALITY RESPONSE PATTERNS

Deviant classroom behavior becomes more difficult to manage as the student develops characteristic defensive mechanisms which serve as integrated response patterns. It is probable that deviant classroom behavior is based on large-scale social alienation. The alienation takes the form of a recognizable pattern of character disorder, the pattern being directly developed by social pathological conditions which are a normal part of the socialization process for millions of children. Julius Horwitz wrote in the *New York Times* (January 31, 1965):

There are 69,000,000 children in the U.S. under the age of 18 [of whom] 12,000,000 live in absolute poverty, which means just enough milk, bread, meat, clothing, and shelter to keep from starving to death or freezing to death. The intellectual and moral starvation is catastrophic. We now know that in a given census tract of a large city, a sizeable proportion of the infants are predestined for a stunted existence unless intervention takes place long before he sees the dirt, the drunks, the drug addicts, the spilled garbage of the slum; the damage takes place when the . . . mother brings her infant home from the hospital and realizes she hates him for being alive.

These social conditions lead to cognitive and perceptual deficits which may be very difficult to change by the time the child enters the first grade. Benjamin S. Bloom has argued that human development is increasingly difficult to influence with increase in age:

The individual not only becomes more resistant to change, as the characteristic becomes stabilized, but change, if it can be produced, must be made at greater emotional cost to the individual . . . It is less difficult for the individual and for the society to bring about a particular type of development early in the history of an individual than it is at a later point in his history.[7]

Various writers state that these social pathological conditions are directly responsible for limiting the social and intellectual potential of millions of children. They are the result of the

impact of disadvantaged environment on learning, resulting in nonorganic mental retardation. Four and one-half million of the retarded (in the U.S.) have no organic pathology and are retarded because of exposure to an environment that destroys the learning capacity of an otherwise normal child.[8]

The deficits created by poor and inadequate environments are multiple. They include physiological impairments, language disorders, pathological effects on personality, and a host of other crippling conditions. By way of illustration, the following combination of typical circumstances is characteristic of what is frequently associated with deviant classroom adjustment. The student is generally hostile and suspicious of the outside world. His experiences with his parents and other adults have conditioned him to expect manipulation and personal rejection. He feels that violence and its expression are a commonly accepted means of resolving conflict situations.

[7] Benjamin S. Bloom, *Stability and Change in Human Characteristics*, John Wiley and Sons, New York, 1964, p. 230.
[8] Julius Horwitz, *New York Times Magazine*, January 31, 1965, p. 52.

His conscience is undeveloped and his morality is unique to his group. He is more inclined to express his actual feelings when provoked than to manage, control, and repress them—quite the reverse of his teacher! His strong concern for virility results in early sexual experience and a more primitive approach to heterosexual involvement. His group does not sanction equal sharing of family control, nor the complex and academic relationship characteristic of white-collar marriages. To him, highly verbal males are "chicken" and lack the "guts" for action. The world he has experienced approves, whenever possible, direct and immediate gratification of impulses. The idea of delay, of planning for advanced goals, has no place in the real world he inhabits.

Most of the teacher's activities involve relating symbolic concepts and utilizing abstractions as learning devices. As Bernstein has pointed out, the development of abstract language is a long-term cognitive process. It is a matter of early auditory conditioning, of imitation and of learning to value symbolic behavior in an intrinsic self-rewarding manner. This opportunity is not available to the deprived child whose language patterns, values, and learning processes are geared to action rather than conceptualization. The emphasis is on an overly simplified vocabulary, and negative feeling is attached to careful verbal articulation. The child's observations are conditioned to concrete items in his perceptual field. His conceptual growth is poorly developed, for he has had little experience with abstract ideas. He was fortunate if he was able to survive his home and neighborhood without being involved with narcotics, crime, early sexual involvement, and delinquency of various kinds.

From the very beginning of school this child experiences an alien world rarely adjusted to his unique learning problems. To help him, the attempt is usually made to lighten his curriculum. Specially developed curricula and teachers for children of this type are occasionally found. What is needed, however, are teacher-training and recruitment programs designed to equip teachers with conceptual and methodological approaches for these children.

The culturally and economically deprived child enters school lacking adequate motivation, creativity, and general knowledge—these have been stunted in his development. Yet he is expected to compete with children with wider and much richer experiences. He soon feels failure, his teacher's expectations drop, often assuming that he is a "slow learner." Of course he feels this rejection, and both school and teachers reinforce his anxieties about what he accurately perceives as a punitive adult world.

For many advantaged children, of course, the rigid curricula and dullness of the teaching make for considerable boredom, but they are able to handle it. They have been more or less conditioned to passive acceptance of adult punitiveness and have internalized the extrinsic reward system utilized by their parents. However, the deprived child has not learned to do this. He sees his failure and boredom as further evidence of his own incapacity. Thus the school adds a final day-by-day destructive touch to his already alienated personality.

SOME IMPLICATIONS FOR ACTION

Poverty children cannot be "managed" within the traditional school structure and curricula. Specially designed teaching materials and methods are required. One thing the deprived child needs is experience in achieving success, something his family or depressed surroundings have usually been unable to provide. This will require the schools in urban and rural poverty areas to make radical changes in their present ritualistic and unimaginative programs.

A recent issue of *Maclean's Magazine* (March 5, 1966) presented a picture story of a new kind of school for immigrant Canadian children. Located "in a shabby building in the east end of Toronto" the Main Street school is an attempt by the Board of Education to meet the special needs of these newcomers to Canada. According to the article, this experiment is viewed as a "radical" departure from the more accepted school formulas. The school provides flexible programing, tutorial services where needed, frequent field trips, involvement of parents in the classroom, multilingual social workers, close and informal contacts between teachers and pupils, and a general atmosphere which is free of the rigid structure often found in many junior and senior high schools.

The interesting point is that this school is viewed as "a radical change" that might be a worthwhile model for immigrant youth. But the fact is that this approach is far more effective for all students—to say nothing of alienated and deprived children!

It has long been known from model school programs and from research studies that drastic changes in elementary and secondary school programs are needed to deal more effectively with students from depressed socio-economic areas. These studies and experimental programs were worked out far back in the 1920's and 1930's but were simply never applied. The *Maclean's* article mentions this very point, saying that the Main Street school "may turn out to be just another elaborate experiment in progressive education."

The key point is that the kind of changes that are needed to reduce deviant classroom behavior are fairly well known and have been for quite some time. What matters is how to get these changes implemented. And it is more than that, more than just reducing deviant classroom behavior. It is one of squarely and honestly facing the problem and eliminating it. But how does one get frightened and insecure adults to cross professional disciplines and honestly confront these and other major social problems?

TEACHER TRAINING AND PLACEMENT

Another area needing attention is that of teacher training and placement. Special training programs should be set up by faculties of education which place a particular teaching emphasis on the social, physical, and psychological backgrounds experienced by poverty children.

The placement of teachers in deprived areas should be based on specific personal and educational qualifications. And the very prevalent system of placing new teachers in these areas on a sort of "time-serving" basis should certainly be discontinued. Not only are teachers and administrators needed here that have a special understanding of their pupils, but they must also be those with a personal interest in this kind of professional challenge. Let me explain what I mean.

It has been more or less traditional practice for urban boards of education to place new teachers in poverty areas and then, after several years, to reward the conforming and noncritical teacher with a preferential placement in a more desirable area. It is obvious that such a policy cannot build an effective staff.

The result is that over the years the poverty-belt schools become characterized by an apathy and inertia which is a direct reflection of these policies. It is common knowledge among school people that the teachers in these schools are a very different group from those in the more desirable neighborhoods. They are generally made up of young and inexperienced teachers in their first job; old timers who have no desire for change; committed and concerned teachers who have chosen to work with deprived children; those who find it easier and less taxing to teach in these areas because they have little, if anything, to do with parents and because of the absence of high academic expectations for the students; and lastly, those who feel that the opportunity for becoming an administrator is greater because of the severity of the problems and the lack of identity and concern by the staff for the welfare of the school. This last factor is important because the poverty school, unlike the one in suburbia, does not involve the staff in any meaningful way in the daily life of the school —a factor noted earlier and of particular importance in any program seeking to enrich the educational life in poverty areas.

DRASTIC ALTERATIONS NEEDED

Much of this could be changed if school boards were to drastically alter their dreary and unimaginative personnel policies and develop programs based on a diagnostic and prescriptive approach to the academic and social problems which characterize the student population of a deprived area. As already mentioned, the key would not be a military type of operation, but a highly flexible and adaptive program involving staff who were constantly seeking new ideas and effective ways of motivating and interesting their students. It would involve small classes of ten and fifteen students, tutorial and remedial work, a heavy emphasis on basic language and reading skills, a program of cultural enrichment, and a general level of excitement and concern by the entire staff.

A school board could engender this kind of staff feeling and support if it deliberately chose to develop the ideas and approaches already being utilized in the Toronto Main Street School. Also, since people do not generally seek to work under adverse and hostile conditions unless there are specific and positive reasons for doing so, the staff of these schools should be provided with salaries and working conditions which make their jobs more attractive.

Mention has already been made of the need for special training and selection methods for teachers. This would include far more careful screening of a teacher's interests, values, and background for this work. Furthermore, school boards need to make it quite clear to teachers that these assignments are highly regarded. Staff would also be regularly evaluated, appropriately rewarded or transferred as their performance indicated, thus demonstrating that this type of teaching was only for selected and highly able teachers, rather than the inexperienced and alienated.

In summary, broad-scale deviant classroom behavior in poverty areas is essentially a problem of the inappropriateness of school programs. Standard academic procedures and expectations are applied to grossly divergent school populations. The result is academic failure and increased social alienation for thousands of children in deprived areas. What is needed is not individual clinical and therapeutic counselling for deviants, but radically redesigned school programs specifically structured to work directly with children in poverty.

PART 3

Dissent and Agreement in Society and Education

EDUCATION AND
NATIONAL ISSUES

The last section treated social class and the problems of the poor. Both of these topics are directly related to the nature and function of various economic systems and subsystems. A primary factor in any society is its economic operations. As this section indicates, there are agreements and dissent among scholars, politicians, and the interested public over the appropriate economic structure for a democratic society. Some form of capitalism seems to be the agreed upon economic theory, but much dissent occurs in determining the specific form and in establishing its operation. Free enterprise is viewed as providing incentive for the ambitious and resourceful as well as allowing freedom from governmental restriction. Private ownership of production is also viewed as a means of exploiting workers and creating monopolies which are not in the best interests of the consumer. By the same token, government ownership or regulation of public utilities is viewed both as a positive protection for the public and as a sign of creeping socialism. The delicate balance of private sector and public sector economics is the area of greatest dissent.

The problems of unemployment arising from the rapid evolution of technology and automation have refocused attention on the balance of private and public economics. Can private ownership provide for the technologically unemployed while competing for technological progress? Can the government become the employer of these unskilled workers without unfairly competing with private business or creating loss of individual initiative? The national issue of internal economics is a major issue in today's society and, thus, in contemporary education.

A second major national issue in which there is considerable agreement and dissent is that of foreign policy. While there is agreement on the need for peace; there is disagreement as to the best means to achieve this objective. Between the polarities of peace at any cost to peace on my terms only lie a series of alternatives, none of which is proven beyond logic or history. In these decisions logic may not be adequate since wars seem to defy logic and impose emotionality. History is also suspect since it cannot be used as a predictor due to its lack of scientific validity as a result of varying interpretations of events by historians. As in the domestic national issue of economics, the problems of attaining peace involve a delicate balance of international affairs. Both issues are the result of and are dependent upon the dynamics of human society. As such they are included in this text to serve as areas for developing understanding of social problems and the role of education in coping with them.

The schools in American society have both public and private nature and function. Private schools differ in purpose, if not in function, from public schools. Public schools produce citizens for a largely private enterprise society. The schools also provide a value framework that encourages or discourages nationalism and/or internationalism. The treatment of Germany or Japan in school materials during the Second World War, or the treatment of Russia and China in many contemporary schools, makes it evident that education serves to inculcate values which have lasting significance. Should the schools deal with the national issues of economics and peace?

Since it is agreed that the teacher is of major importance as a transmission agent for the general culture of a particular society, are the values she transmits agreed upon in that society? There are a large number of major social, economic, and political questions upon which there is major national disagreement. Some of these questions involve the future direction of the economy, the limiting or expansion of government involvement in the private sector of the economy, and the issue of America's role on the international scene. Are the boundaries of our moral and economic interest the boundaries of the world, or are they the boundaries of the territorial limits of American possessions? Will the society prosper or suffer from major transition toward the automated society? Is the poverty and destitution of millions of our own citizens our main national concern, or is this same problem throughout the world one of our responsibilities? Should the mass media in our society be sales agents and manipulators of public tastes, or should the government and public agencies provide alternative choices and place limits on commercial activities in television, newspapers, radio, and the major forms of public entertainment? Within the schools themselves what direction should the curriculum, textbooks, and the purpose of the school assume? Should the school serve primarily as a transmission belt or selected propaganda agency within the society as in Germany during the Third Reich?

When the schools deliberately perpetuated only specific dogmas and doctrines and viewed any offer of alternatives or heresy, they were acting consistently with the society at that time, but inconsistently with social progress. Yet, in form and substance many critics argue that public education today perpetuates only a very limited form of inquiry and intellectual stimulation within the schools. Which approaches are valid for the schools in our society? Major critics have in recent years denounced the whole purpose and function of public education and have demanded a totally different approach than has been currently and traditionally practiced. Do these criticisms of the schools stem from basic concern for the intellectual and social development of the child or is it basic fear and competitive anxiety over the effectiveness of American schools compared with Russian schools? In recent years the government has seen fit to pour millions of dollars into public education for the purpose of improving and enlarging the quality and direction of the educational system. Will the educational establishment that controls the operation of the school and the organizations that speak for the teachers be able to make the drastic changes which are required in a drastically changing society?

Technology and Progress

While society's concern with poverty might seem somewhat anomalous in light of America's mounting affluence, there is, as Robert L. Heilbroner discusses in the following article, a valid reason for emphasizing the negative aspect of an upward economic trend. Technology and automation have had a negative as well as a positive effect on our economy, and we must recognize and be prepared to deal with the crucial problem of unemployment that promises to grow to staggering proportions if left unchallenged.

What role can education play in providing for added leisure time, for the unemployed, for preparation of an automated society? Should the schools adopt more or less vocational programs? How will education absorb the impact of increasing numbers of students for increasing lengths of time?

New Horizons in Economics

ROBERT L. HEILBRONER

It is curious how rapidly economic fashions change. A few years ago the economic word *en vogue* was affluence, and the problems economists talked about were those of abundance and leisure. Today we hear instead about the twenty, forty, or seventy million Americans who are poor, depending on whether we define poverty as subsistence, adequacy, or minimal comfort. One would think from the trend of public concern that the country must have been declining in the intervening years. Yet, for all our current preoccupation with poverty, average incomes have risen by an eighth over the past five years, and we are appreciably more affluent a

Reprinted from *Saturday Review*, Vol. 47, August 27, 1964, pp. 31–32, by permission of the publisher and the author.

society than in 1958, when J. K. Galbraith's influential book was written. To take a figure that I find astonishing, one-quarter of all nonfarm families have now crossed over the $10,000 income line, and nearly half of them over the $7,500 line.

To talk of poverty in the face of such statistics is to risk appearing to be a professional hypochondriac. Yet there is a reason to accent the negative, even in the face of such positive indications. For the forces that are exerting their powerful hydraulic lift do not operate equally—nor even equitably—on all sections of the American public alike. Some are by passed. Worse yet, some are actually pulled downward in the backwash of the forces of propulsive momentum.

The bypassed portion of our society is one which we have become sporadically aware of throughout our history; we are in such a spasm of recognition at the moment. For it became clear during the great boom of the 1950s that currents of the great stream of purchasing power barely penetrate into certain reaches of the American economy, whose poverty remains stubbornly undissolved by the general prosperity. The old, eking out their days on a stingy Social Security allowance (62 percent of all income recipients over age 65 get less than $1,000 a year total income); the Negro family condemned by discrimination to an average standard of living that totals only 52 percent of white earnings; the family struggling along without a male earner (at the same income disadvantage as the nonwhite); the Mississippi farmer who makes only a fourth as much as a California farmer; and the Appalachian family on relief who may receive only a fourth as much as a Mississippi farmer—these are the "pockets" of poverty that defy the general advance. They do not defy it entirely; bit by bit the stagnant backwaters are drawn out into the main channel. But the pace is agonizingly slow.

Hence, if we are looking into the economic future, we shall have to count the not-so-newly poor side by side with the newly affluent. But this static sector is not what is most disturbing about the prospects ahead. Much more unsettling, because it is much more dynamic, is a problem about whose implications we are still loath to think clearly. This is the re-emergence of unemployment in the midst of the longest sustained climb the economy has ever known, and, more serious yet, the possibility that this unemployment is the sign of a fundamental challenge to which nothing less than the opening of a new frontier will be the answer.

We are still unused to the extent of this unemployment and reluctant to tally it fully. There is a considerable temptation to dismiss the unemployment problem as affecting "only" about 5.5 percent of the labor force, compared with an unemployment rate of 4.5 percent in the boom years from 1947 to 1957. A gain of one percentage point does not seem unduly alarming, even after we have been told that it means an increase of 1,000,000 in the number of men and women unable to find work.

But this is still only the "visible" unemployed—those who declare to the Department of Labor poll-takers that they are actively looking for work and cannot get it. To these 4,200,000 visibly jobless during 1963 we must add another 2,300,000 who sought full-time work but could get only part-time work. And even that is not the full count. There are in addition an indeterminate number, estimated at perhaps 2,000,000, who do not declare themselves "unemployed" to the poll-taker because they have simply stopped looking for work. Many lower-income housewives, for instance, would work if there were work to be had, but because they know that a search for a job is likely to be fruitless they stay at home.

Hence, there is reason to be concerned over the unemployment situation, even though on the surface it is not "bad." For if we add to the official unemployment rate of 5.7 percent for 1963 the unemployment represented by part-time work and by stay-at-homes, we get a total rate that is very close to 10 percent. Ten percent of the labor force is still very far away from the terrible days of the Depression, when an equivalent calculation would have revealed a rate of at least 30 percent. But it is sizable enough to represent a cause for deep concern.

How can we account for this slowly worsening problem at a time when so many in the nation have been experiencing a continuous prosperity?

It is usual to place the blame on the fact that our total dollar output, our Gross National Product, has not been growing fast enough. And it is true enough that our rate of growth of dollar output since 1958 is slower by perhaps a third than pre-1958. It is also true that if we could find ways of making our rate of growth increase considerably—let us say to the level of Western Europe or of the USSR—we would undoubtedly find jobs for many millions more Americans. And yet talk about the rate of growth in some ways obscures rather than clarifies the problem. For it hides the crucial fact that one of the main causes for such growth as we do have is also a primary cause for the unemployment we are suffering. That double-acting cause—both adding to our rate of output and subtracting from our rate of employment—is the extraordinary technology of the late 1950s and early 1960s, a technology to which we have given the name "automation."

It is worth our while to take a moment to see this new technology in perspective. After all, there is nothing new in the entry of inventions and improved techniques into our economic process, nor in the thrust that this entry has given to our output. In what way, then, is the present situation different from the past?

To answer the question we must back off far enough to be able to encompass a century in a single glance. For if we then look over the steady technologizing of America, two impressions stand out. The first is that technology has not entered our lives at random, pouring its blessings on all industries impartially. On the contrary, it has been much more concentrated in certain areas of economic activity than in others. In farming, for instance, it has wrought miracles—in fifty years the number of man-hours required to raise 100 bushels of corn has dropped from 147 to four or five. In manufacturing it has made advances nearly as dramatic: the man on the factory floor today outproduces his grandfather six to one. But in one important area of economic activity—the area of trade, service, administration—technology has been laggard. The doctor, lawyer, salesman, clerk is not appreciably more "productive" today than he was at the turn of the century.

To this impression we must now add a second. It is that with few if any exceptions we have never utilized to the hilt the productive possibilities inherent in the technology we introduced. The reason is very simple: output depends not only on productivity but on demand, and demand for the products of industries where technology made possible huge jumps did not immediately grow as fast as potential output. As the corn farmer gradually gained the power to multiply his output thirtyfold, he found that the demand for corn was not going to increase by anything like thirty times. And as the output of each particular industry raced out ahead, its entrepreneurs would find, at least for a while, that supply was outrunning demand.

Hence the traditional use we have made of technology has been a mixed one. Partly we have taken advantage of its ability to increase output, and this is a major cause of our rising productivity and wealth. But partly we have also used its powers to reduce the length of time at work, thereby not only gaining leisure, but holding back an otherwise redundant flow of output. And perhaps most important of all, we have taken advantage of the uneven entry of technology, and of our inability to match demand quickly to its new productive possibilities, by shifting our working efforts to other areas where our expanding purchasing power wished to turn next.

The table below shows this vast process of internal migration and redirected purchasing power very clearly:

Percent Distribution of Employed Workers

	Agriculture, forests, fisheries	Manufacturing, mining, transportation, construction, utilities	Trade, professional, and personal services, state, local, and federal government
1900	38	37	25
1963	8	36	56

Concealed within the table is a dramatic fact. Somewhere during the past sixty years—in fact, during the late 1940s—the number of people actually engaged in services surpassed the numbers engaged in making or handling goods. A society primarily concerned with production gave way to one primarily concerned with administration and distribution.

But the main lesson of the table is anything but concealed. For at least sixty years (and in fact much longer) technology has been bringing about

a gradual redirection of the economic pattern of society, draining manpower away from employment in the field and sending it into the factory,
and then draining it from the factory and sending it into the office and the
store. By way of recent illustration, note that between 1950 and 1963 farm
output rose by 10 percent while farm employment fell by 25 percent, and
that total manufacturing output rose by 30 percent while manufacturing
employment remained steady. And the only reason that manufacturing employment did remain steady was that the office force in manufacturing rose
fast enough to offset the manpower decline on the factory floor.

This résumé of recent history brings us back to the present and to a new
perspective on automation. To some extent, as we can now see, automation
is only a continuation of the past—a thrust of new techniques that will
push men from field to factory and from factory to office. But the new
technology, with its humanoid sensory devices and its uncanny capacities
to "learn" and to correct and guide itself, has an additional potentiality as
well. For the first time it threatens to invade the office as well—*to mecha-
nize the service and administrative branches of work and thereby to bring
to an end their steady growth as a source of work*. Anyone who has visited
a modern bank or insurance company or corporate office and seen batteries
of silent computers and clunking electric printers do the work of file clerks
and shipping clerks and bookkeepers and office managers has seen this new
technology in action. What he has also seen is the belated entry of technology into the last major field of economic activity, where it will once
again play the role it has already performed in agriculture and industry.
This time, however, where shall our unneeded labor go?

There remains one last twist to the problem. The new service-performing
technology in itself poses a substantial enough threat to our economy. But
to make matters worse, it is cutting into our employment base, both on the
factory floor and in the office, at the very time when requirements for new
jobs are reaching record heights. The huge crop of one-time war babies,
having burst through the nation's high schools and inundated its colleges,
is about to emerge onto the market place for jobs. By way of giving some
idea of how many jobs will be needed, consider that between 1950 and
1960 the young labor force, aged fourteen to twenty-four, increased by half
a million. Between 1960 and 1970 it will increase by 6,000,000.

Already we can feel the first effects of this rapidly expanding labor supply. Last year the jobless rate among white teen-agers looking for work
was 15.6 percent. Among nonwhite teen-agers it was 30 percent. And the
full impact is yet to come.

Automation is not, of course, the only economic problem of the future.
No one can look ten and twenty years ahead without asking worried
questions about disarmament and its impact on our overmilitarized economic machine; about our relations with the underdeveloped world, at
once so inescapable and so frustrating; about our growing competitive
struggle with Europe; about affluence itself, with its prospects for an orgy

of commercialism, a Saturnalia of advertising. Yet in many ways the problem of automation lies at the center of things, not alone in its human impact but in the larger implications of its challenge.

That challenge is to find a new frontier of employment to take the place of the disappearance of the service sector, the last great expansive area of private employment. But where can this frontier be? Where can we still use the skills and strengths of millions of Americans, some trained and some not, some young and some not so young? If one asks the question seriously, it is not difficult to answer it. America cries out for work to be done. The cities, ugly and rotten, must be rebuilt. The schools, still fearfully inadequate to their all-important task, must be expanded. The recreational space of the nation, cramped and undermanned, must be enlarged. The growing numbers of the old must be given homes, even villages, with nurses and companions. The public safety and the public convenience, both shockingly neglected in America, must be attended to. And not least, the poor must be guided out of their poverty and, where that is not possible, at least given the dignity of adequate support.

So there is no dearth of wants, no satiety of needs, no lack of work that might be done. But—and this is the crucial thing—all these wants and needs and employments will have to be initiated and financed and supported by the public sector. These are not goods or services that the market can provide. They are, without exception, matters that the community will provide through its public agencies, or that the community will not have.

There is more here than just a series of remedial measures to provide some necessary jobs. The provision of the public well-being represents, I believe, the next stage of economic activity to which a society naturally turns once it has begun to fulfil the demands of the private well-being. This is not to say that the sphere of private wants will not grow or that the private sector will not remain dominant in our economic life. But the challenge of the future does not seem to me to lie any longer in the private zone. It is the public zone that is still small and mean and dingy and poor —and increasingly important. Here is where the horizons are big.

Whether we shall meet this challenge with boldness it is difficult to say. Without doubt we shall hear the cry that it is socialism and the warning that the expansion of the public facilities will destroy the remaining vestiges of our personal liberties. But we can also be certain that the impersonal forces of the economy will be pushing us steadily into the new terrain where human labor, in its traditional places of work, becomes ever more redundant. Before this pending content of an old ideology and a new reality it would be fatuous to offer bland assurances or dire warnings. It is enough to brace ourselves for what is likely to be the central controversy of American political and economic life for at least the next decade and maybe more.

Patterns of Prosperity

*In the following review of an earlier book, Thurman W. Arnold describes
the economic alterations which have occurred in the past quarter century
—the rapidness of industrial change, the intricacies of the cold war, international economic arrangements, and the relation of public to private enterprise. His major concern lies in the fact that our economic theories have
not undergone comparable alterations to accommodate these new phenomena.*

*What is this "folklore of capitalism" that is stifling economic growth in
America? What is its effect on society and on education? Do the schools
perpetuate the folklore, or is it not folklore?*

Preface to *The Folklore of Capitalism*

THURMAN W. ARNOLD

This book [*The Folklore of Capitalism*] was written to describe the frustrating effects, in times of revolutionary change, of ideals and symbols
inherited from a different past. It therefore may be useful to describe what
has happened to our folklore since 1937 when this book was published, a
quarter of a century ago.

Since that time the greatest war in history has been fought. That war
pulled us out of the stagnation of the depression. It forced us to utilize our
industrial resources to the utmost and to expand them at a rate which
would have been considered impossible twenty-five years ago. We came
out of the war far richer in terms of real wealth, by which I mean productive capacity, than when we went in. We became the richest nation the
world has ever known.

For a short time after that war we were a confident nation, sure of our
destiny. We believed that we were at the beginning of a new age of world
order based on fundamental principles acceptable to all civilized nations.
The symbol of that belief was the United Nations, which represented

From the Preface to *The Folklore of Capitalism* by Thurman W. Arnold, 1962 ed.,
pp. iii–xxiii. Reprinted by permission of the publisher, the Yale University Press, New
Haven, Conn.

world unity under a new kind of international law. The first step we took to dramatize the ideal of international law and order was the Nuremberg trials. The purpose of those trials was to establish a great legal precedent which would outlaw forever the kind of aggressive war Germany had forced on the Western world. And so the United States, England, and Russia set up a joint international tribunal to clothe the ideal of international order with a judicial opinion which would be a guide for the indefinite future. The Nuremberg verdict was designed to teach Germany a lesson it would never forget and to be a permanent warning to all future Hitlers that the new world would no longer put up with military aggression.

With the twin symbols—the United Nations, where international disputes were to be resolved, and the Nuremberg trials, establishing a new principle of international morality—we believed we had achieved an enduring foreign policy. The age-old dream of all utopians—that if we can get men to agree on a principle, institutions and social organizations will arise which will adhere to and carry out that principle—was the basis of short-lived optimism and confidence which followed the destruction of the German empire.

In saying this I do not mean to imply that the United Nations has not made a tremendous contribution to world order. It was the first formal recognition in our history that the industrial revolution of the twentieth century had created a world in which even a nation as large as the United States could no longer exist as an isolated economic or political unit. It would have been indeed a tragedy had the United States rejected the ideal of which the United Nations was a symbol. The significance of the United Nations was the fact that it marked the end of a century of isolationist thinking.

Nevertheless we expected too much of it. The apparent agreement between the Soviets and the Western democracies expressed in the Nuremberg trials, that international aggression was abolished as a matter of international law, coupled with a new organization designed to unite every nation in the world in a common humanitarian purpose, lulled us into a sense of false security. And so we cheerfully dismembered Germany into four zones, French, British, Russian, and American, so that all could be partners in eliminating the menace of another Hitler. To have established a corridor giving access to Berlin would have shown distrust of our Russian partner and disturbed that atmosphere of confidence and cooperation which was to remove the threat of future wars.

The disillusionment that followed the collapse of these shining symbols of peace and international morality gave rise to fears and anxieties about the stability of our own institutions at home which grew to a national neurosis. Somebody had to be blamed for our short period of amity with Russia. The idealistic attempt to establish in cooperation with Russia some sort of world order could only have been caused by the infiltration of local

Communists into our own government. The idea spread over the entire nation that the American Communist Party, through devious and secret ways, had the potential power to overthrow the government of the United States. The real danger to our institutions was not Russian power abroad but Communist infiltration at home.

We became more afraid of ideas than realities. This fear increased in intensity as the Cold War proceeded. It wasn't enough to discharge suspected persons from government service. A public badge of infamy had to be pinned on them. We had to celebrate our achievements in ridding the country of its internal dangers by a public ceremony. And so President Truman established a hierarchy of quasi-judicial institutions clothing the hunt for subversives with the sanctity of judicial process. It was in this atmosphere that Senator McCarthy rose to power and was able to dictate to the President who should be discharged and who should be retained. Any idea which did not conform to the McCarthy pattern was sufficient to destroy the career of a liberal in government if by some accident his name got into the files of a congressional committee.

It soon became apparent that there weren't enough Communists to keep the costly and rapidly expanding bureaucracy of security officers, hearing boards, and congressional committees supplied with victims. Most of the material they had to work on was hearsay and secret reports by professional informers. To use such material as evidence was contrary to every American ideal of a fair trial. Indeed, an American tribunal in Germany had convicted German judges on the ground that the use of secret evidence was an international crime.

But this ideal of a fair trial had to give way in order to keep the vast bureaucracy in business. And so it was determined that accused individuals could be convicted on secret evidence given by faceless informers whose identity was unknown to the accused. Nor was the accused permitted to see and rebut the secret evidence given against him. This process tremendously enlarged the supply of game which the security system could track down and shoot. The Supreme Court of the United States gave its tacit approval to the use of this sort of evidence by affirming the conviction of Dorothy Bailey on secret evidence in a four-to-four decision. And from then on, for years, the most publicized policy of government was the rooting out of subversives in government and industry.

Our Cold War with Russia assumed all of the aspects of the religious wars of the Reformation. Both the Soviets and the United States engaged in worldwide propaganda appealing to the hearts and souls of men to adopt the only true religion. The preaching of each side was as violent as any delivered during the Reformation. The only difference was that in the Reformation hell was in the next world. In the religious war of the twentieth century the respective hells of communism and capitalistic imperialism were in this world, just around the corner. Millions were spent by the United States on the Voice of America, and counter-millions were spent by

Russia in jamming its broadcasts. And so for years we believed that our national salvation depended on preaching the glories of capitalism abroad and the rooting out of subversives at home. This is the kind of phenomenon which always occurs when a religious war is being fought.

Today we have fixed our attention on Russian power instead of internal subversion. Yet the essentially religious character of the Cold War still continues. Neither Russia nor the United States is pursuing materialistic objectives. It is indeed a battle for the minds and hearts of men in which symbols are still more important than realities. For example, we have planted our flag in Berlin and are prepared to defend it even at the risk of an atomic war. Berlin is a symbol of the reunification of Germany. The ideological conflict could be resolved, at least with respect to that city, if the United States would recognize the legality of the East German government. Few intelligent men believe that as a practical matter reunification of Germany is even a remote possibility. Yet concessions by either side would be a moral victory for the other with far-reaching psychological consequences in Germany and Western Europe. When wars are fought over markets or for trade advantages they can be ended when they appear too costly. When they are fought for the minds and hearts of men, when it is a struggle between the Catholic and the Protestant churches, or between Communism and Capitalism, neither side can risk defeat on the issue of any symbol which dramatizes its faith. This is true even though defense of that symbol might possibly mean the extinction of half the human race. From a rational point of view this may seem like nonsense. From an anthropological point of view, however, we must recognize that such symbols as Berlin are the cement that holds Western society together, that holds the promise of unity, both political and economic, for Western nations. To abandon such a symbol might utterly defeat the brightest promise of the future. The risk must therefore be taken.

Out of this risk there is emerging a new ideal, and a new set of symbols. The European Common Market, which seemed completely utopian only a few years ago, has become a reality. An international court has been set up to adjudicate the trade practices of the citizens of independent sovereignties. An international code of antitrust laws after the American model has been enacted and is being enforced by the European international court. The United States and England are seeking to join that international economic union.

And here in the Western Hemisphere we have accepted the ideal of the economic unity of the United States and Latin America. That ideal has been embodied in an organization called the Alliance for Progress. The basic concept of that organization is expressed in a treaty by which the United States and Latin American nations committed themselves to an acceleration of economic growth, a more equitable distribution of the fruits of economic development, and recognized the need for tax, land, and institutional reform and new investment capital. In the language of the treaty of Punta del Este these nations and the United States agreed "to unite in a common effort to bring our people accelerated economic progress and broader social justice within the framework of personal dignity and political liberty."

These words could not have been written without a storm of outraged protest when *The Folklore of Capitalism* was published in 1937. No such treaty could possibly have been approved by the Senate of the United States at that time.

In those times Henry Wallace was being denounced as a man who wanted to give a bottle of milk to every Hottentot because of ideas which were insignificant in scope compared with the Alliance for Progress. And yet the Alliance for Progress, which goes further in assuming responsibility for the poverty and economic chaos of Latin American nations than anything Henry Wallace ever dreamed of, has become a political reality supported by liberals and conservatives alike.

Another tremendous change in our ideals and symbols that has taken place since this book was written is in our personification of great corporations as individuals. We no longer feel that government control of industry is something that will end in the destruction of individual liberty. My chapters on "The Personification of Corporation" and "The Ritual of Corporate Reorganization" are largely obsolete today. The amount of regulatory interference with business today which is represented by our vast government bureaus would have been unthinkable to a conservative in 1937. Now these tremendous bureaucratic hierarchies have lost their radical tinge. They have obtained an almost invulnerable place in the hierarchy of our institutions. Our courts, which before the great depression were accustomed to review decisions of administrative tribunals with meticulous care, now affirm them if there is the slightest supporting evidence.

The ideological doctrine which supports the immunity of our present administrative tribunals from judicial review is the theory that they are composed of experts in their particular narrow lines. Under the cloak of this doctrine many of the evils and oppressive bureaucratic practices which were protected by conservatives in 1937 have become a part of our administrative machinery. Yet so securely has our system of administrative tribunals become entrenched that there is no effective protest made today against bureaucratic aggression. This is indeed a revolutionary change since 1937 in our ideas of the proper function of government.

The chapter entitled "The Effect of the Antitrust Laws in Encouraging Large Combinations" needs comment in the light of what has happened since the book was published. That chapter was written after ten years of nonenforcement of the Sherman Act when the total appropriation for the Antitrust Division was less than $250,000. Today it is over $5 million. The decisions of the Supreme Court of the United States since 1937 have tremendously broadened the enforcement of antitrust policy. As Milton Handler said in a recent article (*Columbia Law Review*, Vol. 60, p. 930):

"In few areas of the law is a mature jurisprudence reinforced by so power-ful an arsenal of investigative powers and remedies."

That was not true when I wrote in Chapter IX of this book, page 212: "The actual result of the antitrust laws was to promote the growth of great industrial organizations by deflecting the attack on them into purely moral and ceremonial channels." This is no longer true today.

And even more astonishing from the point of view of one writing in 1937, when the ideal of the antitrust laws was recognized in no other coun-try in the world except the United States, is the fact that the antitrust ideal has spread to Europe. The system of domestic and international cartels which in 1937 was legitimate in Europe is under heavy attack, though not completely abolished, in the European Common Market—a development no one would have dreamed of in 1937 before the Second World War.

In the field of monetary and fiscal policy, however, nineteenth-century economic symbols still cloud the realities of the twentieth-century indus-trial revolution and frustrate American economic progress. Just as during the depression we were unable to utilize our full productive capacity be-cause of a lack of consumer purchasing power, so today we are still unable to utilize it for the same reason. Since 1953 our annual economic growth has not been enough to keep up with our tremendously increasing labor force. The top of every curve in the roller coaster of booms and depres-sions on which we have been riding since 1953 has shown greater un-employment than the top of the last curve. During this period of nearly ten years our economy has been stagnant and sluggish in growth. During the same period France, Germany, and Italy have been advancing, in terms of goods and services produced, more than twice as fast as we have. We are accumulating an increasing number of unemployed. During the same period France, Germany, and Italy have had an actual shortage of labor.

The actual cost in terms of goods and services resulting from our failure to utilize our full industrial capacity has been estimated by Leon Keyser-ling to amount to the stupendous sum of $387 billion from 1953 to the middle of 1962. This enormous wealth was available to us but we could not use it because there was not enough purchasing power in the United States economy to absorb the products which our industrial plant was able to produce.

And thus under the same economic symbols and rituals that we had dur-ing the great depression we are developing today the same symptoms that prolonged that depression. The only time we were free from the tyranny of these nineteenth-century economic images was during the Second World War. Then, for the first time since the depression began, we were able to use and to expand our production to the full limit of our industrial ability. As a result we came out of that war richer in our productive capac-ity than at any time before. But after the Second World War the old religion took over. Since 1953 we have been progressively slowing down and increasingly unable to sustain the economic growth necessary for full employment.

Today we write about ourselves as an affluent society. But in 1960 there were almost 10½ million families (households of two or more persons) with annual incomes of under $4,000 before taxes. This means that one family in every four was living in poverty in the United States in 1960. Out of this group of families with under $4,000 a year over 3,000,000 were living in actual deprivation with incomes of under $2,000 a year, and as for the unattached individuals almost 4,000,000 had annual incomes of under $2,000. These figures are taken from Leon Keyserling's pamphlet *Poverty and Deprivation in the United States,* written for the Conference on Economic Progress. To sum up, Leon Keyserling concludes that there were living in poverty 34,000,000 people in families and 4,000,000 unattached persons. There were living in deprivation 37,000,000 people in families and 2,000,000 unattached persons. This makes a total of 77,000,000 people who are unable to attain what we like to think of as an American standard of living. They are unable to buy the products of our industrial economy. As a result the nation has lost in goods and services a staggering total of $387 billion in the last ten years.

Yet the *Wall Street Journal,* in a typical editorial (July 26, 1962) attacking government spending in a period when our industrial plant is 75 percent idle, says with absolute religious conviction: "There is no visible lack of purchasing power today . . ."

Under this set of beliefs we have been unable to realize the full productivity of our twentieth-century industrial economy except during the Second World War. If we could only achieve an economic philosophy which would permit the realization of our full capacity, as Leon Keyserling points out (*Poverty and Deprivation in the United States,* p. 78):

We have the potentials, by 1965, to reduce the number of families living in poverty from almost 10½ million in 1960 to less than 2 million in 1965, and to about one-half million by 1970. We can reduce the number living in deprivation from almost 10⅓ million to about 7 million, and then to 3½ million. This would mean that, allowing for population growth, the number of families living above the deprivation level would increase from about 24½ million in 1960 to more than 40 million in 1965, and to more than 49 million in 1970.

We can reduce the number of unattached individuals living in poverty from almost 4 million in 1960 to less than 2½ million in 1965, and to about one-half million by 1970. The number living above the deprivation level can be increased from nearly 5 million in 1960 to almost 7 million in 1965, and to more than 10 million in 1970.

Our failure to realize these potentials has occurred during a period when Western Europe has no problem of unemployment and has been operating its industrial plant, in many ways superior to ours in efficiency, at full capacity. This is today a constant source of bewilderment to Europeans. Gunnar Myrdal, a famous Swedish economist, recently visited the United

States. On his return to Stockholm he reviewed the economic conditions in America. He stated that the stagnant condition of the American economy was a menace to the prosperity of the Western world. He regarded it as inexcusable for so rich a country as ours to have so many slums, obsolete houses, inadequate schools, and inadequate social services. He attributed it to the illiteracy of our economic thinking. When asked to comment on Myrdal's observations all President Kennedy could say was the following (*New York Times,* July 24, 1962):

Well, I think it is regrettable that we have not been able to develop an economic formula which maintains the growth of our economy. If we were moving ahead at full blast today, of course, you would have full employment.

In July, when the President made his comment that a formula had not been found to maintain the growth of our economy, the rosy January predictions of his economic advisors had collapsed. The Gross National Product, though it was the highest in our country's history, was billions of dollars short of the January prediction. There had been no change whatever in the problem of unemployment.

The reason why no acceptable formula has been developed to achieve full utilization of the tremendously increased capacity of the twentieth-century industrial revolution is that the majority of our respectable and conservative citizens are still obsessed with the economic picture of the nineteenth century which I have attempted to analyze in this book.

That folklore consisted of a series of very simple mental pictures. The government was pictured as the thrifty head of the family who balances his budget and saves money for the future. If he does not do so he goes bankrupt and his children suffer. The national debt which had been constantly increasing since the First World War was a mortgage on the property of every citizen, which sooner or later would have to be paid by the next generation. Prosperity and full employment could only be forthcoming by balancing the national budget and taking the burden of taxation from the backs of our taxpayers. The money and credit necessary to operate our economy and full employment would then be produced by private industry and our economy would begin to grow and expand, as it did in the nineteenth century. The idea that government credit or government debt could be used to create the purchasing power necessary to distribute the products of the twentieth-century industrial revolution was unsound, radical, crackpot, dangerous, and subversive. It was leading us straight to socialism. Such was the economic folklore of 1962.

When the President said that we had been unable to develop an economic formula which would maintain the growth of our economy he meant that we had no such formula which was consistent with our theology of balancing the fiscal budget. It was an admission that there was no way under the folklore of capitalism existing in 1962 in which we could maintain full employment and full utilization of our resources. We had to go on losing about $10 billion in goods and services every year, which wealth we might have had had our folklore allowed us to distribute it. The principle of balancing the fiscal budget was so sacred that any other course was economic sin and would inevitably lead to some sort of unspecified economic or social hell.

It was not true that no formula had been developed to maintain economic growth. It was only true that no *respectable* formula had been developed. For years a group of economists led by Leon Keyserling had advocated balancing the economic budget rather than the fiscal budget. By this they meant that on one side of the balance sheet the President should estimate the productive capacities of our national industrial plants. On the other side there should be listed the demands on that productive capacity for necessities such as schools, public works, water conservation, health, and so on through a long list. Congress could then formulate programs which would not put an inflationary burden upon our productive capacity but at the same time would utilize it to its fullest extent. France has such a plan. Germany though without a formal plan has for years thought in terms of production rather than money. In other words, balancing the economic budget consists in the establishment of economic goals and the implementation of those goals by practical methods.

But the trouble with this practical approach toward the problem of maintaining economic growth is that there is no automatic fiscal principle by which it can be carried out. Of course the practical ad hoc approach is the one we use in time of war. In the last war we were able to allocate production between the war effort and consumers' goods. We not only maintained our economic growth but expanded it tremendously. Indeed, it was only the enormous spending of the World War which pulled us out of the depression. We also have no difficulty in applying the concept of balancing the economic rather than the fiscal budget in our program for the Alliance for Progress among Latin American nations. Here economic goals are set. Economic planning is the key to the solution; the economic budget rather than the fiscal budget is the center of the program.

But the approach to the problem of economic growth which is possible in time of war, or is freely used in the Alliance for Progress, is as yet impossible in the domestic economy of the United States in time of peace. We are obsessed with the dream of an automatic economy which operates without planning, and the center of the whole thing is the balanced fiscal budget. Given a balanced fiscal budget the private economy is supposed, through credit mechanisms which it creates without government interference, to supply the purchasing power to operate the industrial plant of the twentieth century at full capacity. The fact that it has not been able to do so since 1929 is in conflict with this theory and, therefore, is ignored because it is inconsistent with our folklore.

The central idea of the economic folklore which frustrates our ability to use the capacity of the modern industrial revolution may be expressed as follows: Private enterprise with its tremendous variety of credit devices is able to supply the purchasing power which will not only utilize our full productive capacity but enable it to expand. It is the duty of the government to prevent that expansion from proceeding too rapidly. The government performs that duty by balancing the budget.

This was true prior to the First World War. But since the end of the First World War it has become increasingly apparent that private credit mechanisms are not by themselves sufficient to distribute the tremendously increased industrial capacity created by the twentieth-century scientific revolution.

The persistence of the idea that through the expansion of private credit alone the economy of the twentieth-century revolution can grow and be utilized to its fullest capacity is illustrated by a recital of our popular economic thinking during the boom of the twenties and through the depression. Prior to the First World War sound economic opinion estimated that a national debt of $500 million was all that our economy could safely absorb. But during the war our national debt grew from less than $1 billion to the incredible sum of $26,600,000,000 in 1919. We followed our accepted theory. The sole function of government was to balance the budget. The Republican Administration reduced the national debt in ten years by $9 billion, saving about $1 billion a year. And so, following our accepted theory that the sole function of government was to balance the budget and pay off the national debt the Republican Administration by 1929 had reduced the national debt from $16 billion to $9 billion.

Then came the crash of 1929 and the depression which followed. There was not enough purchasing power to begin to take up the productive capacity we had achieved. But our economic folklore prevented us from seeing this outstanding fact. Roosevelt ran for office on the tried and true principle of balancing the budget. It was not lack of purchasing power but rather lack of business confidence that was supposed to be the cause of prolonging the great depression.

Roosevelt was forced to abandon his devotion to the principle of a balanced fiscal budget in favor of measures which were absolutely required to keep people from starving. He was bitterly attacked on the ground that these measures were leading to inflation and would inevitably result in the destruction of the capitalistic system. The fear of inflation haunted the business community throughout the entire depression in spite of the fact that a realistic appraisal clearly showed that the only thing we had to fear was continued deflation and a sluggish, nonexpanding economy.

In 1937 Roosevelt did succeed in balancing his cash budget, that is, in taking out of the economy more money than the government was putting in. There followed the recession of 1938. But that recession was still not attributed to lack of purchasing power. Conservative economists and bankers pointed out that it was due to lack of business confidence as a result of Roosevelt's attack on the Supreme Court.

The war pulled us out of the depression. It gave us the greatest industrial plant the world has ever known. In spite of gloomy predictions to the contrary which were made by conservatives at the end of the Second World War the country enjoyed an unprecedented boom. Then in 1953 the conservative Republican Party took over, determined to combat inflation and to balance the national budget, and finally to stop inflation by stopping the money supply.

But it soon appeared that the program was impossible. The failure of the conservatives in power has been described by Edwin Dale, Jr., financial editor of the *New York Times,* in a brilliant book *Conservatives in Power: A Study in Frustration* (pp. 209–10):

After five years of trying, the regime had produced (or found itself with), in fiscal 1959, the biggest budget deficit in peacetime history and the first really serious wave of "inflationary psychology" in modern times.

The only answer seemed to be more conservative than ever. Squeeze the budget—Russian challenge and depressing slums and dirty streams to the contrary notwithstanding. Stretch out the national debt at every opportunity—at the risk of even more uncertainty in the bond markets. Keep money tight and interest rates high—even with nearly five million people out of work in the winter of 1958–59. Keep trying to return functions to the states to relieve federal finance—even with the State of Michigan so tightly pinched for money that it had to appeal to large corporate taxpayers to pay in advance.

And given their view of the world and the dollar, the conservatives were right. The only cure for the disease was a stronger dose of the familiar medicine.[1]

And so Eisenhower achieved through his budget-balancing policies the greatest peacetime deficit in our history and the greatest peacetime inflation.

The real difficulty is that we have failed to realize the tremendous productive capacity of the twentieth-century scientific revolution. That capacity is so great that the credit mechanisms invented by the private sector of the economy cannot fully employ it. Those credit mechanisms, which we will call the private printing of money, have never before in our history pumped as much money into the nation's purchasing power. The automobile companies print the money for even the lowest income groups to buy cars. FHA prints the money for private organizations to build houses. Never before in our history has the down payment on houses been so little or the mortgages so long that they outlast the houses themselves. Almost anyone can get an unlimited letter of credit for travel by joining something like the Diners' Club. Department stores are printing the money their customers use to buy goods through revolving credit accounts and whatnot. No one has to pay cash for anything but food. In fact, anything which can be capitalized and on which a dollar income may be attributed can be financed. And this financing, though fantastically unsound according to nineteenth-century standards, is actually working. It is a new type of currency based on faith that the consumer will have a job and pay the installments on his debt. And by and large that faith has been justified.

But this new reservoir of credit, vast as it is, has only kept our industrial plant running since 1953 at about 75 percent of its capacity and $10 billion a year in goods and services has been lost. We are as yet unable to think of our national wealth in terms of productive capacity. We are unable to utilize that productive capacity for pressing national needs such as schools, health, and education because it would unbalance the fiscal budget.

The Potomac River is a good illustration of this folklore. It is an open sewer. A vast recreation area badly needed has gone to waste. The more the sludge accumulates the greater will be the burden on posterity. We have the productive capacity to clean up this river and all the other rivers. But we cannot do so because it would be an intolerable burden on our taxpayers. According to our folklore there is only one economic situation which would justify cleaning up the Potomac, and that is if Washington, D.C., became a depressed area. In that case, perhaps, we might clean it up, not because the job itself was worthwhile doing but because the expenditures might prime the pump and get Washington on its economic feet again. But until Washington becomes a depressed area it is better to let the Potomac fill up with sludge so that it will remain a handy way of priming the pump in the future.

There seems no way, according to our present folklore of capitalism, to utilize our productive capacity to clean up the Potomac because it is a very necessary thing to do with respect to the health and recreation of our nation's capital.

In the nineteenth century our productive capacity was not enough for such public projects. To have engaged in them might have been inflationary. Today, when our productive capacity is so great that only 75 percent of it can be absorbed by the purchasing power created by private credit, we still consider it inflationary to utilize that capacity. We cannot accept as a rational plan for ourselves the basic formula which even the conservatives have been willing to accept for Latin America.

And thus the old folklore of capitalism which I have attempted to describe in this book still frustrates our economic growth. The fact that Western European economies are not so frustrated is a continuing source of bewilderment to us. We are presently sending economists to Western Europe to find out why those countries have no unemployment and are moving ahead at more than double our speed. I suggest that nothing will come of such economic inquiries. Each inquiring economist will look at Western Europe through the spectacles of a preconceived theory. He will then disregard all the facts which do not fit in with that theory. Finally he will come back with the report that the lesson we must learn from the booming economies of Western Europe is to balance our fiscal budget at home. Many reports of this character are already being published in our conservative journals. To paraphase Karl Marx, "Economic theology is the opiate of the middle classes."

Each year more and more goods can be produced with less and less labor. For the past ten years we have been able to use only about 75 percent of what we can produce. As a practical matter it would not be difficult to avail ourselves of that unused production. As an ideological matter it is a present impossibility to carry on the public works and services which our economy could so easily afford. This is because private money and credit are not available for such things as conservation of our water supply, our health, our recreational facilities, and so on through a long list of public necessities. Things which cannot be bought and sold for dollars on the marketplace cannot be financed by private credit. Therefore, we must do without them even though this means a colossal waste of our real productive resources.

If it were just a matter of wasting resources perhaps we could live with it. The nineteenth century was an era of colossal waste. But the present industrial revolution is gradually destroying the purchasing power necessary to distribute its productive ability. This is in spite of fantastic credit schemes which provide private credit that a nineteenth-century banker would consider insane. And so the backlog of unemployment grows as our labor force increases. A new phrase has become part of our economic vocabulary, "structural unemployment." It means that an incredibly rich country can find no ideological way of providing its citizens with the standard of living which it is physically capable of giving them.

The problem is a psychological one, not to be solved by either preaching or learning. It involves a recognition that things without a dollar value on the marketplace are nevertheless national assets of incalculable value. A trained scientist, engineer, or physician is an asset. The university that trains him is as valuable to our economy as a General Motors plant. An unskilled laborer, or an unemployed person, is a liability. A public debt owed by a nation to its own citizens is not a mortgage which their children must pay off. The building of necessary public works is an asset both for the present and the future.

It is this central idea that gives the Russian economy such strength as it has. It is the rigid and inflexible philosophy that such assets cannot be built or maintained by private enterprise that is the principal weakness of Russia. Budgets of course have to be balanced. But the budget of the twentieth century is a balance between productive capacity and the effective demands which are made on that capacity. When those notions become part of our folklore of capitalism the only limit on American progress will be the extent to which modern science can expand productive capacity.

How will this change come about? I expect that the process of the adjustment of inherited economic images to the reality of the vast potential productive capacity of the twentieth century may turn out to be as painful as it was during the great depression when we finally became acclimated to social security, unemployment relief, guarantee of bank deposits, the TVA, control of security markets, and so on through a long list of changes for which Roosevelt was so bitterly denounced. Basic economic beliefs are religious in character. We are struggling today through a period more like the period of the Reformation than any other period in history. This book attempts to study the frustrating effects of religious economic beliefs in a period of revolutionary change.

International Policies in Conflict

These following two selections deal with the highly complex problem of peace and international understanding. George F. Kennan describes the problem in terms of an answer to those who advocate destruction as opposed to peaceful coexistence. His view is not that of pacifism nor of militancy.

While Robert Strausz-Hupé's view, like that of Kennan's, is neither pacifistic nor militaristic, he differs markedly from Kennan in analysis of the problem and in suggested tactics. The selection of these two pieces was not to show the extremes of alternatives, but to indicate the variance within more subtle presentations.

What values underlie each position? Which are the values accepted by society and transmitted through the schools? Which should be?

The Rationale of Coexistence

GEORGE F. KENNAN

What I should like to talk about today is the familiar subject of coexistence, which lies at the heart of this whole matter. There is a great and real issue here. It is the question whether it should be the goal of our national policy to achieve the early and total destruction, everywhere, of everything that calls itself Communism, even if this goal has to be pursued

From *On Dealing with the Communist World*, by George F. Kennan, Harper & Row, New York, 1964, pp. 5–20. Reprinted by permission of the publisher and the Council on Foreign Relations.

at the expense of our chances for living with Communist power successfully so long as it is not destroyed. Or whether it should be our goal to find
acceptable ways of living with it, and influencing it, even if this has to be
done at the expense of our chances for destroying it entirely.

For many years I was under the impression that the first of these views
—the one that despairs of living successfully with our adversary and seeks
only his destruction—had been debated and tried in earlier times and that
there had crystallized among us an adequate consensus to the effect that
this was not the most hopeful way to approach our problem. From 1933
to the late 1940s this was, I think, the case. But during the past ten years
we have witnessed the resurgence of a body of opinion which takes the
other line, which rejects in effect the whole concept of peaceful coexistence
and which would commit us to a policy of "we or they"—a policy which
sees no issue to the present contest except in the final and complete destruction of one side or the other.

Both of the views I cited earlier as evidences of historical shallowness
fall, as you will note, into this category as well. And they are not isolated
examples. Such outlooks are held by a great many people around the country. They have a strong and growing hold on much of our student youth.
There are entire geographic regions where they have almost a clean sweep,
and where to challenge them at all is to court resentment, misunderstanding, and obloquy. They have rarely affected the attitudes of those who,
confronted with over-all responsibility for the conduct of foreign policy,
have had to look at these matters long and hard and to take the rap for
their decisions. But they have made deep inroads on those aspects of our
national behavior which are directly subject to Congressional action or
influence—such things as security procedures, visa and passport controls,
trade restrictions, export and shipping controls. In this way they have often
served to cancel out or to weaken the policy the executive branch was trying, at the moment, to follow. So strong is now their prevalence in Congress
and certain other segments of government in Washington that it is not an
exaggeration to say that we have today two wholly different and mutually
contradictory foreign policies being pursued simultaneously in that city,
and you can find whichever of them you want, depending on which door
you want to put your head in.

No one will be under any doubt, I am sure, as to my own position with
relation to these two alternatives. This is not the first time I have had occasion to raise my voice publicly against these counsels of despair which
persist in viewing Communism as the only serious evil in the world, which
refuse to recognize in it the elements of either change or differentiation,
which insist on treating it as a single conspiratorial force, dedicated only
to our destruction and beyond the range of any human appeals, and
which, accordingly, would willingly see us sacrifice all the positive values
of life to the struggle against it. Naturally, I have to regret that such views
still exist and still have the wide currency they do.

But what worries me even more is the combination of amused contempt, or cynicism, or dreamlike complacency, with which I find this outlook treated by most of my friends. I do not think this body of thought can be disposed of by silence or by ridicule.

The question it raises is not a disrespectable one. There *is* this thing called Communist power. There *is* this problem of its hostility toward us. It is a great problem. And if to myself and to many of those who hear or read these lectures, the basic considerations affecting our answer are reasonably obvious, there are plainly a great many people to whom they are not. If these people ever knew the reasons why something called "victory," in the sense of an early and complete elimination of "Communism," is not the answer, they have forgotten them. And I sometimes suspect that many of us who think that we understand these reasons very well might be hard put to it to recall exactly what they were.

Let us therefore take up this question once more. Let us accept the fact that we have this sharp and serious challenge, and let us ask ourselves, as though we had never asked it before: Why, indeed, coexistence? Why not victory?

No objective historian would deny, I think, that the attitude with which the Soviet leaders initially approached the societies and governments of the West was an outrageous one, full of prejudice and intellectual arrogance and intolerable hostility. It was not the same kind of challenge, to be sure, as those common to international life up to that point. It corresponded to none of the established concepts of international hostility. It was aimed, in theory, only against certain classes in the West, not against entire peoples. It did not envisage overt and full-fledged international hostilities. But it did involve attitudes which were insulting and menacing to the Western societies, which had as their aim the violent destruction of the political systems of those societies, and which were clearly unacceptable on any normal standards of international life.

There could be no question in 1918, and there can be none today, of the moral right of a society to defend itself against such designs: to take measures for the disarming and control of subversive elements within its own citizenry, and to take measures of military precaution insofar as these might be responsive to the nature of the challenge.

But it became clear at an early date that if you went beyond this defensive effort, as some of our allies halfheartedly tried to do in the various interventions of 1918 to 1920, and as many people in this country wanted us to do, and made it your objective to overthrow the Soviet Government, you got yourself into a very messy business indeed, even from the standpoint of moral and political responsibility. There were unclarities and ambiguities in the relationship of the Soviet régime to the Russian people which constantly confused the issue. You discovered that the attitudes of people to régime—and particularly the question whether people really wanted to be liberated from it—depended largely on what they thought were, at any given point, the possible alternatives. But these alternatives were often highly obscure. The two greatest non-Communist political parties which had existed in Russia prior to the Communist seizure of power there, hated each other, unfortunately, at least as much as they hated the Communists. It was out of the question that they could ever get together; and neither, as it happened, was capable of governing alone. Those who spoke, therefore, of overthrowing the Soviet Government had no very convincing answers as to what would be put in its place. The problem was not disposed of merely by saying that democratic procedures would be permitted to prevail. This principle had been tried in 1917; but the understanding for democratic procedures among the Russian people had turned out to be not very widespread. A single ruthless minority had easily pushed through the entire parliamentary system. It was not even certain that some of the opponents of Bolshevism had a much greater devotion than did the Bolsheviki to democratic ideals.

Not only that, but you found that a very considerable part of the Russian people preferred to take their chances on adjusting peaceably to Communist rule rather than to have someone try to liberate them by force and in this way compel them to accept all the hardships and dangers and, above all, the excruciating political choices that go with a civil war and particularly one in which foreigners are involved. It was questionable, in fact, how many people in Russia you were going to be benefiting by such an interference into their political life. That some would be pleased to have this effort made was clear; but that many others would not was also clear. On balance, it was a real question whether such an undertaking, even if successful in the negative sense of bringing about the expulsion of the Communists from the seats of power in Moscow, would have been a blessing for the people as a whole or merely a new source of hardship and horror. One should remember that even the half-hearted and futile little military expeditions which the allies did dispatch to Russian soil in 1918 got vast numbers of people into very serious trouble; the executions that followed them numbered in the tens of thousands.

But aside from all these questions of the political propriety and usefulness of such an endeavor, it was clear that in the sheer physical sense it was an extremely unpromising undertaking. The Russian Communist Party, having had years of experience in the techniques of ousting others from the seats of power, showed from the start an extraordinary mastery of the science of clinging to these seats itself. Once the Communists had established the monopoly of their rule, they had little difficulty in spiking in the bud any really serious attempts at armed opposition. It was plain that they could be removed from the seats of power only by a major insertion of outside force. But any such outside intervention was bound to confuse the very political situation to which it was addressed; for nobody, however opposed to his own government, really feels very comfortable associating himself with foreign military forces coming onto the territory of his country. And the task, in the sheer military sense, was bound to be an enormous one. What was involved, if the intervention was going to do any real good, was not just driving the Communists from power in Moscow. This alone would not have finished them. They were not that breed of cat. They were skilled, as few political movements in history have ever been, in the arts of underground political activity. They knew exactly how to go underground. They would have had to be pursued to the ends of the vast Russian land; and nothing suggests that foreign armies endeavoring to accomplish that pursuit would have ended up in any better position than did, say, the Japanese in the Communist-penetrated areas of northern China during the last war—riveted to the railways, harassed and bled at every turn by guerrillas having closer links with the people and knowing precisely how to exploit those links to the discomfort of an outside force. And this is not to mention the two great subjective questions as to whether, if this were conceived as a joint western undertaking, allied unity would ever have been sufficient to sustain it (it certainly was not in 1918), or if it were to be done by a single Western power, what Western public would ever have consented to bear for long a burden of this nature.

I mention these things simply in order to make the point that even in the early days of Bolshevism, when the Soviet régime was relatively weak and inexperienced, the idea of its overthrow, as a direct goal of Western policy, was never a promising one—either from the standpoint of military feasibility or from that of political effectiveness. Think, then, by comparison, what it would be today, when the Soviet régime has enjoyed a monopoly of power in Russia for nearly half a century; when it has behind it several decades of political and administrative experience; when it disposes over some of the strongest armed forces in the world; and when it has unquestionably achieved a far higher degree of acceptance than was the case in those early years; when large segments of the Soviet population, in fact, have never known any other political system and would be incapable of conceiving of any alternative to this one. The moral is that even if the nature of Russian Communism had undergone no change—even if it represented exactly the same sort of challenge to us that it did forty years ago (which incidentally is what our ardent liberationists all seem to assume), I should have deepest misgivings about any concept of policy which envisaged, as a sort of an end-product, the overthrow of Soviet power either by the direct use of our forces or by incitement of subject peoples to revolts which we would be vaguely expected to back up if they got into trouble.

I am sorry to have to plunge this way into what seem to be murky and somewhat speculative depths, but these unhappy realities seem to lie at the heart of our problem; for it is hard to conceive of any liberationist policy which would not, sooner or later, run up against them at some point. We are told, for example, by prominent protagonists of the liberationist view, that to achieve the downfall of Communism, we would not have to occupy Russia or China. The vast majority of people in these countries, they assure us, are not Communists. "They will, with proper guidance, take care of their own freedom once they are released from the iron grip of Communist dictatorship." But such a statement raises more questions than it solves. Who, first of all, is to release them from their iron grip? They, themselves? Scarcely. Popular revolt against a ruthless, experienced modern dictatorship, which enjoys a monopoly over weapons and communications, which has its own armed forces under tight control, and which retains its unity and its will to power, is simply not a possibility in the modern age.

And could the peoples of these countries be depended upon to "take care of their own freedom" even if, by some miracle, that grip *was* loosened? This only raises again the tedious question of the possible alternative to Communism. There are no opposition parties in Russia today. There is no fund of political experience outside the Communist Party itself. Russia's previous experience with the concepts of Western democracy was pathetically brief and shallow; and the people who would remember it are mostly gone. The organized political force that could replace the Soviet Communist Party in that vast area today is simply not visible. I would know of no assurance that whatever might conceivably come in place of what is there now would be any closer to liberal ideals. Are we, then, to take moral responsibility for this incalculable change, which may or may not be for the better from the standpoint of the average Russian?

I personally believe that political change will continue to come to Russia; and important change at that. But if it is a question of our own time, I can conceive of its coming, as to some extent it already has, only on the foundation of and within the framework of the present political system, which is now firmly established and which has shaped the political outlooks and assumptions of an entire generation.

But while we are on this subject of political change in Russia, there is one further wrinkle of which I think we should take cognizance. We have here in this country, among the opponents of coexistence, people who argue with great vehemence that there *is* indeed a political alternative to the Soviet régime; that it exists in the form of the non-Russian minorities within the traditional Russian state. These elements, they claim, are thirsting for independence. We could bring about the overthrow of Soviet Communism by supporting them politically—by encouraging them to fight for their independence with the implicit promise of our support—by encouraging them, in other words, not only to destroy Communist rule in Russia but indeed to achieve the permanent break-up of the traditional Russian state.

There can be no denying that the multi-national composition which has characterized both the former Russian Empire and the Soviet Union—particularly the Soviet Union since 1945—is an important political fact. Unquestionably, the unhappiness of non-Russian elements had much to do with the final break-up of Tsardom. It is not at all silly to suggest that this factor may well have an important bearing on the political future of the traditional Russian area. But this is about all one can say with any degree of certainty.

Yet the thesis with which we are now confronted on the part of many of these American "liberationists" goes far beyond this. It asserts with a great show of definiteness that there are known to be a whole series of national groups within the Soviet Union which have long desired independence and which dispose over the necessary prerequisites for an independent existence but which were deprived of that independence by the Soviet régime. They even name a number of entities which allegedly correspond to this description; the list will be found in the so-called Captive Nations Resolution, to which a majority of the members of our Congress—many of them having only the dimmest ideas of the places or peoples involved—were induced to subscribe in 1959.

It is not to deny sympathy for the national feelings of certain of the peoples concerned if I point out that as a question of fact this claim is grossly exaggerated, and in some respects entirely spurious.

There are indeed instances—and I am thinking here particularly of the Baltic states—where a good case could be made for the validity of such claims. But there are other instances in which the whole thesis is fictitious and ludicrous. Certain of the national groups whose names appear in the Captive Nations Resolution as those of nations thirsting for a lost independence never existed at all in this quality; and it is incomprehensible that the Congress of the United States should have been led to commit the policy of this country formally to something called their liberation. Finally, there are still other instances in which we simply do not know the facts. We are often told, for example, that the Ukrainians are all thirsting for complete separation from the traditional Russian state. Perhaps so. But who knows? There has been, and could have been, no proper formal test of opinion on this point over these past forty-five years. The Ukraine never was really independent. History bears no evidence that the majority of the people of the Ukraine have at any time desired a total separation from the main body of the Russian people. And those who assure us that this is the case are for the most part people who have had no personal contact with the central regions of the Ukraine for many years, if ever.

Even should these claims be far better substantiated as assertions of objective fact than they actually are, I can think of nothing more catastrophic than that the policy of our government should be committed to the break-up of the traditional Russian state. Remember that nothing of this sort could be carried forward except at the cost of the violent and total estrangement of the Russian people, at the cost of their embittered armed opposition, at the cost, in fact, of a Russian civil war which would make that of 1918–1920 look like child's play. Nor would the chances of the non-Russian elements be favorable in any such encounter unless they had the foreign assistance on a massive scale. The Great Russians may or may not constitute a majority on the present territory of the Soviet Union, but they constitute by far the strongest national group; they command the traditional seats of political power; they command the centers of transportation and communication. In many of the areas where other nationalities predominate, Russians are heavily intermingled with the non-Russian population. Not only would outside force have to be invoked on a massive scale in order to bring about any such dismemberment of Russia in the first instance, but this outside force would have to remain indefinitely in occupation in order to enforce the maintenance of a *status quo* so violently unacceptable to the strongest national group in the area.

If the dream of popular revolt in the Soviet Union is today unreal in any case, which it is, it becomes doubly unreal if you think of it as hinged to an American commitment to the dismemberment of traditional Russia; for in this case all hope of the achievement of a peaceful consensus among the inhabitants of the region would have been lost; the strongest national element would have been wholly antagonized; and once again, the hatreds engendered over issues not connected with Communism would overshadow any resentment felt towards the Soviet régime.

We have, finally, among the arguments against coexistence, the insistent assertion that the Soviet leaders are largely bluffing and could easily be brought to desist from their undertakings or to yield ill-gotten gains if only we had the gumption to tell them that the alternative is war. This is a thesis which has received a specious appearance of substantiation from the fact that the Soviet government, confronted [in 1962] with a choice between withdrawing certain of its installations in Cuba or becoming involved in a war with the United States, preferred to withdraw the installations, and did so at some cost to its prestige.

I can only warn in the strongest way against attempting to draw inferences of this sort from the Cuban crisis. Whatever else may be said of the Russian Communists, history affords no substantiation for the suggestion that they are cowards. If every gesture of prudence or moderation on their part is to be hailed as proof of their faint-heartedness, and cited as an argument for bolder military pressures from our side, I shudder to contemplate the implications for the future course of Soviet-American relations.

The Soviet government is a great power, with a far-flung and complex pattern of international interests, involvements, and commitments. Like any other great power, it can be put on the spot. It can be placed in situations where to yield to bald military threats or ultimata would involve consequences disastrous and unacceptable. Nothing in the long history of its behavior suggests that it would yield, or could afford to yield, to this sort of open intimidation. In general, that school of American political thinking which views the East-West conflict in terms of apocalyptic visions of someone achieving a momentary superiority in weaponry and then saying to others, "Now you do what we say or else . . ." reflects a very shallow under-standing indeed of what makes this world go around. We would not react to this sort of thing, and neither would the others.

The fact is that all these ideas for some sort of violent and short-term disposal of the Soviet problem—disposal of it in ways that would spare us the necessity of talking and dealing and compromising with people whose views we don't like—all these ideas lead sooner or later to war. Let there be no mistake about this. It is going to be hard enough, in the best of cir-cumstances, to preserve the peace. Let no one suppose it will be easier to do so if the very idea of accommodation is ruled out. There is always some point between the undertaking and completion of these militant schemes at which the outbreak of hostilities would become inevitable. And it must be emphasized that the moment we get to this point there become valid and operable, once more, all those ambiguities and uncertainties which were discussed earlier in connection with the very idea of overthrowing the Soviet government by force. Because war has to have an object. There have to be war aims. If you conduct military operations, you have to be willing to state what you would settle for. And what would our war aims be? Is there any likelihood that, once involved in hostilities, we would be inclined to settle for limited aims—for anything less than the complete destruction of Soviet power? The experience of two world wars would not suggest it. In each of these cases we heeded the demands of the hotheads and the super-patriots, and we insisted in fighting the conflict to its final and ultimate conclusion of the total destruction of the enemy's military strength and his political system: in one case, at the cost of installing the Communists in power in Russia; and in the other case, at the cost of turn-ing over to them half of Europe. And during both of these contests, people in our midst who suggested a compromise peace, as did Lord Lansdowne in 1917, were treated as little short of treasonable.

Now there are two things I have refrained from mentioning up to this point, not because they were not germane to the discussion, but because I wanted, if I could, to make my points without them. The first is the ele-ment of change in the Soviet Union. It affects what I have said because it is this that tells us that these desperate and militant policies are not only unpromising but also unnecessary.

This is a great subject in itself. I shall only say here that I find it amazing that men can seriously discuss today these questions of our attitude toward Communist power without taking account of this factor. One can argue about the exact nature and extent of this change; but I do not see how anyone can dispute the difference between the weak and isolated Soviet state of the 1920s and the 1930s and the great power we have before us today, with its far-flung interests and involvements, its embarrassments of empire, its obligations of alliance, its new personalities, and its evolving internal problems. This, surely, is something far more like the traditional, established great power of "Russia" than like the fanatical political personality we faced in the Soviet régime of Lenin's time or the nightmarish totalitarian despotism of Stalin.

We have no need to be thrown off balance by such things as Khrushchev's statement that he would bury us. This does not really mean that he expects to finish us off within his time. He is too much of a realist for this. This, as I see it, was simply a prediction: that his political system would live to assist at the funeral of ours, not vice versa. This is a prediction basic to the Marxist outlook. He cannot do other than to reiterate it. He cannot explain publicly that this is all he means by it; he is a political person and his dogmatist critics would take advantage of it. But there is no reason we should not recognize it for what it is.

I find a great deal that is troublesome in the ideas and behavior of the present Soviet state. There is still a great deal in the way of established procedure and inherited prejudice that Moscow will have to get over before the Soviet Union can coexist tranquilly with other nations. But if I had to choose between dealing with this one or the one we faced thirty years ago, I would take this one any day. While its evolution may not proceed at the pace we would like, it has proceeded at a pace which affords no grounds at all for the total abandonment of all hope that it may some day take an acceptable place in the family of nations. And nothing in the state at which it has arrived justifies us in viewing it as something so far outside the range of ordinary experience that we are entitled to cast aside all the decencies when we deal with it.

The second point I have delayed mentioning, or invoking as an argument, is that enormous multiplication of the dangers of war, and of the unsuitability of war as a weapon of policy, which we have before us in the phenomenon of the nuclear weapon of long-range destructive capacity. I have deliberately refrained from introducing this subject; for what I wish to emphasize is that the concept of destroying Soviet power entirely, as a major goal of policy, is and has always been inherently unsound, quite aside from the nuclear factor. It was unsound in 1918 when the allied expeditionary forces went to Russia. It was unsound in 1941 when Hitler's vast conventional armed forces launched themselves upon the Soviet Union. It did not take the atomic weapon to produce this situation. We only confuse ourselves when we ascribe that quality to the weapon.

The presence on this earth today of systems of weaponry suicidal in their implications strikes me as being only a sharp and impatient reminder by the Almighty of a reality which ought to have been visible to us all long ago, which ought, in fact, to have been visible on the example of World War I, but which we stubbornly refused to see: and this is the very narrow and limited degree to which force can ever be the main solution for problems that involve the states of mind—the outlooks and convictions—of great masses of people on this planet. I am startled and disturbed when I hear it said, as I sometimes do, by our military strategists and commentators, that our purpose in war is simply to "kill Germans" or to "kill Russians" or to "kill" whomever else it may be considered to be our enemy. Is this really the purpose of warfare? Are we really served—do American purposes really prosper—just because a life is extinguished, somewhere on this earth, in the agony of battle? And do they prosper in proportion to the number of lives thus extinguished? I cannot believe it. The sources of tragedy in international life lie in the differences of outlook that divide the human race; and it seems to me that our purposes prosper only when something happens in the mind of another person, and perhaps in our own mind as well, which makes it easier for all of us to see each other's problems and prejudices with detachment and to live peaceably side by side. The question is not: Why not victory? The question is: What does the word "victory" mean?

I am not preaching a spineless pacifism. Such is the stubbornness and recalcitrance of human nature that the use of force cannot always be foreign to the process of persuasion. Force, too, has its place as an argument, but only a limited place. Force can never be the main argument, or the only one. With it must come, if it is to have any eloquence at all, such things as understanding and patience and the willingness to persuade and, above all, the readiness to restrict force to minimum dimensions and to stop it at the right time.

The trouble with all these proposals for the angry, the militant, the punitive approach is that they ignore the dialectics necessarily involved in every great effort to exert influence on the international scene. They neglect the fact that the hopeful approaches have always to be dialectical ones, embracing contradictory elements, embracing both repulsion and attraction, pressure and conciliation, the readiness to defend where defense is the only answer, but also the readiness to receive, to listen, to concede, to be generous, to take chances, and to give confidence, even while defending.

These suggestions that we should solve our problem by getting angry, by getting tough, by doing something drastic and abrupt, are invidious not just because they involve procedures and concepts which are unpracticable and unfeasible and from which the authors would themselves be obliged to desist, if they ever found themselves in positions of responsibility—they are invidious in an even worse way because they crowd and damage and deflate the hopeful approaches, rob them of their effectiveness and their credibility. The Captive Nations Resolution has freed no captive nations, nor is it likely to do so. But it has irritated and misled and estranged a great many people, including numbers who were by no means Communists. It has given a serious misimpression to our friends as well as our adversaries. It has played into the hands of the hotheads and fanatics on both sides. It has complicated the task of everyone in our government who has been working to avoid the catastrophe of war. And the same could be said for many other of the manifestations of the *simpliste,* die-hard psychology which it reflects. My principal charge against this outlook is not that it is itself without hopeful perspectives, though this too is true. My charge is that, uncorrected, unchallenged, and permitted to have the currency it has in this country today, it cripples the hopefulness of any other approach.

This is why I think it high time that the country clarified its mind on the basic issue of coexistence. If we genuinely wish to avoid the catastrophes of a nuclear war and to find solutions to our differences with world Communism which will render redundant and dispensable the tremendous burden of armaments now resting on mankind, it will not do to let a great part of the vocal segment of our society go on talking as though the search for possibilities of accommodation were unnecessary and undesirable, and anyone who facilitates it were unpatriotic. I submit that a constructive and hopeful policy toward the Soviet Union cannot be conducted against the background of so massive a failure of understanding—against the background of such irresolution and such divided counsel as mark this country today. This is not a question of Russia alone. Behind the Soviet Union there stands as well the great problem of relations with Communist China, to which all the considerations adduced in the lecture will some day be relevant, if they are not now.

If what we require is a new national debate, and something like a public showdown, to clarify these questions and permit this country to speak with a clear and unequivocal voice in world affairs, then let us not postpone this debate any longer. This is a question of fundamentals. Whichever way you cut it, someone—and by that I mean one of two great bodies of thought in our country—is terribly, tragically, and intolerably wrong. If we are to move ahead effectively, the country will have to make up its mind which it is.

The Protracted Conflict

ROBERT STRAUSZ-HUPÉ

In the conflict between the United States and the U.S.S.R., two alien systems confront each other. This confrontation takes place in space and in time; the contest is over the domination of the earth—and, now, its outer space—and over the future of human society. It is the climactic phase of the systematic revolution through which the world has been passing ever since 1914. It is thus a struggle of power politics as well as a social contest, a war as well as a revolution.

From *American Strategy for the Nuclear Age*, by Robert Strausz-Hupé, Doubleday Anchor Books, 1960, pp. 16–31. Reprinted by permission of the author.

In the language of politics, the term "revolution" stands for a certain kind of historical change: an old order dissolves and a new one emerges; old rulers are replaced by new ones; men feel that the tempo of events is quickening and that, willingly or unwillingly, they are breaking with the past; and the transition is enlivened by more or less spectacular bursts of violence. Indeed, these were the characteristics of the French Revolution and the Russian Revolution, the most familiar examples of "revolution" in modern history. Both these cataclysms lasted for known spans of time; both were national, insofar as they occurred within historical states. It is plausible to say that the two world wars were revolutionary wars. It is easy to identify the milestones of the "Revolution of Our Times." It is more difficult to relate these discrete events—national revolutions and international revolutionary wars—to a general development which, in different ways, occurs in all countries, affects all men, and lasts over an indefinite period of time.

THE SYSTEMIC REVOLUTION

Cycles of history completed long ago afford us a better insight into the nature of the unfolding world revolution than do the more recent happenings which we call revolutions and which are, in fact, mere tremors, albeit sometimes momentous ones, of a vast and lasting disturbance. Such a vast and lasting disturbance seems to have shaken the ancient world. It started with the Peloponnesian War and reached its climax in the Roman Civil Wars, which pitted first Pompey against Caesar and then Caesar's heirs against one another. The revolution, although its most celebrated stages were Athens and Rome, was not confined to any one city or country. It rolled over the entire Mediterranean region—the universe of the ancients. We may call it a systemic revolution. When it had run its course of four centuries, the state system had changed from one of many city-states into one of a single universal empire. A new order had been established, not only for Rome or Athens, for Italy or Greece, but for all peoples of the Mediterranean region, and even for those peoples who had never known the rule of the city-state. Then again, at the time of the Renaissance and Reformation, Europe was recast. The emergent system of nation-states marked a break with feudalism as radical as that which sundered the universal Roman state from the polis of antiquity.

In each of these systemic revolutions, states fought great wars among one another. These wars between states were also civil wars, for the disturbance of the system spread into all its parts, erasing the distinction between civil and external, national and international. Each of these great upheavals traced a definite pattern of events that baffled the participants although it became meaningful to posterity. The design of the systemic revolution, like that of the business cycle, is woven from the actions of masses of men who neither understand nor desire what they are about to fashion. Design there is, but it is a design that is neither conscious nor rational.

THE PRESENT PARADOX

This generation faces a bewildering and unprecedented paradox: new and virtually unlimited resources are within our reach, and we stand at the threshold of a new rich and universal civilization; yet the survival of civilization itself has been put in doubt. So terrible is our dilemma and so pressing are the demands of the hour that we incline to mistake each bend of the road for a historic turning point. Unique as is our situation, it is but the latest episode of a long story. No one knows how this story will end and whether the leading characters of the current installment will figure in the next. We can but surmise that destiny has placed us in the midst of a revolutionary epoch, comparable, on a global scale, to those which embraced the passing of the city-state, the "fall" of Rome, and the breakdown of European feudalism. For many decades, historic institutions and their sustaining faiths all over this earth have swayed and broken under the impact of revolutionary forces. The nature of the process is still largely veiled to our eyes, for the complete returns are still not in and our judgment is clouded by passion. We may trace, with some semblance of accuracy, this or that root cause: the truths unlocked and the powers unleashed by the natural sciences; the global spread of industrialization; the rapid growth of populations; and the ever accelerating mobility of men, ideas, and things. Yet the political and social crisis of this century remains as ineffable as the human condition to which it has given rise.

The conflict between the United States and the Soviet Union now holds the center of the historical stage. Yet this confrontation is the mere contemporary expression, the vast powers arrayed in each camp notwithstanding, of pervasive conflict that encompasses all lands, all peoples, and all levels of society. The United States and the Soviet Union are now the leading protagonists; the struggle, which is civil as well as international, cleaves all societies. Hence any effective strategy for waging the ubiquitous protracted conflict must be, by necessity, a revolutionary strategy: to wit, a strategy that puts to its own use the revolutionary forces "on the loose" in politics, economics, culture, science, and technology and denies their exploitation to the enemy. Insofar as Communist strategy has been able to do just that, it has been effective. The Communists have benefited from the errors of their opponents who let themselves be bemused by the Marxist myth of revolution and remained blind to the realities of revolutionary strategy.

THE SCAVENGERS OF REVOLUTION

Marxist thought is rooted in a concept of dynamic historical change. The Russian Communists, saturated with a dynamic philosophy of history and astride a formidable territorial base of operations, saw what the West did not: that "the august, unchallenged, and tranquil glories of the Victorian age," tarnished by World War I, were to depart forever amid the rising commotion of Asia and Africa.

The West's rapid expansion to all continents challenged gravely the authority of all the world's surviving civilizations. Western society pressed its forms upon all societies; it planted everywhere the seeds of its creativeness—and of its own dissensions. Thus, revolutionary change within the historic West is inextricably linked with the transformation of the non-Western societies. The concurrence of the crisis of the West itself and the impact of Westernization upon the rest of mankind impart irresistible force to the secular and universal, the systemic world revolution.

Far from being revolutionaries in the commonly accepted sense, the Russian Communists have excelled in capturing nascent revolutionary movements launched by others. The Communists have scored their most significant successes wherever an existing "revolutionary situation" offered them opportunities for conspiratorial "boring" from within and military blackmail from without.

The Russian Communists did not create the "revolutionary situation" in Asia; that "situation" had been taking shape for a long time. The Communists, however, were quick to exploit it and "to push what was falling." First hampered by ideological preconceptions, they soon adjusted their sights to political realities: the colonial peoples would forge the political idea which they had received from the West into instruments for dislodging the Western powers from their imperial holdings. Although the incipient breakdown of the colonial system would be paced by economic and social transformation, the prospect of proletarian revolution held, for the Kremlin, less attraction than the strategic prize: to inflict upon the Western powers, who were, in point of time, the principal opponent of the Soviet Union, heavy losses in political prestige, market and raw-material resources and to weaken them through the debilitating effects, military, economic, and moral, of colonial wars of attrition.

THE POLICIES OF LENIN AND STALIN

Lenin's singular contribution to Communist theory was the conversion of Marxism from an abstract doctrine of conflict between classes into a highly effective instrument of conflict between nations. Lenin projected the class struggle from capitalist society—which Marx had assumed implicitly as being confined by the boundaries of a national state such as nineteenth-century France or England—into world politics. Lenin discerned in the clash of rival imperialisms the swan song of capitalism. By analogy, the competition between capitalism within a state evolves dialectically into a competitive struggle between capitalist states.

The Congress of the Peoples of the East, convened at Baku in 1920, affords a preview of a Communist strategy designed to outflank, so to speak, the capitalist order by carrying the revolution to the colonial empires. At Baku, the Bolshevik leaders met with the national revolutionaries of Asia. The Congress resolved dutifully upon a program for the subversion of the European colonies. The fact that many of the participants played, up until the present, leading roles in Asia's revolutionary movements bespeaks the importance of the Baku Congress. The immediate results of Baku disappointed the Bolsheviks. During the 1920s, one revolutionary attempt after the other ended in failure, partially because the Communists had not allowed sufficient time to prepare the professional core of trained revolutionaries so essential to their method. The Bolsheviks could no longer blink the fact that the resources of Russia were grossly disproportionate to the task of spreading the global revolution and even to the task of keeping communism alive in its first historic abode, namely, in Russia. The eclipse of the ideologists had become a necessity. Stalin assumed the management of Russia and bent the energies of his reluctant countrymen to the establishment of socialism in one country, namely, in their own.

Stalin was no ideological purist. Outside of Russia, the Communist Party was expendable. In Europe, Stalin sanctioned cheerfully such ambiguous devices as the Popular Front and outright alliances with fascism. Outside of Europe, Communist initiative was limited to the oblique and far from generous support of Communist movements that had managed to survive the defeats of the 1920s and the recurrent purges of their respective commands by Stalin. Only in one respect did Stalin prepare the ground for the resumption of the offensive in Asia and Africa: he launched a long-range program for the training of native Communist cadres, to be deployed under more favorable circumstances.

After World War II, Stalin set out to repair the damages caused by German invasion and to modernize the Soviet armed forces. Soviet strategy in the immediate post-World War II period was essentially defensive. Stalin's principal objective was to deter the West from contesting the Soviet gains in eastern Europe and from thwarting, by means of a preventive war, the Soviet Union's gigantic effort to close the military-technological gap. Until Stalin's death, Soviet policy remained relatively inactive throughout the rimlands of Asia, including the Middle East and the Arab world. Although it can be argued that Stalin pursued a positive policy in China, there is strong evidence that Mao Tse-tung often took his own counsel and even proceeded sometimes in opposition to Stalin's wishes.

CONTAINMENT AND THE COMMUNISTS'
TACTICAL SHIFT

American foreign policy, from the late 1940s onward, was presumably designed to counter the Stalinist policy in Europe. American policy sought to contain what it conceived to be the main thrust of Soviet expansionism directed at central and western Europe. Its principal tools were the Marshall Plan and the Atlantic Alliance. Although the bland doctrine of containment was cast in a global mold, its principal objective was to stop the Russians in Europe.

In January 1954, American policy, by reinforcing the doctrine of containment with the doctrine of "massive retaliation," sought to redress the strategic balance in Europe and signified implicitly the United States' determination to fight for the preservation of the *status quo* in Europe as well as in Korea.

The policy of deterrence forced the Communists to desist from such direct challenges as they had presented in Korea and to devise more subtle modes for the penetration of the "gray areas." Neither John Foster Dulles' "massive retaliation" nor, for that matter, the doctrines of "limited war" advanced by his critics coped adequately with Communist strategy, which now had shifted into new political and paramilitary dimensions. Moreover, the growing nuclear power of the Soviet Union put in doubt the United States' readiness to invoke "massive retaliation" unless confronted by a direct threat to national survival.

The 1955 Geneva summit meeting was made possible, if not unavoidable, by prevailing Western public sentiment—weariness with the exactions of the cold war and a characteristic craving for final and formal settlements—and by mounting disagreements among the Western allies.

The Soviet leaders, although they were fully aware of Western motives and integrated them in their own calculations, prompted the encounter at Geneva because of considerations fundamentally different from those inducing their Western opposites to meet with them at the summit. With the demise of Stalin disappeared a formidable obstacle to liquidating a number of demonstrably unproductive ideological positions. The thesis of capitalist economic crisis could now be put conveniently into storage. The petty feud with Tito had been composed, and the Yugoslav leader's alleged heresy could be turned from an ideological liability into a diplomatic asset. More important still, the long overdue reorganization of the Communist system, blocked by Stalin's personal idiosyncrasies, could now be launched under comparatively favorable conditions. By conceding that "many roads lead to socialism," the Soviets hoped to attract the Afro-Asian neutrals, whom Stalin had neglected and whose aversion to totalitarianism sprang not so much from rooted democratic convictions as from distaste for Stalin's unsophisticated methods. By shifting the international cadres of communism from close-order to open-order drill, by purporting to loosen the reins of Moscow's control over the Communist parties outside Russia, the Khrushchev "collective" sought to check the West's military build-up and occasional psychopolitical stabs at the Soviet empire in eastern Europe.

It is doubtful that the summit meeting at Geneva marked a turning point of history. In the protracted conflict between two vast systems, no single event, be it conference or battle, can be decisive. The real significance of the Geneva meeting seems to lie not so much in the importance of the issues under negotiation as in the insight it afforded into mental states: the Western statesmen, whatever might have been their private reservations, were carried to Geneva on the crest of their peoples' perennial hopes for a settlement with finality and surcease from strife; the Soviets came to establish another position of maneuver in the protracted conflict. The Soviets adroitly avoided, as they always had done before, a showdown with Western strength and shifted their weight, as they always had done before, to bring it to bear against Western weakness. The West's key position—NATO—was too strong to be taken by frontal assault; the Communists moved to outflank it. The chosen field of maneuver was the area not explicitly covered by the system of Western alliance treaties. The first probing thrust, which was launched shortly after the vacuous Geneva communiqué, was the Czech arms shipment to Egypt. By the time the numbness induced by Geneva had worn off, the West saw itself confronted with a phenomenon unprecedented in modern history: the emergence of Russia as a Middle Eastern power.

In the West, the summit meeting at Geneva was vested with a meaning that transcended the reticent phrasing of the declarations issued by the assembled statesmen: the United States and the Soviet Union, having recognized the catastrophic horrors of thermonuclear war, had reached a *de facto* agreement to renounce force. If this had been indeed true, a new epoch of international relations would have opened at Geneva. The idea that the Soviets now eschewed all violent conflict in favor of "peaceful" competition was pleasing to the Western mind. To the Western mind, conflict as a conscious, managed struggle, the goals of which are mutually incompatible, is an unpalatable idea, for it does not fit the Western image of modern civilized society. By contrast, regulated competition, because it is impersonal and unconscious in its operation among individual groups bidding for a share of economic goods, is conducive to economic welfare and, if conducted with propriety, to good feeling. After Geneva, the West construed the phrase "peaceful, competitive coexistence" in the light of its own concept of competition, just as in the past it was willing to accept other samples of Communist semantics, such as "popular democracy," "free elections," "imperialism," and "colonialism," as though they meant the same thing to the Soviets as they did in Western parlance.

A DIALECTICAL THEORY OF CONFLICT

Classic Marxian economics is dead; nowhere is it probably taken less seriously than in Russia. Yet communism has outlived its intellectual sterility as well as its moral bankruptcy. Communism now draw its vigor from a dialectical theory of total conflict of indefinite duration between world political systems.

The salient characteristics of the doctrine of protracted conflict are: the total objective, the carefully controlled methods, and the constant shifting of the battleground, weapons systems, and operational tactics for the purpose of confusing the opponent, keeping him off balance, and wearing down his resistance. The doctrine of protracted conflict prescribes a strategy for annihilating the opponent over a period of time by limited operations, by feints and maneuvers, psychological manipulations, and diverse forms of violence. In Communist theory, various techniques of political warfare and graduated violence are so co-ordinated as to form a spectrum that reaches all the way from the clandestine distribution of subversive literature to the annihilating blow delivered with every weapon available.

We can now see how the Communists have applied this doctrine to the strategic situation confronting them from 1945 to 1957. The problem was to annul the Western democracies' technological and strategic superiority while presenting them with no challenge sufficiently decisive to trigger that type of response which Hitlerian strategy forced upon them. At first, the American atomic monopoly deterred Russia from presenting the United States with a forthright military challenge. Later, even after they had developed their own nuclear power, the Western air-base system, which formed a ring around the Communist heartland, kept them at a strategic disadvantage. Through this period, they confined their military challenges to the indirect and irregular type, employing proxies to do their work.

In June 1950, the troops of the Communist puppet regime of North Korea, striking across the 38th Parallel, put to the test the firmness of American intentions in the Far East. Moscow parried the affirmative American response to that aggression by persuading the Chinese Communist regime to enter the war. Even though the U.S.S.R. supplied arms to the North Korean–Chinese forces, the Russians did not allow themselves to become drawn directly into the war. When, after a year of combat, the Communist forces in Korea were unable to win new ground and the American–South Korean build-up permitted potentially decisive offensive operations, the Russians, far from threatening the West with a general war, suggested, in 1951, that negotiations for a truce be opened.

After the Communists had worn down the West's will to fight in Korea by two years of devious armistice discussions and had blanketed the Free World with their peace propaganda, mounted elaborately and financed largely by the contributions of Western Communists, fellow travelers, and pacifists, the Korean truce signaled a stepping up of the operational pace in Indochina. Here France fought an "old" war, heavily encumbered by ambiguous political and moral issues which militated against any vigorous Western response. The Soviet Union thus embroiled the West in Asian wars waged by its Korean and Chinese as well as its Malayan and Indochinese protégés. Their barefaced connivance notwithstanding, the Soviets dodged the responsibility for the actions of their proxies. In this farce, they were assisted by the legal-mindedness of the Western nations and the political naïveté of many of the "uncommitted" Asians.

Following the Soviet forced march into the realm of thermonuclear power, the Kremlin leadership felt capable of introducing important innovations into its postwar tactics. Initially, the Soviets sought to penetrate contiguous areas. In this endeavor, they depended upon the Sino-Soviet superiority in conventional armies and guerrilla-warfare methods. Now, for the first time in their history, the Soviets were able to "leap over" the Western treaty barriers into the more remote areas to which they had always been denied strategic access. By cannily devising proxy arms deals, the Soviet Union was able to extend its influence to Guatemala, Egypt, Syria, and, through Egypt, to Algeria.

Since 1945, the Communists have succeeded in their efforts to confine, on the whole, the cold war to the "war zone" of the non-Communist world, while keeping the "peace zone," namely the Communist bloc, virtually closed to Western intervention and, incidentally, the ministrations of the United Nations. The West was willing to give a round and take a round. If the West won a round, as in Korea and Jordan, for example, it was in the defense of the *status quo*. When the Communists won a round, as in Czechoslovakia, China, Indochina, and the Middle East, they gained access to ground previously closed to them. At best, the West stood its ground; but the Communists, in winning their rounds, made a net gain. At Geneva, the West accepted, together with the "balance of terror" thesis, the Communist-devised rules of the game, namely, to play it anywhere but in the Communist "peace zone" and to content itself with winning and losing the alternate rounds elsewhere.

IMPLICATIONS OF RUSSIA'S
TECHNOLOGICAL LEAP

The integration, in the early 1950s, of nuclear striking power into the Communist military establishment marked the first significant closing of the gap between the Communist and Western military-technological power. The acquisition of atomic capabilities and delivery systems signaled several important and, for the West, ominous changes in the Communist strategy of protracted conflict. These changes have been not so much in the kinds of techniques used as in the degrees of pressures brought to bear upon the West.

Ever since the Communists had to abandon their hopes for a simultaneous world revolution, they relied primarily on the psychopolitical modes of protracted conflict. Their strategy, in the broadest terms, has been to eschew the massive use of hardware and to produce psychological disturbances within the West, while at the same time keeping the uncommitted nations uncommitted or drawing them into the Communist orbit.

Whatever the pace and intensity of Soviet strategies in a given period, Soviet objectives remain the same. They are, in the short run: first, to force the withdrawal of the West from its strategic footholds, especially from the SAC network of bases; second, to compel the West to divert vital economic and military resources from Europe; third, to take Western pressure and attention off eastern Europe; and fourth, to exacerbate the divergencies within the Atlantic Alliance. The long-run Soviet objectives, too, are the same: namely, to isolate the West, deprive it of its sources of strategic raw materials and markets, and to encircle it via Asia, the Middle East, and Africa, until the West, its economic roots having withered, will fall under its own weight.

THE BATTLEGROUND OF THE "GRAY AREAS"

The West is bent upon the crucial problem of its survival in the face of the Communist threat. The West thus offers a ready and profitable target for blackmail. The "backward peoples' common, albeit naïve, admiration for Communist performance, especially for the Soviets' short cut in industrialization, has been deepened by the Soviet's recent technological triumphs and the West's patent discomfiture. The neutrality of Asian countries such as India, Indonesia, and Egypt tend toward diverse shadings of benevolence toward the Soviets. This brand of neutralism is quick to take offense at any Western initiative—except the West's proffer of gifts "without political strings."

In most of Asia and, to some measure, in most underdeveloped lands, the "forces of history" are not on the side of the West; they favor the Communists. In the short run, at least, Western chances of effecting a decisive improvement in Eastern standards of living are slim. Conceding even the dubious thesis that economic improvement stands in any palpable relationship to the growth of democratic institutions or, for that matter, of any political institutions, it is unlikely that whatever the West manages to accomplish within, let us say, the next twenty or thirty years in assuaging the aspirations of the underdeveloped peoples will alter significantly the power relationship between itself and the Communist bloc. At best, the Communists will not grow stronger; the West will not grow weaker.

The increase of international trade and investment and the more rapid economic growth of Asian and African lands are desirable ends in themselves. As great as are the West's economic and strategic stakes in Africa and Asia, its moral stakes are even more important: the West has accumulated a vast capital of good will among all non-Western peoples. Indeed in all noncommitted countries large numbers of individuals, including public officials, intellectuals, and members of the professions, are deeply committed to Western values; not a few chafe under the ambiguities of their governments' non-commitment. But hardly anywhere have such pro-Western sentiments sufficed to reverse official policy or, for that matter, the deeper currents of mass hostility.

In the non-Western world, the West's strategy cannot be more than a holding action. There, the task must be to gain time, to avoid fixed commitments, to improvise, and to abstain from action for action's sake. The idea that large-scale and long-range economic aid—a vast program for the development of the underdeveloped countries—can reverse, within the foreseeable future, the verdict of 300 years of history is born of *hubris*. Unseemly pride has led, in the past, many a mighty nation to perdition. It might have been possible after World War I, when the West's power was still unchallenged and the forces of nationalism in Asia were relatively weak, to transform gradually the social and economic order of the underdeveloped lands and to provide an economic basis for stable governments. The very existence of Communist power makes this now impossible. For no matter how much the West is willing and able to invest in the development of the "uncommitted" countries, there will always be a gap between the Western contribution and native expectations. The Communists need only move into this gap, be it even with the most modest resources, in order to divert to themselves whatever credit the recipient peoples might have been willing to accord a foreign giver.

In the area outside of the system of Western treaties of alliance—in the world of ex-colonial peoples and of the colored races—the Communists have learned that they can proceed with impunity and with a minimum of direct or even indirect involvement. Everywhere in this world, powerful forces inimical to the West have been rising. All the Communists need to do is to fan the fire. In most of Asia and Africa, the economic theories of Marx are even more irrelevant than they are in the highly industrialized West; the Leninist theory of imperialism, however, is alive in Communist strategy and, as a doctrine of conflict, marches from victory to victory. In the battle for the "uncommitted" peoples, the West can only expect to hold the ground which it has not as yet lost; it cannot force a decision in the protracted conflict with the Communists.

TOWARD AN UNDERSTANDING OF THE CONFLICT

The West can hope to defeat the Communists only by giving battle on its own chosen terrain. It must carry the battle to the vital sectors of Communist defense. To do that it must learn to counter the strategy of protracted conflict—to manage conflict in space and in time.

The development of proper Western attitudes toward protracted conflict will be immensely difficult. The Communists possess a mentality that is much better suited to protracted and controlled conflict than that of the Western peoples. The West has neither a doctrine of protracted conflict nor an international conspiratorial apparatus for executing it. What is more, we do not want such a doctrine or such a political apparatus, for it would be a tragic piece of irony if the men of the Free World, in trying to combat the Communists, should become like them. Some of our "weaknesses" vis-à-vis the Communists are irremediable: we cannot turn ourselves into a conflict society, nor can we assign to the government and, in the last resort, to the police the discipline of our conscience. It is within these limitations—which are the ramparts of civilized self-restraint—that we are forced to cope with Communist perversity.

Pericles long ago was confronted with a similar problem. As the leader of the open society of Athens, locked in an irreconcilable conflict with the garrison state of Sparta, he recognized a relatively simple fact which many of the theorists of war in the nuclear age have overlooked, namely, that there are subtle alternatives to the risky and blunt strategy of engaging the enemy in direct and decisive military action. In the protracted conflict known as the Peloponnesian War, Pericles chose to pursue an extended strategy which was designed to avoid a showdown battle while wearing down, by a campaign of economic, political, and psychological attrition, the enemy's will to resist. Liddell Hart pointed out that the Periclean plan was simply a war policy aimed at "draining the enemy's endurance in order to convince him that he could not gain a decision."[1] In today's protracted conflict the United States must maintain and use its power for the same ultimate purpose: to turn the tide of battle against the Communists, to induce them to overextend themselves, to exploit the weakness of their system, to paralyze their will, and to bring about their final collapse. Within the framework of mutual deterrence, both sides can employ the strategy of protracted conflict, and we can do so quite effectively without the dispensation of a jealous and demanding dogma of conflict for conflict's sake.

A psychopolitical offensive, directed against the Communist citadel itself, offers the West its best chance for winning the battle for its own survival and for spoiling the Communist strategy for the subversion of the

[1] B. H. Liddell Hart, *Strategy*, Praeger, New York, 1954, p. 31.

uncommitted world. Although the currents within the uncommitted world are running against the West, the West need not despair of holding its remaining positions once it has forced the Communists on the psychopolitical defensive by engaging them on the most favorable terrain, namely, the Communists' own "peace zone."

It is rather in the psychological arena than in its technological workshop that the West has displayed its most alarming shortcomings. Objectively, Western strategy has been far more effective than the sensational charges of its critics will have it. It is improbable that either side from now on will be able to achieve decisive technological superiority for more than a temporary, even brief, period. No doubt, our military posture is susceptible to a great deal of improvement. But an exaggerated zeal for improvement, especially when it is triggered by pained surprise at the latest ploy of Communist psychological warfare or considerations of domestic political advantage, might prove to be "counterproductive" in developing our real range of power. Do not let us pour the baby out with the bath water. What we need now more than anything else is an understanding of the comprehensive, complex, subtle, and consistent strategy of our opponent— and the calm resolution to draw the practical consequences.

THE SCHOOL AND
CONFLICTING SOCIAL VALUES

Consideration of basic values in cultures was begun in Part 1 of this text. The intent was to show the conflicts of values on a broad scale. This section is presented as an illustration of social-value conflicts in a more narrowly defined scope. Not all of the problems and issues of American culture are presented, but selected issues are covered to illustrate the nature of value conflicts in society and the influence they exert upon the school as a social institution.

The previous section viewed two general and basic national issues—economics and foreign policy. This section offers a look at the diverse subjects of censorship and its effect upon education, anticommunism classes, the right-wing political movement and its educational activities, the new status of religion in American life, the problems of curriculum, and the mass culture problem in mass education. In each of these issues there are several positions. This text has not attempted to present all sides of each conflict, or even the complete presentation of one side. The purpose for including the following selections is both to illustrate the issue involved and to provoke the readers' interest in further study and analysis. The introduction of these topics should lead to thoughtful questions about the schools of an open society.

What value system supports restraints imposed upon the schools through censorship of books, films, speakers, and ideas? How should the schools deal with propaganda from any political force—left, right, or middle? Who should decide what subjects are suitable for study in the schools? What changes are evident in the relation of religion to education? How should mass education treat mass media and mass culture?

Censorship in the Schools

The stereotyped picture of the teacher, free to open any doors of inquiry and beholden only to the conscience of knowledge, is shattered by this forthright analysis of censorship in teaching materials. Harry Bach describes the means by which books are banned from libraries and schools, and offers some answers for an enlightened consideration of the problem.

The issue essentially amounts to a conflict over the purpose of education, for books are a primary means to knowledge. Plato advocated censorship in the society he proposed because the philosopher-king knew the truth and therefore it was his duty to keep falseness from the people by censoring out false material. Which of the censors of today knows the truth? Does the public need censorship in education to protect itself from alien ideas? Can the public be assured that freedom to inquire is coupled with responsibility? Is intellectual freedom a right or a privilege in an open society?

Censorship of Library Books and Textbooks in American Schools

HARRY BACH

On January 9, 1963 the Lowndes County, Georgia, school board banned John Steinbeck's *East of Eden* from all libraries in the county school system. The novel was described as "vulgar trash" by objecting parents. Members of the school board admitted they had not read the book.

In 1963 a bill was introduced in the Texas House of Representatives, H.B. 852, which would penalize public school librarians who deposit in their libraries literature containing language which in the local school board's opinion could be considered to be obscene.

At El Segundo High School, California, some two years ago [in 1963], *The Reporter* and *The New Republic* were suspended from classroom use

Reprinted from the *Journal of Secondary Education*, Vol. 40, No. 1, January, 1965, pp. 3–15, by permission of the publishers, the California Association of Secondary School Administrators.

and six social studies teachers were reprimanded by school district trustees for publicly protesting administrative practices. The school board ruled that the two magazines would be kept in the school library for use only by those students who had a teacher's permission to do so. Board President Charles Schumann chastised the teachers for raising the question of book-banning which he claimed "subjected the community and board to ridicule and criticism."

Charges of communist subversion in the Los Angeles school curriculum were made to the Board of Education on October 29, 1962 by Mrs. Lucinda Benge, who cited six social science textbooks as containing planned communist subversion. The board asked Superintendent Jack P. Crowther to evaluate the charges and report later. Books in question were the *Real People Series* used in 7th grade; the *Present in Perspective* and *Background of World Affairs* used in 12th grade; *Documents of American History* and *Heritage of America* used in the 11th grade.

In November, 1961 two citizens of Meriden, Connecticut, named Casy and Dobson charged that the city's two high schools were brainwashing the students. They stated in their report that after careful examination of the social science texts they reached the conclusion that Meriden parents were indeed financing the subversion of their own children in their own public schools. The report defined subversion as anything tending to undermine "faith and allegiance." The two critics objected to such subtitles in books as "Industrialization Brings Problems as well as Benefits"; and "Congress Attempts to Curb the Trusts." They found fault with books and articles by novelist Pearl Buck because Miss Buck, they said, in 1941 had appealed for help "on behalf of the Russian peoples." Fortunately, a vigilant press and education officials took a strong stand and were able to silence the censors before the latter's ardor reached the book-burning stage.

Are the above accounts isolated incidents? Evidently not. According to Nelson's *The Censors and the Schools*, from the early part of 1957 until the end of 1962, textbooks came under fire in nearly a third of the legislatures in states as far apart as California, Illinois, Texas and Florida.[1]

In California in 1957 State Senator Hugh P. Donnelly introduced a bill to prohibit the use of schoolbooks judged at variance with "morality, truth, justice or patriotism." Donnelly's colleagues in the legislature, however, wondering just who would pass on all those virtues, killed the bill in committee.

The Texas legislature in 1962 established a textbook investigating committee. The duty of the committee of five was to hold public hearings on charges that books now used, or planned for future use in the state schools are subversive. The resolution which established the committee was some-

---

[1] Jack Nelson, *The Censors and the Schools*, Little, Brown & Co., New York, 1963.

what vague: "The House expresses its desire that the American history course in the public schools emphasize in the textbooks our glowing and throbbing history of hearts and souls inspired by wonderful principles and traditions." Following were some of the demands from the right:

Banish books that describe the United States as a democracy rather than a republic

Remove books with favorable descriptions of the New Deal, the United Nations, the Tennessee Valley Authority, and federal aid to just about anything

That Webster's *New World Dictionary* not be used because its definition of communism does not call it "a world menace"

Remove the name of Albert Einstein from textbooks

Eliminate those books which "glorify" government control of economy and use only those which praise the virtues of capitalism

Protest books which give "casual" treatment to Douglas MacArthur or contain too little material on Nathan Hale, Patrick Henry and David Crockett

Oppose books which refer students to books of Eugene O'Neill, Pearl Buck, William Faulkner, Ernest Hemingway, Sinclair Lewis, Theodore Dreiser and historians Charles A. Beard, Henry S. Commager and Bernard De Voto[2]

The extreme expression of distrust was perhaps reached by the Alabama legislature in 1953 when it passed a bill prohibiting the use of any textbooks unless the authors, contributors, or authors cited were certified by the publishers as having no communist affiliations. The act, however, was declared unconstitutional one year later.

Censorship of books is no new phenomenon in American society, or any society for that matter. As Blanshard points out, every group in a nation which has strong convictions concerning the subject matter taught in public classrooms wants to use the schools to indoctrinate the children with those convictions. In one generation it is the slavocracy of the South that insists on indoctrinating Southern children with a flattering representation of slavery and "Southern values"; in the next it is the orthodox leaders of Christian fundamentalism who would eliminate the "heresy" of evolution. Then it is the turn of the anti-British segments to have their day. In the 1920's, socialism was a subject to be omitted from history textbooks altogether. At the same time, however, public utility corporations of the country initiated a drive to rewrite textbooks in such a way that children would appreciate the philosophy of American private enterprise.

Perhaps it might be well at this stage to examine more closely the meaning and nature of censorship. According to Gellhorn, censorship embraces group activity aimed at eliminating particular works or kinds of works, or limiting their availability after publication. He goes on further to make a distinction between official censorship and unofficial censorship. The former based on law or administrative regulation, usually observes the forms of legal procedures, though its permissible content has sometimes been

[2] *Newsletter on Intellectual Freedom*, Vol. 11, No. 2, July, 1962, pp. 1–8.

defined so vaguely that the attendant procedures have given little real protection; the latter derives its force not from legal mechanisms, but, at its best, from persuasion and, at its worst, from implacable economic or political pressure abetted by misuse of police authority. Censorship, says Gellhorn, rests in one or another degree upon the belief that those who are qualified to identify evil and mistake should be empowered to prevent their dissemination. The censors, of course, fail to realize that if choice is foreclosed by another's judgment about what is virtuous or wise, freedom is lost. More importantly, the chances of discovering what really is virtuous or wise diminish when experimentation and disagreement are impossible. John Stuart Mill in his *On Liberty* observes: "All silencing of discussion is an assumption of infallibility. While everyone well knows himself to be fallible, few think it necessary to take any precautions against their own fallibility, or admit the supposition that any opinion of which they feel very certain, may be one of the examples of the error to which they acknowledge themselves to be liable."[3]

To restate the above in different terms: Censorship, in one view, aims at reserving freedom (in the United States, at least) through reinforcing what its proponents regard as the true values and beliefs. Opposition to censorship, in the other view, does not derive from hostility to the virtues the pro-censors cherish, but reflects rather, a conviction that in the end the values of a free society will be attained through freedom rather than repression. The advocates of censorship, in other words, regard it as a means by which to prevent debasement of the individual virtues, the cultural standards, and the common security of democracy. Its opponents regard it, by contrast, as a danger to the freedom which fosters those virtues and standards, and without which democracy cannot survive.

From the legal point of view Justice Black finds censorship of any kind unconstitutional according to the First Amendment's clear statement, "Congress shall make no law ... abridging the freedom of speech, or of the press." If curbs are placed on freedom of the press, these curbs must be based on a clear and present danger of a substantive evil from the publications. Only the courts and not private literature reviewing organizations are the proper tribunals for determining the existence of such danger. In this connection Federal Judge Ernest Tolin, faced with the perplexing question of what constitutes obscenity, discovered fourteen different judicial definitions of the term. Obviously few people can agree upon its essential nature. In any event, says Justice Tobriner of the California Supreme Court, "a legal prescription cannot constrict artistic creation. Man's drive for self-expression which over the centuries has built his monuments, does not stay within set bounds; the creations which yesterday were the

[3] John Stuart Mill, *On Liberty; Representative Government; the Subjection of Women,* Oxford University Press, New York, 1933.

detested and obscene become the classics of today."[4] "We can be pretty sure," adds Everett Moore, 1964 President of the California Library Association, "that even the most hated and feared book of any age will not evoke the same hatred and fear in another time."[5]

The premises underlying legal censorship—that curbs placed on freedom of the press must be based on a clear and present danger of a substantive evil from the publications—have never been fully tested by empirical research. Hence it cannot be unequivocally demonstrated that books do not promote juvenile delinquency, sexual perversion, sadism and the other evils the censors fear will flow from reading. Such objective evidence as does exist, does not sustain the fear. So far as disclosed by the most exhaustive study of juvenile delinquency yet made in America, reading seems to be of small moment in shaping antisocial tendencies. According to George W. Smyth, for many years one of the nation's outstanding children's court judges, reading difficulty was among the 878 causative factors that had had effect upon the troubled children before him; reading, no matter of what, found not a single place in his list. Reading, like other environmental factors, may modify an individual's personality predispositions, though unlikely in itself to make a "bad" man out of a previously "good" one. As Gellhorn points out, unless all children are to be wrapped in cotton batting and utterly removed from the world, we cannot hope to immunize every one of them against contact with something that might conceivably energize his savage side. Even if it be true that reading matter may activate the impulses of some twisted individual, can this possibility justify repressive policies that affect all alike? Could anyone imagine a convict being led into the gas chamber turning to the attendants—or, who knows, a national T.V. audience—to say: I am going where I am going because I have read *Catcher in the Rye!*

Incidentally, while parents, educators, organized groups, etc., may be alarmed lest a few words found in certain recent novels corrupt American children, they seem to show much less concern when every day, right under their noses, they witness whole industries—fashion and advertising, perfume and cosmetics—work very hard at stimulating sexual desires! Furthermore, if we wish to prevent the deterioration of our young people's morals, perhaps we should abolish the draft and also the armed forces! From one or two GI bull sessions the uninitiated will probably "learn" more than from the complete works of a Henry Miller! This is not to say, of course, that an 8th grader should be assigned to report on the *Tropic of Cancer*. It is to say, however, that the matter of reading assignments should be left to the instructor's good judgment and the librarian's policy of adding books to his collection that will enrich the quality of thought and expression. *Tropic of Cancer* could conceivably become suggested or as-

---

[4] Quoted in an article by Everett T. Moore, "A Dangerous Way of Life," *Illinois Libraries*, Vol. 46, No. 3, March, 1964, pp. 165–74.

[5] *Ibid.*

signed reading in an advanced American literature course for the gifted at
the senior level, if the instructor holds the conviction that the book is good
literature which will benefit the serious student and can present it as such
to his class.

Censorship, like other forms of activity, has always flared most dangerously in times of heightened uneasiness, tension, and frustration, when
people reach out for apparently easy solutions to complex problems, flail
the handiest strawman, and burn in effigy the most visible or vulnerable
enemy.

Since the end of the Second World War, many people in the United
States have been uneasy over the revolutionary changes occurring in the
world, especially the growth in the power of the Soviet Union and the
consequent tensions of the Cold War. At home, they are attempting to deal
with the great social problems of racial integration and accelerated urbanization, with all their dislocating effects. Both challenges, external and internal, have aroused passions and anxieties, and fostered unreasoning
violence.

Censorship, therefore, has been held out as a convenient and simple
weapon readily available to people who feel deprived of an effective voice
through democratic means, a club with which to defend and enforce their
own views on public issues, a means of destroying liberty in the name of
liberty. It seems, to many, so easy: the removal of "subversive" books from
the library is a blow against the international Communist conspiracy, removal of "obscene" books from book shelves will put an end to juvenile
delinquency. In this perspective, "undermining the morals of youth" becomes part of the Communist plot against America; the loyalty of librarians,
teachers and authors is suspect; and publishers are either "agents of the
Kremlin," "purveyors of filth for profit," or ironically both. The temptation
to take unilateral, authoritarian counteraction, especially on the part of
people impatient with legal procedures and court decisions, becomes
strong; and books, because they have never been more accessible, and because they are feared as well as respected, become the victims.

In a democracy, all naturally have the right to voice their opinion, to
criticize a book or anything else, if they so desire. Textbooks cannot be
above the judgment of the community; admittedly, the more criticism
there is, the better. But criticism should be honest and informed. According to Blanshard, however, most agitators who have been making trouble
for local school boards have not been independent citizens expressing their
own convictions but mouthpieces of a reactionary movement against public education. These vocal minority groups seem to regard as treason any
slight suggestion that the United States was ever in the wrong or that there
is anything about it that could be improved. They are evidently ignorant
of the fact that what improvement there has been in the American text-

book in the past quarter century has been primarily in response to professional criticism rather than pressure groups.

Brainwashing in the High Schools, by E. Merrill Root, billed as an objective analysis of eleven American history textbooks paralleling the Communist line, published in 1958, seems to be the bible of these ultra-conservative groups. It catapulted Root into the forefront of the assault on public education. The main thesis of the book is that the United States is losing the Cold War and that the blame rests with history textbooks which "brainwashed" students by distorting the truth and indoctrinating them with collectivist ideas! The Daughters of the American Revolution also have been joining the battle against subversive textbooks. Of two hundred and fourteen titles examined by them, only fifteen met their minimum standards. The D.A.R. unearthed what they considered subversion even in books on music, geography, arithmetic and biology. In music, for instance, they found too many work tunes and folk songs, as distinguished from native and national airs. Many books were pronounced "guilty of special pleading from the liberals and internationalists" because writings by people such as Ruth Benedict, Theodore H. White, Alan Lomax, Langston Hughes, Margaret Mead, Louis Untermeyer, Bill Mauldin, etc., were listed for supplementary study.

In 1958, an organization called "America's Future" launched its "Operation-Textbook." According to Rudolf K. Scott, president: "No American textbook publishers have stooped to subversion. There is no evidence of that and I don't like extremism. The whole thing of liberalism in the textbooks has been an evolution, taking place over the past decade or two. But we are going to change that. We have already had some influence and we ultimately will exercise a very considerable force in textbook publishing. Publishers have had a free hand too long. There were no qualified persons criticizing them. Now we are hurting the publisher where it hurts —in his pocketbook." By late 1962 "America's Future" had mailed out thousands of copies of reviews of more than two hundred high school texts. The reviews went to educators, school board members, and numerous organizations dedicated to censoring subversion from texts. The same theme runs through all of these reviews: protests against material on the income tax, Social Security, T.V.A., liberal authors, labor unions, the United Nations, Democratic presidents, etc.

Approximately a year ago, Edwin Castagna, a well-known American librarian, attributed the following characteristics and forms of behavior to reactionary censors:

1. A threatening attitude
2. A belief in personal superiority, a conviction others would be gravely injured by what he wants to suppress

3. An absolute lack of a sense of humor. To the censor a witticism is an indication of treason!

4. A tendency to making the part stand for the whole and making it seem that incidental factors are true for the whole book

5. Lack of knowledge

Censors, he says, often are incredibly ignorant, without the slightest understanding of the creative mind

6. No understanding of history, a lack of realization that their game is one of the oldest and most unsuccessful in the world, that about every classic including Homer, Socrates, the Greek dramatists, the Bible, Chaucer, Shakespeare, Mark Twain, Walt Whitman, at one time or another, have been expurgated, mutilated, suppressed and censored

7. Absence of belief in freedom of expression

8. A tendency to bypass and disregard well-established policies and procedures, an unwillingness to be confronted with obstacles in the way of policies, regulations and well-established practices[6]

However, it must be noted that the superpatriots are not the only censors. There are many conscientious, honest decent parents and citizens who are concerned too. They are wondering what is happening and if they can be certain that the charges are based on fact. In her now famous *Book Selection and Censorship Study*, Marjorie Fiske also brought forth the shocking fact of widespread self-censorship among California librarians and school administrators.[7] Evidently, the existence of extremist groups and a press campaigning against certain books and authors have resulted in a marked effect on school administrators and librarians, who, in order to avoid controversy, have been seeing to it that there is nothing on their library shelves to complain about. Fiske found that two-thirds of the school personnel reporting "no complaints" from book users had restrictive attitudes toward book selection. Nearly one-half of the librarians interviewed in the study expressed unequivocal "freedom to read" convictions. In actual practice, however, as stated above, two-thirds of those who had a say in book selection reported instances where the controversiality of a book or an author resulted in a decision not to buy. One-fifth habitually avoided buying any material which was known to be controversial or which they believed might become the subject of controversy. Librarians also listed reasons widely acknowledged as legitimate (such as reading level and the necessity to supplement the curriculum) for avoiding material. A school librarian working in a metropolitan system, according to Fiske, was not as likely to order controversial material as a school librarian in a smaller city. Not size of city itself but degree of bureaucratization seemed to be the decisive factor. Books complained about, Fiske further reported, were placed on restricted shelves. School librarians, the study revealed, felt like second-class members of their own profession and like

[6] Edwin Castagna, "Courage and Cowardice," *Library Journal*, Vol. 88, No. 3, February, 1963, pp. 501–06.

[7] Marjorie Fiske, *Book Selection and Censorship*, University of California Press, 1959.

second-class members of their own faculties. Thus a feeling of defensiveness on their part, in many cases, led to capitulation to pressures. Librarians and school administrators would do well, therefore, to remember Thomas Braden's words that the trouble with censorship is that there is never a logical place to stop. "If you ban one book," Mr. Braden says, "equally good reasons can be provided for banning another. If you ban a book on moral grounds, then why not on political grounds? If one citizen's complaint that a book is objectionable is satisfied by removing it, then it is fair to satisfy other citizens who may find other books equally objectionable. Censorship is a seamless web."[8]

What are some of the effects of censorship in addition to intimidating teachers, school officials and librarians and creating a climate of fear? Nelson claims that no state escapes the effects of the attacks on textbooks. Book censors in one state, he says, will force a publisher to alter a textbook and that book is sold, as altered, in other states. But more important perhaps is the impact the widespread attacks have on textbook publishers, who are highly competitive. Publishers themselves acknowledge they must walk a narrow path to avoid controversy and offending any special interest groups. As a result, writes A. Alexander, a textbook analyst of the Board of Education of the City of New York: "Many of the textbooks are strangely dull, lifeless, and bear a striking resemblance to each other. Critical of neither the past nor the present, they encourage little respect for the historian's craft . . . they betray a basic lack of confidence in presenting this country full face because some of the warts may show. Many books present few or no serious problems."[9] Henry S. Commager, who agreed with this appraisal, added: "The whole purpose seems to be to take out any ideas to which anybody might object and to balance all sections and interests."[10] Textbooks and library books that avoid offending various interests and levels of authority and legitimate and not-so-legitimate pressure groups eliminate the discussion of controversial issues. (In one case, a publisher deleted an entire chapter on the United Nations from an eighth-grade civics book.) By omitting or glossing over controversial issues, Krug asserts, textbooks fail to provide students with opportunities for critical thinking, for gaining insight into historical or civic problems, for learning the skills needed for problem solving, which alone can prepare young people for the intelligent choice making required of citizens in a democracy. It is democracy itself, at its center, which is strengthened whenever a free choice of books is made available to the student population.

Librarians, more and more, when under attack, have been falling back

[8] Thomas Braden, "Trouble with Censorship," *California Librarian*, Vol. 24, No. 4, October, 1963, pp. 235–38.

[9] Albert Alexander, "The Gray Flannel Cover on the American History Textbooks," *Social Education*, Vol. 24, No. 1, January, 1960, pp. 11–14.

[10] Quoted in an article by Fred Hechinger, "High School History Textbooks Play It Safe by Avoiding Tough Issues," *The New York Times*, February 14, 1960, p. E-9.

on two basic documents: the *Library Bill of Rights* adopted June 18, 1948 and amended February 1, 1961 by the Council of the American Library Association and the *Freedom to Read Statement* prepared by the Westchester Conference of the American Library Association and the American Book Publishers Council, May 2–3, 1953. The former has been called a magnificent charter of literary freedom for American libraries. It has been used very effectively against censorship claques in a number of cities. One of its primary principles is that "in no case should any book be excluded because of the race or nationality, or the political or the religious views of the writer." It goes on to say:

There should be the fullest practicable provision of material presenting all points of view concerning the problems and issues of our times, international, national and local; and books or other reading matter of sound factual authority should not be proscribed or removed from library shelves because of partisan or doctrinal disapproval.

Censorship of books, urged or practiced by volunteer arbiters of morals or political opinion or by organizations that would establish a coercive concept of Americanism, must be challenged by libraries in maintenance of their responsibility to provide public information and enlightenment through the printed word. . . . A book should be judged as a book. No art or literature can flourish if it is to be measured by the political views or private lives of its creators.

The *Freedom to Read Statement,* among many other things, declares:

We believe that free communication is essential to the preservation of a free society and a creative culture. We believe that these pressures towards conformity present the danger of limiting the range and variety of inquiry and expression on which our democracy and our culture depend. . . . The freedom to read is guaranteed by the Constitution. Those with faith in free man will stand firm on these constitutional guarantees of essential rights and will exercise the responsibilities that accompany these rights.

We therefore affirm these propositions:

1. It is in the public interest for publishers and librarians to make available the widest diversity of views and expressions, including those which are unorthodox or unpopular with the majority

2. Publishers and librarians do not need to endorse every idea or presentation contained in the books they make available. It would conflict with the public interest for them to establish their own political, moral or aesthetic views as the sole standard for determining what books should be published or circulated

3. It is contrary to the public interest for publishers or librarians to determine the acceptability of a book solely on the basis of the personal history or political affiliations of the author

4. It is not in the public interest to force a reader to accept with any book the prejudgment of a label characterizing the book or author as subversive or dangerous

5. It is the responsibility of publishers and librarians, as guardians of the people's freedoms to read, to contest encroachments upon that freedom by indi-

viduals or groups seeking to impose their own standards or tastes upon the community at large

6. It is the responsibility of publishers and librarians to give full meaning to the freedom to read by providing books that enrich the quality of thought and expression. By the exercise of this affirmative responsibility, bookmen can demonstrate that the answer to a bad book is a good one, the answer to a bad idea is a good one.

Into these ringing declarations, Ervin J. Gaines, a librarian with a column on intellectual freedom in the *ALA Bulletin* injects a note of caution. Would-be censors, he says, are not interested, it seems, in the academic niceties of a free press. Rightly or wrongly, they are alarmed by a tendency toward immorality that frightens them. Like frightened men they react with force.[11] Nelson in his book quotes William E. Spaulding, former president of the American Textbook Publishers Institute as saying: "There is nothing to be gained by blaming the present situation on the small but highly organized group of professional agitators who have sold a phony bill of goods to the American public. Lash back at them as hard as you please, but the fact will remain that for lack of understanding large segments of the American public have accepted their program in the name of patriotism and as one means of defense against communism."[12]

The failure of the nation's communications media, Nelson continues, to give full reports on textbook controversies and pressure groups has permitted censorship activities to flourish with little organized opposition. If newspapers, television and radio can be called delinquent in their responsibilities, so can many school administrators, teachers, and publishers. As a matter of fact, among the publishers there has been such a noticeable lack of cooperation in meeting the attacks that in some cases book salesmen have taken advantage of unfounded attacks on a competitor's texts to increase the sales of their own firm's publications. Authors and publishers, whom one might expect to be the first line of defense, seem to have decided that disaction is the better part of valor. The authors of books under attack have said very little in reply to their critics, and their silence is apparently dictated by the publishers. This being the situation, it may be fortunate that on February 1, 1962 the Council of the American Library Association passed a resolution giving practical advice to teachers, librarians and administrators regarding ways and means of resisting censorship.
books used in their programs. In view of this fact, it seems desirable to set forth

Libraries of all sizes and types have been under increasing pressures from persons who wish to use the library as an instrument of their own tastes and views. Such individuals and groups are demanding the exclusion or removal of books to which they object or the inclusion of a higher proportion of books that support their views. Similar attacks have been made on schools in connection with

[11] Ervin J. Gaines, "Intellectual Freedom," *A.L.A. Bulletin,* Vol. 57, No. 3, October, 1963, pp. 317–18.
[12] Nelson, *op. cit.*

books used in their programs. In view of this fact, it seems desirable to set forth a few basic principles that may help librarians, trustees, and school administrators in preserving the freedom and professional integrity of their institutions.

Every library or school should take certain measures to clarify its policies and establish its community relations. These steps should be taken without regard to any attack or prospect of attack. They will put the institution in a firm and clearly defined position if its books policies are ever called into question.

As a normal operating procedure, every library, and the administration responsible for it, should establish certain principles.

1. There should be a definite book selection policy. This should be in written form and approved by the board of trustees, the school board, or other administrative authority. It should be stated clearly and should be understood by members of the staff. This policy should apply to other materials equally, i.e., films, records, magazines, and pamphlets.

2. A file recording the basis for decision should be kept for titles likely to be questioned or apt to be considered controversial.

3. There should be a clearly defined method for handling complaints. Any complaint should be required to be in writing, and the complainant should be identified properly before the complaint is considered. Action should be deferred until full consideration by appropriate administrative authority.

4. There should be continuing efforts to establish lines of communication to assure mutual understanding with civic, religious, educational, and political bodies.

5. Newspapers of the community should be informed of policies governing book selection and use. Purposes and services of the library should be interpreted through a continuing public relations program, as should the use of books in the school.

6. Participation in local civic organizations and in community affairs is desirable. The library and the school are key centers of the community; the librarian and school administrator should be known publicly as community leaders.

If an attack does come, remember the following:

1. Remain calm. Don't confuse noise with substance.

2. Take immediate steps to assure that the full facts surrounding a complaint are known to the administration. The school librarian should go through the principal to the superintendent and the school board. Full, written information should be presented, giving the nature of the problem or complaint and identifying the source.

3. Seek the support of the local press immediately. The freedom to read and the freedom of the press go hand in hand.

4. Inform local civic organizations of the facts and enlist their support where possible.

5. Defend the principles of the freedom to read and the professional responsibility of teachers and librarians rather than the individual book. The laws governing obscenity, subversive material, and other questionable matter are subject to interpretation by the courts. The responsibility for removal of any book from public access should rest with this established process. The responsibility for the use of books in the schools must rest with those responsible for the educational objectives being served.

6. The ALA Intellectual Freedom Committee and other appropriate national and state committees concerned with intellectual freedom should be informed of the nature of the problem. Even though each effort at censorship must be met at the local level, there is often value in the support and assistance of agencies outside the area which have no personal involvement.

Whether or not attempts at censorship in the schools will let up in years to come is understandably impossible to predict. We do not know what the political climate will be; we do not know what the moral climate will be; we do not know whether the American public will have a better understanding of the problem. We do know, however, that with the help of more and more books on the subject of censorship and publications such as the *Library Bill of Rights,* the *Freedom to Read Statement,* and the statement on *How Libraries and Schools Can Resist Censorship,* school administrators, teachers and librarians ought to be able to stand up to their destructive critics. Rather than capitulate or impose self-censorship as they have done in too many cases, let them make it impossible for any future study to reach the conclusion that public pressure for censorship of books and magazines appears to be a "prominent part of school life" as it did in Wisconsin recently. Let them not be afraid of the Mrs. Jane Alexanders who said she might charge the trustees of the Sequoia Union High School District, California, with contributing to the delinquency of minors for having the *Dictionary of American Slang* in the six schools under its jurisdiction. Let them remember that if pressure groups rather than qualified educators are allowed to determine the content of books, teaching in American schools will degenerate into indoctrination. The antidote to authoritarianism is not some form of American authoritarianism. The antidote is free inquiry.

Teaching About Communism—
Indoctrination Versus Education

The issue of teaching about communism in American schools has been evident for some time. Not long ago the subject of communism was not allowed to permeate the solid walls of schools on the pretext that teaching about communism was itself subversive. Many school districts would not permit teachers to discuss communism, and some even imposed restrictions on other international studies to the extent that at least one major city school district refused to allow study of UNESCO and another district passed a regulation requiring board of education approval for any teaching materials which included Russia.

More recently, school districts and state educational departments have recognized a need to teach about communism in order to provide for an enlightened citizenry. Their recognition of the need, however, conflicted with the fear of subversion and the possibility of students seeing advantages to communism. The result, typically, was a curriculum designed to stress the positive values of American life and the negative values of communism.

Outside of the school there has been a strong movement to impress the same ideas upon the public through various anticommunism classes and organizations. Professor Metcalf presents a view of these means to teach about communism and suggests some alternatives.

Can critical thinking be encouraged if the schools are denied the opportunity to practice it?

Anti-Communism in the Classroom
Education or Propaganda?

LAWRENCE E. METCALF

For years high school teachers have not been permitted to teach an understanding of communism. Powerful interest groups have opposed any treatment of the subject that might fail to convey an appreciation for right-wing interpretations of free enterprise. The dominant view of these groups has been that "It is all right for young people to think about communism only as long as they reach the right conclusions." In this kind of atmosphere, most teachers have chosen to ignore communism rather than risk having their students draw the "wrong" conclusions.

A recent *New York Times* survey suggests that a growing number of communities are insisting that public high schools reverse this longstanding hands-off policy. Unfortunately, it is an insistence that the schools engage vigorously in rightwing indoctrination, clearly labeling liberals, the welfare state, the U.N., NATO, foreign aid and the income tax as evidences of creeping communism. The shift from neglect to indoctrination is suggested by the new stance of the American Legion. Once opposed to any treatment of communism in the public schools, the organization is reported to be cooperating with the National Education Association in the design of a

Reprinted from *The Nation*, Vol. 194, No. 10, March 10, 1962, pp. 215, 216, 224, by permission of the editor.

"model" course. Reports indicate that rightist groups all over the nation have shifted their position similarly. The result is already apparent: the offering of courses which amount to outright anti-Communist indoctrination, with the facts often sacrificed on the altar of "patriotism."

Typical developments may be found in the South, the Midwest and in certain parts of California. Louisiana, for more than a year, has been requiring students in American history to spend thirty hours on the study of communism. The general drift of the course is right-wing, with an emphasis on such ideas as "There can be compromise with international communism, no coexistence," and "Socialism and the welfare state are way stations on the road to communism." The guide for the course recommends forcefully that teachers use the film, *Communism on the Map*, which implies that Spain, Switzerland and the United States are the only non-Communist countries in the Western world (not even Portugal qualifies for membership).

The Florida legislature has just passed a bill requiring all high school seniors, beginning this fall, to take a similar course. In Houston, Texas, plans for injecting a "disguised" course on communism have aroused considerable controversy. A curriculum bulletin, prepared by the supervisor of world history and economics, has been circulated among the teachers as a recommended syllabus. Known as Curriculum Bulletin No. 59CBM9, it purports to outline a high school course in economics. Its stated purpose is to teach students to appreciate "the good things in the American economic system." But the projected course would seem to violate one of the good things in the American public-school system: the freedom of students to learn the truth about contemporary society and its problems. The list of recommended collateral reading, for example, includes only a few items about economics written by economists, even though the public commonly believes that a major difference at issue in the cold war is over economic systems. Most items are pamphleteering in tone, obviously intended for use in indoctrination programs. A characteristic note is struck in the bulletin's introduction, which exhorts the reader to believe that "the great mansion and small cottage differ only in size rather than basic quality."

A group known as the Houston Association for Better Schools, after a careful reading of the bulletin and its bibliography, doubted its educational value, and asked economists at nine major universities to comment upon it. The economists were specifically asked whether they thought that an economics course based on this guide would contribute to good college preparation. Typical responses:

I consider it an unsatisfactory syllabus because it is designed to present a certain point of view toward economic policy rather than an understanding of the economy.

As a matter of fact, a student would probably be better off not to have had this course.

A large percentage of the material is predominantly propaganda rather than objective analysis of our economic system. This is definitely a slanted list of references and, employed as suggested in the course outline, will lead to serious misconceptions regarding the structure and operation of our economy.

No labor materials are included among the pamphlets. Ultraconservative views by non-economists are well represented but no ultraliberal views. I would favor omitting all interest group items and teach economic principles, not views.

Many will dismiss the Houston bulletin as another example of extremism made in Texas by Texans. But it is common knowledge that many teachers and administrators all over the country see nothing wrong with indoctrination; for them, the choice is merely between anti-Communist and pro-Communist indoctrination. Given such a choice, what American would be anything but anti? As long as educators regard suppression of knowledge as a normal function of the American high school, they will be unable to make much sense of the issues raised by the economists who criticized the Houston bulletin.

Events in Los Angeles, Berkeley and other parts of California further suggest the educational philosophy of anti-Communist propagandists. In Los Angeles, the division of instructional services issued a twenty-five-page bulletin about the teaching of communism which was severely criticized because it recommended the viewing of the McGraw-Hill award-winning film, *Face of Red China*. The film shows school children in Red China smiling; was this not making life under communism appear to be attractive? During a three-day period, the Director of Audio-Visual Programs, who had been instrumental in drawing up the list of recommended films, received anonymous telephone calls at almost ten-minute intervals, and was finally forced to submit the bulletin to review by a special committee.

If indoctrination of the young is to succeed, their teachers must be properly prepared. In Berkeley, a lecture series on "Facts on Communism" provided a forum for professional anti-Communists. Scholars at the University of California were not invited to participate, but public school teachers who attended were given credit toward pay increases by the Berkeley Board of Education.

The idea for the lectures originated with two members of the local Rotary Club who had been stirred to action by a U.S. Navy officer whom they had heard speak at a luncheon. The two men convinced the school board to offer the lecture series under the auspices of the Berkeley Evening School, an adjunct of the public schools. One of the men pointed out that the lectures would help to correct the "pinko" reputation Berkeley had in the outside world; the other summed up his argument with a question: "How can we expect people to vote against the welfare state if they don't understand communism?"

Dr. Ephraim Kahn, president of the Emerson School Parent-Teachers Association, protested the motives of the sponsors, and the lack of educational qualifications of two of the six scheduled lecturers who, he said, were professionals who made a living attacking communism from lecture platforms.

Elaborate plans for kicking off the lecture series with bands, invocations, and color guards included invitations to the Boy Scouts, Girl Scouts, Campfire Girls, and children and nuns from two Catholic schools, whose presence was intended to lend a proper patriotic and religious air to the opening ceremonies. Although the PTA could not bring about a change in the panel of speakers, its protests moderated the circus atmosphere that had been planned, and the presence of an American Legion color guard at the first lecture was not repeated at subsequent meetings. The presence of 600 observers from the PTA, and a third of the Berkeley police force, constituted another restraint.

Five of the six speakers on the Berkeley program also appeared on a similar program at West Contra Costa Junior College. On this occasion, Drummond J. McCunn, Superintendent of the Contra Costa Junior College District, commended the John Birch Society for its exposure of communism. Scheduled to speak to the California Association of School Superintendents on the subject of teaching about communism, Mr. McCunn told a press conference that many textbooks were "slanted" toward socialism, and that others washed out our history by failing to mention the utterances of John Paul Jones and Nathan Hale. Asked to name "slanted" textbooks, he reportedly declined by saying, "I have no documentation before me." Asked to give one instance of Communist influence on textbooks or schools, he answered, according to press reports: "I don't have it at my finger tips today." He then went on to say that music was a particularly dangerous area in school curricula, and when a reporter from Los Angeles asked for his opinion of the song, *Swing the Shining Sickle,* he drew a connection between the words of the song and the Communist flag. Informed that the song had been written in 1897 to celebrate the American harvest at Thanksgiving, he is said to have laughed off the observation by commenting, "You've tripped me up. Maybe I've been brainwashed against the song."

The movements in California and the South are matched in vigor and flavor by Survival Over Communism, an Indiana organization devoted to promotion of youth clubs and study groups. A published manual on how to organize an SOC club includes a sample constitution, sample letters to Congressmen and courses of study of varying length. A full list of instructional materials available for purchase includes tape-recorded lectures as well as films, pamphlets and books.

Much of the listed material can be purchased only from the Christian Anti-Communism Crusade, an organization that helped to found SOC [see "The Cold War Sells Razors," by Phil Kerby, *The Nation,* November

4, 1961]. A textbook for high school students, *You Can Trust the Communists,* by Fred Schwarz, head of the Christian Anti-Communist Crusade, is SOC's recommended bible. SOC claims that a copy of this book is being sent to every high school in the nation. Glenn Martin, chairman of the Social Studies Department of Jackson Central High School, Arcadia, Indiana, has been praised by SOC for his course on communism in which the Schwarz book is used as a text.

Schwarz has been described by Tristram Coffin as an Australian physician, neither American nor economist nor theologian, who uses a quasi-religious, evangelical approach to teaching Americanism in his seminars on communism. According to an observer from *The Christian Science Monitor,* Schwarz attacked in a single seminar, "liberals, modernists, John Dewey, Kirtley Mather, Harvard students, high school students, the San Francisco Chamber of Commerce, textbooks, the American Friends Service Committee, pacifists, the book sections of *The New York Times* and *Herald Tribune,* public libraries, beatniks, the National Committee for a Sane Nuclear Policy, and naive ministers." His pet lecture, says Coffin, is "Why Millionaires, College Professors, and Ministers Become Communists."

The various reports from the South, the Midwest and California reveal the ease with which administrators, teachers and board members can lend themselves to political indoctrination of a certain kind if it is offered as a form of anti-communism. A teacher of social studies who used his classroom as a forum for advancing his liberal views would soon find himself without a job, no matter how anti-Communist he asserted his liberalism to be. But he and his administrators, board members and fellow teachers can boldly support and spread extreme right-wing political views. They can even see to it that knowledge of communism is withheld from students if it would create student doubt as to the truth of certain right-wing premises.

What is most needed in the schools is an objective study of comparative political and economic systems, such as was recommended in a recent report of a committee of the American Economics Association. This comparative approach would serve no political party or faction, and would give students an opportunity to understand communism, both as a theory and as an existing system. The premises that right-wingers would have students embrace as divine truths would be treated as issues or ideas to be examined and appraised reflectively. The habit of regarding ideas reflectively best characterizes what most thoughtful citizens mean by Americanism, and this meaning of Americanism cannot be indoctrinated by the methods of fanatical anti-Communists.

A Threat to the Schools?

American public education is susceptible to all forms of social, political, and economic pressures. By virtue of the charge to educate, with public financing, all of the children, the schools become easy targets for all types of criticism. One of the most recent attacks has been by the political force known as the radical right. In the following essay, Maurice Blanken examines radical right criticisms of public education.

Are the schools prime targets of a conspiracy, either left wing or right wing? What educational policies would likely emerge from radical right leaders? How can teachers recognize attempts from extreme groups to influence curriculum, teaching materials, or school structure? How should such attempts be dealt with in the public schools? Is evidence of irrationalism in society the result of inadequate education? What should be the criteria of legitimacy for attacks on the schools? To what extent are the schools caught in the paranoia of society? Can fear be useful as a means for positive learning? Should we teach children to fear conspiracy?

American Education and the Challenge of the Two R's

MAURICE C. BLANKEN

The American public schools, when confronted by their honest critics, have nothing to fear. However our schools are presently beset by a dangerous and insidious irrationalism. It behooves us, teachers and administrators alike, to learn our two new R's—the Radical Right. The prevalence of this new irrationalism within our society is undeniable. The President himself felt called upon to speak out against it last fall (in November, 1961) during a western tour.[1] The power of the Radical Right, particularly in the South and Southwest, is devastating. It has affected elections in the

Reprinted from *Clearing House*, Vol. 37, No. 1, September, 1962, pp. 15–17, by permission of the editor.

[1] See the New York *Times*, November 19, 1961, for the text of President Kennedy's Los Angeles speech. *Time*, December 8, 1961, and *Newsweek*, December 4, 1961, carried feature articles, and *Life*, December 1, 1961, gave a full-page editorial on this subject. The reader is also advised to see the *Reporter*, July 20, 1961, and the New York *Times* magazine section for November 26, 1961, carrying an article by Alan Barth.

West and held back integration programs in the South. The cudgel of "communist taint" is so successfully employed that adherence to the U.N., advocacy of fluoridation of drinking water, and membership in the National Association for the Advancement of Colored People have become to many prima facie evidence of un-Americanism.

It is not our intent in this article to reveal completely the social psychology of this movement. It should suffice to say that the Radical Right represents a purely negative approach, a movement without purpose other than to oppose positive programs elsewhere. Its roots rest in ignorance and fear. It is anti-Negro, anti-labor, anti-immigrant, and isolationist. Its favorite targets are social legislation at home and our State Department policies of international cooperation abroad. Our concern centers upon its anti-intellectual, anti-public education attitudes. Here its most absurd contention is that our schools are overrun with liberal teachers and administrators dedicated to the goal of preparing our youth for welfare statism. (The favorite claim of the Radical Right illogicality is that liberalism is socialism, communism is liberalism, and therefore socialism is communism.) When we couple such arguments with the anti-tax and anti-progressive education attitudes of the movement, we can see elements sufficiently dangerous to destroy public education as we now know it.

The irrational criticism of public education is not new. Attacks go back to the early 30's with Easley's National Civic Federation, Elizabeth Dilling's *Red Network*, and the special Hearst series on education in 1936. The Hearst articles were based on half-truths, slipshod assertions, and sweeping generalizations. There has been a revival of this technique as seen, for example, in the *Saturday Evening Post* article of November 11, 1961.

However such essays as this and the Admiral Rickover thesis are moderate in comparison to charges against education made by the Radical Right. Moreover, the Radical Right is better organized, is more heavily financed, and has a fanatical determination to effect its program of destruction. A tie-up between the military, political, industrial, business, and conservative religious leadership makes the movement extremely powerful. It has quasi-government support in such items as publications of the House Un-American Activities Committee, Senate Internal Security Subcommittee, and in the film "Operations Abolition," disseminated by military indoctrination programs that flourished before the General Walker controversy.

During the McCarthy period, irresponsible charges of "communism" were leveled against the teaching profession. Unfortunate as this may have been to individuals, these charges appeared to have only limited political consequences at that time. However, education's defense of itself proved to be too feeble to convince the public fully that McCarthyist insinuations concerning public education were completely false. Consequently, the suspicion of disloyalty on the part of the teacher and the administrator remained dormant. Today the Radical Right is capitalizing upon the mood of the 50's. The charges it now makes and solutions it advocates are more violent than ever. Both are grounded in an irrationalism that makes them almost impossible to counter. Public education is to a large measure on the defensive and can ignore its present plight only with peril.

It becomes difficult to assay the strength of the Radical Right. Their leaders claim fantastic numbers. Welch, of the Birch Society, spoke of 100,000 and a goal of a million by 1962.[2] [Still listed in *News Dictionary* 1965 as 100,000.] The strength of the movement lies in the ability of its leadership to magnify the latent frustrations and discontents of many within society. The stalemate of the Cold War which prohibits a speedy and final solution to our international tensions, the growth of numbers and complexity that makes us yearn for more simple mores and values, our fears of a frightening unknown future, make many within our society look backward rather than ahead. The Radical Right would have us return to the ideal confident years of Teddy Roosevelt. This is the comfortable appeal of the Radical Right to bewildered, uncertain, immobilized Americans. It is also recognizable that this nostalgia contains the roots of a native fascism. It would be most profitable for teachers to make comparisons of present American frustrations with those within the Weimar Republic that ushered in the Nazi regime. Perhaps this explains the fascination found over Shirer's *The Third Reich.*

Any society demands explanations for its present state of affairs. An understanding of the pressures of population, technology, and ideologies is too difficult, too involved for the land of the "swift and total solution." A "scapegoat" mentality develops. One of the "sinners" becomes public education, for it becomes obvious that the schools have failed in their responsibility of preparing the citizenry of the future. It was the "liberal notions" of educators that failed to keep pure our good old-fashioned "Americanism." Flirtation with such nonsense as "progressive education" did it all. Children who could no longer spell, write, count, or read, still were indoctrinated with "creeping socialism." John Dewey and our teacher's colleges are the "arch culprits" in this conspiracy to sap the moral fiber of our youth.

Responsible to public opinions, as it must be in our democratic society, the public school is extremely vulnerable. It has little defense against popular opposition, regardless of how misinformed or misled the opposition may happen to be. While most reject its political extremism, the Radical Right's dubious criticism of public education finds warm soil within con-

---

[2] A Los Angeles rally held by Fred Schwarz's Christian Anti-Communism Crusade saw a three-day gathering of over 12,000 persons, with four million TV onlookers. Those present pledged $200,000 to the crusade! Millions are involved in financing the Radical Right with such men as A. P. Sloan of General Motors and H. L. Hunt of Texas oil millions serving as generous supporters. Birch Society dues run from $18 per man to $12 per woman, which gives it an income close to a million, the expenditure of which is not made accountable to the membership. [According to John Rousselot, publicity director of the 1965 *News Dictionary,* the budget is now $3–4 million.]

servative America. Consequently public education has no alternative but to engage in a struggle against the Radical Right. The school's side of the story must be made known. It must educate, teach, and explain the why, wherefore, and consequences of a Radical Right victory over the freedom to teach in our public schools.

There is the possibility that this essay represents an inaccurate analysis of the threat of the Radical Right. Still if the public schools do not enter the fray to defend themselves, they are ignoring a grave responsibility. Our public schools are involved in the very heart of the democratic process. They cannot "sit this one out."

The Value of
Interdisciplinary Study

A continuing social issue reflected in the schools is the determination of what should be taught. The last two selections treated this issue by focusing on subject and critic. The following article by Henry Winthrop suggests that a revision in what is taught must take account of the ever-widening scope of knowledge. Because the quest for knowledge in our complex society is disclosing new interdisciplinary fields, the schools will need to re-examine the curriculum to determine which of the traditional subjects and which of the new disciplines should constitute the curriculum of the future.

If there is a need in society for intellectual synthesis, how can the schools provide for it? Should the schools give up the study of history, English, art, and science in favor of zetetics, cybernetics, and systems theory? Which reflect and which mold society?

Contemporary Intellectual Ferment and the Curriculum of the Future

HENRY WINTHROP

THE RISE OF THE INTERDISCIPLINARY APPROACH

Just as it has been said that trade follows the flag, so it may justly be said that education follows the needs of society. We live in a world which is growing increasingly complex socially and education must be geared to deal with that complexity in many ways. Three of these ways are of major importance. First, politically and socially education must be prepared to deal directly with the task of acquainting the citizen with the range of information and the depth of skill which modern citizenship in a complex society demands. This is essential if the voter is to participate meaningfully in the democratic process. Education must also be prepared to *measure the degree* to which such readiness exists in the average voter, by types of achievement tests which do not even exist at present.

The second major task which must be faced by professional educators who take their curricular responsibilities seriously, is to reorganize the curriculum of higher education so as to reflect the new *interdisciplinary* emphases which are changing the face of the contemporary world. The newer disciplines of which I speak, whose protagonists have been sensitive to the emergent needs of our time, are by now past the stage of being lusty infants. They include cybernetics, automation in all its forms, whether in industry or education, operations research, general systems theory, bionics, linear programming, input-output analysis, information theory and decision theory, data-processing and computer technologies, administration and organization theory, human engineering and human factors analysis, space age technologies and the rich plenum of interdisciplinary approaches which has been called *Zetetics*.[1] If this seems a long list I want to assure the reader that it represents only a very few of the new and emerging interdisciplinary areas which are bound to occupy an increasing place in the curriculum of higher education in the future. Elsewhere I have dealt with the two problems just mentioned, and I believe it is quite important that both secondary and higher education deal with these seriously. The

Reprinted from *The Social Studies*, Vol. 46, No. 3, March, 1965, pp. 83–88, by permission of the editor.
[1] Joseph T. Tykociner, *Research as a Science—Zetetics*, Electrical Engineering Research Laboratory of the University of Illinois, 1959.

major emphasis, however, will have to occur within the precincts of higher education itself.

Space forbids any extended discussion of these new interdisciplinary fields. However, I should like to characterize a few of them here, allowing the interested reader to fall back upon a library and his own intellectual resources, in trying to familiarize himself with the objectives and content of each of these.

The term *cybernetics* has several meanings but one of the widest of these has to do with studies of all sorts which compare the performance of the nervous systems of man and animals to the functions of control and communication in computers, in information-handling machines and in physical analogues and models of complex processes and structures which simulate nervous systems and which therefore greatly increase our understanding of them. Norbert Wiener's[2] popular discussion of the subject constitutes a good introduction to it. Cybernetic theory has been chiefly applied to the study of the functioning of the nervous system, but it has also contributed to advances in biomedical science and diagnosis through the development, for example, of simulacra of the eye and the circulatory system and through machines for the logical diagnosis of ailments. Cybernetics has also been employed in the construction of models which simulate large social systems, complex economic systems and complete business firms. It has even been employed for the simulation of international relations and diplomacy. Its future applications to all areas of learning seem to be unlimited. Its impact on curricular change, with which we are more immediately concerned, can already be noted from new types of interdisciplinary courses in cybernetics which have been instituted in many academic institutions throughout the country. Some of these are being given in a rather semi-popular vein, with no technical background required. The New School For Social Research in New York City, for instance, is one of the institutions which is experimenting with a semi-popular version of this new interdisciplinary field. A good deal of exploratory ferment is occurring in this direction and educators and their student clientele can look forward to some rather significant developments along this interdisciplinary line—developments which cannot escape being translated into curricular innovations in the near future.

Bionics, which in some senses represents a special phase of cybernetics, is concerned with efforts on the part of scientists to use biological systems as models for machines. This generally leads to attempts to describe the functions of various organisms mathematically and a subsequent effort to produce a machine which will exhibit the behavior described by these equations. In short, the aim of bionics is to produce machines which can adjust themselves and adapt to unforeseen conditions, just as biological

[2] Norbert Wiener, *The Human Use of Human Beings. Cybernetics and Society,* Doubleday, New York, 1956.

systems do. Many scientists today who are working in the new interdisciplinary area of bionics, hope that within a decade we will have machines which read, report, hear and understand. We are listing two references to this new field, further on in this article, and the interested reader can therefore pursue the matter further, if he so desires. What the discoveries and the mathematical methods of bionics will do in transforming the traditional curricula of higher education, however, staggers the imagination.

General Systems Theory, although closely related to the preceding two interdisciplinary areas, places the focus of its attention upon the formulation, derivation and development of those principles, theories and relationships which are valid *for all sorts of systems*. It is particularly interested in self-regulating systems. Workers in this interdisciplinary area hope to understand phenomena which are now the concern of specialties within the natural, social, behavioral and management sciences, by finding mathematical models and mathematical system-descriptions, which will be applicable to phenomena in all these areas. In effect, then, the interdisciplinary bridge-building which, it is hoped, will be accomplished by general systems theory, will be largely, though not wholly, mathematical in nature. The end result, of course, will be to provide perspectives, albeit from a mathematical viewpoint, which will indicate that the understanding which is to be achieved, of processes and relationships within traditional subject-matter areas ordinarily regarded as disparate, will be precisely identical in all of them. The yearbooks of the Society For General Systems Theory constitute the best source material for the reader. Here again the gains to be made from revamping the curriculum so as to reflect this discovery, economize effort and cost, and gain latitude in the educational process, are indeed impressive.

Operations research, an excellent account of which has been given by Churchman and others,[3] may be defined in several ways. One definition would explain it as the scientific study of complex organizations aimed at identifying problems and giving decisionmakers a quantitative basis for decisions that will increase effectiveness in achieving objectives. Another definition would lay a somewhat larger stress on method and define operations research as the application of scientific methods, techniques and tools to problems involving the operations of a system, so as to provide those in control of the system with the optimum solutions to their problems. Operations research is interdisciplinary both in *method* and *content*. Although much wider than either linear programming alone or input-output analysis alone, both of these can, in a certain practical sense, be regarded as interdisciplinary approaches within the domain of operations research. The author has had professional experience in these latter two areas and therefore feels justified in stressing the degree to which they can be re-

[3] C. West Churchman *et al.*, *Introduction To Operations Research,* John Wiley & Sons, Inc., New York, 1957.

garded as a new interdisciplinary science of *scheduling*, using the term "scheduling" with the widest possible latitude and using it to apply to any context to which some sort of a scheduling structure applies.

Once again, from the educator's standpoint, the important thing to emphasize is the large variety of human and social phenomena, of both theoretical and practical interest, to which the same types of operational research methods are applicable. From an educational standpoint these identities lend themselves to intellectual integration. Because they do, by the same token, they make possible forms of curricular revision which will be revolutionary in nature. These can provide so much increased comprehension and saving of time in the educational process, that to neglect the task of undertaking such curricular revision in the future would be—if I may use a metaphor which, I hope, is neither unreasonable nor exaggerated—like rejecting educational salvation on a silver platter.

The basic reason which has prompted the rise of interdisciplinary effort in our time is the fact that our major problems, whether in the natural, social or management sciences, are becoming so complex, that they require a special type of treatment. They require this special treatment in two senses. In one sense, it was necessary that we recognize that no problem comes to us labeled as strictly economic, strictly sociological, strictly biological·or medical, strictly legal, etc. There are, in fact, few purely disciplinary problems any more, where by the phrase "purely disciplinary," we refer to problems whose complete solution can be effected solely within the framework of a traditional specialty. The second sense I have in mind is this. A serious attack on major problems, particularly in the social sciences and the life sciences, involves the convergence of information and analytic skills from many of the traditional disciplines. This converging information and these supplementary skills have to be woven together into systematic and unified attacks upon the problems to which they are so distinctly relevant. The full force and truth of this point can be gathered from a reading, for instance, of the contents of the yearbooks of the Society for General Systems Research, published by the Mental Health Research Institute of Ann Arbor; from the transactions of the various conferences which have been held on cybernetics under the auspices of the Josiah Macy, Jr. Foundation; from the first and second symposia on bionics;[4,5] from the papers published in *Operations Research*, the journal of the Operations Research Society of America; or from two such random contributions to welfare economics and problems of value as are represented by the

[4] Bionics Symposium, *Living Prototypes—The Key to New Technology*, WADD Technical Report 60–600; Dayton, Ohio: Directorate of Advanced Systems of Technology, Wright Air Development Division, Air Research and Development Command, United States Air Force, Wright-Patterson Air Force Base, December, 1960.

[5] Eugene E. Bernard and Morley R. Kare, *Biological Prototypes and Synthetic Systems*, Vol. 1. Proceedings of the Second Annual Bionics Symposium, Plenum Press, New York, 1962.

distinguished volumes of Rothenberg[6] and Churchman.[7] It is because these newer interdisciplinary methods, perspectives, theories and results are so pertinent to the problems which we shall all have to face as citizens in the world of tomorrow, that the second major task to which I have alluded becomes a matter of central concern for curricular revision in higher education.

The third major task for higher education revolves around the recognition that this intellectual ferment which I have been describing requires a new type of institution for higher education; namely, The Institute of Intellectual Synthesis, whose functions will be manifold. Let me mention a few of these functions here. First, such an institute will have to encourage interdisciplinary scholars to tackle problems which are either currently neglected because they are missed when seen from the vantage point of the specialist or because they are bound to be neglected when they cannot be fitted into the Procrustean beds of traditional subject-matter. Second, such institutes can assist in the task of acquainting curriculum-builders in higher education with a rough orientation to the substantive nature of the newer interdisciplinary fields, so that curriculum-builders may be able to do a creditable job in the revision of both undergraduate and graduate programs—a revision which is today a crying and still much neglected need. These needed orientations may, of course, be established by many methods, but the 6-8 week workshop has in recent years become a starting point along these lines. Third, the members of such institutes will be in an excellent position to develop new types of methodology appropriate to the peculiar nature of many of our interdisciplinary problems—problems which require the tying together of academic loose ends by approaches which would often be wholly irrelevant to traditional subject fields. Finally, members of such institutes can help to build bridges between the traditional disciplines, so that specialists in our complex society, alienated from one another by the language barriers of the technical terminologies of their crafts, can truly once again become a company of scholars without the drastic secession from the total community, recently recommended by Paul Goodman.[8]

THE SPECIAL FUNCTIONS OF AN INSTITUTE OF INTELLECTUAL SYNTHESIS

A number of scholars in our time have sounded the alarm over the need to integrate intellectually the fruits of proliferating specialization. Kahler,

[6] Jerome Rothenberg, *The Measurement of Social Welfare*, Prentice-Hall, Englewood Cliffs, N.J., 1961.

[7] C. West Churchman, *Prediction and Optimal Decision. Philosophical Issues of A Science of Values*, Prentice-Hall, Englewood Cliffs, N.J., 1961.

[8] Paul Goodman, *The Community of Scholars*, Random House, New York, 1962.

Bertalanffy, Meier, Reiser, and the members of the Behavioral Science Council, to name but a few, regard such intellectual integration as one of the major tasks of modern education. Figures such as these may be voices crying in the educational wilderness but they are bound to make their impact within the next decade. The educational parochialism of our time is becoming increasingly worthless. The tendency to try to settle complex issues and attack major problems, via the thinking habits of the humanities and the law, is being increasingly called into question. Both C. P. Snow[9] and George Lundberg[10] have stressed the anachronistic aspects of the language and thinking habits of a classical education, and the unfitness, as well as the incompleteness, of such an education for trying to deal seriously with the problems of a complex society such as ours. Without some acquaintance with the presuppositions, methods and findings of modern science, without some familiarity with mathematical method, functional thinking and some understanding of the distinction between the *representative* language of science, mathematics and logic, on the one hand, and the *expressive* function of literature and the arts, on the other, only cultural blindness can result. Without these emphases, the college-educated citizen of tomorrow will be an intellectual alien in a world whose basic social and cultural landscape is due largely to the impact of science, technology and invention. It is in such institutes that the deepest values and vision of both the humanities and the sciences, can be truly merged. The value of Institutes of Intellectual Synthesis lies precisely in the degree to which they can make these matters part of the intellectual and spiritual warp and woof of the college-bred citizen, through their ability to collate the efforts of scholarship, research and education, and restore significance once again to the task of seeing life steadily and seeing it whole.

It would be of value, I believe, to mention ten separate tasks, out of a much larger possible number, which could be performed by an Institute of Intellectual Synthesis—tasks whose values are beyond question. I should therefore like to mention these tasks at this point, without elaborating upon them. Such institutes might:

1. Examine interdisciplinary journals for the types of interdisciplinary problems being discussed therein and seek to develop interdisciplinary research teams to work on some of these problems.

2. Study the new methodologies of various interdisciplinary fields, such as *general systems theory*, and organize a classification and substantive treatment of the types of problems which are being tackled by these methods. Members of such institutes might begin an attack on the as yet neglected problems in these fields and try to develop a roster of such neglected problems.

3. Develop a roster of pressing problems which require an interdisci-

---

[9] C. P. Snow, *The Two Cultures and the Scientific Revolution,* Cambridge University Press, New York, 1959.
[10] George A. Lundberg, *Can Science Save Us?* Longmans, Green, New York, 1961.

plinary approach and try to build new courses and new curricula around properly classified aggregates of such problems.

4. Develop a manual or syllabus of *new specialties* which are a result of interdisciplinary work—specialties like that of economic sociology, as developed by Fourastie, and try to develop some courses around these new areas in order to make them a proper part of higher education.

5. Cooperate with the work of The Behavioral Science Council and inaugurate research which will parallel the objectives of this council. In addition the same *type of objective* as that with which The Behavioral Science Council is concerned, might be pursued by such institutes, but for problems which are not economic, social or political. Such institutes might also concern themselves with all these types of problems on other than national levels.

6. Take responsibility for the publication of edited studies (or studies done locally) which deal with interdisciplinary attacks on important scientific and social problems.

7. Take responsibility for the publication of *plans and remedies* drawn up for national or local problems which are based either on local studies or studies done elsewhere. The emphasis here is clearly on *solutions* over and above the task of research and exploration.

8. Develop subsidiary Institutes of Planning which specialize in interdisciplinary planning for all levels of our national life, based upon familiarity with the problems on these levels.

9. Try to extend the work and research on Zetetics, so ably started by Tykociner.

10. Take responsibility for the formation of one or more journals devoted to interdisciplinary studies. They might also spell out in these journals, as a continuing project, the nature and the meaning of the phrase "interdisciplinary studies," and act as centers for the distribution of such journals, so as to widen public consciousness among the educated concerning the nature and importance of interdisciplinary knowledge, research, planning and education.

It is my own firm conviction that one of the next great developments in higher education will be the Institute of Intellectual Synthesis. It seems to be in the cards not only because of the pressing need to provide some sort of unity for the intellectual ferment of our time but also because of the fact that a renovated philosophy of education has to encourage all efforts to redress the balance against the continuous intellectual and educational fragmentation of our age. Those universities over the next decade or two, which assume the pioneering tasks in this direction will, it seems to me, be assured of their place in the educational sun. The spirit in which such an enterprise should be undertaken can best be conveyed in Lincoln's immortal words "new times demand new measures and new men."

Of one thing we can be sure. Curricular change will have to move in the direction of restoring educational wholeness and discouraging the educa-

tion of fractional men. Lest I be misunderstood here, let me say that I
would fight to the death, to paraphrase Voltaire, for the right of the average person to receive vocational training, for whatever that training is
worth in a world in which automation is making both skilled and unskilled
callings obsolescent. I would likewise fight to the death for the right of the
better student in academia to pursue the *professional* specialization which
he so often desires. Finally, I would be prepared to fight for the right, and
even more the necessity, of the academic specialist to teach his subject,
pursue research, and enlarge the horizons of every one of us with respect
to the social importance, intellectual fascination and the as yet unsolved
problems inherent in his subject matter. In the sense that it is the specialist
who piles Pelion on Ossa and slowly accumulates the basic knowledge
without which men could form no sense of community, intellectual adven-
ture or self-transcendence, the specialist is the salt of the earth, the *sine
qua non* of man's forward movement, culturally and intellectually speaking.

However, from time immemorial education has meant what the Greek
concept of *paideia* was intended to convey; namely, the process of bringing to fruition *all the elements in man,* all his rich potentialities, talents and
aptitudes, in all the dimensions along which man is able to move—the
intellectual, the spiritual or value-seeking dimension, and the social, aesthetic and religious dimensions. Within the framework of the Greek concept of *paideia,* man has sought to enlarge all his horizons of awareness
and to pour extended meaning into life. It is not an accident that certain
astute writers, like Teilhard de Chardin and Childe have emphasized man's
educational self-responsibility. This educational self-responsibility must in
part be fulfilled by the type of intellectual fare we offer the student. In
academic circles the *menu* is called the curriculum and that curriculum will
have to be increasingly interdisciplinary if it seeks to come to terms with
the environment, to borrow a phrase from psychoanalysis. The world "from
here to eternity" is not the world which formed the background of consciousness of our forbears. It is a world in which hard culture, that is,
science, technology, invention and mathematics, is changing the face of the
globe and the ground rules for social intercourse and personal development. Fortunately, it is also a world in which soft culture—the arts and the
humanities, philosophy and the quest for value, our designs for living and
what may be called the unbought graces of life—are even more important.
No education is worth a tinker's damn, which fails to operate in the liberal
tradition of (1) ministering to the whole man and (2) making hard culture
serve soft culture—not the other way around.

In this process the interdisciplinary curriculum of the future will be extremely important as well as indispensable. It will be tomorrow's educational answer to the intellectual ferment of today. For the reasons I have
mentioned above, I have never been able to understand the specialist's

resistance to the interdisciplinary approach. This resistance seems to be one of the comic-opera aspects of modern education. In contemporary educational thinking and philosophy, our teachers, scholars and scientists will wholeheartedly and with complete sincerity of conviction, support the wholeness and variety of outlook involved in liberal and general education, and then go right ahead, after they have acquired their own Ph.D's, and retreat intellectually into the shells of their own specialties. There they will strive to learn more and more about less and less. It seems that wholeness of vision and breadth of culture are good intellectual medicine for the undergraduate, but quite toxic for the Ph.D. with tunnel vision. But all this too shall pass away. The restoration of unity in being, outlook and purpose, which is the educational birthright of all of us, cannot be delayed much longer. In the process of achieving this restoration, I feel certain that the curricular developments of the immediate future will play a major role. When, and only when, *interdisciplinary* content is added to the professional core of our present curricula, shall we be able to say that we are turning out students and citizens who are prepared to see life steadily and see it whole.

The New Status of Religion

The topic of religion is a social issue in virtually every society. In a society in which there are legal barriers to the union of church and state, religion becomes a key social issue. Out of the tradition of a theocratic society, which characterized most of the American colonies, came the first amendment to the U.S. Constitution which prohibited the establishment of any state religion in America. This fine line of separation of church and state has had an impact upon society and education since its inception. The questions of federal aid to church-affiliated schools and Bible reading and prayer recitation in public schools are examples of current social problems regarding religion and education.

Will Herberg, in the following reading, stresses his concern for the altered role of religion and the new sense of religiousness in twentieth-century American culture. Are the village atheists an artifact of the past? Many critics of education, and more particularly of the Supreme Court cases which eliminated prayer and Bible reading from public schools, have decried the schools as Godless. What meaning does this have in light of Herberg's analysis of religion? Can the secular and the sectarian coexist without turmoil?

Protestant, Catholic, Jew

WILL HERBERG

The new status of religion as a basic form of American "belonging," along with other factors tending in the same direction, has led to the virtual disappearance of anti-religious prejudice, once by no means uncommon in our national life. The old-time "village atheist" is a thing of the past, a folk curiosity like the town crier; Clarence Darrow, the last of the "village atheists" on a national scale, has left no successors. The present generation can hardly understand the vast excitement stirred up in their day by the "atheists" and "iconoclasts" who vied for public attention less than half a century ago, or imagine the brash militancy of the "rationalist" movements and publications now almost all extinct. Religion has become part of the ethos of American life to such a degree that overt anti-religion is all but inconceivable.

The same factors that have led to the virtual disappearance of overt anti-religion have also made for a new openness to religion and what religion might have to say about the urgent problems of life and thought. In many ways the contemporary mind is more ready to listen to the word of faith than Americans have been for decades.

Yet it is only too evident that the religiousness characteristic of America today is very often a religiousness without religion, a religiousness with almost any kind of content or none, a way of sociability or "belonging" rather than a way of reorienting life to God. It is thus frequently a religiousness without serious commitment, without real inner conviction, without genuine existential decision. What should reach down to the core of existence, shattering and renewing, merely skims the surface of life, and yet succeeds in generating the sincere feeling of being religious. Religion thus becomes a kind of protection the self throws up against the radical demand of faith.

Where the other-directed adjustment of peer-group conformity operates, the discrepancy becomes even more obvious. The other-directed man or woman is eminently religious in the sense of being religiously identified and affiliated, since being religious and joining a church or synagogue is, under contemporary American conditions, a fundamental way of "adjusting" or "belonging." But what can the other-directed man or woman make of the prophets and the prophetic faith of the Bible, in which the religion

From *Protestant, Catholic, Jew,* by Will Herberg, pp. 259–61, 265–69. © 1955, 1960 by Will Herberg. Reprinted by permission of Doubleday & Company, Inc.

of the church he joins is at least officially grounded? The very notion of being "singled out," of standing "over against" the world, is deeply repugnant to one for whom well-being means conformity and adjustment. Religion is valued as conferring a sense of sociability and "belonging," a sense of being really and truly *of* the world and society, a sense of reassurance; how can the other-directed man then help but feel acutely uncomfortable with a kind of religion—for that is what biblical faith is—which is a declaration of permanent resistance to the heteronomous claims of society, community, culture, and cult? . . .

Religion is taken very seriously in present-day America, in a way that would have amazed and chagrined the "advanced" thinkers of half a century ago, who were so sure that the ancient superstition was bound to disappear very shortly in the face of the steady advance of science and reason. Religion has not disappeared; it is probably more pervasive today, and in many ways more influential, than it has been for generations. The only question is: What kind of religion is it? What is its content? What is it that Americans *believe in* when they are religious?

"The 'unknown God' of Americans seems to be faith itself."[1] What Americans believe in when they are religious is, as we have already had occasion to see,[2] religion itself. Of course, religious Americans speak of God and Christ, but what they seem to regard as really redemptive is primarily religion, the "positive" attitude of *believing*. It is this faith in faith, this religion that makes religion its own object, that is the outstanding characteristic of contemporary American religiosity. Daniel Poling's formula: "I began saying in the morning two words, 'I believe'—those two words *with nothing added* . . ."[3] (emphasis not in original) may be taken as the classic expression of this aspect of American faith.

On the social level, this faith in religion involves the conviction, quite universal among Americans today, that every decent and virtuous nation is religious, that religion is the true basis of national existence and therefore presumably the one sure resource for the solution of all national problems. On the level of personal life, the American faith in religion implies not only that every right-minded citizen is religious, but also that religion (or faith) is a most efficacious device for getting what one wants in life. "Jesus," the Rev. Irving E. Howard assures us, "recommended faith as a technique for getting results. . . . Jesus recommended faith as a way to heal the body and to remove any of the practical problems that loom up as mountains in a man's path."[4]

As one surveys the contemporary scene, it appears that the "results" Americans want to get out of faith are primarily "peace of mind," happi-

---

[1] Reinhold Niebuhr, "Religiosity and the Christian Faith," *Christianity and Crisis,* Vol. 14, No. 24, January 24, 1955.
[2] *Ibid.*, Chap. 5, pp. 84–85.
[3] Daniel A. Poling, "A Running Start for Every Day," *Parade: The Sunday Picture Magazine,* September 19, 1954.
[4] Irving E. Howard, "Random Reflections," *Christian Economics,* March 8, 1955.

ness, and success in worldly achievement. Religion is valued too as a means of cultural enrichment.

Prosperity, success, and advancement in business are the obvious ends for which religion, or rather the religious attitude of "believing," is held to be useful. There is ordinarily no criticism of the ends themselves in terms of the ultimate loyalties of a God-centered faith, nor is there much concern about what the religion or the faith is all about, since it is not the content of the belief but the attitude of believing that is felt to be operative.

Almost as much as worldly success, religion is expected to produce a kind of spiritual euphoria, the comfortable feeling that one is all right with God. Roy Eckardt calls this the cult of "divine-human chumminess" in which God is envisioned as the "Man Upstairs," a "Friendly Neighbor," Who is always ready to give you the pat on the back you need when you happen to feel blue. "Fellowship with the Lord is, so to say, an extra emotional jag that keeps [us] happy. The 'gospel' makes [us] 'feel real good.'"[5] Again, all sense of the ambiguity and precariousness of human life, all sense of awe before the divine majesty, all sense of judgment before the divine holiness, is shut out; God is, in Jane Russell's inimitable phrase, a "livin' Doll." What relation has this kind of god to the biblical God Who confronts sinful man as an enemy before He comes out to meet repentant man as a Savior? Is this He of Whom we are told, "It is a fearful thing to fall into the hands of the living God" (Heb. 10.31)? The measure of how far contemporary American religiosity falls short of the authentic tradition of Jewish-Christian faith is to be found in the chasm that separates Jane Russell's "livin' Doll" from the living God of Scripture.

The cultural enrichment that is looked for in religion varies greatly with the community, the denomination, and the outlook and status of the church members. Liturgy is valued as aesthetically and emotionally "rewarding," sermons are praised as "interesting" and "enjoyable," discussions of the world relations of the church are welcomed as "educational," even theology is approved of as "thought provoking." On another level, the "old-time religion" is cherished by certain segments of the population because it so obviously enriches their cultural life.

But, in the last analysis, it is "peace of mind" that most Americans expect of religion. "Peace of mind" is today easily the most popular gospel that goes under the name of religion; in one way or another it invades and permeates all other forms of contemporary religiosity. It works in well with the drift toward other-direction characteristics of large sections of American society, since both see in adjustment the supreme good in life. What is desired, and what is promised, is the conquest of insecurity and anxiety, the overcoming of inner conflict, the shedding of guilt and fear, the translation of the self to the painless paradise of "normality" and "adjustment"!

[5] Roy Eckardt, "The New Look in American Piety," *The Christian Century*, November 17, 1954.

Religion, in short, is a spiritual anodyne designed to allay the pains and vexations of existence.

It is this most popular phase of contemporary American religiosity that has aroused the sharpest criticism in more sophisticated theological circles. The Most Rev. Patrick A. O'Boyle, Catholic archbishop of Washington, has warned that although "at first glance piety seems to be everywhere . . ." many persons appear to be "turning to religion as they would to a benign sedative to soothe their minds and settle their nerves."[6] Liston Pope emphasizes that the approach of the "peace of mind" school is not only "very dubious on psychological grounds," but its "identification [with] the Christian religion . . . is of questionable validity."[7] Roy Eckardt describes it as "religious narcissism," in which "the individual and his psycho-spiritual state occupy the center of the religious stage" and piety is made to "concentrate on its own navel."[8] I have myself spoken of it as a philosophy that would "dehumanize man and reduce his life to the level of sub-human creation which knows neither sin nor guilt."[9] It encourages moral insensitivity and social irresponsibility, and cultivates an almost lascivious preoccupation with self. The church becomes a kind of emotional service station to relieve us of our worries: "Go to church—you'll feel better," "Bring your troubles to church and leave them there" (slogans on subway posters urging church attendance). On every ground, this type of religion is poles apart from authentic Jewish-Christian spirituality which, while it knows of the "peace that passeth understanding" as the gift of God, promotes a "divine discontent"[10] with things as they are and a "passionate thirst for the future,"[11] in which all things will be renewed and restored to their right relation to God.

The burden of this criticism of American religion from the point of view of Jewish-Christian faith is that contemporary religion is so naively, so innocently *man-centered*. Not God, but man—man in his individual and corporate being—is the beginning and end of the spiritual system of much of present-day American religiosity. In this kind of religion there is no sense of transcendence, no sense of the nothingness of man and his works before a holy God; in this kind of religion the values of life, and life itself, are not submitted to Almighty God to judge, to shatter, and to

[6] Address at the forty-first annual meeting of the Association of American Colleges held in Washington, January, 1955, as reported in the *New York Herald Tribune*, January 12, 1955.

[7] Address at the dinner meeting of the broadcasting and film commission of the National Council of Churches, New York City, March 1, 1955 (unpublished). See also Hutchinson, "Have We a 'New' Religion?" *Life*, April 11, 1955, pp. 147–48; Hutchinson calls it the "cult of reassurance."

[8] Eckardt, *op. cit.*

[9] Will Herberg, *Judaism and Modern Man: An Interpretation of Jewish Religion*, Farrar, Straus, and Young, New York, 1951, p. 29.

[10] Warren Weaver, "Peace of Mind," *The Saturday Review*, December 11, 1954.

[11] Ernst Renan is reported to have described the "true Israelite" as a man "torn with discontent and possessed with a passionate thirst for the future."

reconstruct; on the contrary, life, and the values of life, are given an ultimate sanction by being identified with the divine. In this kind of religion
it is not man who serves God, but God who is mobilized and made to
serve man and his purposes—whether these purposes be economic prosperity, free enterprise, social reform, democracy, happiness, security, or
"peace of mind." God is conceived as man's "omnipotent servant,"[12]
faith as a sure-fire device to get what we want. The American is a religious man, and in many cases personally humble and conscientious. But
religion as he understands it is not something that makes for humility or
the uneasy conscience: it is something that reassures him about the essential rightness of everything American, his nation, his culture, and himself; something that validates his goals and his ideals instead of calling
them into question; something that enhances his self-regard instead of
challenging it; something that feeds his self-sufficiency instead of shattering it; something that offers him salvation on easy terms instead of
demanding repentance and a "broken heart." Because it does all these
things, his religion, however sincere and well-meant, is ultimately vitiated
by a strong and pervasive idolatrous element.

Mass Culture and Educational Choice

*Mass culture is an area of social controversy which reaches directly into
the schools since American education is a mass system. The issue at stake
in a discussion of mass culture is whether or not the common man is capable of cultural improvement and whether that improvement is at the
sacrifice of culture itself. The categories used to describe the various levels
of culture are high culture to connote the arts, appreciated and perpetuated by an elite few; mass culture or midcult to represent the common arts;
and folk art to express the simple, homespun endeavors. One position on
mass culture holds that attempting to popularize the arts only demeans
them and high culture suffers. If the artist, the painter, sculptor, novelist,
musician, or other highly creative individual, becomes attracted to mass
production of his works because of the commercialism of mass culture, it
is feared that high culture, which is the lasting culture, will fade to the*

[12] Jules Masserman, "Faith and Delusion in Psychotherapy: The Ur-Defenses of
Man," *The American Journal of Psychiatry*, Vol. 110, No. 5, November, 1953.

*lowest common denominator of the mass artist. Thus, the position con-
tends, mass culture drains high culture.*

*An opposing view holds that common man is capable of gaining appre-
ciations and understandings of art, and that in order to improve the society, mass culture must be expanded. Many scholars have attempted the
popularization of knowledge in the same vein—to assist in the enlightenment of the general populace. The main theme of mass education is consistent with the idea that all citizens need knowledge in order to support
a democracy.*

*These two opposing views on mass culture become apparent upon ex-
amination of the mass media and its critics. No one seems to be happy with
the utilization of the mass media. Highbrow shows don't attract large
enough audiences to attract sponsors; the shows with high viewer ratings
tend to be maudlin, noncreative and anti-intellectual; and the proportion
of time and space spent on cultural enrichment via television, radio, and
newspapers is vastly inferior to the time and space spent on general trivia.
All this is significant because mass culture is disseminated by mass media.*

*The three articles following treat the issue of mass culture by viewing
the mass media and the artists. Can the school system adopt any but a mass
culture belief? How can the schools prepare youth to be discriminating
consumers of cultural life?*

The Mass Media in American Culture

TAHER A. RAZIK

A stranger in an American city need make no more than a five-minute stop
to be easily convinced that American civilization is a mass-media culture
par excellence. If he stays longer, he will soon realize that it is becoming
more, rather than less, so. If the American himself is not conscious of this,
it is not because he has not been so informed, for, along with other phases
of mass production, these media are constantly being "pointed to with
pride" or "viewed with alarm"—both with some reason.

The technical excellence which goes into the construction of the instruments of communication and their continuous improvement are generally
singled out with pride; the content, quality, or design of the message conveyed by the instrument creates the alarm.

The mass media boom now taking place in Western Europe will probably go a long way toward proving that the problems which exist are not

Reprinted from *AV Communication Review*, Vol. 2, No. 4, July–August, 1963, pp.
141–44, by permission of the publisher and the author.

strictly American, but are inherent in the nature of the media. Technological progress allows almost everyone to possess the instruments, and every such improvement puts more instruments into the hands of a greater number of people—people whose interests are supposedly cruder, less trained, simpler, and more childish as the bottom of what we call the socioeconomic barrel is approached.

Countries in which far-reaching censorship is a normal practice (and even some democratic countries in which broadcasting is more or less a government monopoly) can easily subsidize either political propaganda—as in Russia or Cuba—or media presentations considered to be of good quality without paying undue attention to popularity ratings, as the British "Third Program" and its imitators attempt to do. But in parts of the world where the value of a given message (newspaper, film, etc.) is judged entirely on the basis of the number of persons constituting its audience, one is likely to find the general level of the fare mediocre or worse.

In the United States, advertisers who purchase radio-TV time try to outdo each other in the speed, glibness, and effectiveness with which they can present an acceptable image of "the average American."

Often based on the findings of commercial audience research organizations, the average American (male) is generally depicted as a moderately successful man, very extroverted, overflowing with good humor, and extremely naïve—especially in his response to mass media. He lives in a small, but bright, clean, and cheerful frame house in the suburbs, almost indistinguishable from the house next door. He parks, in the driveway, a late-model car whose condition is of considerable concern to him. He is a white-collar worker of some mysterious variety, since he always wears a white shirt and tie and occasionally mutters something about the importance of "getting the 'Blank' contract." He cannot enjoy his breakfast because it coincides with the arrival of the morning newspaper. A few minutes later, on his way to work, he will continue to soak up news, predigested for him by some commentator, over his car radio (cheap transistor sets have permitted the spread of this practice to buses as well) until he arrives at his office. Once at work, he is assumed to be free from the media until he returns home to relax lazily before his TV set in the evening. There may or may not be an evening paper.

While this man is away at the office, his wife supposedly has the time to catch up on the latest in the TV soap opera series, as her electrical push-button machines do the bulk of her washing, cooking, and house-cleaning chores. Over her TV or radio outlet, national manufacturers inform her of the latest improvements in household equipment, and local advertisers tell her where she can get these for "less."

The children of this couple are not as yet interested in soap, washing machines, shaving cream, or golf clubs, but they must eat something relatively harmless for breakfast, and advertisers have learned that most American children visit the supermarkets with their parents. The clown, cartoon, and "little animal" programs, generally televised between 3:30 p.m. and suppertime, have been chosen to attract this group. Children are informed by their cartoon friends that they can procure pictures of them— or masks, stories, and the like—on the back of a certain cereal box. A great deal of advertising is presented directly to the children in this way.

Advertisers seem to be succeeding in spite of the fact that a great deal of fun is made of commercials in general—in some cases, the producer of the program is allowed (perhaps encouraged) to make light of the sponsor's product. In many families commercial interruptions are used by members of the family to leave the room, make telephone calls, empty ashtrays, or prepare food or drinks to be consumed while watching the remainder of the program. Yet advertisers still seem to sell their goods, perhaps because one must buy either *this* or *that* brand or none. One wonders what would happen if all products ceased advertising simultaneously.

It is possible to believe that the American (average or otherwise) has found at least a partially successful psychological defense against this barrage, since he cannot escape it altogether. It is doubtful that his reflexes, his logic, or the nature of his responses have been drastically affected, although he probably loses a great deal of psychic energy in repelling these attacks, energy which might otherwise be used for productive purposes. Advertising can reach nuisance proportions, but there are more dangerous attitudes developed by the mass media.

The free flow of information, commentary, and fantasy available at the flick of a switch creates a pleasant, cozy, seminarcotic atmosphere which rarely enlists the active cooperation of the individual, but instead threatens to make him completely passive. What he reads in the paper or views on television which does not lead to some independent thought or behavior on his part tends to do this, but there is a kind of frustration often created by the mass media, which only superficially resembles this passivity. Any book, for example, which makes a public impression is likely to be seized upon, condensed, advertised, quoted, excerpted, lectured about, and dissected by TV or radio panels, even before the un-average American (who is not necessarily passively disposed toward such matters) has had the opportunity to visit the bookshop. Treated in this fashion, even some extraordinarily worthwhile books are "too soon alive" and "too soon dead," simply because serious reading is not done at breakneck speed. Contrast also the critiques of books, plays, music, etc., which appear in the morning paper, and which are presumably written in a few hours of the previous night with critiques (sometimes of the same book, etc., by the same critic) which, it seems, generally appear in book form and are written at the author's leisure. In the first instance, the book suffers from being cast into a time pattern that is strange to it. The reader suffers, too, and may feel that he has no time to read it; he has seen the movie or has sampled what *Time* has said about it. Whatever the excuse, he probably feels that somehow he and the book he had intended to read do not exist in the same time world. He may have procured the book at the height of all the clamor about it, only to find that it had become a dead issue, untimely or obsolete before he had digested the preface.

Here, passivity is merely relative; the would-be reader is not necessarily more lazy or more lacking in energy than his father or grandfather. What appears to be passivity is often caused by the fact that the speed of the recording and the speed of the transmission of the recording of events have reached or passed the limits of human response.

Devices such as printing presses and automatic binders with their time-collapsing capabilities are to be valued for their positive functions in the service of human life and happiness, but they can help only when they are brought into a range receivable by humans. In this problem of machine speed vs. human speed, the United States still leads the world, but there is nothing specifically American about the situation. Other civilizations will have to face it when their mass media systems reach sufficient numbers and a similar level of efficiency.

There is a response to certain mass-media presentations which better deserves to be called passivity. The passive man allows others to do his thinking and his choosing for him. There may be several degrees of passivity. He may grumble in his own living room about the terrible quality of the programs on television, but not write the station a nasty letter about it. He may be too passive to grumble, or his passivity may be nothing but tolerance carried to an extreme. The trouble with passivity is not that the viewer surrenders himself willingly to be entertained pleasantly for an hour or two by a TV show. The trouble is that after watching television, he does not get out of his easy chair refreshed, relaxed, and energetic enough to resume active participation in the affairs of the world about him. Passivity cultivates passivity, and the passive reader, viewer, or listener tends to carry the trait with him, even in the face of danger to himself, his family, or his country or in the presence of opportunities whose benefits he will miss because of it.

What can those who manage the mass media do about passivity except help to foster it and exploit it? They might let the audience suggest some of the answers. They might be content to give the facts as they are known and let the viewer make the interpretations. They might try to be subtle enough to create a little intellectual challenge, and they might look for new forms of presentation and employ them without apology. They might assume that the people who constitute the audience are their intellectual equals—at least long enough to see what happens.

A very serious and often justified charge leveled at the mass media, and at television in particular, is that they have by their contents adversely affected the morals and tastes of the people. They have been accused of putting a halo around sin and crime and of presenting poor models of conduct to young and old alike. Those responsible for the accused media can always answer that they are simply being realistic; that they are attempting only to give a true and accurate account of a state of affairs which they have found existing in the society. It is difficult to prove they are wrong, but it is possible to tell them that if they can improve the state of affairs in the society, they have the right and the responsibility to do so.

The mass media have also defended themselves on the basis that they give the people what they want—that if they did not do this, they would have no audience. The remark made by Gilbert Seldes when he spoke at the Ohio State University's Conference on the Humanities in 1961 seems to dispose of this plea rather adequately: "Audiences," he said, "do not exist per se. They have to be created."

The mass media, one would like to believe, have been and can always be a boon to American society. The leveling off is better than the absence of knowledge, and the level itself can be brought up by the proper use of the mass media in education.

Mass Culture and the Creative Artist
Some Personal Notes

JAMES BALDWIN

Someone once said to me that the people in general cannot bear very much reality. He meant by this that they prefer fantasy to a truthful re-creation of their experience. The Italians, for example, during the time that De Sica and Rossellini were revitalizing the Italian cinema industry, showed a marked preference for Rita Hayworth vehicles; the world in which she moved across the screen was like a fairy tale, whereas the world De Sica was describing was one with which they were only too familiar. (And it can be suggested perhaps that the Americans who stood in line for *Shoe Shine* and *Open City* were also responding to images which they found exotic, to a reality by which they were not threatened. What passes for the appreciation of serious effort in this country is very often nothing more than an inability to take anything very seriously.)

Now, of course the people cannot bear very much reality, if by this one means their ability to respond to high intellectual or artistic endeavor. I have never in the least understood why they should be expected to. There is a division of labor in the world—as I see it—and the people have quite enough reality to bear, simply getting through their lives, raising their children, dealing with the eternal conundrums of birth, taxes, and death.

From *Culture for the Millions*, Norman Jacobs, editor, 1961, pp. 120–23. Reprinted by permission of the publisher, D. Van Nostrand Company, Inc., Princeton, N.J.

They do not do this with all the wisdom, foresight, or charity one might wish; nevertheless, this is what they are always doing and it is what the writer is always describing. There is literally nothing else to describe. This effort at description is itself extraordinarily arduous, and those who are driven to make this effort are by virtue of this fact somewhat removed from the people. It happens, by no means infrequently, that the people hound or stone them to death. They then build statues to them, which does not mean that the next artist will have it any easier.

I am not sure that the cultural level of the people is subject to a steady rise: in fact, quite unpredictable things happen when the bulk of the population attains what we think of as a high cultural level, i.e., pre-World War II Germany, or present-day Sweden. And this, I think, is because the effort of a Schönberg or a Picasso (or a William Faulkner or an Albert Camus) has nothing to do, at bottom, with physical comfort, or indeed with comfort of any other kind. But the aim of the people who rise to this high cultural level—who rise, that is, into the middle class—is precisely comfort for the body and the mind. The artistic objects by which they are surrounded cannot possibly fulfill their original function of disturbing the peace—which is still the only method by which the mind can be improved—they bear witness instead to the attainment of a certain level of economic stability and a certain thin measure of sophistication. But art and ideas come out of the passion and torment of experience; it is impossible to have a real relationship to the first if one's aim is to be protected from the second.

We cannot possibly expect, and should not desire, that the great bulk of the populace embark on a mental and spiritual voyage for which very few people are equipped and which even fewer have survived. They have, after all, their indispensable work to do, even as you and I. What we are distressed about, and should be, when we speak of the state of mass culture in this country, is the overwhelming torpor and bewilderment of the people. The people who run the mass media are not all villains and they are not all cowards—though I agree, I must say, with Dwight Macdonald's forceful suggestion that many of them are not very bright. (Why should they be? They, too, have risen from the streets to a high level of cultural attainment. They, too, are positively afflicted by the world's highest standard of living and what is probably the world's most bewilderingly empty way of life.) But even those who are bright are handicapped by their audience: I am less appalled by the fact that *Gunsmoke* is produced than I am by the fact that so many people want to see it. In the same way, I must add, that a thrill of terror runs through me when I hear that the favorite author of our President is Zane Grey.

But one must make a living. The people who run the mass media and those who consume it are really in the same boat. They must continue to produce things they do not really admire, still less, love, in order to continue buying things they do not really want, still less, need. If we were dealing only with fintails, two-tone cars, or programs like *Gunsmoke*, the situation would not be so grave. The trouble is that serious things are handled (and received) with the same essential lack of seriousness.

For example: neither *The Bridge On the River Kwai* nor *The Defiant Ones*, two definitely superior movies, can really be called serious. They are extraordinarily interesting and deft: but their principal effort is to keep the audience at a safe remove from the experience which these films are not therefore really prepared to convey. The kind of madness sketched in *Kwai* is far more dangerous and widespread than the movie would have us believe. As for *The Defiant Ones*, its suggestion that Negroes and whites can learn to love each other if they are only chained together long enough runs so madly counter to the facts that it must be dismissed as one of the latest, and sickest, of the liberal fantasies, even if one does not quarrel with the notion that love on such terms is desirable. These movies are designed not to trouble, but to reassure; they do not reflect reality, they merely rearrange its elements into something we can bear. They also weaken our ability to deal with the world as it is, ourselves as we are.

What the mass culture reflects (as is the case with a "serious" play like *J.B.*) is the American bewilderment in the face of the world we live in. We do not seem to want to know that we are *in* the world, that we are subject to the same catastrophes, vices, joys, and follies which have baffled and afflicted mankind for ages. And this has everything to do, of course, with what was expected of America: which expectation, so generally disappointed, reveals something we do not want to know about sad human nature, reveals something we do not want to know about the intricacies and inequities of any social structure, reveals, in sum, something we do not want to know about ourselves. The American way of life has failed— to make people happier or to make them better. We do not want to admit this, and we do not admit it. We persist in believing that the empty and criminal among our children are the result of some miscalculation in the formula (which can be corrected), that the bottomless and aimless hostility which makes our cities among the most dangerous in the world is created, and felt, by a handful of aberrants, that the lack, yawning everywhere in this country, of passionate conviction, of personal authority, proves only our rather appealing tendency to be gregarious and democratic. We are very cruelly trapped between what we would like to be, and what we actually are. And we cannot possibly become what we would like to be until we are willing to ask ourselves just why the lives we lead on this continent are mainly so empty, so tame and so ugly.

This is a job for the creative artist—who does not really have much to do with mass culture, no matter how many of us may be interviewed on TV. Perhaps life is not the black, unutterably beautiful, mysterious, and lonely thing the creative artist tends to think of it as being; but it is certainly not the sunlit playpen in which so many Americans lose first their identities and then their minds.

I feel very strongly, though, that this amorphous people are in desperate search for something which will help them to re-establish their connection with themselves, and with one another. This can only begin to happen as the truth begins to be told. We are in the middle of an immense metamorphosis here, a metamorphosis which will, it is devoutly to be hoped, rob us of our myths and give us our history, which will destroy our attitudes and give us back our personalities. The mass culture, in the meantime, can only reflect our chaos: and perhaps we had better remember that this chaos contains life—and a great transforming energy.

Parallel Paths

FRANK STANTON

The mass media are tempting targets: they are big, they are conspicuous, they are easily distorted, they invite bright and brittle condemnations—and they do have built-in limitations of their virtues. They have shown themselves inefficient warriors, and on the whole have tended to be too little concerned with what the intellectuals have had to say.

On the other side, the fondest attachment of the intellectuals is to theory not to practice; more importantly, there is among many intellectuals an uncongeniality with some of the basic ingredients of a democratic society and, in many cases, a real distrust of them. Democratic procedures, to some extent even democratic values, necessarily involve quantitative considerations, about which intellectuals are always uneasy. This uneasiness is not restricted to cultural matters. For example, it influences their view of the legislative processes and of economic interplays in our society. The intellectual is highly impatient of much that is imperfect but also inevitable in democracies. But despite these differences between intellectuals and the mass media, I think that they have something in common, that their efforts are fundamentally going toward the same general goal but along different paths.

I take it to be the distinguishing characteristic of civilized man that he is concerned with the environment and destiny of himself and his kind. The end of all scholarship, all art, all science, is the increase of knowledge and of understanding. The rubrics of scholarship have no inherent importance except in making the expansion of knowledge easier by creating system and order and catholicity. The freedom of the arts has no inherent

From *Culture for the Millions*, Norman Jacobs, editor, 1961, pp. 85–91. Reprinted by permission of the publisher, D. Van Nostrand Company, Inc., Princeton, N.J.

value except in its admitting unlimited comments upon life and the materials of life. There is no *mystique* about science; its sole wonder exists in its continuous expansion of both the area and the detail of man's comprehension of his physical being and his surroundings.

The ultimate use of all man's knowledge and his art and his science cannot be locked up into little compartments to which only the initiate hold the keys. It cannot be contemplated solely by closeted groups, or imposed from above. If vitality is to be a force in the general life of mankind, it must sooner or later reach all men and enter into the general body of awarenesses. The advancement of the human lot consists in more people being aware of more, knowing more, understanding more.

The mass media believe in the broad dissemination of as much as can be comprehended by as many as possible. They employ techniques to arrest attention, to recruit interest, to lead their audiences into new fields. Often they must sacrifice detail or annotation for the sake of the general idea.

Although it may be presumptuous, perhaps I can suggest a general contrast in the position of the professional intellectual: he feels that knowledge, art, and understanding are all precious commodities that ought not to be diluted. He believes that if things were left to him this dilution would not happen, because the doors of influence would be closed to the inadequately educated until they had earned the right to open them, just as he did. His view is that if standards remain beyond the reach of the many, the general level will gradually rise.

In this respect, I dissent from Mr. [Leo] Rosten's conclusion that the intellectuals "project their own tastes, yearnings, and values upon the masses." I do not believe there is such an irreducible gap between the tastes, yearnings, and values of the intellectuals and those of the masses. The difficulty is that the intellectuals do not project at all to the uninitiated. Their hope is to attract them, providing that it is not too many, too fast. They would wait for more and more people to qualify to the higher group, although they themselves want to stay a little ahead of the new arrivals.

This accounts, I believe, for the intellectuals' fear of popularization. The history of the Book-of-the-Month Club illustrates this point. Intellectuals have repeatedly made statements (not entirely characterized by a disciplined array of evidence), that the book club would bring about an "emasculation of the human mind whereby everyone loses the power of his determination in reading," and that the club's selections were "in many cases, not even an approximation to what the average intelligent reader wants." Yet a study by a Columbia University researcher found that over an eighteen-year span the reaction of reviewers, critics, and professors to the Book-of-the-Month Club selections was far higher in terms of approval than their reaction to random samples of nonselections.

By comparing the two heaviest book selections of the club in 1927 to their two lightest ones in 1949 (without other evidence) Stanley Edgar

Hyman suggests that the standards of selection are deteriorating. Yet he makes no mention of the fact that in 1949 the Book-of-the-Month Club for the first time in its history distributed a serious contemporary play, *Death of a Salesman*, that it distributed a serious discussion of a vital issue in Vannevar Bush's *Modern Arms and Free Men*, that it put it put into hundreds of thousands of homes William Edward Langer's *Encyclopedia of World History*, that it brought to its subscribers George Orwell's *Nineteen Eighty-four*, Winston Churchill's *Their Finest Hour*, and A. B. Guthrie's Pulitzer-Prize novel, *The Way West*.

Let me press what Mr. Hyman regards as evidence of "deterioration" of the Book-of-the-Month Club selections to the conclusion at which he himself arrived, that in the decade since 1949 "the selections seem to have continued to deteriorate." Even a glance at the evidence would refute this slashing generality. Indeed, the books distributed by the club throughout the 1950's suggest some high levels of excellence: in fiction there have been three books by William Faulkner, three by James Gould Cozzens, two by John Hersey, seven plays by Shaw, six by Thornton Wilder, Eugene O'Neill's *Long Day's Journey into Night*, novels by Feuchtwanger, Salinger, Thomas Mann, Hemingway, John Cheever, and James Agee; there have been eight historical works by Churchill, two by Schlesinger, two by Van Wyck Brooks, others by Morison and Nevins, Dumas Malone, Bernard DeVoto, Catherine Drinker Bowen's life of John Adams, Toynbee's *Study of History*, two of Edith Hamilton's studies of ancient Greece, and Max Lerner's *American Civilization;* in poetry, Stephen Vincent Benet, and *The Oxford Book of American Verse;* from the classics, Bulfinch's *The Age of Fable*, Frazer's *The Golden Bough*, the Hart edition of Shakespeare, a new translation of *The Odyssey*, works by Dostoevsky, Gustave Flaubert, and Mark Twain; in art, Francis Henry Taylor's *Fifty Centuries of Art*, John Walker's *Masterpieces of Painting from the National Gallery*, and *Art Treasures of the Louvre;* in reference works, Fowler's *Modern English Usage*, Palmer's *Atlas of World History*, Audubon's *Birds*, and Evans' *Dictionary of Contemporary American Usage*.

To turn to television, I hear over and over such generalities as, "There is nothing but Westerns on television," or "Television is all mysteries and blood and thunder." Such charges usually come from people who do not look at television, but that does not modify their position. As in the case just cited, there is no uncertainty about this exaggeration; one can look at the actual record.

Let us take by way of example the week of February 15 to 21, 1959, on the CBS Television Network, because that week had nothing exceptional about it. During the preceding week, there were such outstanding broadcasts as Tolstoy's *Family Happiness* and a repetition of the distinguished documentary, *The Face of Red China*. In the following week, the programs included the New York Philharmonic and the Old Vic Company's *Hamlet*. Returning to the unexceptional week of February 15, about 4½ hours, or

$\frac{1}{18}$ of CBS Television's total program content of 75½ hours, were devoted to Westerns; about 5 hours, or $\frac{1}{15}$, were taken up by mysteries. On the other hand, 7¾ hours, or about $\frac{1}{10}$ of the total number of hours, were devoted to news and public affairs. Altogether, some 78 percent of the evening programing was occupied by drama, fairly evenly divided among serious, comedy, mystery, Westerns, and romance-adventure.

Looking at the record for the first five months of 1959, I find on the CBS Television Network alone four Philharmonic concerts; 90-minute-long productions of plays by Shakespeare, Barrie, and Saroyan, adaptations of Shaw and Ibsen, full-length productions of *The Browning Version*, Melville's *Billy Budd*, Henry James' *Wings of the Dove*, Hemingway's *For Whom the Bell Tolls*, and many distinguished original dramas; thirteen conversations with people of such diverse minds and talents as James Conant, Sir Thomas Beecham, and James Thurber; nine historic surveys of great personalities or developments of the twentieth century; and nine specially scheduled programs inquiring into major issues in public affairs, such as the Cuban revolution, the closing of integrated high schools, statehood for Hawaii, and the Geneva Conference.

I am citing these for two purposes. One is to show how, by using selected examples, it can be as easily proved that television is exclusively instructive as that it is exclusively diverting. My other purpose is by way of considering a practical response to the complaints that the intellectuals voice about all the mass media.

What do the intellectuals really want? Do they want us to do *only* serious programing, only programs of profound cultural value? Or do they just want us to do more? And if so, what is more? Do they want the Book-of-the-Month Club to distribute only heavy reading, or just more? Does the club do harm because it has included books of humor among the thirty to forty selections, alternates, and dividends it distributes each year? Is there any serious belief anywhere that among the paperback books we ought to censor what we consider culturally insignificant and allow only what we consider culturally enriching? Or do not the intellectuals really want to stake out reserves, admission to which would be granted only on their terms, in their way, at their pleasure?

Television occupies the air waves under the franchise of the American people. It has a threefold function: the dissemination of information, culture, and entertainment. There are different levels and different areas of interest at which these are sought by a hundred and fifty million people. It is our purpose—and our endlessly tantalizing task—to make certain that we have enough of every area at every level of interest to hold the attention of significant segments of the public at one time or another. Therefore we do have programs more likely to be of interest to the intellectuals than to others. We can try to include everybody somewhere in our program planning, but we cannot possibly aim all the time only at the largest possible audience.

The practice of sound television programing is the same as the practice of any sound editorial operation. It involves always anticipating (if you can) and occasionally leading your subscribers or readers or audience. The "mass of consumers" does not decide, in the sense that it initiates programs, but it does respond to our decisions. A mass medium survives when it maintains a satisfactory batting average on affirmative responses, and it goes down when negative responses are too numerous or too frequent. But so also does the magazine with a circulation of five thousand— as the high mortality rate of the "little magazines" testifies. Success in editing, whether a mass medium or an esoteric quarterly, consists in so respecting the audience that one labors to bring to it something that meets an interest, a desire, or a need that has still to be completely filled. Obviously, the narrower and the more intellectually homogeneous your audience, the easier this is to do; and conversely, the larger it is and the more heterogeneous, the more difficult.

I must dissent from the unqualified charge that "advertisers today . . . exercise their most pernicious influence in television." The basis of this charge is that, while an advertiser buys space in a magazine with no power of choice as to the editorial content of the magazine, on television he allegedly controls both the commercials and what program goes into the time space. The matter is not so simple.

In the first place I categorically assert that no news or public-affairs program at CBS, however expensive to the sponsor, has ever been subject to his control, influence, or approval. There is a total and absolute independence in this respect.

An advertiser in magazines does have the power to associate his advertising with editorial content by his choice of a magazine. If he makes a household detergent, he can choose a magazine whose appeal is to housewives. In television, he can achieve this association only by seeking out kinds of programs, or, more properly, the kinds of audience to which specific programs appeal. This is of course why a razor blade company want to sponsor sports programs. But this does not mean that the company is going to referee the game or coach the team. In television, for the most part, advertisers are sold programs by networks or by independent producers, somewhat in the sense that space in the magazines is sold by sales efforts based on the kind of audience the magazine reaches. At the same time, we are perfectly aware that in the rapid growth of television the problem of the advertiser's relationship with program content has not yet been satisfactorily solved. It is an area to which we are going to have to devote more thought and evolve new approaches.

I return to a central point: that some sort of hostility on the part of the intellectuals toward the mass media is inevitable, because the intellectuals are a minority, one not really reconciled to some basic features of democratic life. They are an articulate and cantankerous minority, not readily given to examining evidence about the mass media and then arriving at conclusions, but more likely to come to conclusions and then select the evidence to support them. But they are an invaluable minority. We all do care what they think because they are a historic force on which our society must always rely for self-examination and advancement. They constitute the outposts of our intellectual life as a people, they probe around frontiers in their splendid sparsity, looking around occasionally to see where—how far behind—the rest of us are. We are never going to catch up, but at least we shall always have somewhere to go.

As for the mass media, they are always in the process of trying, and they never really find the answers. They also are the victims of their pressing preoccupations, and can undoubtedly improve their performances, better understand their own roles, learn more rapidly. I feel that intellectuals and the media could really serve one another better if both parties informed themselves more fully, brought somewhat more sympathy to each other's examinations, and stopped once in a while to redefine their common goals. We in the mass media have probably been negligent in not drawing the intellectuals more intimately into our counsels, and the intellectuals, by and large, have not studied the evidence carefully enough before discussing the mass media. The mass media need the enlightened criticism, the thorough examination, of the intellectuals. When the latter are willing to promise these, we shall all make progress faster and steadier.

CONTRASTING PATTERNS IN EDUCATIONAL THOUGHT

Serious questions about the status, role, function, and value of schools in society have been raised for a long period of time. Any period of social stress places burdens on social institutions to justify or alter their operations, and the schools become primary targets of attacks from many directions. At one time the attacks on education are to broaden the academic base and include more practical subjects. At another time the major critics propose a classical program to the detriment of practical studies. The schools have also been criticized for allowing too much student freedom and not emphasizing moral education. One group wants education to promote nationalism.

It is difficult to find a social issue more widely discussed in general magazines, newspapers, meetings of chambers of commerce, legislatures, and conversation groups than education. The critics are in every corner, the defenders harried and disunited. In contemporary America, as in the newly developing countries of the world, education is a main social and political enterprise. Aside from the fact that the schools are the largest economic operation in the majority of small communities and among the largest in nearly all cities, the school as a social enterprise involves virtually the entire society over a period of time. Also, since education is generally viewed as a public concern, whether the schools are public or private, questions about the direction of education tend to be taken up in the public forum.

Education, then, is an issue rightly belonging in this section on dissent and agreement. Readings included in this area are provided to show some of the mainstreams of educational thought and their critics. The relation of school to society is evident in this section as social ideas are directly involved in educational theory.

A Criticism of
Educational Critics

A noted philosopher, Sidney Hook, undertakes an analysis of several of the major criticisms of education in the following piece. Modern education may be a term that defies definition, but it suggests the kind of present-day educational system which attempts a comprehensive program for all youth under the tenets of progressivism or pragmatism. Professor Hook examines the writings of some prominent critics of modern education and points out logical fallacies in their arguments. In a crisp style Professor Hook becomes the critic of critics. His basically positive attitude toward modern education is clearly shown in the early and late sections of this article, but he does not become an apologist for educational problems—rather an analyst of them.

Is pragmatism still a viable philosophy for the schools of the space age? What are the positive values of educational critics? In judging the development of education in America, what criticisms of today's schools are valid? How does Professor Hook's analysis differ from Professor Cremin's treatment of the progressive movement in American education as found in Part 1 of this text?

Modern Education and Its Critics

SIDNEY HOOK

The growth of the educational enterprise in the United States has been accompanied, among other things, by a growth in the volume of criticism. This criticism has come from all quarters of the ideological compass. It has been directed against every aspect of American education. The cost of the physical plant; the organization of the schools; the training of teachers; the character of their instruction, whether given or received; the nature of the curriculum; the philosophy or the lack of philosophy behind it—all have been the target of vigorous attack.

Reprinted from the Seventh Yearbook, American Association of Colleges for Teacher Education, 1954, pp. 139–60, by permission of the publisher and the author.

To the extent that such criticisms make the community aware of educational problems and of the enormous stake all citizens have in the proper functioning of our schools, they should be welcomed even when they seem intemperate and ill-informed. For our hopes for more and better schools are more likely to be realized as a consequence of public criticism, adequately met, than of public indifference. After all, no matter how valid we believe our educational objectives to be, there is no reason for complacency when we survey the educational results. And if our very objectives are challenged, we are under a moral and intellectual obligation to offer a rational defense of them.

One thing we know in advance. Not all criticisms can be well-founded. For many are incompatible with each other. On the other hand, it is unlikely that they will all be unjustified. Our very commitment to free inquiry in our schools should lead us to accept the results of such inquiry about any one, or all, of our educational commitments.

Now it is perfectly true that some attacks on modern education are not made in good faith. They are part of campaigns to capture or influence the schools for some partisan goals or programs which are themselves to be exempt from critical exploration through the normal processes of education. Such attacks should be met and repelled, not by the educators attacked, but by their fellow citizens. But until it becomes patent that good faith *is* lacking, educators should be the first to consider the ostensible reasons offered for dissatisfaction with the schools, even if the ostensible reasons are not the real reasons. We must not forget that, in the last analysis, the relevant evidence for the truth or falsity of what a man says does not depend upon his ulterior motives in saying it.

Before considering some of the chief criticisms of American education, it would be well to keep firmly in view some of the chief accomplishments of American education. This is necessary, not only for a proper historical perspective, but also because some of those very achievements are the cause of current difficulties and misunderstanding.

1. The American school and educational system has been the prime agency of achieving a unified democratic nation out of diverse ethnic groups of varied national origins. This result has been obtained without the oppressive measures which usually marked the emergence of great states in the past, and without the forcible imposition of a uniform cultural pattern from one central source.

2. The American educational system has provided an educational ladder on which millions have climbed to a better social life. In the past man's vocations have been closer to what Santayana has called "natural society" than to "free society." That is to say, they have been determined more by the accidents of kinship, association, and inherited social status than by free choice in accordance with talent and inclination. This is still the rule for most of mankind, but it is less so in the United States than anywhere else in the world.

3. Despite its early denominational beginnings and despite the ever-recurrent tendency of religion to bring the glad tidings of salvation into the classroom, the American school system is predominantly secular. Although it permits study of the materials of religion wherever they are culturally relevant, it has remained neutral in the great conflicts of religious faiths.

4. The American educational system has come nearest to achieving a classless school in the entire history of human society. *Morally,* this is its most glorious achievement. *Educationally,* it has created prodigious difficulties and theoretical confusions which we shall subsequently discuss. No judgment, no plan of reform for American education, is likely to be worth examining if it overlooks the significance of the fact that in a nation of 160 millions more than 80% of its young men and women are receiving a high school education: that whereas in 1900 barely 700,000 students were enrolled in high school, in little more than one generation later, over 7,000,000 students were enrolled; that whereas in 1900 fewer than 250,000 students were enrolled in our institutions of higher learning, today over 2,300,000 are enrolled. That these absolute and relative increases do not hold for every group is, of course, true; but if Mr. Paul Hoffman is correct even "The percentage of our negro population at present enrolled in educational institutions above the high school level is greater than the percentage of Britons, French and Czechs—to say nothing of the Russians—who are receiving comparable training."[1] Despite the tremendous inequalities and complexities which still exist, the direction of the development is quite clear.

5. Finally, notwithstanding the tendencies of human inertia, the activities of pressure groups and vested interests, the character of American education has shown a susceptibility to change—disregarding for the moment the wisdom of some of the changes. It has never been doctrinaire and inflexible. It has shown itself hospitable to criticisms and receptive—perhaps too receptive—to needs, claims, and demands from industry and government. Even without external pressure or stimulus, it has initiated a wide variety of experiments. That this capacity to learn and change is a virtue must be granted even by the most hostile of its present-day critics. Otherwise there would be no point in *their* urging changes.

This brings me to my theme: modern education and its critics. There is a certain ambiguity in the phrase "modern education." Some critics mean by it "current education," not all of which should be regarded as modern. Or it may mean progressive or the new education, not all of which is current. But whatever their differences, all the critics I shall discuss find current education on every level objectionable to the extent that it reflects the theory and practice of the new education whose principles have been sketched in broad outline by John Dewey. Some of the critics find conven-

---

[1] Paul Hoffman, *Oberlin Today,* Vol. 2, No. 8, December, 1953. This does not in any way imply, of course, that the characters of these institutions, or their educational quality, are comparable.

tional education, present or past, objectionable, too. But on the whole the burden of their criticism is that modern or new education is so inferior to what it has replaced that it hardly warrants the name of education. And since, despite these detractors, it is spreading, they regard it as the chief enemy of what by definition—by *their* definition—is called "true" education.

I propose to consider some general criticisms of modern education and the assumptions behind them. And I shall proceed in an unprecedented way but one consistent with the principles of modern education. I shall take as points of concrete departure the recent writings of three widely-heralded critics—Mr. Albert Lynd, Mr. Robert Hutchins and Mr. Arthur Bestor—examining in each case some central points in their animadversions against modern education. After assessing the validity of their charges and the worth of their major recommendations—I shall conclude with some critical observations of my own.

To begin with we must distinguish between the substance and the manner of these criticisms. The manner is almost invariably rude and contemptuous. The title of Mr. Lynd's book is *Quackery in the Public Schools.*[2] Professional educators, especially professors of education, are the quacks, and the teachers, with some exceptions, their unwilling or willing victims. The former are pictured as "illiterate," unable to express themselves in effective English or to draw elementary logical inferences. They are "boondogglers," "copper-riveted bureaucrats" and engaged in a dual conspiracy —a *professional* conspiracy—to pile up needless requirements of educational courses (educationally unprofitable to those who take them but financially profitable to those who give them), and a *political* conspiracy to evade the will of the community by imposing their own philosophy of man, God and universe on the schools. Because John Dewey's educational theories have opened the door to these boondogglers and conspirators, writes Mr. Lynd, "I make no apology whatever for the inclusion of his name and doctrines in a volume concerned with 'quackery in the public school.'"[3]

One is tempted to ignore Mr. Lynd or to retort in kind. But he speaks for many who feel and believe as he does, and if we are interested in the truth we must reply to his arguments, not to his abuse. The trouble is that it is difficult to find a coherent argument. He uses the anecdotal method and confuses illustration with proof.[4]

[2] Albert Lynd, *Quackery in the Public Schools,* Little, Brown & Co., Boston, 1953.
[3] *Ibid.,* p. 207.
[4] Although fiercely indignant with modern educators for their unscholarly habits, he devotes the longest chapter of his book to a jeering commentary on the views of Mr. Kilpatrick—not all of whose ideas are accepted by many modern educators—without a single quotation from any of Mr. Kilpatrick's writings. Instead he contents himself with quoting some loose and ungrammatical sentences from a book by one of Mr. Kilpatrick's uncritical admirers.

Let us state his argument for him. His charge is that modern schools have by and large failed to fulfill their proper function. Their proper function is to teach students how to think, to develop their powers of observation, to make them aware of their cultural origins and continuity with the past, and to instill in them a devotion to the heritage of freedom. In the past these ends were achieved by "formal study in skills and abstract principles": in the elementary schools, through conscientious application to the three R's; in the high schools, through the conventional curriculum of mathematics, foreign languages, grammar, Latin, systematic history, and some sciences; in the colleges, through more of the same. The products of our schools today cannot think or observe properly. They are ignorant of history, and impatient of the intellectual and moral discipline necessary to freedom. All this is a consequence of the abandonment of the conventional curriculum. But the cause of the abandonment is the acceptance of the ideas of the new education whose fountainhead is Dewey. Therefore, to the extent that professional educators and teachers profess allegiance to these principles, they are opposed to "true" education; to the extent that our schools are operated on these principles, they cannot impart "true" education.

Nowhere does Lynd consider whether the ends of a proper education—which he fails to see are among the ends of modern education, too—were *in fact* realized by the traditional curriculum, or whether they were more *completely* realized by the traditional curriculum than by current curricula. He simply ignores all the failures of the past and all the successes of the present. By Mr. Lynd's anecdotal method one could make out a very damaging case of widespread failure in the past. But such a method establishes nothing.

Nor do his historical references establish much more. Examine—in the light of historical evidence—the typical, exaggerated claims by critics of this school that the classical curriculum has been the chief and continuing support of freedom in the Western world. After all, the European countries in which the educational curriculum was and still is the most conventional, in which the secondary schools give *all* students instruction in the classical disciplines, so dearly beloved by Mr. Lynd, were the countries which produced—often with the direct connivance or benevolent neutrality of their classically-educated elite—Fascism, Vichyism, Nazism, and Bolshevism.[5]

Now I am far from saying that there is a direct causal connection between the classical curriculum and these movements, although it is hard to imagine them engulfing a nation whose schools were thoroughly imbued with the spirit and methods of modern or progressive education. What I am saying is that the classical curriculum was certainly not a sufficient safeguard against the *emergence* of a new barbarism.

To Mr. Lynd the assumption of a causal relation between the classical

[5] As a movement Bolshevism is the creation of middle-class intellectuals schooled in the classical curriculum of their day.

training of a country's élite and the emergence of totalitarianism is a *post hoc, propter hoc fallacy*. And he is right, because the first can and has occurred without the second. But is it any less of a *post hoc, propter hoc* fallacy to assume that the decline in the ability to read, write and think on any level—assuming that there has been such a decline—is due to a change in curriculum or to new methods of teaching certain subjects rather than to the fact that we are trying to educate a whole people, including those he calls "the slow-witted" and "dullards," instead of a selected group? Mr. Lynd must admit the possibility that, even by his standards, at least *some* of our students can read and write and think as well as the students of the past. Perhaps their number, in proportion to the entire population of school age and not merely to those in school, is just as great today as in the golden age of yesterday, when many were not in school because they were dropped as uneducable. Would it not then be a decided gain, a great gain, if we could teach something of worth to those whom Mr. Lynd's curriculum and methods could teach nothing? There are, of course, natural dullards. But there are others who are dullards in relation only to a specific curriculum or a specific method of teaching. By clinging to the conventional curriculum, Mr. Lynd has no way of distinguishing them.

In appraising the relative claims of the past and present systems of education, conclusions are difficult to establish. Unless we can evaluate the work of groups comparable in native ability, educational opportunity and social background, our results are scientifically worthless. But on an elementary level it seems possible to make not altogether unreliable studies of comparison between the performance of children in the three R's today and one or two generations ago. These comparisons do not show any conspicuous decline. Mr. Lynd refuses to accept the results because "there is at hand formidable evidence that many of the educationists in power today are not qualified to judge children's performance in the fundamentals."[6] But Mr. Lynd regards himself as qualified to judge that graduates of our high schools are illiterate because he found one student, and his business friends found a few others, who couldn't compose a coherent letter.

In the light of this illustration of what a classically-trained mind regards as probative evidence, it is not surprising that Mr. Lynd should caricature what actually goes on in the schools of the country, misinterpret Dewey's recommendation to relate subject matter to needs and interest into a recommendation to dispense altogether with subject matter and misconceive what is said of "felt needs" as if it implied that needs do not exist unless they are felt.

But the main point I wish to make is not that Mr. Lynd has misread the works of modern educators or that his opposition to it flows from inaccurate empirical observations of the practices of modern education. It is

---

[6] Lynd, *op. cit.*, p. 22.

rather that his opposition is *a priori*. It derives from his view that practices of modern education *must* be bad because they are logically bound up with Dewey's philosophy of pragmatism. He believes that if he accepts these practices as valid, such acceptance would logically imply the validity of Dewey's pragmatism. However, since he is convinced that pragmatism is false, he concludes without the necessity of any further examination that the educational theory and practice which logically imply it are also mistaken.

This is a profound error, but one so widespread that I wish to discuss it at some length. For it is this error which is responsible in part for the belief that educational issues are, at bottom, issues of theology and metaphysics.

Although there is an organic connection in Dewey's own thinking between his philosophical ideas and his educational proposals, they are not related as logical premise to logical conclusion. Dewey, of course, believed that the soundness of his proposals constituted some evidence that his philosophical method was fruitful. But he never contended that, before one could determine whether or not those proposals were sound, one antecedently had to accept pragmatism. The soundness of these proposals was to be a matter for independent investigation. As a matter of fact, there have been notable philosophers who have heartily endorsed progressive educational practices *without* endorsing pragmatism as a basic philosophy, e.g., Bertrand Russell and Felix Adler.

One of the great obstacles to an objective judgment of the claims of modern education is precisely the notion, as Mr. Lynd puts it, that "agreement with the basic philosophy of Mr. Dewey is the logical price of agreement with his educational theories."[7]

What, then, is this Deweyan basic philosophy? Says Mr. Lynd, "It excludes God, the soul, and all the props of traditional religion." But since Mr. Lynd is a firm believer in God, the soul, and all the props of traditional religion, he rejects out of hand Dewey's educational theories and the practices based on them. Believing what he does, he *must* hold progressive or modern education to be pernicious, no matter what the empirical results are. For the question is no longer empirical but metaphysical and theological. Mr. Lynd admits this on occasion. He tells us that he would still oppose progressive education "even if the strongest claims of the progressivists about their success with the three R's are true."[8] If he understands his own words he is telling us something more. He is telling us that he would still oppose modern education even if *all* its claims were true.

It becomes necessary, then, to put the question in its proper light. For if it were true that modern education is logically bound up with certain

---

[7] *Ibid.*, p. 203. Elsewhere he says that they are only compatible, which is, of course, another kind of relationship. But Mr. Lynd is not concerned with logical niceties.
[8] *Ibid.*, p. 205.

beliefs about God, immortality of the soul, and transcendental moral law, we can have no more agreement about education than we can about theology.

Now as I understand it, and as Dewey often explained, progressive education is based on two generic principles. The first is that the verified results of scientific psychology should be brought to bear on the processes of learning. The second is that the values and ideals of democratic life should, as far as possible, be introduced at the appropriate levels in the student's own educational experience. Acceptance of either or both of these principles does not entail acceptance of Dewey's technical philosophy of instrumentalism. If it is true that there is no transference of training from one field to another: if it is true that effort is a function of interest; that interest follows perception of meaning; and that involvement, active or imaginative, in a problem multiplies and dramatizes opportunities to grasp meanings—why should these truths not be guides to teaching? If the end of education is the development of independent thinking, is not the psychology of how we learn and how we think of fundamental relevance in achieving this end?

But listen to Mr. Lynd. "If human behavior depends upon patterns of habit and impulse as Dewey believes," he complains, "the instruction by exhortation is largely useless." Well, *does* human behavior depend upon habit, impulse and, as Dewey would add, the redirective cues of intelligence? This is a psychological question. Not so, according to a whole school of critics. This is a metaphysical or theological question. And since Dewey denies that "a soul or self exists apart from its own experiences," Dewey's empirical psychology is unacceptable. But this is a *non sequitur.* If the soul exists, embodied or disembodied, *apart* from its own experiences, nothing follows about how human beings learn *in* and *through* experience. The only item in an educational curriculum which would seem to follow from faith in the substantiality of the soul is instruction in the religious dogmas regarded as necessary for its salvation. Even this is not strictly necessary, for one can believe in the soul without believing that it must be saved, or believe that it must be saved without believing that its salvation is the business of the public schools.

This refusal to evaluate the fruits of modern education on the ground that they all stem from the poisoned roots of pragmatism is also manifested in the discussion concerning the place of democratic and moral experience in the schools. Mr. Lynd and others insist that the stress upon shared experience and democratic participation in setting some intermediate goals of learning, especially in the early years, is wrong because "Dewey insists that human nature itself is the only source of workable moral guides," instead of a "higher" reality, God or some transcendental ideal. Apparently the experience and results of democracy, as contrasted with its alternatives, cannot be assessed or taken as a guide to practice unless democracy is properly grounded in a "higher reality."

Here, too, the argument rests on a demonstrable error. Our whole American experience is testimony to the fact that cooperation and progress on the plane of democratic action is possible without a common belief in first or last things. The same is true for the entire spectrum of human values. We agree on values because of their quality and consequences in experience and yet disagree about their status in the universe. For example, kindness, veracity, conscientiousness recommend themselves to all of us in terms of immediate qualities and observable effects without any necessity for a prior consensus on their alleged ultimate presuppositions. Do we not every day agree on hundreds of truths even though we may completely disagree about definitions of *the* truth?

It is because progressive educators *believe* in democracy, and not because they *disbelieve* in cosmic ultimates, that they wish to develop students capable of self-discipline, thoughtfulness, and willingness to examine other interests when a conflict of interests arises. And that is why they seek to introduce democratic processes into the child's experiences in the classroom. It is easy to caricature this into the statement that they believe everything should be decided by vote with the teacher either not voting or having only one vote. Their true meaning can be better understood by recalling the atmosphere of the convential classroom not so long ago.[9] One can accept the injunction to encourage democratic participation and still recognize distinctions among the matters on which students should be consulted and permitted to decide, the matters on which they should only be consulted, and the matters which they should be permitted only to question—but always freely to question. Any specific classroom procedure should be tested by its observable or anticipated effects as contrasted with the effects of alternative procedures, not in terms of its relation to a cosmic or higher reality.

No matter what "higher reality" is postulated it can be shown that mutually inconsistent programs of experience are compatible with it. This is as true for a program of studies in the school as for methods of teaching and a scheme of values. But if one cannot derive a program of studies from metaphysics and one refuses to follow the test of consequences—what can be done? There is no alternative but to fall back on tradition for one's curriculum—which Mr. Lynd not unexpectedly does.

As a rule the traditional curriculum means the curriculum on which the critic was brought up. But it is always described as the accumulated wisdom of the race. What is overlooked is that we not only inherit a tradition but create it, that tradition consists in large measure of de-

[9] Their true meaning may be more apparent in the light of an incident that I can still vividly recall. Thirty-six years ago almost to a day, a group of Brooklyn high school students proposed, for the first time in those parts, a scheme of student self-government. They were denounced by educators and editorial writers as Red Guards and Black Guards (the colors of the school) intent upon establishing soviets in the educational institutions of the U.S. In those days students asked questions only when they were invited to ask them—which was not often.

partures from tradition, and that the wisdom of tradition establishes its wisdom by its continuing relevance to problems of the present. We cannot escape responsibility for *our* selections and decisions merely by transmitting from our ancestors what they themselves did not always inherit from their own. Merely to transmit tradition is not a counsel of wisdom but of timidity. Speaking of the conventional disciplines, Mr. Lynd says that "there is more wisdom in 'the subject matters' of mathematics, of literature, of history than in any teacher or body of teachers however wise." As one who strongly believes in subject matter and that modern education is not adequate unless it teaches subject matter and that sometimes subject matter has not been sufficiently stressed, I regard this glorification of subject matter *qua* subject matter as absurd. It reverses the wisdom of Socrates, to whom all subjects and subject matters were merely points of educational departure. For Socrates taught that wisdom, begun with a consciousness of our ignorance, is insight into the nature and career of human values as they bear upon the predicaments of men. Subject matter is neither wise nor foolish; it contains only the *materials* for wisdom—as well as for use and enjoyment. That is why neither history nor experience teaches by itself unless an instructed mind is willing to learn from it.

A second type of criticism goes further than that so far considered. It underlines current strictures against modern education but is not content with a return merely to the conventional models. It substitutes a comprehensive conception of education—new in form but perennial in essence—to guide the remolding of our educational institutions. This conception, whose banner-bearer is Mr. Hutchins, has been worked out in detail for liberal education of a specific kind—the only kind there is, we are assured—on the college level. The curriculum of the elementary and high schools is to be reorganized in such a way as to make this kind of liberal education possible for all students.

This view, whose most recent expression is found in *Conflicts in Education* (New York, 1953),[10] is frankly and proudly non-empirical. It makes great play with deductions from axiomatic first principles and proposes to do what I have tried to show cannot be done, viz., validly to derive a desirable educational program from metaphysical premises.[11]

Here I wish only to analyze some of the leading assumptions behind his position. The first assumption concerns the ends of education and how they are derived. The second concerns the curricular means by which these ends are to be achieved. The third, and most important, concerns the

[10] Robert Hutchins, *The Conflict in Education in a Democratic Society*, Harper & Row, New York, 1953.

[11] In my *Education for Modern Man*, New York, 1946, I have examined at length the views of Mr. Hutchins, as well as those of Mortimer Adler, Stringfellow Barr, and Scott Buchanan, as expressed in their writings up to that time.

claim that to deny the adequacy of Mr. Hutchins' curricular means involves a denial of the democratic philosophy itself.

That the *central* aim of education should be the development of man's power of thought is, so far as I know, denied by nobody—provided we do not identify power of thought with a specific intellectual skill. But, whereas most educators justify the emphasis on thought because of its key role in the organization of impulse and feeling, the control of action, and the enrichment of the meanings of experience even when we cannot act, Mr. Hutchins derives it from a definition of man's fixed and essential nature.

Man is a rational animal. He is uniquely different from other animals by virtue of his power to think. Therefore, education must be directed exclusively to the cultivation of his intellect.

Now there are several things wrong with the deduction. First, even if we deny that other animals can think—and not all psychologists agree with this—the power to think is not the only differentiating feature of the human animal. There are other differentiating features. Man is the only animal who makes his tools. Man is the only animal with a sense of humor. If we were to derive our educational aims from these differentia, we should have to say that man's education must primarily be vocational or technological or that it must develop his power to crack jokes.

Second, the nature of a thing is not completely given by what differentiates it. It includes what it has in common with other species in its genus. Man is a creature of emotion, an organism which adapts to and modifies its environment. An education appropriate to the nature of man must be appropriate to the *whole* of man's nature. This would include some things which Mr. Hutchins excludes. The Greeks, whom Mr. Hutchins takes as his model, regarded as the end of education, not exclusively intellectual development, but the harmonious development of all human faculties. For them a life of reason is no more identical with a reasoning life than a joy of life is identical with a life of joy.

Third, what do we mean by thought? Modern education, to the extent that it is inspired by Dewey, interprets it broadly as creative intelligence in the solution of problems which arise in *all* fields of human experience. But Mr. Hutchins seems to identify thought or reason with academic intellectuality, with verbal skills in the interpretation of texts.

This deductive approach from fallible first principles is carried over into discussion of the curriculum of education. Since by definition all men have a common nature, the education appropriate to that nature must be common, and the means of achieving it—the educational curriculum—must be common. Therefore education everywhere, at all times, and for all men (and women) must be the same. Contrast this with modern education which, not by deduction but by inquiry, discovers that men have a great many needs in common and yet vary greatly, that their differences in culture and time reflect themselves in the way their common needs are fulfilled, and that even in the same culture variations among them are appreciable. It therefore stresses the fact that their indisputable common need—the development of intelligence—may be achieved in different ways.

An analogy might make the point clearer. Everyone needs to be healthy. What it mean to be healthy, i.e., the *definition* of health, is the same for all men. We might even concede that the *formal* requirements of a well-balanced diet necessary for health is the same for all men. But who will therefore deduce that all men must eat the same things at the same time, or exercise in the same way, in order to be healthy? If there are differences among men, if they live in different climates and must perform different tasks, to prescribe a *common* dietary regimen is to guarantee that not all of them will be healthy. Just as there are different dietary roads to health, so there are different curricular roads to educational maturity. Great segments of these roads, of course, will be common.

I believe it can be established that to be intelligent men must be able to communicate with each other, understand the cultural past relevant to their present experience, and in so doing acquire certain basic skills and familiarity with certain subject matters. But to be intelligent in the *modern* world, their education must prepare them to cope with the *problems* of that world. How best to do this cannot be derived from definitions but must be discovered by inquiry and experiment, which may not give us absolute or certain truth for *all* time but sufficiently reliable knowledge for *our* time. This is a far cry, however, from Mr. Hutchins' all-prescribed curriculum for all men and women whose model, incidentally, is not so much the Chicago plan as the curriculum of St. Johns College.

Now Mr. Hutchins is very well aware of the diversity and variety of human talents. No matter how intelligence is defined or measured there is an enormous variation in human abilities, particularly the ability to understand the great books of the past, a few of which are confessedly beyond the competence of some of the architects of the St. Johns plan. He has, therefore, hit upon a novel defense of the kind of education he proposes. According to this argument, since every man in a democracy is a voter, he is a ruler. To be himself a ruler or to elect his rulers, he needs the education which has been universally regarded, except by those who differ with Mr. Hutchins, as the best education. This best education is the education which by prescribed studies in mathematics, languages, philosophy and science develops the intellectual powers of man. It has never been fully tried, but the nearest thing to it is the curriculum of studies as it existed in the aristocratic cultures of the past when few were rulers. Since the best is not too good where all men are rulers, it should be adopted today.

Accused in the past of advocating an education irrelevant, if not hostile, to the needs of men in a democratic society, Mr. Hutchins is now contending that only those who agree with his conception of the best education can be considered consistent democrats. To have "strong faith in the political judgment of the masses with strong doubts of their intellectual capacities," i.e., of their intellectual capacities to acquire the best education, writes Mr. Hutchins, is a paradox. And in criticism of those who penned the report of the President's Commission on Education he says, "They most undemocratically assume that the mass of people are incapable of achieving such an education."

What is paradoxical, to put it mildly, about this argument is that Mr. Hutchins is attempting to settle on political grounds a fact which has nothing to do with politics. Even if the masses were able to profit by the curriculum Mr. Hutchins has deduced for them that would not be decisive, because they might be able to profit even more from the study of a better one and one more relevant to our times. But the belief that not all students are capable of profiting by the kind of education that Mr. Hutchins regards as best for them is neither democratic nor undemocratic. It is either true or false. Jefferson was no less a democrat because he believed that intellectual capacities are unequal. Democracy in education is the belief that each person is entitled to the educational opportunities necessary to develop his potential capacities to their highest form. It is not the belief that all persons can profitably read Clerk-Maxwell's *Electricity and Magnetism*, Galois' *Mathematical Papers* or Kant's *Critique of Pure Reason*—and this before their twentieth year!

Apparently Mr. Hutchins believes that by flattering the masses with assurances that they can all profit by his prescribed educational curriculum—assurances incompatible with what is known about learning—his proposals will become more acceptable to them. But there is no reason to believe that what was the best education for the undemocratic rulers of the past—if it was the best—is now the best education for the masses. There is nothing inconsistent in believing that the citizens of a democracy are on the whole the best judges of their own true interests, and in believing that the training appropriate for the intellectual or academic élite cannot be made an educational requirement for all.

What Mr. Hutchins is really saying is this: either accept the rule of an élite or of intellectual experts and give up democracy or admit that the masses are all potential intellectual experts in a democracy and educate them to be experts. But it is not necessary to be an expert to judge the basic policies proposed by experts. One can choose his doctor wisely without a medical education. It is Mr. Hutchins who is inconsistent here. For, in addressing his appeal for the reform of education to the community, he himself admits that wise educational decisions may be made by those who are not educational experts or who have not been nurtured on the great books. If there are any experts in the wisdom of life, they cannot be mass-produced by the same education. It is one thing to say that a healthy democracy rests upon some kind of common education. It is quite another to say that *all* education in a democracy must be common. And it is still something else again to assert that the content of a common education must be unchanging and identical in every respect.

Mr. Hutchins slides much too easily over the fact that the education recommended by him for the preservation of democracy was in the past close to the kind of education found in undemocratic societies. It nurtured an élite which on the whole opposed democracy wherever it appeared. On the other hand, it was the trade unions and the dissenting churches which were the schools of democracy in Europe, not the *Gymnasium*, the *lycée*, or university. Mr. Hutchins is a little embarrassed that Aristotle, whose works and ideas are pillars which support the best education, opposed democracy and held that some men by nature are slaves. He explains that Aristotle did not understand his own doctrines. Presumably that is why Plato and Aquinas, as important as Aristotle in his educational scheme, advocated the death sentence for heretics.

This calls attention to a significant difference in what modern educators call intelligence and what Mr. Hutchins calls intellectual power. If one recommends the study of a subject for the purpose of developing the intellectual powers of students, one cannot believe without deceiving himself that such powers are general and that they can be brought to bear equally well on the problems of all fields. This is the mistake of those who assume that if their employees are slipshod in the use of tools, it is because they did not learn the niceties of Latin or English grammar. The subject matters of different fields are often so far removed from each other that the skills and habits acquired in mastering one field are no index to competence in another. Indeed, do we not often notice today that there is no more agreement about human affairs among those who have developed a common set of intellectual skills in their profession than among those who have not acquired such skills. This would seem to suggest a conspicuous kind of irrelevance between the intellectual skills in language, mathematics and science, however desirable these skills be for enlarging our understanding of the world, and the political wisdom and maturity about human affairs which Mr. Hutchins assures us is best achieved by what *he* regards as the best education. On occasions one is impressed not only by the absence of political wisdom on the part of those so trained but by their lack of political knowledge.

As modern educators use the term "intelligence" it is broader than the exercise of special intellectual aptitudes. It involves judgment of values, of the relation of persons to persons, and of persons to groups. This is the common subject matter of everybody's experience from child to adult. The common curriculum of studies that seems most relevant for a democracy would look quite different from that proposed by Mr. Hutchins. Without neglecting the basic skills and subject matter, it would emphasize elements in the student's personal and social experiences which mirror larger relationships, carry this to higher levels of generalization and complexity, and orient liberal education to a consideration of the great social and political problems of *our* time, on which *we* have to make decisions, instead of the social and political problems of past time.

If Mr. Hutchins really desires a curriculum relevant to democratic living and citizenship, he should give greater attention to the development in students of attitudes and emotions necessary to recognize our interdependences, our collective responsibilities and our concrete individual duties. He should encourage the quest for curricular activities and projects which strengthen a behavior free from the twin faults of egomania and servility, which facilitate imaginative identification with others, which teach that an opponent is not necessarily an enemy and that democracy is also a personal way of life. But it is precisely projects and activities of this kind which Mr. Hutchins and other critics of modern education scorn as serious tomfoolery.

I am not suggesting that the formation of attitudes which enter into moral character should be the task only of the school or that it should be the whole task of the school or even the direct task of the school except on the elementary level. Nor do I see why it is necessary to divorce it from the study of organized subject matters and basic skills. If "education *for* democracy" is not to become a mere phrase, we cannot neglect it. Modern education does not neglect it. If it does not educate for democracy well, the only legitimate criticism is that it must do it better and not that it must cease to concern itself with attitudes, emotions, and social relations.

In discussing Mr. Bestor's *Educational Wastelands*[12] we are moving to another plane of criticism—one which is frankly empirical. Although Messrs. Hutchins and Lynd fortify their indictment of modern education by citing some unhappy experiences, they rest their case on other considerations. We have seen that Mr. Hutchins minces no words about it. Since the metaphysics of modern education is bad, its results must be bad.

Mr. Bestor, however, speaks for a large and ever-growing number of individuals who profess to judge modern education by its results. And he is profoundly convinced that our schools, especially our elementary and secondary schools, are turning out young men and women not only unwilling to think in a disciplined way but unable to do so; not only ignorant about what they should know but, even worse, ignorant of what to do and where to go to repair the deficiencies of their knowledge when they become aware of them. They simply lack the habits of inquiry. "Intellectual training," he says, ". . . has been pushed out to the periphery of the public school program."[13] "Public school educationists have severed all real connection with the great world of science and learning."[14]

The evidence? Some startling quotations from the writings of a school

[12] Arthur Bestor, *Educational Wastelands*, University of Illinois Press, Urbana, Ill., 1953.
[13] *Ibid.*, p. 44.
[14] *Ibid.*, p. 47.

principal or a professor of education, with no confirming evidence that it represents the dominant sentiment among modern teachers or that the results of modern instruction verify it. For example, Mr. Bestor quotes a sentence which, although he characterizes it as extreme, he nonetheless takes as representative of the current mood in American schools. It is a sentence which has been picked up by popular magazines in what seems to be a campaign to scare the parents of the country.

"We shall some day accept the thought that it is just as illogical to assume that every boy must be able to read as it is that each one must be able to perform on a violin, that it is no more reasonable to require that each girl shall spell well than it is that each one shall bake a good cherry pie."

The implication is that this truly horrifying thought is guiding current practices in teaching the fundamental skills in our elementary schools. But what of the studies which show that modern schools do better in this respect than those of the past? All that shows, according to Mr. Bestor, is that, making allowance for improvement in physical conditions and for the increase of the school year, the improvement is not good *enough*. The results of the *Eight-Year Study?* All that shows is that the colleges in which the products of progressive high schools did well were not very good to begin with.

There is some other evidence, but it is difficult to assess. For example, Mr. Bestor quotes some figures from the federal Office of Education which show that smaller percentages of the present student body are enrolled in courses in mathematics and foreign languages than in the past. But today almost everyone is in high school, including groups of children whose intellectual capacities would have been considered in the past as not sufficiently developed for high school and who, had they been enrolled, would have failed their mathematics and language. I am confident that Mr. Bestor would not be willing to degrade the standards of intellectual achievement merely to be able to enroll everybody. What would be more helpful to know is the relative success of teaching mathematics and language today to students of capacities comparable to those who were taught these subjects in the past. Three questions must be kept distinct. Is present-day instruction inferior to that of the past when comparable factors are considered? Can present-day instruction be improved even if it has not deteriorated? Are we failing to give instruction in certain disciplines which would educationally be more profitable to students than the subjects they are now studying?

I do not know the answer to these questions. Mr. Bestor believes emphatically he does. His emphasis, however, seems to me to be disproportionate to the weight of the evidence he submits. I should say in his support that my colleagues in liberal arts colleges are dissatisfied with the quality of the students the high schools send them. I should add, however, that they always have been dissatisfied. I predict they always will be.

Nonetheless, what is apparent from the wide acceptance of Mr. Bestor's charges is that the public does not know what actually is going on in the schools of the country and that they do not understand what modern education is or what it is trying to do. My own reading of the works of John Dewey and other leading exponents of modern education convinces me that their goal is not the substitution of play for serious study or of proficiency in inconsequential activities for learning, but continuing growth in intellectual and emotional maturity and the acquisition of the knowledge and disciplines which make that growth possible. Even allowing for the distortions and caricatures of their detractors, responsibility for the widespread failure to understand the program of modern education rests heavily on modern educators themselves.

Assume for the moment that the true goals of modern education were to become known independently of whether they were approved or disapproved. Two other things would still have to be known: first, the actual extent to which its goals guide instruction and its methods are consciously used in the school systems of the country; second, the degree of success and failure in the use of its methods as compared with traditional methods. We can answer these questions for a few local communities. I have seen no answers for the country as a whole. A great deal of controversial discussion about current educational matters assumes that these answers are known.

Mr. Bestor believes, however, that there is indirect evidence of the true state of affairs and that it can be found in the curriculum of the teacher-training colleges. He contends that teachers' colleges are at best qualified to teach only pedagogical skills—skills that can be taught through relatively few courses. Teaching skills are worthless unless the prospective teacher has mastered the organized subject matter he wishes to teach. This organized subject matter can best be taught by professors of the liberal arts, not by professors of pedagogy in schools of education. These schools, however, not only compel their students to take needless courses in pedagogy for professional advancement, they provide instruction in the subject matter courses given in the liberal arts college. The consequence is that our prospective teachers are ill equipped to teach the subject for which they are licensed. To Mr. Bestor the life of mind is lived only in the liberal arts college: schools of education constitute a kind of intellectual underworld. Since our schools can rise no higher than their teacher source, they cannot educate for intelligence even if they seek to do so. "Across the edutional world," he writes, "stretches an iron curtain which the professional educationists are busily fashioning. Behind it, in slave labor camps, are the classroom teachers, whose only hope is rescue from without." He closes with an eloquent plea that his colleagues in the liberal arts colleges through their professional associations concern themselves with "the scientific and scholarly soundness of every major proposal affecting the content and organization of the public secondary-school curriculum." He urges them also to study programs of teacher education and the laws governing certification in order to determine whether proper training in intellectual discipline is given by the first and enforced by the second.

Mr. Bestor's language is provocative and in places needlessly offensive. Whether true or false—and I for one distrust such sweeping generalizations—his charges are sure to arouse resentment. But whatever their resentments, professional educators should not, I believe, oppose his proposals. On the contrary, they should welcome them as the best way to raise the iron curtain of which Mr. Bestor speaks. They might suggest, however, an addition to the agenda of concern, viz., an inquiry into the effectiveness of teaching in the liberal arts colleges. But even in their original form Mr. Bestor's proposals, if acted upon, are very likely to bear sound fruit. They will at the very least accomplish something which has never been done before, i.e., make the teachers of liberal arts colleges aware of the problems of mass education in a democratic society. Instead of talking about standards in the abstract, they will think about them in the concrete context of wide variations in the natural powers of students, all of whom are capable of some development but not necessarily in the same way. Although he speaks as if teachers' colleges usurped their function, he is well aware that it was the refusal of liberal arts colleges to take problems of general public education seriously which was in large measure responsible for the growth of teachers' colleges.

It is simply not true that the invidious judgments which, Mr. Bestor reports, are often passed by his colleagues on teachers' colleges are the consequence of the *present* character of their goals and curricular content. Unfortunately, these judgments were already reflected in the profound unconcern which liberal arts colleges in the past manifested towards all the great problems of public education. The reason is not far to seek. Until very recently most of the disciplines in the liberal arts college were taught by specialists for future specialists. Chemistry was taught as if all students were preparing themselves for careers either as research chemists or as professors of chemistry. Mathematics and physics were taught as if all students were going to be engineers or college teachers of those subjects. The consequence was that, except for the select few who did become specialists or college professors, there remained no lasting interest in the subject, no sense of its bearing on other disciplines. Even curiosity and the original sense of wonder about the subject was often killed.

The situation has changed somewhat in the liberal arts colleges, partly as a result of the influence of modern conceptions of education. But even to this day I occasionally discover that the cause of concern among some of my colleagues about the education their children are receiving in the public schools is the secret fear that they are not getting an education which will qualify them to be college professors.

Cooperation between faculties of liberal arts colleges and of teachers' colleges has been too long delayed. Such cooperation will avoid unnecessary duplication of courses devoted to subject matter. It will make every liberal arts teacher aware that he is an educator, too. It will destroy the idea that there can be a double standard of scholarship, at the same time that it stimulates the scholar to make his knowledge come alive and grow in the students' experience.

I should like to conclude with some personal observations. Unlike most university professors, I have had practical teaching experience on every level of the American school system with the exception of the kindergarten. If one feels a responsibility only to a subject or to a discipline, teaching is the easiest activity in the world, especially if one enjoys monologue. But if one also feels a responsibility to the student, to each student, teaching is difficult. It grows in difficulty with the recognition of the variation in the students' capacities.

As I understand modern education, its aim does not slight intellectual development. It wouldn't be education if it did. But it takes seriously the moral obligation to develop the intellectual capacities of each student by whatever method or route is objectively best. This involves measuring his progress not by some arbitrary norm but in terms of his ability to do better, to widen his cultural horizon, and to improve his intellectual skills. This is not incompatible with recognizing the social necessity of the students' achieving some fixed minimum norms of proficiency before qualifying for advanced work or preparation for careers. If the phrase "responsibility to subject matter" has any meaning, those who use it should acknowledge that not *all* disciplines can be properly taught on certain advanced levels that will make them assimilable to everyone. Within the range of normal variation, however, certain disciplines which all students need in order to live in a modern world and a democratic society may and should be required. Because that variation is still very considerable, curricula and methods cannot be fixed but must be adapted to place, time, and persons. In approaching this task we must bring all the resources of modern psychology and pedagogy into play, not to eliminate difficult things from study, but to make them better understood. This is why, as John Dewey used to emphasize again and again, "the road of the new education is not an easier one to follow than the old road, but a more strenuous and difficult one." He also predicted that if there is a reaction against its aims and methods, it will be because of "the failure of educators, who professedly adopt them, to be faithful to them in practice." Inquiry, of course, must establish whether this is true. *Theoretically*, it is possible that even when progressive educators are faithful to their aims and methods, they may fail to do as well as or better than others. This is still an open question.

One thing seems clear. If modern education is difficult, the preparation of those who engage in it must be at least commensurate with its difficulty. I do not see how teachers can ever know too much or themselves stop learning. I have never been able to understand why a good liberal arts education should not be a *sine qua non* for teaching on any level no matter how elementary. It is not an automatic qualification, of course, because certain qualities of personality are also essential.

No matter how well teachers are prepared, they will still have to confront a great danger intrinsic to the approach of modern education. This danger arises from the fact that in attempting to get the most out of those who are least naturally gifted, the intellectual development of those who are the most gifted is sometimes cramped. Only a tutorial system for each student could avoid this.

But there is another device which modern educators sometimes use, which is not more widely used because it is feared that it has undemocratic implications. This is the differentiation of students on the basis of their native capacities and achievements in order to prevent the more gifted from being bored by teaching approaches necessary to motivate the less gifted, and in order to prevent the latter from falling behind when the former are given their head. I do not see how this breaches the democratic commitment of modern education in any way. That individuals vary in their musical or athletic prowess is accepted as a matter of course. It is not unfair discrimination to give to those who vary in their learning power different tasks or the same tasks to complete in different times. In many schools this device is widely used. Some high school students cover the course in intermediate algebra in six months; others take a year; a few are encouraged to master the material by self-study. In some English classes four books are intensively studied, in others three. There seems to be no resentment among students who travel at a slower pace, and there is less educational dissatisfaction than there probably would be if they found themselves in the same classes.

This principle can be generalized and applied to colleges, too. In each case, the end of education will be the same—the development of habits of intelligent inquiry. But the curriculum and methods by which the end is achieved do not have to be the same even when certain disciplines are required for all. Some critics of modern education do not object to this so long as institutions which depart from standard curricula are not *called* colleges. But it is unimportant what educational institutions are called. What is important is that genuine learning goes on in them, even if they are not degree granting, and that teachers do not settle for less if better teaching can achieve more.

The best adult education gives us a parallel and many helpful clues. Subjects, methods and levels of instruction vary. But they all justify themselves to the extent that they contribute to individual growth.

One final word. Modern education will always be on the defensive if it waits for criticisms from those who are hostile to its philosophy before facing its problems and correcting its defects. It is the modern educators themselves who should be the foremost critics of modern education.

A New Form of Authoritarianism

It has often been proposed, as a tenet of modern educational theory, that the school serve as a model democracy in order to properly prepare citizens for a democracy. One aspect of the democratic school system that gained acceptance was the lack of authoritarianism and the development of permissive treatment of youngsters. The feeling that the child should develop naturally and as an individual has pervaded progressive educational thought and has led to many forms of permissive teaching. The teacher-structured oral report and the unstructured "What shall we do today" represent the range of approaches employed to encourage freedom of expression in schools.

Fred N. Kerlinger, in the following treatise, examines the consequences of extreme permissiveness as an educational doctrine. He uses democracy as a reference point and analyzes the actual permissiveness in a nondirected classroom.

What is the dogmatism of permissiveness? What is the proper role of the teacher who aspires to develop democratic attitudes in youngsters? What relation does democracy as a social philosophy have to educational philosophy? What would one expect to observe in a school that was labeled democratic?

The Implications of the Permissiveness Doctrine in American Education

FRED N. KERLINGER

The doctrine of permissiveness in education and its relation to democratic ideology have been tormenting problems to American educators. Most thinkers apparently agree on a rather large measure of permissiveness in the education of children. The idea seems basically to be that children, if they are to mature into democratic individuals and citizens, must not be

Reprinted from *Educational Theory*, Vol. 10, No. 2, April, 1960, pp. 120–27, by permission of the publisher and the author.

too restricted in the pursuit of their own interests and needs, since such restrictiveness will somehow have the unfortunate consequence of producing undemocratic citizens. If children are not "permitted" a good deal of freedom—more specifically, decision choice—then they will not mature into autonomous, cooperative, and generally democratic individuals. In short, without permissiveness we run the danger of creating authoritarian individuals and an authoritarian society. Certainly, the argument goes, we now have a generally authoritarian school system which is systematically warping millions of children into undesirable types of human beings, human beings who lack autonomy, maturity, and true democratic potentiality.

That there is much truth in the above argument few educators would deny. The underlying undemocratic and even authoritarian quality of many, perhaps most, American schools and classrooms seems evident, if we are to believe responsible critics. Yet it also seems that a good deal of the older restrictiveness and authoritarianism have been mitigated; improvement, while slow, has occurred.[1] The strong reaction against the older restrictiveness in education which started in the early part of the century has had its effect. Old-line authoritarian educational thinking and methods are becoming more and more disapproved as the contemporary permissive influence makes itself felt. The superintendent, principal, or teacher who wants to play the boss role must now do it in a more covert and subtle fashion.

The purpose of this paper is to speculate on the possibility of a new authoritarianism springing from a relatively *extreme* and basic emphasis on permissiveness. In a previous paper in which the modern origins of permissiveness in American education were traced, it was claimed that the doctrine of permissiveness in education had its origins in the thinking of Freud and Dewey and that the strong impact of these two great thinkers had laid the foundations for modern ideas and practices of permissiveness in education.[2] It was also suggested that a new authoritarianism might be arising, a phenomenon expressed by two concepts which are becoming influential symbols in American education: permissiveness and group dynamics. It was further suggested that possibly there were manipulatory and authoritarian implications of the doctrines many educators are espousing. Finally, the paper hinted at a covert anti-intellectualism springing from permissivist and group dynamics doctrines. The present essay will be limited to an analysis of the implications of the permissiveness doctrine. Group dynamics doctrine was partially explored in a previous paper.[3] Simi-

---

[1] Careful *scientific* studies of authoritarianism in education are scarce, almost nonexistent. This is probably a function of the difficulty of measuring such a complex phenomenon as authoritarianism plus a general touchiness of school people on the subject.

[2] Fred N. Kerlinger, "The Origin of the Doctrine of Permissiveness in American Education," *Progressive Education*, Vol. 33, 1956, pp. 161–65.

[3] Fred N. Kerlinger, "The Authoritarianism of Group Dynamics," *Progressive Education*, Vol. 31, 1954, pp. 169–73.

larly, the anti-intellectual implications of the permissiveness doctrine will not be directly discussed. It must wait for future treatment.

The argument that follows is based on five main points: (1) that the doctrine of permissiveness is more of a reaction against older restrictive and undemocratic educational ideas than it is a *movement for* democratic ideas; (2) that the espousal and implementation of relatively extreme permissive ideas imply and lead to manipulation of the pupil by the teacher and of the teacher by the pupil; (3) that while extreme permissive practices are claimed to be democratic they may be in effect autocratic; (4) that when permissive ideas dominate a teacher, when they form the mainspring of her educational being, they lead to a basic violation of the integrity of the individual; and (5) that when permissiveness is a fundamental and overriding concern of the teacher it leads to a pervasive conformity of the individual to the will of the teacher and/or the class group.

Before beginning the main discussion, an important point should be clarified. This paper is not meant to be a critique of permissiveness in general. It is assumed that a moderate amount of permissiveness is good and that the older educational restrictiveness is bad. The permissiveness to be discussed is the relatively extreme and unilateral doctrine espoused by a number of educational writers, some of whom will be cited. This unilateral doctrine seems to imply a wholesale sort of permissiveness running from the kindergarten through the graduate school, a permissiveness which labels almost any sort of educational direction from a teacher as a sign of autocracy, which says that to lecture is to impose one's will on students and is therefore bad, authoritarian, and to be eschewed by the democratic educator, which says, furthermore, that group processes in the classroom are in and of themselves good, democratic, to be encouraged since they presumably permit the greatest amount of individual expression through democratic interaction with others. In short, it is the unilateral and extreme doctrine of permissiveness which permits nothing but permissiveness and which threatens to become dogma and religion that is the object of scrutiny.

The first point, that a great deal of permissivist doctrine is a reaction *against* the older authoritarianism and restrictiveness in education rather than a movement *for* permissiveness and democratic ideas is apparent from a study of much education literature. One gets the impression from reading permissivist works that nothing in the older education was much good —except the pupils. This reactivity against traditional education accounts for much of the literature's extreme and rather naive quality, and it leads permissivist authors to be somewhat condescending and patronizing when talking about the older education and about practices with which they disagree. Permissivist literature has mainly negative criticism of traditional education as its ideological foundation. When it comes to the task of constructing a positive philosophy permissivists find themselves in a difficult position since they must "permit" anything but restrictiveness. What permissivists have done, therefore, is to attempt to solve the problem by borrowing quite selectively from Dewey and Freud, mainly, and by manufacturing a new metaphysics on the basis of these borrowings. The character of the movement is heavily moral and, as already indicated, seems to derive most of its force from derogation—derogation of the older education, of subject matter, of teachers. The derogation is often concealed by words and rather vague, even mystical, writing. For example, Rasey says, "And we teachers. We teach nothing. We can no more teach than we can learn a child. We are onlookers while life teaches."[4] As with many such statements there is a kernel of truth here. But there is also obfuscation of the teaching-learning problem. A number of examples of derogation can also be found in Cantor's work. One of the best of these is his castigation of instruction which begins with definitions.[5] He implies that any instructor who uses definitions in approaching a subject is, *ipso facto*, a bad teacher. In another place, Cantor, like many other educators, derogates those who lecture. He says, "The instructor who lectures deprives the students of their right actively to participate in their class."[6] He then says, very significantly, "The instructor who is aware of his function refrains from using students for displaying his knowledge. He permits himself to be used, in a professional way, by them."[7]

The argument being advanced is that, if permissivism is basically a reactive doctrine it must also necessarily be essentially negative in tone and practice. The teacher must *not* do anything restrictive; she must *not* do anything—or think anything—traditional. To be deeply concerned with subject matter, for example, is questionable since it leads to "coercion" of pupils. It seems evident that permissivist educators served a very useful purpose during the early days of reaction against the authoritarian practices of the past. (The battle is of course by no means yet won.) To continue to espouse a basically negative and reactive ideology, however, can be a defeat of the hard-won victories of a splendid educational movement.

Perhaps the most serious implication and end-result of extreme permissiveness is that it leads to manipulation of pupils. The very permissive teacher sets up few or no limits for her pupils. Few norms of behavior and learning are supposed to be teacher-determined. But a normless social situation is of course impossible; some norms or rules must always govern behavior. If the teacher does not supply the rules or norms, the pupils will. Fine! says the permissivist, and it is fine—to a certain extent. But the teacher is a basic authority ingredient of any learning situation. Many educators may dispute this and say that the learner, or rather, the learner group should be the basic ingredient. But the teacher is a guide to learning; she is the experienced group member who must take a leading role in

---

[4] Marie I. Rasey, *Toward Maturity,* Barnes & Noble, New York, 1947, p. 231. See also, the same author's *This Is Teaching,* Harper & Row, New York, 1950.

[5] Nathanial Cantor, *Dynamics of Learning,* Foster & Stewart, Buffalo, N.Y., 1946.

[6] *Ibid.,* pp. 145 and 153.

[7] *Ibid.,* p. 174.

directing group activities toward educational goals set at least partly by society. She is society's surrogate who must ensure, by norm and rule-setting, that the societal educational goals are reached. Now when she does not take this function, she puts herself into the unfortunate situation of being forced, consciously or unconsciously, to manipulate her charges. She *must* discharge the societal function; there is, by definition, no alternative. Pupils may take the responsibility adequately; they may decide to teach the societal goals. Then, again, they may not. And this cannot be left to chance, and any teacher knows it. Pupils, even by the age of six, are dimly aware of it, as Piaget's work would seem to indicate. The problem boils down not to whether or not there are norms—there are always norms— but to who sets the norms. Ideally both pupils and teacher should set them. Yet the teacher's role in norm-setting, again by societal definition, must always be dominant. Any other situation is sociologically and psychologically anomalous. To say that this is a violation of democratic freedom is semantic nonsense. Freedom is always relative; it is always bounded by norms and rules for behavior. As Dewey well said, ". . . guidance given by the teacher to the exercise of the pupil's intelligence is an aid to freedom, not a restriction upon it."[8] The argument can be rounded out with another Dewey excerpt.

Sometimes teachers seem to be afraid to make suggestions to the members of a group as to what they should do. . . . But what is more important is that the suggestion upon which pupils act must in any case come from somewhere. It is impossible to understand why a suggestion from one who has a larger experience and a wider horizon should not be at least as valid as a suggestion arising from some more or less accidental source.[9]

The above argument leads to the third point: that extreme permissivism leads to autocratic rather than, as supposed, to democratic thinking and practice. If the permissive teacher acts upon the precepts of a Kelley[10] or a Cantor, she will find herself in a peculiar predicament. If the group will does not point in the socially desirable direction—and, again, any teacher will know this by the very nature of social norms which depend for their efficacy on being interiorized by all or most members of a society—she will be in the unenviable position of manipulating the group so that it will more or less fall into line. The famous expression, "Do we have to do what we want to do today?" while a humorous exaggeration, contains the kernel of this problem. Basically, and somewhat cynically, the teacher who is committed unilaterally to permissiveness must so manipulate the situation, herself, and the pupils that the goals of society which are her goals by definition since she is, at least in good part, a surrogate of society, are achieved. The manipulation comes in when the direction of educational activity

[8] John Dewey, *Experience and Education*, Macmillan, New York, 1938, p. 84.
[9] *Ibid.*, pp. 84–85.
[10] Earl C. Kelley, *Education For What Is Real*, Harper & Row, New York, 1947.

strays too far from the societal goals. It should not be thought that this is a defense of education as a preserver of the status quo. No matter what position is taken on education's function, it still remains a fact, by the definition of education as a cultural phenomenon, that schools must teach at least a basic core of values, attitudes, skill, and facts. Variability will be very great in a democracy, naturally, but the common norm must be there.

In other words, the lines must be drawn somewhere, and it is the teacher acting for and as society who draws the lines. And the lines must be clear and unambiguous. To think or act otherwise is to lay the foundation for social and personal chaos. One good definition of a teacher is that he is a person working to put himself out of a job. This means, of course, that a teacher always should try to have his students develop as rapidly as possible into mature people who have learned what he knows, who have his understandings and more. To give a child too much freedom too soon, to force children to make choices they are really incapable of making, is to defeat this definition because, as Fromm has pointed out, we have to grow to independence through dependence, through self-love to love of others. Learning from teachers always has this symbiotic character. It is not undemocratic; it is natural and inevitable.

That an espousal of relatively extreme permissivism can lead to violation of the integrity of the individual follows from the argument on manipulation. Manipulation of pupils, if practiced systematically, is a violation of the integrity of both pupil and teacher for quite obvious reasons. The integrity, the wholeness, of any individual depends upon acting fairly consistently in accordance with both approved social norms and one's approved self-image. The manipulation is of course usually not perceived as manipulation. The teacher has herself been taught that the ideas she is trying to implement are good—and they are good. Democratic cooperation, participation in the learning process, and the like are good values. But the difficulty is how to achieve them. The group way, she has been taught, is the right way. She is also taught not to impose her will on children but to discover their needs and interests and to use these to achieve the learning objectives. All this, too, is good. But somewhere, some time, she must draw lines beyond which children cannot be permitted to go. To do this she sometimes must use methods which, in a permissivist framework, are not good, she believes. Thus there is a conflict. And the conflict between being democratic and autocratic cannot be resolved, for her at least, by a clear-cut choice. She has no choice: she must be democratic. Yet to be democratic, she has learned, is to be permissive. Her only recourse is to use the permissive methods and still achieve societal objectives. And this often means doing things which are "coercive." She often ends up using "nice coercion." Children soon learn the rules of the game, and, as Riesman points out, they become skilled at conforming to these "nice" demands. They also become skilled at manipulating the teacher. But in the process both teacher and pupil lose some of their integrity since life and the class-room are not always so nice, so cooperative, so democratic, and in order to maintain the "nice" fiction, it is often necessary to practice mild but insidious deceptions on others and on oneself.

To complete the argument, we need to examine the relationship between permissiveness and conformity. When permissiveness is the *fundamental* guide of a teacher's thinking and behavior, pupils must pay the price of conformity. This is perhaps best understood by going through the back door. It can be agreed that in an autocratic setup the social situation is clear to all parties concerned—role relationships are clearly understood as are group norms. The pupils, for example, at least have something concrete to rebel against and, if necessary, to fight. But with the highly permissive teacher, whether manipulatory and autocratic or not, there is nothing to rebel against or to fight. A pupil may have a vague feeling of being used, and he may want to do something about it. But what can he do? Even the other pupils will disapprove of him if he goes against the "nice one." The pressures toward conformity are very strong in such situations. And the conformity goes beyond what was demanded under the outright and open autocratic setup: it is personal and moral as well as behavioral. The pupils should even think like the teacher, or rather, the teacher-pupil group.

Study of a number of contemporary educational writings shows learnings which clearly imply conformity to the group. In fact, permissiveness and group cooperation, as doctrines, usually go hand in hand in much of the writing. They seem to be basic tenets of a new orthodoxy. For example, Kilpatrick, in talking about the effectiveness of group education, says:

How then is good character best built. . . . In the multitudinous social contacts there will inevitably arise situations of social stress. Under wise guidance the group should be led to see the issues involved and conclude as to just disposition of the dispute. Such a group conclusion no individual will permanently dispute. To defy his group seldom satisfies. *In the end he will accept* . . .[11] (Italics mine.)

Comment here is hardly necessary.

Along with these emphases goes a concomitant rather strong emphasis on emotional learnings. One gathers that the basic function of education is to foster proper emotional attitudes and the ability to get along with people. It is here contended that this "sociometric" approach to education, as Riesman has aptly named it, is actually detrimental to democratic education, that it leads in effect, to autocratic practices. When the emphasis in a class is emotional, it is difficult for children to learn objective modes of thinking. They learn to focus on the rather slippery ground of affect and only secondarily learn to handle facts and things. It is not contended here that emotional learning is wrong. But it *is* contended that a *basic* emphasis

[11] William H. Kilpatrick, *Group Education for a Democracy*, Association Press, New York, 1940, p. 130.

on emotional learning is wrong. The emphasis in a classroom should be on work, on things, *and* on attitudes, but work should be central. Only thus is the child free to develop as a democratic human being. When the central emphasis is on feelings, especially feelings toward other persons, objectivity, independence, and autonomy become difficult or even impossible to learn and to achieve. This is because constant preoccupation with one's own and other people's feelings is an unstable and insecure ground on which to build a basis for learning to make objective and critical judgments of problems and issues since all of one's thinking becomes colored and perhaps distorted by interpersonal affect. This is a major defect of much of the practical application of group dynamics as well as of the classroom dominated by feelings. When one learns always to be concerned with the feelings of others and of oneself *as primary* in any situation, then one also learns to be careful and circumspect, to be always concerned with not promoting bad feelings. Such affect preoccupation effectively cripples any budding learning of how to approach problems objectively since one's approach to problems becomes strongly conditioned by irrelevant concerns such as what other people may think of your proposed solution of the problem. Questionable hypotheses, hypotheses that might jar the group and other people's feelings, are entertained timidly if they are entertained at all. Gradually one learns to be sufficiently sensitive to what will or will not disturb other people's feelings. There are always situations, in any problem solution and in any complex learning, in which it may be necessary for someone to say, "You're wrong; this is the right solution." But this is forbidden in the permissive, group-oriented classroom, strange as it may seem. The word "permissive" comes to mean to permit anything but that which will hurt feelings, which will disturb the nice cooperative atmosphere of the class group.

It can readily be seen that permissiveness in education is anything but permissive. Norms, rules of behavior, are set up in any situation. In the traditional classroom they are set up almost entirely by the teacher. In the permissive classroom, they are set up by the group which includes—or may not include—the teacher. In the former situation the norms are usually clearcut and well understood. They may not be liked but they are clear and unambiguous. And traditional classrooms are usually object or subject or problem-oriented. In the latter situation the norms usually lack clarity and definiteness; they are the rather amorphous product of an amorphous social situation where, theoretically, much is permitted but where, in reality, a great deal is restricted. Norms that are amorphous and ambiguous, however, are still rules of behavior, expectations about the right and wrong things to do. The trouble is that no one is clear as to just what is right, only what is wrong. It is wrong to be uncooperative, not a good group member, not nice. Anything else is right, provided it meets the needs and purposes of the group members. Such an inverted value scale is characteristic of extreme permissive groups, and it is no wonder that manipulation also becomes a characteristic. Manipulation is almost demanded by such a topsy-turvy social situation for, as indicated earlier, the group leader is responsible for achieving the external group goals. But she cannot impose her will; this would not be democratic. Thus she must manipulate the group except in the fortunate case when the group's wishes perhaps fortuitously coincide with the external group goals, i.e., with the goals of society.

The individual psychological consequences of permissiveness have been almost entirely ignored in this essay and can only be touched upon now. It was pointed out in the earlier paper on permissiveness that one of the cogent psychoanalytic reasons for permissiveness was to avoid frustrations to prevent the presumed consequences of frustration, aggression, and possibly mental ill-health. Fenichel has cogently discussed this problem, and I will not repeat his argument.[12] Suffice it to say that in the extreme permissive situation there is probably a good deal of frustration which cannot be dealt with since by definition it is not supposed to exist. Nobody is frustrated if almost anything is permitted everybody (except, perhaps, in the adult group when some members want to get the work done), but as we have seen everything is not permitted. There is a wide band of thinking and activity which is not permitted, even though nothing may be openly said about this *verboten* area: don't do or say anything which will hurt other people's feelings, which is undemocratic (or that anxiety-provoking word, authoritarian), which is uncooperative, which will prevent the group from reaching its goals and meeting its needs. Above all, don't be an unnice person who is hard to get along with. The autocratic implications of all this should be obvious. Like consensus unanimity thinking, extreme permissiveness carries within itself the seeds of authoritarianism. Conformity, not rational conformity which is necessary for any social life, but irrational and emotional conformity and loss of freedom are the prices paid for this questionable product. Other prices, while not as high, are devastating to the individual, especially to the teacher. Guilt at not being nice, at not being sociometric, at not being a good guy is probably increasing among content-oriented teachers. Anxiety lest one say or do the "wrong" thing, lest one be undemocratic, lest one hurt someone else's feelings, lest one be obstructive (the older word is "argumentative"), lest one not appear right, or—most crushing to the teacher—lest one not be permissive, lest one not let whole children grow as wholes, lest one not be warm and loving, is also increasing. Again, the ultimate price of the permissive-group complex is freedom of the individual. Permissiveness, as preached in some educational literature, can be a corrosion of individual freedom, the freedom of the individual intellect to wander, to speculate, to be daring, to be imaginative, even to be radical. To permit too much is really to permit very little.

[12] Otto Fenichel, *The Psychoanalytic Theory of Neurosis*, Norton, New York, 1954, pp. 584–89.

Many readers may think that the argument as presented is extreme. And it is. But it is believed that the tendency as outlined exists to an extent little realized by educators themselves. And what is worse, the idea that the philosophy being espoused may be questionable, may be deleterious to children and to teachers, is not even considered. Educators are also often not aware of the metaphysical quality of contemporary permissivist doctrine. Nor are they aware of its dogmatism. As Dewey aptly said, "It is not too much to say that an educational philosophy which proposes to be based on the idea of freedom may become as dogmatic as ever was the traditional education which is reacted against."[13]

A final word is in order. In a healthy democratic classroom the bounds and limits of behavior must be clearly known and understood by teacher and pupils. Pupils must understand authority. Authority of course does not mean authoritarianism. Nor is authority a dirty word. It is an inevitable concomitant of the social process. In the classroom it inheres in the teacher and only seldom in the class group. To be permissive, especially in an extreme fashion, is to blur and confuse the outlines of the class social situation. This does not mean that a teacher should not be permissive. The difficulties mentioned arise when permissiveness is espoused (explicitly or implicitly) *as a basic doctrine* of educational practice and is not something a teacher occasionally is. When it is espoused as a basic doctrine, it, like all other dogmatisms, leads not to democracy but rather to authoritarianism in the classroom.

Social Ideas of American Educators

In the following two selections from Merle Curti's book, the relation of education to society is expressed as a social historian views it. The first selection analyzes the social thought of John Dewey and its impact. This well-documented presentation of various revolutionary positions taken by Dewey in regard to both social and educational issues shows the philosopher's mind at work. It is doubtful that any person has had so profound an influence on American educational thought or as many critics as John Dewey.

The second selection is taken from a newer preface to Social Ideas of American Educators, *in which Professor Curti deals with changes that have*

[13] Dewey, *op. cit.,* p. 10.

occurred since the first printing twenty-five years earlier. What changes of significance to both society and education does this piece neglect? Where will educational leadership come from during the next twenty-five years? Which social ideas of educational leaders have produced the greatest impact on society?

John Dewey

MERLE CURTI

Dewey's conception of education follows naturally from his belief that mind is a function of organic life and conditioned by the totality of that organic life including basic occupational activity, and from his conviction that mind plays a part in controlling, directing, and reforming social organization. The existing pattern of social arrangements, according to Dewey, is based on an orderly system of reactions to existing stimuli; hence that pattern may be modified by an intelligent change of the stimuli. The change is to be achieved by education, or "the continuous reconstruction of experience." Experience, or trying and undergoing the consequences of activity, provides the organism with intelligent foresight and is fundamental in the educative process.[1]

This psychological conception of experience and education is intimately associated with the theory of democracy. In fact, Dewey regarded psychology as a tool both for understanding and attaining that ideal. For him, as for Emerson and Whitman, democracy is far more than a form of government or an expression of popular sovereignty;[2] it is an associated method of living together in such a way as to break down the barriers which separate the class which works with its hands from the class which occupies itself with matters of the mind.[3] It is, in other words, a way of life in which affairs are so ordered that the aesthetic as well as the intellectual and social self-realization of the individual in a community involves necessarily the equal self-realization of every other person.[4] In a democracy, Dewey urges in an early article, the determination of ethical values lies, not in any set or class, however superior, but in the workings of the social

From *The Social Ideas of American Educators,* by Merle Curti, Scribner's, New York, 1935, pp. 518–41. Reprinted by permission of the American Historical Association and the author.

[1] John Dewey, *Democracy and Education,* Macmillan, New York, 1931, pp. 89–90.

[2] Dewey, in discussing political democracy, repudiated Austin's idea that sovereignty could be found in a certain definitely limited portion of society. *Political Science Quarterly,* Vol. 9, March, 1894, p. 42. For a critical discussion of Dewey's pragmatic conception of politics see W. Y. Elliott, *The Pragmatic Revolt in Politics,* New York, 1928.

[3] *Ed. Rev.,* Vol. 21, May, 1901, p. 471.

[4] *Outlines of a Critical Theory of Ethics,* p. 131.

whole.[5] The needs of the moment, in accordance with the ascertained truth of the moment, are to be met through "the free and mutual harmonizing of different individuals," the precaution being constantly taken that every person share in determining the conditions and aims of his own work.[6] When Dewey asserted that psychology is "a conception of democracy" he seems to have had in mind the communicative and participative processes through which individualization proceeds.[7]

The role of education in promoting social change can now be better understood. Every ideal, according to Dewey, is preceded by an actuality; but "the ideal is more than a repetition in inner image of the actual. It projects in securer and wider and fuller form some good which has been previously experienced in a precarious, accidental, fleeting way."[8] The ideal, for Dewey, is never an abstraction. The diversion of intelligence from attaining concrete, particular ends, desirable for the common good, to upholding vague moral ideas, has done more to establish inequality and injustice among men than brute love of power. In reality, he argued, the championship of the bare precepts of categorical imperatives has resulted in the use of intelligence to incorporate class standards of conduct, based upon uncriticized customs and established habits, into professed ideal codes of morals.[9] If intelligence were, instead, freely and effectively used, and tested by concrete results, then it might become far more potent than a force for achieving true democracy.

If the reconstruction of habits be systematically pursued in a new type of education, then the class codes of morals which, under the caption of ideals, sanction the *status quo* would be, according to Dewey, criticized and finally eliminated; new and more democratic habits, based on the same impulses, would arise. Thus new needs of society could be met in an intelligent way. If asked for more specific indications of exactly how psychology and philosophy are to serve these functions, Dewey would refer the questioner to his concrete criticisms of existing schools and to his definite proposals for their reconstruction.

When in 1894 Dewey left Ann Arbor to become head of the department of philosophy and education at the University of Chicago he had already given evidence of his interest in the school. Possibly three years of high school teaching was the foundation of that interest. As early as 1885 in a paper on health and sex in higher education he had applauded the tendency to apply the exact methods of science to the problems of education and had called attention to the importance of environment, broadly speak-

[5] John Dewey, "Psychology and Social Practice," *Psychological Review*, Vol. 7, March, 1900, pp. 105–24.

[6] John Dewey, *The Influence of Darwin on Philosophy*, Holt, Rinehart & Winston, New York, 1910.

[7] *Ibid.*, p. 268.

[8] John Dewey, *Human Nature and Conduct*, Holt, Rinehart & Winston, New York, 1922, p. 23.

[9] *The Influence of Darwin on Philosophy*, pp. 74–76.

ing, in its various relations to education.[10] Four years later he had collab-
orated with James Alexander McLellan in writing *Applied Psychology:
An Introduction to the Principles and Practice of Education*. In Chicago
Francis W. Parker and Ella Flagg Young not only provided him with suggestions for the organization of his own laboratory school but often helped
him translate his philosophic conceptions into their empirical equivalents.[11]
By 1895 he was participating in the discussions of interest, which the
Herbartian movement had aroused, interpreting the culture epoch theory,
which the American disciples of Herbart were popularizing, and showing
an alert interest in the child study movement. A few years later he was
challenging the educational doctrines of William T. Harris, which he believed to be a fairly adequate statement of existing practice.[12]

The upshot of Dewey's criticism of existing practice in school education
was that it overemphasized the mere symbols of knowledge; that it did not
make ample use of positive and first-hand contact with experience; and,
above all, that by failing to equip its pupils with the scientific and cooperative methods by which the spiritual interests of society are conserved,
broadened, and deepened, it fitted the child to the pattern of accepted
social attitudes rather than making him a conscious center for the criticism
and reconstruction of social life. Existing classroom methods only partly
succeeded in helping the small child to develop physically, to get along
with other people, and to develop expanding interest in the new and the
changing. Too much attention was paid, he urged again and again, to the
acquisition of information, and too little to the development of responsiveness and sharing in common and pleasurable tasks.

The dominant position occupied by book learning in school education,
while once justifiable, was, Dewey thought, no longer defensible. When a
single small class had access to the exclusive knowledge of books, it was
natural and justifiable for the new public schools to concentrate on providing the masses with reading and writing, tools essential to their participation in the knowledge of the past. Now, however, the universal diffusion of
cheap reading matter and the democratization of literacy did not justify
such exclusive attention in the schools to mere book knowledge. In former
generations the child, participating constantly in household and commu-

[10] John Dewey, "Education and the Health of Women," *Science*, Vol. 6, Oct. 16,
1885, pp. 341–42; "Health and Sex in Higher Education," *Popular Science Monthly*,
Vol. 28, March, 1886, pp. 606–14. In contrast to Hall, Dewey concluded that the data
at hand did not bear out the common belief concerning the injurious effects of higher
education on women.

[11] John T. McManis, *Ella Flagg Young*, Chicago, 1916, pp. 120–21. Dewey is quoted
as saying, "More times than I could well say I didn't see the meaning or force of some
favorite conception of my own till Mrs. Young had given it back to me—I am referring
even more to association with her as a colleague than when she was a student."

[12] John Dewey, "The Results of Child Study Applied to Education," *Transactions
of the Illinois Society for Child-Study*, Vol. 1, Jan., 1895, pp. 18–19; "Interest as Related to Will," *Second Supplement to the First Yearbook of the National Herbart Society*, 1895, pp. 209–55; review of Harris's *Psychologic Foundations of Education*, Ed.
Rev., Vol. 16, June, 1898, pp. 1–14.

nity activities, almost automatically acquired capacities for self-direction, leadership, and independent judgment. Now, however, social and economic conditions had so changed that he no longer developed these qualities outside the schoolroom, and education must devise new methods to inculcate them.[13]

Although the Herbartians were emphasizing moral education in a new and more realistic way, prevalent practice still assumed that the term "moral" designated some special and transcendental region or portion of life. But Dewey in those years at Chicago developed his doctrine that the school must relate morality to the actual conditions and problems of community life if it is to enable the child to contribute to the betterment of society. Character is to be thought of as social insight, social executive power, and social responsiveness—the organized capacity for social functioning. The common separation between intellectual and moral training must be broken down; the isolation of what is moral in the school must be so transformed as to be identical with what is moral in the social relations of the world.[14]

To effect this end, the school must be made into a social center capable of participating in the daily life of the community.[15] The way to prepare for a moral social life in the world is to engage in a moral social life in school. In its function as a social center the school must, according to Dewey, develop morality by interpreting to the individual the intellectual and social meaning of the work in which he is engaged; it must further provide for bringing people and their ideas and beliefs together in such ways as to lessen friction and to introduce deeper sympathy and understanding. In addition, the school in its capacity as a social center must make up in part to the child for the decay of dogmatic and fixed methods of social discipline and for the loss of reverence and the influence of authority.

This idea of the school as a social center had been at least faintly anticipated by Barnard. For Dewey, as for so many of his predecessors, the school was to break down class barriers and distinctions. The new note is his insistence that these barriers are due to the traditional and false separation between knowing and doing, and that by their fusion such class distinctions can be in part obliterated; and that, particularly, the school is to reconstruct society by concentrating on existing, developing factors in community life which are not yet dominant.

The belief that school rewards and fear of punishments, with their undemocratic and competitive social implications, will not be necessary if children feel the glow of positive achievement in doing things together

[13] John Dewey, "The Primary-Education Fetich," *Forum*, Vol. 25, May, 1898, pp. 315–28.

[14] John Dewey, "Ethical Principles Underlying Education," *Third Yearbook of the National Herbart Society*, 1897, pp. 7–33.

[15] John Dewey, "The School as Social Center," N. E. A., *Proceedings*, 1902, pp. 373–83.

resembles that of Parker. The assumption is that co-operative activity will develop, not only the positive virtues of energy and originality, but also those of sharing and helpfulness.[16]

In Dewey's opinion another crying evil of the day was to be found in the existing curriculum. The Herbartians, as he was aware, had brought to the front questions connected with the material of study, but their attitude reflected the pedagogue's view of life rather than the child's.[17] Slurring over the fact that the environment involves a personal sharing in common experiences, they exaggerated beyond reason, he thought, the possibilities of methods consciously formulated and used in the teaching technique; and one infers that he believed this to be true of their organization of the curriculum as well. The actual interests of the child must be discovered, Dewey wrote, if the significance and worth of his life are to be taken into account, and if his full development, the aim of a democratic and progressive society, is to be achieved.[18]

In his specific considerations of the curriculum Dewey, both on the elementary and secondary levels, has repudiated narrowly utilitarian criteria. Each subject is to be cherished for its capacity to fulfill the present needs of growing children—a principle which Rousseau was probably the first to lay down. The business of education is not, for the presumable usefulness of his future, to rob the child of the intrinsic joy involved in living each single day. Yet coupled with this emphasis on growth as an end in itself is the equally important consideration of the effect which a given subject produces in promoting social insight, interest, and responsibility for social improvement, qualities which bulk largest of all in the individual's full development. The curriculum, in short, like the methods and spirit of the classroom, must be designed to further the mental and moral growth of everyone in the group toward a full and rich personality.[19]

Although no subjects possess inherent value, geography and history, according to Dewey, are the two great school resources for "bringing about the enlargement of the significance of a direct personal experience"—the two most effective means in an education which furthers growth in individual and social terms. Properly taught, geography and history provide "the most direct and interesting roads out into the larger world of meanings." History makes human implications explicit; geography makes natural implications explicit. History is to be an indirect study of sociology, "a study of society which lays bare its process of becoming and its modes of be-

[16] John and Evelyn Dewey, *Schools of Tomorrow*, Dutton, New York, 1915, pp. 298–99.
[17] *Democracy and Education*, p. 83.
[18] *Ed. Rev.*, Vol. 13, April, 1897, p. 363.
[19] *Democracy and Education*, pp. 59–61, 226. "We are no longer concerned," Dewey wrote in *The Educational Situation*, University of Chicago, Contributions of Education, No. 3, 1902, pp. 78–79, "with the abstract appraisal of studies by the measuring rod of culture or discipline. Our problem is rather to study the typical necessities of social life, and the actual nature of the individual in his specific needs and capacities."

coming."[20] Its ethical value, Dewey claimed as early as 1897, is to be measured by the extent to which it develops powers of observing, analyzing, and making inferences with respect to the factors making up a social situation and the agencies through which it is modified.[21] This social conception of history is to be contrasted with that of Harris and the report of the Committee of Fifteen;[22] and it is also to be kept in mind in judging Dewey's conviction that the school may become an agency for the remaking of social institutions.

Dewey is not among the radical educators who, under the influence of the doctrine of specificity and the apparent failure of the social studies to give students a realistic understanding of contemporary problems, support the claims of indoctrination. He has held that neither social nor economic isms should be taught in the social studies; but he has insisted that subject matter be made sufficiently specific and explicit to bring the student into gradual contact with the actual realities and democratic needs of contemporary life.[23]

Although not a pacifist, Dewey has disapproved of chauvinistic patriotism in current instruction in civics. His advanced views on international questions, including·his pioneer work for the outlawry of war, led him in 1923 to favor a school program designed to promote international friendship. For such a program, considering the determined policy of isolation of the federal government and the reactionary nationalism of the K. K. K., friends of peace felt much need; but Dewey hardly went much farther than Mann and Parker in suggesting effective means for realizing the ideal of international peace through the schools.

In commenting upon the important place he gives to science in the curriculum, a place for which the technological character of the age, as well as the influence of leaders such as Spencer, is responsible, Dewey has been on his guard against making a fetich of laboratory methods. Recognizing that they may become a meaningless ritual, he has insisted that the function of science in the curriculum is to modify "the habitual attitude of imagination and feeling" in such a way as to create "an intelligence pregnant with belief in the possibility of the direction of human affairs by itself."[24] Science, in accordance with the philosophy of instrumentalism, is to be applied to social problems for the determination of objectives as well as for discovering techniques. Its findings, as the teacher should make evident, are to be used for the democratic promotion of human well-being.

[20] John Dewey, "History for the Educator," *Progressive Journal of Education*, Vol. 1, March, 1909, pp. 1–4.

[21] *Third Yearbook of the National Herbart Society*, 1897, pp. 22–24.

[22] *Cf. ante*, pp. 337–38.

[23] John Dewey, "The Schools as a Means of Developing a Social Consciousness and Social Ideals in Children," *Journal of Social Forces*, Vol. 1, Sept., 1923, pp. 513–17; "Freedom in Philosophies" in H. H. Kallen, *Freedom in the Modern World*, New York, 1928. For Dewey's most recent and specific attitude toward indoctrination see *The Educational Frontier*, p. 71.

[24] *Democracy and Education*, pp. 262–63.

The dislike of employing scientific knowledge as it functions in men's occupations, Dewey says, is a survival of an aristocratic culture in which "applied" knowledge was held less worthy than "pure knowledge." But in actuality science is one of the most humanistic of subjects, since knowledge is humanistic in quality, not because it is about human products in the past, but "because of what it *does* in liberating human intelligence and human sympathy."[25]

With such a conception of science, and with his insistence that the curriculum is to be evaluated by its contributions to present growth and joy in participation in group activity, Dewey has naturally opposed whatever is narrowly utilitarian in the theory and practice of industrial education.[26] To the chaotic body of opinion regarding the usefulness or harmfulness of manual and industrial training, he brought, largely as a result of the laboratory school he founded in Chicago in 1896, an orderly and constructive theory.

Friebel, Ruskin, and Heusinger had anticipated Dewey in his belief that industrial occupations in the school are psychologically and educationally sound. Dewey argued that, if the child's knowledge began by doing, then industrial education satisfies his native tendencies to explore, to manipulate tools and materials, and to construct and create.[27] But such a training also provides that play for the creative impulse which in the pre-industrial period the home had offered; it affords the child the knowledge of the industrial world and of the fundamental processes of economic life that in times past could be obtained in the community.[28] Industrial training in the schools, as opposed to the factories, further offers a natural and therefore an interesting avenue to the study of the physical, biological, and social sciences.[29] The resulting culture provided by modern industrial occupations, based as they are on the latest discoveries of science, is not necessarily inferior, Dewey held, to that of the traditional disciplines.

Dewey was more original in discussing the social effects that he believed might result from industrial training, which included commercial subjects as well.[30] Motives for acquiring information could be provided which, in-

[25] *Ibid.*, p. 269; N. E. A., *Proceedings*, 1916, p. 734. Dewey's faith in science as an agent for the solution of social problems is well expressed in his remark that "there is no industrial question that has not arisen in some new discovery regarding the forces of nature and whose ultimate solution does not depend upon some further insight into the truths of nature—upon some scientific advance." *The Educational Situation*, p. 86.

[26] For the development of industrial education in the United States see Charles A. Bennett, *History of Manual and Industrial Education up to 1870*, Peoria, Ill., 1926, and Lewis F. Anderson, *History of Manual and Industrial School Education*, New York, 1926.

[27] *Democracy and Education*, p. 368.

[28] John Dewey, *School and Society*, Chicago, 1900, pp. 21–26.

[29] *Democracy and Education*, p. 372. An important aspect of industrial education was found in the fact that it provided a correlating medium for other subjects.

[30] *The Educational Situation*, pp. 76–77; *School Review*, Vol. 10, Jan., 1902, pp. 26–27. "There is nothing in any one study or any one calling which makes it in and of itself low or meanly practical. It is all a question of its isolation or its setting."

stead of leading to habits of competition and rivalry, would result in co-operative planning and sharing. Industrial occupations in the schools, if related to the cultural pattern, would bring intellectual culture within the reach of the masses; and in doing this, would help to break down feudally inherited barriers separating the vast majority who toil with their hands from the few who enjoy the more creative activities of the mind and the spirit.

But Dewey saw grave dangers as well as advantages in industrial training. When industrial interests began to demand special trade schools for the training of skilled workmen he was the first to sound an alarm. Educators, he declared, must insist upon the primacy of educational as opposed to mere industrial values, because the educational values represent the more fundamental interests of a society organized on a democratic basis. The place of industry in education is not to hurry the child of the poorer classes into his individual trade: "the ideal is not to use the schools as tools of existing industrial systems, but to use industry for the reorganization of the schools."[31]

To the argument of the National Manufacturers' Association that secondary and higher education infected students with "Bolshevism," and that therefore they would better be put into trade schools, Dewey made no soft answer. "The moral is evident," he declared. "The sooner the children leave school . . . the more they will be protected from these dangerous bolshevistic college professors, and the less dangerous will they be to 20 percent or more annual dividends in the textile industries of the United States, and hence less dangerous to the future of America."[32]

Fearing that industrial and commercial interests would dominate special trade schools if they were erected into a system separate from the ordinary public schools, Dewey fought tooth and nail the movement for "splitting up the school system."[33] It seemed to be an overt attempt to have the public school system legally and actually recognize the stratification of classes and adapt its administrative machinery, its course of study, and methods of instruction to perpetuate that stratification. The constant references by industrialist champions of a separate system of trade schools to the advantages Germany had derived from such a policy seemed to Dewey to be additional evidence that the captains of industry wished to exploit industrial education in the interests of the employing class and to condemn the children of the less well-to-do to a permanently inferior economic and social status. He believed that unless care were taken, the older divisions of "master and subject class" were about to be reinstated in a new and subtle form. Social and economic mobility, the wide and varied

[31] *Schools of Tomorrow*, pp. 311–13.
[32] *Journal of the N. E. A.*, Vol. 17, February, 1928, p. 62.
[33] John Dewey, "Splitting up the School System," *New Republic*, Vol. 2, April 17, 1915, pp. 283–84; "Industrial Education, a Wrong Kind," *ibid.*, February 20, 1915, pp. 71–73; "Learning to Earn," *School and Society*, Vol. 5, March 24, 1917, pp. 331–35.

distribution of opportunities, the fullest development of the capacities of every individual regardless of his parents' status, these essential characteristics of democracy were, according to Dewey, threatened by the proposed segregation of poorer children in narrowly vocational schools.

A fear that industrial training, if it were segregated from the rounded education of the public schools, would duplicate and perpetuate some of the most unfortunate effects of factory work, also guided Dewey in his insistence on a broad type of industrial education. Schooling must not model itself upon the "automatic repetitiousness of machines." It must be broad and comprehensive, so that, in the inevitable monotonous stretches of work, the imagination might have worthy material of art, literature, and science upon which to feed, instead of being "frittered away upon undisciplined dreamings and sensual fancies." Industrial training, if integrated with cultural education and with progressive methods in the schoolroom, might help produce the type of laborer who would be capable of assuming greater directive power in his work and thus prepare for the democratization of industry itself. Although Dewey recognized that at best certain types of labor must be of a routine character, he believed that even these could be made more significant if the importance of such labor were realized and if those who performed it had greater control over the circumstances of their work.

In short, if the effort to isolate at an early age the children of the less well-to-do in narrowly vocational schools succeeded, if industrial education merely reproduced the automatic and efficient worker, without furthering his knowledge of and control over his work, then education would certainly fail to promote the social and cultural democracy which, at best, it promised. Education alone could guarantee a community of interest and aim, a free circulation of experiences and ideas, a "lively and ardent sense of common life"; for this reason it was the midwife of democracy, which had to be born each generation anew. If it were to perform its function, then the schools must become more, not less, democratic.[34]

Dewey did not stop with a criticism of narrow, vocational education; he has also opposed a close and literal application of science to educational measurements. Without denying the value of ratings, ideals of efficiency, classifications of students and the like, he has pointed out many of the shortcomings of the mania for measurements. Even if it be true that everything which *does* exist could be measured if we only knew how, that which does *not* exist cannot be measured; and it is no paradox to say that the teacher is deeply concerned with what does not exist. Primarily concerned with growth, change, and the transformation of existing capacities and experiences, the school has less interest in what already exists in the form of native endowment and past achievement than with what such

[34] John Dewey, "The Need of an Industrial Education in an Industrial Democracy," *Proceedings of the Second Pan-American Scientific Conference*, Vol. 4, 1915, pp. 222–24.

endowment and achievement may become. Only if we are satisfied with the aims and progress of existing society, only if the schools are to perpetuate the existing order, is the attempt to determine objectives and select subject matter by the wide collection and accurate measurement of data a commendable procedure.[35]

In *The Educational Frontier* Dewey has pointed out that the application of factual science to education in general results in an educational philosophy which simply transmits and reproduces existing institutions, merely making them more efficient. In addition, it has had the effect of reducing personality to impersonal terms—with the result, in practice, of encouraging an anti-social philosophy.[36] In taking the individual out of the medium of associations and contexts in which he lives, in ignoring social bearings, narrowly factual science invites an educational policy in line with "an outworn philosophy of individualism."

Before attempting to evaluate Dewey's faith in the school as an agency for the promotion of the proximate goals which his analysis of contemporary America demands, it is necessary to call attention to the qualifications he himself has made. The schools, although they are formal agencies for producing mental and cultural attitudes and values, do not, in his view, constitute the basic formative force. "Social institutions, the trend of occupations, the pattern of social arrangements, are the finally controlling influences in shaping minds."[37] But while the school changes in a reflex fashion with changing social conditions, it need not passively accommodate itself to exigencies forced upon it from without: it may by accentuating the more desirable of existing attitudes and ideals take a position in actively determining the movement of social forces.[38]

Education and radical social change, in short, are for Dewey correlative and interactive. Every improvement in the social structure releases the educative forces of mankind and "gives them a better opportunity to enter into normal social processes so that the latter become themselves more truly educative." On the other hand, no social change, however slight or however revolutionary, can endure save in so far as education causes it to permeate the desires and purposes of the people.[39] In other words, by searching out and re-enforcing concrete patterns to remake society and enable each individual to realize his full potentiality in the changing and the new society, the school could become increasingly a dynamic, and decreasingly a reflexive, agency.[40]

To exert this leverage, Dewey recognized, along with a host of educational predecessors and contemporaries, that education must be made more

[35] *Progressive Education*, Vol. 5, July, Aug., Sept., 1928, pp. 199–200.
[36] *The Educational Frontier*, pp. 289–90.
[37] John Dewey, *Individualism, Old and New*, New York, 1930, p. 128.
[38] N. E. A., *Proceedings*, 1898, p. 336.
[39] *The Educational Frontier*, p. 318.
[40] *Ibid.*, p. 36.

truly universal. His personal activity as well as his influence was given generously to the movement designed to enlist federal aid for equalizing educational opportunities throughout the land.[41]

But unlike all of his predecessors, save Parker, Dewey insisted that there must be certain fundamental qualitative changes in the schools. The schools on the whole have reflected the prevalent cultural division between knowledge and conduct. "Only the acknowledgement, first in idea and then in practical fact, of the intimate union of theory and practice, knowledge and action, can create a society having foresight and the capacity to plan so as to regulate the inevitable processes of change.[42] Even when lip service is paid to the new educational and social philosophy, Dewey wrote, it too often means simply a new vocabulary for old practices and attitudes and a new means for justifying them.[43] Relegated to a formal plane, even Dewey's new theories were not, as he himself regretted, applied concretely to the America of today.

According to Dewey the teacher must assume social leadership as a fundamental part of her office if she is to promote, through education, the democratic goal. Aware of the difficulty of resisting the pressure of conservative influences in a community, Dewey, in word and deed, urged teachers to organize themselves in associations sufficiently strong and militant to protect their freedom to work for their larger and more difficult purposes.[44] After visiting the schools of Soviet Russia, he became even more deeply convinced that the large part played by personal competition and desire for profit in our economic life is the greatest possible obstacle to the selection of the embryonic forces of democracy for accentuation in the school—a selection and an accentuation necessary if the school is to accelerate the victory of the democratic ideal.[45] Dewey explicitly recognized that the experimental way of life cannot be fully established unless the right of every person to the realization of all his potential capacities, aesthetic as well as social and intellectual, is effectively recognized.[46]

Finally, Dewey himself, in the spirit of his philosophy of instrumentalism, worked for his ideals outside the schools. As an educator and an organizer, his influence was important in the League for Independent Political Action, which embarked on the task of educating public opinion to the need of a realignment of parties, and in the People's Lobby, which has championed progressive policies at Washingon. In an impressive number of journalistic articles he also promoted proximate goals by fighting,

[41] John Dewey, "Nationalizing Education," N. E. A., *Proceedings*, 1916, pp. 183–89; "Federal Aid to Elementary Education," *Child Labor Bulletin*, Vol. 6, May, 1917, pp. 61–66; "Our Illiteracy Problem," *Pictorial Review*, Vol. 31, Aug., 1930, p. 28.
[42] *The Educational Frontier*, p. 302.
[43] *Ibid.*, pp. 33–35.
[44] John Dewey, "Professional Organization of Teachers," *American Teacher*, Vol. 5, Sept., 1916, pp. 99–101.
[45] John Dewey, "Soviet Education" in George A. Coe, *Am I Getting an Education?* New York, 1929, pp. 39–46.
[46] *The Educational Frontier*, p. 317.

as in the Sacco and Vanzetti case, for what appeared to liberals as more humane and democratic solutions of pressing issues.

But even with these qualifications, it has been the school upon which Dewey especially relied to promote his concept of democracy. The analysis made of his specific recommendations for the transformation of the school, in materials and technique of instruction as well as in spirit, suggests that unless these changes become widely prevalent, they can, in themselves, only very inadequately promote Dewey's proximate goals. It is at least open to question whether the schools, representative as they are of dominant interests, can function on an extensive scale in a way sufficiently effective to counteract the opposition inherent in the existing environment to the principles of experimentalism and radical social change.

Critics of widely different points of view have raised their voices against both the aims and methods of instrumentalism and experimentalism.[47] The inclusive, democratic, and socially radical purposes of Dewey's philosophy have been questioned by a wide variety of interests which refuse to accept his fundamental hypothesis of the desirability of these purposes. Those philosophers who have insisted that the primary function of philosophic discipline is to provide a haven of escape from the immediate and actual cruelties of the world represent a considerable body of opinion.[48] Avowed aristocrats and exponents of the genteel tradition have been vigorous opponents,[49] and to the man in the street, as well as to a great number of teachers, the voice of science, as expressed in the work of leading educational psychologists and biologists, seems to condemn as a will-o'-the-wisp the democracy for which Dewey stands.[50]

Conservative individualists, however obsolete their position, were outspoken in condemning Dewey's democratic purposes;[51] and representative Catholics have likewise questioned some of his fundamental aims as well as his methods.[52] His own tilts with manufacturers' associations over the question of industrial education may be taken as a reminder of the fact

[47] *Elementary School Journal*, Vol. 17, Sept., 1916, pp. 13–17; N. E. A., *Proceedings*, 1919, p. 718; Margaret Naumberg, "A Challenge to John Dewey," *Survey*, Vol. 55, Sept. 15, 1928, pp. 598–600; G. Stanley Hall, *Life and Confessions of a Psychologist*, p. 499.

[48] M. Cohen, review of *Essays in Experimental Logic, New Republic*, Vol. 8, Sept. 2, 1916, pp. 118–19. R. B. Perry, in his review of *Reconstruction in Philosophy*, offers another type of philosophical criticism. *Dial*, Vol. 70, April, 1921, pp. 454–57.

[49] Professor W. H. Sheldon, in declaring that "we do not want the 'all-round' growth of everybody" and that Dewey's idea of participation of all in directing would be fatal to unique achievement, the beauty of division of work, and progress, is representative. "Professor Dewey, The Protagonist of Democracy," *Journal of Philosophy*, Vol. 18, June, 1921, pp. 309–20.

[50] John L. Childs, *Education and the Philosophy of Experimentalism*, New York, 1931, reviews and criticizes these arguments.

[51] Warner Fite, in Adams and Montague, *Contemporary American Philosophy, Personal Statements*, Vol. 1, pp. 362–68.

[52] Joseph T. Barron, "Professor Dewey and Truth," *Catholic World*, Vol. 116, Nov., 1922, pp. 212–21; William Turner, "Pragmatism," *Catholic Encyclopedia*, Vol. 12, pp. 333–38; F. De Hovre, *Philosophy and Education*, pp. 103 *et seq.*

that powerful, if not dominant, economic groups conceal beneath a lip service to democracy a fundamental opposition to it.[53]

In addition to the opposition of people who did not agree with his fundamental assumptions as to what is desirable, Dewey also encountered the opposition of liberals who, while in general sharing his objectives, doubted the efficacy of experimentalism as a method for their achievement. Randolph Bourne, for example, in view of Dewey's support of the World War, wondered whether the tentativeness of experimentalism, its very interest in next steps, its concern with methodology, its very freedom from unyielding standards were not responsible for betraying it into a justification of a war which convinced pacifists and doctrinaire Socialists refused to support on the ground either that war under all circumstances is ethically wrong or that this war was in the interest not of democracy but of imperialism, nationalism, and profits.[54]

What has happened once, these critics said, may happen again. A willingness to take what can be got, they feel, often results in obtaining considerably less than is expected. A willingness to accept war in 1917 brought far less than the Wilsonian promises; a willingness to accept Al Smith in 1928 did not prevent the election of Hoover. Willingness to work with powerful forces, to look for next steps, assumes, it is maintained, that there is a strong desire for progress and change on the part of these powerful forces.[55]

Other critics have contended that Dewey underestimated the power of "the cultural lag" and overemphasized the potency of deliberative and intelligent aspects of individual and social life.[56] Overlooking his own criticism of eighteenth century rationalism for its separation of thought and action, they have contended that he offers little more than the "philosophes" who expected reason to reform the world. One may suggest that a more serious obstacle to his conception of education than these critics have urged lies in the hindrances imposed to scientific solving of social problems by the pressure groups and propaganda methods. Dewey, although aware of the sinister character of propaganda, possibly underrated its strength.

Still other critics have seen in Dewey's devotion to the democratic method of promoting human betterment an idealization and prolongation of the tendency of Americans to form mutual associations, such as the log-raising, the sewing bee, and the co-operative harvest, associations which at the time were spontaneous and truly functional. Now, however, it is maintained, commercial interests and pressure groups exploit this habit

<hr/>

[53] Edwin C. Cooley, "Professor Dewey's Criticism of the Chicago Commercial Club and Its Vocational Education Bill," *Vocational Education*, Vol. 3, Sept., 1913, pp. 24–29.

[54] Randolph Bourne, "Twilight of Idols," *Seven Arts Magazine*, Vol. 2, Oct., 1917, pp. 688–702.

[55] For Dewey's denial that his philosophy is opportunistic see *The Educational Frontier*, p. 313.

[56] Ross Finney, *A Sociological Philosophy of Education*, New York, 1928, p. 478.

for the purpose of profits; and urban conditions have transformed the old neighborliness into the objective indifference of apartment-house dwellers. There is a good deal of truth in such a criticism. Indeed, it might be suggested that Dewey, in spite of the originality and great value of his interpretations of American life for the student of the social sciences, underestimated the force of the aristocratic or Hamiltonian tradition in American life. Even the frontier, relatively democratic though it was, very quickly came to know social distinctions based on the differences in economic status of its early pioneers.

Other critics have contended that, with production and distribution based as they are on a desire for profits, Dewey's ideal of breaking down the separation between the more creative and the more routine tasks cannot be realized by so simple a device as a new type of school and adult political education. They have wondered whether unskilled labor, such as the necessary work in sewers, the care of blast furnaces, and the disposal of garbage, to say nothing of the monotonous tending of a machine, could be made as pleasurable as Dewey supposed by enlightening the participants concerning its social value and increasing their control, within the given system, of the conditions of their work. These critics, however, have partly misunderstood Dewey; and he himself became more clearly aware of the obstacles imposed by the profit motive to the realization of his democratic conception of work and life.

Dewey answered his liberal critics with much effectiveness.[57] It may still be questioned, however, whether in view of the power of certain of the conservatives who have challenged his fundamental hypotheses regarding democracy as a goal and intelligence as a means to that end, the cards may not be in some measure stacked against both the objective and the method. At least certain critics have felt that if the hypotheses of democracy and intelligent action are to be given a fair chance in the actual framework of competing situations and forces, a championship more militant than education may be required.

Dewey himself faced this question and gave an answer. Admitting that, in specific instances, to be determined in an experimental way, other and more immediate techniques, including mass action and even revolution, may be utilized,[58] he insisted that judgments in regard to proximate courses of action must be determined, not by prejudged philosophies, but by the best available knowledge of actual conditions and the concrete situations at hand.[59] In other words, goals, to be effective, must be able to guide one to the next mileposts. Ends are continuous with means: ends

[57] *The Educational Frontier*, pp. 310–19. Sidney Hook has also answered the critics of Dewey in an engaging manner. *New Republic*, Vol. 67, June 3, 1931, p. 73.

[58] Dewey has recalled that both Jefferson and Lincoln believed in the right of the people to change their institutions by revolution for the promotion of the common good. *The Educational Frontier*, p. 43.

[59] For Dewey's most recent analysis of American experience in relation to his objectives and methods see *The Educational Frontier*, Chap. 2.

stated without verifiable consideration of the immediate means are utopias to which no known paths lead.

Dewey would admit that the philosophy of instrumentalism, and the weight it attaches to education as the technique of social betterment, involves risky experiments and the possibility of failure. He would admit, with Mann, that sometimes shortrun contingencies arise when the battle of human betterment cannot be fought effectively with formal education as the instrument. But he did not discover a promising revolutionary situation in contemporary America. He was unwilling to say just what means must be utilized to achieve democracy in America. The quest for certainty, he felt, when all is said and done, leads too often to a mistaken and barren kind of assurance. At best, creative statecraft in education, politics, and industry may without revolutionary violence transform the possibilities of the present into the actualities of the future. And Dewey, whether by decree of the gods or by sensitiveness to the American mood, took an optimistic view.

The Last Twenty-Five Years

MERLE CURTI

One explanation of the difficulty of identifying two or three commanding educational leaders has been the increased lay participation in the formulation of educational aims and of ways of realizing them. An especially interesting example of the combined lay factor and committee approach to the discussion of the social aspects of education has been the work of the National Citizens' Commission for the Public Schools. Chartered in 1946 as the result of a suggestion of President Conant and the initiative of the Educational Policies Commission, the new organization enjoyed the effective leadership of its president, Roy M. Larsen of Time, Incorporated. The National Citizens' Commission for the Public Schools stimulated men and women all over the country "to define good education and encouraged them to bring their own local schools up to the standards they themselves set." The leadership urged participants to work actively to make the best in education available to every American child on completely equal terms and, as a means to that end, to arouse in each community the "intelligence and will to improve our public schools."[1]

From *The Social Ideas of American Educators*, by Merle Curti, Scribner's, New York, 1935, pp. xxvi–xliv. Reprinted by permission of the American Historical Association and the author.
[1] *National Citizens' Commission for the Public Schools. Historical Document Series*, New York, no date, 8 volumes, Vol. 1, p. 2.

Another related example of the more active interest of citizens in education is the 1958 publication of the Rockefeller Brothers Fund, a special studies project report entitled *The Pursuit of Excellence. Education and the Future of America.*[2] This was the result of an effort to assess the chief problems and opportunities that are apt to face the United States over the next decade and a half. Its thesis was summed up in the statement that "our society will have passed an important milestone of maturity when those who are the most enthusiastic proponents of a democratic way of life are also the most vigorous proponents of excellence." To these examples of lay participation in educational thinking might be added the publication of a large body of widely read articles and books about education from the hands of such men and women as Agnes Meyer, Fred M. Hechinger, and Admiral H. G. Rickover.

In discussing the social ideas implicit or explicit in educational writing and practice over our whole history, I pointed out again and again the dominant trends and minor eddies in the American economy and society and the influence these shifting forces had on the social thinking of educational leaders. These trends and eddies included the transfer of western civilization to our shores and its modification by the westward movement, immigration, and the slavery controversy, as well as the shift from a commercial-agrarian to an industrial-urban economy and culture, and the vast consequences of civil and world war. I also took into account the impact on the social ideas of those deeply concerned with education, of such movements of thought as Puritanism, the Enlightenment, humanitarianism, Romanticism, evolutionary theory, scientific measurement, and nationalism and democracy. It still seems to hold that all these developments in the economy and culture were so interdependent with the social attitudes of educators that one could not attribute autonomy either to ideas or to economic and social forces, could not say which were causes and which were effects.

To say this is not to say that were I to write the book today the presuppositions and treatment would be exactly what they were then. It is possible that some of the analyses of issues, as these were developed in *The Social Ideas of American Educators,* were too sharply defined, that they reflected too markedly the mood of the early nineteen thirties, a time when almost everyone was very much aware of the interplay of conflicting interests and ideas. It is now fashionable in historical circles to play down the conflicts in our past, to emphasize a more or less constant homogeneity. This tendency no doubt reflects the understandable search for stability and continuity in a time of world-wide revolutionary changes. The current fashion seems to me to have sometimes resulted, in historical writing, in over-corrective interpretations. Today it seems to be as hard as I admitted

[2] *The Pursuit of Excellence. Education and the Future of America.* Special Studies Project Report V, Rockefeller Brothers Fund, New York, 1958, Vol. 9, No. 7.

it was in the preface to my book, to overcome and transcend the impact of the prevailing intellectual fashions and existing situations.

If the method of relating ideas and interests without giving a determining role to either was essentially sound, one might begin a brief retrospective glance at the last twenty-five years by asking what have been the chief social and economic changes that have furnished a background for the thinking of those who have written in these years about American education and its social implications. Most students would agree in emphasizing the economic recovery from the great depression, the implementation of the New Deal, and the expanding powers of the federal government. Of obvious importance has been the challenge of totalitarianism in Italy, Germany, and Japan and the second world war, problems associated with American leadership of the non-communist world in the "cold war," including the fear of Communism, and the issues of civil and minority rights and intergroup relationships at home. On a different level has been the so-called communications revolution. All these have played important parts in educational operations, including pressures for the expansion of the school plant, the growth in enrollment in schools and colleges, and the recruitment, training, and pay of an adequate teaching force. These social and political developments have also influenced the social thinking of educational spokesmen.

Of importance in greater or lesser degree have been movements of thought and feeling associated with these economic, social, and political developments. Most historians would probably agree that social thinking about education has been only slightly influenced, so far, by neo-Thomism (at least outside Catholic circles), neo-orthodoxy, logical positivism, and existentialism.[3] It may of course be too soon to sense, let alone assess, such influences as these movements of thought may be exerting on education.

In the last quarter of a century three major movements of thought that had already become familiar in educational discussion continued, in quite different ways, to figure in the social thinking of those articulately concerned with education.

One, obviously, has been the continuing emphasis, indeed, an increasing emphasis, on science and technology in our culture, including our education. It is not necessary to belittle the importance and truly great achievements of the natural sciences to note that in many eyes the premiums put on scientific achievements and the applications of these, undermined the humanities. Of late there has indeed been a growing realization that the decline of the humanities has carried its hazards. Vigorous voices, including those of well known scientists, have called attention to the importance

[3] Note should be taken of John Redden and Francis Ryan, *A Catholic Philosophy of Education,* 1942, Jacques Maritain, *Education at the Crossroads,* 1943, Henry P. Van Dusen, *God in Education,* 1951, Israel Scheffler, ed., *Philosophy and Education,* 1958, and George F. Kneller, *Existentialism and Education,* 1958.

of the humanities not only in enriching individual lives but also in preserving and extending ethical and social values highly necessary in a free
society.[4] It is too soon to say what the public response will be.

Another continuing movement in thought and culture has been neo-
Marxism. The direct or positive influence of this and of the world-wide
revolutionary movements associated with it had never been of great importance in American educational thought. Outside two or three metropolitan centers only a very small number of teachers looked with sympathy
on Marxism even at the height of the great depression. True, it was common for the Hearst press, the professional patriotic organizations, and the
National Association of Manufacturers to denounce as "Marxists" and
"Reds" the leaders of the *Social Frontier* magazine and its successor,
Frontiers of Democracy. But Marxism was only one, and certainly not the
most important factor in the social thinking of this group.

By the mid-nineteen forties Marxism had ceased to have any significance
in a positive way for the thinking of this or any other group of educational
leaders. The antithesis between almost everything that the Soviet Union
stood for and the democratic values to which the *Social Frontier* group
was dedicated, was increasingly clear. And the achievements of the New
Deal and, presently, the promises of the Fair Deal, together with a high
level of prosperity, confirmed faith in the American democratic means of
moving toward an ever greater measure of social and economic equality
and well-being.

On the other hand, the indirect and negative impact of Marxism and
the revolutionary movements associated with it was of far-reaching importance on the thinking and feeling of those concerned with education in
a social context. It was plain that freedom of teaching and learning was in
grave danger as McCarthyism swept on, and resistance seemed at best to
be timid and ineffective. The danger was exemplified by the methods often
used by Congressional committees in probing into the past beliefs and
affiliations of students and teachers, by the enactment in many states of
special teachers' loyalty oaths, and by the insistence of citizens' pressure
groups that school textbooks be "purged" of anything that raised questions
about American political and economic institutions and purposes. Even
the United Nations and UNESCO were anathema to many such groups.

Educational circles reacted in several ways to this situation. The path
for one clearly defined position was prepared by the *Social Frontier* group
in the later 1930's when it insisted that there was no place for Communists
in the American Federation of Teachers. Building on this, Sidney Hook
and others during the McCarthy era urged that the distinction between

---

[4] Two able but quite different kinds of defense of the humanities were Gordon Keith
Chalmers' *The Public and the Person,* Regnery, Chicago, 1952, the social implications
of which re-enforced the new conservatism, and Howard Mumford Jones' brilliantly
democratic championship of the humanities in *One Great Society. Humane Learning in
the United States,* Harcourt, Brace & World, New York, 1959.

"heresy" and "conspiracy" is a major one. In other words, liberal and radical dissent was one thing, something to be defended and even welcomed, while Communist rejection of democratic means and values was something very different. The rigid, doctrinaire controls over the mind, it was argued, were too tight to enable a Communist teacher to play his role with the integrity and effectiveness that his position required. Another view, espoused by the American Association of University Professors, maintained that mere association with Communist "fronts" or even with the Party itself as long as it remained a legal organization, was not sufficient ground for the dismissal of a teacher. Competence to teach must be the criterion in each individual case. But this view met with widespread opposition both within the educational profession and in the country at large.

Whatever the differences between educators over the issue of Communism and academic freedom, there was pretty general agreement among educators on the need of opposing the irresponsible tendency to label as communists anyone with ideas different from those of the majority. It was clear to many at the time that the extent of genuine disloyalty was vastly exaggerated. It is not possible to say how many teachers and students were frightened into an unwilling conformity or distraught by fear, anxiety, and insecurity—or still are. Nor is it possible to say that the whole issue, as it was resolved in favor of the moderate position, has been permanently solved. Many have certainly learned that freedom of teaching within the democratic frame is indispensable in a democratic society. But one cannot be sure how well the lesson has been learned, or whether a sufficient number of Americans have learned it to prevent another crisis similar to the McCarthyism of the early nineteen fifties.

In still other ways the influence of Marxism and the world revolution associated with it played an indirect influence on the social thinking of those concerned with education. The great gulf between Communism and the western form of democracy has led to the "cold war." This in turn has been in part responsible for the conservative mood of America in the post-war era. It has expressed itself, so far as education goes, in many ways. One has been the closer relations between American business and education. Educational discussion has had little to say about corporations that suggests an older, frequently critical view. And corporations have given generously to institutions of learning, especially to the liberal arts colleges, partly on the ground that in a time of continuing government expansion into all walks of life it is important to strengthen private and voluntary agencies. But the chief example of the relation between the conservative mood of the country and educational thinking has been the retreat of the idea that the school can and should take the lead in initiating and implementing social reform. This idea, it will be recalled, received much publicity in the 1930's when it was a main tenet in the thinking of George S. Counts and the *Social Frontier* group.

It is true that most of this group did not entirely repudiate the position they once so boldly championed. It was reflected, for example, in the mellow exposition of American education and civilization which Counts wrote in 1952. And in *The Challenge of Soviet Education,* the major work of Counts in the last decade, Americans were called on to meet the challenge presented by the amazing advances in Soviet education, all of which reflected the conviction that education is an all-embracing instrument of political control and of building a completely communist mind and society.[5]

The most vigorous and original exponent of the idea that education could and should improve the social order has been Theodore Brameld. In addresses and in systematic writings he has carried on the tradition with important modifications. He has called his position "reconstructionism." It holds that public education, informed with new findings in the behavioral sciences, especially anthropology and psychology, should take sides with forces all over the world that are struggling to make full use of science and technology to create an abundant life for all peoples. While recognizing the existence and indeed the necessity of conflict, Brameld holds that it can be carried on within the frame of democratic means and values. To some the position which was so clearly developed in such papers as "Education for the Emerging Age" seemed to rely too optimistically on the promise of the behavioral sciences and the world revolutionary situation. But the thoughtful attention given to Professor Brameld's writings indicates that the constructive potentialities in the situation as he analyzed them could not be ignored.[6]

The prevailing position, nevertheless, is that social reform is largely or even solely the business of adult citizens. The only proper role of the school in social reform is that of preparing the child in the classroom to make intelligent judgments when he becomes a voting participant in decision-making. This is to be done by supplying the young with accurate information, by pointing to the ways in which further information can be gathered, and by developing habits of careful thinking and judgment. This view has been popularized by Professor Paul Woodring, among others.[7] In some, though by no means in all respects, this position in its relation to education and social reform, resembles the neo-Thomistic view of education which also attaches great importance to intellectual discipline. But neo-Thomism

[5] George S. Counts, *Education and American Civilization,* New York, 1952, and *The Challenge of Soviet Education,* New York, 1957. See also John L. Childs, *American Pragmatism and Education,* New York, 1956.

[6] Theodore Brameld, *Patterns of Educational Philosophy,* New York, 1950, *Philosophies of Education in Cultural Perspective,* New York, 1955, *Toward a Reconstructed Philosophy of Education,* New York, 1956, *Cultural Foundations of Education,* New York, 1957, and "Education for an Emerging Age" in *The Humanist,* No. 3, 1957.

[7] Paul Woodring, *Let's Talk Sense About Our Schools,* New York, 1953, and *A Fourth of the Nation,* New York, 1957, pp. 119–26.

also emphasizes the importance of a humanistic content much richer than that of the so-called essentialists.[8]

One further indirect result of Marxism and the world of revolution of our time must be mentioned. Long accustomed to regarding themselves as superior to any other people in "know-how," Americans were deeply shaken when, in the autumn of 1957, it was clear that the Russians had an edge on us in the use of atomic power in space technology. The American press teemed with articles blaming our backwardness on our education: the schools had not been sufficiently vigorous in teaching mathematics and the sciences. Much general support was forthcoming to those who had long claimed that American education in general was too soft, that it catered too much to the whims and immediate interests of the young, that it had become enmeshed in a superficial, even frivolous "life-adjustment" program.[9] Education, which President Conant of Harvard had said as early as 1948 was a matter of survival, was now proclaimed to be the indispensable means by which the United States could regain and keep supremacy over the Russians in science and technology. Many commentators felt that it was necessary to imitate the Soviet Union's system of "hard" educational training.[10] Others agreed in holding that supremacy in science and technology could alone insure victory in the "cold war" and that American education must look to this major obligation. Some also insisted that America must in addition prove her civilization to be superior to that of the Communist world in political, cultural, and philosophical terms.

The present-day demands for a reassessment of American education, for a tougher school program, can be understood only in terms of a wider frame of reference than the sudden awakening to the achievements of Soviet science and technology. In point of fact, several basic forces in American life in large part accounted for the growing emphasis over the decades on the "life-adjustment" programs, that is, homemaking, community activity, the driving of automobiles, vocational and personal guidance, and interpersonal and intergroup relationships. In becoming increasingly corporate in character American life and values stressed the importance of teamwork, of conformity to the group norm, of reducing conflict in personal and group relations. This was summed up in such slogans as "other-directedness," "the organization man," and "togetherness." The emphasis

[8] Robert M. Hutchins, *The Conflict of Education in a Democratic Society*, Harper & Row, New York, 1953, and *The Democratic Dilemma in Freedom, Education, and the Fund*, New York, 1956, 138 ff. Hutchins proved a staunch champion of academic freedom, a matter of social importance in any period and one of great importance in the changes taking place in America and in the world in the last quarter of a century.

[9] A widely used text which expounds the position under attack is Florence B. Stratemeyer, Hamden L. Forkner, Margaret G. McKim, and A. Harvey Passow, *Developing a Curriculum for Modern Living*, New York, 1957.

[10] See Fred M. Hechinger, *Big Red School House*, New York, 1959.

on the group and on togetherness, though a natural outgrowth of our own American experiences, helped to prepare us to look with more favor on Russian methods of education. Perhaps, many said, America also needed to concentrate more heavily on scientific and technical training to meet national needs. It was taken for granted in many circles that the supreme national need is to dominate or at least hold the balance in world politics and also, for military reasons, to achieve leadership in the mastery of outer space.

In responding to those values which pressure groups and parents themselves often demanded, professional educators were also influenced by two movements of thought which had become important in the decades after the First World War. One was a body of psychological and psychoanalytical theories and findings which emphasized the adjustment of the individual to his environment. Another was the movement known as progressive education. To be sure, John Dewey himself never advocated life-adjustment as the key to school activities despite the fact that many critics of life-adjustment programs thought so. But many educators did cite Dewey and his interpreters as authority for life-adjustment programs even when they misunderstood and misapplied his teachings.

No one can doubt that the main body of psychological, psychoanalytical and clinical writings contributed a good deal to the understanding of human motivation and behavior. Nor can one doubt that, from some angles of vision, these theories as they were applied proved to be wholesome and beneficial to a great many growing children and adolescents. The point is clear enough when the widespread concern over juvenile delinquency is considered. Social workers, civic leaders, and parents looked with considerable sympathy on the therapeutic responsibilities of the school, particularly when Evan Hunter's *The Blackboard Jungle* and Harrison Salisbury's *The Shook-up Generation* dramatized the issue. The feeling that "getting tough" with uprooted adolescents promised less than intelligent understanding and love, gave support to the life-adjustment programs. So did the search for activities which might motivate these adolescents more effectively than the traditional program of studies.

At the same time psychological and clinical emphases also supported the tendency in our culture to other-directedness, to conformity, to getting along by following the cue of the group. To a certain extent conformity is of course necessary both in the interest of the individual and of society. But in some cases the emphasis or over-emphasis in education on adjustment must have checked the full development of individual potentialities, with a consequent loss for a deeply rich personal growth and for social contributions of importance. In any case, the emphasis on adjustment, working with basic forces in our mid-twentieth century economy and culture, has militated against the doctrine of education for social reform.

But it was not this effect that troubled most of the critics of the American public school both before and after Sputnik.[11] At least as early as the 1930's Robert M. Hutchins argued that the intellectual content of the curriculum had been dangerously watered down by the core curriculum which broke up traditional subject disciplines into units allegedly functional to life-solving problems. The core curriculum and the growing emphasis on life-adjustment had, Hutchins and a growing number of fellow-critics held, done even worse. The movement had deprived everyone subject to it of the basic human right of developing to the full whatever intellectual capacities he had. Whether these critics spoke of themselves as classicists or as perennialists or as essentialists, they agreed that training for immediate needs such a personal hygiene, homemaking, and participation in community interests, gave support to regrettable anti-intellectual forces in American life. The American school, they claimed, had become little more than an "educational wasteland." It was responsible for "the diminished mind." On the positive side, these critics urged a return to an emphasis on the 3-R's, on the basic intellectual disciplines of mathematics, language, and science. Such an emphasis, they insisted, must replace the prevailing one of training partly for immediate needs and for life-adjustment, if the American people were not to be further deprived of their rights to the great heritage of systematic knowledge and of intellectual discipline. After Sputnik, these arguments seemed to have an even wider appeal.[12]

In general the critics blamed John Dewey and the progressive education movement, and the professional educationists who had blindly followed in the path marked out, for the sad state of affairs. If Johnny couldn't read, it was their fault. If the city school in the slum or near-slum was a blackboard jungle, John Dewey or William H. Kilpatrick and their disciples were to be blamed. It is true that some followers of Dewey, in the name of progressive education, misunderstood his teaching, ignored his warning that experiences are not all equally valuable, that the teacher must play a positive, constructive role, that reflective thought is an indispensable part of any worth-while activities program. It is also true that some disciples of Dewey and of progressive education ignored the emphasis he had put, not on mere adjustment to environment as it was, but to those parts of the environment that promised to bring out the best potentialities in children and thus to promote the reconstruction of the whole environment in

[11] C. Winfield Scott and Clyde M. Hill brought together representative criticisms in an anthology, *Public Education Under Criticism*, New York, 1954.

[12] In addition to the Scott and Hill anthology, see, for an elaboration of these criticisms, Arthur E. Bestor, *Educational Wastelands*, University of Illinois Press, Urbana, Ill., 1953, "Anti-Intellectualism in the Schools," *New Republic*, January 19, 1953, and *The Restoration of Learning*, Knopf, New York, 1955; Albert Lynd, *Quackery in the Public Schools*, Little, Brown, Boston, 1950 and Admiral H. G. Rickover, *Education and Freedom*, Dutton, New York, 1959. For a quite different presentation and discussion of the criticisms see Vivian T. Thayer, *Public Education and Its Critics*, Macmillan, New York, 1954.

the interest of better individuals and a better society. It is further true that many professional educators justified the life-adjustment programs even when they fell far short of what Dewey had in mind. But critics failed to see, as I have noted before, that this approach seemed a promising means of motivating and of helping "the beat generation." They also failed to see that it was often the parents, not John Dewey, who demanded that the schools teach good manners, hygiene, the home arts, safe driving, that they provide guidance and direct community activities. Too often the critics did not realize that in no country did the local community and parents have as great an influence on the schools as in America. All these points were made in the more sensible and balanced replies to the critics of the public school.[13]

There is, in any effort to evaluate the social ideas explicit and implicit in the criticism of the life-adjustment emphasis in American education, another side of the coin to be considered. For the emphasis on personal relations in living has, together with other factors, strengthened one of the most affirmative social developments in education. This has been the invigorated effort in our time to realize more fully the American tradition of equality of opportunity for minority groups—for the recent immigrants, for Jews, for Negroes. The issue of desegregation in public education is, of course, only one phase of the larger movement for insuring civil and human rights. The roots of this movement lie deep in American history, as *The Social Ideas of American Educators* clearly showed. In our own time, as in earlier periods, the movement for equality of opportunity has been strengthened by an awareness of the inconsistency between our professions of equal human rights for minority groups and the actualities ("the American dilemma"). That awareness owes something to the awkward position which denial of equal opportunities to some has placed us in during our post-war effort to give effective leadership to the "free world" in the struggle against Communism. But this awareness of the American dilemma and the feeling that something should be done to narrow the gap between professions and practice actually rests largely on the conscientious convictions and efforts of countless men and women. These range from little known people in minority and majority groups to the Bureau for Intercultural Education, a pioneer venture which produced a number of basic studies and initiated many school projects.[14] Of importance was the leadership given by Franklin and Eleanor Roosevelt, Harry S. Truman, and, above all, the Supreme Court.

The maintenance of segregated schools in seventeen states was justified on many grounds, hygienic and social as well as "racial." The constitutional

---

[13] For representative replies on the part of educators see R. Will Burnett and Harold C. Hand, "Two Critiques of Educational Wastelands," *Progressive Education*, Vol. 31, No. 3, January, 1954, and *Educational Theory*, Vol. 4, January, 1954, Hollis L. Caswell, *The Attack on the Schools*, Teachers College, Columbia University, 1958.

[14] Leaders in this movement have included W. H. Kilpatrick, Stewart Cole, and L. J. Stiles.

justification was found in the famous *Plessy v. Ferguson* case of 1896 in which the Supreme Court held that state legislation requiring segregated transportation facilities did not violate the Fourteenth Amendment if these facilities were equal. The gradual shift from this position was reflected in a series of decisions which required state supported professional schools to admit qualified Negroes. In 1954, in five decisions involving segregation in public schools in four states and the District of Columbia, the Supreme Court unanimously rejected the "separate but equal doctrine." It is note-worthy that the opinions cited a considerable body of social science writings in support of the legal reasoning of the justices. The Supreme Court placed the responsibility for desegregating public schools "with all deliberate speed" on local communities. These decisions were a milestone in the long struggle for equal opportunity for all people regardless of race and status.

The struggle since 1954 to spell out the directives of the Supreme Court has been a turbulent one. White Councils have been pitted against the National Association for the Advancement of Colored People, to name only two organizations that have figured in the struggle. Every case, in effect, differed from every other. Sometimes schools have been closed to make the process of desegregation impossible; sometimes they were closed after a few Negroes had been admitted. Occasional incidents of violence have taken place. The greatest differences emerging were those between the border states where, with the exception of Virginia, desegregation in general has proceeded as well as could be expected, and the Deep South where, in 1959, no Negroes had been allowed to go to any white public school and where laws and other devices reflected a determined effort on the part of the whites in control to have things their way.

On all sides the discussion has been charged with high emotional content. To quote the words of a Kentucky educator, the early stages of the struggle clearly showed that "integration is more important to Negroes than the white man realizes, and segregation is more important to whites than the Negro realizes."[15] If a distinguished Negro sociologist, Ira De A. Reid, was right in thinking that it was possible to overstress law and law enforcement, and that personal, group, and cultural interplay and understanding were even more important, then a big burden is thrown on education, broadly conceived as fostering cooperation, and mutual adjustment and appreciation.[16]

On various occasions in our history, as *The Social Ideas of American Educators* made clear, the question of the proper relations between public schools and religion has been a concern of educational leaders. In the past quarter of a century this problem continued to be one that concerned

[15] Don Shoemaker, ed., *With All Deliberate Speed,* Harper & Row, New York, 1957, p. 203.
[16] Ira De A. Reid, "Integration Reconsidered," *Harvard Educational Review,* Vol. 27, Spring, 1957, pp. 85–91.

Jewish, Catholic, and Protestant religious organizations, public school administrators and boards of education, state legislatures, the courts, and Congress itself. The growing American interest in religion, which marked the years following the second world war, provided a new context for discussion and decision.[17]

In an effort to diminish further the gap between those parts of the country in which reasonably good schools rested on a prosperous economy and those in which it proved hard to provide adequate local support for public schools, the movement for federal aid was revived. In the discussions thus evoked religion as well as traditional states rights issues figured. On at least two occasions bills for substantially increasing the federal aid given to schools for special purposes passed the Senate despite opposition. In the House the opposition was stiffer. Many expressed the conviction that federal aid should be provided parochial schools, or at least that federal funds might be used for bus transportation of parochial school pupils, for non-religious textbooks, and for health services. But many stubbornly opposed such provisions. The conflict contributed to the defeat of the proposal, to which opposition was also made on the ground that federal support of schools endangered local control (an issue to which Southern members of Congress were especially sensitive).

The controversy over federal aid to private schools also of course involved the larger issue of the traditional American separation of church and state. This issue figured in the efforts of many religious leaders and many parents to have religion recognized as part of the public school program. Some favored non-sectarian instruction in the history and general significance of religion in civilization; others wanted to have the King James version of the Old Testament read daily, with the saying of non-sectarian prayers; still others wanted to have ministers, priests, and rabbis come to the public schools to teach children of their flocks. All these experiments were tried in one or another locality. But many parents and educators opposed all of them on the ground that each in some way violated the constitutional provision for religious freedom and endangered the historic separation of church and state. The Supreme Court finally ruled that if there was no element of compulsion, public school authorities might send pupils at the request of parents to church or synagogue for special instruction during school hours. If interest in religion continues to increase the whole issue may again become a matter of discussion and decision.

Thus in the past quarter century the lively discussion of the social implications of education has continued a long tradition. It is possible to regard the differences and conflicts as regrettable confusion. Or they may seem an unhappy exception to the consolidation of American thought and

[17] Scott and Hill, *Public Education Under Criticism*, pp. 128–148; Vivian T. Thayer, *Religion in Public Education*, New York, 1947, and *The Attack Upon the Secular School*, Boston, 1951.

values which is taking place as we fight Communism. Many take this view. It is also possible to agree still with the analysis John Dewey made in 1939 when he wrote: "All social movements involve conflicts which are reflected intellectually in controversies. It would not be a sign of health if such an important social interest as education were not also an arena of struggles, practical and theoretical."[18] . . .

[18] John Dewey, *Experiences and Education*, Vol. 5, Macmillan, New York, 1939.

Educators' Reactions to Educational Criticism

Education plays a significant role in the life and cultural style of any society. As society is dynamic, so is the school. Additionally, the schools are a social concern and are subject to continued public surveillance. Critics of the formal educational process are, then, exposed to public view for a long period of time as a result of several factors: the socialization responsibility accepted by schools; the changing nature and values of society and the schools, and public interest in the quality of the process. Criticism of schools is not a new social phenomena. The major philosophers of every era have attempted to propose what education ought to be. However, philosophers are not the only members of society who criticize the schools. Since the schools are constantly in need of improvement, they are fair game for any quality of critic.

The following article deals with the reactions of educators to critics and to criticism. Seldom do the writings of defenders of an educational system come into public view. Why haven't educators defended their opinions and ideas in the more popular magazines? Is a lack of defense interpreted by the public as evidence of the truth of the criticism? With widespread dissent among educators about goals and practices, why are the arguments generally confined to the professional journals?

Conservatism and Passivity in American Educational Thought

THOMAS E. LINTON

Both in educational publications and the meetings of educators it is not uncommon to find the expression of a desire for change. Most frequently this desire is stated in terms which bear a strong resemblance to the stated aims of many of the critics of public education. Yet these same educators do not generally work for the adoption of their frequently expressed "ideas."

What causes this apparent lack of active interest in their own "strongly" felt ideas? It is probable that this withdrawal from possible action has several causes. Among these would be the following: (1) While they are concerned with change, and agree with some of the criticisms of public education, they are occupationally concerned over possible retaliative actions by those presently in power positions. (2) They have found it generally easier to agree with the more vociferous critics, and ready to comply, than to challenge the ideas upon which these criticisms are based. (3) They have agreed with the critics on specific points, but generally find their overall value position hard to accept. (4) They do not usually defend "progressive" education and its achievements, or offer alternative ideational programs for the schools, because they have seldom carefully considered the basic differences in values which various educational programs offer. (5) Educators tend to answer the criticisms by demeaning the personalities or motives of the critics making the charges, rather than dealing with the value of the alternative programs they offer. This paper will examine these factors and offer some alternative suggestions which may enable the educators to do more than unhappily retreat from each encounter with the high-riding critics.

(1) The fear of retaliative reactions by the present holders of power. In its simplest form this fear is the individual's worry that his superiors may not like his criticisms of the existing system, and answer his arguments by eliminating him from his source of income. It is only fair to state that this fear is in part realistic, and that one's position or future may be seriously jeopardized by his adverse comments on the presently accepted approach to public education.

Reprinted from *The Educational Forum*, March, 1963, pp. 299–305, by permission of Kappa Delta Pi, an Honor Society in Education, owners of the copyright.

The reasoning of the dissenting educator generally runs along the following line. Surely we've all heard their arguments passed back and forth over coffee breaks hundreds of times. It goes like this:

A. "You can't fight it; the organization has been entrenched for at least forty or fifty years. Originally many of the ideas were excellent, but they've been so distorted that most of the basic values in 'progressive education' have become educational dogmas and are no longer seriously considered as topics for educational research or open questioning."

B. "Yes! But does it have to remain that way?"

A. "I don't know, but what can one person do to change the huge power structure that has grown up over the years?"

B. "You seem to imply that the power structure is solidified and in basic agreement on the means and ends of the educational system."

A. "In general, I think they are. I think there is a large cadre of 'old timers' who have come to be the new 'traditionalists' in that they essentially accept the means and ends of the present system. When someone criticizes their values and beliefs which have tended to reify into dogmas, they feel personally attacked, and will probably retaliate by firing the critic or giving him a 'hard time' by limiting his economic and social opportunities."

B. "But I still don't get it. You've stated before that many of the 'cadre' members are more aware of the political aspects of holding power than they are with a theoretical analysis of educational practice."

A. "That's right, but they are able to bolster their personal ambitions within the power structure by accepting uncritically the new 'traditionalism.'"

B. "Which implies that they are more involved with power than with a value or ideational position. Wouldn't it follow then that they are more open to change if their ambitions aren't directly interfered with? They might readily implement or adjust to change, as long as their power itself isn't limited."

A. "I think that's very possible."

B. "Well, then, why isn't it a fairly safe time for reasonable criticisms and changes? Especially since you feel, as many others do, that there are many 'educators' who actually want the system changed in several ways. If you put together the fairly large group of dissidents with those who are mainly concerned with power, the danger of retaliation would surely be lessened."

A. "Yes, it does seem that now would be the time for action. However, don't overlook the fact that a large number of individuals across the nation represent the new 'traditionalists,' and that they both hold power positions and believe in a value sense that their educational approach is *the* correct one."

From this conversation a central point emerges. This is that action is possible at the present time. It is possible because the dissenters are a fairly large group, though a minority, and because a large number of power holders are more concerned with self-advancement than they are with ideational positions. This latter group will probably not initiate retaliatory action because they realize that change is imminent, and will be inclined to play both sides until they see a victor emerging. The actual danger lies with the "new traditionalists" who hold power and believe in their values which have reified into slogans through the years.

(2) Agreement with the critics, a readiness to comply, rather than challenge their value positions.

Across the nation we see a great number of changes taking place within the public schools. Some of these changes came about slowly, while others were brought about in an abrupt and arbitrary fashion. The abrupt changes indicated a willingness to comply with the critics on an immediate basis.

Most frequently the rapid changes of policy were engendered by drastic actions by the local school board as the result of public pressure brought against the board. In these cases the administrators may have acted to preserve their jobs and pushed through the demanded innovations, rather than question the values which supported the desired changes.

In the schools of education a similar trend is obviously present. During the recent political fight in California which resulted in a bill which basically altered the training of teachers, the educators tended to seek compliance with the major aims of the bill. They did not in general approach the controversy by justifying the previous educational program. Instead they sought to achieve compromises within the legislation itself. In a sense the leading educational lobby, the California Teachers Association, sought to go along with the central aims of the bill, rather than to challenge its basic ideas and suggest a different position. Even though the CTA and the educators appeared to disagree with many of the bill's central aims, the slogan seems to have become, "Adjust, do not offer opposition; the pressure group is very angry, and we must comply with their desires."

This ready compliance by the educators probably reflects their historical timidity and anxiety when facing public pressure of any kind. Public school teachers and administrators, and schools of education, have not been generally known as the leaders of public opinion. They have usually been viewed as the followers of the demands made by the public. This reputation for conservative adjustment, and fear of public reaction has characterized the public schools and many educators for a long period.

However there was a time when the schools of education, and many public school administrators, as well as teachers, were the active leaders of educational thought. This was the case during the period from 1910 until about 1940. In these years much of the older traditional curriculum was replaced by "progressive educational" ideas. The leaders of this movement and their followers were vocal and active in promoting their ideas. However these people have been replaced over the years by a more conservative group who feel that values are seldom a serious matter. The important point is not to get caught disagreeing with the wrong people.

The result is that in their rush to comply with the daily attacks on education they are continuously shifting position. In this shifting process they inevitably jettison many of the most important values and achievements accomplished in the last forty years in the schools. It is possible that some of these gains may be preserved if the educators are willing to defend these achievements. This, of course, implies that they are aware of these achievements, and care enough about them to openly fight for them.

(3) Educators often agree with the critics on specific points, but generally find their overall value position hard to accept. Among these points are the following.

There is too much time spent in the schools on activities not centrally a function of the classroom. Too much emphasis is placed on non-academic achievement, on areas that require little in the way of intellectual capacity. Many teachers are not well grounded in a specific subject matter field; they need more training in a major area. The selection and training of teachers is generally inadequate and geared to low-ability people. Too much time is spent by teachers in taking repetitive education courses for salary increases, rather than for an upgrading in their subject matter areas.

But while many educators feel the need for these and several other reforms, they find it difficult to support critics like Bestor or Rickover whose value position is inimical to their own. Hence their tendency is to withdraw from the current controversy over public education, while continuing to privately complain about teacher training and public educational policy. For if there is a public misconception about educators, it is that they share a single position on education. In fact, there are many areas of deep disagreement, and many who feel that serious reforms are currently needed.

It is granted that there is also a significant group who carefully work to preserve the status quo in the public schools. Among this latter group, there are those who feel that things are essentially "just fine." It is probable that a large number of school administrators fall into this category.

The strong disagreement over values between the educators and people like Bestor, Adler and Rickover may be briefly stated. These individuals are strongly working for a school system which resembles in tone and curriculum a medieval situation. They wish a return to pedagogical methods and values which went out with the hair shirt, and memorized tables of soon-forgotten nonsense. They desire schools to become "serious business" rather than pleasant areas of activity. They want the word of authority and tradition to replace the "interests and needs" of the child. For the child is the recipient of authoritative judgment, rather than the joint participant in the gaining of behavioral insights. They believe that intellectual activity is superior to other forms of human endeavor, and they wish to promote and cultivate a select group of well trained intellectuals.

The dissenting educators generally find this approach deeply repugnant to their own values and educational goals. They view education not as a function of mind alone, in the traditional European sense, but rather as the fullest possible development of the human personality. They grant that this idea has often dwindled into cliché and cant about the "whole child," but they believe that the European elite system in stressing rote authoritative learning has promoted state dictatorship, and living standards more akin to the middle ages than to the present industrial age.

Those European systems which best represent the Bestor and Rickover approach have directly contributed to the rise of Fascism and the suppression of individual liberty. In emphasizing "classical" learning and the importance of the past, these systems have promoted those qualities which perpetuate the social and economic morass in which European life abounds. The whole system is geared to promote and enhance a rigid social class system based on the acceptance of age old values, and the denial of self-expression among the masses. It is a system, like Plato's, geared to promote a special form of human degradation; it is one that replaces the physical weapon of violence with the educational weapon of convincing the masses that they are intellectually inferior, and must deferentially remain in the shadow of the chosen few.

(4) Educators do not usually defend "progressive" education and its achievements, or offer alternative educational programs for the schools, because they have seldom considered the basic difference in values which various programs offer. Before one can answer a criticism on a reasonable basis it is necessary to have a value position which is rationally defensible. Many professional educators lack this kind of coherent philosophic approach. What they possess instead are technical and methodological kinds of information, which are not, necessarily, based on any educational philosophy. Hence they find it difficult to answer the critics for their main concern is the methodological improvement of education, rather than assessing the social rationale upon which public education is inevitably based.

(5) Answering the critics.

Some of the educators react to the criticisms of public education by judging the motives of the critics rather than examining the values inherent in the criticisms. In recent years educators have appeared to be indifferent to social and cultural changes in the society. The strong competition from Russia for world leadership has frequently been by-passed or de-emphasized by the educators as an unworthy basis for educational change. Yet in this same period the public schools have become increasingly hostile toward an open presentation and discussion of Communist ideas and political policies. This position may simply reflect the community's pressures upon the school, but it also indicates the lack of *educational leadership* which further points up the emphasis on skills rather than values in the process of curriculum development.

One frequently hears comments about Admiral Rickover's inadequate naval career, or Bestor's economic motives for writing the things he does. One does not often hear an open discussion of the merits of Rickover's ideas; yet a large number of educators passively agree with several of his statements. The net result of this refusal to examine other points of view leads to a kind of professional entrenchment, and removal from the cultural values of the period. This rejection of the critics has led to a refusal to acknowledge social change, by the very group that has been traditionally committed to an experimentalist view of historical development. The reason for this resistance to change probably lies in the tendency of organized groups to defensively protect themselves, regardless of the conflicts in values which may be involved.

SUMMARY AND COMMENT

There is a minority group among professional educators who believe that many basic and extensive changes are necessary to improve the quality of public education. This group does not act upon their beliefs because they fear retaliatory actions by their superiors. Another group of educators are mainly concerned with holding their current power positions, and adjusting to whatever value system emerges successful. A third group of educators represent the "new traditionalists." They believe that the current policies and practices of public education are essentially sound, and not subject to lay criticism. Their values are deeply entrenched in the public schools and are passed along in the professional schools of teacher training.

The tendency of these three groups of educators has been to withdraw from open participation in the current controversy. Their participation generally involves adjustment and political compromise to the demands of the critical groups. However in this adjustment process they may be overlooking a disturbing consequence.

The current educational controversy is part of a nationwide movement towards the right wing of political values. The entire movement is essentially anti-democratic in spirit and has its value roots, not merely in reform, but in re-establishing a set of authoritarian ideals and values. These values, which have long been a traditional part of the European educational scene, have promoted autocratic attitudes and life styles, as well as having paved the way for the aristocratic social structure which has long characterized European life.

The European educational system, with its one sided cultivation of an intellectual elite, has fostered the paternalistic climate which still is commonly found on the continent. For the ruling elite perpetuates the idea that the past is more important than the present, and that progress does not mean technological and economic betterment for the masses. Rather the elite system is inclined to categorize all activities in individuals in terms of their educational achievements. It is a system which insures the rule of the educated minority over the masses that do not pass the academic examinations. If, in fact, the educated few were made more "liberal" as the result of their "liberal educations" it would be one thing, but their historical behavior has not indicated their lack of interest in tyranny and the conservative control of change.

The American education system has contributed in a major way to the growth of the democratic spirit, and democratic behavior which is commonly associated with the United States. It has significantly advanced the welfare of the total society through a greater socialization of its citizens. It has aided in promoting intellectual and economic opportunities beyond that of most other nations. It has worked deliberately to lessen class lines and unfair distinctions of caste and class. It has been a heavy contributor in the building of a prosperous and stable society—qualities rarely found in many parts of the world.

These are some of the achievements of Dewey's educational reforms. They are part of the values and goals of "progressive education." It is difficult to challenge these qualities as being less than tremendous accomplishments. However the recognition of these achievements does not mean that professional educators should close their minds to further changes in the educational system. It does mean that the educators should be careful not to remove themselves from the changing interests of the society in which they live.

PART 4

Education in a Metropolitan Society

THE URBAN DILEMMA

American affluence is a popular theme of our time. Popular magazines and television programs publicize our national prosperity and the luxuries and pleasures afforded by our consumer-oriented society. It is not difficult to find individuals who deny that our society has major social problems. As a consequence, they may feel that any analysis or presentation of these issues is an alien and hostile attack upon the goodness and efficiency of American life. On the other hand, if one reads about, or examines in person, the nature of urban life in our society, it becomes apparent that there are large-scale social problems confronting our larger metropolitan centers.

Granting this difference in views about our society, what is the meaning of the phrase, the urban dilemma? Traditionally, the city has been viewed as a place of social and economic opportunity and as a stimulating cultural and commercial center. For the most part these conditions remain true, but other factors have been added to the cities' life in an increasingly large scale which directly limit the value and attractiveness of these population centers. These factors are readily apparent in most large cities. Among the conditions which lessen the interest and value of the city as a place to live are the following factors: large and growing slum districts containing substandard living conditions, high crime and violence rates, friction and conflict between ethnic and racial groups, depressed economic areas known as ghettos, and the decay and lack of care of commercial buildings. In addition there are the factors of high taxes, inadequate city services for those living within the city limits, and the lowered quality of education within the inner city areas.

Historically many of these negative conditions have been present for a long time. For example, the deteriorated areas of slum housing and the higher crime rate are not new developments in the larger cities; but both of these conditions have greatly increased. This is partly because of the population growth and partly because of the breakdown of the city as an effective agency in maintaining stable and meaningful control of its own internal problems.

During the period of large-scale European immigration to the United States, these same conditions were found in several of the larger cities. But a major difference has been added to this urban scene. In the earlier period the immigrants were able to find jobs and to essentially improve their life condition. Within one generation many of their children had raised their educational and occupational levels significantly above those of their parents. They frequently moved into better housing and enjoyed a higher standard of living than their parents were accustomed to. Their children attended better schools, and they had far higher expectations for their own children than would have been possible in the countries from which they came. They expected a lot from the new society and in general their utopian hopes for a new and improved life did bear some realistic results.

But in the case of the Negroes, the story differs. The Negroes came to the northern cities as migrants from the South. Like the European settlers before them, they moved into the poorer districts of the cities; and as more Negroes came, the area increased in size and became exclusively a Negro settlement. This kind of racially or ethically segregated district within a city has often been termed a ghetto area. Not only were the Negroes forced to live in these isolated districts, apart from the white community, but they were discriminated against in housing, employment, education, and social opportunity. In this manner, they were prevented from obtaining the rewards and expectations they had hoped to obtain in their northern migration. In contrast to the European immigrants who moved into and out of the slums in one or two generations, the Negroes were prevented from moving out of their own districts and were isolated from meaningful contact with the non-Negro population. As these restricted areas grew in size, they became major parts of the central city, so that in some cities the total public school population was as high as 80% Negro. Further, the extensive discrimination and isolation of the Negro community promoted alienation and hostility toward the white groups maintaining these personally destructive conditions for the Negro population.

A large number of the commercial and professional people who utilize the city in an occupational sense do not support the city financially nor do they fully participate in the life of the urban community. Their lives are spent in two distinctly separate domains. Their commercial and professional lives are spent in the city, while their personal and community concerns are based in the outlying suburban areas. They utilize the city to achieve their economic goals, but abandon the downtown area in the evening. It is in the suburbs that they pay their taxes for more efficient civic services and public school facilities. It is there that one finds a better living and recreational environment for rearing a family. The urban dilemma lies in the discrepancy between what is happening to our major population centers, and the neglect of these centers by those segments of the population most knowledgeable about these problems.

One writer has described the situation of the inner city as containing "social dynamite." By this term, he has attempted to call attention to the explosive social conditions which are present in several American cities. Many writers feel that major changes need to be made in terms of urban planning and in redesigning the educational approaches that have been traditionally used in the disadvantaged areas of the city. The study of urban education has become an important field of research and many experimental school programs have been developed in metropolitan districts.

Over the years, the federal government has become extensively involved along with private foundations, such as Carnegie and Ford, in helping to solve some of the urban problems. This assistance involves research, large-scale financing of innovative proposals, and the development of federal programs which offer direct aid on a nationwide basis. Some of these government and private programs would include the following areas: urban redevelopment and community planning; community organization among the poor; ameliorating social welfare conditions; lessening overt delinquent behavior; increasing the number of cultural and recreational facilities; and providing a large amount of direct financial aid for the improvement of public education in many different areas. From this it may be seen that there is broad local and national concern over these urban problems and that serious efforts are being made to solve these difficult questions.

The articles which follow comment on various aspects of these urban conditions. They provide the reader with a basis for a better understanding of the city's problems. Many of the articles deal with the deprived and the disadvantaged person in the urban setting. This population and the schools they attend are quite different from the suburban groups and their public school milieu.

Cities in Transition

In the opening article of this section, Professor Lohman critically comments on the changes that have taken place in the larger urban centers. He discusses these changes and their meaning in terms of the future of American society. The central problem in his view is that "the public must, in truth, discover itself." It must realize that the major problems confronting the society are created by interrelated social forces which have long been accepted as part of the system's traditional operation.

The increase of movement by whites into suburban areas coupled with the increase of inner city ghettos populated by nonwhites, is rapidly becoming the major urban dilemma. The human value loss in not urbanizing the Negro or educating the white to the needs for a socially integrated culture, is a significant issue for both the society and the school.

By what process can a public discover itself? Is this any responsibility of education? Are there only negative results from mass living? How can man

accommodate himself to living in mass society while advocating strong in-
dividual rights? Should the modern situation of mass man in segregated
communities demand a different perspective as to who should control edu-
cation?

Significant Changes in Our Society: Their Impact on Youth; Their Implications for Education

JOSEPH D. LOHMAN

Today we are confronted with the necessity of changing our attitudes toward the people with whom we are engaged and to whom we would relate, if there is to be afforded us even the smallest opportunity for the modification of their attitudes. This is so important that without it, and in the sight of it, is to be found much that confounds us today. For what confronts us in our classrooms and communities, is the projection of current processes of community life. There are far too many of us, products of an earlier time and a different place, who are too ready to bring upon the present scene our earlier instruction and education, and to insist that the world meet us as it is today, on those earlier terms. The result is that there may be some who, notwithstanding the emphasis in this presentation, will still think of the degree to which they are not equipped to deal with the vexing problem of marginal youngsters that, unfortunately, in increasing numbers are concerning and challenging them.

The truth is that what was once the problem of the marginal youngster, or a condition of underprivilege, is of necessity to be redefined. It is a new statement of the case to speak of children who are culturally deprived, and it represents a change from the traditional conception of the underprivileged child. This is the current condition under which we are addressing what is a newly defined and a newly emergent problem of such proportions and such dimensions, as to require a definition in collective terms, rather than in terms of the individual.

I was looking at a series of new volumes and was intrigued by the titles that they collectively presented. One of them is a new brilliant and insightful work by Frank Riessman, "The Culturally Deprived." Another is titled "The Troublesome One." A third now commonly referred to, is Conant's "Slums and Suburbs." There was a book called "Delinquency and Opportunity;" another was "Kids, Crime and Chaos." These volumes are a sign

From a paper given at the Southern California Conference on Human Relations Education, May, 1962, University of Southern California. Reprinted by permission of the author.

of the times and a measure of the direction and character of the problem that is confronting us today. Their titles indicate the necessity for collective attention to problems that are, for the most part, unprecedented in the history of the land. For we are concerned here, not with a student that can be sent to a special class or to a counselor, but with major portions of the youthful population. We are concerned with the way in which it has come to pass that the major area of urban life that commands our attention, is one that challenges and threatens to override (certainly within the great central cities of the metropolitan area), the task and mission of conventional education.

Between 1950 and 1960 the twelve largest cities of the United States lost over two million white citizens and they gained in their place nearly two million Negro citizens. This cannot be characterized in the language of the past, as merely transition neighborhoods. That was the way we characterized first the accommodation, later the assimilation and effective integration of the nationality groups that came out of Europe to these United States in the latter part of the 19th and the early part of the 20th century. That migration, of enormous proportions as it was, turned to a large extent upon the acceptance of representative contributions of various ethnic and religious groups to existing, previously established, and relatively well ordered social life. We spoke of the integration of those populations as essentially a problem of their transition to conventional, middle class American life. In specific instances we pinpointed the problem and mission of education in terms of the location of neighborhoods which were in transition at certain relatively few points in the central areas of the great major cities. That which confronts us today can no longer be called "neighborhood in transition." It is, in truth, whole cities in transition.

When, today, officials talk about spreading slums, they must coin such new phrases as the development of "widespread gray areas." There is a major foundation that now talks of its mission as "an attempt to come to grips with the vast range of slum deterioration that has become a condition of the life of the major metropolitan areas in the United States." However, the existence of slum and its physical deterioration is now equated with something more than just geography, as it was in the past. For these areas are now inhabited by a single racial group—by the Negro.

When today police remark upon the increasing incidence of juvenile delinquency and teen-age crime, to what do they refer? They refer to juvenile delinquency as it burgeons amongst the non-white population— juvenile delinquency amongst *Negroes*. When welfare agencies talk about increasing case loads, when the debate waxes hot with reference to illegitimacy and the amount of aid to dependent children, what is the ominous undertone?—*the Negro*. When people speak of inadequacy in public housing, and the problem of reclamation of the physical housing plant of the land, what they are implying all too frequently, is that public housing has become the way in which the Negro is housed in the great central cities of America. When municipal authorities talk about the inadequacy of tax resources within the local community; when they speak about the city having beyond its margins persons who, though they do not pay the costs, utilize its services, what are they talking about? They mean the investing of a city with propertyless Negroes who, in the slum and in the deteriorated areas, cannot afford to support municipal housekeeping as it has been done in the past. When health authorities talk about hospital and medical care in the sense in which it becomes increasingly a public challenge, nearly always the ominous undertone is the need of supplying the great masses of the American Negro population who are underserviced in those regards, with minimal hospital and medical care. I have taken the pains to enumerate these references because they are the terms in which the problem is known and experienced and related to, by the population at large; the way in which it is communicated to you by children who come from middle-class homes. They are talking about Negro adjustment to city life in this decade of the sixties.

Cities are not absorbing and are not urbanizing the new breed Negroes as fast as the numbers move in upon them. Why? Because the cities are preoccupied with upgrading city real estate and disregarding correspondingly essential human values. Note the way in which relocation has been done when upgrading of the real estate is underway. In the decade, 80 percent of those who have been relocated were Negroes. And, by whom were they replaced? Notwithstanding salutary experiments of a few groups that attempted to create integrated social life, the ambition has been to create middle-class neighborhoods and since there were relatively few middle-class Negroes, this meant middle class *white* neighborhoods. To remove the slums meant, therefore, not only to level old houses and build new ones, but to remove the Negroes as well; to kick them about, to shuffle them about, to sift and sort them and let them find their own place in the struggle. It is not an overstatement, nor do I aim to create a specter when I suggest that we must, in good conscience, recognize that in America today the urban problem has become the *Negro problem*. We are therefore challenged with the necessity of using every resource to speed up integration and to move the Negro into middle-class social experience.

The problem is not merely a legal one or a social one; not merely a question of economics, of jobs and income; not just a question of educating young people to exhibit graceful middle-class manners and ways. Nor is it the grasping of formal educational knowledge, procedures and methods. Rather it is all of these together, and cannot be any one of them alone. It has been our misfortune that here and there people have seized upon one or the other as a means of addressing and redressing the situation. These efforts have been self-defeating.

In Los Angeles County the Negro population jumped six-fold since 1940, in twenty years, from a population of 75,000 to a population of 464,000. In Chicago, in twenty years, the increase from 277,000 to well over 825,000 illustrates the relentless tendency everywhere, at the call of the great cities, to create a concentration and a separation of the newly arrived migrant non-white, in a situation that is more insulated than any they have previously experienced. Eighty percent of the 825,000 Negroes who make up the non-white population of Chicago live in communities in which 80 percent of the population is non-white. And today, 89 percent of the whites in Chicago live in neighborhoods where only five percent of the population is non-white. This is what is upon us. This is what distinguishes the unique and especially aggravating problem of a culturally deprived group rather than merely individuals who, in some sense, are under-privileged. This organized collective experience poses problems for us much greater and challenging than the necessity for dragging individuals or members of families within the circle of conventional experiences.

You may ask, how can this be distinguished from the experience in America of the acceptance, accommodation and ultimately the assimilation and integration of other ethnic and even racial groups? The point is that none of the others have that condition of identification that is the experi-ence of the Negro. The fact of color, the corresponding high visibility and the opportunity to identify him and retain his relationship to the past, is unparalleled in our experience with other groups. The goals, the road to those goals, in the whole society, were available to the other immigrants. They were not, and are not yet, to the Negro. The earlier relationship between non-white and white in the history of this nation, established conditions of family disorganization, low status, absence of dignity, obvious and apparent conditions of servility, attendant promiscuity, and even the chronic and persistent embracing and entertaining of violence. This is self-borrowed out of an earlier superordinated and subordinated relationship. All of these things represent the conditions of identification and separation that distinguish this present wholesale development from the rather minor accommodations in the experience of other groups in the past.

What I am talking about here is, at one and the same time, the emer-gence of a new way of life, and in that new way of life, of something more than merely the enlargement of population or its more widespread dis-tribution. The metropolitan community is upon us and there are few, if any of us, who are aware of it. If we know it, we know it only as a figure of speech and not in the sense in which each of us are in organic relation-ships to the whole. I am sure that there are many to whom some of the references made here will continue to be remote and distant, and from whose point of view the problem is not yet with us, and it is not likely that it will ever be with us. But the point is, that it is with you now, and has been for some time without your realizing it. For our immediate neighbor-hoods are organic aspects of the metropolitan whole and each of us in his place, is in some measure a part of that whole, responsible for its assign-ment of function and process.

There are none of us who can be regarded as remote from the problem to which I refer, if we are located within the metropolitan matrix. The explosive increase of our population is, of course, the most obvious form in which this may come to us, but it is something more than that. I should like to spend a minute or two talking about the shape and character of the life we are in, and that we are called upon to live, for it seems to me that it is in this context that we can more effectively examine the attitudes that we take, and the degree to which they are or are not relevant to the reconstruction of the attitudes of the people we are talking about, our pupils.

We are living today in mass society. A society which is increasingly characterized by impersonality, by detachment, by separation and submergence of each of us in isolated and distinct experiences, which in turn, make us, in some degree, irresponsible and apart from the whole. Each of us is in some measure alienated; not only those who are delinquent, not only those who are detached from us, but *all* of us are in some measure estranged and alienated from the whole.

In a Phoenix, Arizona paper, I read of a study being carried on in New York City the headline read: "Most City Dwellers Crazy." The article referred to a study conducted by a psychiatrist, a psychologist, a sociologist and some others, at the University of Buffalo and Columbia University. For a number of years they studied a section of Manhattan, to determine the incidence of mental disorder and emotional difficulty. After some eight years, they reached the following conclusion through what they regard as an effective sample: 80 percent of the midtown Manhattan "cliff dwellers," who were regarded as representative of New York, exhibited some kind of mental or emotional disorder; were, in short, mental or emotional "cases." They found everything from simple neurosis to schizophrenia. They found some comfort in the fact that severe symptom classifications made up only 23.4 percent of the population and that 58.1 percent were in mild or moderate categories. We are part and product of something that is new, something that causes us, in traditional terms and by an earlier conceptualization, to appear somewhat queer and abnormal. Only as we can be conceived of in effective relationships to that from which we stem, can we begin to understand that which we really are.

The metropolitan community has been of concern to me because in its context I have had an opportunity to begin to understand the emergence of large numbers of marginal youngsters who get into difficulty with the law. As delinquents and as teen-agers, they require something different than merely being taken into custody or put into institutions. It is important to note the conditions of the metropolitan community, so that each of us in our several schools and places can address this problem as a function of the community to which the school itself relates. In the first place, there is the population explosion which is rapidly presenting us with a society that has a heterogeneity of character and deployment, which is unprecedented. We are getting paradoxically very old and very young at one and the same time. The numbers are important in the sense that they are disproportionately young and disproportionately old.

This, itself, is not nearly as important as might appear in terms of a numerical breakdown by age groups. What we need to understand is that what young people want to do and need, is very different from that which people in their middle years need, and again very different from what people need and seek in their senior years. The most obvious evidence of this that comes to us in our administrative capacities, is the overwhelming demand for new schoolhouses and teachers. This is only a surface indication of the intrinsic nature of the problem that confronts us. What is resident in this expansion of population is the complex of social relationships which are attendant upon such a new percentage-wise distribution of the age groups in the population, to which the metropolitan community is ill-adapted in its organization and administration of essential service.

If we add to this still another dimension, then we can begin to see the sense in which we are further confounded. For even as the population has exploded, it has sought a new place in response to changes in our technology, and in response to the new economic needs of our nation. The concentration of the land-points adjacent to or at the heart of the central cities, represents a phenomenon that is something more than resettling of population. We inherit the way in which the demands of the economy upon the population are met. Of necessity these demands are directed to those elements within the city that are most sensitive and responsive to the invitation to increased opportunity. Consequently, the metropolitan matrix reflects not an equal development of the traditional pattern in terms of the numbers of the racial and class-identified groups, but a disproportionate gathering of the racial, the minorities, the culturally deprived groups at the city's center. Under these circumstances we see that in the cities, a change to a social-class structure in which new groups at the bottom of the pyramid are disproportionately represented. At the same time there are overtones of cultural differentiation of deprived racial blocks which poses for the city a challenge which it has never had before.

In 1948, when a number of colleagues and myself reported a study of segregation in Washington, we remarked upon the fact that the city lived under the threat of what it called a non-white invasion. But this, on closer analysis, was revealed to be a disproportionate expansion of the white population at highly selected points in the metropolitan scene. The truth of the matter was that the white population of metropolitan Washington was increasing at a ratio of three to one over the Negro population; and has continued to the present day. Within the District of Columbia, the whites moved out into the suburbs in accordance with their advanced economic and social status. That left vacant a large number of homes in the city's center, to be occupied by the newcomers. Thus there was a disproportionate increase in the non-white population in the metropolitan center. We predicted at that time, that unless policies and programs were initiated, to prevent stratification of the population in such pronounced terms as were then evident, this disproportionate increase of non-whites in the city would continue and one day would be noted with alarm as the final proof of the non-white invasion of the city.

Today, 55 percent of the population of Washington is non-white and the white population has continued to move to the regions beyond the municipal limits. What has happened here is happening in Chicago where today its population is 23 percent non-white as contrasted with 18 percent no more than ten years ago; the same is true in St. Louis which had 19 percent non-white ten years ago, and today has 33 percent; in Detroit, Pittsburgh, Cleveland, Los Angeles, and San Francisco. Moreover, on the Pacific coast, I discover that the way this problem is addressed, reflects a tragic repetition of the same ideas, philosophy, and judgment that characterized Washington in 1948.

I have the eerie feeling of being somewhat in the position of coming into a movie and saying, "Well, this is where I came in." In a sense, what is happening on the Pacific coast today, represents a reaction akin to that which was experienced in Eastern and Midwestern cities between 1930 and 1950. Many of the errors are being repeated. Many of the trial experiences which ought not to be repeated, are being repeated here, simply because there is insufficient effort to pass on the experience of the Midwest and the East.

The phenomenon that confronts us is the increasing separation on racial lines of the central cities from the suburbs. We witness the realization of the prediction made by Coleman Woodbury in the 40's: "The central cities will become increasingly the place of residence of new arrivals, of non-whites, lower income workers, young couples, and the elderly. The suburbs will become even more the residence of middle-income families and of those of the better paid workers, particularly those families in the middle stages of the family cycle." This has gone so far that many central cities are fast becoming lower class, largely Negro, slums. The 14 largest metropolitan areas of the United States seem to be moving in that direction. So we see that the educational system of the United States, the municipal bureaucratic organization of the United States, the policy making authorities and leadership of the United States, are confronted with a readily apparent challenge which, for the most part, they have been unable to meet and face.

The Negro population, moreover, is increasing faster than the white under the new conditions of their metropolitan location. It is a younger population with lower death rates and increasing numbers of older people. Infant mortality is lessened because of the availability of health services and hospitalization. In fact, in some situations in the United States, even without the influence of increasing migration, the natural increase in those sub-cultural centers will expand and push outward toward the periphery of the city in the very way that was formerly brought on by migration. In the next 25 years, in terms of a conservative projection of population statistics, natural increase, and the migration of people off the land in the south to the central cities of the north, it is probable that Negroes will constitute from 30 to more than 50 percent of the population in the centers of at least ten of the 14 largest cities. They are the most numerous identifiable group. They are correspondingly, insofar as they are segregated and kept apart, a self-identified group. As a self-identified group, they present problems of effective integration of the community as a whole, which are again unprecedented in the history of the land.

Let me note this in a very pointed respect with reference to the problems of delinquency and crime. Fully 50 percent of all the juvenile delinquents and the teen-age offenders in America, come from communities occupied by no more than à fourth of the youth of our nation. The great majority of these are young people living under the cloud of minority group status. While the non-white population makes up roughly one-tenth of our population, the marginal economic and cultural forces under which they must labor, generate amongst them over one-fifth of all of our delinquency and youthful crime. We need only look about us. We do not even need the benefit of critical studies. In the official reports of the agencies that serve us we discover that the highest rates of juvenile delinquency and teen-age crime are in groups who are at a social and economic disadvantage in their adjustment to the community at large. Their search for normal avenues of cultural assimilation and economic improvement is blocked by social barriers against them. Their language, culture and race make it difficult for them to identify with the dominant cultural values of the community. They are employed in marginal and unskilled occupations. They are segregated, isolated, and hence unduly restricted in their participation in the broad free processes of community life.

One of the instructive experiences that I had while Sheriff of Cook County was to find that six out of ten of the delinquents and teen-agers arrested for hostile acts against persons or things (violation of law), on the occasion of their arrest and detention, were of school age, should have been in school, but were *not* in school. We did not detain them merely as truant officers. The point is that these individuals who were violating the law were recruited en masse from amongst those who either had rejected or were rejected by the operating school system of the community. The community was on notice that deprivation generated hostile acts, done to secure for the individual gratification of his wishes and aspirations. But the community merely struck back at them, dealing with them in desperation.

You are well aware, I am sure, that Americans have an excessive disposition to rely on negative methods of arrests and incarceration as a means of dealing with crime and delinquency. If people are asked why is there a lot of crime or why is there a horrible act, the response is that in some way or another, the police are not adequate to their task. The assumption is that the important variable with reference to the incidence and distribution of crime, is the capacity and deployment of police departments. As one who has been in law enforcement and who continues to be associated with it in research and instruction, I must declare that law enforcement is a less important variable with reference to repression of the phenomenon of crime than is ordinarily assumed. For the fact of the matter is, of crime which is committed and known to the police, no more than a third at best is ever cleared up by the police, let alone the vast additional amount which is never even called to the attention of the police. This is the sense in which we rely excessively and abortively on false notions about crime control, and are driven to self-defeating means. From time to time we are shocked into some kind of action by the report of a horrible crime and find in it overtones that associate it with the presence of people, the desirability of whose presence amongst us we seriously question. By the same token, we visit the negative impact of our system of criminal justice upon those who come within the circle of its influence. We turn them back into the very groups, inside of which can be found the cause of their deprivation. There has been foisted coercively, collectively upon them, a solution of their problems which is at odds with that of the society at large. Within these groups, through them and the agency of their influence, is encouraged a further degradation and alienation from the manner and the point of view of that community from which they came.

The arrested and the detained become an active resource for the production of the crimes about which we are disturbed. When they are released by the police from correctional agencies, they return to the narrowly confined communities from which they came. There, they supply the criminal maturity and the sophistication which they have acquired by their exposure to the insensitive machinery of criminal justice. There are more state penitentiaries in America today than I can shake a stick at, in which more than 60 percent of the inmate population is non-white. Moreover, they have been gathered into those institutions in an insensitive and unwitting preparation for the further degradation of the communities to which they will return. Therefore, the system of correction, in a very large sense, becomes part and party to the system of deprivation to which we refer when we designate an individual as culturally deprived. We cannot and will not contain the problem by merely emphasizing the negative treatment of these individuals, or by isolating them from the total life of the community.

The record shows that among juveniles, non-whites are arrested more frequently and for less serious offenses than are whites. They are more frequently convicted and then serve longer sentences. This can only mean one thing. They are more frequently exposed to the secret disabling effects of the community of the rejected, and feed back into the neighborhoods of their origins their accentuated bitterness, their hostility, their alienated and estranged attitudes, their personal distortions, visiting them upon those who as yet are naive and innocent. It is thus that we are confronted by the paradox of a new metropolitan development in which we are constantly moved to employ self-defeating extremes in our desperate and uninformed efforts to keep abreast of the problems, the nature of whose process has not been grasped.

The heart lands of our great metropolitan centers are becoming the provinces of the new minority. They have come out of a segregated, discriminatory experience in search of freedom and opportunity, into a social world in which, in terms of residence, they find themselves even more restricted than in the older pattern. Therefore, it is not only crime that becomes the abortive fruit of our failure. The unwitting processes of the middle-class suburban drift, and the transformation of vast areas of the central city into an enormous racial slum, have profound political implications. In many of our major cities today, it is affecting a change in the balance of political power. We must recognize the coincidence of the development of these great racial blocks with the traditional organization and location of some distressingly monolithic political machines. To ignore the social, economic and cultural disabilities under which these populations labor, and to try to contain their volcanic eruptions with repressive police measures, can only have the effect of fanning the flames which are smoldering at the core of our metropolitan communities.

We are at a critical juncture, in my judgment, in the history of American community development. The resettlement of the American community, the emergence of the metropolitan communities is, as I have suggested, not merely a change in the numbers of our population groups nor of their geographic location. If we are a part of a metropolitan matrix in which this heterogeneity is not immediately evident, it is nonetheless a thing of which we *are* a part and, incidentally, for which we have a responsibility. This is something of greater importance than distribution or numbers. It is, in fact, an essential modification, even requires in many cases the creation of a whole new set of human relations. It is these new human relations that are the task of education, and when I say human relations, I use a non-normative term. They will be either those relationships visited upon us by the unwitting interplay of the forces which are currently giving us this curious segregated concentration, or through the agency of education and responsible governmental and political leadership, they will be a set of human relationships which are consonant with the egalitarian ideal.

May I suggest that the climate inside of which these metropolitan contests are developing, is one of mass life. The individuation and impersonality, the boredom, ennui, the dissociation, the alienation, the estrangement (all the words the scholars use today to describe the sense in which persons are at loose ends), present a heterogeneity of behavior which challenges us in our capacity for order and purpose. Moreover, in the context in which the banner of equality, freedom and the egalitarian ideal has been lifted, the culturally deprived groups are assigned, from birth to death, a subordinate role in the scheme of things which history records they have accepted without too much tension and conflict. This is incompatible in a system which raises high the banner of progress and upward mobility. For if the Southern non-white population could accommodate itself to a status system in which it was born and in which it was called upon to live its life and find its end, in the North it is called upon to find its place in the sun along with all the others. If that place in the sun is not available, then it will look back upon itself, in the heightened self-consciousness which the development of a sub-culture brings upon it, to use its new found political power and opportunity for expression to engage those who hold the seats of power and influence. This fact has not been appreciated soon enough, in some of the highest places in the land.

Success and failure in the last presidential campaign was to a large extent predicated upon the insight which the candidates had about the capacity of sub-cultural groups, to seize political means for the solution of their problems. I venture to say that this will be the issue in even more specific terms, come the campaign for the presidency in another year.

Finally, I would suggest that as a society of people who live in a mass condition, as a society committed to and under the cover of the egalitarian ideal, and in light of the distribution of people in this new metropolitan context, we must see that we are part of the whole inside of which we are immersed. For if we do not, this community of which we are a part will drive us relentlessly in the direction of those who do wield power and influence. If some of us who persist in our suburban middle-class conventional quiet and peace, will continue to insist upon seeing ourselves as persons apart and in communities to ourselves, it will only be to the end that persons in other places who do see our relationship to the whole, will exercise disproportionate power and influence in the decisions of the community as a whole. This will give us a relationship and a condition of life that many of us do not bargain for.

The dilemma of today is a dilemma of every one. Unless someone asks you whether you want to give up control of the school on the local basis, or control of the resources of government on the local basis, you must searchingly, as leaders of the community ask yourself and them, what in this metropolitan context is *yet* local. Only that which is truly local, only that which grasps essentially the dimension and character of the community, can win for itself whatever advantage is to be had, in giving service to the notion of local control and influence. But if we act in a way which does not give us identification with the community of which we are a part, we shall have only been caught up in a semantic, rhetorical snare; trapped by our language and failing to see in the newly emergent world the community of which we are a part.

The public must in truth, discover itself. It can only discover itself when we recognize that the byword of our day, is the byword of a community which is of such dimensions as to set forth within its perimeters, the true character of the interdependence which makes these unwitting and witting claims upon us.

The metropolitan community is a new community. The problems that we experience are projections of that new community. Just as crime is the lengthened shadow of the community, so is it in turn a reflection of the failure to see that community as an interacting whole. In my judgment, the major problem which confronts America today, is recognition of the fact that, as products of social life our datum is the groups from which we spring and the conditions under which they are generated. The great challenge of the 60's is the way in which, in the new metropolitan context sub-cultures are being generated, and in which their product is being treated. The solution of the problem is to see that criminals are deprived individuals, the projections of the groups of which they are products. This is the relevant level and condition of action. This is the condition for education as it is for government, for law enforcement, and for anyone who would contribute to the development of the good life.

Segregation in the School

In the article that follows, Jeremy Larner describes in vivid and dramatic fashion the plight in which the New York City schools find themselves. Many of the conditions which are presented can be found in several of the larger American cities—Los Angeles, San Francisco, Cleveland, Chicago, Philadelphia, St. Louis, Washington, Baltimore, Boston. By no means are these problems unique to the New York area, although some of them are more characteristic of that city.

This article is not presented as an illustration of the nature of the public school in the urban setting. It is presented because it powerfully and clearly describes the central role of the school in affecting the lives of hundreds of thousands of children in these areas and many other cities. The reader should consider not only the social and educational changes which are necessary to lessen the impact of these devastating forces, but also the factors which prevent meaningful social action from taking place in these large cities.

Which specific characteristics of contemporary schools create the inferiority feelings, alienation, and aggressive behaviors of youth as described in the article? Are there any plausible solutions?

The New York School Crisis

JEREMY LARNER

THE CIRCUMSTANCES

UFT Official: Why is it we can get young people to volunteer for the Peace Corps to teach in Ghana, yet we can't get them to teach in public schools in Harlem? Answer: Because in Ghana, there is hope.

Let me start with some statistics. There are 132 elementary schools and 31 junior high schools in New York City whose students are almost entirely (over 90% in the elementary schools; over 85% in the junior highs) Negro and Puerto Rican. In the past six years, while Negro and Puerto Rican enrollment has gone up 53%, white enrollment has fallen 8%, and the number of predominantly Negro and Puerto Rican schools has doubled. Of New York's one million schoolchildren, roughly 40% are Negro and Puerto Rican, 60% "other." Efforts of the Board of Education in the past six years to eliminate blatant gerrymandering and allow some voluntary transfers have reduced by a third the number of schools where Negroes and Puerto Ricans are less than 10% of enrollment. But the problem gets more difficult all the time, as is indicated by the fact that 52%—an outright majority—of the city's 1st graders are Negro or Puerto Rican.

The increase in segregated schools is due to three factors. First, rural minority groups are moving into the city and the middle-class urban whites are heading for the suburbs. Second, discrimination, economic pressures, and lack of effective planning confine the newcomers to ghettoes. Third, cautious whites send their children to private or parochial schools rather than "risk" a neighborhood school where minorities predominate. Over 450,000 New York children attend private or parochial schools, a figure that would represent a staggering percentage even for an exclusive suburb.

Thus New York City suffers from an educational problem which it has come to describe as "de facto" segregation. The Board of Education says the facts are essentially beyond its control; the civil rights groups say they are the facts of a racist society, and must in all justice be eliminated by whatever means possible.

Segregation in ghetto schools is more than racial; there is segregation by economic class as well. Wherever Negro parents reach the middle class, at least some of them send their kids to private schools. Lower-class Negro

Reprinted from *Dissent,* Vol. 11, No. 2, Spring, 1964, pp. 243–44, 246–49, 264–69, by permission of the publisher.

kids find themselves isolated in schools which are understaffed, under-
equipped, overcrowded, demoralized, and conspicuously lacking in the
mixture of cultural backgrounds which can make life in New York such an
educational experience. Many of them are children of parents who are in
effect first-generation immigrants from southern and rural areas; for of
New York's 1,100,000 Negroes, 340,000 have arrived in the last ten years,
630,000 in the last twenty years. Most of the 600,000 Puerto Ricans have
come in the past decade, while the white population has dwindled by
500,000.

Teaching middle-class children the ins and outs of a culture made for
them is obviously easier than struggling with ghetto children, most of
whom are members of a racial group which has never been allowed to
recover from the effects of slavery. Some minority schools have annual
teacher turnover rates of over 60%. Some teachers flatly refuse to take
assignments in such schools; others drop out as the school year proceeds.
Not only is one out of every two teachers a substitute, but some classes may
stay without a regularly assigned teacher all year, defeating one temporary
substitute after another. One can see that the atmosphere in minority
schools is hardly conducive to learning. It is estimated that 85% of the 8th-
grade students in Harlem are "functional illiterates," which means that
their reading is not above 5th-grade level—in many cases it is much below.

Though some authorities, e.g. Kenneth Clark, disagree, it is hard to believe that the social conditions under which most New York Negroes live
are not responsible for some of the difficulty. According to the Harlem
Youth survey, whose figures many observers regard as conservative, only
one-half of Harlem children under 18 are living with both parents, more
than one-quarter of Harlem youth receives welfare assistance, and the rate
of narcotics addiction in the area is ten times that for the rest of the city.

The fact that these kids have been encouraged to describe their surroundings is the first sign of hope that they will be able to change them.
The school should represent that possibility; it should be a fortress of
security in which the children are respected, accepted and developed.
Otherwise they are surrounded, as the little girl says; drug addiction, for
example, will begin to appear in their ranks while they are still in junior
high school—and addiction is only the most dramatic form of withdrawal
and defeat.

Looking around him, the young Negro boy will find few "father figures"
to imitate; for the men of his world have not been accorded the honorable
work men need to earn self-respect. Bitter, confused, withdrawn, violent
against one another, lower-class Negro men do not usually last long with
their women. The families are matriarchal, the children remaining with
their mothers while a succession of "uncles" come and go. There is small
hope of that masculine self-respect which is the traditional basis of family
pride. The little boy is regarded as inferior to the little girl, and has less
chance of survival—by which I mean simply less chance of getting through

life without cracking up, without sliding into some form of self-obliteration.

Dismal to tell, the schools in many ways duplicate the situation of the homes. The classroom confronts the child with the same old arrangement: a woman with too many kids. Far too few of the elementary schoolteachers are men, let alone Negro men. The size of classes, usually around 30 pupils per class, makes individual attention—and thus the development of positive identity and incentive—as unlikely at school as it is at home.

When lower-class Negro children enter elementary school, they are already "behind" in several important respects. In crowded tenement apartments children are in the way from the moment they are born. While the adults of the matriarchal clan unit work or wander, children are brought up by older children, who have reasons of their own to feel impatient or harassed. According to the teacher of a "fast" group of 6th-grade pupils,

. . . middle-class Negro kids need integration. But what the lower-class kids need right now is that somehow we conquer the chaos they live in. They have no stability whatever—no family, no home, no one to talk with them. They live in a world without space or time. I mean that literally. Even by the time these kids reach the 6th-grade, most of them can't tell time. You can't talk to them about the future—say, about jobs—because they won't know what you're talking about. And when you refer to concepts of space, why you can't talk about "somewhere else," tell how far away another city is, how long a river is, or simple facts of geography. Though they're fantastically sophisticated, more sophisticated than maybe they ought to be, about how adults behave, their mental orientation is almost utterly without abstract concepts. Look: they don't even know who pays the welfare! They don't even know what checks are!

Of course this particular teacher will get his kids talking and thinking about time and space and jobs and where the money comes from. But there aren't enough like him, and one year of a good teacher can dispel the chaos for very few. The class he has taken such pains with finds itself a year later without an assigned teacher, and the boy who last year wrote a brilliant autobiography is in danger this year of flunking at junior high, breaking down, and spending his high school years in and out of institutions.

Why don't teachers make more progress with these children? Because they are woefully short of books and materials, especially good readers based on the facts of urban life. Because they have to spend so much time on discipline.[1] Because they get poor support from their principals and from the rest of the top-heavy school bureaucracy. But the truth is that most of New York's teachers are too middle-class, too insensitive or too fragile to teach ghetto children successfully. Not that they are worse than teachers in other places, they are simply less suited to their jobs. Not all of them are bothered by their failure; some stay in slum schools because

---

[1] Discipline as opposed to socialization. The 6th-grade teacher quoted above reports that with a "slow" class he begins with checkers, and that it takes weeks to get the children to play together without turning over the board and having at each other. Then he brings out the readers.

apparently it gives them a sense of security to blame the kids for what they fail to teach them. Others, with the best will in the world, are baffled by children who literally speak a different language. One young white teacher, extremely hard-working and perhaps more honest than most, told me after a grueling day,

I hate these kids. They're impossible. How did they get this way? I never thought I'd become so authoritarian.

Most of the teachers are conscientious: that's one of the hallmarks of the professional person. But the manner in which teachers are trained and chosen—which I will discuss below—is practically guaranteed to eliminate those possessing the imagination and flexibility to get through to slum children.

As for the curriculum, it is hopelessly inappropriate. The readers still current in practically every school are those insipid productions featuring Sally, Dick and Jane, the golden-haired cardboard tots from Sterilityville. One could go on by describing a series of tests and achievement-levels, but tests and levels are irrelevant to children who mostly do not pass or reach them. Let me quote Martin Mayer (from his book, *The Schools*) on what our young tenement-dwellers are supposed to be learning by the time they get to high school:

In New York . . . the major Theme Center for tenth-grade "Language Arts" is "Learning to Live with the Family." . . . The curriculum guide suggests "round-table, panel, and forum discussions" on "questions relating to allowances, dating, working after school, selecting and entertaining friends, choosing a career, minding younger brothers and sisters, helping with household chores, contributing earnings to the family, decorating one's own room, choosing family vacation places, using the family car."

But what difference does high school make? The battle is lost long before then. Perhaps it's already lost by the time 1st graders move to the 2nd grade, when only 10% of them are on reading level.

Yet, when all is said and done, are not these conditions surmountable by individual effort? Is it not possible for the majority of these youngsters to pull themselves up by their own bootstraps, as so many of their 2nd-generation American teachers say that they or their parents did? Or is this problem unique somehow, does it have to do with the unprecedented oppression and separation of a group that has never in the history of this country been free? Is it really true, as the 1954 Supreme Court decision contends, that "Segregation of white and colored children in public schools has a detrimental effect upon the colored children . . . A sense of inferiority affects the motivation of the child to learn"?

In the opinion of this observer, no one could sit for long in Harlem classes without seeing overwhelming evidence of the demoralizing effects of segregation. These children are treated as inferior, just as their parents and grandparents and great-grandparents were—and there is no sense of any possibility that such treatment is ending! In the classroom of a 1st-grade teacher who was a militant supporter of the boycott, I was surprised to find cut-out pictures of white children used almost exclusively as bulletin board illustrations. Later I found the purified faces of Sally, Dick and Jane beaming out at me in ghetto classrooms of teachers Negro or white, liberal or not: as if to say, these are what good children are like.

"5th-grade Lower East Side boy (F)": I have a problem that I am colored. I would like to be handsom but I can't because other people have strait blond hair and they are handsom.

In a 2nd-grade Harlem classroom the teacher, a lively, intelligent Negro woman, has her kids acting out a nursery tale. In front of the class stands a shy, finger-sucking little girl, her hair in pigtails, absolutely adorable and black. From her neck hangs a large square of cardboard, on which an adult has painted the head of a white girl with abundantly flowing golden hair. Caption: "GOLDILOCKS."

In another 2nd-grade classroom, where well cared-for Negro children are industriously and quietly working under the direction of a Negro teacher, I glance up and see a row of self-portraits above the front blackboard. I count: of 23 portraits, 1 red, 1 green, only 2 brown, and 19 white as the paper they're drawn on.

The sense of inferiority runs deeper than skin-deep. I remember a junior-high-school social-studies teacher trying to discuss the school boycott with his 9th-grade "slow" pupils. Most of them are long since lost; they look as though they have drawn curtains across the inside of their eyeballs. It develops that they do not know the words "boycott" or "civil rights," and to them "discrimination" is something that happens down South. And oh the tortured embarrassment with which they answer questions! From beneath the embarrassment there slinks a kind of arrogance, thriving it seems on the mere fact that the teacher is trying to teach them —as if to say, imagine this fool, asking "me" a question! Whereupon they laugh. They have to. And we are all relieved.

Whether they know the word "discrimination" or not, these kids know they are not worth much to the world they live in. Some of them, all too many, are not worth much to themselves, and lash out in self-hating violence at the nearest target, usually someone who reminds them of themselves. Already the white people of America are beginning to dread the day when these children, as some day they surely must, will recognize their real enemies. As they are at last beginning to . . .

West Harlem 6th-grade boy (F): Teacher! In the caveman days, if there were Negro cavemen, did the white cavemen use them as slaves?

SOCIETY AND THE CLASSROOM

The subject of New York's schools and what's wrong with them cannot entirely be discussed in terms of more cash, more teaching and more integration. What is needed for the classroom above all else is a free and democratic, truly revolutionary society based on human value instead of compulsive striving, competition and accumulation. I doubt, for instance, that there is a single public school in this country where children are given a chance to learn at their individual rates of speed and without grading. Even at best our schools educate our young to fit into a world where ability is measured by quantity only. Concepts of art, science, knowledge, creativity "for their own sake" survive at kindergarten level only; the purpose of an American education is to replace these values with symbols of measure. What can be said of a society which reduces its culture to True-False and multiple-choice tests even on the college level? Among other things, that this society rewards cheating, and that the more advanced the competitors the more extensive and complex the cheating will become, until the cheaters finally cheat themselves of the knowledge of what they are doing.

Our ideal should be schools in which each child can develop as an individual, according to his capacities and desires. A good teacher is someone with a talent for getting through to children and letting them get through to him. If a teacher doesn't in some way enjoy being alive he has nothing to teach. What we need is to replace the authoritarian teacher who has traditionally plagued and scourged the children, whether black or white, achievers, nonachievers, or underachievers. We need a teacher who will nourish talent and individuality rather than crush it.

Unfortunately, teaching attracts types who enjoy relations where they have undisputed superiority. Thus the effort to "understand the disadvantaged child" turns out in practice to be the science of patronizing the slum-child without feeling guilty about it. For the disadvantaged child, of course, is really not that at all, no matter what it helps one to know about his background: he is a person, and as such something splendid in his own right even before a teacher gets to him.

In every ghetto school I visited, teachers recommended a book called *The Culturally Deprived Child* by Frank Riessman. Reading this book, they told me, had helped them to understand the nature of the children they had to deal with. Sure enough, I found Riessman's book preaching "a sympathetic, noncondescending, understanding of the culture of the underprivileged." But neither Riessman nor the average teacher realizes how un-noncondescending sympathy delivered from the top can be:

Moreover, self-expression and self-actualization, other aims of education, particularly modern education, are equally alien to the more pragmatic, traditional, underprivileged person.

No! You just can't talk that way about a child entering elementary school. Kids from "underprivileged" homes want to express themselves and realize themselves just as much as anyone else. Maybe the most important thing for them is to have a teacher who will "expect" something from them, let them know there is some authority who cares. The best teacher I met in Harlem had taken a class of bright 6th graders who up to that time were demoralized and undisciplined. Fortunately he did not assume they weren't interested in self-expression. He assumed that they had something to express, the fruits of their own experience, which is in so many ways deeper and more demanding than that of middle-class children. It was a long haul, after eleven years of neglect, but eventually he got them writing and writing well. He read them French translations and they wrote him parables and fables; it seems Negro children are natural-born fable-writers, for as we have seen—they are not likely to pull their punches when it comes to the moral. He read them Greek myths and stories, and they wrote him back their own myths, classic transformations, and one boy even wrote an illustrated history of the Trojan War. (One of the transformations begins, "I was transformed from a poor little infant into a nice boy, and as I grew I was transformed into a magnificent extraordinary deceiving nuisance to the world.") Most of the children wrote novels, and one 11-year-old boy, without having read a single modern novel, began a remarkable autobiography with the sentence, "I am dreaming and crying in my sleep."

This was an ordinary 6th-grade Harlem class; there were some high IQ's, but it was not an "SP" (specially gifted) class and had attracted no special attention to itself. The teacher disciplined them, yes, kept them in order, but did it not to triumph but to show them he cared. He respected them, which is something you can't learn from books. He visited their homes, which is absolutely unheard-of. He worked patiently with each child, and got them to work with each other.

Now it is a year later, the kids are dispersed into a notoriously depressing junior high, and most of them have lost what they gained. Some are flunking; their former teacher bitterly wonders how the life in them can survive. But for one year they produced a body of work uniquely theirs.

THE GROUPING OF GROUPINGS

If conditions within the classroom are bad enough, to look beyond them is to find oneself in a jungle of stumbling and makeshift, where stentorian voices boom from the tops of trees, and clusters of officious missionaries rush about distributing memoranda on the cannibal problem.

First of all, there is the school bureaucracy. According to Martin Mayer, "New York City employs more people in educational administration than all of France." I believe I have alluded to the public relations men on the

Board of Ed staff, but I have perhaps failed to mention the endless associations, commissions, sub-commissions, advisory committees, deputy directors, associate supervisors, district superintendents, co-ordinators, directors, foundations and independent consultants who must be involved in every policy decision. The trouble with such a set-up is that the basic concern on every level points up, toward impressing the higher-ups, rather than down, toward serving the classroom teacher. Would it be heresy to suggest equal salary for every school position? With the present system, the classroom teacher can be in a panic for materials she ordered three years ago, while the assistant superintendent is sincerely assuring the area superintendent that everything is all right in his sub-sector. In such a bureaucracy, the people who move toward the top are the yes-men, the round pegs, whom the public pays to rise away from the children. They have a priority on operating funds, too; if they could not get their paperwork properly submitted and filed, the system would collapse. In fact, despite the teacher shortage, there are a number of employees listed on the Board of Ed budget as classroom teachers who never report to their assigned schools; they are clerks and typists working in the central offices. Ironically, the policy directives they type, like great portions of our public school funds, may never filter down to the classroom; but they do reach the publicity department, from which they are carefully distributed to the newspapers, which in turn describe to us a school system that doesn't really quite exist. Nevertheless, its paper achievements will be proudly recounted by the functionary flown to a conference of "educators" at public expense. Life in the big city goes on somehow, though where it goes no one knows.

The gap between theory and practice is nowhere more striking than among the school principals. Many of them know little of what goes on in their own schools and make no effort to learn. The job of the principal is to spend his time in educational conferences, or addressing committees, or preparing reports for higher-ups, who never come to check. At the Harlem school where the 6th-grade "slow" learners I have quoted attended, the principal assured me,

I don't notice any demoralization on this level. The children are happy, well-behaved and eager to learn.

Small wonder that one of the best teachers at this school could not get enthusiastic about the boycott:

What if the boycotters are successful and get the Board to come up with a plan? Who has to implement it but these same shits!

Then there is the problem of the teachers themselves and their organization, the UFT. It would be unkind to expect too much of an organization so urgently needed and besieged with such difficulties as is the UFT. But it must be said that an excessive concern of teachers both black and white is their own respectability. The most pressing practical issues are submerged in the desire to preserve their "professional image."

For instance, a teacher's license in New York City cannot be obtained unless the applicant has passed the expensive and utterly idiotic education courses offered at teachers' colleges. I never talked to a single good teacher who claimed to have learned anything of value in these courses. Furthermore, they discourage many of the specially talented people gathered in New York City from seeking employment as public school teachers. Bright, educated people who want to try their hands at teaching children can't, not in New York, not even if they have PhD's, unless they are willing to go back to school for their "education credits."[2] Yet the union, although ambitious to work out a joint recruiting program with the Board aimed at attracting Negro teachers from the South, shows little interest in this question. The current teacher's pay scale is based on these pointless credits, and to upset it would invalidate years of useless course-taking.

Finally, there is the conglomeration of civil rights groups, divided and sub-divided within itself, spreading out towards too many separate targets with only the most general slogans to hold itself together. The structure of the rights organizations is chaotic beyond description. Let me say simply that the end effect is too often the mirror image of the bureaucracy they are arrayed against. And the boycott offered no program for the Negro children to realize their own particular talents, no social-action program with which to unite the Negro community in self-respect. Was not the boycott in some sense one more appeal to the great white father to do right by his poor black children?

NO ENDING

Have I captured the confusion? Here is New York City with a mass of black people, most of whom have never been allowed to partake of our civilization. Now they must be allowed that dubious privilege; for there is no other place for them. In previous eras of American life, there was some room for a variegated lower class, which took care of the dirty work and was not permitted entrance into the cultural mainstream. Little by little most groups surfaced into the middle class, leaving behind among unlucky remnants of themselves a permanent body of American Negroes, who, handicapped by years of slavery and oppression, remained what a Negro teacher describes to me as "a colonial people encapsulated 'within' the colonial country." But now automation is chopping away at the colony; we see the natives in the street, shaking their fists. We must open the door and let them in.

The big question is, will they come in having truly changed and puri-

---

[2] Education courses are not the only obstacles in the paths of potentially valuable teachers. Teachers from the South or from Puerto Rico with advanced academic degrees may find themselves disqualified on the interview section of the teachers' license exam for "speaking English with an accent."

fied and reformed our social structure, as some say they must? Will we have to chip away at our stone walls to let them in, as the Trojans did for the Greek horse? Or will the Negro scrape through bloody, bitter and confused, ready to perpetuate the authoritarian ethic he has so far, to his unique credit, managed to evade?

The answer to this question depends in part on our schools. But all school systems are—and have always been—failures. Even Leo Tolstoy, with all his genius, his wealth, his command, and with not a single bureaucrat to hamper him, could not educate his peasants into free men. His failure, our failure . . . the failure is always the same: the failure to educate each man—not for a prestigious "function" or "role"—but to fulfill his own capacities for living, for being alive, for finding and making his own kind of beauty, for respecting the diversity of life without, in his frustration, turning to violence, self-suppression, and the worship of authority.

So what the boycotters are demanding, ultimately (and more power to them!) is a change in the nature of the lives we lead.

6th-grade Harlem girl (S):

I wish that the hold city can chage. and that the governor make new laws that there to be no dirt on streets and no gobech top off and wish that my name can chage and I wish that whether can trun to summer.

6th-grade Harlem boy (F): Fable

Once upon a time there was two men who were always fighting so one day a wise man came along and said fighting will never get you anywhere they didn't pay him no attention and they got in quarrels over and over again. So one day they went to church and the preacher said you should not fight and they got mad and knock the preacher out
Can't find no ending.

The Vicious Cycle
in the Ghetto School

In the following selection Mr. Clark discusses the conditions that are present in the urban ghetto schools and offers alternative educational programs for these students. These articles were taken from Professor Clark's book Dark Ghetto *which presents an excellent analysis of the psychological and social factors involved in these segregated communities.*

It has been suggested that a school is only as good as its teachers and students. Are the ghetto schools different because of teacher failure? Is the social predicament of Negroes in America such that having superior teachers in superior buildings with superior financing would still not rectify the problem? By what means can the schools arrest educational atrophy in the ghetto?

Ghetto Schools: Separate and Unequal

KENNETH B. CLARK

The public schools in America's urban ghettos also reflect the oppressive damage of racial exclusion. School segregation in the South had, for generations, been supported by law; in the North, segregation has been supported by community custom and indifference. It is assumed that children should go to school where they live, and if they live in segregated neighborhoods, the schools are, as a matter of course, segregated. But the educational crisis in the ghettos is not primarily, and certainly not exclusively, one of the inequitable racial balance in the schools. Equally serious is the inferior quality of the education in those schools. Segregation and inferior education reinforce each other. Some persons take the position that the first must go before the second does; others, that the reverse is true. What is clear is that the problem of education in the urban ghetto seems to be a vicious cycle: If children go to school where they live and if most neighborhoods are racially segregated, then the schools are necessarily segregated, too. If Negroes move into a previously white community and whites then move away or send their children to private or parochial schools, the public schools will continue to be segregated. If the quality of education in Negro schools is inferior to that in white schools, whites feel justified in the fear that the presence of Negroes in their own school would lower its standards. If they move their own children away and the school becomes predominantly Negro, and therefore receives an inferior quality of education, the pattern begins all over again. The cycle of systematic neglect of Negro children must be broken, but the powerlessness of the Negro communities and the fear and indifference of the white community have combined so far to keep the cycle intact.

The central questions that lie behind the entire network of problems are these: Are Negroes such—in terms of innate incapacity *or* environmental deprivation—that their children are less capable of learning than are whites, so that any school that is permitted to become integrated necessarily declines in quality? Or has inferior education been systematically imposed on Negroes in the nation's ghettos in such a way as to compel poor performance from Negro children—a performance that could be reversed with quality education? The answer to these questions is of fundamental importance because the flight of whites from the urban public school system in many American cities is based on the belief that the first is true and the second false. If the first is false and the second true—and the centers of power in the white community can be convinced of that fact—one of the basic injustices in American life could be corrected.

THE PUBLIC SCHOOLS: A SEGREGATED SYSTEM?

Unless firm and immediate steps are taken to reverse the present trend, the public school system in the Northern cities of America will become predominantly a segregated system, serving primarily Negroes. It will, in addition, become a school system of low academic standards, providing a second-class education for under-classed children and thereby a chief contributor to the perpetuation of the "social dynamite" which is the cumulative pathology of the ghetto.

In Chicago, 37 percent of the elementary schools (compared with 22 percent in New York) and 18 percent of the high schools (compared with 2 percent in New York) are now segregated; 48.3 percent of the pupils in Chicago are now Negro. In Cleveland, 60 percent of the elementary schools and 58 percent of the high schools are segregated, white or Negro. In Detroit, more than 40 percent of public school children are Negro. In Philadelphia, more than half of the public school children are now Negro. By 1963 the Washington, D.C., public schools, which ten years ago had been one-third Negro, had become more than three-quarters Negro; by 1970, more than nine out of ten children in the public schools in the nation's capital may be Negro.

In the public schools of Manhattan as a whole, 73 percent of the children are already nonwhites. Ninety percent of school age children in Harlem are in public schools; only two-thirds of the children in the rest of Manhattan are—the others have moved into private or parochial schools. Despite the fact that segregation has been illegal in the public school system of New York State since 1902, virtually all the 31,469 children in Harlem's schools (twenty elementary schools, four junior high schools, and no high schools) are Negro. Only two of the elementary schools have less than 89.9 percent Negro enrollment; and all the junior high schools are at least 91.4 percent Negro. This means that the bulk of the community's children in elementary and junior high schools are educated in *de facto* segregated schools although the city's Board of Education has an official policy of full integration.

The trend toward school segregation, in fact, is accelerating. Seventy-eight New York schools below high school became segregated between 1958 and 1963. Open enrollment and the free choice transfer policy, allowing parents to seek the transfer of their children to nonsegregated schools, have done little to improve the situation—less than 3 percent of the non-white students moved to other schools. Many whites point to this apathy on the part of Negroes as evidence that Negro families in general prefer segregated neighborhood schools to unsegregated distant schools. *Any* parent prefers a neighborhood school, all things being equal and often when not all is equal, and no public school desegregation plan that demands voluntary individual decisions is ever accepted by the majority of Negro or white parents. Yet even if more students did transfer out of the ghetto few, if any, whites would move into the ghetto, and while the schools of the ghetto themselves would probably decline in population, they would remain segregated.

The pairing system, often called the Princeton Plan, which merges the populations of two nearby elementary schools, one predominantly Negro and the other predominantly white, also offers little chance of success in complex urban residential patterns and school systems. The New York City Board of Education proposed in 1964 that twenty-one such pairings be made. If all were introduced at once—though the board responded to further reflection and to community pressures by reducing the proposed twenty-one to four—segregation in the city would be reduced by only 1 percent. If twenty schools a year were so paired, an unlikely move, the school system would still be one-quarter segregated in 1970. Sprawling, densely populated cities are not manageable, peaceful suburban communities like Princeton, and because the plan works in one area is no guarantee it will work in another.

In 1963, 45 percent of New York's nonwhite children attended segregated junior highs. The Board of Education proposals to change the system of feeding students from elementary schools into junior highs would reduce this percentage only slightly. At this rate, and providing that the city's population did not itself change, the junior high schools of New York would be desegregated by about 2010. On the other hand, efforts to desegregate the twenty-five schools dominated now by nonwhites would make a difference in a single decade. If important efforts to achieve school integration are not adopted, segregation in the public schools will increase from the 22 percent of the elementary schools in 1963 to 38 percent in 1975; from 19 to 29 percent of the junior high schools; from 2 to 6 percent of the high schools. The schools by 1980 would be three-quarters Negro and Puerto Rican in the city as a whole and in Manhattan would probably exceed 90 percent, though the proportion may be expected to stabilize at that point.

One of the remedies suggested has been long-distance transportation of elementary school pupils, or "busing." This plan seems to offer immediate desegregation, but in many cases it would lead to bad education and, in the end, therefore, to even more segregation. Whites would pull out of the public school system even more rapidly than they are presently doing. In Brooklyn, for example, if real integration were the goal, about 70,000 Negro and Puerto Rican children, under eleven, would have to be transported twice a day, some of them ten miles away. In Manhattan, where schools have an even higher proportion of Negro and Puerto Rican children, even longer travel time would fail to bring about meaningful integration. As the Allen Commission Report said:

It should be obvious, but does not always appear to be, that integration is impossible without white pupils. No plan can be acceptable, therefore, which increases the movement of white pupils out of the public schools. Neither is it acceptable, however, unless it contributes to desegregation.

Therefore, any effective plan must (1) reduce school segregation; (2) bring better educational services; and (3) hold white pupils, even bring more back into the public school system.

One cannot help noting, however, that the interest in neighborhood schools, however valid, seems to have some relation to human hypocrisy. The white Parents and Taxpayers (PAT) groups in New York threatened boycotts over the school system's plan to transfer 383 children no more than a mile and a half for a ten-minute ride. Assistant Superintendent of Schools Jacob Landers noted that 77,000 children, including 25,000 in parochial schools, have been transferred regularly, and not for purposes of integration. The largest number were children in kindergarten and first and second grades, the same age group whose welfare is invoked fervently in behalf of the neighborhood school.

Many who have been themselves deeply damaged by past patterns of racial segregation will continue to resist the demands of the present. The demands of Negroes for desegregated schools will be met by many and continued forms of subtle and flagrant resistance. The school boycotts organized by civil rights groups in New York to force desegregation in the schools were rooted in the belief that such desegregation was immediately possible. But given the timidity and moral irresolution of whites, any such assumption is unrealistic, and the strategy doomed to fail. All white families need to do in event of forced desegregation is to form a countermovement, as PAT did, and threaten to leave the community, as thousands have already done, or shift their children to private or parochial schools.

Whenever minority group membership in a community increases in the neighborhood of a public school, white families who can afford it tend to take their children out of public school and either move to a new community or send the children to the comparative safety of the private and parochial schools. The white protest groups that arrange community boycotts against integrated schools represent the marginal families who can neither move nor pay private school tuition. These groups react out of that despair which Negroes themselves often reflect when they see no alternatives in a threatening situation.

Less than 10 percent of the private and parochial school population in New York is Negro—about 32,000 pupils; the 90 percent who are white students represent 30 percent of the city's white student population. So, while nine out of ten Negro children are in public schools, only seven out of ten white children are. An ironic possibility is that the present middle-class flight from the public schools which is explained in terms of the desire for quality education will not result in quality education at all. It is conceivable that with the proliferation of private and parochial schools in the urban areas, these schools will not be able to obtain the necessary finances and faculty for a truly quality education. They might then have to base their appeal only on status needs.

Most of New York City's private schools are parochial or church-sponsored, Roman Catholic and Episcopalian predominantly, with a few sponsored by Quakers, Jews, Ethical Culture societies, and others. Roman Catholic and certain Jewish schools give primary emphasis to the parents' desire to reinforce their children's religious loyalty. The Protestant and Ethical Culture groups, in particular, give quality of education as the chief reason for the existence of these private schools. But whatever the intent of the sponsors, many parents—some Negroes as well as whites—send their children to these schools not only for religious training or the sake of quality education but also to escape the growing influx of low-income minority group members into the public school system. There is a real question, of course, whether religion is best served by a displacement of a city's leadership into a private school system. There is a real question, also, whether socially insulated education *is* really education for leadership. The middle- and upper-class parents who defend their decision for private schools with the plea: "I won't sacrifice my child," give perhaps less weight to their children's resilience than the evidence would support, and certainly less weight to the importance of democratically based education than the times demand. But such arguments have little weight when parents fear for their child's future. In American life, where education is considered the first prerequisite for adult success, the issue is especially sensitive. When the question of education, therefore, is combined with the even more sensitive question of race, the emotions of persons are aroused as they seldom are by a public question. . . .

EDUCATIONAL ATROPHY: THE SELF-FULFILLING PROPHECY

The most insidious consequence of these assumptions is that they are self-fulfilling prophecies. The fallacy in the assumptions does not mean that a system based upon them will be demonstrated to be ineffective; for once one organizes an educational system where children are placed in tracks or where certain judgments about their ability determine what is done for them or how much they are taught or not taught, the horror is that the results seem to justify the assumptions. The use of intelligence test scores to brand children for life, to determine education based upon tracks and homogeneous groupings of children, impose on our public school system an intolerable and undemocratic social hierarchy, and defeat the initial purposes of public education. They induce and perpetuate the very pathology which they claim to remedy. Children who are treated as if they are uneducable almost invariably become uneducable. This is educational atrophy. It is generally known that if an arm or a leg is bound so that it cannot be used, eventually it becomes unusable. The same is true of intelligence.

Children themselves are not fooled by the various euphemisms educators use to disguise educational snobbery. From the earliest grades a child knows when he has been assigned to a level that is considered less than adequate. Whether letters, numbers, or dog or animal names are used to describe these groups, within days after these procedures are imposed the children know exactly what they mean. Those children who are relegated to the inferior groups suffer a sense of self-doubt and deep feelings of inferiority which stamp their entire attitude toward school and the learning process. Many children are now systematically categorized, classified in groups labeled slow learners, trainables, untrainables, Track A, Track B, the "Pussycats," the "Bunnies," etc. But it all adds up to the fact that they are not being taught; and not being taught, they fail. They have a sense of personal humiliation and unworthiness. They react negatively and hostilely and aggressively to the educational process. They hate teachers, they hate schools, they hate anything that seems to impose upon them this denigration, because they are not being respected as human beings, because they are sacrificed in a machinery of efficiency and expendability, because their dignity and potential as human beings are being obscured and ignored in terms of educationally irrelevant factors—their manners, their speech, their dress, or their apparent disinterest.

The contempt of these children for school is clearly related to the high dropout statistics, the hostility, aggression, and the seeming unmanageability of children in such schools. They are in a sense revolting against a deep and pervasive attack upon their dignity and integrity as human beings.

Educators, parents, and others really concerned with the human aspects of American public education should dare to look the I.Q. straight in the eye, and reject it or relegate it to the place where it belongs. The I.Q. cannot be considered sacred or even relevant in decisions about the future of the child. It should not be used to shackle children. An I.Q. so misused contributes to the wastage of human potential. The I.Q. can be a valuable educational tool within the limits of its utility, namely, as an index of what needs to be done for a particular child. The I.Q. used as the Russians use it, namely, to determine where one must start, to determine what a particular child needs to bring him up to maximum effectiveness, is a valuable educational aid. But the I.Q. as an end product or an end decision for children is criminally neglectful. The I.Q. should not be used as a basis for segregating children and for predicting—and, therefore, determining—the child's educational future.[1]

"The clash of cultures in the classroom" is essentially a class war, a socio-economic and racial warfare being waged on the battleground of our schools, with middle-class and middle-class-aspiring teachers provided with a powerful arsenal of half-truths, prejudices, and rationalizations, arrayed against hopelessly outclassed workingclass youngsters. This is an uneven balance, particularly since, like most battles, it comes under the guise of righteousness.

THE CULT OF "CULTURAL DEPRIVATION"

Among the earliest explanations of the educational inferiority of Negro children was that the poor average performance was to be accounted for in terms of inherent racial inferiority. After the research findings of Otto Klineberg and others in the 1930s came a serious re-examination among social scientists of the racial inferiority explanation.

More recently, it has become fashionable to attempt to explain the persistent fact of the academic retardation of Negro children in terms of general environmental disabilities. Taking their lead from the Klineberg type of research, these explanations tend to emphasize the pattern of environmental conditions as the cause which depresses the ability of these children to learn—economic and job discrimination, substandard housing, poor nutrition, parental apathy. The most recent version of the environmentalistic approach comes under the general heading of "cultural deprivation." The literature on this topic has used a variety of synonyms for this concept. Among them are: culturally disadvantaged, the disadvantaged, minority groups, socially neglected, socially rejected, socially deprived, school retarded, educationally disadvantaged, lower socio-economic groups, socio-economically deprived, culturally impoverished, culturally different, rural disadvantaged, the deprived slum children.

The cultural deprivation approach is seductive. It is both reasonable and consistent with contemporary environmentalistic thought, which seems to dominate social science thinking. Indeed, it is presented as a rejection of the inherent racial inferiority theories of the nineteenth and early twen-

[1] In 1963, on the initiative of top staff of the New York City Board of Education, a policy was adopted to de-emphasize the use of I.Q. scores in placing of pupils in the elementary grades.

tieth centuries. The recent rash of cultural deprivation theories, however, should be subjected to intensive scrutiny to see whether they do, in fact, account for the pervasive academic retardation of Negro children. Specifically, in what way does a low economic status or absence of books in the home or "cognitive deficit," referred to constantly by proponents of this point of view, actually interfere with the ability of a child to learn to read or to do arithmetic in the elementary grades?

What is meant by "cognitive deficit"? How remediable or unremediable is it? If it is remediable, how? Is it merely a jargon tautology which says only what everyone knows: that these children are not learning? In what way does it explain difficulties in learning to read? What are the implications of these cultural deprivation theories for educational prognosis and methods? What is the relationship between the methodology for educating these children suggested by proponents of these theories and the theories themselves? A rigorously objective study of these problems and attempts to answer these questions might provide answers which will not only increase our understanding of problems of education of lower status groups but might contribute to our understanding of problems of education in general—the teaching and learning phenomena. Cultural deprivation theories might also be crucial to the important problem of determining the reasonable expectations and limits of education.

To what extent are the contemporary social deprivation theories merely substituting notions of environmental immutability and fatalism for earlier notions of biologically determined educational unmodifiability? To what extent do these theories obscure more basic reasons for the educational retardation of lower-status children? To what extent do they offer acceptable and desired alibis for the educational default: the fact that these children, by and large, do not learn because they are not being taught effectively and they are not being taught because those who are charged with the responsibility of teaching them do not believe that they can learn, do not expect that they can learn, and do not act toward them in ways which help them to learn.

The answers to these and related questions cannot be found in rhetoric or continued speculative discourse. Speculation appears to reflect primarily the status of those who speculate. Just as those who proposed the earlier racial inferiority theories were invariably members of the dominant racial groups who presumed themselves and their groups to be superior, those who at present propose the cultural deprivation theory, are, in fact, members of the privileged group who inevitably associate their privileged status with their own innate intellect and its related educational success. Such association neither proves nor disproves the theory in itself, but the implicit caste and class factors in this controversy cannot and should not be ignored. Many of today's scholars and teachers came from "culturally deprived" backgrounds. Many of these same individuals, however, when confronted with students whose present economic and social predicament is not unlike their own was, tend to react negatively to them, possibly to escape the painful memory of their own prior lower status. It is easy for one's own image of self to be reinforced and made total by the convenient device of a protective forgetting—a refusal to remember the specific educational factor, such as a sympathetic and understanding teacher or the tutorial supports which made academic success and upward mobility possible in spite of cultural deprivation. The role of empathy, the understanding and identification of a teacher with his students in eliciting maximum academic performance from them, is an important educational question which should be studied systematically. The problems of empathy and identification between Negro students and their teachers are complex in an essentially racist society. It is significant that this relationship, as a systematic examination of the cultural deprivation literature reveals, has been so far totally ignored.

Looked at one way, it seems the epitome of common sense—and certainly compassion—to be convinced that a child who never has had toys to play with, or books to read, who has never visited a museum or a zoo or attended a concert, who has no room of his own, or even a pencil he can call his own, ought not to be expected to achieve in school on a level to match a more fortunate child. His image of himself is certain to be poor, his motivation weak, his vision of the world outside the ghetto distorted. But common sense and compassion may not tell the whole story. The evidence of the pilot projects in "deprived" schools—odd though it may appear to many—seems to indicate that a child who is expected by the school to learn does so; the child of whom little is expected produces little. Stimulation and teaching based upon positive expectation seem to play an even more important role in a child's performance in school than does the community environment from which he comes.

A key component of the deprivation which afflicts ghetto children is that generally their teachers do not expect them to learn. This is certainly one possible interpretation of the fact that ghetto children in Harlem *decline* in relative performance and in I.Q. the longer they are in school. Furthermore, other evidence supports this conclusion: Statistical studies of the relationship between social factors such as broken homes, crowded housing, low income with performance in Harlem schools show a very tenuous link between environment and performance. Depth interviews and questionnaires with Harlem teachers and school supervisors sustain the same observation. There are some school personnel who feel that the learning potential of the children is adequate. Though the majority believed one-fourth or less had potential for college, they did believe the majority could finish high school. One suspects that the children's level of motivation is, to some extent, set by their teachers. One guidance counselor said: "The children have a poor self-image and unrealistic aspirations. If you ask them what they want to be, they will say 'a doctor,' or something like that." When asked, "What would you say to a child who wanted to be a doctor?" she replied, "I would present the situation to him as it really is; show him how little possibility he has for that. I would tell him about the related fields, technicians, etc." One suspects, from this type of guidance reinforced by poor teaching and academic retardation, that the poor motivation and absence of a dignified self-image stem from the negative influence of such teachers more than from the influence of home and community.

The majority of teachers and administrators interviewed, nevertheless, talked of lowering standards to meet what they considered the intellectual level of their students. Assistant principals, who expressed this view with particular frequency, are in a position to influence curriculum. If they view the ghetto students as unteachable, one could scarcely blame the teachers they supervise for adopting a similar skepticism. When schools do not have confidence in their job, they gradually shift their concept of their function from teaching to custodial care and discipline.

DEFEATISM IN GHETTO SCHOOLS

As Haryou gathered data on the schools, it became increasingly clear that the attitude of the teachers toward their students was emerging as a most important factor in attempting to understand the massive retardation of these children. It was necessary to find out what they really felt, and so the schools were asked to recommend teachers to discuss the problems of teachers in slum schools. Interviews were held; group discussions were conducted; questionnaires were distributed. They tended to make clear what a crucial role the teachers really played in the success or failure of their students. The problems of identifying with children of different backgrounds—especially for persons from the white middle class—the problems of rejection of children deemed unappealing or alien, and the problems of achieving empathy are multiple. Courses in educational philosophy and psychology as presently taught do not prepare these teachers for the challenge of their job.

The pattern of teaching in Harlem is one of short tenure and inexperience. Many white teachers are afraid to work in Harlem; some Negroes consider a post outside of Harlem to be a sign of status. Discipline problems pervade a number of the schools, as students show contempt for teachers and principals they do not respect; and, in turn, the emphasis on "good discipline" displaces an emphasis on learning, both in evaluating a teacher's record and in a teacher's estimate of his own effectiveness. Apathy seems pervasive.

A pattern of violence expected from students and counterforce from the teachers creates a brutalizing atmosphere in which any learning would be hard. One teacher reported: "The children are not taught anything; they are just slapped around and nobody bothers to do anything about it."

Some teachers say or imply that Harlem children expect to be beaten:

When I came to school "X," I had never seen anything like that school. I cried, they behaved so badly. I soon learned that the boys like to be beaten; like to be spoken to in the way in which they are accustomed, and when I learned to say things to them that, to me, would be absolutely insulting and to hit them when they needed it, I got along all right and they began to like me. Somehow that made them feel that I liked them. I talked to them in the terms and in the way to which they are accustomed, and they like it.

Another white teacher said:

Here, both the Negro and white teachers feel completely free to beat up the children, and the principal knows it. They know he knows it and that nothing will be done about it. The principal is prejudiced. Because he knows he is prejudiced, he covers it by giving the Negro teachers the best classes. The Negro teachers are the best teachers because they are more stable. Some colored and white teachers ask for the worst classes because they don't want to work. In the worst classes they don't have to work because whatever happens, they can just say, "It is the children." The white teachers are largely inexperienced—the principal does not expect very much from the teachers. He often says, openly, "Why did they put me here?" The Board of Education should have put an experienced principal there. There is a lot of brutality—brutal beatings, and nobody cares—nothing is done about it. The parents, the principal and the teachers don't care.

One teacher told of a teacher who exploited his students:

The teacher should set a good example; not a teacher who comes to class to shave, clean his teeth, and sleep—as does one of the teachers in my school. Then, so that he will be free of responsibility, he tells one of the bullies of the class to strong-arm the class and keep order.

One teacher of some sensitivity commented on the reaction of Negro children to the often severe, even brutal punishment inflicted upon them:

A child won't respond to minor discipline and will more often only respond to a more brutal form of discipline. There is inconsistent discipline and a lot of brutality in the Harlem schools. Many children are immature and, therefore, are extremely hurt by being disciplined. I have had the experience of children running out of the room after they had been yelled at—there seems to be a very low frustration point at which they can take discipline.

It is only in a context of utter apathy that such behavior could be tolerated. If only *one* teacher could talk of children expecting to be beaten, this would be evidence of inhumanity. The fact is that in the ghetto schools many teachers believe that such discipline is necessary for children who come from ghetto homes. In such an atmosphere where the priority is not on superior teaching, it is not surprising to discover that nearly half of the school personnel report that they find their work in the ghetto "more demanding and less satisfying" than work in other parts of the city.

Negro teachers tended to feel that the Negroes in Harlem are better teachers than the whites, in part because they stayed longer and could keep better discipline. One Negro woman teacher said that a white male teacher constantly asked her to restore order in his classroom. Whites, in turn, often feel a Harlem post is a step down. A Negro teacher said Harlem schools are "a dumping ground for condemned white teachers." Some white teachers report that they feel uneasy with Negroes. One white teacher interviewed said, "When I walk through the streets here I feel conspicuous; I would like to be able to blend into the scenery." Yet there are a number of dedicated men and women for whom the job of teaching the many neglected children of Harlem brings satisfaction and reward.

White teachers who feel they are in hostile territory and Negro teachers who resent their presence can hardly be expected to work together without friction. Much of the feeling is repressed, however, and only emerges in depth interviews conducted in confidence. Negroes express the feeling that whites feel and act superior and "cold" even when they are less well educated. Many of the white teachers are Jewish; for some of them this fact brings a sense of identification with another oppressed minority; for others, an impatience with an ethnic group, unlike their own, where the tradition of eager learning has not yet been firmly established. One Negro teacher expressed her view on the subject in these words:

I find that the Jewish people, in particular, will protect their own and are protected by their own. In our school, this young teacher says that the children "just can't be taught" and even when the method used to teach is not a good one, she blames the children for not having the mentality to learn.

Unless she is a lackey, the Negro teacher has a hard road to travel. Mostly, they are doing a good job, but I don't think that there are enough Negroes in the teaching field with the guts to fight against the things that should not be. Negro teachers are too often trying to placate and please the white teachers. Most of the white teachers are Jewish. They respect the Negro who will fight, but if they find that they will not fight, they will walk all over them.

Negro teachers generally prefer not to associate with white teachers. As one said:

I, by choice, try not to socialize with them because I get sick and tired of hearing how our children will never amount to anything, our children are ignorant, the homes they come from are so deprived, these children are nothing, and so forth, and so on. I get tired of hearing this conversation even though I realize there is a problem.

Another Negro implied that friendliness to white teachers was taboo, and would be frowned upon or punished by her Negro colleagues:

I am a person who has been around and I get tired of "Oh, you feel white today, you're eating with the white teachers." "Oh, ha, she's joining their gang, she's turning on us." I won't eat with any of them. You know what, I'd rather go down to the Harlem Embers and eat by myself.

The dominant and disturbing fact about the ghetto schools is that the teachers and the students regard each other as adversaries. Under these conditions the teachers are reluctant to teach and the students retaliate and resist learning.

Negroes seldom move up the ladder of promotion in urban school systems. There are only six Negroes out of more than 1,200 top-level administrators in New York City, and only three Negroes out of 800 are full principals. Practically all of the Negroes are to be found quite far down in the organizational hierarchy—a fact discouraging in the extreme to Negro teachers and indirectly damaging to the self-image of Negro children who rarely see Negroes in posts of authority.

In past attempts to obtain experienced and qualified teachers for the schools in deprived communities, the Board of Education of the City of New York has not used its statutory power to assign teachers to these schools. The implicit and explicit reasons for not doing so were based upon the assumption that, given the "teacher shortage," teachers would refuse to accept such assignments and would leave the New York City school system if the board insisted upon exercising its power to make such assignments. The board, therefore, sought "volunteers" for these schools and flirted with proposals for providing extra bonuses for teachers who sought assignments in them. These methods have not been successful. The Allen Report declared that:

A spurious "reward structure" exists within the staffing pattern of the New York schools. Through it, less experienced and less competent teachers are assigned to the least "desirable" yet professionally most demanding depressed area schools. As the teacher gains experience and demonstrated competence, his mobility upward usually means mobility away from the pupils with the greatest need for skilled help. The classrooms that most urgently need the best teachers are thus often deprived of them.

Schools in deprived communities have a disproportionately high number of substitute and unlicensed teachers. Some of the classes in these schools have as many as ten or more different teachers in a single school year. Although precise figures are unavailable, nearly half of the teachers answering a Haryou questionnaire said they had held their posts for three years or less—far more than the citywide average (20 percent in present post three years or less).

The persistent failure on the part of the New York Board of Education to solve the problem of the adequate staffing of these schools points to the need for a new approach to this problem. It is suggested that teachers be selected for assignment in these schools in terms of their special qualifications, training, and human understanding. Rather than seek to entice, cajole, or bribe teachers into serving in such "hardship or ghetto outposts," the board should set up rather rigorous standards and qualifications for the teachers who would be invited or accepted for this type of service. These teachers should be motivated and recognized as *master teachers* or individuals working toward such professional recognition. Realistic professional and financial incentives must be provided if this professional status is to be other than perfunctory or nominal. Extra pay should be specifically tied to superior skill and more challenging responsibilities. A high-level professional atmosphere of competent and understanding supervision, a system of accountability—objective appraisal of professional performance—and a general atmosphere conducive to high-quality teaching and clear standards for differentiation of inferior, mediocre, and superior teaching with appropriate corrections and rewards must be maintained.

Excellent teaching can be obtained and sustained only under conditions of excellent supervision. The roles of field assistant superintendents, principals, and assistant principals must be re-examined. Those individuals who are assigned to schools in deprived communities must be selected in terms of special competence and in terms of the highest professional and personal standards. It should be understood that they would be judged primarily, if not exclusively, in terms of objective evidence.

EVIDENCE OF EFFECTIVE LEARNING

The schools in the ghetto have lost faith in the ability of their students to learn and the ghetto has lost faith in the ability of the schools to lead. There are two conflicting points of view—one, that the pupils do not learn because they cannot; the other, that they do not learn because they are not taught. The fact is they are not learning. The problem is to see that they do, and only when the attempt is made with enthusiasm and competence will the answer be clear. As the Haryou report said:

Children do enter school with individual differences in experience, skills, and attitudes which make teaching more or less difficult. It is not unreasonable to expect that some of these differences will stem from differences in cultural or economic background. What has not been demonstrated, however, is that these differences constitute a permanent barrier to learning.

How long does it take to learn the colors of the spectrum, or develop the manipulative skills needed in order to do first grade work?

The studies cited by school administrators are silent on this point. Further, the data here presented show that the major deterioration in learning takes place between the third and sixth grades, not in the first and second grades. This leads to the inference that underachievement is the result of an accumulation of deficiencies while in school, rather than the result of deficiencies prior to school.[2]

Given no evidence to the contrary, the assumption can be made that cultural and economic backgrounds of pupils do not constitute a barrier to the type of learning which can reasonably be expected of normal children in the elementary grades—however much of a barrier such back-

[2] *Youth in the Ghetto*, Harlem Youth Opportunities Unlimited, New York, 1964.

grounds are in respect to social problems such as delinquency, emotional stability, and the like. Only when it is permitted to be a barrier does it become a cumulative deteriorating force.

What are the facts that are presently available that would substantiate this point of view? A few examples follow:

1. A "crash program" of remedial reading for one summer month starting in 1955 and continuing until the summer of 1964 (the data available, however, cover only 1955–1959) at Northside Center for Child Development in New York discovered that a child who has one month of extra daily instruction can gain on the average of almost one school year in reading. The children with the least retardation gained the most—those with I.Q.'s of above 110 gained more than two years in reading achievement, but the most retarded gained at least five months. The 104 children helped came eagerly and voluntarily to the program. Attendance never was less than 85 percent. Those who came more learned more.

This study of large numbers of woefully retarded, economically inferior Negro and Puerto Rican students reveals that such children can learn if taught. Nothing was done to change their "cultural deprivation." The only thing that was done was that they were being taught to read by individuals who believed that they could learn to read and who related to them with warmth and acceptance. Under these conditions they learned. And what is more, they sustained what they had learned during the school year. It is ironic, however, that when they returned to school they sustained their summer gains but they did not advance further.

All studies of the problem of education in deprived communities agree in concluding that the central problem in ghetto schools is the fact that the children are woefully deficient in reading. It has been suggested by the remedial reading staff of Northside Center that as a necessary first step in the development of a program to attain educational excellence in the Harlem schools, the Board of Education drop its normal curriculum in these schools for a period of half a school year, or perhaps a full school year, and immediately mobilize all of its resources toward the goal of raising the reading level of all children in the Harlem schools, especially those from the third to the eighth grades. During this *Reading Mobilization Year* the total school program in these schools would be geared toward the improvement of reading. All other school work would be temporarily postponed for those children who are retarded until they are brought up to grade level.

There is general agreement also, supported by Haryou's research findings and by the Board of Education itself, that there is a desperate need for afterschool remedial centers. Space is available in churches, renovated store fronts and lofts, social agencies, and community centers. What is not agreed upon, however, is the most effective type of remedial program. There is serious question whether submitting the child who has already experienced defeat in school to the same teachers, techniques, classroom settings, and general atmosphere is likely to result in any great educational achievement. An effective remedial program would require a revised curriculum, advanced teaching techniques and materials, a stimulating atmosphere, and generally increased motivation.

2. "Culturally deprived" children have learned in those public schools in which they are expected to learn and in which they are taught. Children attending Harlem schools in the 1920s and 1930s had average academic achievement close to, if not equal to, the white norms. Klineberg's study of the performance of Negro children migrating from the South to the North and those already in Northern schools during the thirties can be used as evidence that at that time the discrepancy between norms of white students and those of Negro students was minimal compared with the present gap.[3] It would be difficult to argue and to prove the contention that Negroes at that time were less culturally deprived than they were in the 1950s or than they are now.

3. Junior High School 43 on the periphery of Harlem, like most Harlem schools, was holding largely a custodial program for the "culturally deprived." In 1956, before the pilot project began, the teachers felt helpless to teach. Their students seemed then to be hopeless, and considered themselves failures, their teachers as enemies. Then the school became a pilot demonstration guidance program and what looked like a miracle occurred. Six times as many students went to college (25 percent) than had earlier (4 percent). The dropout rate fell one-half, from 50 percent to 25 percent. Eighty-one percent were judged to have greater intellectual capacity than their earlier I.Q. and achievement scores would have predicted—their I.Q.'s in the eleventh grade went up an average of eight to nine points. In the more than two years during which the tests were made, the average student gained 4.3 years in reading scores compared with 1.7 years during a similar earlier period. When one studies this pilot project, one does not find any revolutionary educational methods. Most of the New York City schools had both curriculum and individual counseling, trips and programs for parents, as did JHS 43, prior to the project.

The "miracle" seemed due primarily to an implementation of the belief that such children can learn.

School personnel were told to adopt an affirmative view of their students and give up their earlier negative views. Therefore, certain educational methods previously considered questionable for lower-class children were now used. Those who had openly blocked changes before became less influential in the wake of the prestige of the new project. Most of the emphasis on discipline was toned down. Teacher responsibility for maintaining order was relaxed. Students felt that they were "special," and that they were expected to achieve and learn. Teachers were evaluated more on their teaching skill than on their discipline. Because the school administra-

[3] Otto Klineberg, *Negro Intelligence and Selective Migration*, Columbia University Press, New York, 1935.

tion was eager for the success of the experiment, it opened many previously clogged channels of communication between itself and teachers, parents, and pupils. Originally this was meant to win their support, but also, the administration was unconsciously stimulated to solve some of the problems and attend to some of the grievances not necessarily related at all to the question of race. Teachers began to consider themselves competent and their students capable. Pupils were told that they were trustworthy and that their teachers were committed to helping them succeed. Parents were advised that they could help in their children's education and progress. There was no attempt, because the task was too formidable, to reverse the environment of cultural deprivation of the community's children.

The cyclic relationship between educational effectiveness and heightened morale is indicated by the fact that a serious program designed to increase educational effectiveness invariably heightens the morale of pupils, teachers, and supervisors; the heightened morale increases the chances of success of the educational program. Conversely, inferior education in a school decreases morale of teachers, pupils, and supervisors, and the decreased morale tends to reinforce the educational inefficiency.

4. The Banneker Project in St. Louis, Missouri, showed similar striking results.

In 1957, St. Louis high schools inaugurated a three-track system of ability grouping based upon standardized I.Q. and achievement scores. Students scoring high on both tests were placed in Track I and given college preparatory courses. Those scoring below average were placed in Track III and given vocational and technical courses. Average students fell into Track II.

The Banneker School District is one of five elementary school groups in St. Louis and is one of two having the largest proportion of Negroes. The neighborhood is characterized by old housing, slums, high crime rate, high unemployment, etc. Of the 16,000 pupils in the Banneker schools, 9,590 are Negro.

The initial test scores for students in the Banneker District showed that only 7 percent had Track I scores, whereas 47 percent went into Track III. The median scores for reading, arithmetic, and language achievement were consistently below grade level. Otis Intelligence Test scores for 1958–1959 showed Banneker children with an I.Q. median of 90.5, with 12.1 percent below I.Q. 79.

The district director, Dr. Samuel Shepard, immediately moved to improve performance, suggesting that the children had not been properly prepared for the testing experience and for that reason did not measure up as well as they might have if well motivated. Shepard initiated a program designed to stimulate teachers to teach students to learn, and parents to facilitate learning. The initial scores were graphically and comparatively represented to teachers, principals, students, and parents. It was made quite clear, however, that the low standing of Banneker children relative to children in other parts of the city was not to be ignored or explained away as the inevitable consequence of underprivilege. Rather, it was to be used to bring about improvement.

Principals were asked to help teachers have a more positive attitude toward the children and their chances for success. Teachers were to visit the homes of their pupils to familiarize themselves with the social and familial situation. In addition, teachers were asked to ignore I.Q. scores and to treat all children as if they had superior ability. As a result of this intensive, yet inexpensive and relatively uncomplicated approach, eighth graders went from 7.7 years in reading to 8.8 in two and one-half years; from 7.6 in language to 9.1; and 7.9 to 8.7 in arithmetic. Children assigned to Track I increased from 7 percent to 22 percent, while Track III assignments fell from 47.1 percent to 10.9 percent. Attendance in one school reached an unprecedented 97.1 percent. The median I.Q. was raised almost ten points.

In spite of the fact that there had been no drastic change in curriculum, instructional technique, or the basic "underprivileged" social situation, improvements were definitely evident. What had changed was the attitude and perspective of teachers which influenced the way in which the students were taught and learned.

5. Baltimore, Maryland, has tried another interesting program—this one a preschool year for sixty children of four years of age in two of the city's most depressed neighborhoods, both Negro, where crime and delinquency rates have been so high that teachers hesitated to make home visits alone or at night. Francis Keppel, U.S. Commissioner of Education, reports that the school administrator in charge, Mrs. Catherine Brunner, has found that: Every child who entered in 1963 began kindergarten the following year, a record their older brothers and sisters had not matched. In kindergarten they did as well as children from middle- or upper-class families. In first grade, they showed better use of language, superior understanding of ideas and problem solving than other children from the same depressed neighborhoods. In the first grade, two-thirds of the original sixty were in the top half of their class; ten in the top quarter. Keppel quotes one kindergarten teacher's "candid and heartwarming judgment" of the project:

I've always been in the habit of dividing my kindergarten classes into two sections—those who come from poor neighborhoods and lack much background for learning, and those who come from better homes and are accustomed to books and cultural experiences in their families. In a sense, this has also seemed a logical division between the dull children, the ones who need help, and the bright ones, who go along very quickly.

But what seemed so logical before the project started now doesn't seem logical to me today. The youngsters who have this new preschool experience, I'm finding, belong among the highest achieving children in my classes and this is where I place them. It makes me wonder now whether many of us in teaching haven't a great deal to learn ourselves.

Despite the evidence of the effectiveness of early childhood education for the growth and development of children, public schools have not made adequate provision for extensive preprimary education. For children who live in disadvantaged circumstances, well-organized centers for early childhood education can partially compensate for lack of opportunities for wholesome development in these formative years.

There are more than 12,000 children between three and six years of age in Harlem. All of the twenty elementary schools in the area have kindergartens which children may enter at the age of five, but there are at least 4,000 children under five who should have preschool education if community pathology is to be resisted. Haryou proposed that in each school zone, two preschool academies be established, each serving 100 children three through five years old. At first, preference would be given to the four- and five-year olds. But preschool experience, however desirable for its own sake, will not lead children to learn basic skills in the primary grades if, when they reach these grades, the schools react to them as though they cannot learn.

One variable held constant in each of these programs is the nature and extent of the cultural deprivation found in the particular group before the program began. The programs' success then would have to be due either to the unlikely fact that the culturally deprived are particularly responsive to a program of education or that their deprivation is less important in their success than other factors—such as the faith of the teachers, the quality of the education. The common denominator in all these successful programs was more efficient teaching—these children can be taught if they are accepted and respected. But how does one transform an apathetic teacher into an empathic, accepting, and enthusiastic one?

If it were assumed on the other hand that teachers could only teach children who came from homes where learning is respected and encouraged, it would be analogous to physicians asserting that they could only help patients who are not too ill, or who are not ill at all.

If the cultural deprivation theories are valid and relevant explanations of the widespread problem, then it would follow that the extent and degree of academic retardation would be constant, that is, the same, under different conditions and at varying periods of time as long as the social, economic, and cultural conditions of the Negro group remained the same. A related hypothesis would be that the degree of retardation would increase or decrease in proportion to similar changes in the status of the Negro. Any evidence showing constancy in the degree of retardation in spite of changes in the economic and social status of the Negro would seem to raise serious questions about the cultural deprivation theories, and it would then be necessary to seek explanations of the academic retardation of Negro children in terms of variables directly related to the educational processes: What is happening in the classroom? Are these children being taught or are they being ignored? What is the attitude of their teachers toward them? Are they seen as primitive, unmanageable discipline problems and burdens, rather than as modifiable human beings who will respond positively if they are reacted to positively? In short, are these children seen as essentially uneducable because they are racially or culturally inferior? In the 1930s, Otto Klineberg, as noted earlier, succeeded in demonstrating that the academic performance of Negro youngsters in the New York City public schools was nearly equal to that of whites. The economic conditions of Negroes at that time were significantly lower than today. To assume that Negro children are inherently inferior or that environmental inferiority is responsible for poor school performance is educationally irrelevant— and even false. The assumption of inferiority might be the controlling fact which restricts the educational responsiveness of children to the alleged educational experience. In this regard, racial inferiority and cultural inferiority have identical practical educational consequences. This might, therefore, be the chief obstacle—the subtle, insidious human obstacle— which must be overcome if lower-status children are to be educated up to a level of efficiency necessary to bring them within a useful and creative role in society.

There is considerable evidence that this can be done. It has been done. The resistance to accepting this evidence and implementing it, the insistence upon labeling these children with euphemistically derogatory terms, might be the key human and educational problems to be studied if our society is to obtain the benefits of the trained intelligence of these children.

This is not to say that a teacher's affirmative attitude toward children is the only relevant factor influencing the performance of children in ghetto schools and that overcrowded classrooms, inadequate plants and facilities, unimaginative curricula, and the like, are irrelevant. All of these influence a child's educational growth. The point is rather that these factors cannot be given equal importance; in the light of available evidence the controlling factor which determines the academic performance of pupils and which establishes the level of educational efficiency and the over-all quality of the schools is the competence of the teachers and their attitude of acceptance or rejection of their students. Competent teachers who have confidence in children strive to achieve the other dimensions of good education also. But without such competence and confidence, children do not learn even if the textbooks are new and the classes small. There are ghetto schools which are brand new. There are some ghetto schools with comparatively small classes and with adequate facilities. But there are few ghetto schools where the morale of teachers and pupils is high and where the teachers truly believe in the humanity and capacity of the children to learn. In those few schools the children learn.

The pilot experiments in St. Louis, New York, and elsewhere are encouraging evidence that children can learn when they are expected to learn. The Negro child, like the Negro teacher, must be held to the same high standards of academic performance as their white counterparts in white schools. Obviously some Negroes, like some whites, will not have the innate capacity to respond. But many will, and each deserves the chance. Negro students cannot be excused for shoddy performance *because* they are Negro. To do so makes more rigid and intolerable the pathology, injustices, and distinctions of racism. There can be no double standards in education, no easy alibi. Schools are institutions designed to compensate for "cultural deprivation." If this were not true there would be no need for schools.

The schools are crucial to any positive resolution of the problems of the ghetto. As long as these ghetto schools continue to turn out thousands and thousands of functional illiterates yearly, Negro youth will not be prepared for anything other than menial jobs or unemployment and dependency; they will continue the cycle of broken homes, unstable family life, and neglected and uneducated children. The tragic waste of human resources will go on unabated.

Unemployment and the
Adolescent Society

There has been a tendency for the mass media to present the unemployment picture and the effects of automation as minor ripples disturbing the efficient and affluent calm of our society. However, some writers on these topics have indicated the dangers inherent in our increasing utilization of automated industrial and commercial techniques. The danger does not lie in the development of automated equipment, but rather in the lack of manpower planning involved in the transfer over to automated production.

Generally, automation affects the unskilled and the poorly educated. Hence the school failures become the unemployed, and if they are employed, their jobs are often automated out of existence. The result is a cycle of unemployment, inadequate education, and minority group status.

The following article describes the "new lost generation" which is the product of these conditions. Federal planning in terms of job corps and re-education centers are minimally essential, but long range concern and planning are requisite if these problems are to be realistically considered.

Is an educational system outside of the formal school the answer to unemployment for noncollege youth? Such systems as the Army, industries,

*poverty programs conducted by business and others have offered this solu-
tion. Why has the school not been able to account for this problem? Does
the middle-class school with teachers who have adopted middle-class
values provide any real opportunities for other than an ornamental education for the students described in the following piece?*

The New Lost Generation: Jobless Youth

MICHAEL HARRINGTON

Every year the number of young Americans uneducated and untrained for jobs
grows. They are people without a future. Who are they, and can they be helped?

The computers which have tabulated the Federal reports on youth unemployment might have been programed by Emile Zola rather than I.B.M.
Their statistics are the quantification of a social tragedy, the description of
a generation lost beyond Hemingway's imagining.

In February, 1963, President Kennedy pointed to the ominous convergence of high dropout rates, chronic youth unemployment and an economy
which was eliminating unskilled and semiskilled jobs. The situation, he
concluded, was "critical." A year later, Lyndon B. Johnson's poverty message described "the young man or woman who grows up without a decent
education, in a broken home, in a hostile and squalid environment, in ill
health or in the face of racial injustice"—and declared "that young man or
woman is often trapped in a life of poverty." More bluntly, Secretary of
Labor Willard Wirtz has said the failure to come to grips with this problem
is a form of "economic suicide."

But perhaps the most poignant index to the chaos of an entire sub-
generation in American life was given by the Administration when it explained what it hoped to accomplish under the education programs proposed in the projected Conservation Camps. These will seek to raise the
young volunteers up to a minimum reading level of the seventh grade.
And they will literally undertake to teach these young citizens how to
speak their own language—"to be understood in employment and other
conventional situations, and to understand directions."

What is the dimension of this problem in which young Americans must
be Federally schooled in order "to understand directions"? What is the
look of the faces behind the figures? And where is there a basis for hope,
both for them and for the society which bred them?

Reprinted from *The New York Times Magazine*, May 24, 1964. © 1964 by the New
York Times Company. Reprinted by permission of the publisher and the author.

In the Administration's presentation of the Economic Opportunity Act of 1964, one finds this frank statement: "In October of 1963, there were 730,000 young men and women between the ages of 16 and 21 who were both out of school and out of work. This figure had increased 22 percent in a one-year period. But this unemployment figure for a specific week in October does not tell the whole story. Many others are employed only in low-paying dead-end jobs which are beneath their potential abilities.

"Left to itself, the problem will multiply. . . . If the current trends continue, in five years we will have almost 1½ million unemployed youth— without education or training, without jobs and without a future."

There are Government figures which state the crisis even more broadly. During the sixties, there will be some 26 million new entrants into the labor force in consequence of the post-World War II baby boom. Of these, it is estimated that 7.5 million will not have finished high school—and 2.3 million will be under the eighth-grade level. This vast influx of the untrained will take place in a technological setting which will probably require the minimum of a high-school diploma as the prerequisite for a moderately decent job.

But it is not necessary to speculate on the future; the present is plain enough. Between May, 1962, and May, 1963, according to the House committee which reported on the Manpower Development and Training Act, the labor force grew by 1.2 million, while jobs increased only by 900,000. "Nearly the entire impact of this rise in joblessness was felt by the 16-to-19-year-old youth in the labor market," the committee reported. "Their unemployment rate rose to over 20 percent, approximately four times the rate of the adult labor force."

The statistics are conservative. To qualify as officially unemployed, a youth must be in the labor market looking for a job. Yet, according to Labor Secretary Wirtz, there are now more than 300,000 young people who are not in school, not at work and not looking for work. They are simply floating in the society; they have fallen off our misery charts. It goes, almost without saying, that a disproportionate number of this grim lost generation of the sixties is "non-white." Yet it is not true that the majority is Negro or belongs to other racial minorities. The House Labor Committee noted that, in 1962, 57 percent of the non-white youths and 28 percent of the whites between 20 and 24 years old were dropouts. Given the numerical dominance of whites in the nation, this adds up to a problem which is, by a majority, white.

Another important fact about the young poor is that they are largely the children of the middle-aged poor and the grandchildren of the aging poor. The President's Economic Report spells out the hereditary character of American poverty in some detail. Of the families now defined as poor, 64 percent are headed by a person with less than an eighth-grade education; and 67 percent of the fathers of these family heads were without a grade-school diploma.

In the Department of Labor's brilliantly developed and shocking report, "One-Third of a Nation," a study of Selective Service rejectees yielded the same result. About a quarter of the young Americans who appeared before draft boards were rejected because they were not up to the seventh-grade level. Four out of five were dropouts, a third were unemployed and a high percentage were second or third-generation relief cases.

Indeed, the social chances of the dropout and the teen-aged unemployed have become so institutionalized that the Government had to make a frank admission of its failure in even reaching the most desperate among them in the Manpower Development and Training Program.

When this effort began, it was assumed that the great problem would be that of job training. But then it was realized, as a House Committee put it, that ". . . when available job opportunities are discovered and the necessary programs devised, the vast majority of the unemployed cannot pass entrance examinations. In fact, large numbers cannot even be tested, since they are unable to read and write."

So there emerged the incredible fact that, nationally, only one out of eight among the unemployed was even qualified to take advantage of hope when it was offered. This will certainly be true of the 2.3 million youth without an eighth-grade education who will enter the economy during this decade. It is why Sargent Shriver must propose to teach seventh-grade levels of reading and simple spoken English in the training camps. And these are the figures that make the Administration's estimate of a possible million and a half teen-aged unemployed in five years a conservative guess.

Finally, these figures require computation in social, as well as economic, terms. The evidence is overwhelming that youthful hopelessness expresses itself in violence and aimless acts of desperation. In New Haven, for instance, a recent study reported that 18 percent of the high-school graduates and 48 percent of the school dropouts had one or more juvenile arrests. As Abraham Ribicoff testified to the House when he was Secretary of Health, Education and Welfare in 1961, juvenile delinquency among the impoverished youth is not so much individual lawlessness as it is "a system of beliefs and values with a strong and stable tradition of its own."

"Nobody Knows My Name" author James Baldwin called a collection of his essays. When one speaks of these young people as individuals rather than as the raw data of statistics, it is probably true that nobody knows "their" names. Dropouts literally disappear from public view. That is one of the reasons why the Administration says it needs Selective Service—a comprehensive and legally compulsive mechanism—rather than the school system as a way to obtain an introduction to some of the young people it seeks to help. Beyond that, if it is necessary to teach the youth in the conservation camps to talk to the rest of society, who will teach society to speak to them?

I talked to a group of three Negroes, all of them unemployed dropouts. They corroborated more contradictory explanations of their behavior than one could have believed possible; which is to say, I did not feel that I had understood them at all.

"They're living on their wits and their kicks," a civil rights leader had said to me about this kind of youth, lost in the city. They were. When I talked to them, they were high (though on liquor, not narcotics). They were restless, shadowboxing, given to bursts of laughter and comment—energetic like adolescents generally, but more catlike than gawkish. In this persona, their talk was of girls, drinking, fighting, the life of the streets.

If the conversation had stopped there, they could have been defined simply: as filling up their futureless spare time with a desperate, aimless sensualism, living by petty crime and headed nowhere.

Then the talk turned a corner and the three were different people. Edgar Friedenberg, the author of "The Vanishing Adolescent," has argued that the slum kid is the "last aristocrat," "ignorant, often emotionally disturbed to the point of paranoia, dangerous when threatened and parochial. . . . But he has the qualities of his defects: forthrightness, a capacity for real human commitment, more spontaneity. . . ."

The three young men suddenly exhibited these virtues. They had a pride in having borne their miseries, a camaraderie. (On a much more sophisticated level, one hears Negroes in the civil rights movement, sometimes when among friends, use the word "nigger" as an act of defiance against the white world which thus branded them, but also as a stubborn assertion of the community which the brand has evoked.) At this point, they were contemptuous of the attempts being made to rescue them. The whites would certainly do nothing but talk; and anyway, who wanted a place in an office or a factory? There was value enough in a Harlem street.

Their final mood was the most explicitly sociological, and the most ambiguous. In part, it corroborated the wisdom of the song, "Officer Krupke" in "West Side Story"—that some, at least, at the bottom of the society have learned the social-scientific, psychoanalytic, welfare-state clichés about themselves. And in part, it reflected the impact of the civil rights movement in the ghettos of the North. I was not sure whether I was hearing what they thought I wanted them to say, or what they felt—or perhaps both.

Their plight, they agreed, was due to the fact that society was organized against them. They had failed in school, not out of a lack of ability, but because there had been no money at home, no space, no possibility of study. They, in their late teens, were already victims. Maybe politics and the movement would change some things; maybe the Government had been forced into being serious; maybe there was some hope.

And yet, it is a paradox that the very viciousness of American racism has provoked a certain sophistication in the most exploited single group in the society. The Negro unemployed, young and old, have a leadership, a movement; the March on Washington was for jobs and freedom.

Thus, the three Negroes contrasted sharply with some white teen-agers in another city who seemed destined to become dropouts. (It is one of the saddest things about this social underworld that any reasonable person can make a fair guess about the fate hanging over a 13- or 14-year-old long before it happens.) They were already well behind in school, and it was doubtful that any of them would see a grade-school diploma. Yet they did not have the utter cynicism of the older Negro youth, perhaps because their membership in the racial majority allowed them illusions which Harlem simply cannot afford. At least insofar as we communicated with one another, they persisted in dreaming of adult careers that required college degrees.

In short, one knows the statistics about unemployed youth, but not their names. The generalities—that they act out, that they aspire too high and too low, that they form a subculture, and so on—are all true enough and imprecise. One of the problems of the Federal Government will be, not simply to develop a program, but to construct a language for talking to those who are both young and without hope.

Given these massive social determinants of the problem, and its delicate human dimension, is there any reason to think that such youth can be rescued?

The experience of the past is affirmative. Every time there has been a shooting war in the twentieth century, with its concomitant full employment in the advanced nations, hundreds of thousands of "unemployables" have suddenly been discovered to have viable skills. From this point of view, the creation of a full-employment economy is a fundamental prerequisite for doing anything about this new lost generation. A significant number of students, the Government has discovered, drop out of school, not because they want to, but because their parents cannot afford to have them off the labor market. Some of these dropouts become unemployed because they are in the scramble for cheap, unskilled jobs. Federal support for such children—perhaps through some form of the "G.I. Bill" in the war against poverty—and full employment would save many.

Predictably, such a development would rescue the best, the most educated and motivated, of the unemployed youth. But as figures make clear, there are other millions of young people who will enter the economy during this decade who will probably be immune even to the advantages of full employment. (The 2.3 million with less than an eighth-grade education certainly fall into this category; so do many of the 7.5 million without high-school diplomas.)

It is to this problem that the Administration has addressed two new programs in the antipoverty package: the Job Corps (both the Conservation and the Training Camps) for 30,000 to 40,000 young people in its first phase; and the work-training program (in which Washington will, essentially, subsidize some state, municipal and non-profit work for those in school), to extend to 200,000 youth. Both ideas involve special training and education for those at a "structural" disadvantage in the American economy.

It has certainly been demonstrated that such an approach can work. In Chicago, under Raymond M. Hilliard, director of the Cook County Department of Public Aid, basic literacy training was given to welfare recipients. When a source of jobs was found at the Yellow Cab Company, it was discovered that a man could go from illiteracy to paid employment in an amazingly short time. But the qualification in this success story is crucial: when a source of jobs was found.

Here again, unless the basic problem of full employment is met, the Administration's camp program could become a cruel deception; having attracted, motivated and trained young people, it would turn them out two years later into an economy which still could not employ them. This, of course, is not an argument against special training, which is crucial for so many of the youth who are now unfit for the economy. It simply emphasizes the fact that such programs will require the environment of full employment.

Under present conditions, there is no reason to believe that a full-employment economy is around the corner. The tax cut may reduce the jobless rate to 5 percent: it could even bring it down to the 4 percent predicted by some of the more optimistic in Washington. But a work situation that could bring these youth back into the society will require more than that. As proposed by the A.F.L.–C.I.O., it will certainly take a $2-billion investment in accelerated public works in the immediate future; and beyond that, a more basic public commitment to meet the housing, school, hospital, transportation and other needs not only of the poor but of the rest of the society as well.

The Administration has made a beginning, which is in itself a positive accomplishment. It may take the President and Mr. Shriver a while to educate the people on the extent and the critical character of problems like those of the dropouts and the unemployed youth. But time presses and once that is done, much larger steps will have to be taken.

For, typically in this America of midcentury, the Government has admitted the existence of problems it has not yet proposed even to touch. The first installment in the Training Camps will be for some 40,000—and one quarter of the Selective Service rejectees cannot read at a seventh-grade level. There will be over two million young people in this decade, the majority of whom are yet to appear, without a grade-school diploma. Even under conditions of full employment, where will they fit?

As it now stands, the Secretary of Labor has a broad authority to undertake studies of the labor market. Yet there is no effective "early warning system" for automation, such as he has proposed. Without a knowledge of the job needs of the future, of those occupations going into decline and those coming to the fore, it will be next to impossible to develop a rational education and training system for these youth. Among other things, the American prejudice against planning (an irrationality already discarded by most European conservatives) will have to be dropped.

All of these proposals clearly require large changes in American thinking, yet they are necessary to meet the problem of youth as America has defined it. And beyond, the figures suggest that if these young people are to have meaningful lives, perhaps the nation will have to make some new definitions of work (are not the full-time officers of a non-bopping club in the slums "social workers" of a sort?) and of pay (going to school is probably the most productive activity a young person can undertake in this society and, as such, could be compensated for).

In any case, given the Zolaesque underworld of the impoverished youth described by the computers, the Economic Opportunity Act of 1964 is a praiseworthy point of departure. It is, to quote one of the late President Kennedy's maxims, that necessary first step in a journey of a thousand miles.

The City Slums

The next article comments further on the meaning of unemployment, delinquency, and the lack of urban planning in this area. Professor Conant writes that the failure to find employment for major segments of the Negro population should be an important social concern. But while there is a great deal of discussion about the dangers of alienation and enforced poverty on the Negro community, little is initiated in the way of removing the forces which sustain these social conditions.

Does the teacher have any role in urban planning? If the liberal education now offered in schools has contributed to dropout rates, what alternatives exist? Is practical education the answer? Should we train youth for work at the expense of liberating their minds? Are these goals mutually exclusive? Is an urban setting less suitable for study of the classics than a suburban environment? Do suburban schools have problems of dropouts and unemployment?

Schools and Jobs in the Big Cities

JAMES B. CONANT

In preparation for a Conference on Unemployed, Out-of-School Youth in Urban Areas held in May, 1961, a few special studies were conducted in slum areas of large cities to find out what the facts really were with respect to the unemployment of youth in slum neighborhoods. In a slum section composed almost entirely of Negroes in one of our largest cities the following situation was found: A total of 59 percent of the male youth between the ages of sixteen and twenty-one were out of school and unemployed. They were roaming the streets. Of the boys who graduated from high school 48 percent were unemployed in contrast to 63 percent of the boys who has dropped out of school. In short, two-thirds of the male dropouts did not have jobs and about half of the high school graduates did not have jobs. In such a situation, the pupil may ask, "Why bother to stay in school when graduation for half the boys opens onto a dead-end street?"

An even worse state of affairs was found in another special study in a different city. In a slum area of 125,000 people, mostly Negro, a sampling of the youth population showed that roughly 70 percent of the boys and girls ages sixteen to twenty-one were out of school and unemployed. When one considers that the total population in this district is equal to that of a good-sized independent city, the magnitude of the problems is appalling and the challenge to our society is clear.

I do not have to remind the reader that the fate of freedom in the world hangs very much in the balance. Our success against the spread of communism in no small measure depends upon the successful operation of our own free society. To my mind, there is no question that a healthy society requires a sound economy and high employment. Communism feeds upon discontented, frustrated, unemployed people. As I write in June, 1961, the unemployment rate nationwide is something over 7 percent for all age brackets, but unemployment among youth under twenty-one years of age is about 17 percent, or more than twice the nationwide rate for all workers. These young people are my chief concern, especially when they are pocketed together in large numbers within the confines of the big city slums. What can words like "freedom," "liberty," and "equality of opportunity" mean to these young people? With what kind of zeal and dedica-

From *Slums and Suburbs*, by James B. Conant. Reprinted by permission of Educational Testing Service, Princeton, New Jersey. Published by McGraw-Hill Book Co., Inc., New York, 1961, Chap. 2, pp. 33–38.

tion can we expect them to withstand the relentless pressures of communism? How well prepared are they to face the struggle that shows no signs of abating? I am deeply disturbed by the implications that widespread unemployment among the youth of our big cities has for the future of our society.

Although the causes of juvenile delinquency are complex and there is no one solution, employment opportunities are clearly important. A youth who has dropped out of school and never has had a full-time job is not likely to become a constructive citizen of his community. Quite the contrary. As a frustrated individual he is likely to be antisocial and rebellious, and may well become a juvenile delinquent. The adverse influence of the street is largely a consequence of gangs of such youths, out of school and unemployed. I doubt if anyone familiar with slums would deny that, if all the male youth by some miracle were to find employment, the social climate would change dramatically for the better. Some juvenile delinquents would remain, gangs might not wholly disappear, but the attitude of the neighborhood would alter in such a way as to make more effective the teacher in every classroom.

Unemployment is bad anywhere. Adult unemployment, especially in rural areas, towns, and small cities, is grievous because it usually involves the loss of support for an entire family. In such cases, one might say that solving the unemployment of adults has the top priority. But in the slums of the largest cities, the reverse is true. The great need is for reduction of unemployment of male youth under twenty-one.

Consider for a moment the long-run consequence of persistent failure of underprivileged youth to find work. Leaving aside the human tragedies involved in each individual instance and looking at the matter solely in terms of the welfare of our free society, one sees the special position of the large city slums. The boys brought up in slum neighborhoods, even if they come to the big city from the country as children, are conditioned to street life with all that this life implies. Out of work and out of school once they turn sixteen, these youth behave in ways that may have serious political consequences; similar behavior of youth in smaller cities would be far less serious. It is a matter of geography in the last analysis. Three factors are significant: first, group size (the larger the group, the more dangerous); second, the density of the population (the number of frustrated youth per block); third, the isolation of the inhabitants from other kinds of people and other sorts of streets and houses.

If one compares the slum areas in the largest cities with similar districts in small cities, the difference with respect to these three factors is evident. The youth in the big city slums dwell in a mammoth social complex. The surrounding city extends for many blocks. The business and industrial areas hem in the impoverished youth. In the case of the Negro, added to all the negative influences of a slum is the absence of any evidence that there is a pathway out. In spite of the high mobility of the family unit, or perhaps because of it, a tone is set by constant talk and the prevailing attitude of the older people. The tone is not one to encourage education or stimulate ambition. One often finds a vicious circle of lack of jobs and lack of ambition; one leads to the other. It is my contention that the circle must be broken both by upgrading the educational and vocational aspirations of slum youth and, even more important, by finding employment opportunity for them, particularly for high school graduates. It does no good whatever to prepare boys and girls for nonexistent jobs.

The difference between the Negro slum of today and the slums of the Northern seaport cities of sixty years ago is a difference that deserves attention. The worries I have expressed about the continuation of present conditions may appear to be neutralized by contemplating the record of the past. Big cities have always had slums. In the United States in the past it was possible for people to raise themselves by their own bootstraps in the course of a generation. Why be alarmed about the present situation? Such a complacent projection of the past into the obscure future is fallacious for several reasons. First and foremost is the fact that in the past most of the inhabitants of slums were recently arrived white foreign immigrants. They knew that their predecessors for generations had worked their way out of poverty in the cities. They were convinced that they could do likewise. The almost complete lack of such conviction—a consequence of the tragic story of the Negro in the United States—is the outstanding characteristic of youth in the Negro slum. Secondly, a foreign immigrant came from an impoverished but stable society, for the most part a peasant society with its own ancient mores. The pride of family and often strong church connections were social cement that kept the slums from being complete social jungles in spite of the fact that the dwelling conditions were often as bad as they are today. Lastly, for most of the period of our history labor shortages rather than labor surpluses were characteristic of our economy. Particularly, unskilled laborers were in demand. When this was not so, namely, in the depression years, organized society had to step in on a large scale to bolster the tottering social structure. Today automation has affected the employment scene; there is much less demand for unskilled labor. Racial discrimination makes unemployment chronic for the Negro male, North and South. In short, neither in terms of the kinds of people involved nor in terms of the economic and social setting is there much resemblance between the poor city districts of 1900 and those which are the sore spots of our modern cities.

What was especially disturbing to me in my visits to the largest cities was the discovery that the employment of youth is literally nobody's affair. To be sure, there are groups concerned with various aspects of the problem, but no single agency in any of the cities has the data as to the unemployment picture in that city. There is little up-to-date information about youth unemployment even citywide and only the estimate of school people about the slum neighborhoods. Seldom are figures available to distinguish between the unemployed who are high school graduates and those who have dropped out of school before completing the twelfth grade. Most important, it is not possible to say with any accuracy how the unemployed youth are distributed among various neighborhoods. At the beginning of this chapter I cited special studies that were undertaken to ascertain the extent of unemployment among out-of-school youth in slum neighborhoods. These studies corroborated my guess that the situation was bad. There is a great need for reliable information of this sort. Until public opinion demands that the employment of youth be looked at with a microscope, so to speak, neighborhood by neighborhood, we are unlikely to rectify what may be a great hidden danger.

Social Conditions
and Mental Health

The conditions of life in the large urban setting tend to involve greater personal stress and multiple kinds of adjustments which are not characteristic of living patterns in more rural areas. The pressures and changes in which the individual is involved in the city may directly affect his mental health. Do the urban conditions of unemployment, segregation, and poverty lead to mental disorders and emotional maladjustment for many members of the deprived and alienated population? What role could the schools play in lessening the impact of these conditions? The article that follows was selected from a classic study of the relationship between mental disorders and urban living conditions.

Mental Disorders in Urban Areas

ROBERT E. L. FARIS AND
H. WARREN DUNHAM

INTRODUCTION BY ERNEST W. BURGESS,
UNIVERSITY OF CHICAGO

This work, *Mental Disorders in Urban Areas*, by Robert E. L. Faris and H. Warren Durham is a pioneer study in the social aspects of mental disorder. The factual findings are new and many of them are unexpected. They constitute a significant contribution to our knowledge of the mental life of human beings in the large city.

In appraising the contribution of the authors it is important to distinguish between factual findings and interpretations of these findings. This is particularly important in the case of this study, which falls in the borderland between medicine and sociology. As a study in a field between these two disciplines it runs the risk of having unwarranted claims made for it by some readers and all-too-sweeping criticisms by others. The discerning reader will, however, discriminate between the facts presented and the interpretations of those facts. He will, I believe, recognize the value of the factual data as important additions to our knowledge of mental disorder. Those who question the adequacy of the theoretical explanation of the writers may make their own interpretations of the facts in terms congenial to their favorite conceptual systems.

A brief summary of the facts discovered by the authors indicates how definitely and unmistakably the incidence of the chief psychoses are related to the organization of the city.

1. Cases of mental disorders, as plotted by residences of patients previous to admission to public and private hospitals, show a regular decrease from the center to the periphery of the city, a pattern of distribution previously shown for such other kinds of social and economic phenomena as poverty, unemployment, juvenile delinquency, adult crime, suicide, family desertion, infant mortality, communicable disease, and general mortality.

2. Each of the chief types of mental disorder has a characteristic distribution with reference to the differentiated areas found within the large modern city. Each of the following psychoses has its highest rate of inci-

From *Mental Disorders in Urban Areas*, by Robert E. L. Faris and H. Warren Dunham, 1960, pp. ix–xx, 160–64. Reprinted by permission of the publisher, Hafner Publishing Company, Inc., New York.

dence in the indicated type of local community: (a) paranoid schizophrenia in the rooming-house districts of the city; (b) catatonic schizophrenia in the neighborhoods of first immigrant settlement which have a high proportion of their population foreign-born or Negro who are the most recent newcomers to the city; (c) manic-depressive psychoses in areas with higher rentals; (d) alcoholic psychoses in roominghouse and in certain immigrant areas; (e) dementia paralytica in lodging and rooming-house districts and Negro communities; (f) senile psychoses and arteriosclerosis in districts with the lowest percentages of home-owners.

3. There is a high degree of association between different types of psychoses as distributed in different urban areas and certain community conditions, as follows: paranoid schizophrenia with percentage of hotel residents and lodgers; catatonic schizophrenia with percentage of foreign-born and Negroes; manic-depressive psychoses with median monthly rental; alcoholic psychoses with percent of population on relief; dementia paralytica with distribution of vice resorts and with venereal-disease rates; senile psychoses with percentage of home-ownership; senile psychoses combined with arteriosclerosis with percentage of population on relief and with percent of population of native-white parentage.

The association of these different types of psychoses with specific types of communities is a discovery of outstanding significance and the authors might well have been content to establish these correlations and to leave their interpretation to further research.

But with the enthusiasm and courage of pioneers in a new field they have proceeded farther and formulated a theoretical explanation for their findings. Particularly with stress upon the concentration of paranoid schizophrenia in rooming-house areas, they suggest the consideration of the hypothesis that communication is essential for normal mental development and that social isolation makes for mental breakdown.

The authors set forth this explanation as a hypothesis rather than as a generalization established by the study. It is a theoretical position congenial to the sociological student and consistent with a great body of sociological theory.

This hypothesis should, however, be confronted with the entire range of facts now available in the field of mental disorder and be orientated within the group of hypotheses suggested by other theoretical viewpoints. Among the chief facts relative to mental disorder that should be taken into consideration by theories and hypotheses are the following:

1. Certain mental disorders are obviously organic in etiology, as dementia paralytica and alcoholic and senile psychoses. Others, in which an organic origin has not been definitely established, have been called functional, of which the schizophrenic and manic-depressive psychoses are the chief types.

2. Nearly all types of psychoses, whether organic or functional, and especially those involving prolonged mental derangement, manifest more

or less mental deterioration. The manic-depressive psychoses, however, are supposed to be followed characteristically by no deterioration.

3. Mental disorders, as reported by Myerson and others, recur in certain families in the same and/or successive generations, but apparently not always with the same type of psychosis.

4. Behavior in the psychoses is generally of a pattern more or less consistent with prepsychotic behavior.

5. Not all chronic alcoholics develop alcoholic psychoses, nor do all syphilitics develop dementia paralytica.

6. Mental disorders appear to be more prevalant where the population is mobile and heterogeneous than where it is stable and homogeneous and where life-conditions are complex and precarious rather than simple and secure.

7. The financial depression beginning in 1929 was accompanied by little or no increase in mental disorders.

8. Insanity rates for different psychoses vary by race, by nationality, by socioeconomic class, and by occupation.

Not all the foregoing facts are conclusively established, but they represent certain points on which there is more or less general consensus. They constitute, therefore, some of our concrete knowledge about mental disorders which must be taken into account in the formulation of a general theory of mental disorder.

The hypotheses which seek to explain behavior in mental disorder may perhaps be classified under three general heads: (1) constitutional, (2) psychological, and (3) sociological.

1. The constitutional descriptions and explanations of mental disorder proceed from hypotheses of the differences, in comparison with the average, of neural structure, processes, and integrations as basic causative factors. The cause of mental disorders is attributed to congenital or acquired deficiency or disturbance in the neural constitution of the individual.

2. Psychological descriptions and explanations of mental disorder are in terms of hypotheses of psychogenetic disturbances of mental functioning. It is assumed from this standpoint that disturbances in emotional and mental development—i.e., frustrations, regressions, and fixations—are causative factors in mental breakdown.

3. The sociological description and explanation of mental disorders may be concerned with hypotheses upon the role of communication in mental life and upon the effect of isolation upon mental breakdown. This is only one of several sociological explanations that might be formulated. It is the theory, however, that is elaborated by the writers of this study. Mental disorder is interpreted as a phase of personal disorganization arising out of maladjustment in the social relations of the person.

It is at once apparent that the psychological and sociological theories offer no direct explanation of alcoholic psychoses, dementia paralytica, and other organic types of mental disorder. At most, mental and social factors are important only indirectly, as in influencing the formation of habits of alcoholism or in conditioning attitudes and conduct leading to syphilitic infection. Besides indirectly explaining genesis by habits and attitudes, the sociological factors may also be brought into play to explain the evaluations of the person or the group or community of the conduct involved and the corresponding attitudes toward the patient and his role in the community.

The crucial types of mental disorder from the standpoint of theoretical explanation are the so-called "functional" psychoses, i.e., schizophrenia and manic-depressive psychoses. It must be borne in mind that these psychoses may be functional only in the sense that no specific and definite organic basis for them has been established.

There is no doubt that there are both psychogenetic and sociogenetic disturbances in the life-history of persons who later develop a "functional" mental disorder. The crucial question is, however, whether these mental and social disturbances are causal in the mental derangement or only symptomatic of underlying constitutional tendencies. Is the seclusiveness of the precatatonic which appears very early in his life-history a result of the isolation imposed on him in the family circle, or a psychogenetic trait conditioned by an arrest or a regression of the ego in its development leading to isolation, or is it a concomitant of a specific constitutional condition?

Our knowledge at present gives no final answer to this question. Theoretically any one of the three explanations, or some combination of them in varying degrees of significance, may ultimately turn out to be the most satisfactory. The whole evidence is not in. The crucial questions and hypotheses still await the acid test of research.

To many students of mental disorder the recent methods of inducing shock in schizophrenic patients by means of insulin and metrazol give presumptive evidence of the priority in causation to organic factors. At the same time, however, it may be quite possible that a phenomenon may be induced socially and removed organically and vice versa. The specific relationship between the chemical therapy and the course of the "disease" is as yet too little known. It may even be that they work in the form of shock and that psychological and social equivalents for the chemical "shock" may be found.

This recognition of the greater weight of constitutional factors does not mean the minimizing of the significance of mental and social factors in causation. Even if they play less direct roles, they may nevertheless be essential.

In line with these assumptions the following tentative harmonization of constitutional, psychological, and sociological explanations is offered to take account of the facts as outlined above.

1. A constitutional basis is an essential condition for a "functional" as well as for an organic mental disorder. An organic change as a result either of chemical treatment or of physiological processes is necessary for im-

provement of the mental condition of the patient. But mental states of anxiety, guilt, and inferiority may exert an effect upon organic processes, and these mental states may in turn be attributed to existing social factors.

2. The particular psychogenetic type of personality determines not the etiology but the symptoms of mental disorder. The classical Kraepelinian description of psychoses is now regarded by many psychiatrists as a classification of complexes of symptoms and not of specific disease entities. It is possible, though not certain, that certain psychogenetic types may be more predisposed to mental breakdown than others.

A distinction needs to be made between neurotics and prepsychotics who later develop psychoses. Persons with neurotic tendencies may become drug addicts, chronic alcoholics, habitual and excessive gamblers, sexual deviates including homosexuals, pathological liars and swindlers, criminals of the compulsive neurosis type, or psychic invalids, but apparently they do not generally become psychotic.

The precatatonic, preparanoid, and premanic-depressive are perhaps variants on a constitutional basis of distinct psychogenetic types widely represented in the general population.

3. Social conditions, while not primary in causation, may be underlying predisposing and precipitating factors. Situations involving stress and strain of adjustment—such as those of isolation, of migration, of love and marriage, and of frustration in a career may, in the cases of persons constitutionally predisposed, make for mental conflict and mental breakdown.

Any attempted integration of the interplay of constitutional, psychological, and sociological factors in mental disorder should be constantly revised to take account of new findings of research. But at any moment such a systematic general theory may be of assistance in utilizing the findings of the different life-sciences both in research and in treatment. Particularly in the study of prepsychotic cases and in the experiments in the prevention of mental disorders, psychological or sociological aspects of mental disorder may be of great importance. For example, there are not as yet, and may never be, organic tests adequate for identifying prepsychotic individuals, but it may perhaps be feasible to make an accurate description of the psychological types of prepsychotics and of specific precipitation social situations leading to breakdown. On the basis of such descriptions social experiments in the prevention of mental breakdown might be undertaken. If social conditions are actually precipitating factors in causation, control of conditions making for stress and strain in industry and society will become a chief objective of a constructive program of mental hygiene.

In such a program of prevention of mental disorders the findings of this study would be of great assistance. For they indicate not only the local communities with the highest rates of mental disorder but also those psychoses which are prevalent in each type of urban neighborhood. Local community programs of mental hygiene can accordingly be directed to dealing with the indirect and precipitating causes of specific types of psychoses, i.e., syphilis, as in the case of dementia paralytica, or lack of social contacts as with the young precatatonic.

The study by Faris and Dunham makes a contribution not only to our understanding of mental disorder but also to our knowledge of the interrelations of personality types and social organization under conditions of modern city life.

Previous urban studies have demonstrated a dynamic association between the spatial pattern of the city and its moral or social order. They define and describe the city as an entity constituted by the interrelations and integration of its component communities, each of which (1) occupies a territorial area, (2) possesses a specialized function, (3) selects a population with characteristic composition by age, sex, occupation, economic class, and nationality and racial stock, and (4) develops a typical cultural and political order. These earlier studies have also shown that marked differences exist in the various types of local communities of the city in general intelligence, educational status, and social distinction, as well as in the incidence of social problems.

The present study is the first, however, to indicate a striking relationship between community life and mental life. It shows that urban areas characterized by high rates of social disorganization are also those with high rates of mental disorganization. It demonstrates, further, that specific types of psychoses are concentrated in certain types of local communities.

These findings stimulate many interesting speculations. Only two of these will be briefly developed here.

The first one proceeds from the assumption that the syndromes of symptoms that underlie Kraepelin's classifications of mental disorders are not disease entities. The assumption is rather that these symptoms describe the psychogenetic type of personality of the individual who experiences a mental breakdown. If this be the case, then it may be further assumed that in certain of the functional psychoses the incidence of specific mental disorders may be taken as an index of the distribution in the city of its associated psychogenetic type of personality. It may then turn out that human beings in a large city tend to be segregated according to personality types. This hypothesis becomes then a subject for further study.

The second speculation is upon the role of movement both in the placing of people within the city and in the concomitant problems of social and mental adjustment. There is evidence in this study that the distribution of types of mental disorder bears some relation to the migration and the movement of population into and within the city. Hobohemia, the area where homeless men concentrate, has a disproportionately large number of cases of paranoid schizophrenia. Studies indicate that a high percentage of hoboes are egocentric. It is highly probable that they are persons who have failed to adjust to conditions of life in other communities and so have drifted downward and collected in Hobohemia.

The distribution of manic-depressives seems to indicate a movement in the opposite direction to that stated for paranoids. Their movement appears to have been into areas of higher economic status and into the better-grade apartment-house and apartment-hotel areas. The assumption is that the person of the psychogenetic type with manic-depressive predisposition puts forth more effort for success than does the average individual and so for a time rises in the economic scale. Those, therefore, who experience a mental breakdown tend to be found in communities of higher economic status.

Even more important than migration itself is the effect of movement upon the social and the mental adjustment of the person. Precipitation factors in mental breakdown may perhaps be found in the difficulties of adjustment to a new situation. In the light of the points suggested by this study, research in migration into and within the city takes on new aspects.

The significance of a pioneer study lies to a considerable degree in the extent to which it opens up promising and significant problems for future research. Judged by these standards, the present work will achieve a high rating.

HYPOTHESES AND INTERPRETATIONS
OF DISTRIBUTIONS

The establishment of the fact that there are great differences in the patterns of rates for different psychoses in the natural areas of the city is in itself a complicated task. The interpretation of the meaning of these facts is a separate problem; different methods of study are necessary for this part of the research. The distributions of certain psychoses can be fairly successfully explained; others are more difficult and explanations can only be suggested.

It is necessary before discussing the meaning of the configuration of rates for the different psychoses to examine certain possible flaws in the method. It may be possible that insanity is not concentrated, and that it appears to be so only because of some statistical illusion. Several possible explanations for the appearance of concentration are discussed below.

An obvious possibility is that the concentration of cases in certain areas of the city may be due to chance. This suggestion has been made by Professor Frank Alexander Ross, with reference to the computation of rates based on data for a single year. Using a formula to test the chance variation of a rate, he tested whether each rate was significantly different from the rate in an adjacent community. In some cases he found differences were not significant and in other cases they were. By combining two communities and computing a rate he was able to show more definitely that the concentration of rates could not be due to chance alone. The logic of this procedure has been questioned by Charles C. Peters, who pointed out the fact that many rates combined into a pattern greatly increased the statistical significance of the pattern itself, and that the possibility that chance variation alone could produce such a pattern is too small to be considered. Since this preliminary study was made, much larger numbers have been used, further decreasing the possibility that the patterns could be due to chance. It was therefore considered necessary to use the formula for testing chance variation only once—in the study of foreign-born rates of schizophrenia. In those maps which show a clear pattern of distribution, the conclusions are drawn from the pattern and not from differences between adjacent communities. It seems permissible to dismiss the possibility that these patterns are due to chance variation.

A second possibility is that the patterns of rate distribution represent only a concentration of cases of mental disorder which have been institutionalized because of poverty. If the actual incidence of mental disorder is equal in all parts of the city and if those in the higher-income classes are more frequently cared for at home or sent out of the state, the hospitalized cases would show a bias toward the lower-income classes and therefore toward the slum section of the city. An attempt is made to minimize this bias by including in the rates all the cases from the regional private hospitals as well as from public hospitals. Because of the small number of patients in the private hospitals, the rates were only slightly affected by the addition of these cases. No way has been found to estimate the amount of bias in the rates caused by the practice of caring for some patients in the homes. It is possible that there is an income selection in such cases. But it appears unlikely that such an effect dominates the patterns of distribution, because of the fact that different psychoses show different patterns of distribution. If a poverty concentration were the only, or the principal, factor in producing these patterns, they should be reasonably similar for all psychoses.

Another possibility is that the apparent concentration of cases is due to a statistical error or failure to adjust the rates for transiency. That is, if the cases from an area taken during the period of a year are divided by the population taken as of a single day, the rate may be regarded as too high if the population during the year had turned over enough to make a significantly larger population than was present on the one census enumeration day. Professor Ross made this point in the discussion previously mentioned. No satisfactory method was found to make a direct adjustment for this criticism. It is known, however, that in the hobo and rooming-house areas, which show very high rates for several types of mental disorder, the population is transient enough to turn over, perhaps two or three times or more. Ross made the suggestion that in such cases the rate be reduced to one-half or one-third. To justify this, however, it would be necessary to know where the excess population was the rest of the year and what the chances of hospitalization were wherever the people were. Only if it is true that the other cities and towns in which this transient population spends a part of the year do not take their quota in their hospitals, should the rate be adjusted. It seems significant, here, to point out that if the rates in the hobohemia communities for all types of mental disorders were divided by three, the resulting rates would still be two of the highest in the distribution of the rates. These considerations appear to be important in the statistical criticism presented by the factor of mobility.

An interpretation frequently made of the concentration in the center of the city of insanity rates, and the schizophrenia rates particularly, is that persons who are mentally abnormal fail in their economic life and consequently drift down into the slum areas because they are not able to compete satisfactorily with others. Such a process is, of course, possible, although the explanation does not appear to be valid in the case of the manic-depressive patterns. Many of the cases of schizophrenia consist of persons who were born in and have always lived in deteriorated areas. These did not drift into the high-rate areas. There are also cases that are hospitalized from high-income areas, persons who developed a mental disorder before their failure had caused them to drift to the slums. It is a question whether this drift process, which undoubtedly contributes something to the apparent concentration of rates, is anything more than an insignificant factor in causing the concentration. No decisive material on this point was obtained in this study. Some relevant findings should be stated, however.

One method of testing this drift hypothesis is the comparison of the distribution of young and old cases. For this purpose the paranoid and catatonic types of schizophrenia were selected because of the radical difference in both the pattern of the rates and the age distribution. Since those who are first committed at an advanced age have had a longer time in which to fail in their economic life and consequently to drift toward the slums, the distribution of the older cases should show a sharper concentration than the younger cases. There is a concentration of the paranoid schizophrenia cases between the ages of fifteen and twenty-nine years and between the ages of thirty and sixty-four years, respectively. The younger cases, mostly too young to have had much time to drift, are concentrated in the central areas in much the same pattern as the older cases. Both show roughly the same degree of concentration.

A somewhat similar result emerges from a comparison of young and old catatonic cases. Both young and old cases are concentrated, although in this instance there is an indication of some possible drift. The central business district, which has a low rate of younger cases, has a high rate of older cases. The lack of similarity of the patterns is shown by the fairly low coefficient of correlation, .41 ± .07. Except for this, however, the main pattern does not appear to be the product of drift.

A possible interpretation of the concentration of rates in the central areas might be that this measures the racial tendency to mental disorders of the foreign-born populations that inhabit these areas. It has been pointed out, however, that rates for foreign-born cases divided by foreign-born populations are distributed similarly to the rates for all cases. Likewise, rates for Negroes show a variation, being high in the central disorganized areas not populated primarily by members of their own race and low in the actual Negro areas. Some factors other than being foreign-born or Negro are necessary to explain these patterns that are the same no matter which race or nationality inhabits the area. Furthermore, not all psychoses are concentrated in foreign-born areas. Although the correlation of several psychoses with percentages of foreign-born and Negro population is high or medium, such as catatonic schizophrenia (0.86), epilepsy (0.53), and alcoholic psychoses (0.48), others such as paranoid schizophrenia (0.11), manic-depressive psychoses (0.14), general paralysis (0.15), and senile psychoses (0.17), show little or no correlation. The supposed tendency to mental disorders of the foreign-born populations, then, does not appear to explain the rate patterns.

The last possibility to be discussed is that the patterns of rates reveal that the nature of the social life and conditions in certain areas of the city is in some way a cause of high rates of mental disorder. If there is any truth in this hypothesis, it will be necessary to find separate explanations for each psychosis, since the distributions of rates differ both to a large and to a small degree for each psychosis.

Although the distributions are not exactly alike, the explanations of the concentration of general paralysis, drug addiction, and alcoholic psychoses rates according to this hypothesis are roughly similar. Different combinations of social factors, however, are no doubt functioning in the case of each of these psychoses. The general paralysis rates are highest in the hobo and rooming-house areas and in the Negro areas. These are the areas in which there is little family life, and in which the sex experience of the men is in large part with casual contacts and with prostitutes, who are relatively numerous in these districts. These conditions make for the spread of syphilitic infection and hence for general paralysis. The dispensing and the use of drugs is very much of an underworld activity and this is reflected by the high rates in the zone of transition. Lack of normal social life may underlie the dissatisfactions which cause the use of drugs to be felt as a release, hence the slight rise in rates in the upper-income hotel and rooming-house districts. Also, for the use of alcohol to become an appealing habit, basic dissatisfactions are often essential. High rates of alcohol consumption and of alcoholic psychoses are in the foreign-born and rooming-house areas and may be caused by such conditions of life as monotony, insecurity, and other problems difficult to solve, from which alcohol may be a temporary relief. The significant variations of rates according to nativity and race in the different housing areas of the city indicate the greater chances for mental breakdown and personality disorganization in relation to these psychoses especially when a person is living in an area not primarily populated by members of his own group. This fact alone would appear to be the beginning for further research in these mental disorders. In the case of the alcoholic psychoses it would seem to indicate the presence of other important factors in addition to the use of alcohol.

Another group of psychoses, namely, senile psychoses, psychoses with arteriosclerosis, and epilepsy, show unusual patterns of distribution and so make interpretation difficult. These psychoses are generally regarded by psychiatrists as having organic bases, and this might account for the absence of the typical ecological pattern. In the case of the psychoses of old age it did appear, however, that poverty was a basic factor in the selection for admission to the state hospitals.

The undiagnosed distribution and the distribution of cases referred to as "without psychoses" are difficult to interpret since the nature of the abnormal behavior is not indicated by the labels. It is suggested, however, that since both distributions resemble that of schizophrenia cases, it is possible that these are disorders of a similar nature.

Perhaps the most provocative finding in this study resulted from a comparison of the distribution of the manic-depressive and schizophrenic rates. The great contrast between these two patterns seems to imply that some valid distinction has been made in classification. The absence of any pattern in the manic-depressive series makes the interpretation of this distribution extremely difficult, although certain leads for further research might be definitely indicated. The absence of any pattern combined with the absence of skewness in the manic-depressive distribution might suggest that social factors are unimportant in relation to this disorder. If such proved to be the case, there would be a certain justification for asserting the priority of the hereditary and constitutional factors. This of course would be in line with the statistical studies of heredity in the functional psychoses which universally show that biological inheritance is more significant in manic-depressive psychoses than in schizophrenia.

While the ecological and statistical evidence does not bring out any relationship between this disorder and the social milieu, it does not follow that there is no such relationship. Manic-depressive psychoses may be connected with a different type of social process than is the case with the schizophrenic disorders. A possible sociological explanation of the manic-depressive pattern might be found in the suggestion that precipitating factors are causal in relation to these psychoses. Such precipitating factors occur in all social and economic levels of life and consequently are not so likely to have a definite connection with the community situation but rather with the interplay of personality and psychological factors of family relationships and intimate personal contacts. Such a theory tends to connect the manic-depressive disorder with extremely intimate and intense social contacts. This apparently is just the opposite from the situation of the schizophrenic, where isolation from such contacts appears to be an associated condition.

In contrast the schizophrenic rates are arranged into very definite patterns which follow closely the ecological structure of the city and the concentration of all types is very marked. With the exception of the catatonic type, which differs from the others in several respects, the high rates appear to be related to areas of high mobility and, in somewhat less degree, to foreign-born and Negro areas. In the following paragraphs is suggested a possible explanation of the relation between the social life of these areas and the abnormal behavior of the schizophrenic. The hypothesis is that extended isolation of the person produces the abnormal traits of behavior and mentality.

If the various types of unconventional behavior observed in different schizophrenic patients can be said to result from one condition, it appears that extreme seclusiveness may be that condition. The hallucinations, delusions, inappropriate action, silliness, and deterioration may all result from the fact that the seclusive person is completely freed from the social control which enforces normality in other people. For example, such hallucinations as "hearing voices" and "seeing visions" may result not only from sensory disturbances, but also from the inability of the seclusive person to communicate. Some investigations have revealed that patients who claim to "hear voices" may admit on further questioning that it is a "quiet voice" or "not really a voice, nor even a whisper, but a sort of silent whisper." Many such persons have some basis in their experience for such a belief. A patient who had spent a period in jail believed people were calling him "jailbird." A school-girl patient who had been the victim of a rape believed that people were talking about her. For isolated persons who feel that they could not know directly what persons might be whispering, such thoughts are not entirely unreasonable. The powerful feeling of embarrassment, disgrace, and helplessness may give rise to the conviction that other persons are discussing them. The statement that they hear voices may be in the nature of a metaphorical means of expression, used because it is felt that such a means is the only way to communicate the strength of the feeling. Thus, the hallucination of "hearing voices" may be seen as the hopeless attempt of an outcast or disgraced person to communicate his feelings to persons too normal to understand.

Similarly, the statement by a patient that he is Christ may mean that he feels himself to be a very special person, as important as Christ. Only the form of statement that he *is* Christ could communicate the strength of his feelings.

Silliness is a sign of abnormality only when it is inappropriate to the social situation. Collective silliness is a common occurrence. The willingness to be silly when others are solemn or indifferent may be merely a sign that the person is seclusive or isolated enough to be indifferent to the opinions of others. Similarly, other traits may be seen to proceed from the one condition of extreme seclusiveness.

If seclusiveness is the key trait of the schizophrenic, the explanation of the disorder lies in the cause of the development of this trait. It is important to determine whether the seclusiveness is due to an innate lack of sociability or to experiences which destroyed the sociability. An examination of one hundred and one consecutive cases of schizophrenia in an eastern state hospital by one of the authors revealed that twenty-seven were definitely reported to have been normally sociable in their childhood. Only twenty-one were reported never to have been sociable. In the remaining fifty-three cases, there was not enough evidence to decide. The cases reported as formerly sociable showed three typical stages in the development of their seclusive personality: (1) sociably inclined, making attempts to get the companionship of others; (2) being excluded by the others, but continuing to make the effort to establish intimate social relationships; (3) accepting defeat, changing the interests, and building up a system of rationalization. After this third stage, a sort of "vicious circle" process begins to operate. The acceptance or failure to mix with others and the development of a certain profile of personality traits makes the person less acceptable to others than before and more than ever liable to exclusion and, in the case of boys especially, more liable to actual persecution. The treatment in turn furthers the development of the schizophrenic traits. Of the one hundred and one cases included in this study, forty-eight contained sufficient data to reveal the isolating factors. Twenty-nine of these persons were reported to have been "spoiled children." Many of these became the victims of practical jokes at school, and were subject to a considerable amount of persecution. Four cases were discovered with no evidence of being spoiled but with very strict moral and religious training. Each of these four had a strong sense of guilt because of sex experiences and had delusions referring to them.

In addition, there were four cases which showed hallucinations and delusions due to the isolation brought on by deafness. Other cases showed such isolating factors as the inability to speak English, not being allowed by strict parents to play with other children, and sensitivity because of disfiguring physical deformities.

Any factor which interferes with social contacts with other persons produces isolation. The role of an outcast has tremendous effects on the development of the personality. Lack of sufficient self-confidence and the consciousness that others do not desire one's company may act as a serious barrier to intimate social relations. The individual who feels that he is conspicuously ugly, inferior, or in disgrace may be isolated through this conception of himself.

The hypothesis that such forms of isolation are significant factors to account for the high rates of schizophrenia in certain parts of the city is strengthened by the studies which have shown that the conditions producing isolation are much more frequent in the disorganized communities. Especially significant is the connection between the rates of schizophrenia, excepting the catatonic type, and indices of mobility. In addition, the fact that rates for Negro, foreign-born, and native-born are all significantly higher in areas not primarily populated by their own members tends to support this isolation hypothesis. When the harmony of all these facts bearing on the isolation hypothesis is considered, the result is sufficiently impressive to make further pursuit of this lead appear to be worthwhile.

Public Assistance
and Human Welfare

Attendant upon this large scale poverty and unemployment is the problem of public welfare in the urban areas. Millions of dollars are spent annually in the form of public assistance. This assistance is given in the form of public housing, food, clothing, transportation, and other basic living necessities. Many of the families receiving these funds have been on public welfare for more than one generation. There is a regular cycle of low educational achievement, school dropout, unemployment, poverty, and becoming a ward of the vast public welfare system. The traditional social welfare approaches need to be seriously re-examined, for the present picture is one of extensive public support of a sizable group in our society who tend to become permanently dependent on public welfare.

The following article presents the problems inherent in the public assistance programs utilized in New York State. This article does not describe all the legal and technical aspects of the problem, but it does help the reader to understand the nature of a major problem confronting most American cities.

What effects does extensive welfare have on local schools? Do schools in welfare areas exist merely as educational stopgaps as the author indicates? Where and how should corrective action occur? Can education be meaningful in the world described in the following article?

The Grim State of Welfare

JULIUS HORWITZ

Only 32 cities in the United States have total populations greater than the welfare population of New York City. Of 360,000 New Yorkers receiving public assistance, 200,000 are children. Another 20,000 children wander in and out of public-welfare institutions like New York sparrows looking for the spring. Who is responsible for these 220,000 children? How do they live? And who will dare face them 15 years fom now?

The Department of Welfare of the City of New York is responsible for the care of all persons eligible for welfare aid within the five boroughs of the city. Nine thousand employees, including a social-service staff of 4,000, work for the department. Many of the social-service workers are in the process of resigning; the conflict between the utopian aims of New York State's Social Welfare Law and the realities they face daily in their territories has left them shattered and helpless.

In 1963, the Department of Welfare spent $300 million. It provided food, shelter, clothing, medical care and a pot-luck of sociological stew to an army of people who, through loss of money or inability to earn money, could not otherwise survive. The dollar cost is shared by local, state and Federal authorities. The moral cost is immeasurable.

The Social Welfare Law of New York State is a marvelously conceived document that spells out the American dream of total security. It charges the state with complete responsibility for all the needs of life, excepting Golden Books for children and contraceptive information for adults. New York City's *Handbook for Case Units in Public Assistance* specifically budgets money for more than 70 services, collectively designed to create for the have-nots the normal climate of 20th-century life.

For many of the aged, the disabled and the unemployed, public assistance is an immediate alternative to catastrophe. But what happens to the lives of tens of thousands of children, the aged and the disabled is so contrary to the law that the "dream of security" becomes a terrifying nightmare. And as long as inexhaustible funds are available to house children —if house is the word—to spoon-feed the aged into canvas mortuary sacks, to prop up the disabled and to file away the unemployed, 360,000 human beings will continue to be paraded as statistical icons by the Department of Welfare. Why? Because the Department of Welfare has not dared to admit, publicly and with candor, the enormity of the social problems it

Reprinted from *Look*, Vol. 27, No. 6, March 26, 1963, pp. 72–80, by permission of the William Morris Agency, Inc., New York.

faces, problems for which it has assumed a fatuous and dangerous responsibility. In self-defense, Welfare buries that responsibility in case records, in bureaucratic secrecy, in private guilt, in what John Dewey called "riotous glorification."

What really happens in the public-assistance world of New York City? No one can possibly know without taking the black notebook of a social investigator under his arm and walking into the rotting ghettos of New York: the great blocks of Harlem, East Harlem, the West Side, blocks so horrible that they would have awed the missionaries of the 19th century. The black notebook has become a symbol of living death to tens of thousands of New Yorkers. It lists the families for whom simple words like love, home, work, father are devoid of meaning. It lists families whom the rest of us have ruthlessly dumped into oblivion, to be hidden from our sight and banished from our thoughts.

These are the families who fall early prey to the drug pushers, the addicts, the muggers, the purse snatchers, the elevator thieves, the psychologically castrated men whose only proof of manhood is an out-of-wedlock baby, and the morally castrated drifters who have brought panic to New York, a panic that pulses through thousands of brownstone blocks, where white, Negro, and Puerto Rican families plot escapes with the same inner frenzy that infected Londoners during the bubonic plague.

For seven years, I carried the black notebook. There are many names in it. The names used in this article are not from my notebook. They are fictitious. The situations are not. They are composites of actual case histories. The black notebook is immediately recognized on the stoops of the sprawling slums of the East and West Side. That notebook brims with requests for beds, shoes, teeth, eye appointments, winter coats and the forbidden contraceptives. That notebook is a "fenómeno" to thousands of Puerto Rican families in New York. That notebook is more destructive to the American Negro than all the segregation laws of the South. That notebook has spawned the special "landlords" who swarm into the welfare offal like the worms that five-year-old Paula Rivera saw crawling into the mouth of a Mr. Clark during the three days he lay dead "in the single-room occupancy" brownstone owned by a Mr. Sheck. Paula's mother took her screaming out of the building; they slept on a friend's floor in East Harlem rather than return to Mr. Sheck's building.

You must walk through the West Side buildings to know what it's like to have Mr. Sheck for your landlord.

I've known Mr. Sheck as long as I've carried the black notebook. He owns five buildings on the West Side. The five hold a total of over 200 families, if you count as a family any single, unattached person with one or more children. All the people in his houses are on welfare, except for an occasional tenant, unable or unwilling to move. Rents are $15 a week for a cube called a room, and $27.50 to $32.50 a week for a two-room furnished apartment, designed to house families with four or more children when no one else in New York City will house them. These two-room furnished apartments have been "decontrolled." This means that, for a start, the landlord can charge any kind of rent, and beyond that, anything goes.

Who would pay $30 a week for two rooms chopped out of a railroad flat, with broken walls, vermin, furniture that belongs in an incinerator, a front door through which rats enter as freely as the swarming children? Who would pay $30 a week, $65 semimonthly, $130 a month? The City of New York would and does. Why? The landlords know the answer. And the answer makes them inviolate. One of them said, "I run a pigsty for the City of New York. We're partners. See? The city pays me to keep these people off the street and out of everybody's sight, period. They aren't people. They're drunken, filthy, baby-producing pigs, and as soon as they die off, there are more to take their places. Nobody in City Hall would dare mention 'birth control.' They might lose votes, but they don't care about losing the whole city to these pigs. Nobody down there knows how these people live, because if they did, they would scream in their sleep. Me? I sleep, because I'm doing everybody a favor. I give the pigs four walls, and the city appreciates it, or, instead of paying me so well, they'd close me down tomorrow, just like they close down bookie joints and hustlers. But they won't, because there's no place else to put the 150 babies I've got urinating in my halls."

Slums are not a new story in New York. As soon as it took shape, the city became a massive slum. But the institutionalized slum, the publicly supported, high-rental slum, the slum that houses only welfare families, the slum that a child cannot forget, not in sleep, not in the ping of heroin, not in Rockland State Hospital, this is the new social-welfare slum.

Wilma Gilbort is one of Mr. Sheck's tenants. Open the door to Mrs. Gilbort's two rooms. You squeeze between the edge of the door and the edge of the stove and enter a dark hall that is a bedroom for five children, whose faces look at you with shattered innocence. Leonard, William and Thomas sleep in the three-quarter bed. Deborah and Judy sleep in the single bed. Deborah has asthma. William is retarded. Thomas screams in his classroom. Leonard is in a PS 600 school, a kind of educational stopgap for children who are apt to fling themselves at our throats. The living room where Roberta sleeps on a cot, hasn't seen sunlight since 1905.

Roberta is 14, and pregnant. Mrs. Gilbort is 41 and pregnant. This is Roberta's first pregnancy. It is Mrs. Gilbort's 16th. Her ten living children (one, Louis, is in prison) had seven different fathers—all with whereabouts unknown, except for George Williams in Pilgrim State Hospital and John Green in Manhattan State Hospital.

"I got caught this time, Mr. Horwitz," said Mrs. Gilbort. "I didn't mean to let it go this far."

I could see her stomach pushing out of the skirt held together by a diaper pin, a stomach that has heard 16 human monologues, five silenced by the probing of a clothespin.

"Generally I get rid of them, Mr. Horwitz, you know that from my old record. I don't see any reason for bringing more of them into the world."

"Where are you going to put this one? There's no room left for a second crib."

"In the dresser drawer. She'll grow up all right."

I opened my black notebook. "Who's the father?"

Mrs. Gilbort looked at me, trying to remember. Her mind strained for a name, a presence, a real man. She didn't remember, or she didn't know.

Roberta spoke up. Her slipper scraped on the floor. I thought it was the scratching of a rat. I did see a rat run under the crib. Charles saw the rat and smiled secretly at me. Charles is six.

"You know it was that super's helper on West 103rd Street," Roberta told her mother.

"Yes, I'm sure it was him," Mrs. Gilbort told me, relieved.

"Who's him? I need a name."

"He didn't have much of a name. They called him Pim. But that's not his real name. He's from Jersey. I don't know anything about him except that he was a super's helper."

"Did he actually work as a super's helper, or did he just sleep in the basement?"

"I think he just slept there more of the time."

"Did you tell him you were pregnant?"

"He wasn't around when I knew for sure."

"All right, we'll put the baby on the budget when it comes." The budget now is $172 semimonthly, or $344 a month, plus unlimited medical care, plus a clothing grant that can total $225 a year, plus household replacements as needed, plus the secure knowledge that each additional baby will be provided for out of the common treasury and buried in a common grave. (Mrs. Evins in Apartment 2B rushed into the buildings on West 104th Street begging for money to bury her six-year-old daughter Ellen when she died of a concussion, rather than see her dropped into a pauper's grave on Hart Island.)

I went upstairs, up the green hallway, newly painted for the housing inspectors, past the children rushing down into West 101st Street. Were they children? Every girl in Sheck's building over the age of 13 was pregnant, or had delivered a baby, or was imminently in the process of initiation. Like little girls playing with dolls everywhere, they believed their babies were real. The babies weren't real! The babies were hunks of flesh, laid down in dark rooms to age like meat, to be eaten when their taste appealed to rats, sodomites, drug pushers. And if they survived to the age of 18, they could expect to receive their own crisp IBM-processed public-assistance check, payable with the proper yellow identification card.

Mrs. Ringate lives on the first floor. Her door opens right into her toilet. The kitchen is a dark hole with a tiny refrigerator and a makeshift sink drained by leaking rubber hoses. Her two rooms hold five beds and two cribs, and cost $135 a month. The two cribs hold two babies born seven months ago on the 5th and 15th. Mrs. Ringate had her baby on the 5th. Her daughter Gloria had hers on the 15th. Gloria is 17. Mrs. Ringate is 37. Gloria "graduated" from a training school. Mrs. Ringate's oldest son Lawrence is in Dannemora prison. He threw a bottle of lye at his mother; it ate into her face and blinded her in one eye, almost blotting out her vision of him. I looked at Gloria and saw that she was pregnant again.

"Who this time?" I asked Gloria. The father of the first baby was Juan Martinez. He signed the form 384b admitting paternity, then vanished into the brownstones. Gloria told me that she wouldn't go looking for him, because she had heard he was pushing dope on West 88th Street. I could tell by Gloria's eyes that she heard only about every fifth word I uttered, and probably understood about as many as a well-trained cocker spaniel.

"I need a name for the record," I said to Gloria.

"Put down any name this time, Mr. Horwitz. I don't know his name for sure, and that's a fact. And it doesn't make any difference who's the father as long as you give me the checks." Gloria went into the toilet to comb her hair.

Mrs. Ringate showed me the letter from Dannemora advising her that her son would be discharged as soon as he was no longer capable of throwing lye in his mother's face.

"Will they let Lawrence out for real, Mr. Horwitz?"

"They might if they find the right pills."

"What do I do then?"

"Call the police and get an order restricting him from coming to your house."

"You know that won't keep him away. He'll come up the fire escape. He kicked the door in one time. One time, when I had the door blocked with the crib, he started to break in the wall. He'll do it again."

"Why?"

"You must know, Mr. Horwitz, you must know. I think if they let Lawrence out of that hospital, I'm going to take him South and show him his father's grave. Then at least he'll know he had a father once. He's a sick boy. I guessed that when I first saw him laying next to me. His eyes just looked like he shouldn't be looking out on this world. His eyes didn't have the surprise of a new baby. This is no place for him, not this world. He'll get shot in the head by the police or beaten to death in a street fight if they let him out. And if they keep him, then they've got to feed him all those years and watch him to see that he doesn't kill anyone in that hospital. Just send the checks, Mr. Horwitz, as Gloria says. She hasn't the good sense of a three-year-old baby, but she knows about the checks, your checks. Do you know what she told me last night? I tried to talk to her about what she was going to do with her first baby and the coming baby, because she can't stay here—there's no room for us to breathe or for all of us to sit down and eat at the same time. Do you know what Gloria told me? 'Shut up, you pig. I'm getting my own check, ain't I?' "

Mrs. Ringate spoke in a whisper, as though she believed her other children might survive if they didn't hear, but they lay on their beds, stiff, silent, straining, and they already knew.

I went into Anna Domingo's room on West 94th Street. Her mother, Rosa, lives in 2F. Anna lives in 4D. Her mother is a drug addict who has managed to fill two Department of Welfare case folders in eight years. Anna had to quit school. She had her first baby at 16 and now has a second baby. Her room is big enough to hold two cribs, a single bed, one chair, a table. The cooking is done in the community kitchen, and her babies' food is carried through trash-strewn corridors. Anna's brother lives with her mother in 2F. He sleeps with his mother. Incest would be the least of his mother's preoccupations.

"When are you going to get out of here?" I asked Anna.

"I look, Mr. Horwitz."

"I said, 'When are you going to get out of here?' You'll have another baby in ten months."

"I won't have any more."

"How do you know?"

"I'll go to church and tell God that I won't have any more babies. I'll tell Him that I'm not His seed any more."

"But you still have to get out of here."

"I will, Mr. Horwitz. If I get to be like my mother, I'm going to stick my head in an oven."

"Is she sleeping with your brother?"

"I don't know. I don't know what she does. She's high as soon as the check comes on the first and the 16th. I try to feed her after that. I don't know how she lives. I only know she's my mother because we used to be on the same welfare budget. I want to get off the budget. Mr. Horwitz that's what I want to do more than anything else in the world. I hate being on welfare. I know I can't prove it to you now, but that's what I want to do, and that's what I *will* do. I'm looking for someone to take care of my babies. If I find someone, I can go out and work like the other people I see on the street."

"But, in the meantime, you're in this damn building."

"On check day, I'll move. I'll take my check before the landlord cashes it. He always takes his rent money first. He always says I owe him money for extra days. Why does he need *more* money from me, if the money I get is only enough to feed me and my babies for 15 days? I'll move on check day. I'll run."

I watched Anna "run" from Apt. 4D to Apt. 3C.

How do you stop the institutionalized welfare slums, the slums that turn New York's classrooms into bedlam, the slums that turn 220,000 children into potential criminals and their teachers into terrorized bureaucrats? How do you fight the institutionalized welfare slums frequently disguised as Broadway hotels? What do you do with welfare slums hidden in blocks of crumbling, hacked-up, emasculated apartment houses, when they are protected by the guilt and fear of the Department of Welfare? A few sacrificial blocks and separate houses have been fed to the bulldozers. But what do you do when the shiny, vertical replacements are almost immediately befouled by the same forces that poisoned the tenements? What do you do when the cancer of welfare slums spreads to nursing homes, turning them into charnel houses? What do you do with the welfare slums that breed schizophrenia in children faster than the slums of the 19th century bred tuberculosis? And what of the welfare slums that are burgeoning all over the American urban landscape? For example, in 1961, Westchester County spent $11,806,990 on direct assistance, which was 27.5 percent of the total county expenditures, and Westchester is considered a prime refuge from the panic created by New York's welfare situation.

How do we stop the insensate drift toward impenetrable welfare slums? How do we smash an atom? Or place 12,000,000 men under arms? Or wipe out polio? Or send a chimpanzee to talk to the man in the moon? How?

Ethnic Groups in
New York City

The next article is a review of a very interesting study titled Beyond the Melting Pot: The Negroes, Puerto Ricans, Jews, Italians, and Irish of New York City *by Nathan Glazer and Daniel Patrick Moynihan. It is a provocative book on a topic of major importance—the status of ethnic groups in New York. The review which follows questions whether the conditions of life in New York City, for the ethnic groups studied, are similar to those in other large urban centers in the United States. Further, it is generally assumed that America is the great "melting pot" for a large number of diverse ethnic and racial groups. The study questions the reality of this widely accepted belief, presenting the alternative of ethnic and racial groups not assimilating into the mainstream of American life.*

Is the melting pot a part of American mythology? Is de facto segregation, not only of Negroes but also of other major ethnic groups, a social problem that can be solved by or through education? Is the teaching profession an unmelted pot in major cities?

New York's Unmelted Pot

D. W. BROGAN

Somewhere in this most remarkable book is an account of the once famous
play by Israel Zangwill, *The Melting Pot*. It is made plain not only how
bad, how irrelevantly romantic the play was, but we are asked to consider
the important fact that shortly after writing *The Melting Pot*, Zangwill
became an ardent Zionist and Zionism denies the basic premise of *The
Melting Pot* that the United States is on the way (with the rest of the
world following suit) to a happy state when "there shall be neither Jew
nor Gentile." That day has not come and, if it is possibly coming, it will
be a long time before it comes, as this study of "ethnic" groups in New
York is meant to demonstrate. Indeed, the authors seem to imply that what
will come is three different types of American, oriented around ancestral
religions, Protestant, Catholic and Jewish, all very American and internally
homogeneous but not groups only faintly distinguished one from the
other. Where the Negroes, overwhelmingly Protestant as they are, will be
in this set-up, the authors wisely refuse to prophesy.

The merits of this book are so great that it is candid to begin by stating
a methodological doubt. What we are given here is a picture of ethnic
groups in New York and, by an implied extrapolation, what is true of New
York is assumed to be true of the whole country. There are several reasons
for doubting this. In the first place there is the *size* of New York, an important difference on which the authors lay stress. New York is twice as
big as the next biggest American city (Chicago) and its ethnic blocs are
bigger than the ethnic blocs in other cities even if they are relatively
smaller. Thus New York has more Negroes than any other city even if they
represent a smaller share of the population than they do in, say, Washington, D.C., a city ignored by Messrs. Glazer and Moynihan. This statistical
fact (possibly to be coupled with the unusual geographical setting of New
York, after all Manhattan *is* an island) makes it risky to equate New York
with Chicago and still more with St. Louis, San Francisco, Detroit. With
everything said in this book, well, with nearly everything, I am in agreement, but I have doubts about seeing in New York a microcosm of the
nation.

First of all, there is no real equivalent in any other city to the great
Puerto Rican colony. The Puerto Ricans are now spreading outside "El

Reprinted from *Encounter*, Vol. 22, June, 1964, pp. 55–60, by permission of the publisher and the author.

Barrio," but the great mass is still in New York and the fantastically high net reproduction rate has provided New York with an ethnic group unparalleled in any other city. Soon there will be a million people whose home tongue is Spanish, who are American citizens by birth, who have their home country close at hand, a short (and cheap) plane ride away. It is not at all certain that the New York school authorities would not be well advised to begin the teaching of literacy in Spanish in many of the public schools of the city. So the Puerto Ricans are a case in themselves, a case admirably studied here.

Then New York is the home of the greatest Jewish urban centre in history. Other cities (say, Philadelphia) may have as many Jews in proportion, but they do not give the impression of being Jewish as Manhattan does. There are no Philadelphia equivalents of *The New York Times,* Macy's (or Gimbel's), *The Evening Post,* Lehman Brothers, City College— but the list could be prolonged beyond the reader's patience. The Italian colony is perhaps not proportionately bigger than the Italian colony in Boston, but it seems to have survived better. The Boston North End has suffered more from "improvement" than have the traditional Italian quarters of New York and the Italians have, I think, done better in New York city politics than the Italians have in Boston politics.

Then there are the Negroes. "Bronzeville" in Chicago may be more organized, more coherent, better integrated with the governing machine, but Harlem is still the Zion of the aspiring Negro and it is in New York that some of the most intractable forms of "the colour question" show themselves most obviously.

And the Irish, the oldest of the groups, for long politically the most potent, with the best balanced distribution of wealth, children of a city that *was,* in many ways, Irish long before there were more than a handful of Jews, Italians and Negroes on Manhattan and long before Puerto Rico was even a name? They are not, *pace* Mr. Moynihan, a representative sample of the Irish and still less of the American Catholics. For good and ill, they are New Yorkers, old New Yorkers, not Bostonians or Chicagoans and still less San Franciscans or St. Louisians. (I have freely coined some ugly adjectives.)

Because these groups are so large, they can create and maintain their own ethos, refuse to melt, and put up barriers in front of those members of the group trying to escape or to be merged in an undifferentiated "American" mass, that is, in a White Anglo-Saxon Protestant (w.a.s.p.) American mass. They probably couldn't become "Wasps" if they tried, but their communities, notably the Jews and Italians, have been very successful in keeping the exits closed or difficult of access.

New York, then, consists of these groups plus, of course, the numerically small but economically and socially very powerful White Protestants, plus groups less important or less vocal than they used to be, such as the

Germans. (It is worth noting that two of the immigrant groups that are helping to increase Catholic numbers nationally, Poles and "Canadiens," are poorly represented in New York.)

What has New York made of them and what have they made of New York? As I have suggested, it is probably the Jews who have made the most visible mark and that from a slow start, for it is not the small and distinguished Sephardic congregations that have existed from the seventeenth century, or even the much more numerous German Jews of the mid-nineteenth century that have made New York "Jewish"; it is the mass immigration from the Polish Pale and from Russia. And the success story here is the rise in three generations from the sweat shops and push-carts of lower Manhattan to the smart Jewish districts, the smart Jewish suburbs, the "Borscht" circuit in the Catskills, the immense increase in the number of professional men and women who are both the pride and despair of their parents and grandparents. (Mr. Glazer notes the decline in importance of the Jewish doctor and the rise in community status of the scientist. He does not quote, however, the story current in New York, that the Jewish mother doesn't any longer cry out, "Captain, Captain, my son, the doctor, has fallen overboard," but "Captain, Captain, my son the atomic physicist has fallen overboard.") Despite doubts that I have known distinguished Jews express, the Jewish passion for learning, or if not for learning, for high professional accomplishment, does not seem to have been eroded by the New York experience. And it is their great superiority over the other "ethnics" that they have this passion for academic achievement, lacking in all the other groups. And the Jews are the wealthiest group in New York (apart, of course, from the "Wasps"). But all is not well.

First of all, Jews still suffer from certain social and business disabilities. They are victims of social and business anti-Semitism. They can't (on the whole) be members of the "best" clubs—where so much business is done. They are not welcome in the very best suburbs even if they are very famous. They find entrance to the great corporations, the great law firms, the great banks difficult or worse. They suffer much the same disabilities as Irish Catholics do in Boston but *not* in New York. (It was for this reason that Mr. Joseph Kennedy moved his family, for a time, from a Boston suburb to a New York suburb.) Moreover, being a Jew is so ambiguous a thing. It does not mean being religiously committed to the God of Abraham. New York, or at any rate Manhattan, does not much encourage religion. It is different in the suburbs and Jews tend of their own will, as well as from *force majeure,* to congregate together and, in the suburbs, the synagogue or temple may play much the role a "good" Protestant church does in a Gentile suburb. It will be a means of social identification if not of religious edification. But being a Jew is a matter of origin and a matter of environment. Possibly the older, better educated, more opulent New York Jews would have separated themselves from the newcomers as, it is suggested in this book, the middle-class Negroes do from the Negro masses, but for the impact of Hitler. The triumph of the emergence from the Ghetto was seen as transitory. As a writer in *The New Republic* put it thirty odd years ago, it was like being in a zoo looking calmly at a tiger in a cage and suddenly realising that the bars were down. Then Jews began to ponder the truth of Harold Laski's law, "Anybody is a Jew that the Gentiles think is a Jew." So Jews are people who give to Jewish causes, who display often exaggerated touchiness about affronts or injustices, who are anxious to get Judaism (whatever it may mean) given the same respectful attention as is given automatically to various forms of Christianity. So they may fight for the most rigorous exclusion of *any* religious symbolism in schools since it won't, in any event, be Jewish symbolism. (The success of Jewish department stores in celebrating both Christmas and Chanukah with the same window dressing suggests that the Jewish leaders are too pessimistic.) They are loyally "liberal," far more loyal to the Democratic party than the Irish now are. But, unfortunately for the mass of New York Jews, the community, if it can be described as that, has to live down the fact that while few Jews were Communists, many Communists were Jews. The only mass "fellow-travelling" movement in recent American history was the Henry Wallace "Progressive ticket" in 1948 and most of the mass was provided by New York Jews. And that is one of the causes of the Irish *v.* Jewish feuds that have so weakened the Democratic Party in New York.

Many of the genuine grievances of Jews a generation ago are no longer important. The "Ivy League" colleges no longer impose an open or covert *"numerus clausus."* Medical school doors are now open. The New York Jewish community is less and less proletarian. No doubt there still are "Jews without money," to quote from Mike Gold, but there are far fewer of them. No doubt there are relics of the old Ghetto life of the Pale like the "Rebbes" in Brooklyn who carry on the old traditions and occasionally descend on London to be welcomed by London Jews of a type not frequently met in Hampstead. But the New York Jew is well inside the American fence if he, partly by choice and partly by necessity, crops his own corner of the pasture.

The uneasiness of the New York Irish has other roots. It is partly the uneasiness caused by the loss of control of what was one of the big Irish businesses, politics. The causes and results of that loss are admirably described, and it is a sad fact that the New York Irish have not produced a serious politician since Al Smith. True, they are well represented in the Reform section of the Democratic Party along with many more numerous Jews and "Wasps," but the reformers tend to come from Harvard, not from the Fulton Fish Market or even a Catholic college. They are Kennedy types, not the natural heirs of even the creditable Irish leaders of the past. There hasn't been a successful Irish boss in Manhattan since the death of

Commissioner Murphy whom Mr. Moynihan calls alternately "Mr." Murphy or "Frank Murphy." (His name was Charles Francis. Did anybody ever call him Frank?)

But the Irish unease is not merely due to the decline of Irish politicians, boxers, entertainers. It is due to an alienation from the contemporary world. Here Mr. Moynihan pulls no punches. He fully justifies Dr. Johnson's dictum: "The Irish are a fair people. They never speak well of one another." So Mr. Moynihan points out that many Irish failures are due to the booze. Jews and Italians don't produce alcoholics or even heavy drinkers. The Irish do. I seem to see a hint that the Irish male takes to the bottle as a substitute for sex to which he is traditionally indifferent. Maybe; but the Scots, who don't come far behind their cousins in their fondness for whisky, are certainly not indifferent to sex. But whatever the cause, Irish alcoholism, like Negro improvidence, is a handicap from which rival groups, Jews and Italians, profit.

But it is bad education rather than the bottle that Mr. Moynihan blames for the stagnation of the New York Irish. Education becomes more and more important, more and more expensive. The policy of the American bishops is to build up, at vast expense, from the kindergarten to the graduate school, a Catholic system of education. The results may be morally magnificent; at any rate they represent an immense and creditable effort, but all the academic tests that can be applied suggest that, at college level, the Catholic student is not getting the teaching or the equipment he needs. This is not surprising when we find Cardinal Cushing of Boston boasting that not a single cardinal, archbishop, or bishop is the son of a college graduate. When we consider the number of Catholic college graduates, the number of wealthy Catholics, this is a significant admission—or boast.

Mr. Moynihan suggests that many Catholics would like to give up the struggle to keep the school system going and concentrate on the Catholic colleges. I think this is very doubtful. For the increasingly prosperous Catholic middle class and the quite large wealthy class send their children to "good," that is non-Catholic, colleges. Even people like Mr. William Buckley of The National Review didn't go to Fordham or to Georgetown, but took the risks of Yale. The Catholic who has had a purely Catholic education is as handicapped as a graduate of Yeshiva University. He finds dialogue with his non-Catholic countrymen, in what is an overwhelmingly secular society, very difficult. The clergy, beginning with prelates like Cardinal Spellman, find it impossible. American Catholicism, as seen from the outside, is a society in which the equivalent of Father Martin D'Arcy, S.J., is Bishop Fulton Sheen. To give the names is to state the problem.

But—and it is an important but—Mr. Moynihan writes as if the Catholic Church in America was purely Irish in its upper echelons and that the image cast by Cardinal Spellman of New York (or Cardinal McIntyre of Los Angeles) is the only image. But in the Middle West (and in parts of the South as in Texas, near the L.B.J. ranch), it is German. The only cardinal to be a national figure since the death of Cardinal Gibbons was Cardinal Mundelein of Chicago. In the Vatican Council there are stories of a division between Cardinals Spellman and McIntyre and Cardinal Ritter (of St. Louis) and Cardinal Meyer (of Chicago). Mr. Moynihan should go and live in St. Louis for a time or read Mr. Powers of Minnesota (and *The New Yorker*)!

One last valid point is made by Mr. Moynihan that will be resented by many "liberals." The wide-spread support that Irish-American Catholics gave to Senator Joe McCarthy did not do any credit to their heads and not much to their hearts. But the Irish were having their revenge. They had been attacked for not being uncritical supporters of a Spanish Republic that tolerated the wholesale murder of priests and nuns. They were accused of being unduly suspicious of that great ally, Stalin, who had murdered the Poles at Katyn Woods. (He had also murdered Ehrlich and Alter, as a good many old-fashioned Jewish Socialists in New York remembered.) True, no American "liberal" magazine except possibly *The Nation* descended to the depths of imbecility (if that is what it was) of *The New Statesman*. But the Irish would have been more than human if they had not rubbed in the point that a very high proportion of Communist agents and sympathisers were Jews or "Wasps." It was not Fordham (the Jesuit University in the Bronx) which produced the real or alleged traitors of the McCarthy era. The Federal employees turned away from the Fort Monmouth installation were overwhelmingly Jews. And it is one of the revenges that the New York Irish and other Irish-Americans find gratifying that Harvard graduates are investigated by Fordham graduates since a large part of the F.B.I. staff come from that rapidly growing institution. Compared with Boston, the New York Catholic community is very open, but even so you can find complaints among the Irish of the ghetto mentality of the clergy. But we must not despair. The American Jesuits, including those at Fordham, are much more enlightened and much more learned than they were a generation ago. And Cardinal Spellman is not immortal, one is glad to think. If he were succeeded by someone like Bishop Wright of Pittsburgh, the whole character of the New York archdiocese would change, and even the diocese of Brooklyn could be carried screaming some way into the world of John XXIII and Paul VI.

The situation of the Italians is discussed with a great deal of sagacity and sympathy. Again, we must differentiate between the small and distinguished Italian colony from northern and central Italy, whose most notable member in the history of New York was Lorenzo da Ponte, and the great mass of Neapolitans and Sicilians. It is the Neapolitans and Sicilians who provide the votes, the labour force, the new Italian middle class, and of course the gangsters. The old and small north Italian colony is not very sympathetic to its southern countrymen—but it is not very sympathetic in Italy either. On a lesser scale, something of the same division can be seen in Glasgow between the small group of *Lucchesi* and the Neapolitans. But the New York Italians (like the Italians everywhere in the United States) have greatly changed and improved their position in the last generation. Most of them are now native-born Americans, although a number of their political leaders were in fact born in Italy or in Sicily. Then a phenomenon which I have noted but have not been able to explain until I read this book: the American Italians have returned to the Holy Roman Catholic and Apostolic Church in overwhelming numbers. When I first went to America 40 years ago I was told, and I believed, that there were more Italian ministers than Italian priests in the United States. This is no longer true, and whatever chances there were of the Italians becoming Protestant have now been lost, for a reason which Mr. Glazer hints at, but does not state dogmatically enough. The American Protestant finds it hard to welcome "lesser breeds without the law"; the Church does not. And in New York (and still more in very Italianate cities like New Haven), becoming a good Catholic, as most Italian Americans were not a generation ago, is one way to Americanisation. For an Italian girl to marry an Irish boy is an even more effective way to Americanisation, and it is a quite common form of mixed marriage. There are still no great Italian business figures in New York like Mr. Giannini of California, but the whole character of the community is changing. As among the Jews, Italian family feeling is very strong, even excessively strong. It is only recently that the Italian population of New York has begun to realize that it has any duties outside its family loyalties. There is therefore nothing of the proliferation of charitable and other philanthropic societies which marks the Jewish and the Irish Catholic communities. If the New York Italians want to boast of their *italianità* they put up a statue to Verazzano and get a new bridge called after him. They do not start a boys' club or a home for orphans. Mr. Glazer makes a great deal of the fact that there are comparatively few Italian priests and, like Mr. Moynihan, he tends to over-estimate the Irishness of the Church in New York. His explanation of the scarcity of vocations among the Italians is ingenious but implausible. He thinks it is due to the fact that Italians find controlling sex extremely difficult and therefore find celibacy impossible, whereas many Irishmen find sex impossible—or so it is said. But the old criterion of Catholicity, the willingness to provide priests, is not necessarily valid any longer. For example, no one can doubt that West Germany is far more Catholic in any realistic sense than is France, but it produces fewer priests. And rich Irish-American Catholic families do not often produce priests for the secular clergy, although they do produce priests for the religious orders.

I suggest that the scarcity of Italian priests reflects the low economic, intellectual and social status of priests in southern Italy and may change as the Italians begin to appreciate the high social and financial status of a priest in the United States. But the Italians are on the way, as the Irish and then the Jews were before them. From providing mayors, they will soon go on to providing senators, bankers, and bishops.

But what of the group which causes most perplexity and has had its problems made world-wide by *West Side Story*—the Puerto Ricans? Ten years ago I was living in Manhattan on the edge of the Puerto Rican district and I read both the Spanish daily papers, of which *El Diario* catered specially for the immigrants from Puerto Rico. At that time, I thought they were bound to remain at the bottom of the totem pole. They suffered from illiteracy in English and, indeed from near illiteracy in Spanish. They suffered from poor physique and bad health as well as from the absence of easily marketable skills. I thought they would replace the Negroes as "Low Man on the Totem Pole." I was wrong. For one thing, their health is much better in Puerto Rico than it was, thanks to the enlightened government of Señor Marín. Then a great many of the tropical diseases they suffered from in Puerto Rico do not thrive in New York. They are beginning to vote and their votes are beginning to be treasured and used. They are developing very rapidly a small business class, showing a great deal of commercial initiative and talent. Their interests in New York are watched over by the vigilant commonwealth government of Puerto Rico and although they suffer from low wages, horrible housing, and a family structure not adjusted to Manhattan—above all, not adjusted to the freedom given to girls in Manhattan—they are on the way up, still behind the Italians, but not staying at the bottom, as I thought they would.

Alas, the people staying at the bottom are the Negroes. The account of the Negroes given here is intelligent and courageous. It involves, in passing, some caustic comment on the effects of public housing and the failure to create real communities in the vast subsidised skyscrapers. "Urban renewal" may do much less than nothing for the poor of Manhattan, however profitable it is to the Jewish *entrepreneur* who does very well out of it. We all know from reading Mr. James Baldwin and Mr. Alan Lomax and, indeed, a host of others, how many genuine grievances the Negroes have —above all, the grievance of their disability, colour. It is, for example, one of the assets of the Puerto Ricans that the great majority are classified as white. This classification baffles geneticists and sociologists, for a century ago nearly half the Puerto Ricans were classified as Negroes! But Puerto Ricans know very well the advantages of being classified as white, and this has given them a lift which American Negroes cannot get except for the very few who "pass" into the white world.

But the novelty of this book is not in its repetition of the handicaps and hardships from which the New York Negro suffers. It is its bold suggestion that some of these handicaps and hardships are the fault of the Negroes. When everything has been done in the way of explanation, the *damnosa hereditas* of slavery, the brutality of the police, the badness of the schools, the fact remains that some of the Negro troubles are Negro-made. For example, as has been said often, the badly handicapped Puerto Ricans have developed their own middle class, mainly composed of small shop-keepers. In this area, Negroes have not only not gone forward, they have gone backward. They have also gone backward relatively in the professions. Although there are far better facilities for training Negro doctors than there were a generation ago, there are hardly any more Negro doctors now than there were then. The Negro in Harlem is almost always an employee of some kind or another. The Negro middle class is professional, and the profession is often that of being a government official, local or federal. The leadership of the Harlem Negroes is still in the hands of Negro ministers (although by an unfortunate misprint this truth is reversed). No one can pretend that the Reverend Representative Adam Clayton Powell is a satisfactory spokesman for the "race" to which it is asserted that he has in the past denied that he belongs. Yet to criticize Congressman Powell is to betray racial bigotry.

Mr. Glazer is not censorious: he can understand the resentment of the Negroes when reformers cracked down on the Borough President of Manhattan, the Honourable Hulan Jack, for a piece of quite minor graft. Why had the rules been tightened up just as Negroes began to get good city jobs? They have, in fact, been tightened up for everybody: no one can now make a fortune in New York politics, as Croker did, but one can see the grounds for the Negroes' irritation.

Yet it is possible to think that not all New York Negro grievances are the fault of the white world. It may be the result of slavery that the illegitimacy rate is so large, but it is a social fact about the New York Negro community which depresses its level, socially and economically. The fact that the Negro man (one hesitates to say husband) does not admit his responsibilities to his family, as all other groups in New York do, is a regrettable fact about Negro society. The Negroes have a theoretical passion for education, but it compares very badly with the genuine Jewish passion and its results. If there are hardly any Negroes in the Bronx High School for Science, this is not entirely the result of racial bigotry.

It may be, as Mr. James Baldwin tells us, that the sex life, the emotional life, of the New York Negroes is far superior to that of their white brothers. But if the New York Negroes want what the whites have, a high economic status, they will have to imitate the whites in various unattractive ways.

This is an old story. When the Gaelic League was trying to revivify Ireland after the fall of Parnell, it preached not only "the Language" but all sorts of social salvation such as cleanliness, industry, and pride. It preached, in fact, English habits. One of its mottoes was, "For as we are shall Banba (Ireland) be." And an Irish Jesuit has recently been preaching to his Catholic countrymen the desirability of their attempting to imitate some of the good habits of their Protestant countrymen. Mr. Glazer believes that everything that the law can do to promote racial equality in New York has been done, and in addition to the law there are a great many whites whose consciences are touched, especially among Jews. But the anti-Semitism which marks so many New York Negroes, although it is often justified by their encounters with Jewish shopkeepers and Jewish landlords, has a less attractive side: why are there no Negro shopkeepers or Negro landlords? It is not a matter of "race"—there have been many successful business tribes in West Africa. What Negro enterprise there is comes, Mr. Glazer tells us, from the West Indians, above all the Jamaicans.

Bernard Shaw pointed out a long time ago that one of the greatest handicaps of oppressed peoples was that they always had an excuse for their own faults—the brutal Saxon or the even more brutal American white. Both the brutal Saxon and the American white have a great deal to repent of, but one of the big signs of progress in Ireland is the willingness to believe that Irish troubles to-day are the result of Irish faults and not of English faults; and perhaps the New York Negro might be better off if he could admit that some of his troubles are self-made.

I have said earlier that I do not think New York is a representative sample of the American ethnic system. I think the melting pot does melt much more outside New York than it does inside the city. Class and religious barriers are much harder to retain in a small town than in the vast megalopolis of New York. To grow up in a small, unaccepted religion on the wrong side of the tracks in Abilene is not as great a handicap, as General Eisenhower and Dr. Eisenhower show, as to grow up on the wrong side of the tracks in Manhattan. Yet the authors of this book note that in Manhattan there is a much easier mixture of groups and races than anywhere else in the United States. There are more white and Negro affairs and marriages, and so less contempt or, indeed, comment than in any other part of the United States. One of the few charms Manhattan has for me is its nearly complete freedom from one of the most annoying of American habits: impertinent curiosity about other people's affairs.

Perhaps we ought to have a number of other studies—of Chicago and San Francisco, for example—before we make up our minds whether the melting pot is doing its job or not. Meantime, here is a book of great interest and great intelligence. It is full of the most fascinating information, such as the fact that the Jewish leaders of one of the big unions employ Sephardic Jews speaking archaic 15th-century Spanish to deal with the new Puerto Rican workers' unions. In fact, I have learned a great deal about New York—above all about Manhattan. What they will learn is, on the whole, encouraging. For we can no longer make the innocent assumption that only America has race problems, or that Labour politics or Communism automatically abolish race prejudice.

Schools in Suburbia

Up to this point, the articles have dealt with the quality of urban living and education in the lower income districts of the cities. What differences between urban living and behavior patterns which are more characteristic of suburban life are pointed up in the following two articles?

In the first article, Dr. Conant discusses the high academic quality of the suburban schools and the parental insistence that the school's primary purpose is to prepare these children for college. These schools are significantly different from the schools in the lower-income areas of the city. Their physical facilities are more elaborate and more carefully designed for prescriptive approaches to teaching. The ratio of students to teachers is lower, and the students at all academic levels are exposed to many different teaching specialists. There is a larger number of auxiliary personnel available to the students such as counselors, nurses, reading specialists, coaches, and art and music teachers. In general these schools are marked by a high degree of stability and staff involvement. Frequently the staff in these schools has been there for many years, and the students often enter the school and continue in the same community through graduation. In these suburbs the schools serve as an important force in the life of the community.

The College-Oriented Suburbs

JAMES B. CONANT

To drive a car or to ride a train through a wealthy suburb and then through a city slum is for many people an everyday experience. As seen from the car or train window, the basic contrast is one of housing, the congested city blocks contrasting with the more spacious and attractive suburban homes. Although sensitive Americans might find the comparison painful, it is as nothing when compared with the profoundly shocking experience of going from a high school that serves a wealthy suburb to one

From *Slums and Suburbs*, by James B. Conant. Reprinted by permission of the Educational Testing Service, Princeton, New Jersey. Published by McGraw-Hill Book Co., Inc., 1961, Chap. 4, pp. 80–84.

that serves a slum. The social conditions in the slums or large cities are reflected in the schools. As a vivid contrast, let me now turn to the problems in the suburban high school, with which far more readers will be familiar as a result of their own experience.

I shall not stress the contrast in the buildings or the physical facilities, though they are startling enough. For, to be quite frank, I am not at all convinced that in terms of education the dazzling attractiveness of the spacious buildings of some suburban schools I know are as much of an asset as they seem, though I hasten to add that many large city schools should be torn down and replaced by modern structures. The real contrast is evident only to a visitor who will take the time to visit classes, talk to the principals and teachers in both schools, examine the relevant statistics, and ascertain the completely different educational aspirations of the families.

The problems besetting the teachers and guidance officers in the schools in the low-income areas in the big city have been discussed. These problems to a large extent reflect the cultural level and parental ambitions of the homes from which the children come. So, too, do the tasks facing the staff of a high school in a wealthy suburb. But they are almost the reverse of those presented to the teachers in many large city schools. The overriding consideration in the type of community I wish to consider is the parental demand that their offspring obtain admittance to a four-year college. Indeed, a convenient index of the social composition of a school district is the percentage of high school graduates who go on with full-time education. The percentage is remarkably constant year by year if a community is not undergoing marked expansion, contraction, or social change. Nationwide, some 50 percent of high school graduates go on for some kind of further education. In the suburbs the figure may run from 50 percent to over 90 percent.

The heavily college-oriented suburb is the subject of this chapter. When one finds a high school from which 80 percent or more of the graduates regularly enroll in some four-year college or university, one can be certain that a relatively homogeneous residential community is at hand. In such a suburb the vast majority of the inhabitants belong to the managerial or professional class; the average level of income is high; the real estate values are correspondingly elevated. In these wealthy communities, one is likely to find effective school boards, great parental interest in the public schools, high expenditure per pupil. Since the citizens are interested in good schools and ample resources are available, the public schools are as good as the professionals know how to make them.

One could name a dozen or two communities in the large metropolitan areas of New York, Philadelphia, and Chicago where schools of this sort exist. These schools have become nationally famous for their excellence and are sometimes referred to as "lighthouse" schools, beacons lighting the way toward educational progress. There can be no doubt of the excellence of the teaching in the schools in the lighthouse school districts. Large school budgets enable the superintendent and the principals of the schools to recruit a corps of first-rate teachers; the level of the salaries is far higher than in many other districts. Furthermore the size of the staff in proportion to the size of the student body is as much as 75 percent greater than in the corresponding schools in the nearby large central city. Physical facilities are usually the envy of those who live in less prosperous school districts. In short, the high costs per pupil are an essential factor in assuring the excellence of these schools.

Yet it would be a mistake to assume that the high expenditures are the only factor. In addition to a top-flight teaching staff, the lighthouse schools are fortunate in the nature of the student body. The vast majority of pupils come from homes that are by no means typical in the United States. The attitude of the parents toward education, toward music, art, drama, litera-ture, and politics is far different from that of the average American family. Most of the fathers and many of the mothers are college graduates. Shall we say the cultural level and degree of social sophistication are extremely high? Taking the community as a whole and comparing it with most other school districts of comparable size, I think some such description to be warranted.

Many of these well-to-do families who some years ago would have sent their children to private schools now find the costs prohibitive and admis-sion difficult because of increasing selectivity at the better-known private schools. Consequently they look to the public schools to provide the same degree of academic excellence and the same assurance of college admission that the top prep schools traditionally have provided. The result is that the public high schools in these heavily college-oriented communities have reverted to the sole function that most high schools had at the turn of the century; namely, that of preparing youth for college. As I travel about the country, I sense that the public schools in many suburban communities have accepted this challenge. What it amounts to is a stronger academic emphasis than has been present in American public education in some time. To my mind, it is still insufficient in many otherwise excellent schools, particularly with regard to the breadth of the education open to the bright students.

Suburban schools today are challenged to "get" boys and girls into top-flight colleges and consequently to maintain high standards in the aca-demic courses. These schools are also faced with a dilemma. The problem comes in cases where the parental ambitions outrun the offspring's ability; that is, where the boy or girl has difficulty mastering academic work in a school with high standards and yet is expected by his parents to attend a prestige college. If the student with limited ability fails to gain admission to a prestige college, the parents are likely to blame the public school, little realizing that the same student in a private school would probably fare no better. The situation has changed since the time when by dint of hard work and extra tutoring even a dull boy could be admitted to Harvard, Yale, or Princeton. Not that such a boy today is prohibited from admission to college. Far from it. There are colleges today for every kind of student with every degree of ability.

Anxiety in the Suburban Family

The suburban family, by definition, is often one that has high standards of social and occupational achievement. The parents pass these expectations along to the children either verbally or by their own behaviors. These parents are usually well educated and very competitive in terms of their financial and social goals.

When their children share these goals and are highly successful in school, the parental anxieties are lessened. But when the child deviates from the clearly established family values and selects a nonachieving, noncompetitive role, serious concern and anxiety may be aroused. It is probable that the patterns of conformity are greater for the suburban child, in terms of the stronger parental expectations placed upon him for specific kinds of achievement. In the following article, David Riesman discusses the anxieties found in suburban parents and their apparent inability to calmly enjoy their leisure. Their lives are often surrounded by self-generated pressures and guilt over their level of achievement.

This article has many implications for teachers. On the one hand teachers frequently become suburban parents and may reproduce the patterns that Riesman discusses. Also the students in these schools are under very specific pressures from their parents and these pressures in turn create anxieties for the teacher. Do these feelings help to engender a school climate which is altogether different from a school in a less affluent neighborhood?

Some Observations on Changes in Leisure Attitudes

DAVID RIESMAN

Let us look at a concrete example. A friend and former colleague, Professor John R. Seeley, is now engaged in directing a large research project on the relations between school and community in a wealthy, upper-middle-class suburb. It is a suburb which has one of the finest public school systems on this continent, one which is often held up as a model to others; in fact, the magnificent new modern high school dominates the community, even physically, as the cathedrals did in the Middle Ages. The very fact that this elaborate research is going on there—it is to take a period of at least five years before any final conclusions are reached—is indicative of the alertness of the school officials, the school board, and the other community leaders. Yet, from my own very limited observation and from what has been reported to me, it is plain that the community, despite all material advantages, is not happy. The parents have neuroses; the children have allergies; and the teachers—well, I don't know. What has gone wrong?

If we follow the life of the children after school, we can perhaps get some clues. They are being prepared now for their later careers and their later rather hypothetical leisure. Their parents want to know how they have fared at school: they are constantly comparing them, judging them in school aptitude, popularity, what part they have in the school play; are the boys sissies? the girls too fat? All the school anxieties are transferred to the home and vice versa, partly because the parents, college graduates mostly, are intelligent and concerned with education. After school there are music lessons, skating lessons, riding lessons, with mother as chauffeur and scheduler. In the evening, the children go to a dance at school for which the parents have groomed them, while the parents go to a PTA meeting for which the children, directly or indirectly, have groomed *them,* where they are addressed by a psychiatrist who advises them to be warm and relaxed in handling their children! They go home and eagerly and warmly ask their returning children to tell them everything that happened at the dance, making it clear by their manner that they are sophisticated and cannot easily be shocked. As Professor Seeley describes matters, the school in this community operates a "gigantic factory for the production of relationships."

Since, moreover, the same interpersonal concerns dominate life within this "plant" and outside it, there is no sharp change of pace between work and play, between school and home activities. The children and their mothers—the fathers who work in the city at least make a geographical shift and also something of an emotional one—are characterized by a pervading anxiety. This is connected, I think, with the fact that the older, clear goals of achievement have been called into question, and these family units must decide not only how to get what they want but also what it is they should want. To answer this question, the community makes much use of professionals—the school principals and teachers themselves, who have a very high standing; child guidance experts and mental hygienists; and the packaged professionalism which can be bought in books or over the radio. The result is a well-known paradox: here is a suburb devoted to the arts of consumption and leisure, where these arts are pursued with such dogged determination that leisureliness as a quality of life is very largely absent. While all the appurtenances of variety are present, life is monotonous in the sense that it is steadily gregarious, focussed on others, and on the self in relation to others. As I have observed among some students, at Harvard and elsewhere, even casualness can be an effortful artifact.

Yet it is all too easy to deride these parents and children and assorted experts, to urge them—as some people are now doing in the anti-progressive education movement—to drop all this new-fangled nonsense and get back to hard work and traditional curricula and nineteenth-century or classical "values" generally. It is perhaps not surprising that both aristocratic and working-class stances towards leisure combine in this derision. When, for example, this suburban community was recently discussed in my seminar on leisure, many people, both faculty and students, took the position that what these suburbanites needed was more direct and uninhibited aggression, more toughness and less talkiness. They compared the community unfavorably to a working-class community where, for reasons I indicated a moment ago, leisure is undoubtedly more casually dealt with. What they admired was aristocratic or artisan insouciance, as against upper-middle-class anxiety and preoccupation. Yet I do not know by what standard of value one prefers a broken nose to asthma, or lumbago or gout to ulcers. There is no doubt that the suburb in question, and others like it, is anxious and vulnerable, individually and collectively; otherwise, it would not be quite so receptive to a team of researchers. But I think that overadmiration for toughness is part of a romance which the middle class, in Europe as well as in America, has been carrying on with the lower class for a good many years now. Like the romance which many anthropologists have been carrying on with preliterate tribes, or many historians and philosophers and literary men with the Middle Ages, it narrows our sympathy for the problems of contemporary life and our awareness of the values which may, underneath anxiety and awkwardness, currently be emerging in it.

Thus I think we can look at the people of this suburb rather differently from the way I have been doing so far, or from the way my seminar reacted to them. We can see them, for one thing, as explorers. Whereas the explorers of the last century moved to the frontiers of production and opened fisheries, mines, and mills, the explorers of this century seem to me increasingly to be moving to the frontiers of consumption. They are opening up new forms of interpersonal understanding, new ways of using the home as a "plant" for leisure, new ways of using the school as a kind of community center, as the chapel of a secular religion perhaps. But frontier towns are not usually very attractive. And frontier behavior is awkward: people have not yet learned to behave comfortably in the new surroundings. There is formlessness, which takes the shape of lawlessness on the frontier of production and of aimlessness on the frontier of consumption. In both instances, the solid citizens who stayed home are likely to feel superior, both to the formlessness and to whatever may be emerging from it, just as most Europeans of the educated strata have felt superior to most aspects of America throughout most of our history. The move to the suburb, as it occurs in contemporary America, is emotionally, if not geographically, something almost unprecedented historically; and those who move to any new frontier are likely to pay a price, in loneliness and discomfort. When the physical hardships are great, as they were for earlier generations of pioneers, the psychological hardships may be repressed or submerged—though we cannot be too sure even of that, for, as Oscar Handlin makes clear in his book on immigration to America, *The Uprooted*, the most devastating strains on the newcomers were in fact the emotional ones, rough though the physical conditions were.

To carry my analogy further, I do believe that discoveries are being made on the frontiers of consumption. Take the American diet, for instance. Once upon a time, and still in many quarters, this was in charge of the nutritionists, the exponents of a balanced meal, adequate caloric intact and colonic outlet, and plenty of vitamins. These good people bore the same relation to food that recreationists do to leisure: they want it to be uplifting, salubrious, wasteless. But now, among the better income strata at any rate, their work is done: it is incorporated into the formulae of bakers, into the inventories of chainstores, the menus of restaurants, and dining cars. We have, as I sometimes like to put it, moved from the wheat bowl to the salad bowl. In consequence, in the suburb I have been describing, and elsewhere throughout the country, there is an emphasis, which was once confined to small sophisticated or expatriate circles, on having the right responses to food, on being a gourmet. Save for a few cranks, the housewives are not concerned with having enough wheat-germ, but with having enough oregano, or the right wine—and more than that, with having the right enjoyment of the wine. In the middle of the shopping center in this suburb is a store which stocks a stupendous array of delicacies, spices, patisseries, delicatessen, and European gadgets for cooking; the casserole replacing the melting pot!

Now, as I have indicated, the residents of this suburb are anxious about food and their attitudes towards it. They want to be knowledgeable about it and also to enjoy it, but they are not yet easygoing in the matter. Among men particularly, the demand that one must enjoy food, and not simply stow it away, is relatively new, and again these pioneers are awkwardly self-conscious. (Let me make clear in passing that I am not talking about old-fashioned conspicuous consumption. I am not talking about the hostess' fear of making a gastronomic *faux pas*, or fear that her children's table manners will disgrace her; no doubt these fears may still exist, although greatly muted, in the group I am describing. No, these parents are afraid that they are missing some taste experience, which in turn reveals the lack of a basic personality attribute.) We are observing these families, it appears, in a time of transition, when they have left old food-conventions behind and are exploring, without settling on, new ones. They are, in effect, paying the society's costs of research and development.

And can there be any doubt but that the result will be—in fact, has already been—an addition to the stock of American leisure bounties and benefits? The self-service supermarket, with its abundance of foods capably displayed, where the shopper's caprice and imagination can roam without interference from officious clerks or sabotage from indifferent ones, seems to me as significant an invention on the side of consumption as the assembly line on the side of production. But the invention would be meaningless without a "labor force," without a group of experimentalist families prepared to develop new casuistries of food, new combinations of color and taste. And here enters still another service industry: the cookbook and recipe industry, which has ransacked the world's cuisines and produced a host of books and newspaper columns, as well as those restaurants which serve as pilot plants. I think there can be no doubt that the children of the children now growing up in our demonstration suburb will be reasonably free of fears, guilts, and awkwardness about food prepared as a matter of course for the pursuit of happiness in this area of existence. In fact, I see only one caveat: the return of the nutritionist ghost in the craze for reducing, which makes not only women but men choose between food and figure, with one eye on mortality tables and the other on the way one appears in the hall of mirrors which is society. Even so, the reduced diets on which these figure-chasers bravely live are, item for item, unquestionably superior to anything known before in the American provender—which a generation ago made our food, like our bootlegging, an international joke. Moreover, the cult of one's figure, as of one's dress and one's coiffure, is certainly not an illegitimate one for one's happiness and aesthetic sense.

I could, if there were space, go through a number of areas of current pioneering in leisure—in the fields of music, painting, and literature; in the whole subtle field of sociability and conversation; in sports; in the changing style of vacations—and show how the pioneers are paying in financial and emotional outlay, and particularly in anxiety, the exploitation costs of their discoveries—without, however, the offset of the depletion allowance which the federal government allows to the wildcatters for oil and gas. I have already raised the question of whether our intellectual and literary culture is not too severe and derisive about the middle-class vice of anxiousness, compared with its benign tolerance for the aristocratic and lower-class vices of brutality and indifference. Such very general questions of value judgment are of great importance in determining contemporary attitudes towards leisure. I think, for example, that we make life and leisure harder for the already anxious person—whose anxiety is in fact thoroughly understandable in the light of our discussion so far—by making him also anxious about his anxiety, so that we heap on him a cumulative burden. Like the college student who came to see me not long ago, worried because she had a few of the sexual inhibitions she would have been worried about not having a generation ago, teachers also feel it compulsory not to be anxious, but to be always easygoing, warm, and relaxed—what a burden this puts on teachers in the better public and private schools! —whereas lack of discipline and firmness would have worried teachers in an earlier day. I am inclined to think we should form a union of the anxious ones, to defend our right to be anxious, our right to be tense, our right to aspirin and to our allergies. I was shocked when one of my colleagues remarked, after our seminar had had a description of life in the suburb I have here used as a case, that children were worse off there than they had been under the *ancien regime*. Historical amnesia had blinded him, as it blinds many now-fashionable critics of progressive education, to the brutalities and savageries in the treatment of children a hundred years or so ago. Then children were harnessed to the engine of society with often little concern for their own development. Many were too frightened or too cowed to be anxious; anxiety is on the whole a luxury and a sign of luxury. I urged my condescending colleague to read some nineteenth century memoirs, to read *Father and Son,* Edmund Gosse's recollections of his awed and prayer-filled but rarely playful childhood; to read *The Way of All Flesh,* or Dickens, or the reports of health commissioners.[1] I have myself no doubt that the work of such reformers as Ellen Key ("The Century of the Child"), Lucy Sprague Mitchell and of course John Dewey, has been a very great advance.

[1] Stephen Spender's remarkable novel, *The Backward Son,* and George Orwell's account of his schooldays, "Such, Such Were the Joys" (which appeared in *Partisan Review* since the above was written), can remind us that even a generation ago the English public school could still treat the sensitive young with ferocious bullying. Likewise, the fictional hero of Salinger's *Catcher in the Rye* might have profited from some of the humaneness and sensitivity introduced by the now maligned progressivists.

THE NEGRO IN SOCIETY

What is the state of Negro life in American society? The previous section presented material on the changes that have taken place in the large metropolitan areas. Several of the selections commented on segregation, education in depressed areas, and the growing separation between the central city and the suburban districts. But these articles were not primarily focused on the various social forces which are directly involved in the segregation issue.

The articles in this chapter were chosen because they present clear and direct discussions of the conditions of Negro life in America. These conditions have promoted segregation, personal alienation, and a deep separation between the language of democracy and the reality of social, educational, and economic opportunity for the Negro citizen.

What alternatives other than the present state of separate and unequal treatment are available to the society and the educational system? What seem to be the implications for the schools of the contemporary development of the concept of "Black Power"? How has the introduction of Black Power altered the sociology of politics and thus of the schools?

The Threat of Violence

The theme of the introductory article is that two major problems in American society may seriously threaten the future of the democratic state. First is the historic and continued denial of freedom to the Negro in American society. Second, modern technology is creating a vast amount of chronic unemployment and poverty which will continue to grow unless large-scale social and economic changes are undertaken. These two conditions are viewed as interrelated in that the Negro suffers most heavily from unemployment and discriminatory practices.

If the feelings of alienation and resentment resulting from these conditions are not checked, America will find itself enmeshed in a vicious cycle of violence. How can this tendency toward violence be stemmed? Are the schools an answer to the problem? Do the schools foster attitudes of violence? Is it possible for the school to provide outlets for aggressive behavior which will transfer to the society? How can the schools compensate for the lack of equality now suffered by Negroes?

The Coming Test of American Democracy

HANS J. MORGENTHAU

What is disquieting in our present condition is the contrast between the gravity of the two great domestic problems that require solutions—race relations and unemployment—and the complacency permeating the thoughts and actions of government and public alike.

After dictating that sentence, I was informed of President Kennedy's assassination. Returning after a week of horror and sorrow, pity and shame to the task of discussing these two issues, I find their timely gravity accentuated, if anything, by the tragedy of dual violence through which we have just passed. Interrelated as they are, these issues threaten American democracy with a dissolution of the consensus on which it rests; and if that consensus should ever be dissolved, violence must replace it. Violence from below, actual or threatened, would call forth violence from above, or vice versa, and American democracy would transform itself—in all probability imperceptibly and gradually rather than in one glaring breakdown of constitutional processes—into a police state. This alternative to government by consent of the governed is inescapable; for government must rest on one of two foundations: either consent or violence.

The unequal condition of the American Negro has been an endemic denial of the purpose for which the United States of America was created and which, in aspiration and partial fulfillment, has remained the distinctive characteristic of our society: equality in freedom. That unequal condition has been, in Jefferson's words, "a moral reproach," a "condition of moral and political reprobation." The first step toward eliminating this evil and complying with the American purpose was taken a hundred years ago with the emancipation of the slaves. We have tended, in view of the present unequal condition of the Negro, to underrate the practical importance of that emancipation and to look upon it as a mere change in legal status which had only a small effect on the actual conditions of life. But we should remind ourselves that a slave was a piece of property, like

Reprinted from Commentary, Vol. 37, No. 1, January, 1964, pp. 61–63, by permission; copyright © 1964 by the American Jewish Committee.

a chicken or a chair, without any attributes of legal personality. He could not marry and had no right to his children. He had no rights in court and was devoid of all other legal protection: he was, like a dog, subject to the master's punishment. In most slave states it was a criminal offense to teach slaves how to read and write. Thus, in order to assess correctly the present status of the Negro in America, it is necessary to compare that status not only with the ideal of equality in freedom, but also with the status of slavery of a century ago. Emancipation transformed the Negro from a thing into a man—a precondition not only for what he has achieved and can hope to achieve in the future, but also for awareness of himself, of what he is and can become.

The problem which American society faced a century ago in the form of slavery posed itself in quite different and much simpler terms than does the issue of segregation today. On the legal plane, solution of the problem of slavery required only a single act: the Emancipation Proclamation. On the level of actual enforcement, the task was first to contain slavery within a circumscribed territory and then to eliminate it altogether through a victorious war. By contrast, the problem which faces us today in the form of segregation cannot be solved by legal enactment, even though legal enactment is a precondition for its solution. The Supreme Court decision of 1954 declaring segregation in public schools unconstitutional, by itself made hardly a dent in actual segregation. After a protracted period of perfunctory compliance and widespread defiance and evasion, it was the spontaneous initiative of the people themselves, Negro and white alike, supported by the full powers of the federal government, which started to compel real compliance with the Supreme Court decision as well as with the principle of integration in other fields of social interaction.

Furthermore, and most importantly, the problem of segregation is not geographically localized, as was the problem of slavery, even though it is posed in certain Southern states in different terms than elsewhere. In consequence, segregation cannot be contained and sealed off, as was slavery. Slavery was a localized cancer which could be cut out; segregation is a metastasized cancer to be treated by more complex and uncertain means. There are no segregationist and integrationist states, as there were slave and abolitionist states. All states of the Union are segregationist in different degrees, with regard to different activities, and by virtue, or in spite, of different legal arrangements. Even where the law requires integration in all fields of social interaction, segregation is still a social fact.

It is a fact, moreover, which is all-pervasive and resistant to change; by no means does it apply to Negroes alone. Less than thirty years ago I had to deal with American consuls who considered it their patriotic duty to violate the law in order to prevent the immigration of Jews, and once I was here, I could not find a place to sleep in the White Mountains of New Hampshire until I registered under my wife's maiden name. Less than twenty years ago I could not get service at the Dartmouth Inn in Hanover,

New Hampshire. And even today Jews, like Negroes, are barred from owning property in one of the best residential districts in Washington, D.C.
Thus segregation is a general social phenomenon, nourished by social
myths, fear of what is different, actual social differences, and incompatible
interests, real or fancied. These factors on which segregation thrives are as
such impervious to legislation, although legislation can provide levers with
which to contain and weaken them through the application of irresistible
pressure.

In the face of the foreseeable persistence of segregation as a social fact,
the Negroes of America have at their disposal four courses of action: passive acceptance of a slightly improved status quo; peaceful agitation and
pressure; alienation; violence. In view of the high hopes which are being
placed upon the practical consequences of legislative enactments, especially
on the economic plane, militant alienation and violence—and alienation
ultimately means violence, too—are bound to attract large masses of
Negroes. Violence, since it cannot organize itself against a rational political
objective, is bound to appear as anarchy, a completely unmanageable
breakdown of law and order. No less real for not being deemed fit to print
stories about, that anarchic violence already terrorizes many of our streets
and schools. I have been told that in one Chicago school in one week of
November 1963, more than twenty students were attacked by fellow students with deadly weapons, one teacher was hit on the head with a bottle
by a student, and one teacher was raped. The student who hit the teacher
was only suspended for three days by a frightened school administration,
whereupon her father went to school to complain about the treatment his
daughter had received!

Such violence, spreading unchecked, is bound to call forth counter-vio-
lence by those who feel themselves threatened. While the progress the
Negroes are likely to make in their actual conditions of life will be too small
to integrate them into the main body of American society, and hence meet
their aspirations, it will be significant enough to threaten, or at least appear
to threaten, the social position of masses of white members of the lower
middle class. This problem is being aggravated by the large-scale migration
of Southern Negroes to the North; the Negro population of Mississippi, for
instance, has decreased from 51 percent of the total in 1950 to 42 percent
in 1960 and 36 percent in 1963. Here will be an additional incentive to the
kind of violence that has traditionally been employed by a low stratum of
American society that feels itself threatened by a still lower but rising one.
We have had a foretaste of things to come in the protracted violence (inadequately reported or not reported at all) which has accompanied or
prevented the attempts of Negroes to move into white neighborhoods.
Thus we are facing the prospect of a three-cornered relation of violence:
the Negro against the government, the white lower middle class against
the Negro, and the government against both.

This prospect will be gravely accentuated by the persistence and the probable spread of unemployment. The permanent unemployment we have been unable thus far to cope with is different in nature from the mass unemployment of the 30's. The latter was the result of a temporary maladjustment, a consequence of the natural fluctuations of the business cycle, to be remedied by the techniques of Keynesian economics. The unemployment of our day is the result of structural defects due to technological innovations, to be cured only by radical structural changes.

Technological innovations have affected the structure of our economic system in three different respects. Automation is replacing human labor with machines; machines are making unskilled labor permanently unemployable and are assigning to skilled labor an ever more limited scope; and machines are increasing productivity far beyond the ability of a market economy to consume. In consequence, an enormous and ever expanding productive apparatus and the ever shrinking segment of the population profiting from it find themselves face to face with an ever increasing segment of the population permanently severed from the productive processes and kept on a level of bare subsistence only through the benevolent intervention of the state.

Both economic theory and economic practice have been helpless in confronting the gap which technology is opening up between a productive majority and a permanently unemployable new proletariat, which may well become a majority tomorrow. What is needed to close that gap is not the half-hearted application of Keynesian remedies, devised for quite different circumstances, but a revolution in our economic thinking and practice commensurate in its magnitude with the changes modern technology has wrought in our economic circumstances. Such a revolution will have to recognize two fundamental facts, one economic, the other moral.

Economically, we are in the process of acquiring a productive capacity which is transforming our economy from one of scarcity into one of abundance. Morally, we have accepted the obligation to provide all citizens with a modicum of economic well-being and security as a precondition for having an equal opportunity to realize their human potentialities in freedom. It is only outmoded economic theory and practice which stand in the way of our using our productive power for this moral end. Once we have overcome this cultural lag by bringing our economic thinking up to date, we will have to subject our economic system and social organization to a radical transformation.

The two great issues with which American democracy must come to terms—equality in freedom for the American Negro and the restoration of a meaningful economic and social order—are thus interconnected. The former cannot be fully achieved, and might even be ultimately jeopardized, without the latter. For even if the Negro were to come into full possession of legal and social equality, he would still be exposed to the disabilities of a contracting labor market. As an unskilled laborer, regardless of discrimination, he is likely to be permanently unemployed. But even as a skilled worker competing without discrimination for ever scarcer jobs, he would still be threatened with unemployment. The resentment of Negroes whose new equality revealed itself as meaningless in economic terms would be a source of alienation from America and an incentive to violence against it. The resentment of the ever swelling mass of white unemployed would be a source of alienation from the political and social status quo and an incentive to violence against both the Negro and the government. One resentment would be pitted against the other, fanning anew the enmity of races and jeopardizing the ability of the government to govern without the continuous use of violence.

The government, thus deprived on a large scale of the consent of the governed, would have to resort to violence in order to be able to govern. It is at this point that the political order of the states of the Deep South acquires a crucial relevance for the future of American democracy. The governments of these states are already deprived of the consent of the governed, for their legitimacy reposes upon the myth of the natural inequality of the races, a myth unacceptable to the politically conscious Negroes and the white moderates alike. Thus these states can only govern by violence, and it makes a difference only for the modalities of application but not for the substance of the case whether that violence is exerted through the instrumentality of a lynch mob, of an unpunished murderer, of arbitrary police brutality, or of an equally arbitrary administration of justice which destroys life and liberty even more effectively than a mob does.

What is worse, this government by violence is not limited to the Deep South, but rules the nation as a whole through the Southern bloc's domination of Congress. The Southern Congressional leaders cannot afford to support the integration of the Negro into American society since their very political power derives from a denial of the Negro's natural equality. And allied as they are with the most feudalistic sector of the American economy, from which the economic sustenance of their power flows, they cannot even contemplate the radical structural changes in our economic system that technology has made necessary; for them an obsolescent Keynes is a symbol of unacceptable radicalism.

Thus we are in the presence of a dual paradox. On the one hand, a minority which governs its territory through violence rather than the democratic consent of the governed is able to thwart the will of the majority of the nation which seeks to enable American society to cope with the problems of race and permanent unemployment. On the other hand, if it succeeds, that minority will make inevitable the extension of its own methods of government by violence to the whole nation. A century ago, slavery was contained and extirpated through civil war. Today, we face the danger that government by violence may engulf the whole nation through the manipulation of the levers of political power by those who once defended slavery and now can govern their own states only through violence.

Who really won the Civil War? The Union has been preserved, but on whose terms? The house that was divided against itself a hundred years ago is still so divided. It still stands but it has begun to wobble. If the explosive mixture of racial discontent and economic deprivation were ever firmly lodged in its foundations, it could be held precariously together only by the cement of violence.

Education as an Agent
in Social Revolution

The next article deals directly with the importance of educational programs for the unemployed, the disadvantaged, and the Negro population. Mr. Lyford presents the argument that the issue is not centrally one of racial discrimination, but rather a broader-based question of unavailable jobs and a lack of adequate educational programs for the alienated youth in our cities. Even if the Negro ghettos and discrimination were eliminated, millions of adolescents would still be faced with the larger problems of unemployment and educational failure. He believes that what is needed is large-scale social and economic planning by the public and private sectors of the economy. In addition, the schools should offer more innovative and specially adapted programs for the vast number of unemployed, out-of-school youth.

How should we decide on the appropriate kind of education for life? Can we succeed in social reform through educational programs? Is there a solution to the dilemma posed here? If education is the "first order of business," why does society resist massive financing and support for the schools?

Proposal for a Revolution

JOSEPH P. LYFORD

PART 1—NEGROES, EDUCATION, AND THE TWO-EDGED SWORD

In the course of his struggle, the Negro has presented Americans with a basic education about themselves. He has demonstrated that the majority of white Americans, in the South and out of it, are in varying degrees violently or silently opposed to the universal application of the Bill of Rights. By interposing his own body he has shown, beyond any reasonable doubt, the inability of the government of the people to guarantee the freedom of all the people or even protect the safety of their persons if they happen to be of an unusual color. The Negro has made it fairly clear that the Protestant churches in America have countenanced the subversion of fundamental Christian principles about as often as they have advanced the idea of human brotherhood.

But the Negro has done a great deal more than expose the contradictions between the actual and professed beliefs of the American citizen. His battle for freedom has established the fact that the Negro cannot win equality of opportunity until American society as a whole develops some way of dealing with the rise of mass unemployment and the growing ineffectiveness of our political and educational system. What we call the "Negro revolution" is a preview of a much bigger crisis to come; it is forcing us to take a closer look at certain extremely unpleasant developments that are going to transform or destroy the traditional institutions and habits of all of us, black and white. If we fully understand the significance of the Negro's present experience, we will realize how great a stake we have in his success. Given the recent past, however, it seems more likely that we will react by building "monstrosities," as Arnold Toynbee calls them. A "monstrosity" is an ugly construction set up by a society to deal with the effects of a problem it is unwilling to solve, current examples being our public welfare program and the proliferation of mental hospitals.

Paradoxically, some Negro leaders do not seem to be fully aware of what they are up against—at least they have not broadened their attack on the problems of the Negro. They continue to concentrate almost entirely on desegregation, the right to vote, fair employment practices, and the

Reprinted from *Saturday Review*, October 19, 1963, pp. 19–22, and October 26, 1963, pp. 25–28, by permission of the publisher and the author.

breaking down of all types of racial discrimination. The means of reaching these objectives still seem to be mainly a matter of picketing, protest, pressure, and litigation. Perhaps this is all the civil rights groups are able to do. If so, the Negro badly needs a new type of organization that will work on his more general problems. Negro leaders and their white allies may win battle after battle for Constitutional rights only to find that these rights have little practical meaning for the majority of American Negroes under present conditions. The entry of a pair of Negro children into an all-white Birmingham school is an important victory for a fundamental principle, but it carries no immediate hope for Negro children, who will continue to starve to death educationally in the still-segregated schools of the South and hundreds of thousands more who are overcrowding classrooms in the slum-area schools of the North. Forcing open a Jim Crow construction union in New York City to a handful of Negro apprentices is a step forward for decency, yet it has almost no bearing on the employment prospects of hundreds of thousands of teen-agers and millions of adults—white and Negro—who are sinking to the bottom of a society that may very well have 14,000,000 unemployed by 1970. A clean sweep of housing discrimination will not wipe out a single slum or ghetto. The Negro who cries "now" is having to face these facts.

The white man has to face these facts, too. If he thinks very much about joblessness and the state of our educational system, it must occur to him that the Negro is struggling against forces that are undermining white society as well. The Negro has begun to react before anyone else because, being economically in the most exposed position, he is far more sensitive to the shock signals that are traveling through the country. But there should be no assumption on anybody's part that his fate can be divided from the rest of America's. If the Negro does not prevail over the forces that are driving him downward, the white American will go down with him. The issue is the survival of an entire people whose basic educational, political, and economic arrangements are on the verge of breaking down.

It is now just about official that mass unemployment can be added to death and taxes as an inevitable part of the American way of life. Like most inevitable things, they are also totally mysterious. Ed Lahey, an irreverent Washington reporter who has spent most of his time poking into economic riddles, says that there are only three people—he declines to name them—who can understand our tax laws. There is almost as much confusion about unemployment and what it is about to do to us. Our ignorance is becoming more and more apparent at the very moment automation is wiping out 200,000 jobs annually in factories alone and we are trying to figure out what to do about the demands of the Negro for fair and adequate employment.

The most ominous fact about our attitude on unemployment is not that we have failed to discover a solution. It is that we have been unable to come to any sort of agreement in Congress, industry, or labor about what we are dealing with. We have not made the essential connection between unemployment and the breakdown of our system of public education. We have not accepted the fact that the Negro cannot become a part of American society until we find some answer to unemployment. We have not even decided whether 5,000,000 unemployed and 35,000,000 more underemployed are the result of gross economic mismanagement or whether mass idleness is an integral part of a new economic system based on a technological revolution.

Our reaction to the spread of unemployment bears some resemblance to the psychological paralysis that attacks us when we consider the threat of war. In both situations we face problems that have been with us so long they seem permanent, and permanent problems easily become incurable diseases. So, as Jerome Frank has said, we pretend that the diseases don't exist and transfer our attention to such matters as moon shots and the decline of British morality.

While we have postponed a persistent and scientific examination of unemployment, our ignorance has increased as the crisis has worsened. An investigation into the various devices we use to measure unemployment reveals that we have only a cloudy notion of how many people are out of work. Generally accepted estimates tend to understate the problem, partly because unemployment figures are a political issue filtered through governmental agencies and partly because we have no psychological tests to use on people to find out whether they can work, want to work, and have looked for work. Our detection devices are also unreliable: there are thousands of drifting, anonymous people who have become so isolated from American society that they are invisible even to the census-taker. We have only the sketchiest impressions about the attitudes of the unemployed —Negro and white, young and old—toward their situation and a society that finds no practical use for their services. Yet these attitudes may very well cause a major political upheaval if they continue to ferment.

We are also in the dark about the capacities and potentialities of our unemployed and the many millions of others who inhabit the impoverished "other America" described by Michael Harrington. For example, last year the President's Council of Economic Advisers reported that racial bias has prevented us from utilizing the existing or potential skills of the Negro and that the annual loss to the country is between $13 and $17 billion a year. But discrimination is only one cause of our failure to use manpower efficiently. A random sample of the relatively few job-training programs now in effect indicates that we do not know how to find out what people can do, regardless of what color they are, or how to train them or what to train them for.

Without necessarily saying so, we generally assume that when a man is out of work it is because he is lazy or because there is nothing useful he can do. We feel that because the Negro has always been at the bottom of the educational ladder (69 percent of the Negroes in New York City have not finished high school), it is natural for him to end up on welfare and spend the rest of his life looking for odd jobs. At the same time we ignore the fact that 61.6 percent of whites in the same city also do not have a high school diploma but are twice as successful in earning a living. Our thinking about unemployment is largely speculation; and in all of our speculation there is the more or less subconscious conclusion that the middle-aged Negro, the Kentucky miner in the Cumberlands, the aging migrant worker are, economically speaking, multiple amputees who will have to be written off or absorbed into some sort of relief program. We then turn our attention to the children and hold sporadic discussions about saving them from their parents' fate, thereby entering a new realm of misconceptions about a new generation. Our approach to all the above-mentioned matters is fitful, disorganized, and superficial.

Certainly there is little evidence that our political and governmental officials, our labor unions, management, or individual economists have done much more than throw up their hands, blame automation for reducing us to a state of inactivity, and say, "That's life. It's the price of progress." We accept the inevitability of mass unemployment and propose five-hour weeks and salaries for everybody, or we make a few experimental doodles with retraining programs we know are either unworkable or prohibitively expensive and tinker with our educational system in the hope it will get around to producing repairmen for a world of pushbuttons, electronic brains, and dial systems. Beyond this, there is almost nothing. Since glaciers are not melted by cigarette lighters, the freezing process continues.

We cannot afford to resign ourselves to the situation, and there is no need to. We have been given an opportunity by our improved technology to concentrate fully on some of the really important business of living for the first time in our history. In order to get at this business, we need to recognize that it is legitimate and important even though it pays no profits to stockholders or management. We are going to have to junk traditional attitudes about what constitutes the proper business of government before anything of importance happens in the attack on unemployment. We have to redefine the meaning of urgent and necessary work to include jobs that promote the general welfare even to the exclusion of private profit. We are going to have to get rid of political, business, and labor leadership that says—although it doesn't believe what it says—that government has no role to play in the economic sphere except to act as an umpire for private quarrels and create regulatory bodies that regulate nothing but the critics. Unemployment is a massive problem, with massive effects on our future and it will not yield to anything but a massive attack. The direction of this attack, since it has not and cannot be assumed by labor and business, should be undertaken by government.

The private areas of our economy should be cooperating partners in the attack, if not voluntarily then under duress. It has always been fashionable to protest against government compulsion but there will be compulsion from somewhere even if it does not come from government. We already have had innumerable demonstrations of such compulsion; the government's intervention in the rail situation, with the support of U.S. industry, is only the most recent example. If unemployment continues to grow, there will be other, far more explosive pressures compelling us to act. The discontent of those people for whom our republic indicates it has no use will be more than economic. Robert Weaver writes that, for the first time in our history, we now have "class" unemployment. The discontent will be class discontent, and circulating through it will be the inflammable antagonisms between the Negro who finds himself the most expendable part of the system we still refer to as free, private enterprise, and the unemployed white with whom he is competing for dwindling job opportunities.

What is the important business of America that remains to be done, now that we have buttons and levers handling the garbage and ready-to-make automobiles? The first order of business is education. This is a process in which every American can participate, whether as a teacher, a student, a bricklayer, a parent, or a taxpayer. It is a business which up to now has been regarded chiefly as an annoying and expensive sacrifice of public funds. When one compares the magnitude of the need for a broadened program of public education with the size of our commitment, it is fair to say that we are still living in the pre-education phase of American history. Walter Lippmann has pointed out that in 1900 the U.S. government spent $1 for education to every $2 for other purposes, while more than fifty years later we are spending $1 out of every $6, despite the fact that the importance and complexity of education are greater today than ever before.

The old squabbles over infinitesimal financial increases in our educational commitment and the eventual adoption of some token federal aid to education and a few $5-a-week raises for teachers have no relevance anymore. We will have to expand our educational coverage to the point at which every educable person will receive a high school diploma. This means raising the limit for compulsory school attendance from sixteen to eighteen. At the same time we have to intensify the educational experience of the individual pupil, not to the point at which all our class sizes are below thirty children, but to the point at which the ratio of teachers to pupils is one to fifteen, or even less, and where special services are available to children who start their education with severe economic, psychological, or cultural handicaps. A revolutionary expansion of our public education program to three or four times its present level can be financed once we have accepted its necessity. We have been able to mobilize far greater amounts for the construction of weapons and the subsidy of weapon makers and their shareholders. At this point, more and better education is more important to our national security than bigger and cleaner bombs. An uneducated, unemployable population is becoming the greatest threat to our national equilibrium. Education must become one of America's major occupations in the years ahead.

Underlying any expansion of our educational system must be a philosophy of education that meets the needs of the people in it to achieve an independent position in adult life and to distinguish between sentimental fairy tales about America and current realities. Such an educational philosophy would enable us to produce people who could read, write, understand arithmetic, have ideas, and who would be emancipated from the sort of tribal attitudes that have turned Birmingham, Alabama, into a fratricidal society. It would also help produce a nation that can improve itself and anticipate change instead of simply starting violently whenever something jolts the status quo. It would help generate a social and political atmosphere in which people consider technological and social and political changes as promises or opportunities instead of "menaces," "threats," and "impending catastrophes." We would gradually condition ourselves to the point where we would shed our old skins as soon as they ceased to fit, instead of enduring them until the itching drove us crazy.

We might recognize more generally the fact that the misuse or disuse of human beings is caused by miscalculations and poor education and not by immutable economic "laws." If we wish to write off the Negro "problem," as it is called, as insoluble because we think Negroes are generally disqualified by lack of education and the attendant lack of incentive, we also have a responsibility to provide an educational system that is able, among other things, to deal with the causes of these misfortunes. If, in contrast, we consider that racial discrimination against Negroes is responsible for a great deal of their joblessness, an educational system should be able to handle that situation, too. If we view somebody without a job as a casualty of a mindless technology, we can set about the task of putting a mind back into the technology.

Apparently the only way of getting Americans to think seriously about education is to frighten them into it. This should not be difficult in the atmosphere of today's Negro discontent. There is no question that racial tensions are eventually going to make life impossible for all of us unless we develop an educational program that enables the Negro to enter our society and the white man to place a high value on his entry. It should be fairly obvious that education is the only method by which we can overcome our institutionalized system of cheating Negroes, halt the growth of a public welfare community, and slow down the emergence of a new group of aliens, the teen-age school dropouts. We are either going to broaden the boundaries of America to include the exiles, or most of us are going to be joining them.

PART 2—THE FIRST ORDER OF BUSINESS

In addition to undermining a feudal social order, the nonviolent movement to desegregate the South has produced some problems for the civil rights movement elsewhere. Northern integration leaders, with a history of association with both the Negro and white communities, reacted defensively to the growth of a dramatic Southern movement based almost entirely on the Negro, especially when it seemed as if Martin Luther King and the other Southern militants might dominate the integration struggle and attract financial support that might otherwise go to the older civil rights groups in the North. Some Northern integration leaders for a while even attempted to discredit King's motives and belittle his efforts. However, the most enduring and unfortunate result of their defensiveness was an apparent decision that they had to compete with King by imitating him, by reconstructing the atmosphere of the Southern revolt in a Northern setting.

The effect of the Northern groups' resolution to be aggressively and spectacularly militant has been that in city after city, from Portland, Oregon, to Boston, civil rights campaigns have often tended to obscure or ignore the major problems of the Northern Negro and the causes of his special difficulties. Demonstrations seem to have been based mainly on the assumption that for every injustice there is a guilty party and that once the culprits are disposed of, the problem is solved. The assumption is far more realistic in Mississippi than it is in New York City, but it explains why civil rights groups have freely charged that the educational problems of the city's Negroes are mainly the result of a Board of Education that is deliberately segregating the school system along racial lines. Pinning the blame on someone for a situation may make it easier to organize a picket line and issue releases, but in many cases the operation has turned out to be a waste of time and energy that might have been spent on developing workable programs to get the urban Negro out of the slum, into the job, and onto a voting list.

Picketing, protest, and pressure are obviously necessary to the civil rights movement. Direct action should certainly not be de-emphasized, but it could be applied more selectively so that well-meaning people are not sent out to lie down on highways because a city's park department hasn't hired enough Negroes. In both South and North the demonstrations have, in somewhat different ways, spearheaded the drive for racial justice. Aimed at the construction unions, discriminatory landlords and employers, and ineffective public officials, direct action has cracked a number of Northern roadblocks to theoretical equality for the Negro. The fact remains that real equality depends on his achieving political and economic power. In the North the biggest and most intractable obstacle to gaining that power is no longer racial discrimination; it is a general crisis of unemployment and a breakdown of our system of public education. This fact explains why, unless conditions are changed, relatively few Negroes have benefited or will benefit in their lifetime from the civil rights victories that are being won. At present the Negro "revolution" is not a revolution at all: it is a limited action carried on within the framework of a stagnating economic and political system that is incapable of letting the Negro live like a free man even when it finally recognizes his right to do so.

What is the Negro's situation today, twelve years after the Supreme Court's ruling on school desegregation? For one thing, he is steadily losing ground to the white man in terms of annual income. In 1950 the average Negro family income was $1,519 less than the white, while in 1961 the gap had increased to $2,662. More than 75 percent of Negro families earn less than the $5,981 average annual income of whites, and 60 percent of Negro families earn less than $4,000 per year. Employment prospects of Negroes are declining at an accelerating rate because of educational difficulties and the spread of automation. Factory and service jobs, the Negro's chief source of employment, are being automated out of existence at rates estimated to be anywhere from 17,000 to 40,000 a week. Despite token integration of the schools in the South and a slowly growing awareness of the Negro's educational needs in the North, the school system in which most Negro children are caught is just about as inadequate and black as it was before "separate but equal" schools were called unconstitutional. The probability is that the schools are even worse, because of the increasing shortage of classrooms and teachers, and the growth in school population.

A particularly disturbing development is the growth of an enormous colony of unemployed adolescents in our large cities. Thomas J. Watson, chairman of the board of International Business Machines, gives this thumbnail sketch of the problem:

The United States today [1963] has 800,000 teen-agers out of school and out of work—a number approximately equal to the population of San Francisco. Many of these are Negroes, who, in addition to youth and lack of skill, have the further burden of racial discrimination to bear in their search for work—a burden which helps make their rate of joblessness double the national average.

To continue this kind of discrimination is eventually to invite violence, such as we have witnessed in Birmingham and Nashville, and not only in the cities of the South, but in the slums of the North. And to continue to permit unemployment to grow among all teen-agers is to risk disillusionment at best and an explosion of violence at worst. If present trends continue, by 1970 the United States will have in its cities more than a million and a half young people untrained, unemployed, and frustrated to the point of danger. This fact constitutes an indictment of our society—we have somehow failed in our educational responsibilities.

There are other ominous facts. Unemployment, poor education, and hopelessness have seriously interfered with efforts to activate the Negro politically. The *Wall Street Journal* recently reported that Southern integration leaders feel that voter registration drives are having almost as much trouble with Negro apathy as they are with institutionalized white resistance. The problem is not confined to the South. A confidential study of Negroes in an Eastern state, made by John Kraft, Inc., one of the country's leading public opinion research organizations, has found that at least 30 percent are not registered and that 50 percent will probably not vote in the next national election. The finding is especially significant since half of the Negroes in the sample have incomes of more than $5,000, as compared to a national average for Negroes of $3,000. In New York City it is estimated that as many as half a million Negroes who are eligible to vote do not do so. The problem, of course, only begins with apathy. Even when the Negro does register and vote, South or North, he is forced to choose between two parties that have shown either a remarkable indifference to him or downright hostility.

It would seem from all this that the Negro in the black Northern slum needs a new kind of leadership that will stand much closer to him than his traditional leadership has done, and broaden the attack on the immediate causes of his discontents and frustrations. He needs a leadership that will work out a national policy on education, a national policy for rehabilitating our economy, and a national political program to force changes in the structure and standards of both political parties. If the Negro is ever to live like a free man, it is time to turn the rebellion into a revolution and open up a second front in his war of independence.

The most likely place to broaden the attack is in education. What are some of the needs here? More and more emphasis should be placed on guidance in and out of school to create greater incentive and motivation among teenagers so that they would do more than simply inhabit schoolrooms until discharged. Guidance should also attempt to give the student a far better idea about the special paths open to him. More should be done to provide him with information about specific career opportunities and where and how he could obtain financial support for post-high school education and prepare himself for these careers.

Our emphasis on vocational training programs in the high schools themselves should not be increased; if anything, it should be de-emphasized in order to concentrate much more heavily on the general intellectual development of the child and on his reading, writing, and mathematical skills. The miserable failure of so many job-training programs out of school can be directly traced to the trainees' inability to read and write. Expansion of guidance work should supplement the general curriculum, and should give additional meaning and hope to the child whose economic background is such that he is constantly laboring against pressures to become a drop-out.

Perhaps the greatest educational need is more intensive and specialized reading programs both in and out of schools. There are some developments taking place rather quietly in this area of education that may suggest new ways of helping the Negro child of the slums to help himself. The Northern Student Movement, originally organized at Yale, has put hundreds of college undergraduates into the slums of Detroit, Chicago, and New York, where they have set up reading centers for Negro children, during both the regular school year and the summer vacation. Last summer [1962] 200 of the students worked in Harlem. The Associated Community Teams, a federally sponsored Domestic Peace Corps group, is also giving Negro children extra educational training with success. A reading center for dropouts established by the government's Mobilization for Youth on the Lower East Side of New York has enabled many teenagers to achieve the reading skills necessary to get a job. The New York City Board of Education has announced that it will establish 232 after-school reading centers to supplement the regular school programs of the slum areas.

The federal government ought to do far more to extend the educational life of the child in the school system. It could initiate a national program to encourage young people to prepare themselves after high school for elementary and secondary school teaching, nursing, social work, and government service, and for advanced training for science, law, medicine, and university teaching. The government is justified in making a serious financial investment in an educational program for these professions because it would not only open up employment opportunities to people who otherwise will end up looking for nonexistent factory or white-collar jobs, but it would also provide badly needed trained personnel. It should also be pointed out that a shortage of highly trained persons is one of the main obstructions to an increase in our economic growth. There is no reason why, through a system of free tuition and scholarships for teachers, nurses, and social workers, for instance, the government shouldn't emulate our largest corporations, most of which have their own job-training programs. Such programs would have the advantage that, unlike the advanced professions of law and medicine, the student would not necessarily need to take graduate work after college. If a training program were available to the Negro teenagers in New York City, for example, and there were sufficient personnel who could maintain their interest in education, it would be possible to direct large numbers of them into "community service professions." In my interviews with Negro teenagers, I have found that many of them are thinking of these professions as a preferred career, rather than employment in a factory, in business, or in trades. It might be pointed out that the period of post-high school training for the "community service" professions would be nowhere as long as the apprenticeship training periods in most trade unions.

A proposal for a new type of federally backed job training program, supported by an argument that might even interest Harry Byrd, has been advanced by James S. Coleman of Johns Hopkins. Pointing out that two-thirds of our trainees are preparing for blue-collar occupations where unemployment is getting worse all the time, he recommends the experimental high school for dropouts conducted by Encyclopedia Britannica in Chicago and suggests that the federal government invest in such "educational entrepreneurs" throughout the country. These entrepreneurs would "take the culls of the system and teach to get results (not, as in many high schools at present, merely to maintain discipline)." Mr. Coleman explains:

If paid according to results, with students tested by government examiners, I suspect that capitalist enterprise would produce some remarkable successes. The government, in turn, would not be spending its money unwisely, but would be investing in a profit-making enterprise, since every successful student would mean removing a person from a status of dependence on society, and allowing him to move into a high-demand sector of the economy, where he would pay back in taxes and in contributions to economic growth many times the money invested in him in his youth.

Without attending to education as the first order of business, it is useless to discuss anything else. On the assumption that we do attend to it, what are some of the other areas of necessary and unfinished business? There is the matter of conserving and expanding our natural resources before they are wasted away in the manner we are wasting human beings. The business at hand may return no financial profits to anybody in particular—if properly undertaken it may deprive some people of profits—but it advances the future economic welfare and productive capacity of this nation and means useful employment for hundreds of thousands of Americans. Reforestation, soil conservation, flood control, park and recreation area development, creation of new water resources, the elimination of air, sea, and river pollution, the supervision of private operations in the public domain, and the improvement of agricultural techniques are all areas in which the public interest has had little voice and little effect. Much of the work could be done by people who have become superfluous in those urban areas where factory and service work is declining or disappearing. The establishment of small, racially integrated population centers to carry on this work could be, literally, a new frontier for volunteers who have been stranded in our congested cities without work and without decent housing. There is no reason why America cannot create its own version of the Kibbutz, especially since our technology is making present population patterns obsolete.

The "frontier" would also offer the Negro a chance to break out of the big city—Dr. Martin Luther King's "airtight cage of poverty"—and thereby take the first significant step in becoming integrated with the rest of America. Despite the commotion about integration outside the South, the low-income Negro's mobility in the city has been generally restricted to moving from one slum to another, or into a public housing project. The patterns of "de facto" segregation remain the same. Meanwhile, the concentrations of Negroes and other minority groups in the metropolitan centers intensify and the white populations diminish.

If meaningful integration does not proceed outside the great cities, the possibility exists that the large cities may take on the political coloration of the race as well as of an economic group. The prospect of political confrontations between black cities and white towns and suburbs is not promising for our country, especially when one considers the animosities that already exist between city and "up-State" even without the "poor versus rich" or "black versus white" identification.

Of course any government-sponsored proposals for a large program of work in the public interest will be described as socialistic and statist by a great majority of newspaper editors and the Congressmen who read their papers. What is proposed is aimed at preserving human and natural resources that are currently being destroyed and neglected, and unless we find constructive ways for people to support themselves, we can be sure that an increasing body of Americans, and their children after them, numbering in the millions, may very well become lifelong inhabitants of a "poorhouse state."

For those who wish to be briefed on the benefits a welfare-ridden society brings to our republic, Harry Caudill, an Eastern Kentucky lawyer, offers this description of what has taken place in his part of America:

> In most Kentucky Mountain counties the population is so impoverished that between one-third and two-thirds of the people are on the commodity dole and receive public assistance checks. Thus they are charges of the government and dependent upon the government for their daily bread.
>
> In effect the federal government provides the money and the state and local officials deliver the benefits to the people. Local political machines of immense power and efficiency have been organized by and sustained by almost endless amounts of federal money. With the increase in automation and mechanization additional millions of Americans are likely to be reduced to these tragic circumstances. The question arises as to how well democracy can function when the democratic government becomes the custodian and guardian of a majority of the people in a region.

I think it is probably true, from what I heard in interviews in preparation of a study of a section of the West Side of Manhattan, that there has been a tendency to overestimate the extent to which racial discrimination has lessened the employment opportunities of the low-income Negro. His difficulties in getting work seem to result mainly from the fact that, because of a lack of education and of work skills, he is not able to find job opportunities. His educational disadvantages are multiplied by the fact that technology's impact upon factory and service work, where the majority of Negroes are employed, has been especially severe: the jobs themselves are disappearing. His situation deteriorates at a faster and faster rate as a result. This is not to say that discrimination has not played a great part in depriving him of employment. First, the educational disadvantages he suffers occurred largely because of racial discrimination. Second, there is little question that qualified low-income Negroes are often written off as prospective employees by major business institutions the minute they walk in the door; some New York banks are among the worst offenders. Third, the craft unions have in the past closed, and continue to close, their ranks to Negro apprentices for a variety of reasons, some of which have a racist smell about them. Fourth, the Negro who does present educational and professional qualifications for higher-paying jobs invariably finds it difficult to gain employment in financial institutions, publishing, and many other professional areas. His troubles are increased by the fact that a heavy majority of employment agencies throughout the country discriminate against him, according to a recent survey by the American Jewish Congress.

The fact remains that a large proportion of Negroes cannot get far enough in the hiring process to find out if discriminatory considerations are at work, simply because jobs are getting scarce. Stanley Sheinbaum, an economist on the staff of the Center for the Study of Democratic Institutions, writes:

As long as the general unemployment remains acute, all talk about the race issue is as if in a vacuum. Equality in employment will only be achieved in a full employment situation; we all know how discriminatory the labor unions are, the more so the higher the level of unemployment. Both the union members and their officials will protect their own first, and to hell with the race problem. Therefore, as long as unemployment remains high, the minorities are not going to be able to get a fair shake at jobs. The removal of unemployment is absolutely a necessary condition for the resolution of this aspect of the race issue.

Sheinbaum is also critical of government inactivity. He writes:

There is no sign that either the administration or the Congress is interested in doing anything about the job problem. Only recently the Federal Reserve raised the discount rate to one-half per cent, which will further restrict monetary demand. Even if the President's tax proposal does pass, it is far from sufficient to affect the unemployment problem, which fact is a reflection of the administration's lack of interest in the problem. Certainly the Congress has manifested no concern to the extent of taking action.

The same theme is voiced by Robert Theobald in *Free Men and Free Markets*.

Joe Seldin, labor specialist for the now defunct New York *Herald Tribune* put it this way:

You talk to people in vocational rehabilitation or training guidance and ask: Will these programs solve the problems of youth employment? And they say frankly no, they won't. Obviously the problem of youth employment is a segment of the over-all problem of employment in this country. Nobody really has come up yet with a brilliant answer to the problem of unemployment in this country. The best the President is proposing at the moment is a tax cut, which he says is going to stimulate the economy. Last year he tried to do it with allowances for new machinery, which were supposed to stimulate all kinds of things. There was no demonstrable effect. The people in the field tell you the problem is not going to be solved without some over-all approach to the total economic problem of the country. But even if we did come up with such a total solution to the economic problem of the country, you would still need a counseling and guidance and retraining program to make underprivileged kids in the city of New York employable. If employers were begging for help you would still have to produce kids who can read, you would still have to teach them something about work habits and how to apply for a job in order to get them employed.

Seldin's comment is characteristic of him. A labor reporter, he usually ends by talking about education.

Another important and neglected aspect of unemployment is the state of mind of the people undergoing the experience. It is extremely important to know something about this because, whether their ideas are right or wrong —and in many cases they are based on a lack of understanding—the views of the unemployed are going to have a determining effect on the political, social, and economic climate of this country if unemployment isn't checked. Herbert Harris, the labor historian, thinks that the unemployed may some-day be the biggest voting bloc in the country and that they will include not just ex-factory hands but also most of the ex-white collar workers, whom he calls the "Casper Milquetoast isolates." I cannot report generally about the attitudes of the unemployed, but I have conducted many inter-views with unemployed Negroes in my West Side study, and have con-sulted with investigators working in other parts of the city.

One thing that is significant is that the unemployed Negro is resistant to the idea that automation is a major cause of his difficulties. He feels that this is a "dodge" presented by those people in the white power structure of the country to cover up built-in, reflexive hiring practices based on racial bias. He acknowledges the fact that he is handicapped desperately through educational background in a quest for the secure and steady and better-paying jobs, but he doesn't think this explains his difficulties. He has ex-perienced situations in which he has applied over and over for jobs which he knows he can perform—simple unskilled construction jobs, for instance —and he has been told no job is available, only to discover that others who are white have been hired subsequently. His attitude toward unions has been increasingly unfriendly because their apprenticeship programs have been closed to him as a rule and because non-discriminating unions show an indifference to him because of his low earning capacity. He has support for his suspicions even inside union officialdom: a recent publication of the Center for the Study of Democratic Institutions, entitled *Labor Looks at Labor,* quotes United Auto Workers officials as saying that the low-salaried worker and the unemployed worker are neglected by the union movement.

One executive declares, "We have been forgetting the guy way down below, who is really getting kicked in the face. Nobody is doing anything about him except Hoffa." It happens that a great percentage of these "guys down below" are Negroes.

Nor does the Negro feel grateful to the educational system that presumably prepared him for a special trade, when he finds after leaving a vocational high school that he cannot pass the tests to qualify for employment. He compares the obsolete equipment in his vocational school with that used on the outside. He also learns quickly that he has been the victim of obsolete methods of instruction. This experience, plus many others, underlines his distrust of almost all training programs. The Negro who is approached with an offer to retrain for some unseen job reacts with disinterest and cynicism.

A sociologist who has been studying Negro attitudes in the Bedford-Stuyvesant area of Brooklyn offered me this conclusion:

I found little variation between Negroes in their feeling that the common explanations of unemployment are not real as far as Negroes are concerned. I found an alienation, a feeling that the country's unwillingness to get training programs off the ground was due to the fact that the 'wrong group' of people were unemployed. And I am finding, for the first time, a greater degree of unification among Negroes and more of a feeling of disassociation from the body politic than ever before. Sometimes this feeling also hits out at the traditional leadership of the Negro movement, especially if this leadership seems to have come about with white support.

There may be some argument as to how justified these attitudes of the unemployed Negro are. I happen to feel that there is some sophistication in their conclusions because, even though the economic reasoning may be unsound, there is an air of pragmatism in them. Groundless or not, the attitudes are there and they influence action. Perhaps some knowledge of these attitudes and the manner in which they are expressed even to a random interviewer would convince a few Congressmen that the Negro is not inclined to accept any excuses from a society that has left him jobless. He is not going to be permanently counted out of anybody's plans for a future America. Nor are the 40,000,000 or more whites who are also members of our steadily growing and integrated race of the poor. They have the numerical capacity to overturn the American establishment. Whether they will use their power remains to be seen.

The Negro Subculture

The following well-documented article will help the reader to gain an understanding in depth of the Negro's position in American society. It reveals the life condition of the Negro and the psychological problems created by segregation on a nationwide basis. In order to relate these conditions directly to the educational question, the reader should carefully study the selection in the text by Kenneth B. Clark, "Ghetto Schools: Separate and Unequal."

St. Clair Drake describes the social, economic, and political box into which American society has put the Negro. The ghetto-box has many dimensions: a socially unique class system, a ceiling on employment and position within employment, a related disparate income range, sickness and death rates out of line with the rest of the culture, lack of self-concepts, the resulting denial of social, political, or economic power, and an educational system which perpetuates the ills of the past. Each of these factors is treated in this article.

Is the city becoming more ghettoized as a result of suburbanization by whites? If education is a solution to Negro inequality in American society, why can't Negroes with equivalent education obtain equivalent social, economic, and political status with whites? Is there a similar problem in the teaching field in regard to Negro teachers? Are white teachers engaged in a flight to the suburbs?

Folkways and Classways Within the Black Ghetto

ST. CLAIR DRAKE

Black Ghettos in America are, on the whole, "run down" in appearance and overcrowded, and their inhabitants bear the physical and psychological scars of those whose "life chances" are not equal to those of other Americans. Like the European immigrants before them, they inherited the worst housing in the city. Within the past decade, the white "flight to the sub-

Reprinted by permission from *Daedalus*, published by the American Academy of Arts and Sciences, Brookline, Massachusetts. Vol. 94, No. 4, *The Negro American*, Fall, 1965, pp. 777–814.

urbs" has released relatively new and well-kept property on the margins of some of the old Black Belts. Here, "gilded ghettos" have grown up, indistinguishable from any other middle-class neighborhoods except by the color of the residents' skin. The power mower in the yard, the steak grill on the rear lawn, a well-stocked library and equally well-stocked bar in the rumpus room—these mark the homes of well-to-do Negroes living in the more desirable portions of the Black Belt. Many of them would flee to suburbia, too, if housing were available to Negroes there.

But the character of the Black Ghetto is not set by the newer "gilded," not-yet run down portions of it, but by the older sections where unemployment rates are high and the masses of people work with their hands —where the median level of education is just above graduation from grade school and many of the people are likely to be recent migrants from rural areas.

The "ghettoization" of the Negro has resulted in the emergence of a ghetto subculture with a distinctive ethos, most pronounced, perhaps, in Harlem, but recognizable in all Negro neighborhoods. For the average Negro who walks the streets of any American Black Ghetto, the smell of barbecued ribs, fried shrimps, and chicken emanating from numerous restaurants gives olfactory reinforcement to a feeling of "at-homeness." The beat of "gut music" spilling into the street from ubiquitous tavern juke boxes and the sound of tambourines and rich harmony behind the crude folk art on the windows of store-front churches give auditory confirmation to the universal belief that "We Negroes have 'soul.'" The bedlam of an occasional brawl, the shouted obscenities of street corner "foul mouths," and the whine of police sirens break the monotony of waiting for the number that never "falls," the horses that neither win, place, nor show, and the "good job" that never materializes. The insouciant swagger of teen-age drop-outs (the "cats") masks the hurt of their aimless existence and contrasts sharply with the ragged clothing and dejected demeanor of "skid-row" types who have long since stopped trying to keep up appearances and who escape it all by becoming "winoes." The spontaneous vigor of the children who crowd streets and playgrounds (with Cassius Clay, Ernie Banks, the Harlem Globe Trotters, and black stars of stage, screen, and television as their role models) and the cheerful rushing about of adults, free from the occupational pressures of the "white world" in which they work, create an atmosphere of warmth and superficial intimacy which obscures the unpleasant facts of life in the overcrowded rooms behind the doors, the lack of adequate maintenance standards, and the too prevalent vermin and rats.

This is a world whose urban "folkways" the upwardly mobile Negro middle class deplores as a "drag" on "The Race," which the upper classes wince at as an embarassment, and which race leaders point to as proof that Negroes have been victimized. But for the masses of the ghetto dwellers this is a warm and familiar milieu, preferable to the sanitary coldness of middle-class neighborhoods and a counterpart of the communities of the foreign-born, each of which has its own distinctive subcultural flavor. The arguments in the barbershop, the gossip in the beauty parlors, the "jiving" of bar girls and waitresses, the click of poolroom balls, the stomping of feet in the dance halls, the shouting in the churches are all *theirs*—and the white men who run the pawnshops, supermarts, drug stores, and grocery stores, the policemen on horseback, the teachers in blackboard jungles—all these are aliens, conceptualized collectively as "The Man," intruders on the Black Man's 'turf.' When an occasional riot breaks out, "The Man" and his property become targets of aggression upon which pent-up frustrations are vented. When someone during the Harlem riots of 1964 begged the street crowds to go home, the cry came back, "Baby, we *are* home!"

But the inhabitants of the Black Ghetto are not a homogeneous mass. Although, in Marxian terms, nearly all of them are "proletarians," with nothing to sell but their labor, variations in "life style" differentiate them into social classes based more upon differences in education and basic values (crystallized, in part, around occupational differences) than in meaningful differences in income. The American caste-class system has served, over the years, to concentrate the Negro population in the low-income sector of the economy. In 1961, six out of every ten Negro families had an income of less than $4000 per year. This situation among whites was just the reverse: six out of every ten white families had *over* $4000 a year at their disposal. (In the South, eight out of ten Negro families were below the $4000 level.) This is the income gap. Discrimination in employment creates a job ceiling, most Negroes being in blue-collar jobs.

With 60 percent of America's Negro families earning less than $4000 a year, social strata emerge between the upper and lower boundaries of "no earned income" and $4000. Some families live a "middle-class style of life," placing heavy emphasis upon decorous public behavior and general respectability, insisting that their children "get an education" and "make something out of themselves." They prize family stability, and an unwed mother is something much more serious than "just a girl who had an accident"; pre-marital and extra-marital sexual relations, if indulged in at all, must be discreet. Social life is organized around churches and a welter of voluntary associations of all types, and, for women, "the cult of clothes" is so important that fashion shows are a popular fund raising activity even in churches. For both men and women, owning a home and going into business are highly desired goals, the former often being a realistic one, the latter a mere fantasy.

Within the same income range, and not always at the lower margin of it, other families live a "lower-class life-style" being part of the "organized" lower class, while at the lowest income levels an "unorganized" lower class exists whose members tend always to become *dis*organized—functioning in an anomic situation where gambling, excessive drinking, the use of narcotics, and sexual promiscuity are prevalent forms of behavior, and violent interpersonal relations reflect an ethos of suspicion and resentment which suffuses this deviant subculture. It is within this milieu that criminal and semi-criminal activities burgeon.

The "organized" lower class is oriented primarily around churches whose preachers, often semi-literate, exhort them to "be in the 'world' but not of it." Conventional middle-class morality and Pauline Puritanism are preached, although a general attitude of "the spirit is willing but the flesh is weak" prevails except among a minority fully committed to the Pentecostal sects. They boast, "We *live* the life"—a way of life that has been portrayed with great insight by James Baldwin in *Go Tell it on the Mountain* and *The Fire Next Time*.

Young people with talent find wide scope for expressing it in choirs, quartets, and sextets which travel from church to church (often bearing colorful names like The Four Heavenly Trumpets or the Six Singing Stars of Zion) and sometimes traveling from city to city. Such groups channel their aggressions in widely advertised "Battles of Song" and develop their talent in church pageants such as "Heaven Bound" or "Queen Esther" and fund-raising events where winners are crowned King and Queen. These activities provide fun as well as a testing ground for talent. Some lucky young church people eventually find their fortune in the secular world as did singers Sam Cooke and Nat King Cole, while others remain in the church world as nationally known gospel singers or famous evangelists.

Adults as well as young people find satisfaction and prestige in serving as ushers and deacons, "mothers," and deaconesses, Sunday-school teachers and choir leaders. National conventions of Negro denominations and national societies of ushers and gospel singers not only develop a continent-wide nexus of associations within the organized lower class, but also throw the more ambitious and capable individuals into meaningful contact with middle-class church members who operate as role models for those talented persons who seek to move upward. That prestige and sometimes money come so easily in these circles may be a factor militating against a pattern of delaying gratifications and seeking mobility into professional and semi-professional pursuits through higher education.

Lower-class families and institutions are constantly on the move, for in recent years the Negro lower class has suffered from projects to redevelop the inner city. By historic accident, the decision to check the expansion of physical deterioration in metropolitan areas came at a time when Negroes were the main inhabitants of substandard housing. (If urban redevelopment had been necessary sixty years ago immigrants, not Negroes, would have suffered.) In protest against large-scale demolition of areas where they live, Negroes have coined a slogan, "Slum clearance is Negro clearance." They resent the price in terms of the inconvenience thrust upon them in order to redevelop American cities, and the evidence shows that, in some cities, there is no net gain in improved housing after relocation.[1]

At the opposite pole from the Negro lower class in both life styles and life chances is the small Negro upper class whose solid core is a group in the professions, along with well-to-do businessmen who have had some higher education, but including, also, a scattering of individuals who have had college training but do not have a job commensurate with their education. These men and their spouses and children form a cohesive upper-class stratum in most Negro communities. Within this group are individuals who maintain some type of contact—though seldom any social relations—with members of the local white power élite; but whether or not they participate in occupational associations with their white peers depends upon the region of the country in which they live. (It is from this group that Negro "Exhibit A's" are recruited when white liberals are carrying on campaigns to "increase interracial understanding.") They must always think of themselves as symbols of racial advancement as well as individuals, and they often provide the basic leadership at local levels for organizations such as the N.A.A.C.P. and the Urban League. They must lend sympathetic support to the more militant civil rights organizations, too, by financial contributions, if not action.

The life styles of the Negro upper class are similar to those of the white upper *middle* class, but it is only in rare instances that Negroes have been incorporated into the clique and associational life of this group or have intermarried into it. (Their participation in activities of the white upper class occurs more often than with those whites who have similar life styles because of Negro upper-class participation as members of various civic boards and interracial associations to which wealthy white people contribute.) Living "well" with highly developed skills, having enough money to travel, Negroes at this social level do not experience victimization in the same fashion as do the members of the lower class. Their victimization flows primarily from the fact that the social system keeps them "half in and half out," preventing the free and easy contact with their occupational peers which they need; and it often keeps them from making the kind of significant intellectual and social contributions to the national welfare that they might make if they were white. (They are also forced to experience various types of nervous strain and dissipation of energy over petty annoyances and deprivations which only the sensitive and the cultivated feel. Most barbershops, for instance, are not yet desegregated, and taxi drivers, even in the North, sometimes refuse Negro passengers.)

The Negro upper class has created a social world of its own in which a universe of discourse and uniformity of behavior and outlook are maintained by the interaction on national and local levels of members of Negro

[1] The issue of the extent to which Negroes have been victimized by urban redevelopment is discussed briefly by Robert C. Weaver in *The Urban Complex: Human Values in Urban Life,* Doubleday, New York, 1964.

Greek-letter fraternities and sororities, college and alumni associations, professional associations, and civic and social clubs. It is probable that if all caste barriers were dropped, a large proportion of the Negro upper class would welcome complete social integration, and that these all-Negro institutions would be left in the hands of the Negro middle class, as the most capable and sophisticated Negroes moved into the orbit of the general society. Their sense of pride and dignity does not even allow them to imagine such a fate, and they pursue their social activities and play their roles as "race leaders" with little feeling of inferiority or deprivation, but always with a tragic sense of the irony of it all.

The Negro middle class covers a very wide income range, and whatever cohesion it has comes from the network of churches and social clubs to which many of its members devote a great deal of time and money. What sociologists call the Negro middle class is merely a collection of people who have similar life styles and aspirations, whose basic goals are "living well," being "respectable," and not being crude. Middle-class Negroes, by and large, are not concerned about mobility into the Negro upper class or integration with whites. They want their "rights" and "good jobs," as well as enough money to get those goods and services which make life comfortable. They want to expand continuously their level of consumption. But they also desire "decent" schools for their children, and here the degree of victimization experienced by Negroes is most clear and the ambivalence toward policies of change most sharp. Ghetto schools are, on the whole, inferior. In fact, some of the most convincing evidence that residential segregation perpetuates inequality can be found by comparing data on school districts in Northern urban areas where *de facto* school segregation exists.

Awareness of the poor quality of education grew as the protest movement against *de facto* school segregation in the North gathered momentum. But while the fight was going on, doubt about the desirability of forcing the issue was always present within some sections of the broad Negro middle class. Those in opposition asked, "Are we not saying that our teachers can't teach our own children as well as whites can, or that our children can't learn unless they're around whites? Aren't we insulting ourselves?" Those who want to stress Negro history and achievement and to use the schools to build race pride also express doubts about the value of mixed schools. In fact, the desirability of race consciousness and racial solidarity seems to be taken for granted in this stratum, and sometimes there is an expression of contempt for the behavior of whites of their own and lower income levels. In the present period one even occasionally hears a remark such as "Who'd want to be integrated with *those* awful white people?"

Marxist critics would dismiss the whole configuration of Negro folkways and classways as a subculture which reinforces "false consciousness," which prevents Negroes from facing the full extent of their victimization,

TABLE 1

Comparison of White, Integrated and Negro Schools in Chicago: 1962

| | Type of School | | |
Indices of Comparison	White	Integrated	Negro
Total appropriation per pupil	$324.00	$320.00	$269.00
Annual teachers' salary per pupil	256.00	231.00	220.00
Percent uncertified teachers	12.00	23.00	49.00
No. of pupils per classroom	30.95	34.95	46.80
Library resource books per pupil	5.00	3.50	2.50
Expenditures per pupil other than teachers' salaries	86.00	90.00	49.00

Adapted from a table in the U.S. Commission on Civil Rights report, *Public Schools Negro and White*, Washington, D.C., 1962, pp. 241–48.

which keeps them from ever focusing upon what they could be because they are so busy enjoying what they are—or rationalizing their subordination and exclusion. Gunnar Myrdal, in *An American Dilemma*, goes so far as to refer to the Negro community as a "pathological" growth within American society. Some novelists and poets, on the other hand, romanticize it, and some Black Nationalists glorify it. A sober analysis of the civil rights movement would suggest, however, that the striking fact about all levels of the Negro community is the absence of "false consciousness," and the presence of a keen awareness of the extent of their victimization, as well as knowledge of the forces which maintain it. Not lack of knowledge but a sense of powerlessness is the key to the Negro reaction to the caste-class system.

Few Negroes believe that Black Ghettos will disappear within the next two decades despite much talk about "open occupancy" and "freedom of residence." There is an increasing tendency among Negroes to discuss what the quality of life could be within Negro communities as they grow larger and larger. At one extreme this interest slides over into Black Nationalist reactions such as the statement by a Chicago Negro leader who said, "Let all of the white people flee to the suburbs. We'll show them that the Black Man can run the second largest city in America better than the white man. Let them go. If any of them want to come back and integrate with *us* we'll accept them."

It is probable that the Black Belts of America will increase in size rather than decrease during the next decade, for no city seems likely to commit itself to "open occupancy" (although a committee in New York has been discussing a ten-year plan for dismantling Harlem).[2] And even if a race-free market were to appear Negroes would remain segregated unless dras-

[2] A report appeared on the front page of *The New York Times*, April 5, 1965, stating that a commission was at work trying to elaborate plans for "integrating" Harlem by 1975. Columbia University was said to be cooperating in the research aspects of the project.

tic changes took place in the job ceiling and income gap. Controlled integration will probably continue, with a few upper- and upper-middle-class Negroes trickling into the suburbs and into carefully regulated mixed neighborhoods and mixed buildings within the city limits.[3] The basic problem of the next decade will be how to change Black Ghettos into relatively stable and attractive "colored communities." Here the social implications of low incomes become decisive.

SOCIAL IMPLICATIONS OF THE JOB CEILING AND THE INCOME GAP

Nowhere is direct victimization of Negroes more apparent than with respect to the job ceiling and the income gap; but indirect victimization which is a consequence of direct victimization is often less obvious. For instance, it has been mentioned that family incomes for Negroes are lower than for whites; but family income figures are inadequate tools for careful sociological analysis unless we know which, and how many, members of a family labor to earn a given income. In 1960, half of the white families were being supported by a husband only, while just a few more than a third of the Negro families could depend solely upon the earnings of one male breadwinner. In six out of ten nonwhite families where both a husband and wife were present, two or more persons worked; yet less than half of the white families had both husband and wife working. But even in those families which commanded an income of over $7,000 a year, twice as many nonwhite wives had to help earn it as white. One not unimportant consequence is that a smaller proportion of Negro than white wives at this income level can play roles of unpaid volunteers in civic and social work, a fact which should be remembered by those who criticize Negroes in these income brackets for not doing more to "elevate their own people."

One of the most important effects of the income gap and the job ceiling has been the shaping of social class systems within Negro communities which differ markedly in their profiles from those of the surrounding white society. Negro class structure is "pyramidal," with a large lower class, a somewhat smaller middle class, and a tiny upper class (made up of people whose income and occupations would make them only middle class in the white society). White class profiles tend to be "diamond shaped," with small lower and upper classes and a large middle class. Unpromising "life chances" are reflected in inferior "life styles," and Black Ghettos are on the whole "rougher" and exhibit a higher degree of social disorganization than do white communities.

The job ceiling and the income gap do not create classways—for these reflect educational levels and cultural values, as well as the economic situa-

[3] A successful experiment in "controlled integration" has been described by Julia Abrahamson in *A Neighborhood Finds Itself,* Harper & Row, New York, 1959.

tion—but job ceiling and income gap do set the limits for realization of class values. It is a fact of American life (whether one approves of it or not) that as long as Negroes are predominantly lower-class they will, as a group, have low esteem. Yet, Negroes are victimized in the sense that the job ceiling and the income gap make it more difficult for them than for whites to maintain middle-class standards equivalent to those obtaining among whites. A given life style demands a minimum level of income, but it is evident that Negroes are victimized in the sense that their effort as reflected in the acquisition of an education does not bring equal rewards in terms of purchasing power, for they have less to spend than their white counterparts at any given educational level. Nonwhite family heads in 1960 had a smaller median income than whites for every educational level. (See Table 2.)

TABLE 2

*White and Nonwhite Median Family Income by
Educational Level, 1960: U.S.A.*

Amount of Education in Yrs. of School Completed	White	Nonwhite
Elementary School Less than 8 years	$3,656	$2,294
8 years	4,911	3,338
High School—1–3 years	5,882	3,449
4 years	6,370	4,559
College—1–3 years	7,344	5,525
4 or more years	9,315	7,875

In a sense, getting an education "pays off" for Negroes as for all other Americans; but while some individuals "get ahead" of other Negroes, education has not yet raised their earning power to the level of whites with equivalent training. In fact, the average income for a nonwhite family with a male head who had finished high school was less than that of a white male head who had finished only the eighth grade. Since any aspects of the caste-class system which make it more difficult for Negroes than for whites to achieve middle-class norms of family behavior retard the process of eventual "integration," the income differential and the necessity for more members of the family to work operate in this negative fashion. Even more serious in determining deviations from general middle-class family norms is the manner in which both income distribution and the occupational structure function to reinforce the number of families without fathers and to lower the prestige of Negro males *vis-à-vis* their mates, prospective mates, and children. Thus a pattern of male insecurity which originated under slavery persists into the present. In fact, the struggle of Negro men, viewed as a group, to attain economic parity with Negro women has, up to the present, been a losing fight. Norval Glenn, in an exhaustive study of this problem,[4] has concluded that "Among full-time workers, non-white females were, in 1959, less disadvantaged relative to whites than were non-white males." Women were obtaining employment at a relatively faster rate than men and sustained a more rapid proportionate increase in income between 1939 and 1959. According to Glenn, there was an actual reversal in the income growth pattern of Negro males and females during a twenty-year period, and he notes that if their respective rates remain the same it will take twice as long for Negro males to catch up with white males as for Negro women to catch up with white women (93 years to achieve occupational equality and 219 to achieve equality of income). This is a case of *relative* deprivation, of course, but is significant nevertheless. An impressive body of evidence indicates that rather serious personality distortions result from the female dominance so prevalent in the Negro subculture since the general norms of the larger society stress the opposite pattern as more desirable.

The interplay between caste evaluations and economic and ecological factors has tended not only to concentrate a low-income Negro population within ghettos, but has also concentrated a significant proportion of them in vast public housing projects—sometimes "high rise." In the 1930's public housing projects were often exciting experiments in interracial living, but there has been a tendency in many cities for them to become ghettos within ghettos. Within housing projects as well as out, a small hard core of mothers without husbands and a larger group of youth without jobs are developing a pattern which social psychologist Frederick Strodtbeck has called "the poverty-dependency syndrome." Here and there an integrated program of professional family services has proved its usefulness, but, in general, family case-work becomes a mere "holding operation."

Only the future will tell whether a large-scale "Poverty Program" co-ordinated through federally sponsored agencies will break the interlocking vicious circles which now victimize urban Negro populations. The dominant pattern in the American economic system has never been one of racial segregation. In fact, the racial division of labor has always involved considerable close personal contact, while demanding that Negroes play subordinate occupational roles carrying the lesser rewards in terms of economic power and social prestige. Doctrines of racial inferiority originated as dogmas to defend the use of African slave labor and were later used by white workers to defend their own privileged position against Negro competition. Trade union restrictionism reinforces employer preference in maintaining a job ceiling. Often, even when an employer decided it was profitable to use Negro labor, white workers used intimidation or violence against both white employer and black employee.

Access to new roles in the economic structure has occurred during periods of a great shortage of labor, as in the North during both world wars.

[4] Norval D. Glenn, "Some Changes in the Relative Status of American Nonwhites: 1940–1960," *Phylon*, Vol. 24, No. 2, Summer, 1963.

Negroes entered at the bottom of the hierarchy, but were "last hired and first fired." Yet the job ceiling *was* raised, and, beginning with the organization of industrial unions in the 1930's and reaching a climax in the civil rights movement of the 1960's, ideological factors have reinforced economic interest in breaking the job ceiling. Now, for the first time in American history the full weight of top leadership in labor, industry, and government has been thrown in the direction of "fair employment practices," and public opinion is tolerating an all-out drive against job discrimination (partly because the economy is still expanding). Yet so drastic are the effects of the past victimization of the Negro that any decisive alteration in the caste-class structure without more drastic measures seems remote. Thomas Pettigrew, after an analysis of recent changes, concludes:

At the creeping 1950–1960 rate of change, non-whites in the United States would not attain equal proportional representation among clerical workers until 1992, among skilled workers until 2005, among professionals until 2017, among sales workers until 2114, and among business managers and proprietors until 2730![5]

"IN SICKNESS AND IN DEATH"

The consequences of being at the bottom in a caste-class system are revealed clearly in comparative studies of morbidity, mortality, and longevity, the latter being a particularly sensitive index to the physical well-being of groups. Comparing Negroes and whites with respect to longevity, Thomas Pettigrew notes that:

At the turn of this century, the average non-white American at birth had a life expectancy between 32 and 35 years, 16 years less than that of the average white American. By 1960, this life expectancy had risen from 61 to 66 years . . . But while the percentage gain in life expectancy for Negroes over these sixty odd years has been twice that of whites, there is still a discrepancy of six to eight years . . .[6]

In other words, Negroes were "catching up" but, as a Department of Labor study pointed out in 1962, they ". . . had arrived by 1959 at about the longevity average attained by whites in 1940."[7] They were twenty years behind in the race toward equality of longevity.

Differences in longevity reflect differences in morbidity rates. Among the communicable diseases, for instance, the Negro tuberculosis rate is three times greater than that of whites, and the rates for pneumonia and influ-

[5] Thomas F. Pettigrew, *A Profile of the Negro American*, Van Nostrand, Princeton, N.J., 1964, p. 188.

[6] *Ibid.*, p. 99.

[7] Marion Haynes, "A Century of Change: Negroes in the U.S. Economy, 1860–1960." *Monthly Labor Review*, U.S. Department of Labor, Bureau of Labor Statistics, December, 1960.

enza are also higher. The incidence of venereal disease is substantially higher among Negroes, although the Public Health Service figure of a syphilis rate ten times larger than that for whites has been questioned in Dr. Ann Pettigrew's study. Twice as many Negro children per thousand as white children suffer from measles, meningitis, diphtheria, and scarlet fever. Given such differences between Negroes and whites in the incidence of specific diseases, it is not surprising to find that the *death* rate from childhood diseases is six times higher among Negroes than whites and that the tuberculosis death rate is four times higher in all age groups.[8]

The analysis of mortality rates provides one tool for studying the effects of the caste-class system which victimizes the Negro population. A United States government report for the year 1963 noted that "The age pattern of mortality . . . as in previous years, is similar for each of the color-sex groups—high rates in infancy, lower rates until the minimum is reached during grade-school age, then rising rates for the older age-groups." Although the *pattern* was the same, there were racial differentials in the actual rates; for instance, "The relative increases in the 1963 death rates over the prior years were slightly greater for non-white persons than for white . . ." There were other differentials too.

The death rate among mothers at childbirth in 1963 was four times greater for nonwhites than for whites (96.9 deaths per 100,000 live births to 24.0.) The death rate of nonwhite babies during the first year after birth was almost double the rate for white babies (46.6 per thousand to 25.3 per thousand for males and 36.7 to 19.0 for females). Prenatal hazards were, as in previous years, greater for nonwhites than for whites. Up to the age of five the nonwhite death rate was twice that for whites, and for older age-groups varied from two to four times the white rate.

Using broad categories of classification, the U.S. National Center for Health Statistics reported in 1963 that "the three chief causes of death— diseases of heart, malignant neoplasms (Cancer), and vascular lesions affecting central nervous system account for three fifths of all deaths. They are also the chief causes of death for each color-sex group." Here, too, racial differentials exist, the nonwhite to white death ratios being: (a) diseases of heart (333.9/100,000 to 277.9); (b) malignant neoplasms (145.2/100,000 to 123.7); (c) vascular lesions of central nervous system (133.4/100,000 to 71.3). A comparison of deaths from specific diseases and from other causes also reveals racial differentials and the pattern of indifferences suggests a relationship between high rates and low socio-economic status.

If the ten leading causes of death in 1963 for nonwhites and whites are compared by sex, the results of indirect victimization of Negroes are apparent: Those diseases which rate highest as causes of death are found disproportionately among lower-class families, those who suffer from poor

[8] The rates are cited from Pettigrew, *op. cit.,* Chap. 4, "Negro American Health." Dr. Ann Pettigrew collaborated with her husband, Dr. Thomas F. Pettigrew, on this chapter.

nutrition, overcrowded housing; hazardous occupations, and inadequate medical care. Table 3 presents rates for ten leading causes of death for males:

TABLE 3

The Ten Leading Causes of Death: Males, U.S.A., 1963

Causes of Death	Nonwhite		White	
	Rate	Rank	Rate	Rank
Diseases of the heart	330.6	1	444.8	1
Vascular lesions of Central Nervous System	116.8	2	100.5	2
Certain diseases of early infancy	81.8	3	34.3	7
Influenza and pneumonia	70.6	4	39.3	5
Hypertensive heart disease	61.1	5	24.1	9
Accidents other than motor vehicle	57.9	6	37.8	6
Cancer of digestive organs	51.1	7	54.1	3
Symptoms—senility and ill-defined conditions	42.1	8	10.9**	—
Motor vehicle accidents	36.7	9	34.4	8
Homicide	35.7	10	3.9**	—
Cancer of respiratory system	34.5*	—	43.7	4
Diabetes mellitus	13.9*	—	14.2	10

* Not among first ten for nonwhites.
** Not among first ten for whites.

Among males, certain causes of death directly related to standard of living affect nonwhites two to four times more frequently than whites: (a) certain diseases of early infancy (2.38X); (b) influenza and pneumonia (1.79X); and (c) "symptoms-senility and ill-defined conditions" (3.86X). The last named "cause" does not even appear among the first ten for whites. (See Table 4.)

Two causes of death on the list for nonwhite males are probably directly related to the caste situation. The death rate for hypertensive heart disease is over twice that for whites and ranks fifth as a cause of death, compared to ninth for whites. Thomas Pettigrew, commenting on all types of hypertension, notes that some students feel that it is related to "psychosocial influences" and that, with regard to the high rates for Negroes, "the problem of repressing hostility against whites . . . may be an important factor."[9] A homicide death rate nine times higher than that for whites, and appearing among the ten leading causes of death for nonwhite males, reflects the overt terror in the Black Belt, the explosions of in-caste aggression, and the anomic lower-class situation, as well as the distinctive ethos of the Negro subculture where crimes of passion among the lower-class are not condemned to the extent that they are in some other segments of American society.

[9] Pettigrew, *op. cit.*, p. 96.

Of the ten leading causes of death among nonwhite males, eight are also leading causes of death for white males, but in the case of six of these the nonwhite rate is higher (diseases of the heart and cancer of digestive organs being the exceptions). The extent of the difference is indicated in Table 4.

The prenatal period is much more serious for nonwhite male babies than white, death rates for "certain diseases of infancy" (birth injuries, infections, and so forth) ranking seventh as a cause of death for white males, but only third for nonwhites.

The section of Table 4 dealing with females indicates that nonwhite women are also more vulnerable to death from pneumonia and influenza,

TABLE 4

Comparison of Death Rates for Nonwhites and Whites, by Sex, for the Ten Leading Causes of Death for Each Color-Sex Group

Degree of Difference Between Rates	Males		Females	
	Cause of Death	Ratio of Nonwhite to White Rates	Cause of Death	Ratio of Nonwhite to White Rates
Very much higher for Nonwhites	Homicide**	9.14	None	
Considerably higher for Nonwhites	Symptoms— Senility, and ill-defined conditions**	3.86	Symptoms— Senility, and ill-definied conditions**	4.35
	Certain diseases of early infancy	2.38	Certain diseases of early infancy	2.56
	Hypertensive heart disease	2.12	Hypertensive heart disease	2.09
Somewhat higher for Nonwhites	Influenza and pneumonia (except pneumonia of newborn)	1.79	Influenza and pneumonia (except pneumonia of newborn)	1.68
	Accidents other than motor vehicle accidents	1.37	Diabetes mellitus	1.38
	Vascular lesions affecting central nervous system	1.16	Cancer of genital organs	1.17
	Motor vehicle accident	1.07	Accidents*	1.15
			Vascular lesions affecting central nervous system	1.08
Lower for Nonwhites	Diabetes mellitus*	.97	Diseases of the heart	.84
	Cancer of digestive organs	.94	Cancer of digestive organs**	.71
	Cancer of respiratory system*	.78	Cancer of the breast	.67
	Diseases of the heart	.73		

* Among ten top-ranking causes for whites but not for nonwhites.
** Among ten top-ranking causes for nonwhites but not for whites.

hypertension, diseases of early infancy, and "senility and ill-defined conditions" than are white women and to the same degree as nonwhite males. Deaths from "deliveries and complications of pregnancy, childbirth, and the puerperium" are not a major cause of death for any American women but for the 1,466 cases reported for 1963 the nonwhite rate was over five times that for whites (5.6 to 1.0). Anemias, too, are not prime killers, but non-white women have more than their share of death from this cause (3.0/1,000 to 1.7), with the same situation obtaining from asthma (3.2 to 1.8), and gastric ailments (7.2 to 3.9). Table 5 summarizes the data

TABLE 5

The Ten Leading Causes of Death: Females, U.S.A., 1963

	Nonwhite		White	
Causes of Death	*Rate*	*Rank*	*Rate*	*Rank*
Diseases of the heart	262.2	1	312.1	1
Vascular lesions of central nervous system	120.4	2	110.9	2
Hypertensive heart disease	67.0	3	32.0	5
Certain diseases of early infancy	58.1	4	22.7	9
Influenza and pneumonia	51.0	5	30.3	6
Accidents	38.1	6	33.0	4
Cancer of digestive organs	32.1	7	45.5	3
Symptoms—Senility, & ill-defined conditions	30.9	8	7.1**	—
Cancer of genital organs	28.2	9	24.0	8
Diabetes mellitus	25.4	10	19.2	10
Cancer of the breast	18.2	—*	27.0	7

    * Not among first ten for nonwhites.
    ** Not among first ten for whites.

for the ten leading causes of death among women. The diseases of infancy rank fourth as a cause of death among nonwhite women and ninth among white women, a similar situation to that involving males. On the other hand, while the nonwhite female hypertension rate is twice that of whites, the rank order as a cause of death is not very different.

In addition to an analysis of the ten leading causes of death, other 1963 death rates reflect the low socio-economic status and the influences of the Negro subculture. Of the 6,835 who died from tuberculosis, three and one-half times as many nonwhites as whites succumbed. Only about 2,000 deaths from syphilis occurred, but nonwhites were over-represented four to one.

As for a group of deaths from children's diseases, the pattern of over-representation for nonwhites also prevails. (See Table 6).

It was once both fashionable and scientifically respectable to explain these differences in terms of differential racial susceptibility to various diseases, but as Thomas Pettigrew points out:

The many improvements in his situation since 1900 rendered a dramatic incre-
ment in the Negro's health, providing solid evidence that corrosive poverty and
inadequate medical care were the reasons for his short life span in the past . . .
This difference (between Negro and white rates) can be traced to the diseases
which are treatable, preventable and unnecessary.[10]

TABLE   6

Number of Deaths and Rates for Whites and Nonwhites,
for Certain Children's Diseases: U.S.A., 1963

Diseases	Cases	Nonwhite	White
Whooping Cough	115	.3	.0
Scarlet Fever	102	.1	.0
Diphtheria	45	.1	.0
Measles	364	.4	.2

This is now the generally accepted view among serious students of the
problem, and "corrosive poverty" and "inadequate medical care" are aspects of the victimization to which Negroes have been subjected. Further
improvement in the health status of Negroes depends upon the eradica-
tion of poverty and all its accompanying side effects as well as upon access
to adequate medical care.

Much of the "corrosive poverty" has been associated with life in the
cotton fields, the logging camps, the mines, and the small-town slums of
a poverty-stricken South. Conditions were bad for most people, and the
caste-system made them worse for the Negro. Dr. Ann Pettigrew has
presented convincing evidence that the massive shift of Negro population
into Northern and Western cities during the past two decades has resulted
in some health gains for the Negro, and these gains have been due
largely to greater access to medical advice and medical care. But, the
differentials are still large, even in the North, especially for tuberculosis,
pneumonia, and venereal diseases. "Ghettoization," with its associated
overcrowding, has been one important factor in keeping these rates high;
but for these, as well as for other ailments, hospital discrimination is a
primary factor limiting access to adequate medical care.

Patterns of discrimination and segregation by hospitals are prevalent
throughout the country. A report prepared in 1962 for circulation to members of the National Medical Association (an organization of Negro
physicians)[11] summarized the hospital situation in a sentence, "Things are
bad all over," and the report included the bitter comment that "Hospitals
under religious auspices have been the most vicious in discrimination."

[10] Ibid., p. 99.
[11] It has been demonstrated with data drawn from six southern states that Negro
mothers occupying private rooms in hospitals had a lower death rate among their infants
than white mothers in the wards. Bee H. Black, H. Lippett, B. Redner, and D. Hirsch,
"Reduction of Mortality in the Premature Nursery," Journal of Pediatrics. Vol. 41, No. 3,
September, 1952, pp. 300–04.

Conditions were worst in the South where the caste-system has not yet been shattered. In Birmingham, Alabama, for instance, a city of 750,000 people half of whom are Negro, only 1,100 beds were available for whites, and only 500 for Negroes. In Atlanta, Georgia, the South's most progressive city, 4,000 beds were available for whites, but only 600 for Negroes. (Nonwhites were 22.8 percent of the population of the metropolitan area.) In Augusta, Georgia, a smaller city, twelve beds were set aside for Negroes in the basement of the white hospital but there were no beds for Negro pediatrics or obstetrics patients. The Hill-Burton Act under which federal funds may be secured for aid in building hospitals has a non-discrimination clause, but, generally, it has been evaded or ignored in the South. In one large Texas city a new $6,000,000 hospital constructed with federal aid refused to admit any Negroes until threatened with a suit. (The National Medical Association report emphasized that it was a Catholic hospital.) In Richmond, Virginia, a new "treatment center" accepted Negroes only as out-patients. By 1962, about 2,000 hospitals had been built in the South with federal assistance, and of these 98 would accept no Negroes, while the others stayed within the letter of the law by providing as little space for them as possible. In the few places where Negro physicians are practicing, they usually find it impossible to have their patients hospitalized under their own care since they cannot become members of hospital staffs. (In Elizabeth City, North Carolina, a Negro physician was recently taken on a staff after thirty-two annual applications.) Most Southern local medical societies bar Negroes from membership. (In South Carolina, however, twenty-five of the sixty-five Negro doctors belong to the state medical association, but must hold separate sessions. They can join local societies only if they will agree in advance to stay away from social functions.)

In the more fluid ethnic-class system in the North, patterns of discrimination and segregation vary from city to city. At one extreme is Pittsburgh, Pennsylvania, of which the National Medical Association report simply says, "No hospital problems." A similar assessment is made of Philadelphia. In Gary, Indiana, after a prolonged fight, 85 percent of the Negro physicians were placed on the staff of some formerly all-white hospitals. When the National Medical Association says that "There is no hospital problem" in these cities, what it really means is that Negro physicians no longer find it difficult to have their patients hospitalized. But the Negro masses still face other problems; for, insofar as they are disproportionately represented in low-income groups, more of them are "charity" patients and must face the more subtle forms of victimization which the poor face everywhere in American hospitals—less careful attention to their needs, psychological and physical, than private patients receive. There is substantial evidence from studies made in one Northern city that such patients are more frequently handled by medical students and interns than by fully trained doctors, and there is reliable statistical evidence indicating that more infants die on the wards than in the rooms of private patients. As important as it is to insist upon the right of Negro doctors to take their patients into hospitals which formerly barred them, other aspects of the Negro health problem must be dealt with, too.

The city of Chicago, with its 900,000 Negroes rigidly segregated into ghettos, reveals the full dimensions of the problem. As recently as 1960 there were no more than 500 beds available to Negroes in private hospitals —one-half bed per 1000 Negroes as compared with 4.5 beds per 1000 whites. A distinguished Negro physician serving as Chairman of a Committee to End Discrimination in Medical Institutions released a statement to the press in October, 1963, in which he said that only thirty-three out of eighty private hospitals admitted Negroes and that:

> Many of these do so on a segregated and discriminating basis . . . Some hospitals which do admit Negroes place them in the oldest rooms, in basements, in all-Negro wings and often have a quota system limiting the number of Negro patients they will accept . . . when a Negro becomes ill, he knows he will be accepted at County hospital and is in no mood to have to fight to gain admittance to a private hospital where he will be discriminated against.

The Negro physicians, however, did take up the issue by insisting upon staff appointments so they could take their own patients into these hospitals and insure adequate care for them.

The fight began seriously in 1955 with the passage of an anti-discrimination bill in the City Council and a plea for compliance by Cardinal Stritch. In 1960, after five years of publicity and pleading, only twenty-one of the two hundred fifteen Negro physicians in Chicago held appointments on any private hospital staff outside of the Black Belt, these being at twenty-one of the sixty-eight hospitals of this type. At this point the Mayor appointed a special committee to work on the problem, and a group of ten Negro doctors filed suit under the Sherman and Clayton anti-trust acts against fifty-six hospitals, the Illinois Hospital Association, the Chicago Medical Society, the Chicago Hospital Council, and the Illinois Corporations operating Blue Cross and Blue Shield medical prepayment plans. They took this action, they said, "to thwart the more subtle and sophisticated techniques" being used to evade the issue.

In response to these pressures (and to the general atmosphere regarding civil rights), forty-two of the sixty-eight hospitals in the city had given one hundred two staff appointments to sixty-four of the city's two hundred twenty-five Negro doctors by 1965. (Only eighty-eight of these, however, "permit the physician to admit his private patients.") The downward trend in the number of Negro physicians choosing to practice in Chicago was arrested. For a city which ranked only fourth from the bottom among fourteen cities on degree of hospital integration, the breakthrough has been a major victory. One measure of the extent of the Negro's victimization is the fact that scores of physicians had to spend their money and invest time which could have been devoted to research or professional development in fighting for access to hospital facilities.

The victory of the Chicago Negro doctors has alleviated the plight of paying patients who now have a wider choice of hospitals, though not necessarily closer to their homes. (Because of the fear of being "swamped" by Negro patients, some hospitals, near the Black Belt have interposed stronger barriers against Negro doctors than have those farther away.) As early as 1949, a health survey of Chicago pointed out that "A serious problem faced by the Blue Cross Plan for hospital care in this area is its inability to fulfil its obligations to the 50,000 Negro subscribers, since they are not accepted by all the member hospitals . . . Many of the subscribers must be admitted to Cook County Hospital under the guise of emergencies . . ." Six years later, the Packinghouse Workers Civic and Community Committee complained that "Our union has struggled and won hospital benefits for all our members, but a great number of UPWA–CIO members who are Negroes are being cheated out of those benefits . . ." With over 100,000 insured Negroes and less than 1,000 beds available to them in private hospitals they are still being cheated, and not they alone.[12]

Chicago Negroes have been forced by hospital discrimination to use the facilities of four or five hospitals within the Black Belt and the large but overcrowded Cook County Hospital which should be serving only those who cannot pay and emergency cases. By 1960, almost two-thirds of all the Negro babies delivered in a hospital were being born at Cook County. Some white hospitals near the Black Ghetto closed down their maternity wards rather than serve Negroes. A prominent white physician delivering an address in 1960 in favor of widening access to hospital care stressed that this was unfair both to the paying patients who were denied the right to choose and to the indigent who were being deprived of space at the Cook County Hospital by Negroes who could pay. He said:

> Cook County Hospital is even being used to absorb a large number of Negro patients unwanted by the voluntary hospitals even though they may be able and willing to pay . . . the Chicago public would not tolerate this misuse of a tax-supported hospital . . . for an equivalent number of non-Negro patients . . .[13]

Placing Negroes on the hospital staffs has not solved the fundamental problem of the shortage of beds available to a rapidly expanding Negro population. To build new hospital facilities in the Black Belt *before* eliminating segregation in *all* hospitals would be considered bad strategy by most Negro leaders and a "sell-out" by the militants. The Chicago paradigm has general relevance and is not applicable only to the local scene.

Hospital discrimination is only one facet of a complex process involving both direct and indirect victimization which leads to a lower level of

[12] Summarized from documents on file with Chicago Urban League.
[13] Dr. Franklin C. McLean, "Negroes and Medicine in Chicago," on file with Chicago Urban League.

physical and mental well-being among Negroes and which is reflected in morbidity and mortality rates. Health hazards for most of the Negro population begin even before birth, and they affect both mother and child. These hazards are greatest in the rural South, but they exist in urban situations as well, both Northern and Southern. Premature births occurred 50 percent more frequently among Negroes than among whites during 1958–1959 and maternal mortality rates among Negroes were four times higher. A higher proportion of Negro mothers failed to receive prenatal care, and a higher proportion died in childbirth. The most authoritative testimony on the disadvantaged position of the Negro expectant mother has been supplied by an eminent obstetrician, Dr. Philip F. Williams, who has called attention to the fact that "one survey of maternal mortality is cited which found errors in judgment and technique as well as neglect on the part of the physician, as much as fifty percent more frequently in the case of Negro than white mothers." He pointed out, too, that Negro women who were pregnant and those who had babies were victims of a set of interlocking conditions which included a lack of concern by husbands and putative fathers, a relatively high exposure to gonorrhea and syphilis, and, in the South ". . . a scarcity of physicians that has resulted in an inferior grade of attendance at birth (the untrained midwife) . . ."[14] In both North and South, hospital facilities are still inadequate and all of these factors combine to create a situation ". . . more or less adversely affecting the chances of survival of the Negro mother at childbirth." They affect the chances of the baby's surviving, too. Studies made soon after World War II revealed that, for Negroes as compared with whites, fewer Negro babies were delivered in hospitals and therefore more of them died at birth or during the first year after (and more died before they could be born, too). Immunization of children was less common among Negroes and childhood diseases more prevalent and more often fatal. Negro children, on the average, received fewer of the benefits of deliberately planned feeding, and fewer parents, in proportion, ate according to the more advanced nutritional standards.

Insofar as the job ceiling, the income gap, and Ghettoization preserve and reinforce lower-class behavior patterns among Negroes to a greater extent than in the general society, the general health status of the Negro will be affected. For instance, a less adequate nutritional level than is found among whites is one factor often cited in accounting for the poorer average health status of Negroes. It is conceivable that Negroes could improve their nutritional status immediately by altering their present patterns of food consumption, but this is likely to occur less as a result of education and propaganda than as a by-product of changes in the caste-class situation. Except in wartime or during depressions, food habits are among the most difficult to change, unless change is related to mobility

[14] Dr. Philip F. Williams, "Material Welfare and the Negro," *Journal of American Medical Association*, Vol. 132, No. 11, November 16, 1946, pp. 611–14.

strivings. Maximizing the opportunity for Negroes to achieve the values and norms of the general American middle class is likely to do more to change the eating habits of the Negro population than all of the written or spoken exhortations of home economists or the most seductive of television commercials. A shift in social class supplies the motivation to change, and such a shift is dependent upon an increase in the number and proportion of Negroes entering white-collar occupations.

Maintaining a style of living consonant with any occupational roles demands a minimum level of income. Success in improving the health status of the Negro population may ultimately depend upon an indirect rather than a frontal assault. One student of the problem gives us a clue to the strategy when he observes that ". . . the much lower income level of the American Negro, to the extent that it is a measure of standard of living, explains, in part at least, the differences in health status and longevity between whites and non-whites in the United States."[15] Carefully controlled studies "point up the intimate relationship between physical illness and economic . . ."[16] to use Dr. Ann Pettigrew's expression. Economic factors do not only partially explain, or serve as indices of, the causes of divergent morbidity and mortality rates, but they also give us the clues to a strategy for change, namely, working toward a continuously rising standard of living. Whether hope or pessimism is warranted depends upon the possibility of drastically changing the economic status of the Negro over the next decade, of eliminating economic "victimization."

Closing the income gap is crucial, or alternatively, the provision of a subsidy for medical services. Large masses of Negroes will never become members of the white-collar class, but better job opportunities in commerce and industry will place many of them in a position to benefit from privately sponsored health and insurance plans. These will be of maximum benefit, however, only if hospital discrimination is eliminated. Also, the wider extension of adequate medical care to all citizens through the use of public funds, and the more effective use of social workers and educators, will automatically benefit those Negroes who are not upwardly mobile.

Chronic illness, as well as frequent periods of sickness, not only results in loss of man-hours of production, but also increases stress and strain in interpersonal relations and deprives individuals of the maximum amount of pleasure to be derived from a sense of physical well-being and from recreation and pleasurable interaction with other human beings. Insofar as

[15] Marcus S. Goldstein, "Longevity and Health Status of Whites and Non-Whites in the United States," *Journal of the National Medical Association,* Vol. 46, No. 2, March, 1954, p. 83.

[16] Dr. Ann Pettigrew cites a study carried out in Chicago, using 1950 data, in which, when Negroes and whites of the same economic level were compared, mortality rates were about the same although the rates for Negroes as a group when compared with those for whites as a group were higher. Other studies using the same body of data indicate sharp differences in mortality rates as between laborers and skilled workers among Negroes, a situation similar to that found among whites (Pettigrew, *op. cit.,* p. 98).

the general health level of Negroes is lower than that of whites they suffer more from these deprivations. Tendencies to escape from pain and its consequences by habitual use of alcohol and drugs, or the anodyne of excessive preoccupation with the supernatural world, may be related to the general health situation within the Negro lower class. These less tangible and immeasurable disabilities are as real as the financial burdens imposed by sickness.

THE IDENTIFICATION PROBLEM

Some of the most damaging forms of indirect victimization manifest themselves at the psychological level. The Black Ghetto and the job ceiling are the key variables in accounting for differences in morbidity and mortality rates, and for the persistence of subcultural behavior patterns which deviate from middle-class norms. At the subjective level they also determine the crucial points of social reference for the individual Negro when answering the questions "Who am I today?" and "What will I be tomorrow?" The Black Ghetto forces him to identify as a Negro first, an American second, and it gives him geographical "roots." The job ceiling is an ever present reminder that there are forces at work which make him a second-class American. But the Black Ghetto and the job ceiling are only two components of a caste-class system now undergoing revolutionary transformation—an institutional complex which includes the courts, schools, church, voluntary associations, media of mass communication, and a network of family units. Like all other persons, the individual Negro receives his orientation to this social nexus first from his family and later from his peer group. Exposure to schools and the mass media continues the process of socialization and personality formation while membership in voluntary associations provides a tie to the class system and constitutes an aid to upward mobility.

The white middle class is the reference group for those who are mobile; yet the entire system operates to emphasize identity with "The Race," since defensive solidarity must be maintained against the white world. Inner conflicts are inevitable; and conventional, as well as idiosyncratic, adjustments to this situation have been thoroughly studied. Ann Pettigrew suggests that ". . . the perception of relative deprivation, the discrepancy between high aspirations and actual attainments . . . is a critical psychological determinant of mental disorder. And certainly racial discrimination acts to bar the very achievements which the society encourages individuals to attempt."[17] A disparity in psychosis rates reflects this discrepancy, but for most Negroes the reaction to oppression is less severe. Neither insanity nor suicide is a *typical* Negro reaction.

[17] *Ibid.*, p. 80.

Both Negroes and whites are "victims" of one persisting legacy of the slave trade—the derogation of "negroidness." The idea that a dark skin indicates intellectual inferiority is rapidly passing, but at the esthetic level derogatory appraisal of thick lips, kinky hair, and very dark skin is still prevalent. That many Negroes reject their own body image is evident from advertisements for skin lighteners in the major Negro publications,[18] and Negro children in experimental situations begin to reject brown dolls for white ones before the age of five.[19] The ever present knowledge that one's negroid physiognomy is evaluated as "ugly" lowers self-esteem and, therefore, weakens self-confidence. The rise of the new African states has given a psychological "lift" to those American Negroes who still look more African than *metis*, but extreme Negro physical traits are still a source of inner disquiet—especially for women. (There is no equivalent in America of the African cult of *negritude* whose poets idealize the black woman.) These negative esthetic appraisals are part of a larger stereotype-complex which equates Africa with primitiveness and savagery and considers Negro ancestry a "taint." A frontal assault on a world-wide scale is necessary to undo this propaganda of the slave era which still exists as a form of cultural lag which has lost even the excuse of the functional utility it once had in rationalizing an integral part of the Western economic system—Negro slavery.[20]

Negroes in America, as a numerical minority, always have a feeling of being "on the outside looking in," of not being "in the main stream." Yet, the mere fact of being only one in ten does not automatically generate this feeling; the "victimization" flows, rather from the values of the majority who refuse to accept every individual upon his own merit, but insist upon ascription of status on the basis of membership in a racial group. (Bahia, Brazil, presents an interesting case where the opposite is true, where individual achievement can almost completely over-ride racial origin.)[21] This sense of alienation is reinforced by traditional or deliberate omission of Negroes from the decision-making process. That they are absent from the boards of major corporations is not surprising; but it is surprising that they

[18] *Ebony*, a well-edited, widely circulated, popular weekly magazine which concentrates upon the display of what its editor calls "Negro achievement" carries skin-lightener advertisements routinely. *Ebony's* African imitator, *Drum*, also carries such advertisements.

[19] The classical study in this field is Kenneth B. Clark and Mamie P. Clark, "Racial Identification and Preference in Negro Children," which has been made widely accessible through T. M. Newcomb and E. L. Hartley's *Readings in Social Psychology*, Holt, Rinehart & Winston, New York, 1947, pp. 169–78.

[20] Analyses of the genesis of the derogatory stereotypes of Africa and Africans may be found in Kenneth Little, *Negroes in Britain*, K. Paul Trench, Trubner, London, 1948, and Philip Curtin, *The Image of Africa*, University of Wisconsin Press, Madison, Wis., 1964. See also "Toward an Evaluation of African Societies," by St. Clair Drake, in *Africa Seen by American Negro Scholars*, Presence Africaine, Paris, New York, 1958.

[21] The extent to which the pattern in Bahia, Brazil, differs from that in the United States is analyzed by Donald Pierson in *Negroes in Brazil*, University of Chicago Press, Chicago, Ill., 1942.

are virtually absent from the boards of foundations and professional associations. Only in the realm of public administration and the world of sports
and entertainment are Negroes present in sufficient numbers to be "visible,"
and to serve as role models for Negro youth.

These omissions are particularly crucial in a society where numerous
illustrated publications function as the image-makers. A Negro child seldom sees a person like himself in an advertisement or in illustrations accompanying fiction. The children in the textbooks are all white. The image
of the powerful, the desirable, the admirable is set very early as "white."
There is an increasing awareness of the seriousness of this problem, and
by 1964 the television industry was making a half-hearted attempt to use
a few Negroes in commercials, and one or two Northern cities were experimenting with "integrated textbooks." But still, Negro newspapers and
magazines alone cater to this hunger to see the Negro image in print.
These publications also give prominence to whatever interracial participation is taking place, but they cannot eliminate the feeling of resentment
over exclusion from the collective representations of the larger society.

Leaders in the civil rights movement frequently refer to the process of
desegregation and integration as having the goal of "bringing Negroes into
the main stream." This sense of isolation from "the main stream" was given
poetic expression by the late Dr. W. E. B. Du Bois in the 1890's when he
spoke of living behind, or within, "The Veil." This isolation not only generates distorted perceptions of the total society and occasionally bizarre
definitions of situations, but it also results in cognitive crippling. The communication flow needed to provide data for rational decision-making is
often impeded. Incomplete information is available for "playing the game"
the way it is played in various segments of the larger society, and in a
highly mobile society it is all-important to know "who is who" and "what is
what." There is some evidence, for instance, to indicate that lower-middle-
class and lower-class Negro parents often have high aspirations for their
children but have no clear idea how to realize them. Negro students in
segregated colleges and high schools are also often woefully ignorant of
opportunities and techniques for succeeding.

One cannot be mobile without learning the professional codes and the
folkways of other social strata. It was this which the Supreme Court had
in mind when it ruled some years ago that a separate law school for
Negroes cut the student off from those contacts which were necessary to
make a person a first-class lawyer and therefore could not meet the criterion of equality. It is this contact which most Negro physicians are
denied. Also, in a society where the social ritual is so much a part of the
business world, Negroes are generally not in a position to secure the cues
and tips needed for competition on a basis of complete equality. If they
cannot meet their peers at professional meetings and in the informal
gatherings of persons who pursue similar occupations and professions,
they, of necessity, will see only "through a glass darkly." Very clever and

ambitious individuals (and persistent ones) sometimes rip aside "The Veil," but such persons are rare within any ethnic group. Most individuals remain victims of the communication blockage, and special efforts will be necessary to open the channels of communication. Participation across race lines with persons in similar occupations is the first step toward structural integration.

In a social system which forces Negroes to think of themselves *first* as Negroes and only second as Americans, a problem of "double identification" is posed for those who are partially integrated. Guilt feelings sometimes arise over the charge hurled by others that they are "running away from the Race." Negroes who represent the country abroad are exposed to the criticism of Africans and Asians as being "the tool of the white man." Personnel officers, political leaders, and work-supervisors are always open to the charge that they are "Uncle Toms," have "sold out," or have "forgotten the Race." This problem will be intensified if the process of integration at upper levels of power and prestige is not accompanied by the complete disappearance of racial barriers to upward mobility, or if the masses of Negroes are doomed to be America's permanent lower class. In the meanwhile, the rise of Malcolm X and the appeal of the Black Muslims and various local Black Nationalist groups suggest that the lower classes and lower middle classes can work their way out of the problem of double identification by rejecting "white" values and by proudly proclaiming their psychological independence. Such a solution is not available to the more sophisticated Negroes, but the possibility is not to be excluded that, since America insists upon limited integration rather than complete acceptance, increased identification of educated Negroes with some aspects of the Negro subculture and with the cultural renaissance taking place in Africa may become the norm.

THE CONDITION OF POWERLESSNESS

The problem of "identification" is crucial, but Charles Silberman, in *Crisis in Black and White,* puts his finger upon the most critical aspect of Negro-white relations in the United States when he stresses the psychological effect of being "powerless." Negroes realize that, as a minority in "the white man's country," they do not set the rules of the game. Unlike Negroes in Africa and the West Indies they do not fight for national independence, but rather for "desegregation" and "integration," and they can attain these goals only if the white majority sanctions them as legitimate and desirable. "Integration," in the final analysis, also means that the Negro community must increasingly become more middle-class in values and behavior if it is to win respect and approval. Negroes do not determine the ends for which they struggle, nor the means. The most they can expect is an increasingly greater share in the *joint* determination of their future.

THE NEGRO IN SOCIETY

The problem of maintaining dignity and some autonomy in such a situation is, for sensitive personalities, a continuous one, even within the civil rights movement, for white friends, even in liberal-left circles, often strive to bend Negroes to their will and not to ask their advice as co-workers.

In the past, this sense of "powerlessness" to determine their own destiny or to change their position in the caste-class system has been one important factor in accentuating in-group aggression among lower-class Negroes, in the division of energy and financial resources into the over-elaboration of the church-voluntary association complex, and in the development of those styles of life which E. Franklin Frazier portrayed so unsympathetically in *Black Bourgeoisie*. Black Belt crime, juvenile delinquency, and cynical exploitation have also been interpreted by some sociologists as one reaction to a state of "powerlessness." Within the lower class and lower middle class, hostility and resentment become "socialized" for a few in the form of Black Nationalism and take organized form in movements such as the Black Muslims.[22] Among the rootless masses, the anger flowing from frustration bursts forth periodically in verbal abuse and violent assault, in arson and looting, in attacks upon policemen and property—thus the tragedy of Harlem, Rochester, and Philadelphia in 1964 and of Los Angeles and Chicago in 1965. The feeling of having made the conquest of power, of being in control of their own fate, if only for a moment, is symbolized in a widely circulated photograph of jubilant Negroes giving the V-for-Victory sign on top of a shattered police car in Los Angeles. But these Black Belt explosions underscore a basic fact—that no revolution can follow the storming of the Bastille by Negroes in America. Camus and Sartre, not Marx, provide the key for understanding these events.

Conventional politics has been the most realistic approach to gaining at least the semblance of power. Recent demographic trends, including the flight of whites to the suburbs, have placed some Negro communities in a strategic position to play "balance of power" politics more effectively, and the civil rights movement may result in increased political power for Negroes in the South. Yet, all Negro leaders know the limits of their ability to wield decisive political influence. (And in the world of "big business" their influence is even less.) Silberman has suggested the importance—cathartic and practical—of grass-roots movements, with "middle-level" leadership, fighting for limited goals where results can be achieved, and Thomas Pettigrew has stressed the psychologically liberating effect of participation in the civil rights movement.[23] The feed-back in terms of an increased incentive to secure more education or to get better jobs can be sustained only if society actually provides the rewards in terms of ex-

[22] See Essien-Udom, *Black Nationalism: A Search for an Identity in America*, Chicago, 1962; and Charles Eric Lincoln's *The Black Muslims in America*, Boston, 1961. Reactions to the deaths of Patrice Lumumba and Malcolm X among a segment of the Negro American lower-class reveal the not-to-be-ignored depth of Black Nationalist feeling in the U.S.A.

[23] Pettigrew, *op. cit.*, pp. 161–68, "The New Role of the Equal Citizen."

panded occupational mobility. The sense of being powerless can disappear, however, only if the social system eventually changes to the extent that Negroes will not need to organize *as Negroes* to defend their interests and if color ceases to be a factor in membership in the "power structure." Riots will cease only when Americans allow Black Ghettos to dissolve.

THE MYTH OF "SEPARATE BUT EQUAL"

Negroes have been "victimized" throughout the three hundred fifty years of their presence on the North American continent. The types of social systems which have organized their relations with whites have been varied—over two hundred years of slavery and indenture, ten years of post-Civil War Reconstruction in the South, and eighty years of experimentation with a theory of "separate but equal" ostensibly designed to replace caste relations with those of class. The "separate but equal" doctrine has now been repudiated by the federal government and a broad section of public opinion as unjust and inimical to the national welfare. The period of desegregation has begun. Yet, the legacy of the past remains. As a transition to some new, and still undefined system of race relations takes place it is relevant to examine the extent to which victimization persists. An estimate, too, should be made of whether or not what Merton has called "the unintended consequences of purposive social action" carry a potential for new forms of victimization.

By 1900 the doctrine had become firmly established that it was desirable for Negroes and whites to be members of two functionally related segments of a bi-racial society in which families, intimate friendship groups, and voluntary associations (including churches) would be separate, although members of both races were participating in a common economic system and political order. Both Negro and white leaders emphasized the point that "social equality" was not a Negro aspiration, and Booker T. Washington's famous Atlanta Compromise address delivered in 1895 made this point very explicit with his symbolism of the five fingers, separate and distinct, but joined together at the palm.

The theory of "separate but equal" visualized a future in which Negroes would gradually acquire wealth and education on such a scale as to develop a social-class system within the Negro community paralleling that of the white community. Then, as the sociologist Robert Park once phrased it, Negroes and whites would "look over and across" at each other, not "up and down." Defenders of "bi-racialism" believed that although institutional life—including schools and neighborhoods—should remain separate, Negroes should be allowed to compete freely for jobs and should gradually acquire the full voting rights which they had lost in the South after 1875. It was considered unwise, however, to make a frontal assault upon segregation in public places since the key to the ultimate dissolution or transformation of the caste system lay in the acquisition of education and economic well-being—not in protest. The "correct" behavior of an enlarged Negro middle class would eventually win acceptance by the white middle class. The doctrine of "separate but equal" was given legal sanction in a number of Supreme Court decisions, the most famous being that of *Plessy vs. Ferguson,* and it became the operating ideology among Southern white liberals between the two world wars.

During the first decade after World War II the doctrine of "separate but equal" was abandoned as a guide to the formulation of public policy insofar as the armed forces, public transportation, public accommodations, and public schools were concerned. Experience between the two world wars had demonstrated that, while it might be theoretically possible to achieve equality within the framework of a segregated school system in the South, it seemed impossible in actual practice. In the field of public transportation, no matter how many shiny new coaches replaced the old rickety "Jim Crow" coaches, Negroes did not consider them "equal," and they never ceased to be resentful that there were two American armies instead of one. The cost of duplicating facilities to make public accommodations and schools truly equal would have been exorbitant even if Negroes welcomed the idea. Thus, a demand for change was in the air when the historic 1954 decision requiring school desegregation was taken, and the Court cut through to a fundamental question which had often been evaded: whether or not it was possible to maintain any kind of *forced* segregation in an open society without pejorative implications. Did not the very insistence upon separation imply inferiority? The caste-class system organizing race relations was recognized for what it really was—a system which, irrespective of the intent of individuals, resulted in the victimization of Negroes. Makers of national policy have now embarked upon a thoroughgoing program of desegregation coupled with an assault upon all institutionalized forms of racial discrimination. But the white public has not accepted the concept of "total integration."

SOME PARADOXES OF PROGRESS

The abandonment of the doctrine of "separate but equal" has forced consideration of many provocative questions, such as: "Can the victimization resulting from unequal treatment of Negroes in the past be eliminated without preferential treatment for present-day victims?" There are those who contend that justice demands more than equality, that it requires a "revolutionary break-through" in the form of preferential hiring, distinctive programs of education, and special scholarship schemes. The existence of entrenched patterns of residential segregation also raises the question of the desirability and probability of the persistence of Negro neighborhoods and institutions. If *forced* separation eventually disappeared would sep-

arateness cease to be an index of victimization? Would it then lose its pejorative implications? Would the right to choose, if it ever came, mean that
some Negroes will choose *not* to be "integrated" except in the economic
and political order?

New types of victimization are emerging which are not only indirect but
are also unintended consequences of actions designed to eliminate victimization. For instance, in several Northern cities an earnest effort is being
made to facilitate and speed up the process of residential desegregation
at the middle-class level. Negroes whose incomes and life styles approximate those of the white middle class are accepted into neighborhoods and
apartment buildings in limited numbers in order not to excite fear and panic
among white residents. The goal, as one Chicago neighborhood association
states it, is "an integrated neighborhood with high community standards,"
to reverse the process of ghettoization. However, without a commitment to
"open occupancy" at the city level, attainment of this goal demands a
neighborhood-by-neighborhood approach, which calls for studying "tip-
ping points" and setting up "benign quotas" in order to maintain a "racial
balance." It may also involve a program which forces all lower-class residents to leave irrespective of their color, while integrating a small number
of middle-class Negroes into neighborhoods or specific apartment buildings. One effective technique has been clearance of slums followed by re-
building at a high enough rent level to keep the proportion of Negroes
automatically very low. This process is frequently called "controlled integration. Actions such as these often result in the concentration of many
lower-class Negroes into almost completely segregated public housing projects. What is gained for some in terms of better physical surroundings is
lost in increased "ghettoization." Other displaced persons increase the degree of overcrowding in already overcrowded neighborhoods or filter into
middle-class Negro neighborhoods and disorganize them.

Serious problems also arise within the middle class at the psychological
level. Insofar as Negro families have to cooperate actively in setting and
maintaining quotas on the number of Negroes who enter, and in eliminating lower-class Negroes from the neighborhood, they become vulnerable
to attack by other Negroes. Some sensitive individuals suffer from a feeling
of guilt over-manipulating the situation to maintain exclusiveness; others
feel a loss of dignity in carrying on continuous discussion about race with
white people. They dislike dealing with themselves as "a problem." A few
people simply withdraw from such "integrated" situations into the comfort
of the middle-class "gilded ghetto." This situation is only a special case of
a more general problem confronting some Negroes in this Era of Integration—how to reconcile being a "loyal Negro" or a "Race Man" with new
middle-class interracial relations or new occupational roles.

Rapid and fairly complete "integration" of middle-class Negroes into
neighborhoods, churches, and voluntary associations could have a profound

effect upon Negro institutional life "skimming off the cream" of the Negro elites to the disadvantage of the larger Negro community. This would result in a kind of victimization of the Negro masses which would be permanent unless the conditions of life for the lower classes were drastically changed.

Unfortunately there are few signs of hope that the Negro masses will profit from current economic changes, for at the very moment when the civil rights movement has been most successful, and when access to training is being made more widely available to Negroes, forces are at work which could render these gains meaningless. Whitney Young, Jr., of the National Urban League, emphasizing economic problems facing Negroes, stated upon one occasion: "Unless we identify these problems and take steps to meet them, we will find the masses of Negroes five years from today with a mouthful of rights, living in hovels with empty stomachs."[24] About 12 percent of the nonwhite labor force were unemployed in 1960, twice the rate for white workers. In some urban areas it was between 15 and 20 percent. It was higher for Negro men than for women. Unemployment rates are particularly high for Negro youth. In 1961, nonwhite boys and girls between fourteen and nineteen had the highest unemployment rate of any age-color group in the nation, while the unemployment rate for Negro high-school graduates between the ages of sixteen and twenty-one was twice that for white youth and higher than the rate for whites who had *not* attended high school. One out of five Negro high-school graduates were unable to find jobs. If high-school graduates face such a situation, the plight of the untrained Negro is likely to be even worse. It was estimated in 1964 that automation was wiping out about 40,000 unskilled jobs a week, the sector of industry where Negro workers are concentrated. This trend is likely to continue for some time.

If Negroes are not to become a permanent *lumpen-proletariat* within American society as a result of social forces already at work and increased automation, deliberate planning by governmental and private agencies will be necessary. Continued emphasis upon "merit hiring" will benefit a few individuals, but, in the final analysis, structural transformations will have to take place. There are those who feel that only a radical shift in American values and simultaneous adjustments of economy and society will wipe out, forever, the victimization of the Negro. If such a situation does occur it is not likely to be the result of any cataclysmic proletarian upheaval, but rather through drift and piece-meal pragmatic decisions. One straw in the wind has been raised to test the temper of the time. Gunnar Myrdal and twenty-nine other scholars, writers, and political scientists have released a statement on "The Cybernation Revolution, the Weaponry Revolution, and the Human Rights Revolution." In discussing the need for adjustment to the effects of largescale automation, they made a revolutionary suggestion:

[24] Quoted by James Reston in a column, "The Ironies of History and the American Negro," *The New York Times,* May 15, 1964.

We urge, therefore, that society, through its appropriate legal and governmental institutions, undertake an unqualified commitment to provide every individual and every family with an adequate income as a matter of right . . .

Should this ever happen, Negroes, would, of course, profit even more than whites, but demands for radical reforms of this type have not arisen from within the Civil Rights Movement whose leaders generally accept a middle-class work ethic which is incompatible with such a solution.

The Value of Teaching Negro Culture

It has been stated by many critics that the public school curriculum does not adequately or fairly present the position of the Negro in American life or history. This has been changing in recent years, but it is still an important issue. Because one of the most, if not the most, vital means we have for dispelling prejudice is that of "educating against it," the schools must take up the gauntlet and work toward a new enlightenment for both Negro and white students.

What kind of curriculum materials and how much coverage should be given the various racial and ethnic groups in the society? While the following article deals specifically with the teaching of Negro culture in the schools, the reader should bear in mind this same question as it relates to other racial and ethnic groups.

Teaching Negro Culture in High Schools—
Is It Worthwhile?

WILLIAM G. PICKENS

CULTURAL TRAINING AND METHODS
USED TO TEACH IT

There seems to be controversy over the teaching of Negro culture, literature, and history in our high schools. Perhaps most school systems assume
that this is already being done, but, if so, they are mistaken, it seems. This
sort of material is hardly being taught on any level, elementary, secondary,
or collegiate.

There are strong reasons for the failure, we suspect, reasons that lie deep
in the fabric of the American society, reasons that have appealed to Negroes and whites alike, though perhaps in different ways. Whatever the
reasons, it seems clear that until justice is done in this area, high schools
will continue to turn out Negro and white students who are warped by
a false picture of the history of their forebears.

It is our purpose in this paper to attempt to provide a peek at the causes
and effects of social and school curriculum policies that fail to treat adequately the role of the Negro in American society and history, because it
is "controversial." Our further purpose is to suggest a remedy.

This is not to say, however, that *all* school systems fall into this class.
The author himself attended a secondary school system that did teach this.
It *is* to say, however, that Negro culture is not generally taught and is not
generally learned. Even when it is treated, this is not always done from the
proper motivation, under the proper circumstances, and with the proper
degree of thoroughness. Our basic premise is that the proper teaching of
Negro culture and history is one of the few effective ways to motivate
Negro students to higher levels of achievement, and at the same time help
whites to remove some of their false values, based on ungrounded concepts
of their racial superiority. It is one of the few ways of helping both groups
toward a greater appreciation of the Negro as a human being, and toward
a better understanding of themselves and each other.

Throughout the whole world, cultural training seems to have always
been one of the chief functions of societies from time immemorial. No

From the *Journal of Negro Education*, Vol. 34, Spring, 1965, pp. 106–13, by permission
of the publisher.

claim has been made that either geography, climate, epoch, degree of civilization, topography, wealth, race or any other factor or group of factors has gotten in the way of this activity of all human societies. Historically, it appears that every means available to one generation to impress on younger ones this cultural continuum has been employed, and more or less effectively.

In our own times, cultures have benefited and continue to benefit from all of these earlier methods. New ones have been developed or utilized, however, as the genius of man has expanded. Therefore it is commonplace to see links made directly or indirectly with the past by such means as photographs, recordings, radio and television stories, movies and dramas. Furthermore, pamphlets, newspapers, periodicals, books, and school courses play dramatic roles in this effort. In short, societies seek to transmit the cultural impetus from earlier times by many different approaches, and in depth. Why? Perhaps it is indisputable that one of the key reasons is to promote a feeling of association with earlier generations, to promote a feeling of gratitude and reverence for the heritage that has been passed down. In this way we feel a part of something; we belong to something. We can identify.

To this end, then, millions of dollars are spent annually in historical research and analysis, in such fields as archaeology, geology, anthropology, biology, and the arts. On another level millions are spent for genealogical and historical research by various public and private societies and individuals. A billion dollar business has developed from concentrated commercial efforts to rehash, relive, and glamorize the high achievements of some Western civilizations from the time of the fall of Rome to the latest "shoot-em-up" triumphs over the Indians. So the people of this country use every favorable scrap of information available to them about their predecessors, in order to have this feeling of identification and worth.

This is good, and works fine for the majority. But we find a sharply contrasting picture as it regards the Negro minority in America. Ironically, the forces most to blame, we feel, are the same ones just shown to be so solicitous of their own identification with a glorious past.

THE NEGRO AND THE CONSEQUENCES

The Negro American has been stripped of his heritage. He is like Esau without his birthright. He has been placed in the position that, except in a strictly biological sense, he can hardly lay claim to even having an ancestry at all. He has largely been uprooted and sundered and shorn from his cultural tradition. He has been kidnapped and ransomed in every sense of the word imaginable, and culturally murdered. He has been ordered to stand aside and build the road over which the army of history has swept, a history, again ironically, that was begun apparently by his forefathers in his own original homeland. This cleavage has been accomplished so successfully that it is the unusual mature American Negro who has any faint notion as to just who his great grandfather was, except to know that he was very likely white.

This situation has been long apparent, and the sociologists of the thirties and forties, while not the first, did spell it out. The label Negroes bear as the "culturally deprived" really takes the meaning "deprived of their culture."

This has been no accident at all. A very limited analysis of the evidence reveals that as far as treatment of Negro culture and history in America is concerned, three types of sins have been committed. They are sins of commission, of omission, and of distortion. In short, American history has been mistaught as it concerns Negro Americans. It is hard to escape the conclusion that Meyer is correct in his feeling that this mis-teaching is primarily chargeable to the desire of some white Americans to insure and perpetuate "white supremacy."[1] "Strip the Negro of his sense of worth and belonging," the theory must have gone, "and you'll have a manageable chattel." To a large extent, if this was the theory, it appears to have worked.

Aside from all of the separating, punishing, etc., in the first place, whites, aided and abetted later by the U.S. Bureau of the Census, made the social decision that "one drop" of Negro blood determined a Negro. This was a sin of commission. Further, whites decided long before the courts added their approval that the Negro, neither male nor female, had no rights that a white man was bound to respect. It was easy then to inflict on the Negro any and every form of bestial treatment that the imagination and lusts and whims of the slave-owners, slave-merchants, over-seers, guests, and police authorities could devise. Starvation, death, promises, threats, demoralization, disunity, and even some religious teachings had succeeded in changing humans into property.[2]

At the same time, the sins of omission were in motion. For instance, the rulers concealed the fact that it was not in 1619 when Negroes had first come to the New World (and even then as indentured servants and workers, not slaves), but at least as early as 1512, with the Spaniards. This was 108 years before the "Mayflower." Substantiation comes from Franklin,

Thirty Negroes, including Nuflo de Olano, were with Balboa when he discovered the Pacific Ocean. Cortes carried Negroes with him into Mexico, and one of them planted and harvested the first wheat crop in the New World. Two Negroes accompanied Velas in 1520. When Alvarado went to Quito, he carried

[1] Howard N. Meyer, "The Neglected Tool," *The Crisis*, Vol. 70, November, 1963, p. 529.
[2] The reader can perceive that details of how this was all accomplished are easily obtainable despite efforts of Negroes and whites alike to suppress them. See standard Negro history texts.

two hundred Negroes with him. They were with Pizzaro on his Peruvian expedition and carried him to the Cathedral after he was murdered. The Negroes in the expeditions of Almagro and Valdivia saved their Spanish masters from the Indians in 1525.[3]

It was concealed that in the centuries prior to the founding of America, Africans had developed the first civilizations. It was concealed "that Africans first domesticated the sheep, goat, and cow, developed the idea of trial by jury, produced the first stringed instruments, and gave the world its greatest boon in the discovery of iron."[4]

It is still concealed that ancient and famous names like Hannibal, Queen Nefertari, Cleopatra, Aesop, Makeda, Queen of Sheba, and Simon the Cyrenian were those of "Negroes." It has been concealed that famous names of more recent times, like St. Benedict, St. Augustine, Alexandre Dumas (*pere* and *fils*), those of three popes, at least one U. S. president, and perhaps even that of the greatest personage in world music, are names of "Negroes."

The full extent of what has been concealed is probably infinitely more shocking to Negroes than to whites, since it is whites who have done the major part of the suppression of such facts. Even when a name has been mentioned in our texts of a prominent person of Negro ancestry, whites have at *these* times often avoided the racial tag. In this regard we think, for instance, of Pushkin, Frederick Douglass, and Crispus Attucks.

It served the interests of the slave owners much, in addition, to omit reference to facts of Negro history and culture bearing on mutinies, revolts and plots, massacres of whites, the Haitian Revolution, Negro minutemen, and Negro participation in all of the nation's wars (even being the deciding balance of power in both the Revolutionary and Civil wars), lynchings and atrocities, promiscuity, miscegenation, tactical indolence, purposeful sabotage, and the Abolition Movement.

Sins of distortion have also been rampant, it would appear. Here again the generalizations and stereotypes enter, like those of the lazy, happy-go-lucky Negro buck. Odum (who since has changed his opinion) was one of the powerful early twentieth century writers guilty of this sin. Herskovits quotes him as saying,

The Negro has little home conscience or love of home. . . . He has no pride of ancestry . . . has few ideals . . . little conception of the meaning of virtue, truth, honor, manhood, integrity. He is shiftless, untidy and indolent. . . . The migratory or roving tendency seems to be a natural one to him. The Negro shirks detail and difficult tasks. . . . He does not know the value of his word or the meaning of words in general. . . . The Negro is improvident and extravagant; . . . he lacks

[3] John Hope Franklin, *From Slavery to Freedom*, Alfred A. Knopf, New York, 1960, p. 46.
[4] Carter G. Woodson, *The Mis-Education of the Negro*, The Associated Publishers, Inc., Washington, D.C., 1933, p. 21.

initiative; he is often dishonest and untruthful. He is over-religious and super-stitious . . . his mind does not conceive of faith in humanity—he does not comprehend it."[5]

Other examples of these sins are easy to come by.

What have been the consequences of these sins of commission, omission, and distortion? Certainly they have had an effect on all American citizens. The hopelessness and helplessness of the modern day Negro in the face of current discriminatory practices in housing, employment, politics, and education is shattering. This is the fruit of about 345 years of oppression in America. The conception that this is a "white man's country" is nearly correct, at least in the sense of where the power lies.

One consequence has been the self-depreciation of the Negro. "Throughout the Negro's stay in America," offers Vontress, he has been misrepresented, misjudged, and maligned.[6]

Wolff agrees,

The group stigma as a means of enforcing a negative self-evaluation on the individual was used with greatest effect against the Negro in American history. . . . The Irish, Jew, Italian, Greek, Chinese, and even Puerto Rican found in himself and in his relationship to the beauty of his land of origin as well as to the glorious history of his group, the strength to counteract and overcome the effects of the stigma.[7]

Africa, the root of degradation for the American Negro, has been rejected by him, therefore. He has felt, until very recently, no kinship with Africa or with Africans. He has retained, Herskovits notwithstanding, few if any vestiges of the ancient and highly developed cultures of Africa and has come to the view of his overlords here that Africa is the "dark continent" in both senses. Having lost his cultural attachments to African societies and been denied access to those of the dominant groups here, the American Negro has been hard put to maintain a sense of psychological balance. Some have not succeeded.

We must begin to realize how many warped, twisted, and distorted personalities there are who will never become inmates of institutions . . . but who will continue in their daily lives exhibiting every form of destructive activity, sabotaging, and defeating human needs and values and obstructing social order

[5] H. W. Odum, "Social and Mental Traits of the Negro," *Columbia University Studies in History, Economy and Public Law*, Columbia University Press, New York, 1910. Quoted in Melville J. Herskovits, *The Myth of the Negro Past*, Harper & Row, New York, 1941, p. 22.

[6] Clemmont E. Vontress, "The Negro Against Himself," *Journal of Negro Education*, Vol. 32, Summer, 1963, pp. 237–41.

[7] Max Wolff, ed., "Toward Integration of Northern Schools," *The Journal of Educational Sociology*, Vol. 36, November, 1963, p. 242.

while existing under stress and strain and tensions that progressively undermine
their health and their capacity for living.[8]

The wonder is that Negroes have been able to adjust to the extent that
they have. This self-depreciating and escapist tendency on the part of
many Negroes is not likely to subside because of automation, osmosis, or
any other mechanistic, scientific or materialistic device. It has made Negroes ashamed to be Negroes, that they count for so little, that they are so
despised. They are ashamed because they do not know, for the most part,
that they do have cultural roots. They have not learned what they are,
and whites have denied or ignored them. This is why Negroes, in order
to be "accepted," have acquiesced into feelings of unworthiness even
though privately they do feel pride when they learn of Negro accomplishments, so long as they are those of Negroes with whom they are not in
immediate competition for white favors and esteem. In this last respect the
Negro again proves that he, too, is human. But he is still confused. He
often waits to make sure that the white man approves before he dares
make any public sign of approbation. It is what James Baldwin describes
as a tendency for the Negro, instead of looking upward, to look into the
face of the white man, when he is asked if it is raining. This accounts,
perhaps, for Warren's experience. He quotes a Negro teacher in Louisiana:

> You hear some white men say they know Negroes. Understand Negroes. But it
> is not true. No white man ever born ever understood what a Negro is thinking.
> What he's feeling. . . . And half the time that Negro . . . he don't understand
> either.[9]

Aside from the long term of bondage and involuntary servitude itself,
these sins of commission, omission and distortion have further served to
attack directly the ego itself of all these generations of Negroes. This attack
is constant and often even unrealized consciously by the whites who make
it. Sometimes the defensive mechanisms of the Negro prevent his conscious
discernment too of the constancy of such attacks, but the ego never mis-
interprets. The ego registers every one. It registers the slurring remarks,
the hastily withdrawn hand, the expressions of avoidance and annoyance,
the platitudes of friendship and concern, the hiring and promotional policies, the "racial" job assignments. All form a frontal and formidable attack
on his ego.

Nor have these been the only consequences. The ravages on the personality and ego of the Negro show only one side of the coin. Some writers
feel that whites have also been "damaged" by the sort of cultural and historical teachings that we have been discussing.

---

[8] *Mental Health in the Classroom*, The Department of Supervisors and Directors of
Instruction of the National Education Association, Thirteenth Yearbook, Washington,
D.C., The Department of Supervisors and Directors of Instruction of the N.E.A., 1940,
p. 3.
[9] Robert Penn Warren, *Segregation*, Random House, Inc., New York, 1956, pp. 16–17.

[They are] being taught to gain personal status in an unrealistic and non-adaptive way. . . . The culture permits and, at times, encourages them to direct their feelings of hostility and aggression against whole groups of people, the members of which are perceived as weaker than themselves.[10]

James Baldwin, in a talk that he called "The Negro Child—His Self Image," made similar comments.

If . . . one managed to change the curriculum in all the schools so that Negroes learned more about themselves and their real contributions to this culture, you would be liberating not only Negroes. You'd be liberating white people. . . .
What passes for identity in America is a series of myths about one's heroic ancestors.[11]

Perhaps, then, these sins of historical training, while causing *delusions* among Negroes have caused *illusions* among whites, both damaging to the mental health of the nation. One illustration of the latter possibility might lie in the frustration of many white liberals who cannot understand "why the Negroes can't seem to produce enough good leaders." There are Negroes who might reply that at the same time that these "liberals" are making this complaint, the white power structure, of which they are often a part, is doing everything in its power to render completely ineffective— by bribery, blackmail, threat, force, or murder—any leader worthy of the name.

THE REMEDY AND THE CONCLUSIONS

What is the remedy? As suggested earlier and hinted at periodically the remedy probably lies in education. If miseducation has done the damage, perhaps education can undo some of it, if permitted.

Curriculum changes should be encouraged that would simply teach the truth. Then students, Negro and white, would learn the facts about the Negro in the arts, in general and American culture, in general and American history. Even a small start is something. For instance, one history department distributed to its teachers a fact sheet of dates, names, and events with the request that teachers work the information into their regular presentations. For it seems clear that if teachers are to teach more, they must first learn more. Perhaps an in-service education program is indicated, for both white and Negro teachers, wherever needed.

Thus, by selecting from all of the resources at our disposal for disseminating learning—radio, television, art, literature, ceremonies, recordings,

[10] Kenneth B. Clark, "Segregated Schools in New York City," *Journal of Educational Sociology,* Vol. 36, No. 6, February, 1963, p. 246.
[11] James Baldwin, "A Talk to Teachers." From a speech delivered in New York City on October 16, 1963. Published in *Saturday Review,* December 21, 1963, p. 44.

photographs, lectures, newspapers, periodicals, textbooks, and courses—certainly the teacher can soon find *something* to use as a resource.

One other understanding that the teacher must have, though, concerns his attitudes about the intelligence and capability of the Negro and particularly of the ones classified as "culturally deprived." Many writers, like Reissman, have cast doubt on the reliability of IQ tests as true measurements.[12] Another recent scientific study goes further, in a different direction:

> There is not sufficient evidence to justify the conclusion that there are native differences between the intelligence of whites and Negroes. The nature of intelligence tests is such that they are incapable of identifying genetic differences between any two groups.[13]

That teachers must be careful how they label groups is further illustrated by a classic example from Senior. He asks, "What group do you think is being discussed?"

> They are satisfied with poor living conditions. . . . They don't want modern facilities. . . . They won't use bath tubs. . . . They don't want to change their standards. . . . They're destructive and overspend money. . . . We've known about any number of illegitimate children who have moved into already overcrowded homes with mother. I recall a family with thirteen children of its own. Sister has four illegitimate children. . . . —and so forth.[14]

Senior answers his question by revealing that this discussion is "of the purest 'Nordics' in the United States: the white, Protestant, individualistic Southern mountaineer, in Cincinnati. . . ."[15]

If teachers will teach more of the truth, the solution is perhaps in sight, for this may lead to a corresponding rise in the Negro's self-esteem. With greater self-esteem the Negro secondary school youth may become more teachable, the white youth more understanding and appreciative. This is not guaranteed, but is it worth a try?

But the questioner asks, "Why can't the Negro child's parents teach him his history and give him motivation?" It's a good question, but overlooks the fact that many Negro parents can't. They can't teach what they don't know. They can't motivate what they don't feel. One writer calls them "only an older generation of the disadvantaged. . . . The problem of the educator is to break the vicious circle."[16]

---

[12] Virgil A. Clift, Review of *The Culturally Deprived Child and His Education,* by Frank Reissman, *Journal of Negro Education,* Vol. 32, Spring, 1963, p. 152.

[13] Melvin M. Tumin, *Race and Intelligence—A Scientific Evaluation,* Anti-Defamation League of B'nai B'rith, New York, 1963, pp. 13–33.

[14] Clarence Senior, *Strangers—Then Neighbors: From Pilgrims to Puerto Ricans,* Anti-Defamation League of B'nai B'rith, New York, 1961, p. 17.

[15] *Ibid.*

[16] Ronald Rousseve, "Teachers of Culturally Disadvantaged American Youth," *Journal of Negro Education,* Vol. 32, Spring, 1963, p. 114. To a remarkable degree the Jews, with stronger economic resources and unbroken traditional heritage, have been able to do this in the synagogue and in the home.

The Negro teachers alone cannot accomplish this, if for no other reason than that they are too few. Woodson offers a more potent reason.

Taught from books of the same bias, trained by Caucasians of the same prejudices or by Negroes of enslaved minds, one generation of Negro teachers after another has served for no higher purpose than to do what they are told to do.[17]

This statement, whether true or not, runs the risk of inflaming many a Negro teacher. Undoubtedly, however, few Negro teachers have had the chance to learn very much of Negro culture and history.

What about the mental health of the teacher, Negro and white alike? With apparently little or no help currently available, in terms of what to do for the disadvantaged youngster, is the teacher's mental health unassailable? The problem looms particularly for the "white, college youngsters having the advantages of economic and family security, early primed for middle class success,—who in great numbers will teach in the 'slum schools.'"

To combat the corrosive effects of centuries of human bondage, denial, and the ghetto, what other practicable alternative have we? Is this suggested program, to incorporate the teaching of Negro culture in the secondary school curriculum, worthwhile? Shall we try it and see? One thing is certain. Even if this were to work, it is extremely doubtful that this alone would suffice. Our educational system and our society must do all of the other things at the same time.

CONCLUSIONS

1. Cultural training is basically important to good social and educational adjustment.

2. Society normally uses many means to effect this sort of training.

3. In the case of the Negro, society has been remiss. Consequently, the self-esteem of the Negro has nearly been bred out of him, while on the other hand whites have been led into an ungrounded sense of superiority. Both of these conditions are damaging to the mental health of the country.

4. One effective remedy may be to incorporate such training into appropriate places in the secondary school curriculum.

[17] Woodson, *op. cit.*, p. 23.

The Psychosocial Basis of Racism

It is a common approach to consider the position of the Negro in American society as a part of what is often termed "the Negro problem." This point of view focuses on the life style of the Negro family, the history of the Negro in the U.S., and the descriptive conditions which differentiate the Negro community from the non-Negro areas. Another way to look at the discrimination issue is to observe the non-Negro, who is essentially responsible for "the Negro problem." What economic, social, and psychological factors operating in the white community perpetuate this problem? By examining these factors and the conduct and attitudes they evoke, the reader can more easily understand why racial and ethnic segregation is practiced.

How do the texts used in schools treat the history of racism? Are the schools, through books and teachers, continuing the psychological need for racism? How can the racism motif be destroyed? Is it a universal occurrence?

The Nature and Function of Racism: A General Hypothesis

JAMES A. TILLMAN, JR.

Racism may be viewed as the active commitment to and basic use of race as the central component in the generalized system of criteria by which the individual makes ultimate judgments concerning other people.

Racism permeates and suffuses the whole fabric of Western culture. It is supernational, i.e., it has a universality that transcends national boundaries. The *compulsion* to practice racism also afflicts Catholics, Jews, and Protestants as well as the unchurched and nonbelievers. Moreover, it is found in all classes in Western culture. Its manifestations differ from country to country and from region to region within the same country; but, at bottom, its basic nature and its fundamental psychosocial function remain the same. Wherever and whenever practiced, racism is a

Reprinted from the *Journal of Human Relations*, Vol. 13, First Quarter, 1964, pp. 50–59, by permission of the publisher.

form of behavior by which the individual attempts to mitigate the difficulties, uncertainties and fears attendant upon his own moment in history by seeking an ultimate identity and a basic security that he is not required to earn by objective achievement; that is to say, racism is a basic manifestation of Western man's refusal to stand alone and his self-defeating attempts to flee the awesome responsibilities and the unavoidable tensions and uncertainties that inherently characterize the fluid and potentially open society. *Racism, for Western man, is a manifestation of his attempt to escape from himself.*

RACISM IN HISTORIC PERSPECTIVE

When the historic antecedents of contemporary Western society are examined—Egypt, Greece, Rome, pre-Crusade Europe and feudal Europe—it becomes overwhelmingly clear that racism, which underpins the segregated society, is a peculiar and unique function of a certain type of social and economic system; a highly fluid commercial and industrial system that, during its incipient phase, depended upon the subjugation and exploitation of overseas labor markets.

A critical examination of the antecedents of Western society, as we know it today, reveals that racism did not exist prior to the overseas expansion and exploration of Europe. In no other society, ancient or contemporary, do we find a labyrinth of legalism devoted to defining the "place" of various groups along racial lines.

In both Egypt and Greece, for example, the relationships between different groups were those of captor and captive—or, more precisely, master and slave. It is true that the Greeks knew some Negroes as slaves, but most slaves were racially the same as the Greeks. The relationship between being Negro and being a slave was not sufficiently consistent and constant to give rise to the association of a special physical type with that of slave status. Moreover, there can be no doubt that the most basic distinction that the Greeks made between themselves and other peoples was essentially cultural: any barbarian could remove himself from Greek exclusion by adopting Hellenistic culture.

Slaves among the Romans were drawn from Germans, Britons, Ethiopians, Nubians, and Africans. Romans spoke contemptuously of all peoples they conquered irrespective of race. Initially, marriage between Romans and barbarians was stoutly discouraged. Citizenship, not race, was at the bottom of this objection. Such unions, it was contended, flouted the custom of marriage between citizens. It should be noted, however, that in time even this prohibition passed away under the successive influence of the Stoics and the early Christians.

Rome's successor, the Catholic Church, in time became an instrument of international order demanding that all be brought under its administrative and theological umbrella. Out of this motivation, the Catholic Church waged "holy wars" against Muslims and pagans. Religion in this situation thus became the ultimate criterion of division and the basic source of antagonism among men. Muslims were enslaved by Christians because they were viewed as enemies of the faith. The rigid and systematic definition of the unbeliever as a member of the *outgroup* developed to its fullest on European soil between the First Crusades and the discovery of America.

Following the initial explorations by Europeans, this method of dividing humanity into the *ingroup* and *outgroup* was taken over by the colonizing powers and a racial content was substituted for the original religious content.

There was a compelling pragmatic reason for substituting race for religion. As the Europeans expanded and commercialism grew, there developed among the explorers the necessity for free and cheap labor. Since the missionary and proselyting spirit of Christianity made it possible and desirable for heathens to become Christian and thereby members of the *ingroup,* it became necessary for European settlers and explorers to create a new ideology with which and by which to justify their exploitation of the natives. In other words, the natives—in spite of the fact that many became Christians—had to be rendered *outgroup members.* This definition of the natives the Europeans arrived at by resorting to racism, which in time replaced both religion and nationalism as mechanisms of exclusion and internal cohesion.

The history of European contacts with non-Europeans from the beginning of the period of exploration is a history of Europe's attempt to depersonalize and dehumanize whole groups of non-Europeans in order to reduce them to effective instruments of exploitation in the pursuit of wealth and profit. By doing so, Europeans sought to create a *standard* method for rationalizing their treatment of non-Europeans. This, then, is a brief outline of the historic antecedents of today's racism.

Many of the reasons that, in the West's view, necessitated the rise and development of racism have long since passed away with the growth of urban industrialism; but, in time, racism, which grew up originally to justify a specific economic condition, became a *compulsion* and a defense mechanism for many who sought both a stable sense of identity and status in a highly fluid social system.

THE FUNCTION OF RACISM

Many Americans begin their attempt to change both attitudes and conduct by accepting segregation and discrimination as a collective *given* in the field of minority-majority relations. Any attempt to determine the elemental function of this *given* for the majority group is often omitted.

The addiction by majority group members to the "tolerance" and "brother-hood" theses in intergroup relations is a universally standard technique by which majority group members try to avoid an examination of the *function* that the segregationist attitude performs for the personalities of majority group members.

It is important that Americans understand the social and psychological nature of the resistance to the open society. *Briefly, the resistance is symbolic of the American's fear of standing alone in a fluid society where both status and a sense of identity must be achieved before one's in-dividual security can be established.* Repeatedly, those who resist the open society indicate, consciously and unconsciously, that the creation of such a society will, in their view, seriously upset both their sense of iden-tity and their self-defined status in a fluid society.

It is true that racism grew up in the Western world, in great part, to justify and rationalize the violent extension of Western capitalism (and exploitation) to Asia and Africa. And it is also true that in time racism was transformed into a new means by which Western man sought to create for himself a sense of identity and a sense of security. Racism eventually replaced nationalism, which had itself replaced the stability and the sense of identity that the feudal structure provided for Western man.

The experiences of the Greater Minneapolis Interfaith Fair Housing Program indicate that, on the whole, the average white American lives in a state of quiet desperation in regard to both his status and his sense of ultimate identity as an individual.

Rationality and Irrationality. Racism, expressed in resistance to equality of opportunity, serves the essential function of ameliorating the tensions that flow from the American's sense of desperation regarding his identity and his status. The American's fear of standing alone finds expression in the same mechanisms that have served to distinguish the West in many ways from earlier and other contemporary cultures; namely, the unique combination and social application of the matriarchal and patriarchal complexes.

The operation of the patriarchal spirit in Western society since the Renaissance is symbolized by an increasingly rational spirit that has found expression in the growth and development of science. This same patriarchal spirit has also led to irrational nationalism and to racism. Both nationalism and racism involve blind submission of the individual to an overriding mechanism that provides him with a sense of ultimate iden-tity and a symbol of consistent authority.

At the same time, the application of the matriarchal spirit (which is grounded in the idea of man's commonality by virtue of a common ori-gin in and common relationship to Mother Earth) has led to the idea of human equality before the law. On the other hand, we find that this same idea has also led to racism. Cut adrift by the great revolutions from the ties that gave him permanent identity and status in the medieval community, Western man became an isolate; he was required to stand alone or to find new bonds to replace those that operated in the feudal community. He sought escape from the isolation inherent in his new freedom by creating, in turn, new idol gods: nationalism and racism. Racism, which grew up initially to rationalize a specific type of economic pattern, replaced the nationalism that emerged from the ashes of feudalism. It then became a new idol and gave him a new sense of identity. When applied in majority-minority relations, it also gave him a sense of status that he was not required to earn by objective achievement.

These tendencies have been developed and sustained in the United States in a much more systematic way than is the case in Europe where social fluidity is less pronounced than in America.

The Quest for Identity. The fact that the *compulsion* to discriminate along racial and religious lines is so widespread in the Western world suggests that it is related to a problem that universally afflicts Western man. A clue to the nature of this problem can be found in those studies in the psychosocial disciplines that have attempted systematically to examine the relationship between the prejudiced outlook and the nature of social mobility in the West. In a summary fashion, I think it can be said that while there is no clear-cut and consistent relationship between the individual's status at a given time and his addiction to or freedom from irrational and antirational prejudice, a very perceptible and consistently strong relationship emerges when one begins to examine social mobility and prejudice. Studies seem to show that prejudice is found among all classes in Western society and that prejudice is strongest among the most mobile elements in the population. Moreover, it would appear that it does not seem to matter greatly whether the mobility is upward or downward. Prejudice is very high among people who have experienced *upward* mobility and relatively low among those who have remained fairly stable. *Mobility,* then, seems to increase and intensify prejudice; relative *stability* tends, it would appear, to lessen prejudice.

If mobility, per se, *not simple loss of status,* seems to increase prejudice, the logical and unavoidable question becomes this: what basic feature is common to both upward and downward mobility? Again, the literature suggests that mobility inevitably upsets the individual's *self-concept* and brings the person's *identity* into serious question. In Western man's continuous attempt to establish his own individual identity—to acquire and maintain a consistent self-concept—the external social symbols, many of which can be both acquired and lost, are used as supports. His profession, name, established habits and, above all else, his *race,* all tend to define who he is and to establish consistent behavior expectations with reference to his role vis-à-vis the roles of others.

Changes in external circumstances, and these are unavoidable in a society where feudal symbolism is not very strong, necessarily require changes in the person's habitual responses to the world and in the responses of other people to him. *This means, therefore, that changes in external circumstances are likely to change one's sense of identity. This leads to anxiety from which the individual inevitably seeks escape.*

The quest for identity is common to all people, but its consequences seem to be more severe among Western man because of the fluidity and mobility that characterize the West. Information in the areas of sociology, history, anthropology, and psychology tends to substantiate this broad generalization.

The quest for identity first evidences itself in early childhood when the child seeks to substitute a superego for his initial dependence on parental care. Initially, this is accomplished by the child's gradual identification with either or both parents. The cultural function and demands of parenthood in highly organized societies among humans make the process of achieving a self-concept difficult for the child. Before the individual can achieve self-control, autonomy and an appreciation of the need for rules, punishment and disapproval may often induce in him a sense of not being wanted. Confusion with respect to the self-image is inevitable at this stage; but many Western people, unfortunately, never overcome this confusion. For many, it remains throughout their lives a basic feature of their personality.

Case materials in the psychosocial disciplines indicate that persons who are particularly irrational and antirational with respect to race have had a particularly difficult and severe identity conflict. If the individual retains the insecurity attendant upon his early childhood attempts at selfhood, he is likely to view and interpret the apparently sharply defined and precise identity of others as undeniable evidence of his own failure. If he can, by distorting reality and by the use of rationalization, bring himself to believe that the sharply defined identity of others results from their inferiority, he can then live with his own confusion regarding his own identity more easily. He may be wholly uncertain about his own identity, but he can reassure himself that "at least, I am *not* a Negro or a Jew" or he can say: "I *am* free, *white* and twenty-one," if he is an adult.

In his incessant attempt to find some consistently reliable equilibrium and to come to terms with himself, Western man's efforts at establishing sexual identity is vital. Continuing conflicts in this area may become the most common source of anxiety. Normally, when all goes well, the child comes out of his early phase of turbulence at five or six years of age without lasting scars, having developed a strong identification with the parent of his own sex, but with the capacity to love both parents with a full and healthy recognition of the differences between the two. The literature tends to suggest that even when the confusion of sexual roles is apparently routinely overcome, many adults continue to bear scars of this early struggle. These scars seem to manifest themselves in anxiety concerning adequacy in the adult's sexual role. It should not come as a surprise that racial antagonism, a symbol of man's unstable sense of identity, has a strong and vital sex component.

Summarily stated, then, irrational and antirational prejudice today seems to characterize a certain type of personality: the personality that has not been able to overcome unresolved doubts about his own identity. The sex role is vital, not marginal or peripheral, in this conflict; hence the preoccupation with sex and minority relations among highly prejudiced people. This conflict regarding identity is apparently universal among the human species, but the highly prejudiced seem to suffer from this conflict to an exaggerated extent.

Because of its fluidity and the mobility that characterizes it, Western society (particularly the United States) as a social system seems to foster those social forces that apparently make a sense of identity difficult to achieve. Moreover, a sense of autonomy, which permits one to act from inner regulations, is also difficult to achieve; hence the ultimate identification with and reliance upon race that enables the individual to achieve an easy and apparently undeniable identity.

This identification is unhealthy and in the long run self-defeating, because it robs the person of the opportunity to achieve that relative autonomy that characterizes the mature. Consequently, as an individual, he is never the conscious and deliberate subject and object of his own mental processes. He, therefore, never develops a stable and reliable sense of identity and can never fully accept himself as an individual. He seeks escape from (or identity for) himself within a mother and father image called "race."

The Quest for Status. Success and survival in a highly fluid society where status is not determined by feudal considerations require great mobility. America is basically a fluid society where people are required to engage in mobility to achieve in the first instance. *They are also required, in the second instance, to engage in continuing mobility if they are to protect that which has already been achieved.*

In spite of the fluidity of our society, symbols in our culture do acquire and reflect differential and unequal rankings; that is to say, some symbols are more to be desired at a given time than others. Most Americans engage in a life-long pursuit of the symbols that are rated high on our society's rank-order scale of values.

The essential difference between our highly fluid and mobile society and other societies that are relatively static and feudal is to be found in the fact that preferential status symbols can be acquired, with notable exceptions, largely through one's own abilities. These exceptions (caste and racist restrictions) are often significant and help to make general mobility and the resulting anxiety more bearable.

It can be said that American society is basically pyramidal in nature. The number of attainable success symbols decreases as one moves up the vertical scale of mobility. The possibility of failure is therefore increased.

The anxieties related to mobility are constant and ever-present and are often intensified by the recognition that status symbols, like all items of value, are not unrelated to scarcity.

The recognition of this scarcity is made consciously or unconsciously by most Americans. Sooner or later, they recognize that their own abilities and the very nature of our social system impose limitations upon what they can achieve in their own lifetimes. This recognition often leads to frustrations and to aggression that is sublimated or displaced. The existence of lower caste-like groups, which segregated practices make possible, often serves the purpose of providing members of the majority group with a disadvantaged group on which they may displace and sublimate their aggression.

Irrespective of the amount of physical contact that occurs between members of the majority group and members of a minority group, the relationships remain essentially those of superordination and subordination. In such a situation, members of the majority group—irrespective of their general worth and status—enjoy an advantaged position in relation to members of the minority.

Psychosocial ills that damage the whole community result from segregation and discrimination based upon race; for this arbitrary mechanism of exclusivity often becomes the only means by which cohesion is maintained in the superordinate group and by which identity is established in a rapidly changing world.

CONCLUSION

From the previous discussion, it would seem that Americans, on the whole, are resistant to accelerating changes in race relations because racism provides the average American white a universally understood and respectable mechanism for mitigating the tensions, insecurities, and uncertainties incident to living in a fluid society. Moreover, racism provides the average American with an easily accessible method by which both identity and status may be established in a society that is relatively devoid of feudal symbolism.

Attempts to induce the American to become committed to equality of opportunity must rest firmly on the knowledge that lasting and meaningful changes in race relations cannot be achieved unless the majority-group American is given the psychosocial tools that will enable him to accept himself, with his limitations and failures, as well as his assets and successes, and to live with uncertainty.

I suggest that the elimination of racism is central, not marginal or peripheral, to Western man's quest for freedom; for it is clear that he who derives his ultimate identity from his race is not yet prepared to live maturely and responsibly in a free society. Racism nullifies and negates the basic conditions necessary for the birth and growth of the free society. The West can never hope to realize its fullest potential until it sheds the yoke of racism.

The central question before this Conference, it seems to me, is this: How can churches and synagogues *actively* and intelligently participate in and give leadership to programs that can remove the yoke of racism from America with all deliberate speed? In our deliberations, I hope we shall not be shackled and immobilized by yesterday's timidity and lack of vision. We can, if we but desire, take bold and imaginative steps here today. Let it never be said that, in our moments of supreme opportunity, we faltered because we lacked the capacity and the will to see and embrace the future.

The Changing Character of the Civil Rights Movement

The title of the next article, "From Protest to Politics," states very clearly its central theme. It argues that the Negro protest movement by confining itself to active demonstrations will not be able to effectively succeed in its goal—the elimination of pernicious social and economic discrimination against the Negro community. To achieve success on a national scale will require the development of extensive political action by the Negro movement. Similar to the article by Joseph P. Lyford, "Proposal for a Revolution," this article contends that unemployment and poverty are the result of deficiencies in the overall functioning of society. Rustin feels that the resolution to the problems confronting the civil rights movement lies in the acquisition of political power rather than in isolated protest actions.

What effects will the changing nature of the civil rights movement have on society and the schools? If the lower rungs of the economic ladder are being eliminated by the technological revolution, as is stated in the following article, how can the schools alter the educational level of Negroes rapidly enough to keep ahead of the pace?

From Protest to Politics:
The Future of the Civil Rights Movement

BAYARD RUSTIN

The decade spanned by the 1954 Supreme Court decision on school de segregation and the Civil Rights Act of 1964 will undoubtedly be recorded as the period in which the legal foundations of racism in America were destroyed. To be sure, pockets of resistance remain; but it would be hard to quarrel with the assertion that the elaborate legal structure of segregation and discrimination, particularly in relation to public accommodations, has virtually collapsed. On the other hand, without making light of the human sacrifices involved in the direct-action tactics (sit-ins, freedom rides, and the rest) that were so instrumental to this achievement, we must recognize that in desegregating public accommodations, we affected institutions which are relatively peripheral both to the American socio-economic order and to the fundamental conditions of life of the Negro people. In a highly industrialized, 20th-century civilization, we hit Jim Crow precisely where it was most anachronistic, dispensable, and vulnerable—in hotels, lunch counters, terminals, libraries, swimming pools, and the like. For in these forms, Jim Crow does impede the flow of commerce in the broadest sense: it is a nuisance in a society on the move (and on the make). Not surprisingly, therefore, it was the most mobility-conscious and relatively liberated group in the Negro community—lower-middle-class college students—who launched the attack that brought down this imposing but hollow structure.

The term "classical" appears especially apt for this phase of the civil rights movement. But in the few years that have passed since the first flush of sit-ins, several developments have taken place that have complicated matters enormously. One is the shifting focus of the movement in the South, symbolized by Birmingham; another is the spread of the revolution to the North; and the third, common to the other two, is the expansion of the movement's base in the Negro community. To attempt to disentangle these three strands is to do violence to reality. David Danzig's perceptive article, "The Meaning of Negro Strategy," [*Commentary*, Feb., 1964] correctly saw in the Birmingham events the victory of the concept of collective struggle over individual achievement as the road to Negro freedom. And Birmingham remains the unmatched symbol of grass-roots protest

involving all strata of the black community. It was also in this most industrialized of Southern cities that the single-issue demands of the movement's classical stage gave way to the "package deal." No longer were
Negroes satisfied with integrating lunch counters. They now sought advances in employment, housing, school integration, police protection, and
so forth.

Thus, the movement in the South began to attack areas of discrimination
which were not so remote from the Northern experience as were Jim Crow
lunch counters. At the same time, the interrelationship of these apparently
distinct areas became increasingly evident. What is the value of winning
access to public accommodations for those who lack money to use them?
The minute the movement faced this question, it was compelled to expand
its vision beyond race relations to economic relations, including the role
of education in modern society. And what also became clear is that all
these interrelated problems, by their very nature, are not soluble by private, voluntary efforts but require government action—or politics. Already
Southern demonstrators had recognized that the most effective way to
strike at the police brutality they suffered from was by getting rid of the
local sheriff—and that meant political action, which in turn meant, and
still means, political action within the Democratic party where the only
meaningful primary contests in the South are fought.

And so, in Mississippi, thanks largely to the leadership of Bob Moses, a
turn toward political action has been taken. More than voter registration is
involved here. A conscious bid for *political power* is being made, and in
the course of that effort a tactical shift is being effected: direct-action
techniques are being subordinated to a strategy calling for the building of
community institutions or power bases. Clearly, the implications of this
shift reach far beyond Mississippi. What began as a protest movement is
being challenged to translate itself into a political movement. Is this the
right course? And if it is, can the transformation be accomplished?

The very decade which has witnessed the decline of legal Jim Crow has
also seen the rise of *de facto* segregation in our most fundamental socio-
economic institutions. More Negroes are unemployed today than in 1954,
and the unemployment gap between the races is wider. The median income of Negroes has dropped from 57 percent to 54 percent of that of
whites. A higher percentage of Negro workers is now concentrated in jobs
vulnerable to automation than was the case ten years ago. More Negroes
attend *de facto* segregated schools today than when the Supreme Court
handed down its famous decision; while school integration proceeds at a
snail's pace in the South, the number of Northern schools with an excessive proportion of minority youth proliferates. And behind this is the
continuing growth of racial slums, spreading over our central cities and
trapping Negro youth in a milieu which, whatever its legal definition, sows
an unimaginable demoralization. Again, legal niceties aside, a resident of

a racial ghetto lives in segregated housing, and more Negroes fall into this category than ever before.

These are the facts of life which generate frustration in the Negro community and challenge the civil rights movement. At issue, after all, is not *civil rights*, strictly speaking, but social and economic conditions. Last summer's riots were not race riots; they were outbursts of class aggression in a society where class and color definitions are converging disastrously. How can the (perhaps misnamed) civil rights movement deal with this problem?

Before trying to answer, let me first insist that the task of the movement is vastly complicated by the failure of many whites of good will to understand the nature of our problem. There is a widespread assumption that the removal of artificial racial barriers should result in the automatic integration of the Negro into all aspects of American life. This myth is fostered by facile analogies with the experience of various ethnic immigrant groups, particularly the Jews. But the analogies with the Jews do not hold for three simple but profound reasons. First, Jews have a long history as a literate people, a resource which has afforded them opportunities to advance in the academic and professional worlds, to achieve intellectual status even in the midst of economic hardship, and to evolve sustaining value systems in the context of ghetto life. Negroes, for the greater part of their presence in this country, were forbidden by law to read or write. Second, Jews have a long history of family stability, the importance of which in terms of aspiration and self-image is obvious. The Negro family structure was totally destroyed by slavery and with it the possibility of cultural transmission (the right of Negroes to marry and rear children is barely a century old). Third, Jews are white and have the *option* of relinquishing their cultural-religious identity, intermarrying, passing, etc. Negroes, or at least the overwhelming majority of them, do not have this option. There is also a fourth, vulgar reason. If the Jewish and Negro communities are not comparable in terms of education, family structure, and color, it is also true that their respective economic roles bear little resemblance.

This matter of economic role brings us to the greater problem—the fact that we are moving into an era in which the natural functioning of the market does not by itself ensure every man with will and ambition a place in the productive process. The immigrant who came to this country during the late 19th and early 20th centuries entered a society which was expanding territorially and/or economically. It was then possible to start at the bottom, as an unskilled or semi-skilled worker, and move up the ladder, acquiring new skills along the way. Especially was this true when industrial unionism was burgeoning, giving new dignity and higher wages to organized workers. Today the situation has changed. We are not expanding territorially, the western frontier is settled, labor organizing has leveled off, our rate of economic growth has been stagnant for a decade. And we are in the midst of a technological revolution which is altering the fundamental structure of the labor force, destroying unskilled and semi-skilled jobs—jobs in which Negroes are disproportionately concentrated.

Whatever the pace of this technological revolution may be, the *direction* is clear: the lower rungs of the economic ladder are being lopped off. This means that an individual will no longer be able to start at the bottom and work his way up; he will have to start in the middle or on top, and hold on tight. It will not even be enough to have certain specific skills, for many skilled jobs are also vulnerable to automation. A broad educational background, permitting vocational adaptability and flexibility, seems more imperative than ever. We live in a society where, as Secretary of Labor Willard Wirtz puts it, machines have the equivalent of a high school diploma. Yet the average educational attainment of American Negroes is 8.2 years.

Negroes, of course, are not the only people being affected by these developments. It is reported that there are now 50 percent fewer unskilled and semi-skilled jobs than there are high school dropouts. Almost one-third of the 26 million young people entering the labor market in the 1960's will be dropouts. But the percentage of Negro dropouts nationally is 57 percent, and in New York City, among Negroes 25 years of age or over, it is 68 percent. They are without a future.

To what extent can the kind of self-help campaign recently prescribed by Eric Hoffer in the *New York Times Magazine* cope with such a situation? I would advise those who think that self-help is the answer to familiarize themselves with the long history of such efforts in the Negro community, and to consider why so many foundered on the shoals of ghetto life. It goes without saying that any effort to combat demoralization and apathy is desirable, but we must understand that demoralization in the Negro community is largely a common-sense response to an objective reality. Negro youths have no need of statistics to perceive, fairly accurately, what their odds are in American society. Indeed, from the point of view of motivation, some of the healthiest Negro youngsters I know are juvenile delinquents: vigorously pursuing the American Dream of material acquisition and status, yet finding the conventional means of attaining it blocked off, they do not yield to defeatism but resort to illegal (and often ingenious) methods. They are not alien to American culture. They are, in Gunnar Myrdal's phrase, "exaggerated Americans." To want a Cadillac is not un-American; to push a cart in the garment center is. If Negroes are to be persuaded that the conventional path (school, work, etc.) is superior, we had better provide evidence which is now sorely lacking. It is a double cruelty to harangue Negro youth about education and training when we do not know what jobs will be available for them. When a Negro youth can reasonably foresee a future free of slums, when the prospect of gainful employment is realistic, we will see motivation and self-help in abundant enough quantities.

Meanwhile, there is an ironic similarity between the self-help advocated by many liberals and the doctrines of the Black Muslims. Professional sociologists, psychiatrists, and social workers have expressed amazement at the Muslims' success in transforming prostitutes and dope addicts into respectable citizens. But every prostitute the Muslims convert to a model of Calvinist virtue is replaced by the ghetto with two more. Dedicated as they are to maintenance of the ghetto, the Muslims are powerless to affect substantial moral reform. So too with every other group or program which is not aimed at the destruction of slums, their causes and effects. Self-help efforts, directly or indirectly, must be geared to mobilizing people into power units capable of effecting social change. That is, their goal must be genuine self-help, not merely self-improvement. Obviously, where self-improvement activities succeed in imparting to their participants a feeling of some control over their environment, those involved may find their appetites for change whetted; they may move into the political arena.

Let me sum up what I have thus far been trying to say: the civil rights movement is evolving from a protest movement into a full-fledged *social movement*—an evolution calling its very name into question. It is now concerned not merely with removing the barriers to full *opportunity* but with achieving the fact of *equality*. From sit-ins and freedom rides we have gone into rent strikes, boycotts, community organization, and political action. As a consequence of this natural evolution, the Negro today finds himself stymied by obstacles of far greater magnitude than the legal barriers he was attacking before: automation, urban decay, *de facto* school segregation. These are problems which, while conditioned by Jim Crow, do not vanish upon its demise. They are more deeply rooted in our socioeconomic order; they are the result of the total society's failure to meet not only the Negro's needs, but human needs generally.

These propositions have won increasing recognition and acceptance, but with a curious twist. They have formed the common premise of two apparently contradictory lines of thought which simultaneously nourish and antagonize each other. On the one hand, there is the reasoning of the *New York Times* moderate who says that the problems are so enormous and complicated that Negro militancy is a futile irritation, and that the need is for "intelligent moderation." Thus, during the first New York school boycott, the *Times* editorialized that Negro demands, while abstractly just, would necessitate massive reforms, the funds for which could not realistically be anticipated; therefore the just demands were also foolish demands and would only antagonize white people. Moderates of this stripe are often correct in perceiving the difficulty or impossibility of racial progress in the context of present social and economic policies. But they accept the context as fixed. They ignore (or perhaps see all too well) the potentialities inherent in linking Negro demands to broader pressures for radical revision of existing policies. They apparently see nothing strange in the fact that in the last twenty-five years we have spent nearly a trillion dollars fighting or preparing for wars, yet throw up our hands before the need for overhauling our schools, clearing the slums, and really abolishing poverty. My quarrel with these moderates is that they do not even envision radical changes; their admonitions of moderation are, for all practical purposes, admonitions to the Negro to adjust to the status quo, and are therefore immoral.

The more effectively the moderates argue their case, the more they convince Negroes that American society will not or cannot be reorganized for full racial equality. Michael Harrington has said that a successful war on poverty might well require the expenditure of a $100 billion. Where, the Negro wonders, are the forces now in motion to compel such a commitment? If the voices of the moderates were raised in an insistence upon a reallocation of national resources at levels that could not be confused with tokenism (that is, if the moderates stopped being moderates), Negroes would have greater grounds for hope. Meanwhile, the Negro movement cannot escape a sense of isolation.

It is precisely this sense of isolation that gives rise to the second line of thought I want to examine—the tendency within the civil rights movement which, despite its militancy, pursues what I call a "no-win" policy. Sharing with many moderates a recognition of the magnitude of the obstacles to freedom, spokesmen for this tendency survey the American scene and find no forces prepared to move toward radical solutions. From this they conclude that the only viable strategy is shock; above all, the hypocrisy of white liberals must be exposed. These spokesmen are often described as the radicals of the movement, but they are really its moralists. They seek to change white hearts—by traumatizing them. Frequently abetted by white self-flagellants, they gleefully applauded (though not really agreeing with) Malcolm X because, while they admitted he had no program, they thought he could frighten white people into doing the right thing. To believe this, of course, you must be convinced, even if unconsciously, that at the core of the white man's heart lies a buried affection for Negroes —a proposition one may be permitted to doubt. But in any case, hearts are not relevant to the issue; neither racial affinities nor racial hostilities are rooted there. It is institutions—social, political, and economic institutions— which are the ultimate molders of collective sentiments. Let these institutions be reconstructed *today*, and let the ineluctable gradualism of history govern the formation of a new psychology.

My quarrel with the "no-win" tendency in the civil rights movement (and the reason I have so designated it) parallels my quarrel with the moderates outside the movement. As the latter lack the vision or will for fundamental change, the former lack a realistic strategy for achieving it. For such a strategy they substitute militancy. But militancy is a matter of posture and volume and not of effect.

I believe that the Negro's struggle for equality in America is essentially revolutionary. While most Negroes—in their hearts—unquestionably seek only to enjoy the fruits of American society as it now exists, their quest cannot *objectively* be satisfied within the framework of existing political and economic relations. The young Negro who would demonstrate his way into the labor market may be motivated by a thoroughly bourgeois ambition and thoroughly "capitalist" considerations, but he will end up having to favor a great expansion of the public sector of the economy. At any rate, that is the position the movement will be forced to take as it looks at the number of jobs being generated by the private economy, and if it is to remain true to the masses of Negroes.

The revolutionary character of the Negro's struggle is manifest in the fact that this struggle may have done more to democratize life for whites than for Negroes. Clearly, it was the sit-in movement of young Southern Negroes which, as it galvanized white students, banished the ugliest features of McCarthyism from the American campus and resurrected political debate. It was not until Negroes assaulted *de facto* school segregation in the urban centers that the issue of quality education for *all* children stirred into motion. Finally, it seems reasonably clear that the civil rights movement, directly and through the resurgence of social conscience it kindled, did more to initiate the war on poverty than any other single force.

It will be—it has been—argued that these by-products of the Negro struggle are not revolutionary. But the term revolutionary, as I am using it, does not connote violence; it refers to the qualitative transformation of fundamental institutions, more or less rapidly, to the point where the social and economic structure which they comprised can no longer be said to be the same. The Negro struggle has hardly run its course; and it will not stop moving until it has been utterly defeated or won substantial equality. But I fail to see how the movement can be victorious in the absence of radical programs for full employment, abolition of slums, the reconstruction of our educational system, new definitions of work and leisure. Adding up the cost of such programs, we can only conclude that we are talking about a refashioning of our political economy. It has been estimated, for example, that the price of replacing New York City's slums with public housing would be $17 billion. Again, a multi-billion dollar federal public-works program, dwarfing the currently proposed $2 billion program, is required to reabsorb unskilled and semi-skilled workers into the labor market—and this must be done if Negro workers in these categories are to be employed. "Preferential treatment" cannot help them.

I am not trying here to delineate a total program, only to suggest the scope of economic reforms which are most immediately related to the plight of the Negro community. One could speculate on their political implications—whether, for example, they do not indicate the obsolescence of state government and the superiority of regional structures as viable units of planning. Such speculations aside, it is clear that Negro needs cannot be satisfied unless we go beyond what has so far been placed on the agenda. How are these radical objectives to be achieved? The answer is simple, deceptively so: *through political power.*

There is a strong moralistic strain in the civil rights movement which would remind us that power corrupts, forgetting that the absence of power also corrupts. But this is not the view I want to debate here, for it is waning. Our problem is posed by those who accept the need for political power but do not understand the nature of the object and therefore lack sound strategies for achieving it; they tend to confuse political institutions with lunch counters.

A handful of Negroes, acting alone, could integrate a lunch counter by strategically locating their bodies so as *directly* to interrupt the operation of the proprietor's will; their numbers were relatively unimportant. In politics, however, such a confrontation is difficult because the interests involved are merely *represented*. In the execution of a political decision a direct confrontation may ensue (as when federal marshals escorted James Meredith into the University of Mississippi—to turn from an example of non-violent coercion to one of force backed up with the threat of violence). But in arriving at a political decision, numbers and organizations are crucial, especially for the economically disenfranchised. (Needless to say, I am assuming that the forms of political democracy exist in America, however imperfectly, that they are valued, and that elitist or putschist conceptions of exercising power are beyond the pale of discussion for the civil rights movement.)

Neither that movement nor the country's twenty million black people can win political power alone. We need allies. The future of the Negro struggle depends on whether the contradictions of this society can be resolved by a coalition of progressive forces which becomes the *effective* political majority in the United States. I speak of the coalition which staged the March on Washington, passed the Civil Rights Act, and laid the basis for the Johnson landslide—Negroes, trade unionists, liberals, and religious groups.

There are those who argue that a coalition strategy would force the Negro to surrender his political independence to white liberals, that he would be neutralized, deprived of his cutting edge, absorbed into the Establishment. Some who take this position urged last year that votes be withheld from the Johnson-Humphrey ticket as a demonstration of the Negro's political power. Curiously enough, these people who sought to demonstrate power through the non-exercise of it, also point to the Negro "swing vote" in crucial urban areas as the source of the Negro's independent political power. But here they are closer to being right: the urban Negro vote will grow in importance in the coming years. If there is anything positive in the spread of the ghetto, it is the potential political power base thus created, and to realize this potential is one of the most challenging and urgent tasks before the civil rights movement. If the movement can wrest leadership of the ghetto vote from the machines, it will have acquired an organized constituency such as other major groups in our society now have.

But we must also remember that the effectiveness of a swing vote depends solely on "other" votes. It derives its power from them. In that sense, it can never be "independent," but must opt for one candidate or the other, even if by default. Thus coalitions are inescapable, however tentative they may be. And this is the case in all but those few situations in which Negroes running on an independent ticket might conceivably win. "Independence," in other words, is not a value in itself. The issue is which coalition to join and how to make it responsive to your program. Necessarily there will be compromise. But the difference between expediency and morality in politics is the difference between selling out a principle and making smaller concessions to win larger ones. The leader who shrinks from this task reveals not his purity but his lack of political sense.

The task of molding a political movement out of the March on Washington coalition is not simple, but no alternatives have been advanced. We need to choose our allies on the basis of common political objectives. It has become fashionable in some no-win Negro circles to decry the white liberal as the main enemy (his hypocrisy is what sustains racism); by virtue of this reverse recitation of the reactionary's litany (liberalism leads to socialism, which leads to Communism) the Negro is left in majestic isolation, except for a tiny band of fervent white initiates. But the objective fact is that *Eastland and Goldwater* are the main enemies—they and the opponents of civil rights, of the war on poverty, of medicare, of social security, of federal aid to education, of unions, and so forth. The labor movement, despite its obvious faults, has been the largest single organized force in this country pushing for progressive social legislation. And where the Negro-labor-liberal axis is weak, as in the farm belt, it was the religious groups that were most influential in rallying support for the Civil Rights Bill.

The durability of the coalition was interestingly tested during the election. I do not believe that the Johnson landslide proved the "white backlash" to be a myth. It proved, rather, that economic interests are more fundamental than prejudice: the backlashers decided that loss of social security was, after all, too high a price to pay for a slap at the Negro. This lesson was a valuable first step in re-educating such people, and it must be kept alive, for the civil rights movement will be advanced only to the degree that social and economic welfare gets to be inextricably entangled with civil rights.

The 1964 elections marked a turning point in American politics. The Democratic landslide was not merely the result of a negative reaction to Goldwaterism; it was also the expression of a majority liberal consensus. The near unanimity with which Negro voters joined in that expression was,

I am convinced, a vindication of the July 25th statement by Negro leaders calling for a strategic turn toward political action and a temporary curtailment of mass demonstrations. Despite the controversy surrounding the statement, the instinctive response it met with in the community is suggested by the fact that demonstrations were down 75 percent as compared with the same period in 1963. But should so high a percentage of Negro voters have gone to Johnson, or should they have held back to narrow his margin of victory and thus give greater visibility to our swing vote? How has our loyalty changed things? Certainly the Negro vote had higher visibility in 1960, when a switch of only 7 percent from the Republican column of 1956 elected President Kennedy. But the slimness of Kennedy's victory—of his "mandate"—dictated a go-slow approach on civil rights, at least until the Birmingham upheaval.

Although Johnson's popular majority was so large that he could have won without such overwhelming Negro support, that support was important from several angles. Beyond adding to Johnson's total national margin, it was specifically responsible for his victories in Virginia, Florida, Tennessee, and Arkansas. Goldwater took only those states where fewer than 45 percent of eligible Negroes were registered. That Johnson would have won those states had Negro voting rights been enforced is a lesson not likely to be lost on a man who would have been happy with a unanimous electoral college. In any case, the 1.6 million Southern Negroes who voted have had a shattering impact on the Southern political party structure, as illustrated in the changed composition of the Southern congressional delegation. The "backlash" gave the Republicans five House seats in Alabama, one in Georgia, and one in Mississippi. But on the Democratic side, seven segregationists were defeated while all nine Southerners who voted for the Civil Rights Act were re-elected. It may be premature to predict a Southern Democratic party of Negroes and white moderates and a Republican Party of refugee racists and economic conservatives, but there certainly is a strong tendency toward such a realignment; and an additional 3.6 million Negroes of voting age in the eleven Southern states are still to be heard from. Even the *tendency* toward disintegration of the Democratic party's racist wing defines a new context for Presidential and liberal strategy in the congressional battles ahead. Thus the Negro vote (North as well as South), while not *decisive* in the Presidential race, was enormously effective. It was a dramatic element of a historic mandate which contains vast possibilities and dangers that will fundamentally affect the future course of the civil rights movement.

The liberal congressional sweep raises hope for an assault on the seniority system, Rule Twenty-two, and other citadels of Dixiecrat-Republican power. The overwhelming of this conservative coalition should also mean progress on much bottlenecked legislation of profound interest to the movement (e.g., bills by Senators Clark and Nelson on planning, manpower, and employment). Moreover, the irrelevance of the South to Johnson's victory gives the President more freedom to act than his predecessor had and more leverage to the movement to pressure for executive action in Mississippi and other racist strongholds.

None of this *guarantees* vigorous executive or legislative action, for the other side of the Johnson landslide is that it has a Gaullist quality. Goldwater's capture of the Republican party forced into the Democratic camp many disparate elements which do not belong there, Big Business being the major example. Johnson, who wants to be President "of all people," may try to keep his new coalition together by sticking close to the political center. But if he decides to do this, it is unlikely that even his political genius will be able to hold together a coalition so inherently unstable and rife with contradictions. It must come apart. Should it do so while Johnson is pursuing a centrist course, then the mandate will have been wastefully dissipated. However, if the mandate is seized upon to set fundamental changes in motion, then the basis can be laid for a new mandate, a new coalition including hitherto inert and dispossessed strata of the population.

Here is where the cutting edge of the civil rights movement can be applied. We must see to it that the reorganization of the "consensus party" proceeds along lines which will make it an effective vehicle for social reconstruction, a role it cannot play so long as it furnishes Southern racism with its national political power. (One of Barry Goldwater's few attractive ideas was that the Dixiecrats belong with him in the same party.) And nowhere has the civil rights movement's political cutting edge been more magnificently demonstrated than at Atlantic City, where the Mississippi Freedom Democratic Party not only secured recognition as a bona fide component of the national party, but in the process routed the representatives of the most rabid racists—the white Mississippi and Alabama delegations. While I still believe that the FDP made a tactical error in spurning the compromise, there is no question that they launched a political revolution whose logic is the displacement of Dixiecrat power. They launched that revolution within a major political institution and as part of a coalitional effort.

The role of the civil rights movement in the reorganization of American political life is programmatic as well as strategic. We are challenged now to broaden our social vision, to develop functional programs with concrete objectives. We need to propose alternatives to technological unemployment, urban decay, and the rest. We need to be calling for public works and training, for national economic planning, for federal aid to education, for attractive public housing—all this on a sufficiently massive scale to make a difference. We need to protest the notion that our integration into American life, so long delayed, must now proceed in an atmosphere of competitive scarcity instead of in the security of abundance which technology makes possible. We cannot claim to have answers to all the complex problems of modern society. That is too much to ask of a movement battling barbarism in Mississippi. But we can agitate the right questions by probing at the contradictions which still stand in the way of the "Great Society." The questions having been asked, motion must begin in the larger society, for there is a limit to what Negroes can do alone.

Portrait of a Southern Town

The previous articles in this chapter have dealt with the Negro issue in American society in a fairly academic and intellectualized manner. However, apart from all the words, demonstrations, and government attempts to give meaning to the concept of a free society, there is the simple reality of daily life for the Negro and the human feelings that life engenders. The following article, in a highly personalized manner, catches the meaning and significance of the human side of this question.

Have there been changes in the South? What of needed changes in the North, East, and West? Can a Puerto Rican boy go home to New York after serving in the Army, and expect changes? Can a Mexican-American boy go home to California after working on the sugar beet farms and find social acceptance? What part should the schools play in this problem? Personal feelings and attitudes are developed in schools and by teachers. Are they sufficient to counteract the pervading social attitudes or do the schools and teachers reinforce the social attitudes which Mr. Lomax describes?

Georgia Boy Goes Home

LOUIS E. LOMAX

I came home to Georgia by jet. The flight from New York to Atlanta was uneventful, but as the plane taxied toward the terminal I felt slightly uneasy. Georgia had just gone for Goldwater; Georgia was still Georgia. Walking along the corridor to the main lobby, I heard cracker twangs all about me; these, in my childhood, were the sound of the enemy, so that even now I react when I hear them, and I immediately suspect any white

Reprinted from *Harper's Magazine*, Vol. 230, April, 1965 by permission of the publisher and the author.

man who has a Southern drawl. Yet I could see no signs telling me where
I should eat, drink, or go to the rest room. The white passengers seemed
totally unconcerned with me. I could see a change in their eyes, on their
faces, in the way they let me alone to be me.

I was on my way to the Southern Airlines counter to confirm my reservation to Valdosta. Suddenly I saw a brown arm waving at me from a phone
booth. There, in the booth, was Martin Luther King, Jr. Martin's family
and mine had been Negro Baptist leaders in Georgia for almost fifty years;
I first got to know him when I was in college and he was in junior high
school. Now I was on my way home to Valdosta for *Harper's* to write
about the changes in my town and to give a sermon in my uncle's church;
Martin was on the way to the island of Bimini to write his Nobel Prize
acceptance speech.

Martin and I stood in the lobby and tried to talk, but to no avail. We
were continuously interrupted by white people who rushed over to shake
his hand and pat him on the back. I could hardly believe that I was in
Atlanta, that these were white people with twangs, and that they were
saying what they were saying. Many of them asked for Martin's autograph;
a few of them recognized me from television or from the dust jacket of a
book and asked me to sign slips of paper. They were an incredible lot: a
group of soldiers, five sailors, three marines, a score of civilians including
the brother of the present Governor of Georgia, and three Negro girls. One
stately old white man walked up to Martin and said, "By God, I don't like
all you're doing, but as a fellow Georgian I'm proud of you."

My flight home was several hours away, and I had made a reservation at
a motel near the airport. As Martin and I were parting, the loudspeaker
announced that the motel bus was waiting for "Dr. Lomax." A Negro
porter gathered my baggage and led me to the bus; he put my bags on the
ground and I tipped him. A few seconds later I saw the white bus driver,
and I knew I had reached a moment of confrontation. It seemed an eternity
as I glanced up and down, from the white driver to my baggage; I remembered all those years I had spent serving white people as a bellboy, a shoeshine boy, a waiter. The driver, however, couldn't have cared less about
me or my color. He picked up my bags and put them in the bus. This is
what the Republic has done to me and twenty million like me—I never
felt so equal in all my life when I saw that white man stoop down and
pick up *my* bags. "Get right in, sir," he said.

The motel people were the same. They acted as if there had never been
such a thing as segregation. I ate and drank where I pleased. Later I had
to break away from three white men and their woman companion who
latched onto me in the motel dining room and insisted that I party with
them until my plane left.

I came back home to the land tilled and served by my fathers for four
generations. Valdostans, like most people, are children of fixity; as indi-

viduals and as a tribe they find a crag, a limb, a spot of earth—physical or emotional or both—and they cling on for dear life. They change without growing, and the more they change the more they remain the same. What frightens them, as with most people, is the sudden discovery that what they are—how they have lived all their lives—stands somehow in the path of history and of progress.

One can go home again if he remembers and accepts the land of his birth for what it was, if he understands what that land has become and why. The homecoming is more complete if one admits that he and his land have shaped each other, that from it springs much of both his weakness and his strength. Only as I walked down River Street toward the place I was born did I realize how much of a child of this land I am: its mud squished through my toes as I romped on unpaved streets and alleys; its puritanical somnolence settled over my childhood dreams and all but choked me into conformity. It was on the corner of River and Wells Streets, when I was eight years old, that a white man ordered his bulldog to attack me simply because I was a Negro. Judge J. G. Cranford and his wife lived in the big white house on the corner. They saw the incident from the front porch, and Mrs. Cranford ran into the street to my rescue and drove the man away with shame.

River Street has grown old without changing very much. The weed field that stretched between here and Jackson Street Lane is still a weed field; the old warehouse that sat at the edge of the field is now a surplus food distribution center. The houses are the same houses they were when I was a child.

R. F. Lewes, as I shall call him, lived on this block. The summer before my junior year in college I was a handyman in his shop. Mr. Lewes would entertain his customers with dramatic descriptions of lynchings he had attended. His favorite story was about the night three Negroes were killed in a swamp near the Florida line. Lewes would advise his customers to get to a lynching early and stake out a choice spot on the killing ground. "But if the crowd is already there when you get there," he would add, "get down on your all fours and crawl between their legs so you can get up close to the nigger." One night I was cleaning the store when three of Mr. Lewes' cronies came in. "By God," he said to them, "this has been a rough day. Let's get a pint of moonshine and find some nigger bitches and get our luck changed."

Finally the stories became too much, and one day I threw down my shoeshine rag and went home. (After all, I was almost a junior in college and an official in my campus NAACP.) Lewes' son drove to our house and insisted that I return to work. My grandfather, the minister of the Macedonia First African Baptist Church, flatly said I didn't have to work in a place where my race was abused. R. F. Lewes, Jr. assured Grandfather that he would see to it that his father stopped telling lynch stories while I was in the shop. I had hardly returned to work when Lewes walked up to me and put his arms around my shoulders. "Louis," he said, eyeing me as if I were a wounded animal, "I wouldn't hurt *you!*"

During my visit home I saw Mr. Lewes on the street. He is very old and walks with a stick. A few weeks before, a Negro man had sat on a bench on the courthouse lawn next to him. Recoiling in anger, Lewes began jabbing the Negro in the ribs with his walking stick. The Negro called the police, and they told Lewes that the courthouse bench was for all the people, and either to calm down or move on. Mr. Lewes moved on.

Ours was a curious ghetto. Jackson Street Lane was the boundary line between the Negro and white sections along River Street. For one block Negroes lived on the north side of the street; the south side was completely white. To compound the oddness—the kind of thing that keeps the South on the edge of insanity—the first two families in our block were white. I remember how their menfolk ran into the street rejoicing the night Max Schmeling defeated Joe Louis.

The two white houses are still there, but I cannot for the life of me account for the white people who had lived in them. They were of another world; I did not know their names, who they were, or what they did. For that matter, I can't recall a single white person in the entire town whom I *really knew* when I was a boy. There were a few white people—R. F. Lewes and the man whose bulldog attacked me—whom I truly feared and, more than likely, hated. There were a few white people, Mrs. Cranford for example, whom I trusted and, perhaps, loved. But whatever understanding I had of all of these people was based on nothing more than surface encounter.

The house where I was born is torn down, the land covered with brush. The corner grocery store, built by a grocery chain on land leased from my grandfather, is now an eyesore and a public hazard. This land still belongs to us. My Uncle James, now the preacher at the Macedonia Baptist Church, and I are the last of the Lomaxes. Soon we must sit down and decide what to do about the land. Where my grandmother's living room once was, there are wild weeds; thistles cover the place where my grandfather used to retire on Saturday nights to prepare his sermon. There are tall bushes in the potato patch and creeping vines in the bait bed.

There are other changes. The new freeway that runs from Atlanta to Jacksonville has ruined the sucker and catfish hole where Grandfather and I used to fish. The new city hall and its grounds sprawl over the homesites of more than twenty families, Negro and white. The mud swamp on the Clydesville Road is now the airport, and the Dasher High School from which I was graduated twenty-five years ago is now the J. L. Lomax Junior High School, which is named after my Uncle James.

When I walked these streets as a boy I prided myself in the fact that I knew exactly how many people there were in the town—14,592. (My grandfather used to say that this figure included "Negroes, white people, chickens, cows, two mules, and a stray hound dog.") By 1960 the population had more than doubled, and it is predicted that there may be 75,000 people living here by 1980. Since I was a child the number of people working in agriculture has decreased threefold; the corresponding increase in trades, technical, professional, and government employees is expected to continue.

Despite the occasional new sight, Valdosta, like most American cities and towns, is old and tired and falling down. A few weeks ago, not far from my old home, a chimney fell from a dilapidated building and killed a small child. In October of last year the city manager pleaded with the mayor and the city council for power to initiate a comprehensive housing code. His research showed that 33 percent of Valdosta's housing is either dilapidated or deteriorating, that less than half of the town's dwelling units are owner-occupied, and that only slightly more than five hundred new housing units will be erected during the rest of the 1960s. The city manager wanted to force the owners of deteriorating properties to fix them up, the owners of dilapidated buildings to tear them down under the threat that if they don't the city will. He wanted to do something about the lack of recreational facilities for young people. So far he has not succeeded, but he is still trying.

A referendum that would have levied two bond issues for parks and recreation recently was defeated, with about 10 percent of the registered voters participating. But in October a one-million-dollar school bond issue won the voters' approval, although less than two thousand of the city's eight thousand registered women voters bothered to go to the polls.

Apathy plagues the town. The people, both Negro and white, seem to have run out of gas. They simply don't care about civic improvements. The referendum for parks and recreation would have given the city two swimming pools. It was defeated by seventeen votes. Yet one night I walked up and down Patterson Street, the white mecca, and saw scores of boys and girls slinking into darkened store alcoves and alleys. Then I went down along South Ashley Street, the Negro section, and saw even more young people darting into back streets, petting in open lots, dancing to funky music in questionable "soda and ice cream parlors."

As far as public accommodations go, Valdosta is an open town. I ate where I chose and went where I pleased, talking with whomever I wished of both races. Like most Southern towns, this one had moments of racial tension during the first days of integrated cafés, lunch counters, and theaters. But a well-disciplined law force invoked the law of the land. While police chiefs in other Southern towns were rousing the white rabble, the Valdosta police chief was traveling through the swamp farmlands on the town's outskirts telling white men who were most likely to get likkered up and come to town to keep calm. The Negroes were told to eat, not just demonstrate, and the whites were warned to keep the peace. They both did just that. Whenever and wherever Negroes have pressed their case there has been compliance with the Civil Rights Act.

This did not happen all by itself. A loosely organized interracial council arrived at reasonable, step-by-step goals. I think the major preventive act took place when the white power structure yielded to demands for Negro policemen. The sight of Negroes whom they knew and trusted policing their community gave Valdosta's Negroes a pride and a sense of personal security they had never had before. My town has not made ugly national and international headlines because the white power structure, led by three key men, took a long look at the turmoil that confronted so many places in the South and decided it would not happen in Valdosta.

E. M. Turner, the seventy-two-year-old editor of the local paper, took the same position with me. I was both astounded and angry. He had been the editor of the paper since I was a child. I had wanted to be a reporter and a writer, to learn the fundamentals of my craft, but I couldn't even get a job as a delivery boy. The first essay I ever wrote won me an honorable mention in a contest sponsored by the paper; they announced that I was a Negro and they misspelled my name. Yet E. M. Turner sat with me now for almost an hour and a half. He traced the rise of Valdosta from a one-crop town that trembled at the thought of the boll weevil to a town which changed its economy to one based on turpentine, pine trees, and resin. He sketched out the semi-industrial era that lies ahead for the town.

Our talk moved on to the race issue. "I've never had any trouble with nigras," Turner said. "I may not like the Civil Rights Bill, but it's the law of the land and it must be obeyed. But let me tell you this," he said. "I talked to my cook; she is a sweet old nigra woman who has been with us for years and she told me she didn't want her grandchildren going to school with white children."

I heard E. M. Turner well, and I thought to myself that I have yet to meet a white man, in the South or the North, whose cook believed in integration. Yet I wondered how, without integrated schools, such a man as Turner expected us to turn out Negroes equally prepared for the American job market. I decided to ask a significant question:

"Would you hire a Negro reporter if he was qualified?"

Turner did not hesitate. "I've never been faced with the issue," he said. "I'm not sure what I would do."

Later that day, when I had a talk with a local businessman, I saw something of the anguish that afflicts many white Valdostans of my age. His brother-in-law lives in Colombia and is married to a Colombian woman darker than most Negroes. The brother wanted to bring his wife to Valdosta for a visit; the proposed visit was, of course, vetoed with vigor. "Lord, how ashamed I am," he told me. "I'm afraid to have my own brother and sister come to my home."

He is a devout member of a Protestant church in Valdosta. His church raises money each month to keep an impoverished Negro church of the same denomination going. "We raise that money," he told me, "to keep the Negroes from coming to our church. I was just horrified when I saw how my fellow white Christians reacted when the question of integrating the two churches came up."

But it was another realization that really troubled him. "Now take you," he said. "I'd like to have you in my home, to sit down to prayer and break bread with my family. My wife feels the same way. But we'd be afraid to invite you."

"I'd invite you to my home," I told him. "I'm not afraid."

"But I'd be afraid to *come*," he shot back, pounding the desk with anger at his world and himself.

"In other words," I said, "there is a sense in which I, a Negro, have more freedom than you have."

"That's true," he replied. "Everything is so confused down here. They wouldn't bother you and your Uncle James if you invited my family to your home. But they would get after *us* if we came." He turned in his chair, dropping me out of his sight as he faced the wall and let his eyes drift toward the ceiling.

"But I did vote for Goldwater," he added, speaking more to himself than to me. "Somebody has just got to stop the Communists from taking over the world."

The Goldwater victory hung like a frightening cloud over the well-meaning white Valdostans who were trying to find a way out of the racial wilderness. One of the men most responsible for Goldwater's carrying Valdosta was George C. Cook, the seventy-three-year-old owner of the radio station. Cook came to town thirty years ago and became a leader in the business community; he has been president of the Chamber of Commerce and has spearheaded the drive to get more industry—"particularly those that will give these nigger women on relief something to do," he explained to me—into Valdosta. He made his station the voice of Goldwater conservatism and the White Citizens' Council. The week before the election, Cook encountered one of Valdosta's most respected Negroes in the post office. "Doctor," Cook said to the Negro, "I want you to go home and call all your friends and tell them to tune in on my station tonight at seven-thirty. We're going to give the niggers and Jews hell tonight and I sure want you and your people to hear it."

I talked with Cook for more than an hour. "Now I came out for Goldwater, but I ain't no Republican," he said. "I'm a Democrat. That," he went on to say, pounding his chest, "is in here, in my heart. I could no more be a Republican than I could fly. But I just couldn't stomach that Kennedy-Johnson crowd and the way they are taking over the rights of the states and the individual.

"Now as for this integration business, I don't see what all the hell's about. We never had any trouble with niggers. I was against the Civil

Rights Bill but when it became the law of the land I felt we'd better try and live with it. One of my friends called me up and told me he'd gotten word that the niggers were coming to his lunch counter to demonstrate. He said he was going to feed them if they came there. I told him, by God, to feed them niggers and he'd find out that once he fed them, and they had made their point, they would never come back. And you know," he added, bursting into laughter, "that's exactly what happened. Them niggers ate, then they left and ain't a one of them black sonsabitches been back there since.

"Let me tell you something, Louis," he said suddenly. "I lived with niggers all my life; I grew up with them and played with them; there wasn't a bit of trouble. Why a sweet, old black nigger woman helped raise me; she was as sweet a woman as God ever let live. And if and when I get to heaven I'm going to look up that nigger woman and kiss her on the cheek.

"There ain't going to be no trouble here," he said. "A few young niggers and young white trash might try to start something; then the old heads, nigger and white, will keep things under control. What we need in this town instead of agitation is some new industries with nigger jobs, so these nigger men can feed their families, so these nigger women on relief can make a pay check. That's what we need to keep Valdosta going. Why, the niggers are pouring into town by the carloads every day, and if we don't find something for them to do we are going to have one hell of a mess in this town before too long. Yes sir, that's what this town needs: nigger jobs, for nigger men and women."

On the subject of jobs, Comer Cherry, a diametrical opposite to Cook among the business community, feels the same way. Cherry has been president of the Chamber of Commerce and the Rotary Club, and a prime mover behind the biracial commission. He is representative of the new thinking among white Valdostans. "The way I see it," he says, "the economy of the nigra community is the root of the problem. Once the nigra can earn a respectable pay check, most of the agitation will die down."

The median income for a Valdosta white family in 1960 was $4,360; for Valdosta Negro families, $2,364. And there is a chilling prophecy in a recent economic study of the town. The study predicts that by 1980 the median income of Valdosta white families will be $9,500, while the income of Negro families will reach only $4,250—more than twice the present disparity. Comer Cherry and George C. Cook have a point. Somebody, somehow, had better do something about Negro income in Valdosta or there will be real trouble in the future.

I found no tension whatsoever in the Valdosta Negro community. The Negro masses undulate along the streets, oblivious to what is going on in the Congo, in Red China, or in Mississippi. The county hospital has been completely integrated, and the authorities have shut down the old back entrance marked "colored." Yet despite the fact that the leaders have told local Negroes to use the front door, one witnesses the pathetic spectacle of their going to the same place to find a back way in. What mainly struck me is that there are more of them, and that they are growing in geometric proportions. They are the citizens of "Niggertown," the habitués of juke joints, of pig-foot alley and crumbling shanties. Their children pour into school, only to drop out. Talking with these dropouts one comes away knowing that they never really dropped in. They don't know anything; they can't do anything. Here, among the black masses, is the greatest monument to my town's—the South's—wickedness. It is a society which continues to grind out hundreds, thousands, millions who are totally defeated, who are alienated from that society from the day they are born.

The Valdosta black bourgeoisie serve the black masses. They teach them in school, pull their teeth, prescribe medicine for their livers, tell them about Jesus on Sunday morning, sell them life insurance when they are young, and bury them when they die. That is the way it was thirty-five years ago; that is the way it is now. Their only saving grace—and this is true all over the country—is that they are willing to accept, without recourse to background, any person who can traverse the maze that leads from Shantytown to professionalism. I was born to the black bourgeoisie; I stumbled and floundered for twenty years; and there were grave doubts that I would ever validate my heritage. Yet I had schoolmates who were up from the trash pile; some of them made it, and they are now solid members of the Valdosta Negro middle class.

It would be wrong for me to say that they don't care about the black masses. They do care; they care, at times, almost to the point of nervous breakdown. Their problem, essentially, is the same as that of the concerned white men of Valdosta: the monster created by the Southern way of life is so terrifying, and becoming so gargantuan, that nobody knows what to do or where to start doing it.

Meanwhile, the Valdosta black bourgeoisie are becoming more and more comfortable, their world more and more secure. They are the ones who can afford to dress up and go out for dinner once a week to a previously "white only" restaurant, who can travel during their vacations and take advantage of the integrated motels, hotels, and travel facilities. Yet few of them have actually contributed to the Negro revolution that has made these things possible. The Valdosta black bourgeoisie are largely schoolteachers. Despite their new freedom, they must plod away in schoolrooms that are still separate and unequal; they must keep quiet about integration or be fired.

"I'm doing all I can do and still keep my job," one third-grade Negro teacher told me. "When my principal isn't around, I teach my children that four pickets times nine pickets is thirty-six pickets. I just hope and pray they grow up and get the message."

Part of the tragedy of my town is that there is no real Negro leadership to translate to the masses the message this teacher is trying to deliver. Negro leadership in Valdosta is nothing more than ten or twelve men with incomes rooted in the ghetto, who sporadically gather to try to muster general support for programs each of them has presented to the town's white fathers when his fellow Negro spokesmen were not looking. A dozen of these Negro leaders—most of whom I have known since childhood— met with me to discuss the plight of the Valdosta Negro and to describe what they planned to do about it. The more they talked the more it became apparent, as one of them had the courage to say, that Negro leadership was about the same as it was when I was a little boy. There is no NAACP in Valdosta, no Urban League. Nobody would dare let Martin Luther King, Jr., preach in their church, and CORE is something they read about in the newspaper and hear about on television. The Negro leaders, such as they are, turn on each other and accuse one another of being disloyal, apathetic, and indifferent.

What, then, is the next step forward for Valdosta, not just toward integration, but into the world as it really is?

Although the Negro population is 36 percent, not a single public school is integrated in the town. However, the all-white board of education is ready to accept Negro pupils into any schools they can establish their legal right to attend. Moreover, the white power structure knows precisely where these schools are, and the white students have been prepared for the probability that their schools will one day be integrated. Even more, the white students have accepted the idea and wish the Negroes would get it over with so everybody concerned can settle down to learning his lessons.

White Valdosta businessmen have jobs waiting for Negroes; these jobs will never be filled until Negro leaders stop fighting each other and draw up a unified job program to place before the biracial commission.

At a state college located in Valdosta, I was told, there were only two Negro students, and these were financed by some of the Negro leaders who met with me. No other Negroes had enrolled in two years. This could be changed if Negro spokesmen would unify and make the right demands. There is an integrated county technical and industrial school on the outskirts of Valdosta that is begging for Negro students. There are all too few Negro applicants. The brunt of the burden, I regret to say, rests with the town's Negro middle class. But they, like so many of their white peers, are consumed by fear.

The Valdosta Negro middle class, then, is on the verge of becoming a tribe; its members are fiercely proud of themselves and their own; they couldn't care less about socializing with white people. At a large party given for me one night, I was able to locate only one Negro friend—a woman—who had a social relationship with a white person. She and a white woman have a "luncheon friendship," largely at the urging of the white woman. Even that almost collapsed when the white woman invited other white women to join.

"The other white women smiled dryly at me," she said, "and I was ready to say, like, forget it. My husband makes more than her husband and I wasn't about to grovel just to have some white lunch dates."

"I know what you mean," a county school principal said. "These phony white liberals are about a bitch. They say they love us, that they want to cement relations, that they want to overcome the fact that there has been no communication between us and them, and then they get in that damn voting booth and . . ."

"Vote for Goldwater," several people shouted.

"You think you got problems," a doctor broke in. "I was walking down Patterson Street a few weeks ago and a white man fell to the sidewalk with a heart attack right in front of me. I forgot he was white and tried to help him. A crowd gathered and became hostile because I was a Negro!"

"Did you go away and let him die?" somebody shouted from the back room.

"No," the doctor replied, "I did the best I could for the sonofabitch and sent him off to the hospital." Everyone, of course, laughed.

The party music played, but there was surprisingly little drinking or dancing. I was home; these were my brothers and sisters. They knew me and were glad to see me. We talked of the days when we were children, of our fathers and mothers and grandparents who pushed us so far along the way. We told the "in" jokes. Nobody mentioned white people; nobody wanted or needed them there. We would have stayed all night if it had not been Saturday. But at church the next morning one of the school principals was scheduled to sing a solo. One woman was to play the organ, another the piano. Another school principal was to handle the collection, and I was to deliver the sermon.

The next day I stood in the Macedonia Baptist Church pulpit that has been occupied by a Lomax for more than half a century; some of the people who sat in the congregation had known me before I knew myself. Tribal middle-class pride was running high. Just the Sunday before, Calvin King, one of my younger childhood schoolmates who went on to get his doctorate in mathematics, had been the guest preacher. Uncle James had listened with pride as Calvin told of his travels in the Holy Land, of his work in helping launch a new university in Nigeria.

I told the congregation about my experiences in Africa, behind the Iron Curtain, and in American cities where racial troubles had erupted. White Christianity, I said, had become synonymous with white oppression all over the world, and the black Christians were about all Jesus had left. We were the only ones who could now go about preaching the words of Jesus without being suspected of questionable motives. My plea was that we black Christians become more militant, that we take a courageous stand for human rights, to clarify Christ's name if for no other reason.

It is significant that when I had finished there was a loud congregational "amen." A few white people had come to the service, and one of them was crying. Uncle James issued the invitation for the unchurched to come up and join. But that was not the hour for sinners. Rather, I think, it was a time for the believers to reassess what they were in for.

Change is coming. Having seen many of the troubled places of Africa, America, and the Caribbean, I know social dynamite when I see it. But Valdosta will make it peacefully into tomorrow, partly because the whites themselves are slowly changing, partly because the Negroes are not really pushing. Time nudges them both along. They—the black and the white of my town—are now looking across at each other in estrangement against the day when they might join in frank friendship.

PART 5

Teaching as a Social and Professional Vocation

THE TEACHER AS A
CULTURAL AGENT

In most cultures of the world someone serves as the teacher and indoctrinating agent in transmitting the values and knowledge of the particular
culture. Within American society, the teacher passes on the folklore of
American values and traditions of the "western heritage"—the beliefs, the
rituals, and taboos commonly present in our culture. However, within the
framework of passing on the sanctions and taboos of our society there are
great differences between school systems in the latitude and freedom present. The teacher is limited by the parochialness or broadness of his teacher
education, by the depth of interest in his field, by his own ennui or enthusiasm as he engages in classroom presentations. Apart from these factors of
individual background and personality which make a significant difference
in classroom effectiveness, the institutional factors in the school and community directly limit or encourage the free inquiry of the teacher. When a
class in high school social studies is committed by curriculum guides to
covering material rapidly and to relying heavily on a textbook, the vital
dynamism of the social sciences may be destroyed for students. Instead, a
dislike for these human concerns may be engendered. Also courses geared
to state examinations restrict the teacher by confining class study and discussion to only those aspects of the subject typically covered on the exam.

In a similar manner the teacher who wishes to utilize controversial issues
as content in appropriate courses may discover that the community pressure through institutional means becomes too great to be overcome. Although the Scopes trial occured in 1925, Tennessee did not legally permit
teaching the theory of evolution until 1967. In the state of New York a
group of clergymen in one community protested the presentation of *Inherit
the Wind,* the play based on the Scopes trial, in the local high school. The
school relented and the play, according to the newspapers, was not presented. This was in 1965, and in a state which does not legally prohibit the
teaching of evolution. There are many such examples of issues not allowed
open inquiry in schools as a result of formal and informal institutions in
society. Some of these issues are presented in Part 3 of this text.

The effects of social, educational, and political limitations of teachers
are discussed in the following section. In recognition of the teacher as an
agent for transmitting culture, the several readings that follow examine

the relationship of the teacher to society, to ideas, to students, and to education.

What cultural heritage should the teacher be expected to transmit? What limitations are appropriate to cultural transmission? What other cultural agents exist in American society? What relation should exist among these agents? How are the various roles of socialization agents determined?

Teaching in a Democracy

The relation between a political order and an educational system is a topic this text has treated in several ways. A political system based on the rationality of man, such as democracy which provides for self-government, must have an educational system which provides literacy and knowledge for the entire populace. An autocracy, which limits the governing of a society to a select group, would not require so massive or inclusive an educational system. Indeed, the history of educational institutions reveals distinctions between various political forms in terms of the number, level, and types of students permitted into schools. At the present time the distinctions are more difficult since the apparent values of educating large populations, as America has demonstrated, is moving virtually every developing society to adopt mass education in some form.

In the article that follows, John L. Childs presents a view of the progressive teachers in a democracy and a discussion of the interests which should be of major concern to them. Should the teacher be committed to a democratic "welfare state" as Childs suggests? In what ways is the present public school system inconsistent with democratic ideals? What other categories of educational thought can be added to those suggested?

Teachers and the Democratic Struggle

JOHN L. CHILDS

For this special issue on "education and the class structure in America," the editor of *Progressive Education* has asked me to discuss the question: "With what class group, if any, should teachers be identified?" In my opin-

Reprinted from *Progressive Education*, Vol. 27, No. 4, May, 1950, pp. 116–20, by permission of the John Dewey Society.

ion, the question of class collaboration is essentially a problem of *means,* and as such it cannot be significantly explored apart from the purposes or the results which a given group desires to achieve. While it is true that the *means* which teachers employ will condition the outcomes or ends they actually attain, it is equally true that the ends they have in mind will condition their view of the means that should be accepted as necessary and desirable.

Human interests are the soil out of which human purposes or ideals develop. Indeed, an ideal that is not formulated in terms of human interests is either an impertinence or a sentimental indulgence. Hence we can be intelligent about social and educational goals and programs, only as we are aware of the definite human interests we are concerned to defend and promote. Whatever values are designated by the concepts of "impartiality" and "objectivity"—and I believe these concepts have important implications for the work of teachers—they cannot be legitimately construed to imply that teachers should be indifferent to human interests, or to the present clash of interests in American society.

Certainly progressive educators who are committed to the values of democratic education, should not pretend to be indifferent to whatever is required to maintain the health and vigor of our democratic way of life. Loyalty to a democratic program of education necessarily involves loyalty to the democratic civilization which is the ultimate source and foundation of that democratic program of education. I shall therefore begin my discussion with a summary of major interests which, at this time, should be a special concern of American teachers.

PRESERVATION OF THE PUBLIC SCHOOLS
IS A PRIMARY INTEREST OF TEACHERS

One of these primary interests is the maintenance of the institution of the public or common school. Although the democratic principle of equality involves much more than the provision of universal education, it is nevertheless true that the struggle for equality of educational opportunity is a fundamental part of the task of preserving a democratic civilization. The American single-ladder system of public schools clearly ranks as one of the finest products of our democratic way of life. But today the effort to provide equality of opportunity through a system of common schools suffers from a combination of forces. It suffers from economy-minded groups of tax-payers who condemn as "sanctified squander" the expanded school program now required to equip the young for adult responsibilities in our complex industrial and democratic civilization. It also suffers from privileged economic groups who provide for the education of their own children in special private schools, and hence tend to be indifferent about the quality of education the "children of the masses" receive in our public schools. It further suffers from the fact that in our country population and material wealth are unevenly distributed, and as a result the children of certain states receive a radically inferior grade of education.

Equality of educational opportunity also suffers in those districts in which whites exclude colored children from the community school and compel them to attend substandard, racially segregated schools. The United States Office of Education reports that states having segregated school systems expend an average of about twice as much for the education of a white child as for a negro child. The attempt to equalize educational opportunity by special grants from the Federal government is hindered by ecclesiastical groups who are seeking to develop a separate parochial system for the education of their children, and who oppose measures for Federal aid of the public schools unless they also contain subsidies for children enrolled in their system of private schools. Obviously, teachers who are concerned to provide a common educational experience for American children in a system of public schools, must take account of the various forces that are hostile to this program of public education.

FREEDOM OF TEACHING AND INQUIRY MUST BE DEFENDED AND MAINTAINED

But a program of democratic education is concerned to keep our schools open *intellectually* as well as *physically*. A second major interest of American teachers therefore is the maintenance of security for the members of the educational profession—the provision of those elemental conditions which make freedom of teaching and inquiry possible. Whenever the right to inquire and to communicate the results attained through inquiry is abridged, both teachers and society suffer—teachers are robbed of their opportunity to function as morally responsible human beings, and a democratic society is prevented from using its educational agencies to develop that perspective and understanding which is indispensable to its own continuing adjustment. Today the freedom of our schools is threatened. We live in a period of social change and transformation, and powerful groups who have vested interests in the traditional arrangements and practices seek to curb freedom of inquiry and discussion both within and outside our schools.

Thus in this period of transition when it is of the utmost importance that the avenues of inquiry and communication be kept open, our schools are increasingly subjected to pressure by a variety of social groups. Certain economic groups desire to make a sacred dogma out of our inherited private property and enterprise system, and they move in subtle and persistent ways to discourage teachers from inquiring into the democratic implications of our altered modes of living and of making a living. Ecclesiastical authorities are profoundly disturbed by the growing prestige of the methods and the findings of experimental science, and they seek to shield historic theological beliefs from the processes of free inquiry. They even at times call on legislatures to enact laws that will authoritatively prescribe what shall and what shall not be taught in certain areas of human experience, as though truth were something to be determined by the votes of political parties. Militant patriotic groups dominated by inherited and unexamined assumptions about national security and national solidarity frequently demand that authoritarian political creeds be taught in the schools, and they seek to fix rigid boundaries beyond which the search for knowledge and understanding must not go. At times these groups even demand that our young be kept ignorant of alternative systems of economy and government, as well as of the movement of ideas and events in countries other than our own.

It is of course possible to exaggerate the power of these repressive groups. In spite of their determined effort to intimidate teachers and the members of boards of education, our teachers have done much to inform the young of the significance of developments in our own and foreign countries. Indeed, public education has rendered an invaluable service by making it possible for both children and parents to achieve a more adequate orientation to the new world that is in process of formation. On the other hand, the strength of these repressive groups is increasing at the present time, and in many communities teachers feel too insecure in their school positions to conduct necessary examinations into the deeper meanings of changes now underway. Many teachers also feel that it would be unsafe for them to assume normal citizenship roles in the social and political affairs of their communities.

An important evidence of this sense of insecurity and frustration on the part of teachers is found in the ease with which they abandon their educational positions to take on other jobs. Undoubtedly the inadequate salaries paid teachers is a primary factor in this connection, but it is by no means the only one at work. Human beings do not care to be involved in intellectual pursuits when they are forced to act as the agents or the mouthpieces for established systems of thought and behavior in which they no longer have confidence. Teachers are no exception. They develop an enthusiasm for their work as teachers only when they enjoy those conditions of security and freedom which make it possible for them to preserve their integrity as they function in the realm of ideas. Teachers who have a real faith in the future of the educational profession necessarily have a basic interest in the struggle to make our schools sufficiently secure to permit them to function in both the development and the communication of ideas.

COMMITMENT TO A DEMOCRATIC
"WELFARE STATE" IS ESSENTIAL

But the fundamental interests of teachers as teachers are not restricted to the effort to get an adequate material and spiritual support for the public school. Teachers are also concerned with the effort to organize and maintain a society that can make a productive use of the human product of the schools. Education begins to lose its social significance whenever those who have completed its program of study and preparation are denied opportunity to work in socially productive activity. Nor can the responsibility for finding satisfactory employment under existing conditions be exclusively lodged with the individual. In the interdependent America of today, society along with the individual must accept responsibility for maintaining an adequate schedule of socially useful vocations. This problem of the creative use of our human resources is, to be sure, a technological, economic and political problem, but it is also a human problem and no group is more fully involved in its moral aspects than the members of the teaching profession. There is no more certain way of breeding a cynical and unstable generation of young people than to prepare them in attitude, knowledge and skill for constructive service and then to graduate them into an economic and social system that has no real use for their abilities.

In order to provide productive work for the growing numbers enrolled in our schools and colleges, adjustments will have to be made on both sides. Our schools will have to extend their range of educational preparation—vocational and cultural—to include all of the socially useful activities through which the American people provide for their material and spiritual well being. This means that our educational program must be committed to the effort to make all forms of socially necessary work—agricultural, industrial, commercial and professional—into desirable ways of human living, and not merely ways of making a living. In other words, education in democratic America must be premised on the assumption of the essential equality—pecuniary and cultural—of all types of socially useful activity. Education must be designed to develop the scientific, the social, the political, and the cultural possibilities of these varied forms of human livelihood.

But American society must also make a parallel adjustment. To make a creative use of all its people, our country will not only have to affirm the principle of full employment, it will also have to develop a new pattern of social and economic arrangements. This means that America will have to revise its historic view of the nature of productive work. As a number of our leading economists have been emphasizing for some time, we cannot have a full employment America if we stubbornly cling to the idea that the vast majority of our people must be engaged in the material side of production. Technological developments in both agriculture and industry have made the human factor less dominant in material production. For example, whereas at the founding of our Republic over ninety percent of our people lived and worked on farms, today only about twenty percent are thus engaged. The introduction of power machinery and automatic processes have brought about even more revolutionary changes in industrial production. All of this means that we must develop a more sensitive regard for the cultural aspects of human existence, and be prepared to support a vastly extended program of community services. This, in turn, means frank commitment to the "welfare state," and to the planned organization of the productive enterprises of our country. The real issue is no longer one of social and economic planning versus an individualistic system of *laissez-faire*; it is rather one of what forces are to do the planning, by what means are controls to be exercised, and for what purposes. In sum, a functional education must now be associated with the task of the achievement of a more functional society, and teachers interested in democracy have a basic stake in the development of this functional society.

WE MUST BE ON THE SIDE OF A
BOLD DEMOCRATIC FOREIGN POLICY

Thus far our discussion of the interests of teachers has been confined to American domestic affairs. But today our country is part of an interdependent world, and security for the American people is bound in with the effort to develop some form of effective world organization. Unfortunately, at the present time a functioning system of mutual security defines an urgent *human need,* not a developed *human capacity.* Even those of us who believe that the United Nations represents the most promising approach to a system of world security, must admit that its present pattern of functioning does not provide even the minimum essentials of human security. Physically and technologically our world is one; but politically, culturally, and economically it remains divided. This tragic division has resulted in an ominous race in armaments, and in an unprecedented effort to mobilize the scientific, material, and human resources of the world for purposes of total war. Preparation for national and regional defense has now become a controlling factor in our national program, as it has in the program of the Soviet Union. It is folly to suppose that we can continue indefinitely in the pattern of the garrison state and not suffer a decline in standards of living and in the cultural and welfare services, including the service of public education.

America has emerged from the World-War as one of the great power centers of the world. Much depends upon how that power is used. One need not join with the sentimentalists who believe that we can gain security and peace by a program of non-resistance and unilateral disarmament, to recognize that unless our country can exercise a more constructive use of its power for democratic ends the prospect for ultimate peace is not good. In spite of many necessary and admirable features in the present world policies of our country, the fact is that America tends to become progressively associated with the feudal, reactionary forces of the world rather than with those democratic groups who are seeking to build a civilization that can use the productive powers of science and technology for the welfare of mankind. Increasingly the fear develops that our world policies are now being too largely shaped by forces that are seeking to fashion foreign countries into secure and profitable markets for American dominated international corporations and cartels.

Whether our foreign policy can recover a bold democratic initiative depends, in the last analysis, on the groups that control our government. American isolationism is dead, but it is clear that those forces who want to see it reborn in the form of a program of American imperialism are growing in number. Should these groups become dominant in the affairs of state an atomic world war is almost surely to develop. Educators have a great stake in preventing that development, for no one can have any assurance of what kind of a world would survive a third world-war, and this irrespective of which nations eventually gain the victory.

WHERE PROGRESSIVE TEACHERS
MUST STAND IN THE STRUGGLE

In the foregoing, I have outlined four major interests of American educators. Three groups of educators may be distinguished with respect to these social and educational interests. One of these groups affirms the foregoing educational values, but holds that it is utopian to assume that they can be realized through a peaceful, democratic procedure. Accepting the doctrines of historical materialism as interpreted by the world Communist movement, this group asserts that cultural and educational reconstruction necessarily follows economic reconstruction, and that significant economic transformations cannot be attained by reliance on the democratic instrumentalities of the established American social and political system. According to this theory, our so-called democratic state is not a neutral political organ, but is actually the instrument of the capitalist class, and this class will inevitably become more restrictive and repressive as the crisis in the American economy deepens. Believing that peaceful reconstruction of existing institutions is impossible, this group is committed to an alternative strategy of seizure of power by a disciplined revolutionary minority—a minority party which acts for the mass of the people who on their own are unable either to define or to carry through the program required to secure their own emancipation.

Fortunately, the number of American educators enlisted in this movement has never been large, and now that it has been demonstrated that

World Communism operates as the slavish tool of the policies of the Kremlin, very few of our teachers are willing to cooperate in social and educational movements in which Communists have a directing leadership. Organized labor, moreover, in all of its main branches is taking determined steps to eradicate the influence of the Communists from its various trade unions, and in view of present world trends it is unlikely that their program will exert great influence in future American public affairs. Most American educators find the Communist doctrine that "the end justifies the means" repugnant to their moral sentiments, and they have steadfastly affirmed democracy as both social *end,* and as social and political *means.*

A second and numerically large group of American educators does not consider that the resolution of social, economic and political problems is properly the responsibility of educators as educators. This group emphasizes that teachers are servants of the whole public, and that it is undesirable for their professional organizations to take sides on those matters about which the American people are divided. It therefore centers its attention on two educational objectives: the securing of more adequate material support for public education, and the defense of the schools against those who seek to restrict freedom of teaching and inquiry. These educators put their trust not primarily in organized political action, but in the disposition of the general public to do the right and generous thing once the issues have been clarified. They tend to view democracy, not as a process of struggle and adjustment between conflicting interest groups, but rather as a disinterested process of enlightenment in which men of good-will cooperate with one another in the search for the common good.

As the needs of the school have grown more acute, however, this group of educators has been forced to take some account of power factors and to resort to direct political pressure. This pressure has taken the form of organizing support of specific measures that would provide more adequate funds for public education. These educators, for example, have tried for years to get Congress to pass an educational Federal aid bill. In pursuit of their specific objectives they make temporary alliances with such pressure groups as will serve their purposes, but they do not want the cause of public education to become merged with a general program of social and economic reconstruction, and they are also opposed to all efforts to identify teachers with broader social or economic groups.

A third group of progressive educators finds certain weaknesses in the policy described above. This group does not regard the democratic process as an alternative or a substitute for social struggle, for it recognizes the role of power in human affairs. It rather views democracy as an effort to nourish the human attitudes, the loyalties, the procedures, and the institutions which will make it possible for conflicts between different interest groups to be adjusted by orderly and peaceful means. It perceives that at the present time a far-reaching struggle is actually being waged between economic groups or classes in American society. Broadly speaking these groups may be identified by the attitudes they assume toward the principles and the goals of what has come to be called "the welfare state."

This third group of educators believes that in the long run both the material and the spiritual interests of public education depend upon the achievement of a re-organization of our economy. They therefore do not have faith in a policy that insists on teachers working separately as a mere educational pressure group, and which discourages them from uniting with other functional groups in a common effort to develop an economy in which production will be cooperatively planned for the welfare of all. This group of educators also believes that there is an intimate connection between the domestic effort to achieve a more socialized economy and the world effort to develop a democratic system of collective security. In fact, they are convinced that our country would make a contribution to world order and peace of the highest importance were it to succeed in developing an American economy which could sustain a high level of production and employment. Many things which now seem uncertain in the world scene would begin to look more hopeful were America to achieve this domestic transformation.

Educators who share the view that the struggle for a system of democratic education is now an inherent part of the struggle for a more democratic America will not find it difficult to identify the groups upon which they can count in this more fundamental and comprehensive program of social reconstruction. Broadly speaking the groups which are uniting to support the social, economic and political developments which Americans have chosen to describe as the "welfare state" are those who are concerned to achieve a more productive and more democratic America. By identifying themselves with these groups, American educators will be taking the step most needed to preclude a fascist development in our country; they will also be supporting the positive actions which are required to strengthen democracy in America, and through America in the world.

The Teacher as a Conformist

Conformity in social life is both approved and condemned. It is approved as a means of stability as in making certain that all drivers conform to a set of driving rules, but it is condemned as intellectually and culturally crippling as in the case of censoring all ideas so that they conform to an accepted pattern. In the field of education, conformity operates in the same manner. Rules for safe practice in a woodshop are deemed necessary, yet opening areas of literary ideas to unlimited inquiry by students is also considered valuable for intellectual growth. A predicament occurs when the schools confuse the two—when they do not provide proper supervision of youngsters in physical education and restrict materials of instruction in controversial areas in order to provide only safe ideas.

The effects of conformity on education and on the products of that education, and the role of the teacher in fostering free and independent thought in a political system is discussed in the following article by David Spitz, a political science professor. Is censorship a desirable activity in society and education? What social, political, and educational roles does a teacher have in an open society? How should teachers accept the intellectual commitment of an open society? Should they be leaders or followers? Are the schools spokesmen for orthodoxy? Is this especially improper? Do teachers have any role in dealing with the unorthodox in society?

Politics, Patriotism, and the Teacher

DAVID SPITZ

Everywhere custom is king, and everywhere men think themselves free even as they bend the knee to it. They mean to get along; they seek approval and success; they comply, therefore, with customary ways and customary expectations. They do not so much submit as behave, for to submit is to yield one's inclination to custom, and they have no inclinations except for what is customary. And because *they* behave, and are comfortable in doing so, they are disquieted and irked by those who talk and act otherwise than they do.

What is true of men in general is true of teachers in particular. In the folklore of the academy, teachers are the victims of conformist pressures. They are oppressed by governments, harassed by private power groups, and suffocated by a climate of opinion which not only punishes them for unorthodox speech and improper behavior but, more importantly, prevents them, by a well-inculcated fear of probable consequences, from embarking on such speech or behavior at all. And as with all bits of folklore, there is sufficient evidence to make the point credible.

But in reality, teachers are as much, if not more, the creators of conformity. For teachers, though they might be expected to know better, are by and large no different from other men. They too have their vanities and their precious dreams. They too want to be appreciated, nay, applauded and esteemed. They too accept the values and the myths of their com-

Reprinted from *The National Elementary Principal*, Vol. 43, No. 3, January, 1964, pp. 17–22, by permission of the publisher and the author.

munity. Hence they too are annoyed by those among them who disturb their tranquility and repose.

Conformity in education, then, is not merely a matter of pressure from without. It is this, to be sure; but it is also a pressure from within. Thus he who would oppose these pressures must be prepared to dwell always under double jeopardy. He must withstand the external pressures of governments and of private powers, and he must withstand the internal pressures of the teaching profession itself. In each case, moreover, he must understand that even where these forces act in the furtherance of their special interests, they speak always in the rhetoric of idealism. And in these difficult times there is no idealism as appealing as patriotism.

I should like, in these pages, to say something of each of these elements of present-day conformity. They are not, of course, the only elements that matter, but they are surely among the more important of them. If I pose the alternative positions as polar extremes, it is not because two alternatives exhaust a situation (they rarely if ever do), but because polar opposites generally reveal assumptions and consequences in stark and dramatic form, and also because even moderate positions tend toward the individualist or authoritarian extreme.

POLITICS AND THE GOOD LIFE

Consider first the impact of politics on education. Of the two dominant schools of political thought, one relates politics to the good life, or justice; the other, to a struggle for power. Yet each has, with one crucial exception, similar consequences for the teacher.

If, on the one hand, we view politics as the practical attempt to implement the quest for and discovery of the good life, then either the existing society embodies the good life or it does not; and the judgment, along with the criteria for that judgment, is either in the individual—in this case, the teacher—or in a source outside of him.

If we assume, as those who have power in any society generally do assume, that the existing system is by and large the embodiment of the good life, and that the judgment of the rulers is binding on all other men in the community, then the task of the teacher is clear. He is nothing more than a servant of the power system. He is not free to teach what he wants, what he as a teacher thinks is important or right. He must teach as right what the rulers affirm to be right. He must do what those in power want him to do.

This, it is argued, is not an unreasonable demand. Clearly it is not the job of the teacher to communicate evil. And since, in this view, the state is a good state, governed by men who know right from wrong, it becomes the obligation of the rulers to protect the youth from the corrupting influences of misguided teachers. For this reason, Socrates in *The Republic* would censor what is taught and favor exile for the misguided. (Though Socrates, it will be recalled, was in fact the victim of his own policy recommendation when he was later required to drink hemlock.)

But there is another side to this picture. For if we believe that the City of God exists only in heaven, then every actual state is, in some measure, an imperfect state. Every actual state is a mixture of good and evil, however these may be defined. And if, further, we believe that this moral judgment is properly the province of the individual (here the teacher) and not something to be abdicated to the rulers, then we must also accept the teacher as a critic of society. Precisely because he is committed to the quest for the good life, he must condemn the actual state for its shortcomings, if only by calling the attention of his students to the facts. He must not simply inquire into the meaning of the good life; he must also test his society by that standard. He may thus support or oppose the existing order of things. In a society he considers just, or largely just, he will defend the system; but in an unjust society, he will be compelled to attack it.

It is this last consequence—this idea of the teacher as an autonomous social critic—that so agitates those who hold power. For if the teacher condemns the society, or particular institutions or practices within that society, he is likely to be deemed a rebel, an enemy of the state, and may (like that earlier teacher, Socrates) be punished.

POLITICS AS A STRUGGLE FOR POWER

If, on the other hand, we regard politics as a struggle for power, we arrive at a single consequence, though in two dimensions.

At the simplest level, power groups want the schools to inculcate the values and predispositions that will justify them and their policies, even (if not especially) to the extent of perpetuating them in power. They do not think it proper for the schools to subvert them. Hence, the job of the teacher is to indoctrinate in the crudest sense of this term. He is to teach as true what those in power believe to be true. He is to teach as right the values dear to them. It is not his function to challenge the rulers, or their beliefs, or the system that has brought them to the top and now maintains them.

However, this notion of politics as a struggle for power has a redeeming feature. Since, in a democracy, power is multicentered, there are power groups outside the government that insist on their right to carry on their own type of indoctrination. (This is one reason why we have denominational schools.) And since those who currently occupy the seats of political power may someday be out of power, and will then want (hopefully sooner rather than later) to be returned, they are prepared to accept criticism that is leveled at a particular political party or social or economic group or government. But they are not equally prepared to welcome criticism of the system that enables them to exist in such form and to carry on their activities. Hence the teacher must still indoctrinate, albeit at a more general level. Now he indoctrinates not so much in support of, say, Republicans or Democrats, but in support of the democratic system, or what is alleged to be the democratic system, that makes the rule of both parties— either alone or in concert—possible.

This is euphemistically known as education for democracy, or education for citizenship. For the teacher who believes in such indoctrination, there is, of course, no problem. But for the teacher who holds to an anti-democratic philosophy or who, while himself a democrat (with a small "d"), conceives it his function to subject even democratic principles, or political and social practices popularly believed to be consistent with democratic principles, to the test of reason, there may be no end of difficulties.

For it is still true, on any fair reading of the historical evidence, that men in power are motivated less by abstract considerations of justice than they are by the promotion of their conceived interests. Those who teach things that question the value of the interests pursued, or the pursuit of such interests in the established ways, are often deemed to be enemies—not simply of the power groups but of the social order that makes possible, and in that sense sanctions or approves, their power and conduct. Hence, we return to the point that the teacher is expected to indoctrinate one way or the other—either as a defender of the underlying system or as a protagonist of a particular power group. He is not free to teach what he wants. He must teach as he is expected.

Thus, in both theories of politics, there is a demand by society that the teacher become a servant of the power system and not a free and independent thinker. Only in one theory—that which allows a subjective judgment as to the justice of the existing order—can the teacher claim a right to serve as a free critic.

IDEAS ABOUT PATRIOTISM

As there are opposing theories of politics, so there are conflicting theories *about* patriotism and *of* patriotism. All derive from the idea that patriotism means love of nation or of country, but they differ both in what they mean by love of country and in the value they attach to this love. Hence they differ, too, in their consequences for the teacher.

Take, first, the conflict of ideas *about* patriotism. In what I understand to be the dominant (if largely unarticulated) American view, patriotism is that attitude which puts one's nation or country not merely above self but above humanity. It is idle, therefore, to argue—and improper to teach —that unlike dictatorship, where man is said to exist for the state, in democracy the state exists for man. Whatever the claims of individuality, they are less important and less compelling than the claims of nation or country. Whatever the needs of humanity, whatever the democratic teaching affirming the equality of man or the religious teaching affirming the brotherhood of man, the first priority is that of *national* welfare, the first teaching that of *national* superiority. We can see this not merely in the idolatrous worship of national symbols—e.g., the flag, the Constitution, the national anthem—but in the insistence that men go forth to fight, if necessary to die, for the security and glory of their country.

It follows, therefore, from this idea about the exalted value of patriotism —a view which, for purposes of contrast, I deliberately put here in extreme form—that the teacher's duty is to inculcate the primary obligations of citizenship: loyalty to, nay reverence of, the state and obedience to the law. He may, to be sure, have his pupils recite the words, "In democracy the state is for man, not man for the state," for this rhetoric is still esteemed, but he must make certain that they understand (as the citizens of Orwell's *1984* came to understand) that words are not always what they seem.

There is, however, an alternative judgment about the value of patriotism. In this conception the state, the nation, the country are but instrumental to the requirements of man—man as self and man as humanity. The individual is the supreme end; the country but the means to the fulfillment of that end. To argue otherwise, to reverse this order of value, is held to be a perversion of purpose. Consequently, nationalism is regarded from this standpoint as little more than a form of incest, even of insanity. It degrades rather than elevates man. It debases democratic and religious ideas of the value, the significance, of man.

For the teacher who holds this alternative view, the primary obligation of the school is not to the nation but to humanity. And patriotism, which is the cult of nationalism, is necessarily to be scorned. At the very most, it may be defended as a temporary and necessary expedient; but under no circumstances is it to be revered as an intrinsic good. This, however, I need hardly add, is not the value that most of our teachers and the overwhelming bulk of the community attach to patriotism. Hence, the pressures of conformity move rather to sustain the first conception, that which puts love of country above love of man.

THE MEANING OF PATRIOTISM

Men who hold this value *about* patriotism do not, however, always agree as to the meaning of patriotism. Patriotism as love of country may mean— again to state the extreme formulations—either an attachment to whatever that country is or does at a particular time or an attachment to the ideal or ideals historically associated with or symbolized by that country.

If patriotism is conceived in the former sense, what is required is an undiscriminating affection for and devotion to all that a country is or does.

It means, in the familiar words of the schoolboy maxim, "My country right or wrong." It means that the teacher is not seriously to question our country's treatment of the American Indian or the American Negro. He is not seriously to inquire into our motives for particular wars or into our conduct of foreign policy. For him, it ought to be enough that we acted as we did; and the fact that we did it strongly argues, if it does not "prove," that it was basically the right thing for us to have done. His job as a teacher, therefore, is to develop a similar attitude among his students.

But patriotism as devotion to an ideal historically represented by his country means something else. Here the country is not taken to be the land or the government or even the inhabitants; it is rather the symbol, the embodiment of an idea, a moral principle. In the case of America, this has customarily meant the idea of liberty, of equality, of democracy.

Under this conception, the teacher is forced to evaluate both our institutions and our policies by an ideal standard. And since, as I indicated before, an actual state can never be more than an imperfect state, this view of patriotism leads the teacher once again to essay the role of social critic.

One need go no further than to refer to our state and national policies concerning our various minority groups or those who wish to immigrate to this country to see that a teacher who is patriotic in the second sense of this term will run afoul of those who are patriotic in the first sense of the term.

THE FUNCTION OF THE TEACHER

As men disagree on politics and on patriotism, so they disagree on education.

According to the dominant view, the teacher is to teach what is perceptibly useful and right. He must, to be sure, develop (or at least try to develop) certain technical skills on the part of his students: they should, it is generally expected, know how to read and write and execute simple computations with reasonable competence; they should even, perhaps, acquire the virtue of occasional silence. But his primary responsibility is to transmit and thereby to instill in his students a love of—the accepted view of—what constitutes the American way of life.

Only a few years ago, the newly appointed president of a large state university gave vigorous expression to this conception of education. He said:

An understanding of the American way of life, and faith in it, is a necessary requirement [of the teacher]. Without this belief in the freedoms and privileges of the citizens of our own country, how could anyone teach it satisfactorily? The schools are functions of the state and the teachers should be dedicated to the system.

There is, however, as I indicated earlier, a contrary view of the proper function of the teacher. This derives from the principle that the school is a center of intellectual inquiry and that academic freedom means not only the freedom of the teacher to teach but the freedom of the teacher and the student to learn. What are they to learn? Quite simply, the truth; at the very least they must be free to seek the truth.

In this view, the schools are not functions of the state but independent centers of learning. They are centers of free inquiry. They are even, some of us dare occasionally to hope, centers of intellectual leadership.

In this view, the teacher exists to preserve and to enrich the basic idea of education itself, which is to help men learn to think for themselves, and not to parrot the dogmas favored by governments and school administrators.

And in this view, most importantly, the business of the schools is not to produce good *citizens* but to produce good *men*. Here, of course, I but return to Aristotle, who put this persistent problem into classic form. Can the good man, Aristotle asked, be a good citizen? And the answer, of course, is yes—but only in the City of God, only in the just state. In an unjust state, which is always part of the City of Man, the good man may sometimes have to be a bad citizen. For his obligation as a man compels him to be true to those principles he considers just; he cannot, as a good man, do an immoral thing. His obligation as a citizen, however, requires him always to obey the laws, to do what those in power require him to do.

Here, it is evident, the teacher cannot readily bestride these opposing views. He must seek either to encourage unswerving obedience to the law or to invite his students critically to examine the law's moral content and the sometimes distressing consequences of compliance. His model—at least in his questioning—must be Jean Valjean, or Javert. It seems almost superfluous to add that in times of crisis—and somehow we seem to live now nearly always in a time of crisis—the demands of authority are all too easily equated in the public mind with the requirements of justice.

THE TEACHER AS CONFORMIST

The problem of the teacher thus derives—I tend to think fundamentally —from the fact that men hold opposing views of politics, patriotism, and the teacher; and that, in each case, what I take to be the wrong view has moved, by and large, into a position of dominance. This is true not only of those who command positions of power in the realm of politics and of the general state of public opinion with respect to the idea of patriotism, but even, I fear, of those who are teachers themselves.

I would deny, that is to say, the general presupposition that with respect to all these things the teacher stands on one side—the right side (which somehow, in the public mind, is too often construed to be the left side)—and the community on the other. It is my observation that while this conflict between the teacher and the community is very real and never totally absent, it is greatly exaggerated. The fact is that both teachers and community are internally divided; that many teachers think precisely as the dominant sectors in the community think—they share the same values, the same prejudices. Hence the issue is not simply that of teachers versus the community, but of a particular group of teachers who cling to one set of theories, along with a portion of the community that supports them, versus another group of teachers and those in the community who support them.

It is clear, I think, that in the resolution of this struggle, those who cling to the idea of a liberal education are not likely easily to prevail. Not only do they stand today on what may well be the losing side, or at least on that side which is today under the most severe and pressing attacks; what is more important, the opposition to the liberal idea of education is increasingly enlarged by insensitive, because intellectually deficient, products of our schools.

As a result, the essential push of politics and of patriotism on the schools will remain the push to conformity and not the drive for critical and independent thought. We can expect little significant relief from the whole silly business of loyalty or non-disclaimer oaths, of increased censorship or would-be censorship by parent and patriotic and governmental groups, of increased administrative supervision, of released time and religion-in-life week programs, and the like.

What is characteristic of our time is not that these pressures exist, for pressures of this sort have always beleaguered the schools. What is distinctive, and disheartening, is the fact that the schools have not succeeded in defeating, or even (by and large) in opposing, these pressures. This is to be accounted for, in part, by the fact that teachers are often timid and respectable men who dislike to sully their hands in "dirty" politics; so they suffer the consequences of having lesser men rule over them. But it is also to be explained by the fact that some of our teachers themselves welcome these pressures and seek to impose them.

I do not wish to enter here into the controversy about the merits of progressive as against other kinds of education, for such an endeavor would require, among other things, the freeing of John Dewey's teachings from the vulgarizations that often impute to him doctrines he never held. I wish only to make one small, but in this context perhaps important, point. This is, that to the extent that the schools accept the notion of conformity, or of adjustment (as it is more pleasingly and popularly called), they help to destroy their own intellectual and moral foundations; they deny their very *raison d'être*.

For to make conformity or adjustment the goal—to believe that it is most important to produce men who are like other men, who are popular or at least accepted, who belong—is to make a travesty of the idea of education itself, which is to produce a man, a whole man, an individual with a personality and a mind and judgments of his own. To produce a whole man, an educated man, is to produce a reflective and critical intelligence. It is to place a premium on uniqueness; it is to value differences. If the schools abjure this and succumb to the mania for conformity, what will emerge is not the *autonomous* but the *anonymous* man. What will emerge is not a man at all, but a cipher.

I cannot emphasize this point too much, for what is vital is not simply adjustment to life, important as this undeniably is; for life includes the must loathsome forms of hypocrisy and degradation. What is vital is the pursuit of the good life, which includes the life of the mind, the beauties (as well as the agonies) of solitary contemplation, the pursuit of differences which give zest and excitement and bring grandeur and comedy to otherwise drab and penurious lives.

It is indeed a gross commentary on American life—and on its schools—that we have produced a breed of man who values money above beauty, who seeks power and prestige instead of happiness, who dreads the thought of retirement because he does not know what he will do with his time. Is it not a sobering thought that those we have taught to read prefer Spillane to Shakespeare?

THE TEACHER AS EDUCATOR

How, then, are we to resist the push to conformity? (I say resist rather than overcome, for we are not likely ever to eliminate what is surely a universal characteristic of human society, even if it appears particularly pronounced or misguided in our own.)

The answer, I fear, is as simple as it may appear innocuous. This is, that we can do so only by remaining true to our calling as teachers, only by educating men in the proper sense of that term.

This is a simple but not an easy prescription, for it implies that as teachers we must be prepared to raise doubts in the minds of our children, to challenge the intellectual nonsense—the prejudices and the stereotypes—that their parents and elders have put there. But such parents and elders are not, customarily, people who are dissatisfied with their own ways of thought, their own patterns of behavior. On the contrary, they can rarely visualize anything better for their children than that they should be taught to think and to behave exactly as their parents and elders do. The teacher, then, who attempts—and if he is a teacher he *must* attempt—to introduce his students to new ideas, to new or different ways of conduct, must possess a degree of courage commensurate with his learning. He must be prepared to live not merely with the dislike of a portion, perhaps of a majority, of the community, but with the disrespect and inadequate rewards consequently given him.

Yet there remains always the consolation that in creating doubt and wonder where previously unreflective certainty reigned, he gives to his students the supreme gift that it lies within his power to confer: the dignity of intellectual freedom.

Controversy and the Teacher

The social impact of teachers is often judged to be minimal. Teachers themselves tend to discount their own power in a community. It seems to be the exceptional teacher who speaks out publicly on issues, who is politically active, who treats controversy in the classroom. David Riesman provides a rationale for this teacher reluctance based upon tradition and the nature of the school system. What effect does the school's vulnerability have on its teachers? The school pattern of competition and conformity is said to be drawn from the adult society. Where does the teacher stand in relation to this pattern?

Constraint and Variety in American Education

DAVID RIESMAN

In rural areas, matters are again different. Warren Peterson found, in his study of women high school teachers in Kansas City, that many had entered the Kansas City system after sad experiences of rural and small-town politics, where a single shift in the school board might eliminate a school principal and virtually dispossess his teachers; in comparison, a metropolitan school system offered the security of tenure, often enforced by a union, as well as greater opportunity to specialize.

The harassment of the public school teacher has been traditional in the smaller American communities, but this used to take the form (particularly

From *Constraint and Variety in American Education*, by David Riesman, 1956, pp. 112–15, 118–19. Reprinted by permission of the University of Nebraska Press, Lincoln, Neb.

if the teacher was a woman) of policing her private life, her smoking and gallivanting and church-going, without much direct interference in her conduct of the classroom. Today, especially in the larger places, the teacher is much freer to lead her own private life, but what we might term her academic freedom is under a great deal of pressure. Lack of concern over the teacher's private life reflects the general urbanization of America and the decline of puritanical vigilance over teachers, ministers, and other exemplars; meanwhile, however, concern over the teacher as a person has taken on a new aspect; the teacher is required today to be a "good guy," warm and friendly, not too eccentrically dedicated to interests in which the community cannot share. Moreover, the personality of the teacher has become more closely intertwined with the subjects taught: the high schools, which could remain fairly remote from immediate community preoccupations when attended only by a few, are now under a service-minded pressure to teach the social studies, and in many places they are also under pressure to teach a kind of syncretistic and neutral religion, as well as to teach tolerance, democracy and citizenship, and all other good things.[1]

Teaching these topics, which contain more obvious dynamite than the limited traditional curriculum did, however, both draws on what is in the papers and risks getting into them. High school teachers can become labeled by their students as "controversial" as soon as any discussion in the social area gets at all heated or comes close to home.[2] While a college student usually has to take the trouble to write home before he can get a parent steamed up about what a teacher has said in class, and in fact is quite likely to protect his teacher against his less enlightened parents, the secondary school student is still living at home with parents whose jealousy of the teacher is not mediated by distance either of space or of status. The high school teacher has in fact lost relative status in recent years as more and more parents are themselves high school graduates. And while the kindergarten teacher gains admiration because she can control several dozen preliterates whose mothers cannot always manage even one, the high school social studies teacher has a harder time being one-up on American-born parents who can claim to know as much as she about civics or UNESCO.

[1] In smaller communities, as Wilbur Brookover points out in *The Sociology of Education,* the high schools also have in the past borne much of the obligation to furnish entertainment—through sports, debates, plays, music, etc.—a function from which the mass media, the country clubs, and do-it-yourself are gradually relieving them.

[2] A number of investigations have asked high school students what they consider as the qualities of a good teacher; this "consumer research" indicates a preference for clear explanations, good discipline and impartiality (no pets), good grooming, consideration for pupils' feelings, patience and kindness. These are hardly the qualities easiest for the dedicated social science teacher to cultivate! See, e.g., Sister M. Theophane and Arlene Rasor, "Good Teaching as Seen by Junior High School Pupils," *School Review,* Vol. 54, 1956, pp. 72–75.

THE SOCIAL STUDIES AS A CASE IN POINT

Considering this situation in an essay a few years ago, I proposed that social studies be abandoned in the public schools, since they could not, without more protection for the teachers, be taught with any vigor or candor, and that without this they were apt to become sheer piety or, as they are called in one school, the "social slops." Rather than having the teachers assign news-magazines and deal with current debates, or try to show that the Brazilians or even the Chinese are human, too, and live in an interesting way, I suggested they stick to languages, mathematics, and the arts. These are disciplines that can be taught without political compromise (other than that of allowing poor students to pass), and they can be adequately, if sometimes crushingly, taught by a person who is neither courageous nor inspiring.[3]

John Dewey, with his orientation towards problem-solving as the principal basis of thought, and towards the school as a factor in the life of the community, would probably have regarded my view as an unwarranted concession to reaction. He might have pointed out, as many of my critics did, that even today perhaps no more than a quarter of our high school students go on to college, and the rest if social studies were abandoned would get no formal orientation in a confusing world. And, just because the social studies do connect, if not taught too badly, with contemporary themes, they may occasionally help the teacher make contact with students for whom the traditional curriculum seems meaningless and remote— students who would otherwise drop out of school or, what is worse, remain physically present while learning how to evade the school's requirements —thus, in effect preparing themselves to do the same in the jobs they will hold later on. . . .

No Road Back. All these considerations have brought me around to conceding that there is no presently viable alternative to some high school social studies programs—quite apart from the moral and practical problem of abandoning a program, for whatever good reasons, at the same time that it is under attack from conservatives who want to go back to the old-fashioned curriculum and from reactionaries who want the social studies

---

[3] David Riesman, "Some Observations on Intellectual Freedom," *The American Scholar*, Vol. 23, 1954, pp. 9–25.

Patrick Hazard has in correspondence made a point I fully agree with, namely that the arts can, if illuminatingly taught, be quite as controversial—even as "political"—as the social sciences, but for most teachers, regrettably, the invitation to controversy is a latent one in the arts and an unavoidable one in the social studies. I am also aware that teachers of such allegedly non-controversial subjects as French and algebra, basketball and shop, do often manage to convey social attitudes all the more effectively by pretending not to—convey them by side-comments or even by the way they conduct themselves in class; it would often be well to have such unexamined attitudes clarified and counterposed by social studies teachers who make explicit their preference for detached factuality as against side-of-the-mouth indoctrination.

revamped to drill the students in their version of Americanism. For those who are going on to college, the social studies might well be postponed, but for those who are not—and they cannot simply be consigned to vocational courses—the high schools have perforce become an *ersatz* college with all that implies in curricular and extra-curricular patterning. Nevertheless, I cannot comfortably resign myself to a dilemma in which teachers are forced, in a setting far less protected than that even of relatively unfree colleges, to take positions (including text adoptions) that may get them into trouble with vigilante groups on the one side or their own consciences on the other. Some school teachers have felt I was patronizing them in discouraging courageous behavior on their part, but of course I have nothing but praise for those who willingly take the risks involved in intrepid social studies teaching. But no school system can count on possessing even a minority of such teachers—for perhaps the majority, in fact, the dilemmas I have been discussing will scarcely exist, so encapsulated are they in the uncriticized values of their local communities.

The Teacher as an Enemy

Creativity and conformity are bipolar problems for teachers. The schools advocate the development of creative youngsters yet cause students to be molded into a set pattern. It is a strange phenomenon that children seem to exhibit far more creative activity before they enter school than after they have become students. Teachers also manifest this paradox. The means of defining creativity rests on agreement in form, or conformity. That is, the teacher orally encourages creative actions on the part of youngsters, yet is greatly disturbed when creativity is exhibited which does not fit her preconception. The boy who finds a new way to use his textbook for note-taking will probably not be rewarded by his teacher.

The problem is particularly evident in teacher work with gifted youth. Edgar Z. Friedenberg, a sociologist, presents an interesting and provocative analysis of why teachers act and react to creativity as they do. Is the value of conformity sufficient grounds for teachers to deny creativity? What processes in teacher selection and education are needed to correct the following problem?

The Gifted Student and His Enemies

EDGAR Z. FRIEDENBERG

One of the most heavily emphasized themes in current discussions of education in the United States is the search for potential excellence. In the past we have tended to equate academic promise with high intelligence, and to infer that the most serious wastage of young people in school resulted from the school's failure to recognize and reward high academic aptitude in lower-status youngsters. The search for excellence, on these terms, became an extension of the traditional American quest for equality of opportunity, which served as its moral justification. But this defines the issue far too narrowly. Of perhaps more fundamental importance is the effect of the school on kinds of giftedness that may be useless or even disadvantageous in earning good grades and high recommendations in a typical high school milieu. High IQ and diligence do not exhaust the possibilities of superior capacity. Originality and insight, disciplined but impassioned sensitivity, and a highly personal and unique quality of mind contribute as indispensably to human achievement.

In the school, as in much of our society, creative youngsters seem usually to arouse a specific animus. Teachers dislike them, and the students learn quite early that the spontaneity and subjectivity they prize in themselves cannot be expected to lead to success in school or in later life.

What is the source of the animus, and why is the creative student so likely to encounter it? Particularly useful in answering these questions is a concept which, though explicitly introduced by Friedrich Nietzsche, has only recently had much impact on American social thought. This is the concept of *Ressentiment*. The word sounds like a French translation of "resentment," and this does approximate the meaning. But only imprecisely. *Ressentiment* is less completely conscious than resentment, and less focused on the particular real experiences that are its actual causes. In contrast, it is usually rationalized, covert, diffuse, and largely unconscious. Just as one may legitimately refer to "free-floating anxiety" as a decisive element in certain kinds of personality, *ressentiment* is a kind of free-floating ill-temper. It is the syndrome produced by intense hostility intensely repressed over long periods of time. As such, it is familiar enough. Why then is it worth discussing as a *social*, rather than a psychological, disorder? Because of the peculiar and devastating ways in which *ressentiment* has become institutionalized in 20th-century mass culture.

Reprinted from *Commentary*, Vol. 33, No. 5, May, 1962, pp. 410–19, by permission; copyright © 1962 by the American Jewish Committee.

The conditions of contemporary life have reified *ressentiment* into a massive social and political reality. The operation of democratic political institutions—and especially their underlying egalitarian value assumptions —has greatly increased the political influence of the most *ressentient* social groups while weakening the will of more affirmative individuals to resist them.

Public education is one of the social institutions most strongly affected by *ressentiment*. The public schools attract, as teachers, administrators, and counselors, individuals from groups in the population that are particularly subject to it, and for reasons which are likely to influence the selection of the more *ressentient* from among such groups. The school is the traditional avenue—and arena—for social mobility, which many of its clientele appear to conceive as its sole *raison d'être;* one goes to school in order to get ahead, or one drops out; few youngsters are held in school by any real commitment to the cultural values represented by education, and few public schools in fact represent those values adequately. But those who are most anxious about social mobility are also most likely to be *ressentient*.

Those social groups are most prone to *ressentiment* whose members are especially subjected to frustration in their position in life, but who feel so impotent that they do not dare to get consciously angry and rebel and hit back, or strike out for themselves against the actual source of their frustration. Generally, they dare not even recognize it. Instead they identify with and accommodate to the very individuals or social forces undermining their position, and whose strength they tend to admire and exaggerate. By thus exercising their impotence, they increase it; what a less threatened individual would have felt as rage becomes resentment, then a kind of small-shopkeeper's fearful and self-pitying distrust, and finally, perhaps, merely an unconscious predisposition to sanctimonious spitefulness.

Ressentiment therefore ravages most seriously the rootless lower-middle or white-collar classes who give up most in order to be respectable and get least real deference and security in return. The threat to them is much more serious now that Western life permits its lower-level personnel to develop so few real skills. Yet, they cannot attack the system that has made their lives meaningless, for they are in collusion with it and want to rise within it.

It is not merely the economic threat that leads to *ressentiment*, for *ressentiment* is not simply anxiety. The *ressentient*, rather, are those who have given up important human potentialities in making deals with the system, and are now faced with mounting evidence that this is not going to pay off. Thus the German inflation of the 20's, wiping out the savings of millions of petty bourgeois who for a lifetime had slaved to confuse thrift and order with decency, helped pave the way to Nazism, which epitomized *ressentiment* in its Eichmannesque combination of sadism and alienation. The essence of the Nazi position, after all, is that its motives were worthy of the highest traditions of the civil service; one likes to think that the executioners of Joan of Arc, by comparison, at least felt that there was something cheerful about a nice fire. Even hatred is too strong an emotion for the highly authoritarian, who can handle feeling only by bureaucratizing it, so that it emerges as prejudice against classes of individuals rather than open hostility. Good authoritarians never get personal.

But the rigidity, hostility, and alienation that reveal the authoritarian personality in face-to-face relationships are not peculiar to adherents of the political far right. In the presence of the doctrinaire young liberal, the professional Negro or Zionist, the militant opponent of atomic warfare, one often senses the existence of the same animus however strongly one may agree with their views. It does not seem to matter very much—it does matter somewhat—whether humanitarian issues are themselves a central part of the ideology. The aggressively poor young college instructor, flaunting his radical views, minority status, and undisciplined children as explanations of his lack of recognition and status, is no fascist. But he does seem to run on the same fuel. Such a person, feeling helpless to begin with, becomes frightened lest his resentment provoke further punishment, and rationalizes it as a more positive emotion: Christian love, the desire to protect the weak, or to secure social justice. All these are perfectly real emotions that may and do arise as spontaneous responses to real human experiences. It is perfectly possible to wish, through love or compassion, to help a suffering fellow being, whether the cause of his misery be poverty, disease, sheer misfortune, or any combination of evils. It is likewise possible to be moved by his plight to genuine and fierce anger at the persons or circumstances that have brought it about, and to commit oneself wholeheartedly to fight the good fight on his behalf. But this is a very different attitude, and expresses a very different character, from that represented by *ressentiment*—which prizes the victim *because* he is a victim, and loves the suffering while covertly exploiting the sufferer.

No one has expressed this difference more clearly, or evaluated it more precisely, than Thoreau in the following passage from *Walden:*

I would not subtract anything from the praise that is due to philanthropy, but merely demand justice for all who by their lives and works are a blessing to mankind . . . I want the flower and fruit of a man; that some fragrance be wafted over from him to me, and some ripeness flavour our intercourse. His goodness must not be a partial and transitory act, but a constant superfluity, which costs him nothing and of which he is unconscious. This is a charity that hides a multitude of sins. The philanthropist too often surrounds mankind with the remembrance of his own castoff griefs as an atmosphere, and calls it sympathy. We should impart our courage, and not our despair, our health and ease, and not our disease, and take care that this does not spread by contagion. From what southern plains comes up the voice of wailing? Under what latitudes reside the heathen to whom we would send light? Who is that intemperate and brutal man whom we would redeem? . . .

I believe that what so saddens the reformer is not his sympathy with his fellows in distress, but, though he be the holiest son of God, his private ail. Let this be righted, let the spring come to him, the morning rise over his couch, and he will forsake his generous companions without apology. . . . There is nowhere recorded a simple and irrepressible satisfaction with the gift of life, any memorable praise of God. . . . All health and success does me good, however far off and withdrawn it may appear; all disease and failure helps to make me sad and does me evil, however much sympathy it may have with me or I with it. . . . Do not stay to be an overseer of the poor, but endeavour to become one of the worthies of the world.

In the contemporary American high school, *ressentiment* is much more effectively institutionalized in its "philanthropic" than in its authoritarian form. Individual teachers and administrators representing either tendency are common, but one way of expressing a major change in the climate of American education over the past half-century is by saying that authoritarianism has been placed in a thoroughly defensive position, while the "philanthropic" attitude has become dominant.[1]

Teachers and administrative officials of schools come primarily from lower-middle class backgrounds. Many come from families of somewhat higher status, but the folkways of the schools are lower-middle class folkways: the official language, the customs and regulations governing dress— even the food in the school cafeteria. All these tend to be shabby-genteel. They are not forthright expressions of the actual limitations of the schools' financial, intellectual, and social resources, such as peasant life and art express, but cheap reproductions of corporate or academic life, as imperfectly conceived. Schoolteachers by and large have likewise notably resisted, even more than most white-collar workers, identifying with the working class in their own financial interests, as by unionization. One may, of course, dislike joining a union and refuse to do so on a variety of grounds from social ideology to personal taste. But the actual circumstances of the public school teacher's background and vocational life make union membership a promising device for achieving his legitimate economic aspirations. The difficulty seems to be that teachers' economic aspirations are regularly subordinated by their middle-class identifications. Unionization is inconsistent with their insistence that they practice a profession. Fully established professions, like medicine and law, have of course evolved militant organizations to advance and safeguard their economic interests, though these are not called unions. But teachers have not so far created any organization suited to the purpose of direct economic action on their behalf. The life-style of the public high school teacher remains, characteristically, that of the dutiful subordinate awaiting preferment in a niggardly bureaucratic structure.

---

[1] The shift from "traditional" to "emergent" values in the schools discussed by George P. Spindler in his classic paper, "Education in a Transforming American Culture," *Harvard Educational Review*, Summer, 1955, might be expressed with equal validity as a shift from the dominance of authoritarian to "philanthropic" modes of *ressentiment*.

Such a life is the very breeding ground of *ressentiment*. The teacher is linked to his principal, his superintendent, and his peers by a pretense of professional equality that prevents him from either demanding the perquisites of status or the liberty to scoff at it. Within a bureaucratic structure in which one depends not merely for advancement but for personal gratification as well on the endorsement of one's peers and subordinates, open conflict generates intolerable anxiety. Frustration and anger degenerate into malicious gossip, and are absorbed into the general ambience of wariness and cynicism. Ultimately, the consequence is alienation; in such people there is no longer direct connection between their actual experiences, their feelings, and their actions.

Nothing about this is peculiar to the career of teachers in contemporary America; this is rather the familiar catalogue of complaint about life in the organized system. *Ressentiment* probably is less prominent among teachers than among many social groups like waiters or cab drivers, whose work keeps them in constant contact with people visibly enjoying a higher standard of life than they can achieve in a culture that makes it impossible to take pride in performing personal service well—or like social workers, whose "philanthropic" enterprise puts them in a position of unparalleled opportunity to intervene in the lives of other people whose poverty and tendency to act out conflicts make them both particularly tempting and particularly vulnerable to the *ressentient*. And there are many other social groups in which *ressentiment* has become institutionalized under somewhat different conditions: yellow journalism and the pornography of violence, for example. But there are further reasons that are peculiar to the education establishment why the public high school should be the locus of strong *ressentiment*.

The official function of the schoolteacher is still defined in academic and intellectual terms, however irrelevant the definition may be to the daily work a teacher in a slum school actually does. And in academic and intellectual terms, the public secondary school teacher is inferior. This, moreover, is a fact he must consciously face. The elementary school teacher can avoid facing it—if indeed it is a relevant judgment to apply to her—because she is not graded in her professional training in direct competition with people who are going into other work. In other words, she is likely to be—in many states she virtually has to be—an "ed major." High school teachers are not; they are math majors or English majors or history majors and, generally speaking, they are the ones who made poorer grades than those who head into industry, the professions, or higher education on the basis of their specialized study. In graduate school such direct comparisons are again inapplicable, but the norms for graduate students in education on standardized intelligence tests (like the Miller Analogies) are substantially lower than those for graduate students in other academic disciplines. Students are forced into secondary school teaching because they are not able to make the grade in a specialized or scholarly discipline. Finding themselves comparatively impotent academically, they are unwilling to relinquish respectable intellectual pretensions altogether, and settle for something that, in their own view, is decidedly second-rate. It is perfectly possible, of course, to define the function of a high school teacher as an honorable and extremely significant specialty in its own right; and it is also perfectly possible that, if it were so defined, it would have a rather low correlation with conventional academic and intellectual achievement. If high school teaching *were* so defined, the people who go into it would not have a sense of partial failure, and there would be no reason for their academic situation to lead to *ressentiment*. Certainly, neither the early-childhood nor the primary grade school teacher seems so prone to it. The public image of such a teacher as a constricted and punitive spinster has disappeared—though, as usual, more slowly than the reality—to be replaced by the image of the young woman who thinks of herself as, and very often really is, a professional emissary to the private world of childhood. She may not be especially scholarly or analytical-minded, but she knows her job and does it well. The children know that she does; and there is a good deal of mutual respect and affection.

In the later grades and in junior high and high schools the situation is much worse.[2] Subject matter has begun to matter, and so has the fact that the teacher is often incompetent to handle it. There is more to this incompetence than relative ignorance or stupidity. There is also the fact that the school has begun to deal with controversial content and controversial purposes. High school civics, social studies, and biology courses are no place for people who do not know their history, economics, or biology. But they are also not the place for timid or insecure people, for people who are especially anxious to make a good impression on the community or to keep out of trouble. These are, of course, exactly the kinds of people that a principal or superintendent who is timid or insecure himself will try to keep there.

Again, in this context, the feeble persistence of identification with academic norms contributes to the high school teacher's *ressentiment*. The identification is not strong enough to make him a hero.[3] But it is strong enough to make him ashamed of himself, and to add to his feeling of impotence. His impotence is real enough; he generally just does not *know* enough to defend an unpopular position on scholarly grounds even if he had the courage. But until he abandons the professional stance, or ceases

[2] See Martin Mayer, *The Schools*, Harper & Row, New York, 1961, for an excellent treatment of observations dealing with this point.

[3] Not, to be sure, that college and university people, in the social sciences at least, behaved particularly heroically under pressure. See Paul Lazarsfeld and W. Thielens, *The Academic Mind*, Free Press, New York, 1958, for a canny account of the extent of accommodation, from widespread self-censorship to occasional outright betrayal of colleagues, that occurred during McCarthy's dreadful reign.

to link it to academic competence, he cannot accept himself as a part of the local propaganda apparatus either. The statement "You shall know the truth, and the truth shall make you free" is quite false; knowledge can be a dreadful burden. But like pregnancy, knowledge to a teacher is a form of commitment no longer subject to voluntary abridgment without a sense of catastrophic guilt, and to have only a little is no help at all.

I have stated that the most serious consequence of *ressentiment* is alienation. The *ressentient* individual loses the connection between his feelings and the situation in which he is actually living. His emotions, and even his perceptions of reality, are channelled in the directions that cause least anxiety rather than toward the experiences that actually arouse them, either in the past or in the immediate present. All neurosis, of course, has this effect, but *ressentiment* is especially effective because it is the emotion itself—anger, rage, impotence, and fear of retribution—that is the source of anxiety and that must be repressed. So *ressentient* individuals are especially clumsy and insensitive, in contrast to those with other sorts of neurotic difficulty, in using their feelings to help them understand the meaning of their lives and to discipline their moral conduct. This is why they become sentimental; they prefer fake experiences that decorate the actual situation to symbolic evocations of its actuality. This kind of sentimentality has become a negative status symbol, evoking the atmosphere of lower-middle class life as surely as a whiff of H_2S brings back freshman chemistry: the plastic flowers in the apartment house lobby, which insist that this is a place in the sun; the conventional cuteness of the mass-produced, mock-hostile office signs and mock-boastful chef's aprons. The worst thing that could happen, obviously, is that a genius really should be at work.

What happens when one is—even an embryonic one? The essential quality of the creative student, as he is beginning to be defined in the literature, is that his thought is divergent. He doesn't arrive at right answers by deducing them from established premises, but by an intuitive understanding of how the problem he is dealing with really works, of what actually goes into it, and the right answers he arrives at may not be right in the textbook; they will not be, if the textbook has been carefully edited to make it as widely acceptable as possible. He works hard when the problem requires it, and respects facts as a part of reality. But for the creative student, facts are not right answers but tools and components for building original solutions.

How will the high school teacher react to this? If he is a high school teacher because the job gives him joy, and is competent intellectually, with astonished delight. But to the degree that he is *ressentient*, with defensive hostility. Consider the poor mathematician, who manages to salvage enough math to become a high school teacher, or the ninth-grade teacher who hates mathematics and never meant to have any traffic with it at all. Such teachers manage by knowing a set of answers, and a conventional procedure for arriving at them. They maintain their self-esteem by convincing themselves that this is really enough; and the student who really understands mathematics puts them in a dilemma. On the one hand, he may show them up as incompetent. On the other, they don't know but that he may be cheating somehow, and laughing at them for being taken in. They dare not commit themselves either way. If they are authoritarian, they bully him into solving the problems "the way I show you as long as you are in my class." If they are "philanthropic," they respond with studied tolerance and amusement to Johnny's "attention-getting behavior." But in either case they try to make sure that he doesn't embarrass them again by actually getting up and doing mathematics in front of the whole class.

In the humanities the creative student is both more threatening and more vulnerable. He is more vulnerable because there aren't any right answers to support him. He is more threatening because the humanities, if truthfully handled, are themselves threatening to the *ressentient*. It is the job of the humanities to get to the root of human experience, which at best means hewing austere beauty out of some very ugly blocks in such a way that their real character is revealed. This is just what the alienated cannot tolerate. What happens to the adolescent boy or girl who writes a theme about an experience that had deep meaning for him—at this age it will probably be in part a sexual experience—as it really was? For that matter, how does the well-indoctrinated professional educator, suffused with the benign values underlying his course in child development and his belief in the wholesomeness of family living, handle either Medea or Salome?

The position of the social science teacher is more ambiguous. *Ressentiment* is not always such a handicap in the social sciences, which provide a superb eminence from which to look down on one's neighbors while discharging one's scholarly obligations. The convention of objectivity keeps the *ressentient* social scientist from having to face the full responsibility for his hostility and destructiveness; after all, he is just doing his job. The creative student in social studies may therefore get an additional chance. Besides the possibility common to all fields of encountering a superior, *ressentiment*-free instructor, there is the possibility in social studies of finding an instructor who does not clobber the creative even though he is *ressentient*, but identifies with their undisciplined or rebellious disjunctivity and accepts and encourages it as an expression of his own *ressentiment*— taking refuge in academic freedom and his obligation to the truth if detected.

But such teachers are inevitably rare; they are selected out in the process of teacher-training, which requires the candidate to suffer a great deal of nonsense without protest; and administrators get rid of them if they find them out in time as likely to get the school in trouble with intransigent groups in the community. The creative student is far less likely to encounter a social critic on the high school staff than he is teachers with whom he will quickly establish a mutual loathing and who are continually reminded by his freshness of perception that they have consented to devote their lives to teaching what they know to be false or irrelevant; to denying in class that the fundamental experiences of his life can even have occurred. Hundreds of high school teachers can, and do, spend several hours a day trying to teach slum children in civics courses the official syllabus on the American Way of Life. If the children are creative, the questions they raise are difficult to answer, especially after they have given up trying to ask them verbally, and express them directly through their attitudes and behavior in class. One gets used to it, in time, and learns to maintain order. But the job of an assistant warden in a custodial institution is a long step down from earlier expectations.

Overlying the special influence of *ressentiment* on instruction in the separate fields of knowledge and reinforcing its effects is the "philanthropic" ideology of the school. Students, by definition, are subordinate in status to their schoolmasters; they are in a partially dependent position, and the function of the school is to nurture them. It is appropriate that the school devote itself to their needs and attend to and utilize their interests. Its primary purpose is to serve them.

But an institution designed to nurture the relatively weak and dependent presumably does so because it cherishes their potential strength and autonomy. There would be good reason for it to value most highly those youngsters who show most intellectual vigor and originality in the disciplined handling of ideas; as, in some cultures, a father will love his strongest and most virile sons most even though he fears them a little. The *ressentient*, identifying with impotence and resentful of strength, respond very differently. The school, strongly influenced by *ressentiment*, is rather inclined to cherish the weakness of the weak.

Thus one notion that even very poor students of educational sociology grasp eagerly is that schools are generally biased against lower-class students. They certainly are, and this is an important truth. But when the proposition is explored, what it seems to mean in the professional curriculum of education is that middle-class students "have advantages" which they ought to be forced to share more generously. The remedy is to insure that the lower-status students get their share of good grades, scholarships, opportunity for social leadership, and so on.

But these are still conceived almost wholly in middle-class terms. There is no corresponding respect for the lower-status child's own experience of life, his language, and the forms of social organization he spontaneously adopts. It is true enough that the school faces a difficult dilemma; lower-class behavior creates real difficulties in running a formal social organization like a school, quite apart from any question of bias; yet the bias is real and harmful. But professional education both in its curriculum and in its practice tends to respond to the bias as if the chief objection to it was that it gave the privileged too many privileges, rather than with a real, imaginative concern for the quality of life of lower-status youngsters.

This is a major reason why the bias is hard to eliminate. Its most important consequences do not occur in the schools, but in the long run. Giving the children of Southern Negro migrants more high grades even if they don't read or do arithmetic very well is not really going to help them much in getting into medical school. What is needed is something like the original conception of progressive education, which combined an extremely flexible conception of both educational content and instructional technique with a rather rigid adherence to standards of achievement. This is *genuine* acceptance of the meaning of underprivileged life, and real help in mobilizing the youngster's real strengths to either pull himself out of it or learn to live it more richly, at his own choice, Pushed to extremes, this might mean letting the younger brother of the leader of a "retreatist" gang use the backyard marijuana plot as his project in arithmetic and biology, thus utilizing his need for status in the peer group. But what is far more important, it also means giving him an "A" if—and only if—he solves his problems of cultivation, processing, and marketing in such a way as to show high competence in arithmetic and biology—and an "F" if he lets his marijuana go to pot.

So tough-minded a philosophy has, in fact, rather less chance than marijuana itself of taking root in the emotional climate of the American public school. "Philanthropically" inverted, the "emergent" attenuation of progressive education abandons the controversial undertaking of dealing realistically with the experiences of lower-class life. Then, to make up for not taking these children seriously, the school tries to equalize their position by expecting less of them. Simultaneously, it prevents them from learning what they are missing by inflating its credentials and subtly derogating the quest for distinction.

Higher-status children also are discriminated against in the public school, if they attempt to live in school as they do at home and in their social life. They do not share the lower-status youngster's difficulty in earning high grades and scholarships; and they are usually adept enough socially to dominate the extra-curriculum despite the attempts of the school to democratize it, especially if such attempts are enfeebled by the school administration's fear of parents' possible political influence. So the discrimination higher-status youngsters encounter is not comparable in kind to that experienced by the lower-status pupils. But as indications of *ressentiment*, the forms it takes are significant, and are especially likely to stultify creativity. Any mode of expression that is highly individualized, extravagant, or overtly sensual is forbidden or discouraged. It is assumed that it is better for the school dance to be one that everyone can afford than one with an especially good band and refreshments; that boys and girls whom nature has provided, for the time being, with especially splendid bodies ought not to be allowed to dress in such a way as to derive any special advantage from them; that the illumination of the school grounds, if there are any, be such as to discourage courtship rather than to suggest the exquisite delights to which nature may be encouraged.

Adolescence is a time when highly individualized, extravagant, and overtly sensual modes of behavior do crop out, despite the position the school takes toward them. But by its disparagement, the school abandons its opportunity to help youngsters create a style suited to their romantic age. The essential first step in encouraging creativity in secondary school youngsters is surely to link their new sexual energy and their occasionally flamboyant quest for identity to meaningful larger aspects of present and past culture, which is what taste means and disciplined self-expression requires. If the baroque manifestations of adolescence instead elicit an attitude of sulky oppression, the adolescents are thrown back onto resources they have not yet developed. The twist may then be as far as they can get by themselves in the face of official disapproval. Moreover, the ideology of the school grudgingly supports the numerous *ressentient,* lower-middle class youth against the more creative within the youth-culture itself. The school thereby tips the balance in favor of the "teen-age" solution to the problem of adolescence, quietly maintaining support for the unassuming, undiscriminating boy or girl who sees things the way other sensible people do and with other "teen-agers" builds a conventional social group, accepting conventional discipline for occasional stereotyped "teen-age" misbehavior within it. The youngster who is most handicapped by this situation is not the delinquent or the rebel, for both of these are conventional adolescent roles in their own way which society endorses by punishment. It is the innovator who sees things freshly and differently. One does not punish this youngster formally; for to do this would be to admit that he was there and that what he had said was intelligible. Instead, one isolates him by denying him the customary sources of status—that is, recognition for his work and point of view. Then one helps him—helps him to become assimilated with the "teen-age" group. In a little while, it is as if he had never been.

The "philanthropic" refusal to allow excellence to get above itself is not limited to areas, like the fine arts, toward which lower-middle class American culture is generally hostile or suspicious. Within the school even those forms of distinction that are commonly supported within this culture are treated ambiguously. I suspect *ressentiment* is one factor in the continued, and now apparently rising, complaint about overemphasis on athletics in the school. There is a substantial basis for the complaint in many schools, for athletics is sometimes the only activity that is taken seriously at all. But conversely, athletics is sometimes the only activity that is at all serious, and in which any distinction of style or achievement is permitted or recognized. The clue to whether *ressentiment* is at the root of the complaint lies in the terms in which it is couched. Complaints that the emphasis on and preoccupation with athletics interferes with specific aspects of the academic program are serious and legitimate. What are highly suspect, however, are complaints that the emphasis on athletics allows the athletes to become an elite group and gain favor and eminence unavailable to their less glamorous colleagues. Before considering such protests, one would like to be certain that the history teacher encourages a brilliant and resourceful analysis of American foreign policy with as much joy—and technical assistance—as the basketball coach does brilliant and resourceful play-making and backcourt work (for these are not inherently glamorous). It is possible that students respect an elite of athletes because good athletes are encouraged to be proud of themselves for being as good as they can, and that these are the only people left on campus with anything in particular to be proud of.

Among the most important educational consequences of *ressentiment*, then, are failure to recognize the gifted, or to nurture their gifts when discovered; differential drop-out rates among students from different social classes; and fundamental difficulties in curriculum construction that vitiate earnest and costly efforts to adapt the curriculum to the needs of divergent individuals or social groups. *Ressentiment* also influences the total experience of education in ways that are so general that they can hardly even be recognized as problems: the flavor of education itself; whether students will come to think of it as opening their understanding to a wider and deeper range of experiences or as constricting and limiting their range of possible emotional and intellectual response; whether, in the long run, the school tends more to liberate than to alienate. The total social function of education is intimately involved with *ressentiment;* for the secondary school has both a cautionary and a mithridatic function. It is here that one learns to avoid the expression of noble or heroic aspirations in noble or heroic terms, so as not to destroy at the outset the chance that they may be realized. Conversely, it is here that one learns to tolerate without surrender the demands of guilt and humility; to retain, in some measure, the power to continue to enjoy privileges and personal achievements without being disconcerted by the envy they arouse. Now that the differences are neither clearly indicated nor morally defended, many Americans devote their lives to an effort to steal into the first-class compartment without awakening the tourist passengers; and the school is where one first learns how numerous and vigilant they are. The school is where you learn to be an American; and an important part of Americanism is to learn the prevailing norms and limits of achievement and self-assertion and how to maintain them against the encroachments of a mass society that the moral support of a strong egalitarian tradition has made extremely aggressive.

Delinquency and the Classroom Teacher

Development of the self is a pervasive goal in most educational systems. As the preceding article shows, the process of self-realization may be retarded or suppressed by the same forces which offer it as a goal, the teachers. What happens to students who are unable to successfully achieve this goal? Another of the aims of education described in the following piece is that of social utility. What effect does a lack of social utility and understanding of self have upon youngsters?

Professor W. C. Kvaraceus briefly lists the available knowledge about the causes and signs of delinquent behavior and suggests possible approaches and methods the teacher can institute in the classroom to effectively meet this problem.

The Delinquent Challenges the Teacher

W. C. KVARACEUS

The school aims to guide boys and girls to a high degree of self-realization and social utility. To achieve these aims the teacher has intimate and extended contact with the growing child. Just what effects the school contacts will have on the behavior patterns of the child will depend on certain concepts and attitudes of the teacher as well as on the skills he has perfected in bringing about desirable changes in pupil behavior. The nature of these concepts and skills will be discussed from the point of view of the delinquent child or, better, the child who habitually evidences aggressive and unapproved behavior which bothers our dominant society. Since the delinquent child frequently differs only accidentally or slightly from the non-bothersome pupil, these concepts and skills are also considered to have direct application to the wholesome growth and development of all boys and girls.

Reprinted from *Progressive Education*, Vol. 27, No. 3, January, 1950, p. 82–86, by permission of the John Dewey Society.

WHAT IS DELINQUENT BEHAVIOR?

A careful study of the research literature of the past twenty-five years in the fields of causation and treatment of delinquent behavior yields the following concepts and generalizations:

1. Children who develop delinquent behavior are usually confronted by prolonged and severely frustrating conditions which deny the fulfillment of basic needs. These frustrating factors deny, or make it difficult if not impossible for the child to achieve normal growth and development. Conditions which frequently present obstacles to normal growth and development, or which often frustrate growing children, making them susceptible to delinquent conduct include:

poverty,
excessive and continued school failure,
broken or atypical homes,
inadequate personal relationships between family members,
poor imitative patterns of behavior in the home,
family mobility,
retarded mental development,
problems growing out of adolescence,
membership in marginal and minority groups,
residence in delinquency areas,
lack of membership in organized groups,
conflicts within the social class of which the child is a member and
   between social classes,
and the mores of the child's group as they conflict with standards of
   behavior as set by dominant society.

2. Delinquent behavior is always adjustive behavior from the point of view of the child. Most delinquents are trying to solve difficult and serious problems which confront them. The delinquent behavior frequently represents, for the malbehaving child, the only solution possible, and one which usually gives at least temporary relief to the frustrated child. Reacting to the stresses and strains around him, the delinquent child works out for himself the best and sometimes the only solution to his problem.

3. Delinquent behavior is bothersome or disturbing behavior from the point of view of the dominant society. While a delinquent act represents a solution to the child, at the same time it creates another problem, in that his behavior-solution brings him in sharp conflict with what others around him (parents, teachers, police) consider to be better solutions.

4. The delinquent child is one who *habitually* reacts in an aggressive manner to stresses and strains placed upon him, thus bringing himself into conflict with the dominant social group. One transgression or one conflict does not make a child delinquent. A child should not be termed delinquent

until he evidences an habitual pattern which is aggressive and in conflict with the mores of the dominant group.

5. The delinquent child must always be viewed as a specimen in the milieu of his own culture. When a delinquent's behavior is studied in terms of the behavior of his own social group, his conduct pattern is more easily understood and frequently considered normal, natural or acceptable behavior, from that point of view.

6. The importance of the emotional life of the child must be recognized. How the child feels about himself, and the various factors in his environment, plays an important role in delinquency causation. In studying the factors in and around the behaving child only those items of information are relevant which impinge on his feelings.

7. Delinquent behavior is not a twenty-four hour malady. An unbroken thread of continuity in behavior exists from the early post-natal experiences to the child's present expression. In order to understand the present conduct of the pupil the teacher frequently must go back to the earlier life of the youngster. The distinction between precipitating causes, and developmental causes in the genesis of undesirable behavior, must be made. Too frequently the teacher becomes engrossed with the precipitating, or immediate factor, that produces truancy. For example, teachers often disregard the continuity of earlier experiences which have culminated in a set of conditions that enables a slight pressure, or unusual experience, to throw the child in the direction of undesirable or bothersome behavior.

8. The delinquent act is usually social in nature. Less than one fifth of delinquent acts represent solitary behavior. Since delinquent behavior represents a form of group behavior, study and treatment should take into account the psychological factors of group conduct and behavior.

9. There is no single cause, or single pattern of causes, that will explain all instances of delinquent behavior. Individual children show unique patterns of causation. However it is true that certain common inimical factors frequently surround many children who eventually show delinquent behavior.

10. Children frequently give many signs of delinquency proneness. These may be seen either in the personality make-up of the child himself, or in his home, family or neighborhood setting. Early detection of these exposure signs makes preventive measures possible. The teacher is one person in the community who is in a good position to note these signs of delinquency proneness.

11. A large proportion of delinquent behavior is precipitated during the adolescent period. While it is true that much of adolescent malbehavior can only be understood in terms of the pre-adolescent experiences of children, the stresses and strains placed on children growing into manhood and womanhood must be taken into consideration, and relieved, in the prevention and control of delinquency.

12. The teacher should recognize that many stresses and strains are placed on the child in the classroom. These frequently aid and abet the development of delinquency. This is particularly the case when the individual is burdened with unrealistic and highly verbal situations which may beget continuous failure, insecurity, and rejection.

13. Delinquency control and prevention postulates sympathetic understanding on the part of the teacher, rather than blaming, moralizing, and censuring which often surrounds the child who shows bothersome behavior.

14. Only a very few delinquent children (perhaps no more than two percent) constitute a group of compulsive behavior delinquents. The constitutional delinquent, as seen particularly in the psychopath, is a rare phenomenon, although in recent years many children whose behavior has not been easily understood have been erroneously classified in this category.

15. Since the delinquent child is usually one who is putting up a good fight against the inimical factors which surround him, and prevent his wholesome growth and adjustment, there is something wholesome about his straightforward and overt attempt to come to grips with his problem. His behavior is in sharp contrast to that of the child who reacts to the stresses and strains of his environment by withdrawing within himself, and thereby hiding his difficulties from those who might help him. The delinquent gives the teacher many unmistakable symptoms that something is wrong within himself or within his environment. He shrieks that he is in need of help.

16. Most delinquents are normal individuals. They are more like, than different from, their fellow pupils who do not bother society. The differences between delinquent and non-delinquent children are more frequently accidental rather than essential. Many delinquent children who are not apprehended and who are given no outside assistance work out their own problems and become well adjusted adults.

HOW TO DETECT CHILDREN EXPOSED
TO DELINQUENCY

Since delinquent behavior does not develop overnight, the teacher who comes in contact with his pupils over an extended period of time has an unusual opportunity to look for and identify those children who are susceptible, exposed, or vulnerable to the development of delinquent behavior.

The following characteristics taken from the *K D Proneness Check List*[1] have been found to be frequently associated with delinquency behavior.

[1] Reprinted by special permission from *The K D Proneness Scale and Check List*, by W. C. Kvaraceus, World Book Company, Yonkers, N.Y., 1950.

Not all of these signs are necessarily causes of delinquent behavior. They are, however, external signs that usually precede, or accompany, delinquent patterns of behavior. This list must be used with caution and reservations. It should not be applied mechanically, nor used as a basis for official "typing" of pupils as "predelinquent." It may be used as a rough guide in determining which boys and girls might be selected for further study and subsequent treatment in a planned, scientific, and individualized program of delinquency prevention and control.

PERSONAL FACTORS

Boy is between 10 and 16 years of age.

Girl is between 12 and 16 years of age.

Is limited in academic aptitude.

Is in poor health.

Has physical defect.

Reacts to situations in overly-aggressive manner.

Attends the movies twice a week or more often.

Lacks or resists contacts with recognized recreation or character building agencies.

Shows low achievement, or lack of success, in out-of-school activities.

Has previous record of delinquent behavior.

Evidences a philosophy of "good" or "bad" luck.

Plays or associates with children who are vulnerable or who have been delinquent.

Runs with a "gang."

Is the youngest child in large family.

ENVIRONMENTAL FACTORS—HOME AND FAMILY

Birth was unplanned or accidental.

Family is broken or atypical—death, desertion, divorce, other.

Relationships in family life unwholesome.

Emotional conflicts between parents.

Emotional conflicts between sibs.

Emotional conflicts between parents and sibs.

Severe punishment frequently used.

Overindulgence exhibited toward child.

Child feels disliked or unwanted.

There is drunkenness in family.

The family scene presents nagging.

There is evidence of neglect.

The family scene presents overprotection.

The family scene presents intensive sibling rivalry.

The family scene presents extreme parental domination.

There are cultural conflicts between parents and sibs.

Child has brothers or sisters who have been delinquent.

Parents have court records.

The family is large.

The family belongs to a marginal group—negro, foreign-born parentage, other.

Child does not live in his natural home.

Family does not have adequate income to live decently.

Family shows record of welfare agency contacts.

Father is unskilled worker.

Mother is employed outside the home.

The living quarters in the home are not adequate.

Child lives in a multi-family dwelling.

Overcrowding (more than 1.5 persons per room) prevails.

Furnishings are inadequate.

There is no radio.

Home is unsanitary.

Family is mobile or migratory.

Family lives in underprivileged neighborhood.

Family lives in high-delinquency-rate area.

Child has no play opportunities in yard, neighborhood, or home.

Family lives over a store or business establishment.

Family rents their home and pays less than average rent prevailing in community.

FACTORS IN THE SCHOOL

Has limited verbal ability.

Has little interest in work.

Is unsuccessful in grade work.

Has repeated one grade.

Has repeated several grades.

Is in a special class.

Dislikes school fiercely.

Is the oldest in the class.

Transfers frequently from school to school.

Is truant from school.

Intends to leave school as soon as the law will allow.

Feels that he does not belong to the class group.

Takes little or no part in extra-curricular or club activities of school.

SPECIAL SERVICES CAN HELP THE TEACHER

After detecting children who show exposure, or susceptibility, to the development of delinquent patterns of behavior, the alert teacher will utilize the special services within his school system—attendance department, guidance office, testing, medical and nursing services, visiting teachers, special classes, remedial services, etc. These services will enable the teacher to understand the child better and to obtain ideas and recommendations as to what might be done in the classroom to relieve stresses and strains. These services will also help the teacher to utilize the therapy possibilities that abound in the classroom. Moreover, schools have available within the community many youth-serving agencies that can aid and assist the teacher in helping the child to grow and develop normally. The alert teacher knows what child-serving agencies exist; he knows what functions they serve, and he knows how to get individual children who are in particular need of the services of a particular agency in the hands of that agency, at the time the services are needed. Much can be done by the teacher through early discovery of children who are susceptible to delinquency and then making use of agencies which are equipped to help him better to understand the child, to guide him more effectively, and, if need be, to carry on a treatment program. Too frequently classroom teachers are either uninformed about, or unwilling to use, the special services within the community as well as within the school system itself.

SANITARY EMOTIONAL CLIMATE IN
THE CLASSROOM IS ESSENTIAL

Teacher-pupil relations should reflect a democratic, cooperative, and friendly spirit. The teacher should not dominate the classroom scene, or rule by threat or punishment, but rather he should show sympathetic respect and concern for all personalities in the classroom. Meticulous precautions should be taken lest any pupil feel rejected, unwanted or insecure. All children should attain security and satisfaction through successful achievement in classroom endeavors. A variety of activities should be encouraged in the classroom, and the teacher should play the role of a helpful guide in the selection of the learning-teaching activities. Pupils should be given an active part in setting up aims and objectives as well as in the selection of their own learning activities within the level of their maturity. Always the classroom work should be meaningful to the pupil and related to his out-of-school life and experiences. A conscientious attempt should be always made to study and improve the inter-relationships between class members. Failure experiences and rejections should occur infrequently or not at all.

The objectives in the classroom must be envisioned, stated, and pursued in terms of expected modifications and changes in pupil behavior. Unless the learning-teaching activities are appraised in terms of how pupils act and behave, in consequence of their having attended school and having "learned" in the classroom, little positive effects on wholesome growth and development can be expected. If the teacher is content to measure outcomes solely in terms of what pupils say or write, the result will be children who deny the effectiveness of their "knowledge of good and evil, right and wrong" through their daily conduct, in spite of the fact that they may have "learned the right answer" and made high marks on paper and pencil tests. The teacher who is not oriented to the objectives of the school, and to learning as stated and seen in behavior modifications, will feel no concern for delinquent behavior and will have little effect on desirable forms of day-to-day living among the pupils.

PROVISION FOR INDIVIDUAL DIFFERENCES IS ESSENTIAL

Few educational principles have been worn to a platitude faster, and with less effect on classroom practices, than the concept of individual differences. Yet evidence is available, indicating that violation of this principle aids and abets the development of undesirable behavior more than the effects of broken homes or poverty. The systematic use of tests, and other analytical devices, to note the readiness of the individual pupils for various learning experiences must be an integral part of the beginning teaching process. Use of varied and appropriate reading materials, and visual and audio aids, for pupils of differing abilities and interests, together with grouping of pupils in homogeneous units for the learning of skills, will promote more effective learning. Differentiation in assignments and learning activities to meet the abilities and achievement of pupils of superior, average, and low abilities should insure progress on the part of all pupils in accordance with their individual potentials for growth. Adequate recognition of achievement, in keeping with each child's abilities, should characterize the pupil's growth record. Only when the teacher succeeds, through frequent and wise use of the devices and techniques at his disposal, in helping each child make continuous progress, for which he is properly recognized and rewarded, will the classroom be rid of the great hazards to child adjustment.

The Liberal and the Professional in Teacher Education

Teacher education is a social and vocational task which has incurred as much criticism as the field of education itself. Preparing teachers for various types of schools, purposes, students, and environments is a highly complex operation. Critics exist within and without the field of professional education. The arguments over educational goals, treated earlier in this text, involve the nature of teacher education. Arguments over curriculum also extend to teacher preparation. Thus, disputes as to the relative worth of a liberal, as opposed to a professional, education take on both philosophic and practical considerations.

The following two articles deal with problems connected with preparing students to be effective teachers. They do not pose all of the positions presently being argued about teacher education, but some give views that are not readily obtainable in the popular magazines. The selection by George S. Counts, an education professor, stresses the disparity between content and method, and discusses teacher education as a part of the scientific movement. The final treatment by Paul C. Rienert, President of St. Louis University, is a suggestion for uniting the best of liberal and professional education.

What should be the proportions of liberal to professional course work for teachers? What specific learnings are necessary for competent teaching? Where should these be taught, in liberal arts courses or professional education classes or neither? What requirements should be demanded of all teachers and what requirements in specific fields or grade levels?

A Discussion of Teacher Education

GEORGE S. COUNTS

The present program of teacher training continues to reflect the conditions of the past. It still bears marks of the class organization of education developed in Europe during the eighteenth and nineteenth centuries. There the masses attended some kind of folk school distinguished by a meager program and an emphasis on obedience and the acquisition of skills, while the privileged orders were provided with an extended program of intellectual education embracing preparatory school, secondary school, and university. The teachers in these two branches of the educational system differed in social origins and in training. Those in the folk schools came from the masses and were trained in the normal schools, whereas those in the secondary schools came from the classes and were prepared in the universities. The American people, though repudiating the dual educational system of Europe, preserved that system in part in their program of professional training. In general they have prepared their elementary teachers in normal schools and their secondary teachers in colleges and universities.

Reprinted with the permission of Charles Scribner's Sons from *Social Foundations of Education*, pp. 274–79, by George S. Counts. Copyright © 1945 Charles Scribner's Sons; renewal copyright © 1962.

In their curricula and methods of work the normal schools and their offspring, the teachers' colleges, reveal their ancestry. Although various contrary tendencies have been at work, these institutions have fostered the tradition, congenial to a society divided into governed and governing classes, into working and leisure orders, that method may be separated from the content of thought. They have based their programs partly on the assumption that teaching is chiefly a matter of the mastery of method and that education is to be conceived as independent of the body of a given culture. Clearly methodology, if it revolves about its own center, becomes an intellectual operation akin to that of the Sophists of ancient Greece and the minor Scholastics of the Middle Ages; if it advances to the center of the substance with which it deals, it becomes something else, an aspect of purposeful activity. In the former case it is sterile; in the latter it is submerged in thought and philosophy.

Aside from the operation of the deeper social forces, the responsibility for this divorce of method and thought, for the establishment of separate institutions for the training of teachers, must be borne in part by the trends in the higher learning in America. By disdaining concern with educational practice and by becoming immersed in the development of their own specialties, university professors have practiced a form of deception not unlike that practiced by the methodologists. While scorning methodolgy, they have unwittingly become methodologists themselves. But since they refused to assist teachers confronted by the urgent problems involved in instructing increasing millions of children, the teachers were compelled to shift for themselves.

Another force contributing to this divorce of methodology and thought was the growth of teacher training as a vested institutional interest. Following what seems to be a kind of natural law, the normal school, once established, became concerned, like the good court, with a declaration of its independence and an extension of its jurisdiction. Also like all established institutions it had positions, salaries, emoluments, honors, titles, and privileges to distribute to those presumably expert in the mystery or craft of methodology. Moreover, since most of the students it trained were in a hurry on their way to teaching and since society was increasing the demand for teachers, the normal school confronted a dilemma. Thorough instruction in subject matter seeming impossible, it chose the course of specializing in certain tricks of the trade which poorly educated teachers could repeat without much difficulty. Thus, a virtue was made of apparent necessity, and a makeshift became a dominant interest. Method assumed the form of a cult. And teachers who knew little of the fact and thought of their subjects were subjected to the tyranny of an instrument.

As scholars become enslaved to specialty and pedagogues to method, both inquiry and instruction were impoverished. Moreover, the scholar generally ignored the difficulties of the teacher. Sometimes with a pride little warranted the former assumed that a person deeply engrossed in such a matter as the mediaeval manor or the tun-moot in early England was for some reason superior to a person engaged in leading children along paths of knowledge and good living. Thus many university professors scorned such "elementary," but profoundly significant, problems as the instruction of boys and girls and refused to consider the vital question of the relation of their specialties to the schools. Like the pedagogues they had their vested interests which they wished to guard. If specialty is brought into connection with life, its small stature is exposed. They therefore thought it safer to preserve their cult or mystery unsullied by the world.

As the rift widened, as subject matter specialists turned in upon themselves and their specialties, and as methodologists gained increasing power over teacher training and the schools, the latter took steps to fortify their growing vested interest. They brought pressure upon state legislatures and state and local boards of education and secured the adoption of laws and rules requiring applicants for elementary and high school teaching positions in any field or fields to present credentials stating that they had taken and passed a certain number of courses in "education," variously described, sometimes as "the theory and art of teaching" and sometimes as "the science of education." The proportion of hours in this field to the total number of hours required for certification varies. In some cases it is as high as one-fourth; but whether it is one-fourth or one-tenth or one-fifteenth, it is a positive limitation. No matter how competently and widely trained in subject matter the applicant may be, he cannot obtain a teaching certificate without having taken and passed the prescribed number of courses in pedagogy. Schools and professors offering instruction in "education" are thus given a preferred position with reference to a subject which in both theory and practice is loosely defined.

Perhaps the most characteristic development in the sphere of education since the opening of the twentieth century is the effort to create a science of education. Into this movement a tremendous amount of energy has gone. The quantitative method has been applied to the learning process, methods of teaching, and many aspects of school administration. School systems large and small, state and local, have been surveyed; and so-called objective tests, scales, and score-cards, practically without number, have been standardized for the measurement of intelligence, school attainments, teaching ability, administrative efficiency, and almost every phase of the conduct of education. And the prediction has been confidently made again and again that by means of the scientific method all of the problems of education will submit themselves to speedy and impersonal solution.

The results of this development are difficult to appraise at the present time. A great body of facts pertaining more or less to the task of education has certainly been accumulated. A very large proportion of these facts, however, are either comparatively irrelevant or trivial in nature; and the attention of teachers, administrators, and educational leaders has been directed to those aspects of the educative process that lend themselves most readily to the application of quantitative procedures—the more simple, the more mechanical, the less profound aspects of the problem. It is not too much to say that emphasis on the measurement of the more mensurable concomitants of education, regardless of questions of relevance, has provided the profession with a mode of escape from the larger and more disturbing questions that have been raised by the onward sweep of industrial civilization. When the best minds in education might have been devoting themselves to a consideration of the meaning for education in the United States of the shift from the individualistic agrarian economy, they were actually engaged in the fashioning of spelling scales and scorecards for school buildings.

The devotion to measurement has also fostered the view that education is a branch of thermodynamics and is essentially mechanical in nature. All matters involving the selection and rejection of values, which after all must always lie at the center of any educational program, were barred from consideration on the grounds that they were subjective in nature, outside the range of science, and therefore unworthy of consideration by educational science. The consequence of this narrowing of the field of interest and of inquiry was quite generally the acceptance of the traditional framework of institutions, ideas, and values. When the framework crumbled in the great depression beginning in the summer and fall of 1929, those engaged in the scientific study of education were therefore caught wholly unawares. The foundations on which they had been building, without really being aware of the fact, were found to be in a process of disintegration. They had regarded education as primarily a question of method and more or less independent of the course of cultural evolution.

The mechanical conception of education resting on the quantitative method also favored the elaboration of the technique of education. This in turn tended to alter the roles of teacher and administrator. If education is largely a matter of tests and scales and classification, then the process can be guided by persons seated at the center of a given school system. By manipulating the proper levers at the proper time they can direct efficiently the course of learning and teaching throughout the area under their jurisdiction. One need not even know the content of a particular subject which he is supervising, if he has at hand objective tests which, when administered according to carefully outlined directions, reveal as unerringly as a thermometer in its field the precise condition of the learner. If the tests are supplemented by a knowledge of method, the supervisor can pass judgment not only on the product but also on the process of instruction. All of these tendencies have resulted in the reduction of the role of the teacher and the elevation of that of the administrator or supervisor. Under such a regime, for a genuinely gifted person to engage in teaching would appear to be a waste of talents.

The Liberal Arts and Teacher Education

PAUL C. REINERT

When a great cultural heritage flows on from one generation to another, gathering, we hope, strength, power and brilliance as it goes, the channels that carry it are now, as in every other age, the teachers in that culture. Whether they are walking with a young friend through the woods on a quiet afternoon, or lecturing from a proud academic chair in a great university, they are the bearers of the heritage. Sometimes they may be men or women soon to be surpassed in achievement by those now their students; sometimes, though only rarely, they may be great intellectual figures in their own generation—but always they must have caught some spark of the intellectual and cultural tradition that they help to pass along. No one who does not have that spark can be a really effective teacher on any level. And only to the extent that he has caught that spark and developed it within the limits of his own abilities and personality, can anyone be a really effective teacher on any level.

In all the years that the Association of American Colleges has been meeting it has been our proud boast that the liberal arts colleges of this emerging American culture have been the means of generating this spark in the students who have come to us. I do not think that it is too much to say that we have held firmly to the notion that our colleges not only have done this task but are better fitted to do it than any other institutions on the American scene. This is a proud boast indeed, but I think a justified one. Like all such boasts, it brings along with it stern responsibilities. In the language of the street, we can well be challenged to put our money where our mouth is.

And this in two ways: one—that we do the job we pretend to do with those students who come to us; two—that we take special pains to make this great gift available to those in our civilization who stand most in need of it. And who may these be? Who else if not those whose task it is to pass along the spark to the next generation, the teachers of our own age? And can you say that the young woman who introduces the six-year-old to the wonderful world of reading is not passing along this vital spark of culture as significantly as the college professor of literature or physics? If she and any of the other teachers who wage the daily battle against ignorance in our elementary and secondary classrooms are to be effective in their work,

Reprinted from *Liberal Education*, Vol. 51, March, 1965, pp. 20–28, by permission of the publisher and the author.

they themselves must first of all have developed the effective personalities which we claim to be the product developed best by our liberal arts colleges.

Many years ago our colleges generally ignored the need for liberally educated elementary school teachers. The burden of producing teachers to man the elementary schools fell on institutions which have only painfully, if at all, learned the harsh lessons of the qualities needed by an institution which is to give a sound liberal education. For many years, too, the graduates of our liberal arts colleges fell into secondary school teaching with little professional orientation, and with little direct attention paid to the student's eventual role in the classroom. This may have been enough for the unusual, the "born" teacher. That it is enough for the great number of teachers needed to staff our elementary and secondary schools today may be seriously doubted.

What we sorely need is a major effort by the best and most perceptive minds on our liberal arts faculties to make a careful and unprejudiced examination of the qualities needed in the effective elementary and secondary school teacher, and of all the ways in which a sound liberal arts education can be adapted to produce them. In this way, we will not be trying to professionalize the liberal arts but to put the liberal arts into the mainstream of American education, through the teachers that are the channels for that stream.

Instead of such a competent examination of total programs designed to produce effective total personalities to man the classrooms of the next generation, we have had a series of efforts, often well-intentioned and quite helpful, by groups who have had some special interest or some specialized orientation. Their recommendations, as a result, look to strength in particular aspects rather than to total effectiveness. These efforts may be grouped under three headings.

First, there has been a series of quite productive efforts in the various academic disciplines to improve the teaching of those disciplines in the elementary and secondary schools and consequently involving efforts in the training, and especially the re-training, of the teachers of those specialties. Almost always, however, the suggestions include a much more thoroughgoing specialization for the prospective teacher or a much lengthened program or both.

Second, there has been a strong push within the organized teaching profession, particularly under the auspices of the American Association of Colleges for Teacher Education and the National Commission on Teacher Education and Professional Standards, to strengthen the quality of teacher education programs, by encouraging experimentation with a variety of approaches, by emphasizing the general education aspect of teacher preparation, by pressuring the various legal agencies to avoid specific regulations for the content of teacher education programs, and by bringing together representatives of both the academic and the professional faculties involved in teacher education so that misunderstandings could be removed and cooperation fostered. This approach of course tends to take a strongly professional view of the problem and, although the leaders have frequently had a very broad outlook, there is always the tendency in their recommendations to professionalize the liberal arts component in the teacher education programs.

The third type of effort has been that exercised through public pronouncements of journalists like Milton Mayer, public figures like Admiral Rickover and foundation-financed experts of whom the chief is James Bryant Conant. These men have made a more or less careful investigation of the problems of teacher education, have been captivated by various aspects of European education and have their own panaceas for our American problems, usually involving a much higher degree of governmental control of teacher preparation and education generally than is now the case in this country.

The first and second groups of efforts I have mentioned are not sufficient in themselves. They are incomplete and tend to be weighted in one direction or another, thus missing the balance and style which should be the essential marks of the well-educated teacher. The third group of efforts is often superficial, frequently imitative of foreign programs outmoded in the countries of origin, and sometimes positively dangerous in its emphasis on governmental controls. All of these efforts have been important these last several years, but they do not give us the genuine keys to the improvement of our teacher education programs—keys which, I am convinced, are in the hands of the faculty and administrations of our liberal arts colleges, that is, yourselves.

When we analyze the qualities that have made the American liberal arts colleges genuinely productive of liberally educated men over the years, one of the qualities which has been most significant has been the independence of action which our culture has afforded the colleges. The great claim that was so ably defended by Daniel Webster in the Dartmouth case has become the *magna charta* for the independence of thought and independence of action that has made our colleges great. Why is it that they are able to defend the truth against attack, to hold unpopular ideas before the general public is prepared to accept them, to encourage independence of thought in their students and to protect those students against the attacks of those who would brainwash them? Why? Because they are not subject to the dictation of governmental agencies which can tell them what they shall teach, whom they shall teach and when they must keep silent.

Our liberal arts colleges are free institutions in a free society; it is out of this freedom that their strength arises; it is this freedom which makes it possible for them to build into their students the personal qualities which we expect from a genuinely liberal, that is a genuinely free, education. The history of Germany, Italy and Russia show us all too vividly what can happen to institutions of learning that are under the domination of governmental agencies.

Why this emphasis on the freedom of the colleges in a talk on the relationship of the liberal arts colleges with teacher education? Because I think that this freedom is in great danger. There are many pressures which are combining to cause this danger: the pressure of mounting enrolments, the rising costs of higher education, the consequent demands for more and more governmental financial help, the resulting insistence on governmental planning to guide the direction of that help, the pious insistence on efficiency and avoiding waste which is the traditional justification for increasing governmental controls.

But one of the most insidious threats to the freedom of American institutions of higher education comes from those who present themselves as friends of free institutions but continually recommend greater and greater domination by governmental agencies. And nowhere is this attack more prevalent than in the area of teacher education. The attack comes in two directions. One is an attack on voluntary accrediting agencies, the second an attack on institutional autonomy by the encouragement of governmental planning and control of the procedures leading to the licensing of teachers.

One of the ways in which American higher education, up to this point, has been saved from governmental domination has been, I am convinced, through the development of efforts on a voluntary basis for the necessary supervision and encouragement of institutions by their peers. The rise of the regional accrediting associations has challenged the new and inferior institutions to sometimes superhuman efforts to merit recognition by their fellows in higher education, without any appeal to governmental sanctions. This recognition has been given on the basis of criteria framed by those actively engaged in the work of higher education and consequently knowledgeable about and sympathetic with both the problems and the ideals of the collegiate world. Why should this be handed over to government and to what is sure to become, by the inevitable processes of Parkinson's Law, a bureaucratic monstrosity remote from the actual problems of higher education and subject to all the winds of political pressure?

The professional accrediting agencies too have provided a remarkable example of the way in which experienced and knowledgeable people can cooperate in a voluntary endeavor to strengthen and police the procedures by which new entrants to professions vital to our welfare are prepared. Through such agencies, the institutions directly concerned and the professionals who have a personal stake in the quality of their new colleagues can exchange ideas, set appropriate standards and apply the democratic sanction of recognition by peers, in a voluntary fashion free from the threats of governmental empire-builders and the vagaries of political log-rolling.

We are all aware of the weaknesses and inconsistencies of some and perhaps all of these voluntary agencies. That is why, again on a voluntary and free basis, we established the National Commission on Accrediting. But we should improve the agencies, correct the defects and press forward as thinking people able to regulate our own affairs, and not throw out this product of many labors and much good will in favor of the state controls which have proven so inadequate in the history of education.

While no one denies the right of governmental agencies to license teachers—this is after all an extension of the police power in order to protect the children against real incompetence—the attempts by the states until recently have been strongly in the direction of prescribing particular courses which the students preparing to be teachers must take in college. This has been recognized as poor policy by college people and by the teaching profession generally.

The National Education Association, through the National Commission on Teacher Education and Professional Standards, has been trying to get the states to do away with these detailed prescriptions, and has met with considerable success in the last several years. But even where the prescriptions still exist as they do in a number of states, the colleges can still determine the content of the courses bearing the prescribed titles, and so have been able to determine what actually was being offered to and demanded of the student. It has been inconvenient but not impossible to retain appropriate freedom in this situation.

Now our valiant defenders of higher education against the "educationists" want the state to take over not only the prescription of the key element in the education of teachers, the practice teaching experience, but also the direct management of that experience, thus removing the freedom which the colleges were just managing to regain. Without ever mentioning the example of Germany, the design of this so-called "reform" is almost identical to the present practice in Germany, a practice which many German academicians admit to be far from satisfactory.

It is frightening enough that the "reform" proposed is designed to take away much of the freedom of the colleges in the preparation of teachers. Even more frightening is the way in which the reformers intend to bring about their reform. Is it to be adopted by the colleges on the basis of a critical examination of its merits and free choice by the institution concerned? Not if we are to believe James Conant, the most outspoken advocate of this reform. His own description of the process is as follows: ". . . the proponents of the restricted state approved program approach can hardly expect to have their view welcomed with enthusiasm by most college or university administrators or most professors of either liberal arts or education faculties. Indeed, the state may have to exert considerable pressure on teacher education institutions before this particular reform is consummated." (AACTE, Hunt Lecture, 1964, p. 18)

If this is not an appeal for the replacement of free choice in higher education by brute governmental force, I have never heard one. The same author's newest book, *Shaping Educational Policy*, extends this same plea for the replacement of free choice by governmental action in all facets of education, not merely the education of teachers.

The institutions you represent are under a subtle but serious attack. It is their freedom which is threatened. We may not have a Daniel Webster to fight our cause in this particular crisis, but surely we need not abjectly surrender our freedom merely because some vocal individuals demand that we let the dictates of political bureaucracy replace the free choice of mature academic institutions in determining what sort of education we offer all our students, and particularly those whose vocation makes them the channels of our culture to the next generation.

A liberal education, combined with an effective professional orientation, can and should produce the kind of people we need in all our classrooms— people completely at home in what Jacques Barzun calls "the house of intellect"; people vibrantly aware of the riches of their cultural heritage but keenly attuned to the legitimate demands of our contemporary society; people well equipped with the tested techniques of our educational tradition but able to adjust readily to new approaches that will make their effort more effective; people who are well read and continually alert to new ideas; people only a liberal education can produce. And unless our liberal arts colleges show by successful example how it is to be done, who is to lead the way?

Sometimes one gets the impression that liberal arts colleges get into the business of "training" teachers—and I use the term *business* advisedly —because it attracts the students whose tuition furnishes the wherewithal to keep the college operating. But they do it reluctantly, almost shamefacedly, as if somehow forced to go slumming in spite of themselves. To me such an attitude is a major violation of the basic principles for which the liberal arts college stands. Not only are the liberal arts colleges the direct descendants of the faculties of arts of the great universities; not only have they developed a significant role in the total education of the young people of our American society—but they can only justify their riches available to the next generation through its teachers.

In summary, therefore, teacher education *needs* the liberal arts colleges. But what of the liberal arts colleges themselves? Do they have some needs which can be met only by a deep concern for and commitment to teacher education? We would be hiding our head in the sand if we failed to acknowledge that our liberal arts colleges are subject to and often deserving of sharp criticism. That criticism can be summed up in one word: sterility. Where is the life, where is the vigor which should prove that the colleges are vibrant citizens of a throbbing, dynamic, expanding civilization, and not inert prisoners in an ivory tower?

One of the ways I would like to suggest in which such life and vigor can be reintroduced into our liberal arts educations is precisely through a commitment to a sound program of teacher education. Such a program must necessarily put the prospective teacher into direct contact with the children of the next generation, with their hopes, their fears, their frustrations, their boundless optimism. Where better than in such a context can the college student find the personal involvement in humanity's cares and humanity's future which will open the doors of his own inner self to the impact of the natural sciences, the social sciences and the humanities? Without such an opening the knowledge he gains becomes dry bones to rattle or insipid pap to regurgitate. But for one who is open to this impact, the achievements of our culture become tremendously and personally important. The college student must have contact with life; involvement with children can be the means to that contact, and thus be the means for his own completely liberal education.

So we can say with all honesty that teacher education needs the liberal arts colleges. But just as honestly, the liberal arts colleges need teacher education, to keep them vital and productive, to make it possible for them to do their own job adequately.

What kind of a teacher education program should a liberal arts college provide in order to produce the effective teaching personality our classrooms need and at the same time capitalize on and reinforce its own strengths as a college? By all means we should avoid the temptation to list specific courses and credit hours. Each college achieves its effectiveness through the development of its own personality, and this is achieved through the curricular decisions of its own faculty, based on the particular strengths of that faculty and of the institution generally. But we might point out some important characteristics which should be found in our teacher education programs as we look at them on a national scale. I would hope for:

1. *Variety*—an intelligent variation based on the differing personalities of the institutions and within the institutions on the differing abilities and backgrounds of individual students. No single pattern of teacher education can be the best everywhere and always.

2. *Vitality*—achieved by close personal contact between students and faculty members who are scholars in the fullest sense, vitally aware of the relationships of their disciplines with contemporary concerns, vigorously involved in the excitement of significant research, thoroughly responsive in their teaching approaches to their students as individuals and sympathetic with their students' professional and personal goals.

3. *Vigorous commitment*—by the institution to the objective of preparing persons who are suitable as teachers, by the faculty to significant values to guide them in their efforts to help in the personal development of their students, by the students to a sense of dedication in a career of service. And finally,

4. *Freedom*—from unnecessary governmental controls, based on the mature responsibility of free institutions solving their own problems as individuals or as voluntary groups. Only in this atmosphere of freedom can

we possibly build the education designed for free men, which, after all, is just another name for a liberal education.

The liberal arts, or better, a liberal arts education, is not some predetermined sequence of courses, not some pattern sanctified by tradition, but a program of learning experiences which open the mind, enlarge the spirit and challenge the powers of the total personality. Different patterns will have this effect on different student personalities; different institutional personalities will find some patterns more effective means to this goal than others—but different students and different institutions must be free to grow if they are to live, must be able to satisfy the restless, seeking, self-critical drive that marks the free man. Such growth can take place only in an atmosphere of genuine academic freedom, not in one harassed by bureaucratic red tape and governmental big-brotherhood.

I may seem to have strayed from my assigned topic in the emphasis I have put on institutional self-determination. But the future of our society depends in a special way on the teachers of the next generation. If they are to produce free men able to cope with the challenges of our times, they must be free themselves in every good sense of the term. It is the task of liberal education, and therefore preeminently of our colleges of liberal arts, to provide the sound and open atmosphere in which free and vigorous personalities can grow to that high level which alone is adequate for the responsibilities of classroom teaching.

TEACHER ORGANIZATIONS AND THE EDUCATIONAL ESTABLISHMENT

Education *provides* power, education *contains* power, and education *is* power. Power is provided through the exploration and communication of knowledge. Man cannot progress individually or socially without knowledge. In a social system based on man's rationality, education becomes the means to both the maintenance and alteration of that social system.

Education contains power in the way that any natural resource has latent power. In the expansion of knowledge, education provides power; in the availability of an educational system for transmitting change or stability, it possesses latent power.

Education is power in the sense that whoever controls the schools controls the development of the society. This is an extension of the exploration of knowledge and the availability of a system for transmission of cultural values. Power in education is exemplified by the schools in Nazi Germany where education was used as an instrument of national design. Another example is the developing nations of the world where education is seen as the means to industrialization and economic expansion. A third example is the civil rights movement in America where education is seen as a powerful tool for rectifying social inequities.

Power in education transfers to its agents, the teachers. Because power is an important and sought-after condition in a dynamic society, the agents of schools become significant as the schools gain in actual and latent power. The battle between groups seeking to represent teachers in the society can be viewed as a power engagement. Two conditions must be understood to view the struggle in this manner. First, power in itself is not detrimental to society. It becomes negative or positive depending upon the manner in which it is used. The second condition to understand is that the acquisition of power is not the only reason for the battle. Altruistic and ulterior motives also influence the conflict outside of basic power concerns. The sincere betterment of society and the self-preservation of jobs within the organizations both effect the interplay.

This section presents one view of the teacher-organization conflict which has become a major concern to education and society. Both the National

Education Association and the American Federation of Teachers have had gains and losses during the past few decades. Their local teacher-association affiliates have had strikes, negotiations, bargaining, sanctions, and peace at varying times and in diverse places. The limits of each organization's perimeter are becoming more difficult to ascertain. The methods and activities of the groups differ, yet overlap considerably.

Within the educational establishment, power is becoming more important to society.

The Dynamics of
Teacher Organizations

Taking a broad and comprehensive view of American education, Myron Lieberman, a professor of education, analyzes both the AFT and the NEA. He attacks the weaknesses of both in light of their organization, financing, and influence on education. The New York City election, mentioned at the end of this article, was decided in favor of the AFT affiliate, and the NEA affiliates in Oklahoma and Utah have made significant impacts on society since Lieberman's piece was originally published. The figures quoted in this article are no longer accurate, but the analysis remains a perceptive statement of the problems of both groups.

Teachers are required by some administrators to join affiliates of the NEA as a result of internal school pressure in order to be a 100 percent membership school. Other teachers are required to have their interests represented only through collective bargaining arrangements by the AFT affiliated organization. This could lead, presumably, to a union closed-shop system which appears no better than an administrator-enforced membership. Is either approach the appropriate one for teachers? Is there another alternative? The battle between NEA and AFT has had some advantages as well as some disadvantages for teachers. While the organizations split teacher power, they have become much more concerned about teacher welfare. Will a unified organization improve the status of teachers in American society?

The Influence of Teachers' Organizations
upon American Education

MYRON LIEBERMAN

One of the striking characteristics of contemporary American society is the growing influence of occupational organizations. This influence has resulted in what is aptly called "the organizational revolution." Persons who perform the same kind of work, or who are employed by the same employer or kind of employer, usually need some organizational machinery to advance their views and interests in occupational affairs. Unions, professional organizations, and trade associations, to name three kinds of occupational organizations, serve this purpose and, in doing so, play an important role in our society.

PURPOSES AND FUNCTIONS OF
TEACHER ORGANIZATIONS

Most occupational organizations were formed originally to advance the interests of members on bread-and-butter matters, such as salaries and working conditions. As time passed, they recognized that salaries and working conditions were affected by a wide range of factors which had not been considered in their early programs. This recognition led to the development of broader and broader programs having less and less direct connection with occupational affairs.

As an occupational organization becomes involved in issues having little direct bearing on occupational affairs, it usually experiences an increase in intraorganizational disagreement. As a result, its leaders usually encounter great difficulty in maintaining organizational unity and, therefore, find it expedient to discourage the membership's normal tendencies toward an expansion of organizational activities.

On the other hand, there is a tendency for occupational organizations to attain a commanding role over the lives of their members. In extreme form, this practice is reflected in regulations making membership in the organization a prerequisite to employment. Credit unions, housing projects, health and insurance services, and death benefits are some of the other

Reprinted from the *Sixtieth Yearbook of the National Society for the Study of Education,* Vol. 60, Pt. 2, 1961, pp. 182–202, by permission of the Society.

services which tend to make individuals dependent upon their occupational organization. One of the most serious problems in our economy is the way in which pension and retirement benefits become tied to organizational membership. Individuals, if they change jobs, are forced to give up substantial benefits and sever their relationship with their organizations. This situation presents a growing threat to the geographical and occupational mobility essential to our dynamic economy.

In an earlier day, Americans reacted adversely to the company house, the company store, and the company effort to control the political activities of its employees. Today, we must guard against both organizational and corporate domination over the individual.

It is erroneous to assume that occupational organizations operate solely for the self-interest of their members. They are, or can be, instruments for protecting the public interest in occupational affairs that have little to do with salaries, working conditions, or other aspects of employee welfare. The tendency to visualize occupational organizations solely as self-seeking agencies is most unfortunate. It is the inevitable result of our preoccupation with governmental structure and our corresponding failure to recognize that a person's role in occupational affairs is often more important than his traditional civic responsibilities. For example, in voting for someone to lead his occupational organization, the worker or professional person exercises a choice that can be just as important to the welfare of the country as his choice of candidates for political office.

In trying to assess the influence of educational organizations, our first problem is the sheer number of organizations. The U.S. Office of Education publishes its *Education Directory* annually. In 1960, the section devoted to education associations required 128 pages. There are local, state, regional, and international associations; organizations of teachers of particular subjects; religious organizations of teachers; honorary and fraternal associations of teachers; and many other kinds.

Our concern in this chapter will be with comprehensive organizations, that is, organizations which try to enrol and represent all teachers, regardless of subject or grade level. This type of organization bears the responsibility for representing the teaching profession as a whole. It usually has the largest membership and budget of any kind of teachers' organization. Also, most of the specialized organizations are constituent units of comprehensive organizations. For these reasons, comprehensive organizations are the key to an understanding of the influence of teachers' organizations generally in American society.

For all practical purposes, there are only two comprehensive organizations of teachers in the United States, the National Education Association (NEA) and the American Federation of Teachers (AFT), the latter being a teachers' union affiliated with the AFL-CIO. More precisely, these are the only two national organizations of the comprehensive type. In educational literature, the AFT is not regarded as a comprehensive type of organization because it excludes from active membership administrators above the rank of principal. In fact, this exclusion is probably the most important single difference between the two organizations. Nevertheless, with the qualification just noted, the NEA and the AFT can be regarded as the only comprehensive type national organizations on the American scene. Each of these two, but more especially the much larger NEA, has a large number of local and state affiliated organizations.

In order to assess the influence of these organizations, it will be helpful, first, to examine certain aspects of their internal structure and operations. We cannot assert that an organization is influential merely because it has a large membership and budget. Neither can we assert that it is without influence because its membership and budget are relatively small. On the other hand, data on factors such as these provide valuable background for assessing statements about organizational activity and influence.

THE DYNAMICS OF ORGANIZATIONAL MEMBERSHIP

On May 31, 1960, the NEA enrolled 713,994 members out of a total of 1,468,502 instructional staff in public elementary and secondary schools. Thus, as a rough approximation, about 49 percent of the teachers in the country were members of the NEA on that date. The increase in NEA membership from 1959 to 1960 was 46,874, which is 12,307 less than the 59,181 total membership of the AFT on May 31, 1960.

An even greater number of teachers are members of the state and local associations affiliated with the NEA. As of May 31, 1960, 1,317,696 teachers were members of state associations affiliated with the NEA (this figure does not include New York City, where only 749 out of 45,000 professional personnel were NEA members as of May 31, 1960).

No comprehensive statistics on the number of teachers who belong to local associations are available. On the average, city and county associations affiliated with the NEA enrol about 81 percent of their potential membership. However, it is difficult to say whether 80 percent of all teachers are members of local associations affiliated with the NEA. In some communities, there is no local association in existence. While only the smaller communities do not ordinarily have a local association, a smaller percentage of teachers join in the larger cities than in small and medium-sized ones. However, it is likely that more teachers are members of local associations affiliated with the NEA than are members of the NEA itself.

In the AFT, membership in the local federation automatically involves membership in the national federation as well. Where there are state federations, affiliation with them is through the local, not through individual application for membership (except for members at large, i.e, members of the AFT who are not part of any local, usually because there is no local in their community). In effect, AFT policies require the overwhelming majority of its members to have simultaneous membership in local, state, and national federations.

Almost one-third of the total AFT membership is enrolled in its six largest locals, located in Chicago, New York, Detroit, Los Angeles, Cleveland, and Minneapolis.[1] The Chicago local, with over 7,500 members is probably the strongest local organization of teachers in the United States. On the other hand, the AFT has never been able to organize teachers on a broad scale in the South, in rural areas, or in suburban communities, although its prospects in the latter are improving in the North.

In some fields, individuals seeking employment must join a particular occupational organization to be eligible for employment. This was especially true in the building trades and in certain other craft unions. It was also true in education in communities where teachers were forced to join the NEA and its state and local affiliates as a condition of employment. Ironically enough, the "closed shop" still persists, but it is not recognized as such because it prevails in "professional" occupations, such as law and medicine. Thus, in over half the states, individuals must join the state bar association in order to practice law. Many hospitals will not admit to practice physicians who are not members of the American Medical Association. Membership in the AMA is, therefore, compulsory as a practical matter, since a physician who cannot treat his patients in a hospital faces a formidable barrier to successful practice.

The pressures on teachers to join comprehensive organizations vary a great deal from community to community. It is noteworthy that NEA locals which permit unrestricted administrator membership enrol a higher percentage of potential members than associations restricted to classroom teachers. This suggests that administrator pressure is still a factor in maintaining membership in the NEA and its affiliates. Also, administrator opposition must be accounted one of the major obstacles to any sizable increase in AFT membership. Of course, these comments should not be interpreted to mean that teachers join or refuse to join these organizations solely as a result of pressure. Undoubtedly, conventional reasons, such as the desire to secure better salaries and working conditions, play an important role in most cases.

THE DYNAMICS OF ORGANIZATIONAL FINANCE

As is the case in most unions and professional associations, dues constitute the major source of income for teachers' organizations. This is true for all levels of organization. Of the $6,725,146.00 income in the NEA's General Fund (its operating budget) for the year ending May 31, 1959,

[1] The AFT does not publish membership figures for individual locals, but the estimate is undoubtedly a reliable one.

$6,006,143.00 or 89 percent was from membership dues. Most of the assets of the Association, such as its land and buildings in Washington, has come from the sale of life memberships in the Association. Dues probably constitute an even higher percentage of the income in state and local associations affiliated with the NEA and at all organizational levels in the AFT.

The heavy dependence upon dues unquestionably helps to explain the cautiousness of organizational leadership in education. As long as there is little job control by teachers' organizations, organizational leaders are extremely hesitant to recommend policies which might offend a sizable segment of the membership. This attitude is publicly defended as "democratic," but its enduring basis is organizational security. For example, the fear of losing southern members has played an important role in the NEA's passive position toward the problems of school integration. It may be, however, that the Association loses as much in the North as it gains in the South from its timidity on integration. In 1959–60, the NEA enrolled only 749 out of 45,000 professional employees in New York City, only 798 out of 17,788 in Chicago, and only 97 out of 3,278 in Boston, to cite a few extreme cases. Dependence upon dues also helps to explain the uncritical tone of organizational publications and their "look the other way" attitude toward questionable methods of recruitment. However, it does not appear that educational organizations are worse in these respects than most other occupational organizations.

Dues in teachers' organizations are usually much less than dues in most unions and professional associations. NEA dues are $10.00. Dues in its state and local affiliates vary a great deal. A recent study of local associations showed that, in 1957–58, the median annual dues in local associations was between $3.00 and $4.00; in almost half the local associations, average annual dues were $3.00 or less. Thirty of the NEA's affiliated state and territorial associations have annual dues of $10.00 or less, and this number does not include fourteen other state associations which have a sliding scale which starts at less than $10.00. Also, only four such associations had annual dues of at least $20.00, although an additional eleven had sliding scales which required some of their members to pay $20.00 or more in state dues. It is likely, however, that only a small minority of members in these eleven associations paid this much in state dues.

AFT dues also vary, but, on the average, AFT members pay less in dues than NEA members. This is true despite the fact that AFT members pay a small per capita dues to the AFL-CIO and, in many cases, to state and local central labor bodies. The dues payable to the national office of the AFT are 60 cents per month per member. National dues for members at large (i.e., not affiliated with any local) are $12.00 annually. State federations of the AFT existed in only sixteen states in 1959. While these states included most of the membership, the per capita payment for state federations is invariably lower than the dues for the corresponding state association affiliated with the NEA. The only exception appears to be Arizona, where the Arizona Federation of Teachers Unions receives five dollars per month per member and where unified dues in the local and state associations, plus NEA dues, amount to $24.00.[2]

On the whole, there is no doubt that the dues level in education can and should be raised substantially. The NEA raised its dues from $5.00 to $10.00 in 1957 and suffered a decline of 87,122 members the following year. However, by 1960 it had more than regained this loss in membership, and its financial position was much stronger.

Dependence upon dues has always been a difficult problem for occupational organizations. It is especially so in education because of the high rate of turnover. Most educational organizations must spend considerable effort just to enrol members and collect dues. In trying to solve this problem, the NEA and the AFT reveal a typical terminological difference. The NEA presses for "payroll deductions," whereas the AFT pushes hard for the "checkoff." Of course, since so many top-level administrators are in the NEA and prefer their teachers to join it, the NEA and its affiliates are more likely to secure administrative approval for the practice by whatever name is given to it.

For operating expenses, the NEA spends about $7,000,000.00 annually, and the AFT about $400,000.00. As low as the AFT budget is, it is still considerably larger than the operating budget of the American Association of University Professors. The AAUP spent only $272,914.41 out of an income of $321,344.13 in 1959; its 1960 budget called for expenditures of $329,750.00. In view of the fact that there are about 200,000 persons professionally engaged in higher education, of whom about 40,000 are members of the AAUP, it appears that professors in the United States are making a shockingly low investment in organizational efforts to improve their situation.

Almost one-sixth of the NEA's operating budget is devoted to the *NEA Journal,* which has the largest circulation of any educational or professional journal in the United States. It should be noted that, in addition to its operating expenditures of nearly $7,000,000.00, the NEA has almost $8,000,000.00 in its permanent fund. Most of this fund represents land and buildings owned by the Association in Washington. Although the Association is in a comparatively healthy state financially, its assets are still considerably less than those of leading unions. The wealthiest union, probably the United Mine Workers, had over $110,000,000.00 in assets in 1960, not counting its welfare and retirement funds estimated to be in excess of $100,000,000.00. The Teamsters Union, the United Automobile Workers, and other unions, some of which have fewer members and have been in existence a shorter time than the NEA, have considerably more assets. On the other hand, the NEA's annual operating budget is larger than that of any professional association, including the redoubtable American Medi-

[2] There is no summary of local and state dues in the AFT. Statements concerning them are based upon discussions with AFT members.

cal Association. This point is of more than academic interest, since the funds available to an organization are one important indication of the weight it can bring to bear in certain situations.

Recent summary data on the financial status of the state education associations are not available. Unquestionably, they are in much sounder financial condition than local associations. The recent study of its affiliated local associations during 1958–59 by the NEA's Research Division brought out the following facts about them:

1. Eighty-six per cent lacked any office space of their own.
2. Over 90 percent had no paid staff; the paid staff in the others was usually on a part-time basis.
3. About half reported expenditures between $100.00 and $500.00; only 12 per cent spent more than $1,200.00 during the year.

Analogous data concerning state and local federations of the AFT are not available. The AFT is very weak at the state level, even in the northern industrial states where the Federation has its greatest strength. At the local level, the AFT has always been characterized by a large number of small, weak federations. These federations are often established on an emergency basis and then decline as the founders move away or as the school administration attacks the organization. In 1960, less than one-third of the 1,355 local federations chartered by the AFT since 1916 were still in existence.

THE DYNAMICS OF ORGANIZATIONAL LEADERSHIP

At the local level, there are relatively few full-time paid positions of organizational leadership in education. The 1959–60 *NEA Handbook* lists only 26 local associations which employed or planned to employ an executive secretary by September, 1959. This is an extremely low number for an organization of over 700,000 members. It is likely that most of these executive secretaries were teachers who had been active in the local association. Of the 23 persons actually employed when the 1960–61 *Handbook* was published, 4 were women and 19 were men.

At the state level, the pattern in the state associations affiliated with the NEA is for the chief permanent officer to be the executive secretary, with the president, vice-president, and treasurer elected annually, either directly or indirectly, by delegates at state conventions. The larger the association, the more indirect are the controls exercised by the membership. This tendency is especially noticeable in the case of the executive secretary of the NEA. That officer, the chief spokesman for over 700,000 members, is chosen by the NEA's Board of Trustees, which also sets his salary. The board of trustees consists of four elected members and the president of the NEA, *ex officio*. Of the elected members, one is elected annually for a four-year term by the NEA's board of directors. The latter organization consists of two groups. One group, known as the state directors, is chosen by the state and territorial associations affiliated with the NEA. Each state or territorial association is entitled to one state director and to an additional director for each 20,000 active and life members. The other directors consist of the NEA's president, vice-president, immediate past-president, treasurer, chairman of the board of trustees, members of the executive committee of the board of directors (four are elected at large by the NEA's representative assembly), and, as ex-officio members of the board, all former presidents of the NEA who were elected prior to July 1, 1937.

This cumbersome and complex procedure for selecting the chief executive officer stands in marked contrast to practice in AFL-CIO international unions, which usually elect their chief permanent officers at biennial conventions. Since the delegates to the conventions who elect the permanent officers are chosen directly by the membership, the executive officers of these unions are only one echelon removed from direct election by the membership. Interestingly enough, the AFT made its president the chief executive officer in 1952, dropping the position of executive secretary. The president of the AFT is chosen directly by the delegates to the annual convention for a two-year term, with his salary being fixed by an executive council composed of sixteen vice-presidents elected at large by delegates to the annual convention.

Organizational salaries are low with a few exceptions. The NEA does not disclose staff salaries, but its salary scale is competitive with the better universities, though not the very top-rank ones such as Harvard or Yale. The executive secretary of the California Teachers Association receives $30,000.00 a year, probably the highest salary in any organization of public school personnel in the country. In 1958, fourteen of the state executive secretaries received less than $10,000.00 a year. Two of these were the executive secretaries of state-wide associations of Negro teachers in states still maintaining both white and Negro associations.

The top salary in the AFT is paid to the president of its Chicago local, who received $18,000.00 a year in 1960. The national president of the AFT received $14,500.00 in 1959–60. Salaries for field representatives and executive secretaries of state federations are usually under $10,000.00. The lack of funds is undoubtedly a factor in keeping AFT salaries low, but so is the widespread view that the salaries of organizational personnel should not be substantially superior to those of teachers. Whatever the cause, low organizational salaries are a severe handicap in building strong teachers' organizations. Teachers who could be strong organization leaders find it impossible to advance rapidly as teachers, hence they often go into school administration where their chances of getting higher salaries are much better. This process is very similar to that which prevails in industry, where management's ability to outbid employee organizations for able personnel constantly weakens the effectiveness of the employee organizations.

THE EFFECTIVENESS OF TEACHERS' ORGANIZATIONS

Evaluation of the influence of occupational organizations is a difficult task. There is first the factual question: What has the organization done? With teachers' organizations, this is not an easy question to answer because they have not been studied intensively. Furthermore, knowing what they have done is one thing; knowing the impact or influence of what they have done is something else again. If salaries have gone up, it may be practically impossible to disentangle the organizational influence from other factors.

Most of the literature on teachers' organizations is organization-sponsored. This literature is propagandistic and tends to overinflate the activities and influence of the organizations. It also tends to put organizational staff in the best possible light. For example, in 1960 NEA enrolled 49 percent of the instructional staff in public elementary and secondary schools. Should its leaders be complimented on this new high, or should they be criticized because less than half the teachers are enrolled in the association?

There is the further difficulty of assessing the influence of each level of organization. Generally speaking, the broad objectives of local, state, and national organizations are the same. Differences lie more in the way each level of organization contributes to these objectives rather than in the objectives themselves. Thus, all three levels devote considerable effort to improving the economic status of teachers. The national organization works on Congress and subsidizes studies and reports of national interest on this subject. The state associations work with the state legislatures, mainly in efforts to secure state-wide minimum-salary legislation, changes in the state tax structure, and state-wide welfare benefits. Local associations are responsible for negotiations with local school boards intended to secure benefits superior to the state minimums.

The point is that although the over-all results are usually an index to the effectiveness of a local or a state organization, and there are wide differences between locals or state associations, we cannot always delineate the activities and influence of each level of organization in a clear-cut way. A state organization lobbying in the state legislature may rely upon the pressure its locals can bring to bear upon key legislators. A local association will frequently use materials or consultants from both its state and national organizations, hence its success or failure is partly dependent upon the effectiveness of its parent bodies.

With these precautions in mind, let us turn to an analysis of organizational activities and influence. We shall start with the NEA. Certainly, the statistical dimensions of the Association are impressive. It has over 750 employees among its 30 departments, 13 headquarters divisions, and 26 commissions and committees, covering virtually every aspect of education.

In 1958–59, its division of accounts handled receipts in excess of $13,000,-000.00 for all units of the Association. It processed over 116,000 requests for publications alone. The business service division, which handles mailings, sends out 100 bags of mail a day. The inventory of NEA publications lists over 6,000 titles. Over 20,000,000 copies of materials are reproduced every year. Statistics such as these convey only a limited sense of the tremendous scope and volume of NEA activity.

Nevertheless, it is necessary to go behind these organizational statistics, impressive as they may be, to ask: What difference does it all make? Obviously, any answer to this question here will have to be in broad strokes which assume many exceptions and qualifications.

Let us first turn to various focal points of organizational activity and try to assess the impact of the NEA upon them. For several years, the relative economic position of teachers has hovered slightly above the average for all employed persons. This represents an improvement over the war and immediate postwar years but no advance, and possibly a decline when all factors are considered, in the long-range (fifty-year) economic position of teachers.

Professional ethics is another area wherein teachers' organizations have had only a superficial influence. Teachers are not significantly affected by the professional codes which have been adopted by the NEA and its affiliated state associations. The codes themselves are poorly drafted and include many dubious or unprofessional provisions. Indeed, it could hardly be contended that teachers as a group even take seriously the concept of an autonomous teaching profession which assumes responsibility for the competence and integrity of its services.

Control over entry is one of the key objectives of all major unions and professional associations. Teachers as an organized group exercise very little control over certification. In fact, in some states, teachers are excluded by law from the state boards which license teachers, and the trend in this direction seems to be as strong as any toward teacher control of certification.

The impact of comprehensive organizations upon teacher education likewise appears to be minimal. The state associations have been active in promoting legislation calling for minimum standards of preparation, and some type of minimum standard for teaching certificates prevails in every state. We can readily concede that in many states the standards are higher than they would have been without the activities of the state associations. Nevertheless, the level of teacher education and certification is still very low. As evidence for this, we can point to the absence of qualitative standards for a teaching certificate and the fact that state examinations have all but disappeared in education, whereas their use has been expanded in many other fields. We can point also to the fact that, in most states, only public school teachers are required to have a legal certificate, to the tremendous diversity in certification requirements without any research basis, and to the large number of substandard institutions of higher education which are permitted to train teachers.

The NEA, through its National Commission on Teacher Education and Professional Standards, has been instrumental in establishing the National Council for the Accreditation of Teacher Education (NCATE). However, the NCATE does not as yet have the power to protect the public and the profession from substandard programs of teacher education. A few states now require applicants for a teaching certificate to have received their training in an NCATE-approved institution, and there is some apprehension among smaller institutions not yet approved that this movement will grow at their expense. The NCATE is also becoming involved in approving institutions for the training of school administrators, and its activities in this field are likely to force some of the weaker institutions to improve or drop their programs in this area. Nevertheless, this writer does not know of any movement or circumstance indicating that either the NEA or the NCATE has had a major impact on teacher education. As for the AFT, it has yet to recognize teacher education as a major area of concern within the purview of the federation.

Leaving aside the conventional criteria of professional progress, we come to the matter of organizational impact upon public opinion. It may be suggested that teachers' organizations are not successful in setting forth and achieving reasonable professional goals, but how successful are they in responding to the proposals of others? Do teachers' organizations have any veto power, as distinguished from the power to initiate educational policies? This is a particularly important aspect of educational influence in an era of educational challenge and change.

On routine employment matters, it is safe to assert that teachers' organizations ordinarily have little influence in shaping employer policies or in preventing unwarranted interference in educational matters by other groups. From a strictly employment point of view, most teachers' organizations are ordinarily too weak to resist successfully even the most flagrant abuses on the part of school authorities. As we have seen, most local organizations lack the resources to put up any kind of resistance along these lines. The futility of many local associations at present is clear from the fact that during 1958–59 almost half sent no communication to school authorities and almost 70 percent received no communication from them. When teachers' organizations become involved in supporting an individual teacher, it is usually on a post-mortem basis. Comprehensive organizations, especially at the state level, occasionally investigate a situation and issue a report condemning somebody, but they are not routinely involved in the defense of teachers being treated unfairly. Reading the reports of the NEA's National Commission for the Defense of Democracy through Education, nothing is so impressive as its failure to constitute a force-in-being to prevent unfair treatment of teacher personnel. Its main function seems to be the issuance of statements which come too late to help the victims. In this respect, both the NEA and the AFT resemble the AAUP, which has persistently avoided the use of sanctions which can be applied immediately and effectively in grievance situations.

The weaknesses of teachers' organizations extend also to their inability to prevent the miseducational policies and programs advocated by other pressure groups. The same organizational weaknesses that leave teachers helpless in matters of employment leave them equally helpless to defend the public interest, as they see it, in matters pertaining to curriculum, instructional materials, teaching methods, and academic policy-making.

The evidence supporting this conclusion is necessarily diffuse, but some concrete instances can be cited. Curriculum prescriptions by state legislatures have been increasing for years despite widespread agreement by educators as to their undesirability. More so than any other groups, teachers have been forced to accept unprofessional and humiliating loyalty oaths. Studies of textbook content and instruction, especially in the social studies, reveal a widespread neglect of issues dealing with race, religion, sex, economic policy, and other important controversial areas. It is conjectural as to how much of this failure is due to teacher failure to grasp the importance of certain issues and how much is due to restrictions on their freedom to teach as they see fit, but unquestionably the second reason plays an important role in many communities.

All this is not to say that teachers never resist community pressures. They do, but seldom as an organized group. Teacher resistance has made enormously difficult the supervision of large numbers of teachers. Board policy may be one thing, but, when teachers close classroom doors, practice may be another. Teachers may be ordered to teach an extra class without more salary, but it is practically impossible to prevent them from sloughing off on the job if they choose to do so. As in every bureaucracy, policy gets changed and diluted as it goes down the line. In so far as teaching methods are concerned, it is likely that the public furor over them never had any great classroom impact, one way or the other.

The current concern over widespread criticism of public education stems largely from the peculiar employment situation confronting school superintendents. They are usually employed on short-term contracts, rarely over five years in duration and usually two or more years less than this. Since their jobs are so dependent upon public opinion, they magnify the importance of every criticism. In no other way, it seems to me, can one explain the prominence given in educational literature to certain critics, such as those associated with the Council for Basic Education. This organization has three full-time persons, lacks any well-defined membership base or source of permanent financial support. Its regular publication consists of a newsletter which only scratches the surface of the inanities to be found everywhere in American education, and it does not even do this for the inanities of its own members. Nevertheless, educational literature includes repeated references to this organization, as if it were a major pressure group.

These comments have nothing to do with the validity, or the degree of validity, of CBE criticisms. I merely point out that the occupational situation confronting school superintendents (and professors of education, although for different reasons) leads them to exaggerate the political strength of their critics. The average school administrator comes to be much more sensitive to the weight of criticism than to its validity. A valid criticism without popular support will not bother him anywhere near as much as a completely invalid one that does have popular support. The latter poses a threat to his occupational security whereas the former does not.

In this manner, we have come to look upon the school administrator as one who gives the people what they want, educationally speaking. Thus, administration is oriented away from objective measures of educational excellence and toward the techniques of opinion-polling. For every superintendent who takes the initiative in integrating his schools, a hundred ask the board whether or not they want their schools desegregated. And this is true, not just for the deep South where anything but adherence to segregation would be occupational suicide, but to border areas and even in northern states where there is some room for educational leadership on this issue.

The failure of educational organizations to influence public policy or action is most dramatically illustrated by their irrelevance to the course of racial integration in public education. For many years, equality of educational opportunity has been a major rallying cry among teachers' organizations, especially in their efforts to secure federal aid to education. The inequalities due to racial discrimination have been more flagrant and almost as pervasive, yet it cannot be said that educational organizations have been an important factor in the fight to eliminate racially segregated schools. It was the NAACP, not the professional organizations of teachers, which successfully attacked differential salary schedules for white and Negro teachers, the practice of forcing Negroes to go out of the state for certain kinds of professional training, and the obviously unequal facilities for Negro students in the South. Since the Supreme Court decisions in 1954, declaring racial segregation in public education unconstitutional, educational organizations have failed to provide leadership for gaining acceptance of the decision and for implementing the necessary reorganization of teacher-pupil assignments. The NEA did not even endorse the decision in its platform from 1955 to 1959. In the latter year, it got around to appointing a committee to study the problems of integration. The committee report in 1960 included no recommendations for action.

The AFT record concerning integration is much better. It provided legal support for Negro plaintiffs in the suits which overturned segregation in public schools, and it has all but eliminated locals based on race. On the other hand, the AFT has always been very weak in the South, so its more aggressive stand for racial equality does not expose it to any major risk of defection. Indeed, the surprising thing is that the AFT has been so ineffective in using its liberal stand concerning integration to recruit AFT membership in the large urban areas in the North.

The failure of teachers' organizations to have any substantial impact upon public opinion is particularly striking in view of their preoccupation with the public's concern for continued improvement in educational services. Teachers' organizations produce an enormous amount of materials designed to influence public opinion: pamphlets, brochures, flyers, movies, radio and television programs, news releases—all representing school practices designed to induce favorable public reaction to the teachers' educational objectives. In addition, an emphasis upon working with lay groups pervades every level of education. The NEA cosponsors American Education Week. It has joint committees with the American Legion, the American Medical Association, and other groups. The AFT has always asserted that its affiliation with labor enables it to bring the power of organized labor to bear upon its educational objectives. At the local level, citizens' committees on education are endless. Business-education or business-industry-education days under the cosponsorship of the local chamber of commerce and the school system are common. Books and magazine articles devoted to educationist positions are too numerous to be listed.

Despite all these activities, we are left with the conclusion that teachers' organizations are unable to carry out modest programs of educational reform and typically lack even as much power on educational matters as other leading pressure groups. Why is this the case?

In answering this question, it is not enough to point to the low dues level, lack of strong leadership, inadequate resources, or other characteristics of educational organizations. These things are immediate causes of organizational weakness, but they are results as well as causes. What lies behind them?

The following list undoubtedly includes the major reasons:

1. The fact that 90 percent of the local and all of the state associations affiliated with the NEA, and the NEA itself, permit unrestricted administrator membership. As a result, most comprehensive teachers' organizations are employer dominated and oriented away from vigorous action to advance their objectives.
2. A long tradition among teachers of using only nonpolitical means to achieve their goals. This tradition has two major roots. One is the desire of school boards, as employers, to keep their employees weak. The other factor is the broader fear of the American people of intensive political activity by public employees. The feeling that teachers should be objective in their teaching has further contributed to the unrealistic and undesirable belief that they should be nonpolitical outside the classroom.

3. The fact that teaching is predominantly a female occupation, and that pre-dominantly female occupational organizations are usually much less aggressive than predominantly male ones.
4. A false concept of professionalism which has led teachers to ignore the fact that professionalism often imposes an obligation to resist rather than to blindly follow public opinion.
5. In so far as they are active in politics, teachers' organizations have never devel-oped a realistic strategy for political action. They have overstressed the im-portance of action at the level of the local school board, where organizations are weakest, and have relied too much on diffuse appeals to public opinion instead of focusing political pressure on key individuals in government.

It is not possible here to go into these factors in detail. However, I should like to tie some of them together by a reference to the struggle for federal aid for education. Teachers' organizations have supported large-scale federal aid to education for several decades. During the Eightieth Congress, a bipartisan bill calling for $300,000,000.00 annually passed the Senate twice. The bill was cosponsored by Senator Taft, the acknowledged leader of the conservatives in the Senate. Nevertheless, the bill was de-feated in House Committee by a 13–12 vote, with the Chairman of the House Committee on Education and Welfare, John Lesinski of Michigan, casting the decisive negative vote.

In an interesting analysis of this incident, one apparently well-informed observer, D. W. Cox, asserted that the NEA made the following mistakes:

1. It overestimated the influence of the Senate upon the House.
2. It underestimated the power of the House on appropriation bills and delayed too long in bringing pressure to bear on it.
3. It failed to involve the state education associations which might have swung key votes.
4. It ignored the AFT, which sponsored its own bill and, thereby, made it easier for politicians to avoid supporting any bill at all.
5. It failed to utilize the mass media effectively to secure widespread support for the bill.
6. It did not help Congress solve the problem of deciding how much federal aid, if any, should go to parochial schools.
7. It failed to dent the solid front of business opposition to federal aid to education.[3]

Cox also charged that the NEA repeated these mistakes in 1955, when it had strong support in the Senate but again failed to persuade the House Committee to hold hearings in time for House action. He concluded that, "What is needed are men with a fresh and convincing slant on the coun-try's school needs and who are versed in the intricacies of political maneu-vering. The present crop, unimaginative and naïve, is doing as much as any group in the country to retard the progress of our public schools."

[3] D. W. Cox, "The Lobby That Failed," *Nation*, February 18, 1956, pp. 139–40.

Without necessarily concurring in Cox's specific postmortems concerning federal-aid bills, this author would like to concur in this conclusion.

Despite this rather gloomy analysis of the organizational situation in education, this writer is hopeful about the future. The emergence of collective bargaining in public education is likely to be a major step toward the decline of employer-dominated teachers' organizations. This development is close at hand in at least some states and communities; in fact, the New York City Board of Education has just announced an election to choose a bargaining agent for that city's 40,000 teachers. The election will probably be held early in 1961 [vote was for AFT affiliate]. A decisive victory in it for a teachers' organization free of administrator domination could launch the organizational revolution in education, the most important single educational need of our time.

Bibliographic Essay

We have endeavored to present enlightened, provocative readings to assist in understanding the ideas, opinions, and speculations of many who have considered the problems of school and society. It is our intent to stimulate consideration of the relation of culture to education by providing selections of sufficient length to convey complete ideas, by including topics treated by writers of prominence and skill, by directing your attention to the major concerns expressed in each presentation, and by offering additional sources for study. In fulfilling this latter interest, we recognize that the value of a comprehensive bibliography lies in its usefulness. Our personal additions to your potential reading list are included with comments in this section.

Each person who comes upon an enlightening book or article that provides him with a thoughtful and provoking analysis of some dimension of life, wishes that others might enjoy the same pleasures. We have that problem in deciding which of the many excellent works we should suggest as supplementary reading. The following are merely samples of the widely available and valuable materials on school and society.

PART 1

In looking at the history of education, there are several noteworthy books. An early, but soundly researched treatment, is Elwood Cubberley's *Public Education in the United States*. Other educational histories which are very useful in analyzing the changes in education over many years include R. Freeman Butts' *A Cultural History of Western Education*, and Robert Ulich's *History of Educational Thought*. A short, but most informative paperback which traces humanism in schools is Robert Holmes Beck's *A Social History of Education*. The problem of conflicting values is covered in many fields. Two opposing views on relativism and absolutism are well portrayed in C. S. Lewis' *The Abolition of Man*, and Charles Frankel's *The Case for Modern Man*. Of particular importance on the question of values are the Max Weber essays "Politics as a Vocation" and "Science as a Vocation," as found in *From Max Weber*, edited by H. C. Gerth and C. Wright Mills. Values in the social sciences are the subjects of Leo Strauss' *What Is Political Philosophy?;* Howard Becker's *Through Values to Social Interpretation;* and W. H. Werkmeister's "Social Science and the Problem of Value," in *Scientism and Values*.

The area of culture and national character is portrayed in a provocative manner in Margaret Mead's *Coming of Age in Samoa* and Mead and Wolfenstein's *Childhood in Contemporary Cultures*. Ruth Benedict's *Patterns of Culture* will assist in defining cultural systems, as will Clyde Kluckhohn's *Mirror for Man*. National character is denied and defended in a fascinating set of readings collected by Michael McGiffert in *The Character of Americans*. In *The Italians*, Luigi Barzini presents a broad and unusually objective view of national attributes. Margaret Mead's *And Keep Your Powder Dry: An Anthropologist Looks at America* is a stimulating analysis, as are D. W. Brogan's *The American Character* and Geoffrey Gorer's *The American People*. Further reading in this area can be pursued through John Kouwenhoven's work *Made in America*, or Erik Erickson's *Childhood and Society*. Dwight MacDonald's bright and critical writing reveals his subtle perception of the problems of American character. See especially his essay "America, America" as it appeared in *Dissent* magazine. A very appropriate work of fiction to illustrate American culture is Thomas Wolfe's *You Can't Go Home Again*. Conflicts in American culture are presented in Robert Lynd's classic, *Knowledge for What?*. Historians' views of American life include Henry Steele Commager's *America in Perspective*, Oscar Handlin's *Race & Nationality in American Life*, and Richard Hofstadter's *Anti-Intellectualism in American Life*. Another view is offered in Howard Mumford Jones' *O Strange New World: American Culture, The Formative Years*.

PART 2

Social class, poverty, and deprivation are areas of continuing social concern as illustrated in works such as August B. Hollingshead's *Elmtown's Youth*, Robert and Helen Lynd's *Middletown* and *Middletown in Transition*, Charles Walker's *American City*, and Celia Stendler's *Children of Brasstown*. Problems of the poor in an affluent society are expressed in Michael Harrington's *The Other America: Poverty in the United States*. R. H. Tawney's earlier work, *Equality*, shows significant problems of the poor, as does Ben Bagdikian's very recent book, *In the Midst of Plenty*. Relating poverty to education is the widely read *Slums and Suburbs* by James B. Conant. Leon Keyserling gives chilling data on the problem in *Poverty and Deprivation in the United States*. The most touching stories of poverty in depression times are those of James Agee in *Let Us Now Praise Famous Men*.

A very fine set of readings on alienation is *Man Alone: Alienation in Modern Society* edited by Eric and Mary Josephson. Another popular book on this subject is David Riesman's *The Lonely Crowd*. More theoretic considerations of alienation are contained in Emile Durkheim's *The Division of Labor in Society* and *Le Suicide, Etude de Sociologie*, Erich Fromm's *The Sane Society*, Karl Marx's *Economic and Philosophic Manuscripts of 1844*, Marx and Engels' *The German Ideology*, and Robert K. Merton's *Social Theory and Social Structure*. Solomon Lichter *et al.* treat a recurring problem in *The Drop-Outs*. Allison Davis' *Social Class Influences Upon Learning*, Patricia Sexton's *Education and Income: Inequalities of Opportunity in Our Public Schools*, and Frank Reissman's *The Culturally Deprived Child* are good background readings for an understanding of the relation of social class to education and deprivation.

PART 3

Economics as a national issue can be studied in terms of arguments over various economic theories. John Galbraith's influential *The Affluent Society* argues that economic theory based on scarcity is out-of-date. Galbraith's earlier book *American Capitalism* is a major contribution to capitalistic theory. Henry Hazlitt's *Economics in One Lesson* opposes the Galbraith position and restates the Adam Smith theories found in *The Wealth of Nations*. A difficult, but powerful, study of capitalism which has become a classic book is Thorsten Veblen's *Theory of Business Enterprise*. Shorter selections of Veblen are available in *The Portable Veblen*, edited by Max Lerner, and in George Soule's *Ideas of the Great Economists*, which outlines several basic economic ideas. Robert Heilbroner's *The Worldly Philosophers* should not be overlooked as an excellent treatment of economic philosophers and their ideas.

The problems of international conflict are well documented historically in the two volume work by Denna Fleming *The Cold War and Its Origins* which is critical of all sides. Harold Laski's *Reflections on the Revolution of Our Times* is a provocative book suggesting the conflicts that would occur as the result of the breakup of capitalism. A worthwhile analysis of behaviors and foreign affairs is Otto Klineberg's *The Human Dimension in International Relations*. Herman Kahn's writing, especially *Thinking About the Unthinkable*, a frighteningly clear discussion of arms and the sequence of escalation. Temple Wanamaker's concise paperback *American Foreign Policy Today* presents Department of State positions. *In Place of Folly* by Norman Cousins and *The Armed Society* by Tristam Coffin are very readable and most provocative in dealing with the militarism of American Society. A valuable set of papers by insightful scholars in several behavioral science fields is *International Conflict and Behavioral Science* edited by Roger Fisher.

Literature dealing with social issues covers many areas including a concern for the freedom of teachers to deal with controversy. A collection of opinions on this topic is in John S. Brubacher's *Eclectic Philosophy of Education, A Book of Readings*. Although dated, the Howard K. Beale book *Are American Teachers Free?* remains one of the most provocative treatments of the subject. A section on social issues not treated in schools appears in Maurice Hunt and Lawrence Metcalf's *Teaching High School Social Studies*. Relevant readings on the problems of contrasting political philosophies appear in Daniel Bell's *The American Right* and the major problem of an obsessive fear of conspiracy is portrayed in Richard Hofstadter's *The Paranoid Style in American Politics*. The contemporary liberal-conservative distinction can be clarified by a reading of Guido De Ruggiero's *History of European Liberalism*. A shorter statement with fascinating corollary documents is J. Salwyn Shapiro's *Liberalism: Its History and Meaning*.

Some very useful works on religion include George Brantl's edited two volumes of essays titled *The Religious Experience*. The classic application of pragmatism to religion is John Dewey's *A Common Faith*. The church-state problem is well expressed in Anson P. Stokes' *Church and State in the United States*. R. Freeman Butts' *The American Tradition in Religion and Education* is an analysis of the relation of religion to the schools. Alternative positions on education and religion are found in *American Education and Religion*, edited by Ernest Johnson. One of the most clearly defined analyses of this problem is *Religion and the Schools,* published by the Fund for the Republic. A recent statement by the American Association of School Administrators entitled *Religion in the Public Schools* attempts to clarify the issue in light of Supreme Court decisions and federal aid questions. Among the best books on the subject is Leo Pfeffer's *Church, State, and Freedom.*

Mass Culture, edited by Bernard Rosenberg and David Manning White, is a powerful and readable collection of readings in this area of strongly divergent opinions. C. Wright Mills' *The Power Elite,* and Ortega y Gasset's *Revolt of the Masses* are classic works which relate to this issue. A recent consideration of mass culture and education is *Schools in an Age of Mass Culture* by Rudy Willis.

Conflicting views on education are to be found in readings in Henry Ehlers and Gordon Lee's *Crucial Issues in Education,* Bernard Johnson's *Issues in Education: An Anthology of Controversy,* and Scott, Hill, and Burns' *The Great Debate: Our Schools in Crisis.* The basic philosophies of education are treated in *Selected Readings in the Philosophy of Education,* edited by Joe Park. John Brubacher in *Modern Philosophies of Education* clearly analyzes several basic theories about schools. One of the most worthwhile collections of writing on the schools is Robert Ulich's *3000 Years of Educational Wisdom.* In the same way, a collection of documents showing various views on schools and teachers from Plato forward with valuable commentary is *Prologue to Teaching* edited by Marjorie Smiley and John Diekhoff.

Critics of progressive education have written extensively in recent times. Of great influence in society and educational thought are Mortimer Smith's *And Madly Teach,* Albert Lynd's *Quackery in the Public Schools,* Arthur Bestor's *The Educational Wastelands* and *The Restoration of Learning,* Bernard Bell's *Crisis in Education,* and Hyman Rickover's several books including *Education and Freedom.* A reading of John Dewey is essential to an understanding of the theory underlying progressive education. *Experience and Education* is foremost in explaining traditional versus progressive education and is a reaction to criticisms of the practice of progressivism. *Democracy and Education, School and Society,* and *The Child and the Curriculum* are also worthwhile Dewey readings on this topic.

More recent theories on education can be found in George Kneller's *Existentialism and Education,* Israel Sheffler's *Philosophy and Education,* and Smith and Ennis' *Language and Concepts in Education.* Other positions include Robert Hutchins' *The Conflict in Education in a Democratic Society,* Harry Broudy's *Building a Philosophy of Education,* Ernest Bayles' *Democratic Educational Theory,* and William H. Kilpatrick's *Philosophy of Education.*

PART 4

In recent years numerous books have been written about urban and suburban problems. A few of these are presented here as further reading for the interested student.

For articles on the sociology of the city, there is the *Reader in Urban Sociology* by Paul K. Hatt and Albert J. Reiss Jr. Lewis Mumford's *The City in History* gives a historic developmental picture of the city and contains a very good bibliography. Comparative readings on cities are presented in the volume *Great*

Cities of the World edited by William A. Robson, and Jean Gottman's *Megalopolis*, which examines several cities in the Northeastern United States. Louis Wirth, the distinguished sociologist, has a volume titled *On Cities and Social Life*, Lloyd Rodwin edited *The Future Metropolis*, and Thorsten Sellin has a collection of readings on *Metropolis in Ferment*. The waste of manpower and resources in the U.S. is discussed in Stuart Chase's *The Tragedy of Waste*, and Wall Street is viewed in *Madison Avenue, U.S.A.*, by M. Mayer.

Joseph A. Kahl's book *The American Class Structure* is probably the clearest and most readable one available in this area. Provocative, powerful writing characterizes *The Power Elite* and *White Collar* by C. Wright Mills; see also the writings of Daniel Bell and Irving Howe. An excellent collection of articles covering many aspects of urban social structure is *Class, Status and Power* by R. Bendix and S. M. Lipset. On social class and education there is the classic *Who Shall Be Educated* by L. Warner and others.

On specific problems in the metropolitan area the following readings are suggested: *Mental Health in the Metropolis* by L. Srole *et. al.* deals with urban conditions and mental health and should be read along with Faris and Dunham's earlier classic in this field, *Mental Disorders in Urban Areas*. Also very good and recent is *Social Class and Mental Illness* by Hollingshead and Redlich. In the field of delinquency a basic book of readings is Glueck's *The Problem of Delinquency;* see also the writings of A. K. Cohen, C. R. Shaw and H. D. McKay, B. Lander, and Ivy Bennett. Marshall Clinard's *Sociology of Deviant Behavior* is helpful in gaining a generalized overview of social deviancy. The classic study of middle- and upper-class corruption is *White Collar Crime* by E. Sutherland. This should be read by all who believe that crime is a lower-class phenomenon. A broad picture of the extent of organized criminal activities may be found in Estes Kefauver's *Crime in America*. For greater understanding of the impact of culture on personality, see the book *Five Families* by Oscar Lewis, as well as the study *Beyond the Melting Pot* by N. Glazer and D. P. Moynihan. The book *Social Problems in America* by H. C. Bredemeier and J. Toby provides the reader with both an emotional and intellectual understanding of some of the major social problems of our time. A careful study of the skid-row area in large cities is revealed in *Skid Row, U.S.A.* by S. Harris. Very dated but still very interesting as an appraisal of socio-economics by a socialist thinker is Norman Thomas' *Human Exploitation*.

In the suburban area the books *The Vanishing Adolescent* by Edgar Friedenberg, Paul Goodman's *Growing Up Absurd*, and David Riesman's work are original and provocative comments on high achieving, more affluent social groups. James S. Coleman has written good analytic material on the subculture of secondary education, as has C. Wayne Gordon in his *Social System of the High School*. But probably still the most readable and critical is Willard Waller's *Sociology of Teaching*. For a recent work on social class in the suburbs, see the book *Class in Suburbia* by W. M. Dobriner. Provocative and critical of American culture and family life is *Childhood and Society* by Erik H. Erikson, and *The Mask of Sanity* by H. M. Cleckley. For greater understanding of the factory worker's life, values, and feeling of alienation read Ely Chinoy's *Automobile Workers and the American Dream* and Theodore Caplow's *The Sociology of Work*.

On the Negro issue there are several books that should be read. There are the classic studies in Gunnar Myrdal's *An American Dilemma*, Allison Davis and

John Dollard's *Children of Bondage,* E. Franklin Frazier's *The Negro in the United States* and *Black Bourgeoise;* and St. Clair Drake and Horace P. Cayton's careful analysis of the Negro in the large urban area in *Black Metropolis;* see also *The Mark of Oppression* by A. Kardiner, and *Racial and Cultural Minorities* by G. E. Simpson and M. J. Yinger. Journalistic in approach are such books as *Crisis in Black and White* by Charles E. Silberman, *Black Like Me* by J. H. Griffin, *Who Speaks for the Negro* by R. P. Warren, and *Why We Can't Wait* by Martin Luther King. A skillful analysis of *A Profile of the Negro American* was recently written by Thomas F. Pettigrew. In the Fall of 1965, *Daedalus* magazine published a two volume series of articles dealing with the major aspects of the Negro question. The Puerto Rican problem in New York City is well documented in the book *Spanish Harlem* by P. C. Sexton.

Some of the fiction writers in this area convey the feelings of the Negro community more realistically than do the more academic studies. For this approach one should read Richard Wright's *Native Son,* Claude Brown's *Manchild in the Promised Land,* Harper Lee's *To Kill a Mockingbird,* Warren Miller's *The Siege of Harlem,* Ralph Ellison's *Invisible Man,* and James Baldwin's *Go Tell It to the Mountain.* Probably the most readable and thoughtful book that has been done on the Negro in the inner city area is *Dark Ghetto* by Kenneth B. Clark.

On the side of specific social and educational planning in slum areas, there is some very interesting work being done. Saul Alinsky is one of the major figures in terms of community organization. Warren Haggstrom is another important leader in this field of initiating social action programs among the poor. An excellent volume discussing these issues is *The Mental Health of the Poor,* edited by Frank Reissman, Jerome Cohen, and Arthur Pearl. Haggstrom has a chapter in this book titled "The Power of the Poor," which presents his approach to organizing deprived communities.

In the area of education there is Frank Reissman's *The Culturally Deprived Child* and A. Harvey Passow's *Education in Depressed Areas.* The Passow volume has an excellent bibliography and lists and briefly explains various school programs. Martin Deutsch has done extensive work on preschool programs for deprived children. For a comprehensive bibliography and review of the literature on adolescence in urban areas see *Adolescent Behavior in Urban Areas* by David Gottlieb and Jon Reeves. For a presentation of the management of classroom disorders one should read *Conflict in the Classroom* by Long, Morse, and Newman.

The volume *The Schools and the Urban Crisis* by Kerber and Commarito has many excellent readings which examine specific school programs for disadvantaged youth. *The Search for an Educational Revolution* by S. M. Miller is very important in the areas of delinquency and special programs. To gain more insight into the theory and methods of achieving social change in an urban setting, the book *The Planning of Social Change* by Bennis, Benne, and Chin is very useful. In order to understand the basic conditions which are involved in social change, one should read *The Radical Right* edited by Daniel Bell; *Public Opinion and Propaganda* edited by D. Katz *et al.;* and *Reader in Bureaucracy* edited by R. K. Merton *et al.*

For additional articles, books, and projects in the field of urban education, the following three sources would be most helpful: *Urban Education, An Annotated Bibliography* produced by Hunter College, City University of New York; *An*

Inventory of Compensatory Education Projects, 1965 prepared by the Urban Child Center, School of Education, University of Chicago, Robert D. Hess; and *Programs for the Educationally Disadvantaged* from the U.S. Department of Health, Education, and Welfare.

PART 5

Much of the literature on teaching as a profession and its social implications is covered in the writings on conflicting educational theories. However, concomitant with this is the question of how teachers ought to be educated. One of the most critical books on how teachers are trained is James Koerner's *The Miseducation of Teachers*. A more constructive view is James Conant's *The Education of Teachers*, while a description of the problem is presented in the *Education of Teachers* by G. K. Hodenfield and T. M. Stinnett. Several viewpoints on the controversy in teacher education are presented in *Teacher Education: A Reappraisal* edited by Elmer R. Smith.

Myron Lieberman's *Education as a Profession* and *The Future of Public Education* should be read by any student preparing for teaching. The latter book is a particularly good treatment of power in teacher organizations. A collection of readings descriptively titled, *Teaching in America*, edited by Riccio and Cyphert presents a broad coverage of the teaching field. A positive approach to teaching is offered in *Education and the Teacher* by B. J. Chandler. Haskew and McLendon's *This Is Teaching* is a clear introductory text.

Personal, stimulating, and provocative writing about teaching includes Jacques Barzun's *Teacher in America*, Gilbert Highet's *The Art of Teaching*, *Teachers*, by Sylvia Ashton-Warner, and a paperback collection of essays by internationally prominent people on their most inspiring teacher, titled, *Great Teachers*, and edited by Houston Peterson.

Index